Financial Aid
for Asian Americans
2014-2016

RSP FINANCIAL AID DIRECTORIES
OF INTEREST TO MINORITIES

College Student's Guide to Merit and Other No-Need Funding
Selected as one of the "Outstanding Titles of the Year" by *Choice,* this directory describes 1,300 no-need funding opportunities for college students. 490 pages. ISBN 1588412350. $32.50, plus $7 shipping.

Directory of Financial Aids for Women
There are nearly 1,500 funding programs set aside for women described in this biennial directory, which has been called "the cream of the crop" by *School Library Journal* and the "best available reference source" by *Guide to Reference.* 504 pages. ISBN 1588412504. $45, plus $7 shipping.

Financial Aid for African Americans
More than 1,300 funding opportunities open to African American college students, professionals, and postdoctorates are described in this award-winning directory. 502 pages. ISBN 1588412423. $45, plus $7 shipping.

Financial Aid for Asian Americans
This is the source to use if you are looking for funding for Asian Americans, including college-bound high school seniors, undergraduates, graduate students, professionals, and postdoctorates; nearly 950 sources of free money are described here. 356 pages. ISBN 1588412431. $40, plus $7 shipping.

Financial Aid for Hispanic Americans
The 1,175 biggest and best sources of free money available to undergraduates, graduates students, professionals, and postdoctorates of Mexican, Puerto Rican, Central American, or other Latin American heritage are described here. 458 pages. ISBN 158841244X. $42.50, plus $7 shipping.

Financial Aid for Native Americans
Detailed information is provided on nearly 1,400 funding opportunities open to American Indians, Native Alaskans, and Native Pacific Islanders for college, graduate school, or professional activities. 504 pages. ISBN 1588412458. $45, plus $7 shipping.

Financial Aid for Research and Creative Activities Abroad
Described here are more than 1,000 scholarships, fellowships, grants, etc. available to support research, professional, or creative activities abroad. 413 pages. ISBN 1588412512. $45, plus $7 shipping.

Financial Aid for Study and Training Abroad
This directory, which the reviewers call "invaluable," describes nearly 1,000 financial aid opportunities available to support study abroad. 353 pages. ISBN 1588412520. $40, plus $7 shipping.

Financial Aid for Veterans, Military Personnel, & Their Families
According to *Reference Book Review,* this directory (with its 1,100 entries) is "the most comprehensive guide available on the subject." 429 pages. ISBN 1588412482. $40, plus $7 shipping.

High School Senior's Guide to Merit and Other No-Need Funding
Here's your guide to 1,100 funding programs that *never* look at income level when making awards to college-bound high school seniors. 411 pages. ISBN 1588412369. $29.95, plus $7 shipping.

Money for Graduate Students in the Arts & Humanities
Use this directory to identify 1,000 funding opportunities available to support graduate study and research in the arts/humanities. 287 pages. ISBN 1588412296. $42.50, plus $7 shipping.

Money for Graduate Students in the Biological Sciences
This unique directory focuses solely on funding for graduate study/research in the biological sciences (800+ funding opportunities). 241 pages. ISBN 158841230X. $37.50, plus $7 shipping.

Money for Graduate Students in the Health Sciences
Described here are 1,000+ funding opportunities just for students interested in a graduate degree in dentistry, medicine, nursing, nutrition, pharmacology, etc. 313 pages. ISBN 1588412318. $42.50, plus $7 shipping.

Money for Graduate Students in the Physical & Earth Sciences
Nearly 900 funding opportunities for graduate students in the physical and earth sciences are described in detail here. 280 pages. ISBN 1588412326. $40, plus $7 shipping.

Money for Graduate Students in the Social & Behavioral Sciences
Looking for money for a graduate degree in the social/behavioral sciences? Here are 1,100 funding programs for you. 319 pages. ISBN 1588412334. $42.50, plus $7 shipping.

Financial Aid for Asian Americans 2014-2016

Gail Ann Schlachter
R. David Weber

A List of Scholarships, Fellowships, Grants, Awards, and Other Sources of Free Money Available Primarily or Exclusively to Asian Americans, Plus a Set of Six Indexes (Program Title, Sponsoring Organization, Residency, Tenability, Subject, and Deadline Date)

Reference Service Press
El Dorado Hills, California

ISBN 10: 1588412431
ISBN 13: 9781588412430

10 9 8 7 6 5 4 3 2 1

Reference Service Press (RSP) began in 1977 with a single financial aid publication *(The Directory of Financial Aids for Women)* and now specializes in the development of financial aid resources in multiple formats, including books, large print books, disks, print-on-demand reports, eBooks, electronic databases, and online sources. Long recognized as a leader in the field, RSP has been called by the *Simba Report on Directory Publishing* "a true success in the world of independent directory publishers." Both Kaplan Educational Centers and Military.com have hailed RSP as "the leading authority on scholarships."

Reference Service Press
El Dorado Hills Business Park
5000 Windplay Drive, Suite 4
El Dorado Hills, CA 95762-9319
  (916) 939-9620
  Fax: (916) 939-9626
  E-mail: info@rspfunding.com
Visit our web site: www.rspfunding.com

Manufactured in the United States of America
Price: $40.00, plus $7 shipping.

ACADEMIC INSTITUTIONS, LIBRARIES, ORGANIZATIONS AND OTHER QUANTITY BUYERS:
Discounts on this book are available for bulk purchases. E-mail or call for information on our discount programs.

Contents

Introduction

WHY THIS DIRECTORY IS NEEDED

Despite our country's ongoing economic volatility and increased college costs, the financial aid picture for minorities has never looked brighter. Currently, billions of dollars are set aside each year specifically for Asian Americans, African Americans, Hispanic Americans, and Native Americans. This funding is open to minorities at any level (high school through postdoctoral and professional) for a variety of activities, including study, research, travel, training, career development, and creative projects.

While numerous print and online listings have been prepared to identify and describe general financial aid opportunities (those open to all segments of society), those resources have never covered more than a small portion of the programs designed primarily or exclusively for minorities. As a result, many advisors, librarians, scholars, researchers, and students often have been unaware of the extensive funding available to Asian Americans and other minorities. But, with the ongoing publication of *Financial Aid for Asian Americans,* that has all changed. Here, in just one place, Asian American students, professionals, and postdoctorates now have current and detailed information about the special resources set aside specifically for them.

Financial Aid for Asian Americans is prepared biennially as part of Reference Service Press' four-volume *Minority Funding Set* (the other volumes in the set cover funding for African Americans, Hispanic Americans, and Native Americans). Each of the volumes in this set is sold separately, or the complete set can be purchased at a discounted price. For more information, contact Reference Service Press's marketing department or visit www.rspfunding.com/prod_prodalpha.html.

No other source, in print or online, offers the extensive coverage of funding for minorities provided by these titles. That's why the Grantsmanship Center labeled the set "a must for every organization serving minorities," *Reference Sources for Small and Medium-Sized Libraries* called the titles "the absolute best guides for finding funding," and *Reference Books Bulletin* selected each of the volumes in the *Minority Funding Set* as their "Editor's Choice." *Financial Aid for Asian Americans,* itself, has also received rave reviews. *Al Jahdid* called the directory "an excellent resource," the Miami-Dade Public Library System included it in its list of "Essential Titles for the College Bound," and *Small Press* found it both "inclusive" and "valuable." Perhaps *Choice* sums up the critical reaction best: "a unique and valuable resource; highly recommended."

WHAT'S UPDATED?

The preparation of each new edition of *Financial Aid for Asian Americans* involves extensive updating and revision. To make sure that the information included here is both reliable and current, the editors at Reference Service Press 1) reviewed and updated all relevant programs covered in the previous edition of the directory, 2) collected information on all programs open to Asian Americans that were added to Reference Service Press' funding database since the last edition of the directory, and then 3) searched extensively for new program leads in a variety of sources, including printed directories, news reports, journals, newsletters, house organs, annual reports, and sites on the Internet. We only include program descriptions that are written directly from information supplied by the sponsoring organization in print or online (no information is ever taken from secondary sources). When that information could not be found, we sent up to four collection letters (followed by up to three telephone or e-mail inquiries, if necessary) to those sponsors. Despite our best efforts, however, some sponsoring organizations still failed to respond and, as a result, their programs are not included in this edition of the directory.

The 2014-2016 edition of *Financial Aid for Asian Americans* completely revises and updates the previous (seventh) edition. Programs that have ceased operations have been dropped from the directory. Similarly, programs that have broadened their scope and no longer focus on Asian Americans have also been removed from the listing. Profiles of continuing programs have been rewritten to reflect current requirements; nearly 75 percent of the continuing programs reported substantive changes in their locations, requirements (particularly application deadline), benefits, or eligibility requirements since the 2012-2014 edition. In addition, hundreds of new entries have been added to the program section of the directory. The resulting listing describes the nearly 950 biggest and best sources of free money available to Asian Americans, including scholarships, fellowships, grants, awards, and other funding opportunities.

WHAT MAKES THIS DIRECTORY UNIQUE?

The 2014-2016 edition of *Financial Aid for Asian Americans* will help Americans with origins from Asia or subcontinent Asia and Pacific island nations (e.g., Japan, China, the Philippines, Vietnam, Korea, Laos, Cambodia, Taiwan, Burma, Thailand, Malaysia, Indonesia, Singapore, Brunei, Macao, Hong Kong, India, Pakistan, Bangladesh, Tonga) tap into the billions of dollars available to them, as minorities, to support study, research, creative activities, past accomplishments, future projects, professional development, and many other activities. The listings cover every major subject area, are sponsored by more than 750 different private and public agencies and organizations, and are open to Asian Americans at any level, from college-bound high school students through professionals and postdoctorates.

Not only does *Financial Aid for Asian Americans* provide the most comprehensive coverage of available funding (947 entries), but it also displays the most informative program descriptions (on the average, more than twice the detail found in any other listing). In addition to this extensive and focused coverage, *Financial Aid for Asian Americans* also offers several other unique features. First of all, hundreds of funding opportunities listed here have never been covered in any other source. So, even if you have checked elsewhere, you will want to look at *Financial Aid for Asian Americans* for additional leads. And, here's another plus: all of the funding programs in this edition of the directory offer "free" money; not one of the programs will ever require you to pay anything back (provided, of course, that you meet the program requirements).

Further, unlike other funding directories, which generally follow a straight alphabetical arrangement, *Financial Aid for Asian Americans* groups entries by intended recipients (undergraduates, graduate students, or professionals/postdoctorates), to make it easy for you to search for appropriate programs. This same convenience is offered in the indexes, where title, sponsoring organization, geographic, subject, and deadline date entries are each subdivided by recipient group.

Finally, we have tried to anticipate all the ways you might wish to search for funding. The volume is organized so you can identify programs not only by intended recipient, but by subject focus, sponsoring organization, program title, residency requirements, where the money can be spent, and even deadline date. Plus, we've included all the information you'll need to decide if a program is right for you: purpose, eligibility requirements, financial data, duration, special features, limitations, number awarded, and application date. You even get fax numbers, toll-free numbers, e-mail addresses, and web sites (when available), along with complete contact information.

WHAT'S EXCLUDED?

While this book is intended to be the most comprehensive source of information on funding available to Asian Americans, there are some programs we've specifically excluded from the directory:

- *Programs that do not accept applications from U.S. citizens or residents.* If a program is open only to foreign nationals or excludes Americans from applying, it is not covered.

- *Programs that are open equally to all segments of the population.* Only funding opportunities set aside primarily or exclusively for Asian Americans are included here.

SAMPLE ENTRY

(1) **[86]**

(2) **COCA-COLA FOUNDATION APIASF SCHOLARSHIPS**

(3) Asian & Pacific Islander American Scholarship Fund
2025 M Street, N.W., Suite 610
Washington, DC 20036-3363
(202) 986-6892   Fax: (202) 530-0643
E-mail: info@apiasf.org
Web: www.apiasf.org/scholarship_apiasf.html

(4) **Summary** To provide financial assistance to Asian and Pacific Islander Americans who are the first member of their family to attend college.

(5) **Eligibility** This program is open to U.S. citizens, nationals, permanent residents, and citizens of the Freely Associated States who are of Asian or Pacific Islander heritage and the first member of their immediate family to attend college. Applicants must be enrolling full time at an accredited 2- or 4-year college or university in the United States. They must have a GPA of 2.7 or higher or the GED equivalent. In addition, they must complete the FAFSA and apply for federal financial aid.

(6) **Financial data** The stipend is $2,500.

(7) **Duration** 1 year; nonrenewable.

(8) **Additional information** This program is sponsored by the Coca-Cola Foundation and administered by the Asian & Pacific Islander American Scholarship Fund (APIASF).

(9) **Number awarded** Varies each year; recently, 30 of these scholarships were awarded.

(10) **Deadline** January of each year.

DEFINITION

(1) **Entry number:** The consecutive number that is given to each entry and used to identify the entry in the index.

(2) **Program title:** Title of scholarship, fellowship, grant, award, or other source of free money described in the directory.

(3) **Sponsoring organization:** Name, address, and telephone number, toll-free number, fax number, e-mail address, and/or web site (when information was available) for organization sponsoring the program.

(4) **Summary:** Identifies the major program requirements; read the rest of the entry for additional detail.

(5) **Eligibility:** Qualifications required of applicants, plus information on application procedure and selection process.

(6) **Financial data:** Financial details of the program, including fixed sum, average amount, or range of funds offered, expenses for which funds may and may not be applied, and cash-related benefits supplied (e.g., room and board).

(7) **Duration:** Period for which support is provided; renewal prospects.

(8) **Additional information:** Any unusual (generally nonmonetary) benefits, features, restrictions, or limitations associated with the program.

(9) **Number awarded:** Total number of recipients each year or other specified period.

(10) **Deadline:** The month by which applications must be submitted.

- *Money for study or research outside the United States.*   Since there are comprehensive and up-to-date directories that describe the available funding for study, research, and other activities abroad, (see the list of Reference Service Press titles opposite the directory's title page), only programs that fund activities in the United States are covered here.

- *Very restrictive programs.*   In general, programs are excluded if they are open only to a limited geographic area (less than a state) or offer limited financial support (less than $500). Note, however, that the vast majority of programs included here go way beyond that, paying up to full tuition or stipends that exceed $20,000 a year!

- *Programs administered by individual academic institutions solely for their own students.*   The directory identifies "portable" programs—ones that can be used at any number of schools. Financial aid administered by individual schools specifically for their own students is not covered. Check directly with the schools you are considering to get information on their offerings.

- *Money that must be repaid.*   Only "free money" is identified here. If a program requires repayment or charges interest, it's not listed. Now you can find out about billions of dollars in aid and know (if you meet the program requirements) that not one dollar of that will ever need to be repaid.

HOW THE DIRECTORY IS ORGANIZED

Financial Aid for Asian Americans is divided into two sections: 1) a detailed list of funding opportunities open to Asian Americans and 2) a set of six indexes to help you pinpoint appropriate funding programs.

Financial Aid Programs Open to Asian Americans.   The first section of the directory describes nearly 950 sources of free money available to Asian Americans. The focus is on financial aid aimed at American citizens or residents to support study, research, or other activities in the United States. The programs listed here are sponsored by more than 750 different government agencies, professional organizations, corporations, sororities and fraternities, foundations, religious groups, educational associations, and military/veterans organizations. All areas of the sciences, social sciences, and humanities are covered.

To help you focus your search, the entries in this section are grouped into the following three chapters:

- **Undergraduates:**   Included here are 408 scholarships, grants, awards, and other sources of free money that support undergraduate study, training, research, or creative activities. These programs are open to high school seniors, high school graduates, currently-enrolled college students, and students returning to college after an absence. Money is available to support these students in any type of public or private postsecondary institution, ranging from technical schools and community colleges to major universities in the United States.

- **Graduate Students:**   Described here are nearly 400 fellowships, grants, awards, and other sources of free money that support post-baccalaureate study, training, research, and creative activities. These programs are open to students applying to, currently enrolled in, or returning to a master's, doctoral, professional, or specialist program in public or private graduate schools in the United States.

- **Professionals/Postdoctorates:**   Included here are 143 funding programs for U.S. citizens or residents who 1) are in professional positions (e.g., artists, writers), whether or not they have an advanced degree; 2) are master's or professional degree recipients; 3) have earned a doctoral degree or its equivalent (e.g., Ph.D., Ed.D., M.D.); or 4) have recognized stature as established scientists, scholars, academicians, or researchers.

Within each of these three chapters, entries appear alphabetically by program title. Since some of the programs supply assistance to more than one specific group, those are listed in all relevant chapters. For example, the Asian American Architects and Engineers Foundation Scholarships support both undergraduate or graduate study, so the program is described in both the Undergraduates *and* Graduate Students chapters.

Each program entry has been designed to give you a concise profile that, as the sample on page 7 illustrates, includes information (when available) on organization address and telephone numbers (including toll-free and fax numbers), e-mail address and web site, purpose, eligibility, money awarded, duration, special features, limitations, number of awards, and application deadline.

The information reported for each of the programs in this section was gathered from research conducted through the beginning of 2014. While the listing is intended to cover as comprehensively as possible the biggest and best sources of free money available to Asian Americans, some sponsoring organizations did not post information online or respond to our research inquiries and, consequently, are not included in this edition of the directory.

Indexes. To help you find the aid you need, we have constructed six indexes; these will let you access the listings by program title, sponsoring organization, residency, tenability, subject focus, and deadline date. These indexes use a word-by-word alphabetical arrangement. Note: numbers in the index refer to entry numbers, not to page numbers in the book.

Program Title Index. If you know the name of a particular funding program and want to find out where it is covered in the directory, use the Program Title Index. To assist you in your search, every program is listed by all its known names, former names, and abbreviations. Since one program can be included in more than one place (e.g., a program providing assistance to both undergraduate and graduate students is described in both the first and second chapter), each entry number in the index has been coded to indicate the intended recipient group (for example, "U" = Undergraduates; "G" = Graduate Students). By using this coding system, you can avoid duplicate entries and turn directly to the programs that match your eligibility characteristics.

Sponsoring Organization Index. This index makes it easy to identify agencies that offer funding primarily or exclusively to Asian Americans. More than 750 organizations are indexed here. As in the Program Title Index, we've used a code to help you determine which organizations sponsor programs that match your educational level.

Residency Index. Some programs listed in this book are restricted to Asian Americans in a particular state or region. Others are open to Asian Americans wherever they live. This index helps you identify programs available only to residents in your area as well as programs that have no residency requirements. Further, to assist you in your search, we've also indicated the recipient level for the funding offered to residents in each of the areas listed in the index.

Tenability Index. This index identifies the geographic locations where the funding described in *Financial Aid for Asian Americans* may be used. Index entries (city, county, state, region) are arranged alphabetically (word by word) and subdivided by recipient group. Use this index when you are looking for money to support your activities in a particular geographic area.

Subject Index. This index allows you to identify the subject focus of each of the financial aid opportunities described in *Financial Aid for Asian Americans.* More than 200 different subject terms are listed. Extensive "see" and "see also" references, as well as recipient group subdivisions, will help you locate appropriate funding opportunities.

Calendar Index. Since most financial aid programs have specific deadline dates, some may have closed by the time you begin to look for funding. You can use the Calendar Index to determine which programs are still open. This index is arranged by recipient group (Undergraduates, Graduate Students, and Professionals/Postdoctorates) and subdivided by the month during which the deadline falls. Filing dates can and quite often do vary from year to year; consequently, this index should be used only as a guide for deadlines beyond 2016.

HOW TO USE THE DIRECTORY

Here are some tips to help you get the most out of the funding opportunities listed in *Financial Aid for Asian Americans.*

To Locate Funding by Recipient Group.   To bring together programs with a similar educational focus, this directory is divided into three chapters: Undergraduates, Graduate Students, and Professionals/Postdoctorates. If you want to get an overall picture of the sources of free money available to Asian Americans in any of these categories, turn to the appropriate chapter and then review the entries there. Since each of these chapters functions as a self-contained entity, you can browse through any of them without having to first consulting an index.

To Find Information on a Particular Financial Aid Program.   If you know the name of a particular financial aid program, and the group eligible for that award, then go directly to the appropriate chapter in the directory (e.g., Undergraduates, Graduate Students), where you will find the program profiles arranged alphabetically by title. To save time, though, you should always check the Program Title Index first if you know the name of a specific award but are not sure in which chapter it has been listed. Plus, since we index each program by all its known names and abbreviations, you'll also be able to track down a program there when you only know the popular rather than official name.

To Locate Programs Sponsored by a Particular Organization.   The Sponsoring Organization Index makes it easy to identify agencies that provide financial assistance to Asian Americans or to identify specific financial aid programs offered by a particular organization. Each entry number in the index is coded to identify recipient group (Undergraduates, Graduate Students, Professionals/Postdoctorates), so that you can easily target appropriate entries.

To Browse Quickly Through the Listings.   Look at the listings in the chapter that relates to you (Undergraduates, Graduate Students, or Professionals/Postdoctorates) and read the "Summary" paragraph in each entry. In seconds, you'll know if this is an opportunity that you might want to pursue. If it is, be sure to read the rest of the information in the entry, to make sure you meet all of the program requirements before writing or going online for an application form. Please, save your time and energy. Don't apply if you don't qualify!

To Locate Funding Available to Asian Americans from or Tenable in a Particular City, County, or State.   The Residency Index identifies financial aid programs open to Asian Americans in a specific state, region, etc. The Tenability Index shows where the money can be spent. In both indexes, "see" and "see also" references are used liberally, and index entries for a particular geographic area are subdivided by recipient group (Undergraduates, Graduate Students, and Professionals/Postdoctorates) to help you identify the funding that's right for you. When using these indexes, always check the listings under the term "United States," since the programs indexed there have no geographic restrictions and can be used in any area.

To Locate Financial Aid Programs Open to Asian Americans in a Particular Subject Area.   Turn to the Subject Index first if you are interested in identifying funding programs for Asian Americans that are focused on a particular subject area. To make your search easier, the intended recipient groups (Undergraduates, Graduate Students, Professionals/Postdoctorates) are clearly labeled in the more than 200 subject listings. Extensive cross-references are also provided. Since a large number of programs are not restricted by subject, be sure to check the references listed under the "General programs" heading in the index, in addition to the specific terms that directly relate to your interest areas. The listings under "General programs" can be used to fund activities in any subject area (although the programs may be restricted in other ways).

To Locate Financial Aid Programs for Asian Americans by Deadline Date.   If you are working with specific time constraints and want to weed out the financial aid programs whose filing dates you won't be able to meet, turn first to the Calendar Index and check the program references listed under the appropriate recipient group and month. Note: not all sponsoring organizations supplied deadline information; those programs are listed under the "Deadline not specified" entries in the index. To identify every relevant financial aid program, regardless of filing date, go the appropriate chapter and read through all the entries there that match your educational level.

To Locate Financial Aid Programs Open to All Segments of the Population. Only programs available to Asian Americans are listed in this publication. However, there are thousands of other programs that are open equally to all segments of the population. To identify these programs, talk to your local librarian, check with your financial aid office on campus, look at the list of RSP print resources on the page opposite the title page in this directory, or see if your library subscribes to Reference Service Press' interactive online funding database: *RSP FundingFinder.* For more information on that award-winning resource, go online to: www.rspfunding.com/esubscriptions.html.

PLANS TO UPDATE THE DIRECTORY

This volume, covering 2014-2016, is the eighth edition of *Financial Aid for Asian Americans.* The next biennial edition will cover the years 2016-2018 and will be issued by the beginning of 2016.

OTHER RELATED PUBLICATIONS

In addition to *Financial Aid for Asian Americans,* Reference Service Press publishes several other titles dealing with fundseeking, including the award-winning *Directory of Financial Aids for Women; Financial Aid for Persons with Disabilities and Their Families;* and *Financial Aid for Veterans, Military Personnel, and Their Families.* Since each of these titles focuses on a separate population group, there is very little duplication in the listings. For more information on Reference Service Press' award-winning publications, write to the company at 5000 Windplay Drive, Suite 4, El Dorado Hills, CA 95762, give us a call at (916) 939-9620, fax us at (916) 939-9626, send us an e-mail at info@rspfunding.com, or visit our expanded web site: www.rspfunding.com.

ACKNOWLEDGEMENTS

A debt of gratitude is owed all the organizations that contributed information to the 2014-2016 edition of *Financial Aid for Asian Americans.* Their generous cooperation has helped to make this publication a current and comprehensive survey of awards.

ABOUT THE AUTHORS

Dr. Gail Ann Schlachter has worked for more than three decades as a library manager, a library educator, and an administrator of library-related publishing companies. Among the reference books to her credit are the biennially-issued *Directory of Financial Aids for Women* and two award-winning bibliographic guides: *Minorities and Women: A Guide to Reference Literature in the Social Sciences* (which was chosen as an "outstanding reference book of the year" by *Choice)* and *Reference Sources in Library and Information Services* (which won the first Knowledge Industry Publications "Award for Library Literature"). She was the reference book review editor for *RQ* (now *Reference and User Services Quarterly)* for 10 years, is a past president of the American Library Association's Reference and User Services Association, is the former editor-in-chief of the *Reference and User Services Association Quarterly,* and is currently serving her sixth term on the American Library Association's governing council. In recognition of her outstanding contributions to reference service, Dr. Schlachter has been named the University of Wisconsin School of Library and Information Studies "Alumna of the Year" and has been awarded both the Isadore Gilbert Mudge Citation and the Louis Shores/Oryx Press Award.

Dr. R. David Weber taught history and economics at Los Angeles Harbor College (in Wilmington, California) for many years and continues to teach history there as an emeritus professor. During his years at Harbor College, and earlier at East Los Angeles College, he directed the Honors Program and was frequently chosen the "Teacher of the Year." He has written a number of critically-acclaimed reference works, including *Dissertations in Urban History* and the three-volume *Energy Information Guide.* With Gail Schlachter, he is the author of Reference Service Press' *Financial Aid for Persons with Disabilities and Their Families,* which was selected by *Library Journal* as one of the "best reference books of the year," and a number of other financial aid titles, including the *College Student's Guide to Merit and Other No-Need Funding,* which was chosen as one of the "outstanding reference books of the year" by *Choice.*

Financial Aid Programs
Open to Asian Americans

Undergraduates ●

Graduate Students ●

Professionals/Postdoctorates ●

Undergraduates

Listed alphabetically by program title and described in detail here are 408 scholarships, grants, awards, and other sources of "free money" set aside for college-bound high school seniors and continuing or returning undergraduate students of Asian origins (including those of subcontinent Asian and Pacific Islander descent). This funding is available to support study, training, research, and/or creative activities in the United States.

[1]
AAF MINORITY/DISADVANTAGED SCHOLARSHIP PROGRAM

American Institute of Architects
Attn: American Architectural Foundation
1799 New York Avenue, N.W.
Washington, DC 20006-5292
(202) 626-7511   Fax: (202) 626-7420
E-mail: scholarships@aia.org
Web: www.aia.org/education/aiab081881

Summary To provide financial assistance to Asian American and other high school and college students from minority and/or disadvantaged backgrounds who are interested in studying architecture in college.

Eligibility This program is open to students from minority and/or disadvantaged backgrounds who are high school seniors, students in a community college or technical school transferring to an accredited architectural program, or college freshmen entering a professional degree program at an accredited program of architecture. Students who have completed 1 or more years of a 4-year college curriculum are not eligible. Initially, candidates must be nominated by 1 of the following organizations or persons: an individual architect or firm, a chapter of the American Institute of Architects (AIA), a community design center, a guidance counselor or teacher, the dean or professor at an accredited school of architecture, or the director of a community or civic organization. Nominees are reviewed and eligible candidates are invited to complete an application form in which they write an essay describing the reasons they are interested in becoming an architect and provide documentation of academic excellence and financial need. Selection is based primarily on financial need.

Financial data Stipends range from $3,000 to $4,000 per year, depending upon individual need. Students must apply for supplementary funds from other sources.

Duration 9 months; may be renewed for up to 2 additional years.

Additional information This program, established in 1970, is offered jointly by the American Architectural Foundation (AAF) and the AIA.

Number awarded Up to 5 each year.

Deadline April of each year.

[2]
AAFO SCHOLARSHIPS

Asian American Foundation of Oregon
P.O. Box 51117
Eugene, OR 97405
(541) 914-4235
Web: www.aaforegon.org

Summary To provide financial assistance to residents of Oregon who have been involved in Asian American cultural activities and are interested in attending college in any state.

Eligibility The program is open to residents of Oregon who have demonstrated interest and effort in Asian American cultural activities. Applicants must be graduating high school seniors or current undergraduate students at a college or university in any state. They must have a GPA of 2.5 or higher. Along with their application, they must submit a 250-word essay that describes their college plans, career interests,

relationship to and interest in Asian culture, and/or future commitment to the Asian American community. U.S. citizenship is required.

Financial data The stipend is $1,000.

Duration 1 year.

Number awarded 2 each year.

Deadline April of each year.

[3]
AAJUW SCHOLARSHIP PROGRAM

American Association of Japanese University Women
Attn: Scholarship Committee
3543 West Boulevard
Los Angeles, CA 90016
E-mail: scholarship@aajuw.org
Web: www.aajuw.org/scholarship.php

Summary To provide financial assistance to Japanese American and other female students currently enrolled in upper-division or graduate classes in California.

Eligibility This program is open to women enrolled at accredited colleges or universities in California as juniors, seniors, or graduate students. Applicants must be involved in U.S.-Japan relations, cultural exchanges, and leadership development in the areas of their designated field of study. Along with their application, they must submit a current resume, an official transcript of the past 2 years of college work, 2 letters of recommendation, and an essay (up to 2 pages in English or 1,200 characters in Japanese) on what they hope to accomplish in their field of study and how that will contribute to better U.S.-Japan relations.

Financial data The stipend is $2,000.

Duration 1 year.

Additional information The association was founded in 1970 to promote the education of women as well as to contribute to U.S.-Japan relations, cultural exchanges, and leadership development.

Number awarded 1 to 3 each year. Since this program was established, it has awarded more than $100,000 worth of scholarships to nearly 100 women.

Deadline October of each year.

[4]
ABE AND ESTHER HAGIWARA STUDENT AID AWARD

Japanese American Citizens League
Attn: National Scholarship Awards
1765 Sutter Street
San Francisco, CA 94115
(415) 345-1075   Fax: (415) 931-4671
E-mail: ncwnp@jacl.org
Web: www.jacl.org/edu/scholar.htm

Summary To provide financial assistance for college or graduate school to student members of the Japanese American Citizens League (JACL) who can demonstrate severe financial need.

Eligibility This program is open to JACL members who are enrolled or planning to enroll at a college, university, trade school, or business college. Applicants must be undergraduate or graduate students who are able to demonstrate that, without this aid, they will have to delay or terminate their education. They must submit information on their involvement in

JACL and a 2-page essay on a topic that changes annually but relates to Japanese Americans. Selection is based on that essay, financial need, academic history, JACL involvement, school activities, work history, scholastic honors, and community involvement.

Financial data Stipends generally average more than $2,000.

Duration 1 year; nonrenewable.

Number awarded At least 1 each year.

Deadline March of each year.

[5]
ACA/MARTIN LUTHER KING JR. SCHOLARSHIP AWARDS

American Correctional Association
Attn: Scholarship Award Committee
206 North Washington Street, Suite 200
Alexandria, VA 22314
(703) 224-0000 Toll Free: (800) ACA-JOIN
Fax: (703) 224-0179 E-mail: jenniferb@aca.org
Web: www.aca.org/pastpresentfuture/awards.asp

Summary To provide financial assistance for undergraduate or graduate study to Asian Americans and other minorities interested in a career in the criminal justice field.

Eligibility Members of the American Correctional Association (ACA) may nominate a minority person for these awards. Nominees do not need to be ACA members, but they must have been accepted to or be enrolled in an undergraduate or graduate program in criminal justice at a 4-year college or university. Along with the nomination package, they must submit a 250-word essay describing their reflections on the ideals and philosophies of Dr. Martin Luther King and how they have attempted to emulate those qualities in their lives. They must provide documentation of financial need, academic achievement, and commitment to the principles of Dr. King.

Financial data A stipend is awarded (amount not specified). Funds are paid directly to the recipient's college or university.

Number awarded 1 each year.

Deadline May of each year.

[6]
ACT SIX SCHOLARSHIPS

Act Six
c/o Degrees of Change
1109 A Street, Suite 101
P.O. Box 1573
Tacoma, WA 98401
(253) 642-6712 E-mail: tim.herron@actsix.org
Web: www.actsix.org

Summary To provide financial assistance to Asian Americans and other residents of Washington and Oregon who come from diverse backgrounds and are interested in attending designated private faith-based universities in those states.

Eligibility This program is open to high school seniors or recent graduates and planning to enter college as freshmen who come from diverse, multicultural backgrounds. Applicants must be residents of the following regions and interested in attending designated colleges for that region: Portland: George Fox University or Warner Pacific College; Spo-

kane: Gonzaga University or Whitworth University; Tacoma-Seattle: Gonzaga University, Northwest University, Pacific Lutheran University, Trinity Lutheran College, or Whitworth University; or Yakima Valley: Heritage University. Students are not required to make a faith commitment, but they must be willing to explore Christian spirituality as it relates to service and leadership. Ethnicity and family income are considered as factors in selecting an intentionally diverse group of scholars, but there are no income restrictions and students from all ethnic backgrounds are encouraged to apply.

Financial data The program makes up the difference between any other assistance the student receives and full tuition. For recipients who demonstrate financial need in excess of tuition, awards cover some or all of the cost of room and board, books, travel, and personal expenses.

Duration 1 year; may be renewed.

Number awarded Varies each year; recently, 65 of these scholarships were awarded.

Deadline October of each year.

[7]
A.D. OSHERMAN SCHOLARSHIP FUND

Greater Houston Community Foundation
Attn: Scholarship Coordinator
5120 Woodway Drive, Suite 6000
Houston, TX 77056
(713) 333-2205 Fax: (713) 333-2220
E-mail: lgardner@ghcf.org
Web: www.ghcf.org/Recieve/Scholarships

Summary To provide financial assistance to Asian Americans and members of other designated groups who are residents of Texas and attending or planning to attend college in any state.

Eligibility This program is open to Texas residents who are graduating high school seniors or full-time freshmen, sophomores, or juniors at an accredited public 2- or 4-year college or university in any state. Applicants must qualify as a member of a recognized minority group, the first in their family to attend college, or a veteran with active service, particularly service in Iraq or Afghanistan. They must have a GPA of 2.75 or higher and a history of community service. Financial need is considered in the selection process.

Financial data The stipend is $2,500 per year for students at 4-year universities or $1,500 per year for students at 2-year colleges.

Duration 1 year; recipients may reapply.

Number awarded 2 each year.

Deadline March of each year.

[8]
ADDIE B. MORRIS SCHOLARSHIP

American Association of Railroad Superintendents
P.O. Box 200
La Fox, IL 60147
(630) 762-0754 E-mail: aars@supt.org
Web: www.railroadsuperintendents.org/Scholarships

Summary To provide financial assistance to undergraduate and graduate students, with preference given to Asian Americans and other minorities working on a degree in transportation.

Eligibility This program is open to full-time undergraduate and graduate students enrolled at accredited colleges and universities in Canada or the United States. Applicants must have completed enough credits to have standing as a sophomore and must have a GPA of 2.75 or higher. Preference is given to minority students enrolled in the transportation field who can demonstrate financial need.

Financial data The stipend is $1,000. Funds are sent directly to the recipient's institution.

Duration 1 year.

Number awarded 1 or more each year.

Deadline May of each year.

[9]
ADVISORS OF AMERICA SCHOLARSHIP

Hmong American Education Fund
P.O. Box 17468
St. Paul, MN 55117
(651) 230-3634   E-mail: scholarships@thehaef.org
Web: www.thehaef.org

Summary To provide financial assistance to Hmong students who demonstrate a commitment to academic excellence and are interested in attending college in any state.

Eligibility This program is open to residents of any state who identify themselves as a person of Hmong descent. Applicants must be high school seniors, GED recipients, or students currently enrolled full time at a public 2- or 4-year college or university in any state. They must be U.S. citizens or permanent residents and have a GPA of 3.0 or higher. Along with their application, they must submit transcripts, ACT or SAT scores, and a 1,500-word essay on their commitment to education, their financial need (annual household income between $30,000 and $92,000), how this scholarship can help them, and their community service. Selection is based on academic excellence, commitment to helping their community, and financial need.

Financial data The stipend is $500 per year.

Duration 1 year; may be renewed up to 3 additional years.

Number awarded 1 each year.

Deadline March of each year.

[10]
AFPD MINORITY SCHOLARSHIPS

Associated Food and Petroleum Dealers
Attn: AFPD Foundation
5779 West Maple Road
West Bloomfield, MI 48322
(248) 671-9600   Toll Free: (800) 666-6233
Fax: (866) 601-9610   E-mail: info@afpdonline.org
Web: www.afpdonline.org/michigan-scholarship.php

Summary To provide financial assistance to Asian American and other minority high school seniors and current college students from Michigan who are enrolled or planning to enroll at a college in any state.

Eligibility This program is open to Michigan residents who are high school seniors or college freshmen, sophomores, or juniors. Applicants must be members of 1 of the following minority groups: African American, Hispanic, Asian, Native American, or Arab/Chaldean. They must be enrolled or planning to enroll full time at a college or university in any state. Preferential consideration is given to applicants with a mem-bership affiliation in the Associated Food and Petroleum Dealers (AFPD), although membership is not required. Selection is based on academic performance, leadership, and participation in school and community activities; college grades are considered if the applicant is already enrolled in college.

Financial data The stipend is $1,500.

Duration 1 year; nonrenewable.

Additional information This program is administered by International Scholarship and Tuition Services, Inc. The AFPD was formed in 2006 by a merger of the Associated Food Dealers of Michigan and the Great Lakes Petroleum Retailers and Allied Trades Association.

Number awarded At least 10 each year, of which at least 3 must be awarded to member customers.

Deadline March of each year.

[11]
AGAINST THE GRAIN ARTISTIC SCHOLARSHIP

Against the Grain Productions
Attn: Scholarship Committee
Attn: Scholarship Coordinator
3523 McKinney Avenue, Suite 231
Dallas, TX 75204
E-mail: outreach@againstthegrainproductions.com
Web: www.againstthegrainproductions.com/scholarship

Summary To provide financial assistance to Asian and Pacific Island students working on an undergraduate degree in fields of visual or performing arts.

Eligibility This program is open to high school seniors and current full-time students at accredited 2- and 4-year colleges and universities and vocational schools. Applicants must be of at least 50% Asian and/or Pacific Islander ethnicity and U.S. citizens, nationals, or permanent residents. They must be majoring in a field of the performing and/or visual arts (e.g., film, theater, fashion, photography, graphic design, dance, music) and have a GPA of 3.0 or higher. Selection is based on an essay and artistic portfolio, academic performance, leadership and community service, and an interview.

Financial data The stipend is $1,000. Funds are disbursed directly to the educational institution.

Duration 1 year.

Number awarded 2 each year.

Deadline April of each year.

[12]
AHLEF/HYATT HOTELS FUND FOR MINORITY LODGING MANAGEMENT STUDENTS

American Hotel & Lodging Educational Foundation
Attn: Manager of Foundation Programs
1201 New York Avenue, N.W., Suite 600
Washington, DC 20005-3931
(202) 289-3100   Fax: (202) 289-3199
E-mail: scholarships@ahlef.org
Web: www.ahlef.org/content.aspx?id=19468

Summary To provide financial assistance to Asian American and other minority college students working on a degree in hotel management.

Eligibility This program is open to students majoring in hospitality management at a 4-year college or university as at least a junior. Applicants must be members of a minority group (African American, Hispanic, American Indian, Alaskan Native, Asian, or Pacific Islander). They must be enrolled full time. Along with their application, they must submit a 500-word essay on their personal background, including when they became interested in the hospitality field, the traits they possess or will need to succeed in the industry, and their plans as related to their educational and career objectives and future goals. Selection is based on industry-related work experience; financial need; academic record and educational qualifications; professional, community, and extracurricular activities; personal attributes, including career goals; the essay; and neatness and completeness of the application. U.S. citizenship or permanent resident status is required.

Financial data   The stipend is $2,000.

Duration   1 year.

Additional information   Funding for this program, established in 1988, is provided by Hyatt Hotels & Resorts.

Number awarded   Varies each year; recently, 18 of these scholarships were awarded. Since this program was established, it has awarded scholarships worth $588,000 to 294 minority students.

Deadline   April of each year.

[13]
AICPA ASCEND SCHOLARSHIP

Ascend: Pan-Asian Leaders
Attn: Director of Programs
120 Wall Street, Ninth Floor
New York, NY 10005
(212) 248-4888   Fax: (212) 344-5636
E-mail: scholarships@ascendleadership.org
Web: www.ascendleadership.org

Summary   To provide financial assistance to undergraduate and graduate minority accounting students who are members of Ascend: Pan-Asian Leaders and of the American Institute of Certified Public Accountants (AICPA).

Eligibility   This program is open to members of minority groups underrepresented in the accounting profession. Applicants must have completed at least 30 hours of college course work, including at least 6 hours in accounting, at a 4-year college or university in the United States or its territories as a full-time undergraduate or graduate student in an accounting-related field. They must be members of Ascend and AICPA, have a GPA of 3.0 or higher, and be U.S. citizens or permanent residents. Along with their application, they must submit a 500-word personal essay on how they have demonstrated leadership and teamwork in their academic studies, professional career, and/or extracurricular activities and community volunteer work; why they believe those qualities are important to transforming themselves into a better leader; their career goals after graduation; and the role Ascend has played in the achievement of their academic and career goals. They must also be able to demonstrate some financial need.

Financial data   The stipend is $5,000. The program also provides travel and lodging for the Ascend annual national convention.

Duration   1 year.

Additional information   Ascend was formed in 2004 as the National Asian American Society of Accountants. This program is sponsored by AICPA.

Number awarded   1 each year.

Deadline   May of each year.

[14]
AIKO SUSANNA TASHIRO HIRATSUKA MEMORIAL SCHOLARSHIP

Japanese American Citizens League
Attn: National Scholarship Awards
1765 Sutter Street
San Francisco, CA 94115
(415) 345-1075   Fax: (415) 931-4671
E-mail: ncwnp@jacl.org
Web: www.jacl.org/edu/scholar.htm

Summary   To provide financial assistance for undergraduate education in the performing arts to student members of the Japanese American Citizens League (JACL).

Eligibility   This program is open to JACL members who are enrolled in undergraduate study in the performing arts. Applicants should provide a recording of themselves performing, along with published critical reviews and/or evaluations by their instructor. Along with their application, they must submit information on their involvement in JACL and a 2-page essay on a topic that changes annually but relates to Japanese Americans. Selection is based on that essay, academic history, JACL involvement, school activities, work history, scholastic honors, and community involvement. Professional artists are not eligible.

Financial data   Stipends generally average more than $2,000.

Duration   1 year; nonrenewable.

Number awarded   1 each year.

Deadline   March of each year.

[15]
ALAN COMPTON AND BOB STANLEY MINORITY AND INTERNATIONAL SCHOLARSHIP

Baptist Communicators Association
Attn: Scholarship Committee
1519 Menlo Drive
Kennesaw, GA 30152
(770) 425-3728   E-mail: mmdempsey@bellsouth.net
Web: www.baptistcommunicators.org/about/scholarship.cfm

Summary   To provide financial assistance to Asian American, other minority, and international students who are working on an undergraduate degree to prepare for a career in Baptist communications.

Eligibility   This program is open to undergraduate students of minority or international origin. Applicants must be majoring in communications, English, journalism, or public relations and have a GPA of 2.5 or higher. Their vocational objective must be in Baptist communications. Along with their application, they must submit a statement explaining why they want to receive this scholarship.

Financial data   The stipend is $1,000.

Duration   1 year; recipients may reapply.

Additional information   This program began in 1996.

Number awarded   1 each year.

Deadline   March of each year.

[16]
ALICE YURIKO ENDO MEMORIAL SCHOLARSHIP

Japanese American Citizens League
Attn: National Scholarship Awards
1765 Sutter Street
San Francisco, CA 94115
(415) 345-1075   Fax: (415) 931-4671
E-mail: ncwnp@jacl.org
Web: www.jacl.org/edu/scholar.htm

Summary   To provide financial assistance to student members of the Japanese American Citizens League (JACL) who are working on an undergraduate degree, particularly in public or social service.

Eligibility   This program is open to JACL members who are currently enrolled at a college, university, trade school, business college, or other institution of higher learning. Applicants must submit information on their involvement in JACL and a 2-page essay on a topic that changes annually but relates to Japanese Americans. Selection is based on that essay, academic history, JACL involvement, school activities, work history, scholastic honors, and community involvement. Preference is given to students with an interest in public or social service and/or residing in the Eastern District Council area.

Financial data   Stipends generally average more than $2,000.

Duration   1 year; nonrenewable.

Number awarded   1 each year.

Deadline   March of each year.

[17]
ALMA EXLEY SCHOLARSHIP

Community Foundation of Greater New Britain
Attn: Scholarship Manager
74A Vine Street
New Britain, CT 06052-1431
(860) 229-6018, ext. 305   Fax: (860) 225-2666
E-mail: cfarmer@cfgnb.org
Web: www.cfgnb.org

Summary   To provide financial assistance to Asian American and other minority college students in Connecticut who are interested in preparing for a teaching career.

Eligibility   This program is open to students of color (African Americans, Asian Americans, Hispanic Americans, and Native Americans) enrolled in a teacher preparation program in Connecticut. Applicant must 1) have been admitted to a traditional teacher preparation program at an accredited 4-year college or university in the state; or 2) be participating in the Alternate Route to Certification (ARC) program sponsored by the Connecticut Department of Higher Education.

Financial data   The stipend is $1,500 per year for students at a 4-year college or university or $500 for a student in the ARC program.

Duration   2 years for students at 4-year colleges or universities; 1 year for students in the ARC program.

Number awarded   2 each year: 1 to a 4-year student and 1 to an ARC student.

Deadline   October of each year.

[18]
ALTRIA SCHOLARS

Virginia Foundation for Independent Colleges
Attn: Director of Development
8010 Ridge Road, Suite B
Richmond, VA 23229-7288
(804) 288-6609   Toll Free: (800) 230-6757
Fax: (804) 282-4635   E-mail: info@vfic.org
Web: www.vfic.org/scholarships/scholarships_vfic.html

Summary   To provide financial assistance to students (especially Asian Americans and other minorities) who are majoring in designated fields at a college or university that is a member of the Virginia Foundation for Independent Colleges (VFIC).

Eligibility   This program is open to sophomores who are enrolled as full-time second-semester sophomores at 1 of the 15 VFIC member institutions. Applicants must be nominated by their institution. They must have a GPA of 3.0 or higher and a declared major in accounting, biology, business management, business, chemistry, computer science, economics, engineering, finance, marketing, or physics. Selection is based on merit and financial need. Special consideration is given to underserved populations. U.S. citizenship is required.

Financial data   The stipend is $5,000 per year.

Duration   1 year (the junior year). May be renewed for the senior year, provided the recipient maintains a GPA of 3.0 or higher and a record of good citizenship and conduct.

Additional information   Funding for this program, established in 2001, is provided by Altria Group (parent company of Philip Morris USA). Recipients also have an opportunity to apply for paid internships with Altria. The 15 member institutions are Bridgewater College, Emory and Henry College, Hampden-Sydney College, Hollins University, Lynchburg College, Mary Baldwin College, Marymount University, Randolph College, Randolph-Macon College, Roanoke College, Shenandoah University, Sweet Briar College, University of Richmond, Virginia Wesleyan College, and Washington and Lee University.

Number awarded   10 each year.

Deadline   October of each year.

[19]
ALVAN T.–VIOLA D. FULLER JUNIOR RESEARCH FELLOWSHIP

American Cancer Society-New England Division
30 Speen Street
Framingham, MA 01701
(508) 270-3109   Toll Free: (800) 952-7664, ext. 3109
Fax: (508) 270-4607   E-mail: koconnor@cancer.org
Web: www.cancer.org

Summary   To provide funding for cancer research during the summer to undergraduate students (particularly Asian American and other minority students) in New England.

Eligibility   This program is open to residents of New England currently enrolled as juniors or seniors at a college or university in any state. Applicants must be interested in working on a summer research project at a teaching hospital, university, or medical school in New England. They must be interested in working under the supervision of an accomplished cancer investigator. Preference is given to student with advanced science course work, laboratory skills, and an interest in research. Minority students and those with American Cancer Society volunteer experience are especially encouraged to apply.

Financial data The grant is $4,500.

Duration 10 weeks during the summer.

Number awarded 1 or more each year.

Deadline January of each year.

[20]
AMBASSADOR MINERVA JEAN FALCON HAWAI'I SCHOLARSHIP

Hawai'i Community Foundation
Attn: Scholarship Department
827 Fort Street Mall
Honolulu, HI 96813
(808) 566-5570   Toll Free: (888) 731-3863
Fax: (808) 521-6286
E-mail: scholarships@hcf-hawaii.org
Web: www.hawaiicommunityfoundation.org/scholarships

Summary To provide financial assistance to Hawaii residents of Filipino ancestry who are interested in attending college in the state.

Eligibility This program is open to Hawaii residents of Filipino ancestry who are enrolled in or planning to enroll in an accredited college or university in Hawaii. Applicants must be full-time students at the undergraduate level and able to demonstrate academic achievement (GPA of 2.7 or higher), good moral character, and financial need. Along with their application, they must submit a short statement indicating their reasons for attending college, their planned course of study, their career goals, and what community service means to them. They must also submit a 2-page essay on how they plan to be involved in the community as a Filipino American student.

Financial data The amounts of the awards depend on the availability of funds and the need of the recipient. Recently, the average value of each of the scholarships awarded by the foundation was $2,200.

Duration 1 year.

Additional information This scholarship was first offered in 2001.

Number awarded Varies each year.

Deadline February of each year.

[21]
AMELIA KEMP MEMORIAL SCHOLARSHIP

Women of the Evangelical Lutheran Church in America
Attn: Scholarships
8765 West Higgins Road
Chicago, IL 60631-4101
(773) 380-2741   Toll Free: (800) 638-3522, ext. 2741
Fax: (773) 380-2419   E-mail: valora.starr@elca.org
Web: www.womenoftheelca.org

Summary To provide financial assistance to Asian American and other lay women of color who are members of Evangelical Lutheran Church of America (ELCA) congregations and wish to study on the undergraduate, graduate, professional, or vocational school level.

Eligibility This program is open to ELCA lay women of color who are at least 21 years of age and have experienced an interruption of at least 2 years in their education since high

school. Applicants must have been admitted to an educational institution to prepare for a career in other than ordained ministry. U.S. citizenship is required.

Financial data The maximum stipend is $1,000.

Duration Up to 2 years.

Number awarded 1 or more each year.

Deadline February of each year.

[22]
AMERICAN ASSOCIATION OF UNIVERSITY WOMEN CAREER DEVELOPMENT GRANTS

American Association of University Women
Attn: AAUW Educational Foundation
301 ACT Drive, Department 60
P.O. Box 4030
Iowa City, IA 52243-4030
(319) 337-1716, ext. 60   Fax: (319) 337-1204
E-mail: aauw@act.org
Web: www.aauw.org

Summary To provide financial assistance to Asian American and other women who are seeking career advancement, career change, or reentry into the workforce.

Eligibility This program is open to women who are U.S. citizens or permanent residents, have earned a bachelor's degree, received their most recent degree more than 4 years ago, and are making career changes, seeking to advance in current careers, or reentering the workforce. Applicants must be interested in working toward a master's degree, second bachelor's or associate degree, professional degree (e.g., M.D., J.D.), certification program, or technical school certificate. They must be planning to undertake course work at an accredited 2- or 4-year college or university (or a technical school that is licensed, accredited, or approved by the U.S. Department of Education). Primary consideration is given to women of color and women pursuing their first advanced degree or credentials in nontraditional fields. Support is not provided for prerequisite course work or for Ph.D. course work or dissertations. Selection is based on demonstrated commitment to education and equity for women and girls, reason for seeking higher education or technical training, degree to which study plan is consistent with career objectives, potential for success in chosen field, documentation of opportunities in chosen field, feasibility of study plans and proposed time schedule, validity of proposed budget and budget narrative (including sufficient outside support), and quality of written proposal.

Financial data Grants range from $2,000 to $12,000. Funds may be used for tuition, fees, books, supplies, local transportation, dependent child care, or purchase of a computer required for the study program.

Duration 1 year, beginning in July; nonrenewable.

Additional information The filing fee is $35.

Number awarded Varies each year; recently, 63 of these grants, with a value of $670,000, were awarded.

Deadline December of each year.

[23]
AMERICAN HEALTH INFORMATION MANAGEMENT ASSOCIATION FOUNDATION DIVERSITY SCHOLARSHIPS

American Health Information Management Association
Attn: AHIMA Foundation
233 North Michigan Avenue, 21st Floor
Chicago, IL 60601-5809
(312) 233-1175   Fax: (312) 233-1475
E-mail: info@ahimafoundation.org
Web: www.ahimafoundation.org

Summary To provide financial assistance to Asian American and other members of the American Health Information Management Association (AHIMA) who are interested in working on an undergraduate or graduate degree in health information management (HIM) or health information technology (HIT) and who will contribute to diversity in the profession.

Eligibility This program is open to AHIMA members who are enrolled at least half time in a program accredited by the Commission on Accreditation for Health Informatics and Information Management Education (CAHIM). Applicants must be working on a degree in HIM or HIT at the associate, bachelor's, post-baccalaureate, master's, or doctoral level. They must have a GPA of 3.5 or higher and at least 1 full semester remaining after the date of the award. To qualify for this support, applicants must demonstrate how they will contribute to diversity in the health information management profession; diversity is defined as differences in race, ethnicity, nationality, gender, sexual orientation, socioeconomic status, age, physical capabilities, and religious beliefs. Selection is based on GPA and academic achievement, volunteer and work experience, commitment to the HIM profession, quality and relevance of references, and completeness and clarity of thought.

Financial data Stipends are $1,000 for associate degree students, $1,500 for bachelor's degree or post-baccalaureate certificate students, $2,000 for master's degree students, or $2,500 for doctoral degree students.

Duration 1 year.

Number awarded Varies each year; recently, 9 of these scholarships were awarded: 6 to undergraduates and 3 to graduate students.

Deadline September of each year.

[24]
AMERICAN SOCIETY OF ENGINEERS OF INDIAN ORIGIN UNDERGRADUATE SCHOLARSHIPS

American Society of Engineers of Indian Origin
Attn: Southern California Chapter
P.O. Box 18215
Irvine, CA 92623
E-mail: scholarships@aseisocal.net
Web: www.aseisocal.net/12.html

Summary To provide financial assistance to undergraduate students of Indian origin (from India) who are majoring in engineering, computer sciences, or related areas.

Eligibility This program is open to undergraduate students of Indian origin (by birth, ancestry, or relation). They must be enrolled full time at an ABET-accredited college or university in the United States and majoring in engineering, computer

science, or allied science and have a GPA of 3.2 or higher. They must be members of the American Society of Engineers of Indian Origin (ASEI). Selection is based on demonstrated ability, academic achievement (including GPA, honors, and awards), career objectives, faculty recommendations, involvement in science fair and campus activities, financial hardship, industrial exposure (including part-time work and internships), and involvement in ASEI and other community activities.

Financial data Stipends range from $500 to $1,000.

Duration 1 year.

Number awarded Several each year.

Deadline August of each year.

[25]
AMERICAN SOCIETY OF INDIAN ENGINEERS SCHOLARSHIP PROGRAM

American Society of Indian Engineers
Attn: Scholarship Program
P.O. Box 741007
Houston, TX 77274
E-mail: asiehouston@gmail.com
Web: www.asiehouston.org/joboppurtunities.php?id=13

Summary To provide financial assistance to residents of any state who are of Indian origin (from Indian) and are working on an undergraduate or graduate degree in engineering or architecture at a college in the Houston area of Texas.

Eligibility This program is open to residents of any state who are of Indian origin and currently enrolled at a college or university in the greater Houston metropolitan area. Applicants must be working full time on an associate, bachelor's, or graduate degree in engineering or architecture. Along with their application, they must submit an essay about themselves, their achievements, career goals, and activities. Selection is based on that essay (50%), GPA (25%), and financial need (25%). An interview may also be required.

Financial data The stipend is $1,000.

Duration 1 year.

Number awarded Up to 10 each year.

Deadline September of each year.

[26]
ANA MULTICULTURAL EXCELLENCE SCHOLARSHIP

American Association of Advertising Agencies
Attn: AAAA Foundation
1065 Avenue of the Americas, 16th Floor
New York, NY 10018
(212) 262-2500   E-mail: ameadows@aaaa.org
Web: www.aaaa.org

Summary To provide financial assistance to Asian American and other multicultural students who are working on an undergraduate degree in advertising.

Eligibility This program is open to undergraduate students who are U.S. citizens of proven multicultural heritage and have at least 1 grandparent of multicultural heritage. Applicants must be participating in the Multicultural Advertising Intern Program (MAIP). They must be entering their senior year at an accredited college or university in the United States and have a GPA of 3.0 or higher. Selection is based on academic ability.

Financial data The stipend is $2,500.

Duration 1 year.

Additional information This program was established by the Association of National Advertisers (ANA) in 2001. The American Association of Advertising Agencies (AAAA) assumed administration in 2003.

Number awarded 2 each year.

Deadline Deadline not specified.

[27]
ANS/ACCELERATOR APPLICATIONS DIVISION SCHOLARSHIP

American Nuclear Society
Attn: Scholarship Coordinator
555 North Kensington Avenue
La Grange Park, IL 60526-5535
(708) 352-6611   Toll Free: (800) 323-3044
Fax: (708) 352-0499   E-mail: outreach@ans.org
Web: www.new.ans.org/honors/scholarships

Summary To provide financial assistance to undergraduate students (particularly Asian Americans or other minorities and women) who are interested in preparing for a career dealing with accelerator applications aspects of nuclear science or nuclear engineering.

Eligibility This program is open to students entering their junior year in physics, engineering, or materials science at an accredited institution in the United States. Applicants must submit a description of their long- and short-term professional objectives, including their research interests related to accelerator aspects of nuclear science and engineering. Selection is based on that statement, faculty recommendations, and academic performance. Special consideration is given to members of underrepresented groups (women and minorities), students who can demonstrate financial need, and applicants who have a record of service to the American Nuclear Society (ANS).

Financial data The stipend is $1,000 per year.

Duration 1 year (the junior year); may be renewed for the senior year.

Additional information This program is offered by the Accelerator Applications Division (AAD) of the ANS.

Number awarded 1 each year.

Deadline January of each year.

[28]
APCA SCHOLARSHIPS

Asian Pacific Islanders for Professional and Community
  Advancement
c/o Yakun Gao, Scholarship Committee
P.O. Box 2694
San Ramon, CA 94583
(425) 633-4935   E-mail: scholarship@apca-att.org
Web: www.apca-att.org/scholarship.html

Summary To provide financial assistance to Asian Pacific Islanders and other high school seniors from selected states who are interested in attending college in any state.

Eligibility This program offers national scholarships to seniors graduating from high schools in Arizona, California, Colorado, Georgia, Illinois, Michigan, Missouri, New Jersey, Texas, Washington, Wisconsin, and the Washington, D.C. metropolitan area (including Maryland and Virginia). Appli-

cants must be planning to continue their education at an accredited 2- or 4-year college or university or vocational school in any state. They must have a GPA of 3.4 or higher. Along with their application, they must submit a 750-word essay on making a difference in their community. Financial need is not considered in the selection process. Students of all ethnic backgrounds are eligible, but a goal of the sponsoring organization is to promote growth and influence on issues that impact Asian Pacific Islanders. Students who are not awarded a national scholarship are eligible for the National Community Service Award Scholarship or (if they are residents of California, Georgia, or New Jersey) state scholarships. U.S. citizenship or permanent resident status is required.

Financial data National scholarships are $2,000; the National Community Service Award Scholarship and state scholarships are $1,000.

Duration 1 year; nonrenewable.

Additional information This program was established by an organization named the Asian/Pacific American Association for Advancement at AT&T, which offered the 4A-AT&T National Scholarship Program. In 2006, that organization merged with Asians for Corporate and Community Action to form Asian Pacific Islanders for Professional and Community Advancement (APCA). Both the former and current organizations are comprised of Asian Pacific American employees of AT&T, Inc.

Number awarded Varies each year; recently, 19 national scholarships, 1 National Community Service Award Scholarship, and 34 state scholarships (6 in California, 24 in Georgia, and 4 in New Jersey) were awarded.

Deadline February of each year.

[29]
AP-GOOGLE JOURNALISM AND TECHNOLOGY SCHOLARSHIP PROGRAM

Online News Association
Attn: Scholarship Manager
P.O. Box 65741
Washington, DC 20035
(646) 290-7900   E-mail: irving@journalists.org
Web: journalists.org/next-gen/ap-google-scholarship

Summary To recognize and reward undergraduate and graduate students (especially Asian Americans and those from other diverse backgrounds) who propose outstanding projects "at the intersection of journalism and technology."

Eligibility This program is open to full-time undergraduates (at least sophomores) and graduate students at U.S. institutions who have at least 1 year of study remaining and a GPA of 3.0 or higher. Students from diverse backgrounds (defined as ethnic and racial minorities, members of the lesbian, gay, bisexual, and transgender (LGBT) community, and students with disabilities) and those attending rural area institutions are strongly encouraged to apply. Some scholarships are reserved for students who can demonstrate financial need. Applicants must develop original journalistic content with computer science elements; they should explain how their strategy moves digital journalism forward or provides valuable lessons or outcomes. Examples include data visualization, data mining, mobile devices and applications, 3-D storytelling, digital ethics, or microcomputers. In the selection process, emphasis is placed on innovation and creativity. U.S. citizenship is required.

Financial data The award is a $20,000 scholarship, of which half is paid to the winner's institution at the beginning of the first semester and half at the beginning of the second semester, provided the recipient earns a GPA of 3.0 or higher for the first semester.

Duration The competition is held annually.

Additional information This competition is supported by Google.

Number awarded 6 each year.

Deadline February of each year.

[30]
APIO SCHOLARSHIP PROGRAM

Asian Pacific Islander Organization
c/o Gina Schworm, Scholarship Committee Co-Chair
USDA Natural Resources Conservation Service
Coshocton County Service Center
724 South Seventh Street, Room 120
Coshocton, OH 43812-2391
(740) 622-8087   E-mail: gina.schworm@oh.usda.gov
Web: www.apio.org/scholarship.htm

Summary To provide financial assistance to Asian and Pacific Islanders who are studying designated fields in college or graduate school.

Eligibility This program is open to Asian and Pacific Islander students who have completed at least 15 semester hours of credit at an accredited 2- or 4-year college or university. Applicants must be working on an undergraduate or graduate degree in a field related to natural resources (e.g., agricultural business, agronomy, biology, botany, environmental science, forestry, geology, horticulture, plant science, rangeland management, soil science, or agricultural, civil, or environmental engineering). Along with their application, they must submit a 1-page personal statement on their background, personal and career goals, and extracurricular activities. Selection is based on academic achievement, personal strengths, leadership abilities, career goals, and work experience. U.S. citizenship is required.

Financial data The stipend is $1,000, $1,500, or $2,000.

Duration 1 year.

Additional information The Asian Pacific Islander Organization (APIO) was established in 1998 as a professional society of employees of the Natural Resources Conservation Service of the U.S. Department of Agriculture.

Number awarded 3 each year: 1 each at $1,000, $1,500, and $2,000.

Deadline April of each year.

[31]
APPLE PROGRAM

American Psychological Association
Attn: Division 41 (American Psychology-Law Society)
c/o Jennifer Hunt, Minority Affairs Committee Chair
Buffalo State University of New York, Psychology
  Department
Classroom Building C308
1300 Elmwood Avenue
Buffalo, NY 14222
(716) 878-3421   E-mail: huntjs@buffalostate.edu
Web: www.ap-ls.org/grantsfunding/APPLEprogram.php?t=4

Summary To provide an opportunity for undergraduate students (particularly Asian Americans and members of other underrepresented groups) to gain research and other experience to prepare them for future graduate work in psychology and law.

Eligibility This program is open to undergraduate students who are members of underrepresented groups, including, but are not limited to, racial and ethnic minorities; first-generation college students; lesbian, gay, bisexual, and transgender students; and physically disabled students. Applicants must be interested in participating in a program in which they work on research for approximately 10 hours per week; participate in GRE classes and/or other development opportunities; attend a conference of the American Psychology-Law Society (AP-LS); submit a proposal to present their research at an AP-LS conference or in the Division 41 program of an American Psychological Association (APA) conference; submit a summary of their research experience to the AP-LS Minority Affairs Committee chair within 1 month of its completion; and correspond with a secondary mentor from the Minority Affairs Committee to participate in the ongoing assessment of this program. Selection is based on the quality of the proposed research and mentoring experience and the potential for the student to become a successful graduate student.

Financial data Grants range up to $3,000, including a stipend of $1,200 per semester or $800 per quarter or summer, $100 for research expenses, and up to $500 to attend the AP-LS conference.

Duration Up to 1 year.

Number awarded 5 each year.

Deadline November of each year.

[32]
APPRAISAL INSTITUTE MINORITIES AND WOMEN EDUCATIONAL SCHOLARSHIP PROGRAM

Appraisal Institute
Attn: Appraisal Institute Education Trust
200 West Madison Street, Suite 1500
Chicago, IL 60606
(312) 335-4133   Fax: (312) 335-4134
E-mail: educationtrust@appraisalinstitute.org
Web: www.appraisalinstitute.org

Summary To provide financial assistance to Asian American, other minority, and women undergraduate students majoring in real estate or allied fields.

Eligibility This program is open to members of groups underrepresented in the real estate appraisal profession. Those groups include women, American Indians, Alaska Natives, Asians and Pacific Islanders, Blacks or African

Americans, and Hispanics. Applicants must be full- or part-time students enrolled in real estate courses within a degree-granting college, university, or junior college. They must have a GPA of 2.5 or higher and be able to demonstrate financial need. U.S. citizenship is required.

Financial data The stipend is $1,000. Funds are paid directly to the recipient's institution to be used for tuition and fees.

Duration 1 year.

Number awarded At least 1 each year.

Deadline April of each year.

[33]
ARIZONA CHAPTER JAPANESE AMERICAN CITIZENS LEAGUE SCHOLARSHIPS

Japanese American Citizens League-Arizona Chapter
5414 West Glenn Drive
Glendale, AZ 85301-2628
E-mail: arizonajacl@gmail.com
Web: www.jaclaz.org/services.html

Summary To provide financial assistance to graduating high school seniors in Arizona who are of Japanese heritage.

Eligibility This program is open to graduating high school seniors in Arizona who have a GPA of 3.0 or higher. Applicants or their parents must have been members of 1 of the following organizations for at least the preceding 3 years: Arizona Chapter of the Japanese American Citizens League (JACLA), the Phoenix Japanese Free Methodist Church, the Arizona Buddhist Church, a youth group of JACLA, a youth group of the Phoenix Free Methodist Church, or a youth group of the Arizona Buddhist Church. Financial need is not considered in the selection process.

Financial data The stipend is $1,000.

Duration 1 year.

Additional information This program includes the Sara Hutchings Clardy Scholarship Awards, the Joe Allman Scholarship, the Herbert Jensen Scholarship, the Tatsuko and Hiroshi (Nick) Nakagawa Scholarship, and the Betty and George Kishiyama Scholarship.

Number awarded 7 each year.

Deadline February of each year.

[34]
ARSENIO AND CO BIT SIY SCHOLARSHIP

Organization of Chinese Americans-Wisconsin Chapter
c/o Vera Lau, Scholarship Committee
120 North 73rd Street
Milwaukee, WI 53213
E-mail: ocawischolarship@yahoo.com
Web: www.ocawi.org/www/scholarships.html

Summary To provide financial assistance to high school seniors who are children of members or business affiliates of the Wisconsin Chapter of the Organization of Chinese Americans (OCA-WI) and interested in attending college in any state.

Eligibility This program is open to graduating high school seniors whose parent has been an OCA-WI member or business affiliate for at least 2 years and who are planning to enroll full time at an accredited college or university in any state. Applicants must have a GPA of 3.0 or higher or rank in the top 20% of their class. Along with their application, they

must submit a personal statement that includes information on their future college and career plans; a list of scholastic awards, honors, extracurricular activities, and honor societies and offices; and a description of their volunteer service to OCA-WI and their community. Financial need is not considered in the selection process.

Financial data A stipend is awarded (amount not specified).

Duration 1 year.

Additional information This program began in 1993.

Number awarded 1 each year.

Deadline March of each year.

[35]
ARTHUR H. GOODMAN MEMORIAL SCHOLARSHIPS

CDC Small Business Finance
Attn: Scholarship Program
2448 Historic Decatur Road, Suite 200
San Diego, CA 92106
(619) 291-3594   Toll Free: (800) 611-5170
Fax: (619) 291-6954
Web: cdcloans.com

Summary To provide financial assistance to Asian Americans, other minorities, and women who are transitioning from a community college in California or Arizona to a 4-year university in those states and interested in preparing for a career related to community development.

Eligibility This program is open to minorities and women who are residents of or attending school in California. Applicants must have completed 2 years of community college study with a GPA of 3.0 or higher and be ready to transfer to a 4-year college or university. They must be interested in preparing for a career in business, government, nonprofit, public service, or other profession that will improve their community. Along with their application, they must submit a 3-page personal statement on their community involvement and volunteerism, why they volunteer, how it has influenced them personally and their career goals, how their volunteerism has impacted individuals or the community, an individual or event that has influenced their decision to attend college and/or select their desired career, their future goals and how they include community involvement, and why they feel they are a strong candidate for this scholarship. Financial need is considered in the selection process.

Financial data Stipends range from $1,500 to $3,000.

Duration 1 year.

Additional information This program began in 1998 with a fund administered through the San Diego Foundation.

Number awarded Approximately 4 each year.

Deadline May of each year.

[36]
ASCPA EDUCATIONAL FOUNDATION DIVERSITY SCHOLARSHIPS

Alabama Society of Certified Public Accountants
Attn: ASCPA Educational Foundation
1103 South Perry Street
P.O. Box 5000
Montgomery, AL 36103
(334) 834-7650   Toll Free: (800) 227-1711
Web: www.ascpa.org

Summary   To provide financial assistance to Asian American and other minority accounting students at colleges and universities in Alabama.

Eligibility   This program is open to minority (Black or African American, Hispanic or Latino, Native American, or Asian) residents of any state enrolled at least half time at colleges and universities in Alabama with at least 1 full year of school remaining. Applicants must have declared a major in accounting and have completed intermediate accounting courses. They must have a GPA of 3.0 or higher overall and in all accounting classes. Along with their application, they must submit a 25-word essay on why the scholarship is important to them. Financial need is not considered in the selection process. Preference is given to students who have a strong interest in a career as a C.P.A. in Alabama. U.S. citizenship or permanent resident status is required.

Financial data   The stipend is $2,500.

Duration   1 year.

Additional information   This program began in 2012.

Number awarded   4 each year.

Deadline   March of each year.

[37]
ASIAN AMERICAN ARCHITECTS AND ENGINEERS FOUNDATION SCHOLARSHIPS

Asian American Architects/Engineers Association
Attn: Foundation
645 West Ninth Street, Unit 110-175
Los Angeles, CA 90015
(213) 896-9270   Fax: (213) 985-7404
E-mail: info@aaaesc.org
Web: www.aaaesc.org/student-scholarship-application

Summary   To provide financial assistance to members of the Asian American Architects/Engineers Association (AAa/e) who are interested in working on an undergraduate or graduate degree at a school in southern California.

Eligibility   This program is open to student members of AAa/e who are U.S. citizens, permanent residents, or noncitizens enrolled full time at a college or university in southern California. Applicants must be graduating seniors, undergraduates, or graduate students working on or planning to work on a degree in architecture, civil engineering (environmental, geotechnical, structural, transportation), electrical engineering, mechanical engineering, landscape architecture, planning and urban design, or construction and construction management. Along with their application, they must submit 1) a 1-page personal statement on their involvement and service to the Asian Pacific Islander community; 2) letters of recommendation from 2 faculty members or employers; and 3) a sample of their work, which may be a design or research project, a completed project, or a proposed project, including an assignment from a class, a senior project, or an assignment from work. Selection is based on the work sample (65%), personal statements (20%), and recommendations (15%).

Financial data   Stipends range up to $5,000.

Duration   1 year.

Number awarded   Varies each year.

Deadline   May of each year.

[38]
ASIAN AMERICAN COMMUNITY COLLEGE SCHOLARSHIP

Scholarship Administrative Services, Inc.
Attn: MEFUSA Program
457 Ives Terrace
Sunnyvale, CA 94087

Summary   To provide financial assistance to Asian American high school seniors who are interested in attending a community college.

Eligibility   This program is open to Asian American seniors graduating from high schools anywhere in the United States. Applicants must be planning to attend a community college on a full-time basis. Along with their application, they must submit a 1,000-word essay on their educational and career goals, how a community college education will help them to achieve those goals, and how they plan to serve the Asian American community after completing their education. Selection is based on the essay, high school GPA (2.5 or higher), SAT or ACT scores, involvement in the Asian American community, and financial need.

Financial data   The stipend is $5,000 per year.

Duration   1 year; may be renewed 1 additional year if the recipient maintains full-time enrollment and a GPA of 2.5 or higher.

Additional information   This program is sponsored by the Minority Educational Foundation of the United States of America (MEFUSA) and administered by Scholarship Administrative Services, Inc. MEFUSA was established in 2001 to meet the needs of minority students who "show a determination to get a college degree," but who, for financial or other personal reasons, are not able to attend a 4-year college or university. Requests for applications should be accompanied by a self-addressed stamped envelope, the student's e-mail address, and the name of the source where they found the scholarship information.

Number awarded   Up to 100 each year.

Deadline   April of each year.

[39]
ASIAN AMERICAN ESSAY SCHOLARSHIP PROGRAM

Organization of Chinese Americans-New Jersey Chapter
22 West Grand Avenue
P.O. Box 268
Montvale, NJ 07645-0268
(973) 873-8315   E-mail: oca.njedcom@gmail.com
Web: www.oca-nj.com

Summary   To recognize and reward, with college scholarships, high school seniors in New Jersey who are of Asian American descent and submit outstanding essays on what it means to be Asian American.

Eligibility This competition is open to seniors graduating from high schools in New Jersey who are of Asian American descent. Applicants must be planning to attend a college or university in any state. They must submit a 2-page essay on a topic that changes annually but relates to being an Asian American. They must also provide personal information and a list of extracurricular activities. Selection is based on the essay's theme and content (50%), organization and development (15%), grammar and mechanics (15%), and style (10%); and community service and extracurricular activities (10%).

Financial data Awards range from $300 to $1,500.

Duration The competition is held annually.

Additional information Recipients must attend the sponsor's Asian American Heritage Month luncheon in May to accept the award.

Number awarded Approximately 15 each year.

Deadline April of each year.

[40]
ASIAN AMERICAN GOVERNMENT EXECUTIVES NETWORK SCHOLARSHIP

Asian American Government Executives Network
1001 Connecticut Avenue, N.W., Suite 320
Washington, DC 20036
(202) 558-7499   Fax: (202) 296-9236
E-mail: programs@aagen.org
Web: www.aagen.org/ScholarshipProg

Summary To provide financial assistance to Asian American and Pacific Islander high school seniors and undergraduate students who are preparing for a career in government service.

Eligibility This program is open to high school seniors and current undergraduates who support the sponsor's principles of helping to promote, expand, and support Asian American and Pacific Islander leadership in government. Applicants must submit transcripts and information about courses they plan to take and how those will improve their ability to serve at the local, state, and/or federal level. Selection is based on the relationship of their courses or field of study to service at the local, state, and/or federal government levels; academic achievement and excellence (based on SAT or ACT scores and a GPA of 3.3 or higher); school, employment, or extracurricular activities that demonstrate a seriousness of purpose in serving at leadership principles in government; letters of nomination and recommendation; and essays on their interest in public service.

Financial data Stipends are $1,500 or $1,000.

Duration 1 year; nonrenewable.

Number awarded 4 each year: 2 at $1,500 and 2 at $1,000.

Deadline March of each year.

[41]
ASIAN PACIFIC COMMUNITY FUND-VERIZON SCHOLARSHIP AWARDS PROGRAM

Asian Pacific Community Fund
1145 Wilshire Boulevard, First Floor
Los Angeles, CA 90017
(213) 624-6400, ext. 6   Fax: (213) 624-6406
E-mail: scholarships@apcf.org
Web: www.apcf.org/what-we-do/scholarship-fund

Summary To provide financial assistance to Asian and Pacific Islander high school seniors who are residents of or planning to attend college in California, Oregon, or Washington and are interested in majoring in a field of mathematics, engineering, or science.

Eligibility This program is open to high school seniors who are 1) residents of California, Oregon, or Washington and planning to enroll full time at a 4-year college or university in any state; and 2) residents of any state planning to enroll full time at a 4-year college or university in California, Oregon, or Washington. Applicants must have a GPA of 3.0 or higher and be planning to major in a field of mathematics, engineering, or science. They must be able to fulfill the sponsor's goals of meeting the diverse needs of Asian Pacific Islanders.

Financial data The stipend is $1,000.

Duration 1 year.

Additional information This program is sponsored by Verizon.

Number awarded 10 each year.

Deadline January of each year.

[42]
ASIAN PACIFIC ISLANDER AMERICAN PUBLIC AFFAIRS ASSOCIATION COLLEGE SCHOLARSHIPS

Asian Pacific Islander American Public Affairs Association
Attn: Community Education Foundation
4000 Truxel Road, Suite 3
Sacramento, CA 95834
(916) 928-9988   Fax: (916) 928-9983
E-mail: info@apapa.org
Web: www.apapa.org/news/scholarship.aspx

Summary To provide financial assistance to residents of California, especially those of Asian or Pacific Islander ancestry, who are attending college or graduate school in any state.

Eligibility This program is open to residents of California who are currently enrolled as an undergraduate or graduate student at an accredited 2- or 4-year college or university in any state. All students are eligible, but applications are especially encouraged from those who have Asian or Pacific Islander ancestry. They must have a GPA of 2.75 or higher. Along with their application, they must submit a personal statement demonstrating their commitment to the Asian Pacific Islander community. Selection is based on academic achievement, abilities, career goals, civic activities, leadership skills, and demonstrated commitment to the Asian Pacific Islander community. U.S. citizenship or permanent resident status is required.

Financial data The stipend is $1,000. Funds are paid directly to the student's institution.

Duration 1 year; nonrenewable.

Number awarded Varies each year; recently, 14 of these scholarships were awarded.

Deadline February of each year.

[43]
ASIAN REPORTER FOUNDATION SCHOLARSHIPS

Asian Reporter
Attn: AR Foundation
922 North Killingsworth Street, Suite 1A
Portland, OR 97217-2220
(503) 283-0595   Fax: (503) 283-4445
E-mail: arfoundation@asianreporter.com
Web: www.arfoundation.net

Summary To provide financial assistance for college to residents of Oregon and also Clark County, Washington who are of Asian descent.

Eligibility This program is open to 2 categories of students: 1) Oregon residents attending Oregon schools of higher education; and 2) residents of Oregon or Clark County, Washington attending schools of higher education in Oregon or Washington. Applicants must be of Asian descent, have a GPA of 3.25 or higher, be a graduating high school senior or current college student working on or planning to work on an undergraduate degree as a full-time student, have a record of involvement in community- or school-related activities, and be able to demonstrate financial need.

Financial data The stipend is $1,000.

Duration 1 year; nonrenewable.

Number awarded Varies each year; recently, 12 of these scholarships were awarded.

Deadline March of each year.

[44]
ASIAN STUDENTS INCREASING ACHIEVEMENT (ASIA) SCHOLARSHIP PROGRAM

Ronald McDonald House Charities
Attn: U.S. Scholarship Program
One Kroc Drive
Oak Brook, IL 60523
(630) 623-7048   Fax: (630) 623-7488
E-mail: info@rmhc.org
Web: rmhc.org/what-we-do/rmhc-u-s-scholarships

Summary To provide financial assistance for college to Asian Pacific high school seniors in specified geographic areas.

Eligibility This program is open to high school seniors in designated McDonald's market areas who are legal residents of the United States and have at least 1 parent of Asian Pacific heritage. Applicants must be planning to enroll full time at an accredited 2- or 4-year college, university, or vocational/technical school. They must have a GPA of 2.7 or higher. Along with their application, they must submit a personal statement, up to 2 pages in length, on their Asian Pacific background, career goals, and desire to contribute to their community; information about unique, personal, or financial circumstances may be added. Selection is based on that statement, high school transcripts, a letter of recommendation, and financial need.

Financial data Most awards are $1,000 per year. Funds are paid directly to the recipient's school.

Duration 1 year; nonrenewable.

Additional information This program is a component of the Ronald McDonald House Charities U.S. Scholarship Program, which began in 1985. It is administered by International Scholarship and Tuition Services, Inc. For a list of participating McDonald's market areas, contact Ronald McDonald House Charities (RMHC).

Number awarded Varies each year; since RMHC began this program, it has awarded more than $44 million in scholarships.

Deadline January of each year.

[45]
ASIAN WOMEN IN BUSINESS SCHOLARSHIP FUND

Asian Women in Business
42 Broadway, Suite 1748
New York, NY 10004
(212) 868-1368   Fax: (877) 686-6870
E-mail: info@awib.org
Web: www.awib.org

Summary To provide financial assistance for college to Asian women who have demonstrated community leadership or entrepreneurial achievement.

Eligibility This program is open to women who are of at least 50% Asian or Pacific Island ancestry and are U.S. citizens or permanent residents. Applicants must be enrolled full time at an accredited 4-year undergraduate institution in the United States and have a GPA of 3.0 or higher. They must be able to demonstrate either 1) a leadership role in a community endeavor; or 2) a record of entrepreneurial achievement (e.g., founded their own business). Additional funding is available to applicants who can demonstrate financial need.

Financial data The stipend is $2,500. Recipients who demonstrate financial need are eligible for an additional $2,500. Funds are paid directly to the recipient.

Duration 1 year.

Additional information This program began in 2006.

Number awarded 6 each year.

Deadline September of each year.

[46]
ASSE UPS DIVERSITY SCHOLARSHIPS

American Society of Safety Engineers
Attn: ASSE Foundation
Scholarship Award Program
1800 East Oakton Street
Des Plaines, IL 60018
(847) 699-2929   Fax: (847) 768-3434
E-mail: bzylstra@asse.org
Web: www.asse.org

Summary To provide financial assistance to Asian American and other minority upper-division students working on a degree related to occupational safety.

Eligibility This program is open to students who are U.S. citizens and members of minority ethnic or racial groups. Applicants must be majoring in occupational safety, health, environment, industrial hygiene, occupational health nursing, or a closely-related field (e.g., industrial or environmental engineering). They must be full-time students who have completed at least 60 semester hours with a GPA of 3.0 or higher.

Membership in the American Society of Safety Engineers (ASSE) is not required, but preference is given to members.

Financial data   The stipend is $5,250 per year.

Duration   1 year; recipients may reapply.

Additional information   Funding for this program is provided by the UPS Foundation. Recipients may also be provided with the opportunity to attend a professional development conference related to safety.

Number awarded   3 each year.

Deadline   November of each year.

[47]
ASSOCIATED CHINESE UNIVERSITY WOMEN SCHOLARSHIPS

Associated Chinese University Women, Inc.
Attn: Dorothy Mau, Scholarship Committee Chair
P.O. Box 62264
Honolulu, HI 96822
Web: www.acuwhawaii.org/scholarship

Summary   To provide financial assistance to residents of Hawaii who are of Chinese ancestry and interested in majoring in education or Chinese studies at a college in any state.

Eligibility   This program is open to residents of Hawaii who are of Chinese ancestry or interested in Chinese culture. Applicants must be attending or planning to attend an accredited 4-year U.S. college or university as a full-time student with the objective of earning a baccalaureate degree. They must have a GPA of 3.8 or higher and be planning to major in education or Chinese studies (e.g., history, language, music, art, dance, and/or theater). Along with their application, they must submit a personal statement on why they should be awarded this scholarship, including their plans for serving their community after graduation. Selection is based on academic achievement (including GPA and SAT score), character, extracurricular activities, school and/or community service, and financial need. U.S. citizenship or permanent resident status is required.

Financial data   The stipend is $2,000 for regular scholarships or $1,000 for special scholarships.

Duration   1 year.

Additional information   Special scholarships that have been awarded include the Nancy Wong Yee Scholarship and the Chew Yee Janet Lam Scholarship.

Number awarded   Varies each year; recently, 6 of these scholarships were awarded: 5 regular scholarships and 1 special scholarship.

Deadline   March of each year.

[48]
ASSOCIATION OF ASIAN INDIAN WOMEN IN OHIO SCHOLARSHIP

Cleveland Foundation
Attn: Scholarship Processing
1422 Euclid Avenue, Suite 1300
Cleveland, OH 44115-2001
(216) 861-3810   Fax: (216) 861-1729
E-mail: Hello@clevefdn.org
Web: www.clevelandfoundation.org

Summary   To provide financial assistance to Asian Indian high school seniors in Ohio who plan to attend college in any state.

Eligibility   This program is open to graduating high school seniors in Ohio who are of Asian Indian descent. Applicants must be planning to enroll at a college or university in any state. They must have a GPA of 2.0 or higher and be able to demonstrate financial need. Along with their application, they must submit a transcript and a 150-word essay about their goals.

Financial data   The stipend is at least $500.

Duration   1 year.

Additional information   This program is sponsored by the Association of Asian Indian Women in Ohio.

Number awarded   1 or more each year.

Deadline   April of each year.

[49]
ASSOCIATION OF VIETNAMESE AMERICANS SCHOLARSHIP

Association of Vietnamese Americans, Inc.
Attn: Scholarship Committee
8121 Georgia Avenue, Suite 503
Silver Spring, MD 20910
(301) 588-6862   Fax: (301) 576-4502
E-mail: awardspicnic@mdvietmutual.org
Web: www.mdvietmutual.org

Summary   To provide financial assistance to Vietnamese American high school seniors in Maryland who are planning to attend college in any state.

Eligibility   This program is open to Vietnamese American students who are graduating from high schools in Maryland and planning to enroll at a college, university, or vocational school in any state. Applicants must submit transcripts, information on their financial situation, 2 letters of recommendation, a copy of their SAT score, and an essay of 500 to 650 words that touches on 1) how their past and present experiences have inspired them to continue in their education; 2) how their attendance in college will better their community; and 3) how this scholarship will assist them in the achievement of their goals.

Financial data   The stipend is $1,000.

Duration   1 year.

Additional information   This sponsor was established as the Maryland Vietnamese Mutual Association in 1982 and began a scholarship program in 2000.

Number awarded   1 each year.

Deadline   May of each year.

[50]
ATKINS NORTH AMERICA ACHIEVEMENT SCHOLARSHIP

Conference of Minority Transportation Officials
Attn: National Scholarship Program
1875 I Street, N.W., Suite 500
Washington, DC 20006
(703) 234-4072   Fax: (202) 318-0364
Web: www.comto.org/?page=Scholarships

Summary   To provide financial assistance to Asian American and other minority high school seniors and undergraduates interested in working on a degree in transportation or a related field.

Eligibility   This program is open to seniors graduating from high school with a GPA of 3.0 or higher and students currently enrolled as full-time undergraduates. Applicants must be studying or planning to study transportation, engineering, planning, management, or a related discipline They must be able to demonstrate leadership and active commitment to community service. Along with their application, they must submit a cover letter with a 500-word statement of career goals. Financial need is not considered in the selection process. U.S. citizenship or legal resident status is required.

Financial data The stipend is $2,000. Funds are paid directly to the recipient's college or university.

Duration 1 year.

Additional information The Conference of Minority Transportation Officials (COMTO) was established in 1971 to promote, strengthen, and expand the roles of minorities in all aspects of transportation. This program is sponsored by Atkins North America. Recipients are expected to attend the COMTO National Scholarship Luncheon.

Number awarded 1 each year.

Deadline May of each year.

[51]
ATKINS TRANSPORTATION YOU HIGH SCHOOL SCHOLARSHIP

Women's Transportation Seminar
Attn: WTS Foundation
1701 K Street, N.W., Suite 800
Washington, DC 20006
(202) 955-5085   Fax: (202) 955-5088
E-mail: wts@wtsinternational.org
Web: www.wtsinternational.org/education/scholarships

Summary To provide financial assistance to female high school seniors (particularly Asian American and other minority women) who are studying fields of science, technology, engineering, or mathematics (STEM) and planning to attend college to prepare for a career in transportation.

Eligibility This program is open to women who are high school seniors with a GPA of 3.0 or higher. Applicants must be studying STEM fields in high school and be planning to attend college to prepare for a career in transportation (e.g., civil engineering, city planning, logistics, automotive engineering, truck repair). Along with their application, they must submit a 500-word statement about their career goals after graduation and why they think they should receive the scholarship. Applications must be submitted first to a local chapter; the chapters forward selected applications for consideration on the national level. Minority women are especially encouraged to apply. Selection is based on transportation involvement and goals, job skills, academic record, and leadership potential; financial need is not considered.

Financial data The stipend is $1,000.

Duration 1 year.

Additional information Local chapters may also award additional funding to winners for their area.

Number awarded 1 each year.

Deadline Applications must be submitted by November to a local WTS chapter.

[52]
ATSUHIKO TATEUCHI MEMORIAL SCHOLARSHIP

Seattle Foundation
Attn: Scholarship Administrator
1200 Fifth Avenue, Suite 1300
Seattle, WA 98101-3151
(206) 622-2294   Fax: (206) 622-7673
E-mail: scholarships@seattlefoundation.org
Web: www.seattlefoundation.org

Summary To provide financial assistance to residents of Pacific Rim states who are of Japanese or other Asian ancestry and interested in working on an undergraduate degree at a college in any state.

Eligibility This program is open to residents of Alaska, California, Hawaii, Oregon, and Washington who are graduating high school seniors or undergraduates. Applicants must be attending or planning to attend a public or private community college, 4-year college or university, or trade/vocational school in any state. They must have a GPA of 3.0 or higher, be able to demonstrate financial need, and be of Japanese or other Asian ancestry. Along with their application, they must submit a 500-word essay on the most interesting book they have read and how it influenced them.

Financial data The stipend is $5,000 per year.

Duration 1 year; may be renewed up to 3 additional years.

Number awarded At least 1 each year.

Deadline February of each year.

[53]
AT&T FOUNDATION APIASF SCHOLARSHIPS

Asian & Pacific Islander American Scholarship Fund
2025 M Street, N.W., Suite 610
Washington, DC 20036-3363
(202) 986-6892   Toll Free: (877) 808-7032
Fax: (202) 530-0643   E-mail: info@apiasf.org
Web: www.apiasf.org/scholarship_apiasf.html

Summary To provide financial assistance to Asian and Pacific Islander Americans who are entering college for the first time.

Eligibility This program is open to U.S. citizens, nationals, permanent residents, and citizens of the Freely Associated States who are first-time incoming college students and of Asian or Pacific Islander heritage. Applicants must be enrolling full time at an accredited 2- or 4-year college or university in the United States. They must have a GPA of 2.7 or higher or the GED equivalent. In addition, they must complete the FAFSA and apply for federal financial aid.

Financial data The stipend is $2,500.

Duration 1 year.

Additional information This program is sponsored by the AT&T Foundation and administered by the Asian & Pacific Islander American Scholarship Fund (APIASF).

Number awarded Varies each year; recently, 6 of these scholarships were awarded.

Deadline January of each year.

[54]
AVIATION AND PROFESSIONAL DEVELOPMENT SCHOLARSHIPS

Airport Minority Advisory Council
Attn: AMAC Educational and Scholarship Program, Inc.
2001 Jefferson Davis Highway, Suite 500
Arlington, VA 22202
(703) 414-2622, ext. 4   Fax: (703) 414-2686
E-mail: aaron.pope@amac-org.com
Web: www.amac-org.com/scholarships.html

Summary To provide financial assistance to Asian American and other minority high school seniors and undergraduates who are preparing for a career in the aviation industry and are interested in participating in the Airport Minority Advisory Council (AMAC).

Eligibility This program is open to high school seniors and current undergraduates who have a GPA of 2.5 or higher and a record of involvement in community and extracurricular activities. Applicants must be working on a bachelor's degree in accounting, architecture, aviation, business administration, engineering, or finance as preparation for a career in the aviation or airport industry. They must be interested in participating in the AMAC program, including having an endorsement from a current AMAC member, becoming a member if they are awarded a scholarship, and communicating with AMAC once each semester during the term of the scholarship. Along with their application, they must submit a 1-page essay on their career goals and why they have chosen their particular field of study. Financial need is not considered in the selection process. U.S. citizenship is required.

Financial data The stipend is $2,000 per year.

Duration 1 year; recipients may reapply.

Number awarded 4 each semester.

Deadline August of each year for spring semester; April of each year for spring semester.

[55]
BBCN BANK APIASF SCHOLARSHIPS

Asian & Pacific Islander American Scholarship Fund
2025 M Street, N.W., Suite 610
Washington, DC 20036-3363
(202) 986-6892   Toll Free: (877) 808-7032
Fax: (202) 530-0643   E-mail: info@apiasf.org
Web: www.apiasf.org/scholarship_apiasf.html

Summary To provide financial assistance to Asian and Pacific Islander Americans from designated counties around the country who are entering college for the first time.

Eligibility This program is open to U.S. citizens, nationals, and permanent residents who live in designated counties of California (Alameda, Los Angeles, Orange, Riverside, San Bernardino, San Diego, or Santa Clara), New York (Bronx, Kings, New York, or Queens), New Jersey (Bergen or Middlesex), Washington (King), or Illinois (Cook, DuPage, or Lake). Applicants must be first-time incoming college students of Asian or Pacific Islander heritage and enrolling full time at an accredited 2- or 4-year college or university in the United States. They must have a GPA of 3.0 or higher or the GED equivalent and be able to demonstrate financial need.

Financial data The stipend is $2,500.

Duration 1 year; nonrenewable.

Additional information This program is sponsored by BBCN Bank and administered by the Asian & Pacific Islander American Scholarship Fund (APIASF).

Number awarded Varies each year; recently, 36 of these scholarships were awarded.

Deadline January of each year.

[56]
BEHAVIORAL SCIENCES STUDENT FELLOWSHIPS IN EPILEPSY

Epilepsy Foundation
Attn: Research Department
8301 Professional Place
Landover, MD 20785-2353
(301) 459-3700   Toll Free: (800) EFA-1000
Fax: (301) 577-2684   TDD: (800) 332-2070
E-mail: grants@efa.org
Web: www.epilepsyfoundation.org

Summary To provide funding to undergraduate and graduate students (particularly Asian Americans, other minorities, women, and students with disabilities) who are interested in working on a summer research project in a behavioral science field relevant to epilepsy.

Eligibility This program is open to undergraduate and graduate students in a behavioral science program relevant to epilepsy research or clinical care, including, but not limited to, sociology, social work, psychology, anthropology, nursing, economics, vocational rehabilitation, counseling, or political science. Applicants must be interested in working on an epilepsy research project under the supervision of a qualified mentor. Because the program is designed as a training opportunity, the quality of the training plans and environment are considered in the selection process. Other selection criteria include the quality of the proposed project, the relevance of the proposed work to epilepsy, the applicant's interest in the field of epilepsy, the applicant's qualifications, and the mentor's qualifications (including his or her commitment to the student and the project), and the quality of the training environment for research related to epilepsy. U.S. citizenship is not required, but the project must be conducted in the United States. Applications from women, members of minority groups, and people with disabilities are especially encouraged. The program is not intended for students working on a dissertation research project.

Financial data The grant is $3,000.

Duration 3 months during the summer.

Additional information This program is supported by the American Epilepsy Society, Abbott Laboratories, Ortho-McNeil Pharmaceutical Corporation, and Pfizer Inc.

Number awarded Varies each year.

Deadline March of each year.

[57]
BILL BERNBACH DIVERSITY SCHOLARSHIPS

American Association of Advertising Agencies
Attn: AAAA Foundation
1065 Avenue of the Americas, 16th Floor
New York, NY 10018
(212) 262-2500   E-mail: bbscholarship@ddb.com
Web: www.aaaa.org

Summary To provide financial assistance to Asian American and other multicultural students who are interested in working on an undergraduate or graduate degree in advertising at designated schools.

Eligibility This program is open to African Americans, Asian Americans, Hispanic Americans, and Native Americans (including American Indians, Alaska Natives, Native Hawaiians, and other Pacific Islanders) who are interested in studying the advertising creative arts at designated institutions as a full-time student. Applicants must be working on or have already received an undergraduate degree and be able to demonstrate creative talent and promise. They must be U.S. citizens, nationals, or permanent residents. Along with their application, they must submit 10 samples of creative work in their respective field of expertise.

Financial data The stipend is $5,000.

Duration 1 year.

Additional information This program, which began in 1998, is currently sponsored by DDB Worldwide. The participating schools are the Art Center College of Design (Pasadena, California), Creative Circus (Atlanta, Georgia), Miami Ad School (Miami Beach, Florida), University of Texas at Austin, VCU Brandcenter (Richmond, Virginia), Savannah College of Art and Design (Savannah, Georgia), University of Oregon (Eugene), City College of New York, School of Visual Arts (New York, New York), Fashion Institute of Technology (New York, New York), and Brigham Young University (Provo, Utah).

Number awarded 3 each year.

Deadline October of each year.

[58]
BILL DICKEY GOLF SCHOLARSHIPS

Bill Dickey Scholarship Association
Attn: Scholarship Committee
1140 East Washington Street, Suite 103
Phoenix, AZ 85034
(602) 258-7851   Fax: (602) 258-3412
E-mail: assistant@bdscholar.org
Web: www.nmjgsa.org/scholarships.php

Summary To provide financial assistance to Asian American and other minority high school seniors and undergraduate students who excel at golf.

Eligibility This program is open to graduating high school seniors and current undergraduate students who are members of minority groups (African American, Asian/Pacific Islander, Hispanic, or American Indian/Alaskan Native). Applicants must submit a 500-word essay on a topic that changes annually but relates to minorities and golf. Selection is based on academic achievement; personal recommendations; participation in golf, school, and community activities; and financial need.

Financial data Stipends range from 1-time awards of $1,000 to 4-year awards of $3,500 per year. Funds are paid directly to the recipient's college.

Duration 1 year or longer.

Additional information This sponsor was established in 1984 as the National Minority Junior Golf Association and given its current name in 2006. Support is provided by the Jackie Robinson Foundation, PGA of America, Anheuser-Busch, the Tiger Woods Foundation, and other cooperating organizations.

Number awarded Varies; generally 80 or more each year.

Deadline April of each year.

[59]
BONG HAK HYUN MEMORIAL SCHOLARSHIPS

Philip Jaisohn Memorial Foundation
Attn: Education and Scholarship Committee
6705 Old York Road
Philadelphia, PA 19126
(215) 224-2000   Fax: (215) 224-9164
E-mail: jaisohnhouse@gmail.com
Web: www.jaisohn.org

Summary To provide financial assistance to Korean American undergraduate and graduate students who are studying health care or medicine.

Eligibility This program is open to Korean American undergraduate and graduate students who are currently enrolled at a college or university in the United States and working on a degree in health care or a field of medicine. Applicants must be able to demonstrate excellence in community activities and financial need. Along with their application, they must submit an essay on either "Who is Dr. Jaisohn to Me," or "The Significance of Dr. Jaisohn's Ideal to Korean Americans." They must also submit a brief statement on how they can contribute to and be involved in the activities of the Philip Jaisohn Memorial Foundation. Selection is based on potential, passion, and leadership.

Financial data The stipend is $1,500.

Duration 1 year.

Number awarded 2 each year.

Deadline November of each year.

[60]
BOOKER T. WASHINGTON SCHOLARSHIPS

National FFA Organization
Attn: Scholarship Office
6060 FFA Drive
P.O. Box 68960
Indianapolis, IN 46268-0960
(317) 802-4419   Fax: (317) 802-5419
E-mail: scholarships@ffa.org
Web: www.ffa.org

Summary To provide financial assistance to Asian American and other minority FFA members who are interested in studying agriculture in college.

Eligibility This program is open to members who are graduating high school seniors planning to enroll full time in college. Applicants must be members of a minority ethnic group (African American, Asian American, Pacific Islander, Hispanic, Alaska Native, or American Indian) planning to work on a 4-year degree in agriculture. Selection is based on academic achievement (10 points for GPA, 10 points for SAT or ACT score, 10 points for class rank), leadership in FFA activities (30 points), leadership in community activities (10 points), and participation in the Supervised Agricultural Experience (SAE) program (30 points). U.S. citizenship is required.

Financial data The stipend is $1,000. Funds are paid directly to the recipient.

Duration 1 year; nonrenewable.
Number awarded 5 each year.
Deadline February of each year.

[61]
BROWN AND CALDWELL MINORITY SCHOLARSHIP

Brown and Caldwell
Attn: Scholarship Program
201 North Civic Drive, Suite 115
P.O. Box 8045
Walnut Creek, CA 94596
(925) 937-9010   Fax: (925) 937-9026
E-mail: scholarships@brwncald.com
Web: www.brownandcaldwell.com/scholarships.asp

Summary To provide financial assistance to Asian American and other minority students working on an undergraduate or graduate degree in an environmental or engineering field.

Eligibility This program is open to members of minority groups (African Americans, Hispanics, Asians, Pacific Islanders, Native Americans, or Alaska Natives) who are full-time juniors, seniors, or graduate students at an accredited 4-year college or university. Applicants must have a GPA of 3.0 or higher and a declared major in civil, chemical, or environmental engineering or an environmental science (e.g., biology, ecology, geology, hydrogeology). They must be U.S. citizens or permanent residents. Along with their application, they must submit an essay (up to 250 words) on their future career goals in environmental science. Financial need is not considered in the selection process.

Financial data The stipend is $5,000.
Duration 1 year.
Number awarded 4 each year.
Deadline April of each year.

[62]
BUICK ACHIEVERS SCHOLARSHIP PROGRAM

Scholarship America
Attn: Scholarship Management Services
One Scholarship Way
P.O. Box 297
St. Peter, MN 56082
(507) 931-1682   Toll Free: (866) 243-4644
Fax: (507) 931-9168
E-mail: buickachievers@scholarshipamerica.org
Web: www.buickachievers.com

Summary To provide financial assistance to students (particularly Asian Americans, other minorities, women, and those with ties to the military) who are entering college for the first time and planning to major in specified fields related to engineering, design, or business.

Eligibility This program is open to high school seniors and graduates who are planning to enroll full time at an accredited 4-year college or university as first-time freshmen. Applicants must be planning to major in fields of engineering (chemical, computer, controls, electrical, energy, environmental, industrial, manufacturing, materials, mechanical, plastic/polymers, or software); technology (automotive technology, computer science, engineering technology, information technology); design (graphic, industrial, product, transportation); or business (accounting, business administration, ergonomics,

finance, industrial hygiene, international business, labor and industrial relations, management information systems, marketing, mathematics, occupational health and safety, production management, statistics, or supply chain/logistics). U.S. citizenship or permanent resident status is required. Selection is based on academic achievement, financial need, participation and leadership in community and school activities, work experience, educational and career goals, and other unusual circumstances. Special consideration is given to first-generation college students, women, minorities, military veterans, and dependents of military personnel.

Financial data Stipends are $25,000 or $2,000 per year.
Duration 1 year. The $25,000 awards may be renewed up to 3 additional years (or 4 years for students entering a 5-year engineering program), provided the recipient remains enrolled full time, continues to major in an eligible field, and maintains a GPA of 3.0 or higher. The $2,000 awards are nonrenewable.

Additional information This program, which began in 2011, is funded by the General Motors Foundation.
Number awarded 1,100 each year: 100 at $25,000 and 1,000 at $2,000.
Deadline February of each year.

[63]
CALIFORNIA DIETETIC ASSOCIATION FOUNDATION SCHOLARSHIP HONORING BERNICE AARONS

California Dietetic Association
Attn: CDA Foundation
7740 Manchester Avenue, Suite 102
Playa del Rey, CA 90293-8499
(310) 822-0177   Fax: (310) 823-0264
E-mail: patsmith@dietitian.org
Web: www.dietitian.org/d_cdaf/cdaf_outreach.html

Summary To provide financial assistance to residents of California (particularly Asian Americans, other minorities, men, and persons with disabilities) who are members of the Academy of Nutrition and Dietetics (AND) and interested in participating in specified types of programs in any state.

Eligibility This program is open to California residents who are AND members and 1) entering the first or second year of an approved Dietetic Technician Program in any state; 2) entering at least the second year of an accredited Coordinated Program (CP) or Didactic Program in Dietetics (DPD) in any state; or 3) accepted to an accredited Supervised Practice Program in any state to begin within 6 months. Along with their application, they must submit a letter of application that includes a discussion of their career goals. Selection is based on that letter (15%), academic ability (25%), work or volunteer experience (15%), letters of recommendation (15%), extracurricular activities (5%), and financial need (25%). Applications are especially encouraged from ethnic minorities, men, and people with physical disabilities.

Financial data The stipend is normally $1,000.
Duration 1 year.
Additional information The California Dietetic Association is the California affiliate of the AND.
Number awarded 1 each year.
Deadline April of each year.

[64]
CALIFORNIA JAPANESE AMERICAN ALUMNI ASSOCIATION SCHOLARSHIP PROGRAM

California Japanese American Alumni Association
Attn: Katherine Yoshii
P.O. Box 15235
San Francisco, CA 94115-0235
(510) 559-9277   E-mail: scholarships@cjaaa.org
Web: www.cjaaa.org/scholarship.html

Summary To provide financial assistance to undergraduate or graduate students of Japanese American descent who are currently enrolled at campuses of the University of California.

Eligibility This program is open to continuing or returning undergraduate or graduate students of Japanese American descent from California who are attending 1 of the 10 UC campuses. They must be U.S. citizens and may be studying in any field or discipline. A GPA of 3.0 or higher is strongly recommended but not required. Applicants interested in participating in the University of California Education Abroad Program in Japan must have a GPA of 3.5 or higher. Selection is based on academic achievement, contribution to the community, personal attributes, and financial need (in that order).

Financial data Stipends range from $1,000 to $5,000. The Moriaki "Mo" Noguchi Memorial Scholarship of $3,000 is given to the top overall candidate. The George Kondo Award is at least $1,000 and is awarded to the applicant with the best community service record. The Yori Wada Award is $2,000 and is awarded to the applicant with the most outstanding record of public service. The stipend for a student accepted to the University of California Education Abroad Program ranges from $2,500 to $5,000.

Duration 1 year; nonrenewable.

Number awarded 8 to 10 each year.

Deadline April of each year.

[65]
CAMBODIAN HEALTH PROFESSIONALS ASSOCIATION OF AMERICA SCHOLARSHIP

Cambodian Health Professionals Association of America
1025 Atlantic Avenue
Long Beach, CA 90813
(562) 491-9292   E-mail: CHPAAmission@gmail.com
Web: www.chpaa.org/scholarships.html

Summary To provide financial assistance to Cambodian American college students who are preparing for a career in a field of health care.

Eligibility This program is open to Cambodian Americans who are currently enrolled at a college or university in any state. Applicants must be preparing for a career in a field related to health care.

Financial data A stipend is awarded (amount not specified).

Duration 1 year.

Number awarded 1 each year.

Deadline Deadline not specified.

[66]
CAMMER-HILL GRANT

Wisconsin Women of Color Network, Inc.
Attn: Scholarship Committee
P.O. Box 2337
Madison, WI 53701-2337
E-mail: contact@womenofcolornetwork-wis.org
Web: www.womenofcolornetwork-wis.org/scholarship.html

Summary To provide financial assistance for vocational/technical school or community college to Asian American and other adult women of color from Wisconsin.

Eligibility This program is open to residents of Wisconsin who are adult women of color planning to continue their education at a vocational/technical school or community college in any state. Applicants must be a member of 1 of the following groups: African American, Asian, American Indian, or Hispanic. They must be able to demonstrate financial need. Along with their application, they must submit a 1-page essay on how this scholarship will help them accomplish their educational goal. U.S. citizenship is required.

Financial data A stipend is awarded (amount not specified).

Duration 1 year.

Additional information This program began in 1994.

Number awarded 1 each year.

Deadline May of each year.

[67]
CANFIT PROGRAM CULINARY ARTS SCHOLARSHIPS

Communities-Adolescents-Nutrition-Fitness
Attn: Scholarship Program
2140 Shattuck Avenue, Suite 610
Berkeley, CA 94704
(510) 644-1533   Toll Free: (800) 200-3131
Fax: (510) 644-1535   E-mail: info@canfit.org
Web: www.canfit.org/scholarships

Summary To provide financial assistance to Asian American and other minority culinary arts students in California.

Eligibility This program is open to American Indians, Alaska Natives, African Americans, Asian Americans, Pacific Islanders, and Latinos/Hispanics from California who are enrolled at a culinary arts college in the state. Applicants are not required to have completed any college units. Along with their application, they must submit 1) documentation of financial need; 2) letters of recommendation from 2 individuals; 3) a 1-to 2-page letter describing their academic goals and involvement in community nutrition and/or physical education activities; and 4) an essay of 500 to 1,000 words on a topic related to healthy foods for youth from low-income communities of color.

Financial data A stipend is awarded (amount not specified).

Number awarded 1 or more each year.

Deadline March of each year.

[68]
CANFIT PROGRAM UNDERGRADUATE SCHOLARSHIPS

Communities-Adolescents-Nutrition-Fitness
Attn: Scholarship Program
2140 Shattuck Avenue, Suite 610
Berkeley, CA 94704
(510) 644-1533   Toll Free: (800) 200-3131
Fax: (510) 644-1535   E-mail: info@canfit.org
Web: www.canfit.org/scholarships

Summary To provide financial assistance to Asian American and other minority undergraduate students who are working on a degree in nutrition or physical education in California.

Eligibility This program is open to American Indians, Alaska Natives, African Americans, Asian Americans, Pacific Islanders, and Latinos/Hispanics from California who are enrolled in an approved bachelor's degree program in nutrition or physical education in the state. Applicants must have completed at least 50 semester units and have a GPA of 2.5 or higher. Along with their application, they must submit 1) documentation of financial need; 2) letters of recommendation from 2 individuals; 3) a 1-to 2-page letter describing their academic goals and involvement in community nutrition and/or physical education activities; and 4) an essay of 500 to 1,000 words on a topic related to healthy foods for youth from low-income communities of color.

Financial data A stipend is awarded (amount not specified).

Number awarded 1 or more each year.

Deadline March of each year.

[69]
CAPSTONE CORPORATION SCHOLARSHIP AWARD

National Naval Officers Association-Washington, D.C.
  Chapter
c/o LCDR Stephen Williams
P.O. Box 30784
Alexandria, VA 22310
(703) 566-3840   Fax: (703) 566-3813
E-mail: Stephen.Williams@navy.mil
Web: dcnnoa.memberlodge.com

Summary To provide financial assistance to Asian American and other minority high school seniors from the Washington, D.C. area who plan to attend college in any state.

Eligibility This program is open to minority seniors graduating from high schools in the Washington, D.C. metropolitan area who plan to enroll full time at an accredited 2- or 4-year college or university in any state. Applicants must have a GPA of 3.0 or higher and be U.S. citizens or permanent residents. Selection is based on academic achievement, community involvement, and financial need.

Financial data The stipend is $1,000.

Duration 1 year; nonrenewable.

Additional information Recipients are not required to join or affiliate with the military in any way. This program is supported by Capstone Corporation, a minority-owned business incorporated in 1986 by former active-duty Navy officers.

Number awarded 1 each year.

Deadline March of each year.

[70]
CARGILL ASCEND SCHOLARSHIPS

Ascend: Pan-Asian Leaders
Attn: Director of Programs
120 Wall Street, Ninth Floor
New York, NY 10005
(212) 248-4888   Fax: (212) 344-5636
E-mail: scholarships@ascendleadership.org
Web: www.ascendleadership.org

Summary To provide financial assistance to members of Ascend: Pan-Asian Leaders who are college juniors working on a degree in accounting, taxation, or finance.

Eligibility This program is open to members of Ascend who are enrolled as full-time juniors at colleges and universities in the United States. Applicants must have a GPA of 3.0 or higher and a major in accounting, taxation, or finance. They must be U.S. citizens or permanent residents. Along with their application, they must submit a 500-word personal essay on how they have demonstrated leadership and teamwork in their academic studies, professional career, and/or extracurricular activities and community volunteer work; why they believe those qualities are important to transforming themselves into a better leader; their career goals after graduation; and the role Ascend has played in the achievement of their academic and career goals. They must also be willing to interview for an internship with Cargill. Financial need is not considered in the selection process.

Financial data The stipend is $1,000.

Duration 1 year.

Additional information Ascend was formed in 2004 as the National Asian American Society of Accountants. This program is sponsored by Cargill.

Number awarded 1 each year.

Deadline May of each year.

[71]
CARL A. SCOTT BOOK FELLOWSHIPS

Council on Social Work Education
Attn: Chair, Carl A. Scott Memorial Fund
1701 Duke Street, Suite 200
Alexandria, VA 22314-3457
(703) 683-8080   Fax: (703) 683-8099
E-mail: info@cswe.org
Web: www.cswe.org

Summary To provide financial assistance to Asian American and other ethnic minority social work students in their last year of study for a baccalaureate or master's degree.

Eligibility This program is open to students from ethnic groups of color (African American, Asian American, Hispanic/Latino, or American Indian) who are in the last year of study for a social work degree in an accredited baccalaureate or master's degree program. Applicants must have a cumulative GPA of 3.0 or higher and be enrolled full time. They must demonstrate a commitment to work for equity and social justice in social work.

Financial data The stipend is $500.

Duration This is a 1-time award.

Number awarded 2 each year.

Deadline May of each year.

[72]
CARMEN E. TURNER SCHOLARSHIPS

Conference of Minority Transportation Officials
Attn: National Scholarship Program
1875 I Street, N.W., Suite 500
Washington, DC 20006
(703) 234-4072 Fax: (202) 318-0364
Web: www.comto.org/?page=Scholarships

Summary To provide financial assistance for college or graduate school to Asian American and other members of the Conference of Minority Transportation Officials (COMTO).

Eligibility This program is open to undergraduate and graduate students who have been members of COMTO for at least 1 year. Applicants must be working on a degree in a field related to transportation and have a GPA of 2.5 or higher. They must be enrolled at least half time. Along with their application, they must submit a cover letter with a 500-word statement of career goals. Financial need is not considered in the selection process. U.S. citizenship or legal resident status is required.

Financial data The stipend is $3,500. Funds are paid directly to the recipient's college or university.

Duration 1 year.

Additional information COMTO was established in 1971 to promote, strengthen, and expand the roles of minorities in all aspects of transportation. Recipients are expected to attend the COMTO National Scholarship Luncheon.

Number awarded 1 each year.

Deadline May of each year.

[73]
CAROL HAYES TORIO MEMORIAL UNDERGRADUATE SCHOLARSHIP

California Dietetic Association
Attn: CDA Foundation
7740 Manchester Avenue, Suite 102
Playa del Rey, CA 90293-8499
(310) 822-0177 Fax: (310) 823-0264
E-mail: patsmith@dietitian.org
Web: www.dietitian.org/d_cdaf/cdaf_outreach.html

Summary To provide financial assistance to residents of California (particularly Asian Americans, other minorities, men, and individuals with physical disabilities) who are members of the Academy of Nutrition and Dietetics (AND) and interested in working on an undergraduate degree at a school in any state.

Eligibility This program is open to California residents who are AND members and 1) entering at least the second year of an accredited Coordinated Program (CP) or Didactic Program in Dietetics (DPD) in any state; or 2) accepted to an accredited Supervised Practice Program in any state to begin within 6 months. Along with their application, they must submit a letter of application that includes a discussion of their career goals. Selection is based on that letter (15%), academic ability (25%), work or volunteer experience (15%), letters of recommendation (15%), extracurricular activities (5%), and financial need (25%). Applications are especially encouraged from ethnic minorities, men, and people with physical disabilities.

Financial data The stipend is normally $1,000.

Duration 1 year.

Additional information The California Dietetic Association is the California affiliate of the AND.

Number awarded 1 each year.

Deadline April of each year.

[74]
CEA MINORITY STUDENT SCHOLARSHIPS

Colorado Education Association
Attn: Ethnic Minority Advisory Council
1500 Grant Street
Denver, CO 80203
(303) 837-1500 Toll Free: (800) 332-5939
Web: www.coloradoea.org

Summary To provide financial assistance to Asian American and other minority high school seniors in Colorado who are children of members of the Colorado Education Association (CEA) and planning to attend college in any state.

Eligibility This program is open to seniors graduating from high schools in Colorado who are members of a minority ethnic group, defined to include American Indians/Alaska Natives, Asians, Blacks, Hispanics, Native Hawaiians/Pacific Islanders, and multi-ethnic. Applicants must be the dependent child of an active, retired, or deceased CEA member. They must be planning to attend an accredited institution of higher education in any state. Along with their application, they must submit brief statements on 1) their need for this scholarship; and 2) why they plan to pursue a college education.

Financial data The stipend is $1,000.

Duration 1 year; nonrenewable.

Number awarded 4 each year.

Deadline March of each year.

[75]
CENTRAL FLORIDA CHAPTER NBMBAA SCHOLARSHIPS

National Black MBA Association-Central Florida Chapter
Attn: Scholarship Committee Chair
P.O. Box 692696
Orlando, FL 32869-2696
(321) 578-8305 E-mail: scholarships@cflblackmba.org
Web: www.cflblackmba.org

Summary To provide financial assistance to Asian Americans or members of another minority group who are residents of any state working on a degree in business at a university in Florida.

Eligibility This program is open to members of the following groups from any state: African American/Black, American Indian/Alaska Native, Asian American/Pacific Islander, or Hispanic/Latino. Applicants must be enrolled in a business program at an AACSB-accredited college or university in Florida. They must have a GPA of 3.0 or higher. Along with their application, they must submit a 2-page essay on a topic that changes annually but relates to minorities and business. Selection is based on that essay, transcripts, a resume, and extracurricular activities. The highest-ranked applicant receives a named scholarship sponsored by Darden Restaurants.

Financial data The Darden Named Scholarship is $5,000; a total of $10,000 in scholarships is awarded each year.

Duration 1 year.

Number awarded Varies each year.

Deadline October of each year.

[76]
CENTRAL INTELLIGENCE AGENCY UNDERGRADUATE SCHOLARSHIP PROGRAM

Central Intelligence Agency
Attn: Human Resource Management
Recruitment and Retention Center, 4B14-034 DD1
Washington, DC 20505
(703) 371-2107
Web: https:

Summary To provide college funding and work experience to high school seniors and college sophomores (particularly Asian Americans, other minorities, and students with disabilities) who would be interested in working for the Central Intelligence Agency (CIA) after graduation from college.

Eligibility This program is open to U.S. citizens who are either high school seniors or college freshmen or sophomores. Seniors must be at least 18 years of age by April of the year they apply and have minimum scores of 1500 on the SAT (1000 on critical reading and mathematics and 500 on writing) or 21 on the ACT. All applicants must have a GPA of 3.0 or higher and be able to demonstrate financial need (household income of $70,000 or less for a family of 4 or $80,000 or less for a family of 5 or more) and be able to meet the same employment standards as permanent employees of the CIA. This program was developed, in part, to assist minority and disabled students, but it is open to all students who meet the requirements.

Financial data Scholars are provided a salary, an optional benefits package (health, dental, and vision insurance, life insurance, and retirement), and up to $18,000 per year for tuition, fees, books, and supplies. They must agree to continue employment with the CIA after college graduation for a period 1.5 times the length of their college support.

Duration 1 year; may be renewed if the student maintains a GPA of 3.0 or higher and full-time enrollment in a 4- or 5-year college program.

Additional information Scholars work each summer at a CIA facility. In addition to a salary, they receive the cost of transportation between school and the Washington, D.C. area and a housing allowance.

Number awarded Varies each year.

Deadline October of each year.

[77]
CHEN FOUNDATION SCHOLARSHIPS

Asian Pacific Community Fund
1145 Wilshire Boulevard, First Floor
Los Angeles, CA 90017
(213) 624-6400, ext. 6   Fax: (213) 624-6406
E-mail: scholarships@apcf.org
Web: www.apcf.org/what-we-do/scholarship-fund

Summary To provide financial assistance to Asian and Pacific Islander high school seniors in California who plan to attend a campus of the California State University (CSU) system and major in a field of mathematics, engineering, or science.

Eligibility This program is open to seniors graduating from high schools in California who fulfill the sponsor's goals of meeting the diverse needs of Asian Pacific Islanders. Applicants must be planning to attend a CSU university and major in a field of mathematics, engineering, or science. They must have a GPA of 3.0 or higher and a family income below the official California low level.

Financial data The stipend is $2,000 per year.

Duration 1 year; may be renewed 1 additional year, provided the recipient maintains a GPA of 3.0 or higher and remains actively involved in community service.

Additional information This program is sponsored by the Chen Foundation.

Number awarded 5 each year.

Deadline April of each year.

[78]
CHEN-PAI LEE MEMORIAL SCHOLARSHIPS

Chen-Pai Lee Scholarship Fund
P.O. Box 142801
Irving, TX 75014
Web: www.chen-paileememorialscholarship.com

Summary To provide financial assistance to Taiwanese American high school seniors who plan to attend college in any state and major in any field.

Eligibility This program is open to graduating high school seniors who are Taiwanese descendants or who have at least 1 parent who is a Taiwanese descendant. Applicants must be planning to enroll full time at a 2- or 4-year college or university in any state. Along with their application, they must submit information on their work experience, a list of extracurricular activities, information on their community or volunteer service, and a 3-page essay on 1 of the following topics: 1) how they can contribute to Taiwan's progress to help the country achieve greater freedom and democracy; or 2) how they, as a descendant of Taiwanese immigrants, can contribute to U.S. society and make it better for future generations.

Financial data The stipend is $500.

Duration 1 year.

Number awarded 5 each year.

Deadline January of each year.

[79]
CHINESE AMERICAN ASSOCIATION OF MINNESOTA SCHOLARSHIPS

Chinese American Association of Minnesota
Attn: Scholarship Program
P.O. Box 582584
Minneapolis, MN 55458-2584
E-mail: office@caam.org
Web: www.caam.org/?page_id=82

Summary To provide financial assistance to Minnesota residents of Chinese descent who are interested in attending college or graduate school in any state.

Eligibility This program is open to Minnesota residents of Chinese descent who are enrolled or planning to enroll full time at a postsecondary school, college, or graduate school in any state. Applicants must submit an essay on the role their Chinese heritage has played in their work, study, and accomplishments. Selection is based on academic record, leadership qualities, and community service; financial need is also considered for some awards. Membership in the Chinese American Association of Minnesota (CAAM) is not required.

Priority is given to applicants who have not previously received a CAAM scholarship.

Financial data The stipend ranges from $1,500 to $2,000.

Duration 1 year.

Additional information Recipients who are not CAAM members are expected to become members for at least 2 years.

Number awarded 1 or more each year.

Deadline December of each year.

[80]
CHINESE AMERICAN CITIZENS ALLIANCE FOUNDATION ESSAY CONTEST

Chinese American Citizens Alliance
1044 Stockton Street
San Francisco, CA 94108
(415) 434-2222   E-mail: info@cacanational.org
Web: www.cacanational.org/Essay-Contest

Summary To recognize and reward high school students of Chinese descent who write outstanding essays on a topic related to Asian Americans.

Eligibility This competition is open to high school students of Chinese descent. Candidates apply through their local lodge of the Chinese American Citizens Alliance and meet at a site arranged by that lodge, usually on the first Saturday in March. They are given a topic and devote the next 2 hours to writing a 500-word essay, in English, on that topic. The topic is assigned at the time of the competition (always relates to the Chinese and Asian American communities). Selection is based on originality, clarity of thought, and expression.

Financial data Prizes are $1,000 for first place, $700 for second place, $500 for third place, and $100 for merit awards.

Duration The competition is held annually.

Number awarded Varies each year; recently, prizes included 1 first place, 1 second place, 1 third place, and 10 merit awards.

Deadline February of each year.

[81]
CHINESE AMERICAN CITIZENS ALLIANCE FOUNDATION SCHOLARSHIPS

Chinese American Citizens Alliance Foundation
Attn: Scholarships
763 Yale Street
Los Angeles, CA 90012
(213) 628-6368   E-mail: cacafoundation@gmail.com
Web: www.cacafoundation.org

Summary To provide financial assistance to Chinese American undergraduate students at colleges and universities in California.

Eligibility This program is open to students of Chinese descent from California who have completed the sophomore year at a college or university in the state. Applicants must provide information on their volunteer work, accomplishments and honors received in college, organizational membership and offices held, previous scholarship awards, career plans, and how they will benefit from the scholarship. Financial need is not considered. Applicants must be available for an in-person interview in Los Angeles.

Financial data The stipend is $1,000.

Duration 1 year.

Additional information This program, which began in 1971, currently consists of the following named scholarships: the Yoke Quong Jung Memorial Scholarship, the Huan Lin Cheng Memorial Scholarship, the Y.C. Hong Memorial Scholarship, the Collin and Susan Lai Scholarship, the Julius and Eleanor Sue Scholarship, the Robert and Edith Jung Scholarship, the James Bok Wong and Betty KC Yeow Scholarship, and the Stanley and Mary Mu Scholarship.

Number awarded 8 each year.

Deadline June of each year.

[82]
CHRISTIAN COLLEGE LEADERS SCHOLARSHIPS

Foundation for College Christian Leaders
2658 Del Mar Heights Road
PMB 266
Del Mar, CA 92014
(858) 481-0848   E-mail: LMHays@aol.com
Web: www.collegechristianleader.com

Summary To provide financial assistance for college to Christian students (particularly Asian Americans and other minorities) who are from California, Oregon, or Washington.

Eligibility This program is open to entering or continuing undergraduate students who reside or attend college in California, Oregon, or Washington. Applicants must have a GPA of 3.0 or higher, be able to document financial need (parents must have a combined income of less than $75,000), and be able to demonstrate Christian testimony and Christian leadership. Selection is based on identified leadership history, academic achievement, financial need, and demonstrated academic, vocational, and ministry training to further the Kingdom of Jesus Christ. Special consideration is given to minority students.

Financial data A stipend is awarded (amount not specified).

Duration 1 year; may be renewed.

Additional information The foundation, formerly known as the Eckmann Foundation, was founded in 1988.

Number awarded Varies each year.

Deadline May of each year.

[83]
CHUNGHI HONG PARK SCHOLARSHIPS

Korean-American Scientists and Engineers Association
Attn: Scholarship Committee
1952 Gallows Drive, Suite 300
Vienna, VA 22182
(703) 748-1221   Fax: (703) 748-1331
E-mail: admin@ksea.org
Web: scholarship.ksea.org/InfoUndergraduate.aspx

Summary To provide financial assistance to women who are undergraduate student members of the Korean-American Scientists and Engineers Association (KSEA).

Eligibility This program is open to women who are Korean American undergraduate students, are KSEA members, have completed at least 2 semesters as a college student, and are majoring in science, engineering, or a related field. Along with their application, they must submit an essay on a topic that changes annually but relates to science or engineering.

Selection is based on the essay (20%), KSEA activities and community service (30%), recommendation letters (20%), and academic performance (30%).

Financial data The stipend is $1,000.

Duration 1 year.

Number awarded 2 each year.

Deadline March of each year.

[84]
CIC/ANNA CHENNAULT SCHOLARSHIP

Asian American Journalists Association
Attn: Student Programs Coordinator
5 Third Street, Suite 1108
San Francisco, CA 94103
(415) 346-2051, ext. 102   Fax: (415) 346-6343
E-mail: programs@aaja.org
Web: www.aaja.org/apply-for-a-scholarship-now

Summary To provide financial assistance to college freshmen who are studying journalism and demonstrate sensitivity to Asian American and Pacific Islander issues.

Eligibility This program is open to college freshmen entering their sophomore year who can demonstrate academic achievement, journalistic ability, commitment to the field of journalism, and sensitivity to Asian American and Pacific Islander issues. Applicants are not required to be members of the Asian American Journalists Association (AAJA), but they must be committed to its mission and they must agree to become a member if they are awarded this scholarship.

Financial data The award is $5,000, including $3,900 as a stipend for college study and $1,100 as a grant to help cover travel, lodging, and registration costs for attendance at the AAJA national annual convention.

Duration 1 year.

Additional information This program is sponsored by the Council for International Cooperation (CIC). The recipient participates in the Voices student news project at the AAJA convention and is paired with a professional print, online, or broadcast mentor at the convention.

Number awarded 1 each year.

Deadline May of each year.

[85]
CIE/USA-SEATTLE APA SCIENCE, ENGINEERING AND TECHNOLOGY SCHOLARSHIP AWARD PROGRAM FOR COLLEGE STUDENTS

Chinese Institute of Engineers/USA-Seattle Chapter
Attn: Scholarship Committee
15921 N.E. Eighth Street, Suite 200
Bellevue, WA 98008
(425) 653-5589   E-mail: ciescholarship@cie-sea.org
Web: www.cie-sea.org

Summary To recognize and reward Asian Pacific American college students in Washington who have contributed to the fields of science, engineering, and technology.

Eligibility This award is available to students currently enrolled full time at a college or university in Washington who come from a family with an ethnic Asian Pacific background. Self-nominations are accepted, but nominations by teachers and coaches are preferred. Nomination packets must include 1) a 2-page description of applicable science, engineering, or

technology projects, accomplishments, or activities; and 2) an essay by the student that includes a description of past volunteer or community service activities, a statement on their Asian Pacific family background, and a paragraph on future plans. Selection is based on that essay (20%), academic achievement (30%), volunteer and community service (25%), and extracurricular activities and accomplishments (25%).

Financial data Awards are $600.

Duration The awards are presented annually.

Number awarded 2 each year.

Deadline June of each year.

[86]
COCA-COLA FOUNDATION APIASF SCHOLARSHIPS

Asian & Pacific Islander American Scholarship Fund
2025 M Street, N.W., Suite 610
Washington, DC 20036-3363
(202) 986-6892   Toll Free: (877) 808-7032
Fax: (202) 530-0643   E-mail: info@apiasf.org
Web: www.apiasf.org/scholarship_apiasf.html

Summary To provide financial assistance to Asian and Pacific Islander Americans who are the first member of their family to attend college.

Eligibility This program is open to U.S. citizens, nationals, permanent residents, and citizens of the Freely Associated States who are of Asian or Pacific Islander heritage and the first member of their immediate family to attend college. Applicants must be enrolling full time at an accredited 2- or 4-year college or university in the United States. They must have a GPA of 2.7 or higher or the GED equivalent. In addition, they must complete the FAFSA and apply for federal financial aid.

Financial data The stipend is $2,500.

Duration 1 year; nonrenewable.

Additional information This program is sponsored by the Coca-Cola Foundation and administered by the Asian & Pacific Islander American Scholarship Fund (APIASF).

Number awarded Varies each year; recently, 30 of these scholarships were awarded.

Deadline January of each year.

[87]
COCHRAN/GREENE SCHOLARSHIP

National Naval Officers Association-Washington, D.C. Chapter
Attn: Scholarship Program
2701 Park Center Drive, A1108
Alexandria, VA 22302
(703) 566-3840   Fax: (703) 566-3813
E-mail: Stephen.Williams@Navy.mil
Web: dcnnoa.memberlodge.com

Summary To provide financial assistance to Asian American and other minority female high school seniors from the Washington, D.C. area who are interested in attending college in any state.

Eligibility This program is open to female minority seniors graduating from high schools in the Washington, D.C. metropolitan area who plan to enroll full time at an accredited 2- or 4-year college or university in any state. Applicants must have a GPA of 2.5 or higher and be U.S. citizens or permanent residents. Selection is based on academic achievement, community involvement, and financial need.

Financial data The stipend is $1,500.

Duration 1 year; nonrenewable.

Additional information Recipients are not required to join or affiliate with the military in any way.

Number awarded 1 each year.

Deadline March of each year.

[88]
COLGATE "BRIGHT SMILES, BRIGHT FUTURES" MINORITY SCHOLARSHIPS

American Dental Hygienists' Association
Attn: Institute for Oral Health
444 North Michigan Avenue, Suite 3400
Chicago, IL 60611-3980
(312) 440-8900, ext. 204   Fax: (312) 440-6726
E-mail: institute@adha.net
Web: www.adha.org/ioh/programs/scholarships.htm

Summary To provide financial assistance to 1) Asian American and other minority students (females or males) and 2) males of any race who are members of the Student American Dental Hygienists' Association (SADHA) or the American Dental Hygienists' Association (ADHA) and enrolled in certificate programs in dental hygiene.

Eligibility This program is open to members of groups currently underrepresented in the dental hygiene profession (Native Americans, African Americans, Hispanics, Asians, and males) who are active members of the SADHA or the ADHA. Applicants must have a GPA of 3.0 or higher, be able to document financial need of at least $1,500, and have completed at least 1 year of full-time enrollment in an accredited dental hygiene certificate program in the United States. Along with their application, they must submit a statement that covers their long-term career goals, their intended contribution to the dental hygiene profession, their professional interests, and how their extracurricular activities and their degree enhance the attainment of their goals.

Financial data The stipend ranges from $1,000 to $2,000.

Duration 1 year; nonrenewable.

Additional information These scholarships are sponsored by the Colgate-Palmolive Company.

Number awarded 2 each year.

Deadline January of each year.

[89]
COLORADO EDUCATIONAL SERVICES AND DEVELOPMENT ASSOCIATION DIVERSITY SCHOLARSHIPS

Colorado Educational Services and Development
  Association
P.O. Box 40214
Denver, CO 80204
(303) 256-9785   E-mail: kim.medina@jwu.edu
Web: www.cesda.org/664.html

Summary To provide financial assistance to high school seniors in Colorado who are planning to attend college in the state and are either first-generation college students or members of ethnic or racial minorities.

Eligibility This program is open to seniors graduating from high schools in Colorado who are 1) the first member of their family to attend college; 2) a member of an underrepresented ethnic or racial minority (African American, Asian/Pacific Islander, American Indian, Hispanic/Chicano/Latino); and/or 3) able to demonstrate financial need. Applicants must have a GPA of 2.8 or higher and be planning to enroll at a 2- or 4-year college or university in Colorado. U.S. citizenship or permanent resident status is required. Selection is based on leadership and community service (particularly within minority communities), past academic performance, personal and professional accomplishments, personal attributes, special abilities, academic goals, and financial need.

Financial data The stipend is $1,000.

Duration 1 year; nonrenewable.

Number awarded Varies each year.

Deadline March of each year.

[90]
CONNECTICUT EDUCATION FOUNDATION SCHOLARSHIPS FOR MINORITY COLLEGE STUDENTS

Connecticut Education Association
Attn: Connecticut Education Foundation, Inc.
21 Oak Street, Suite 500
Hartford, CT 06106-8001
(860) 525-5641   Toll Free: (800) 842-4316
Fax: (860) 725-6323   E-mail: jeffl@cea.org
Web: www.cea.org/about/cef/minguidelines.cfm

Summary To provide financial assistance to Asian American and other minority college students in Connecticut who are interested in preparing for a teaching career.

Eligibility This program is open to minority students (Blacks, Native Americans or Alaskan Natives, Asian or Pacific Islanders, and Hispanics or Latinos) from Connecticut who have been accepted into a teacher preparation program at an accredited college or university in the state. Applicants must have earned a GPA of 2.75 or higher. Finalists may be interviewed. Financial need is considered in the selection process.

Financial data The stipend is $1,000.

Duration 1 year; may be renewed.

Number awarded At least 1 each year.

Deadline April of each year.

[91]
CONNECTICUT EDUCATION FOUNDATION SCHOLARSHIPS FOR MINORITY HIGH SCHOOL STUDENTS

Connecticut Education Association
Attn: Connecticut Education Foundation, Inc.
21 Oak Street, Suite 500
Hartford, CT 06106-8001
(860) 525-5641   Toll Free: (800) 842-4316
Fax: (860) 725-6323   E-mail: jeffl@cea.org
Web: www.cea.org/about/cef/minguidelines.cfm

Summary To provide financial assistance to Asian American and other minority high school seniors in Connecticut who are interested in attending college in the state to prepare for a teaching career.

Eligibility This program is open to minority seniors (Blacks, Native Americans or Alaskan Natives, Asian or Pacific Islanders, and Hispanics or Latinos) graduating from high schools in Connecticut. Applicants have been accepted at an accredited 2- or 4-year college or university in the state and be planning to enter the teaching profession. They must have a GPA of 2.75 or higher. Finalists may be interviewed. Financial need is considered in the selection process.

Financial data The stipend is $1,000.

Duration 1 year; may be renewed.

Number awarded At least 1 each year.

Deadline April of each year.

[92]
CONNECTICUT MINORITY TEACHER INCENTIVE PROGRAM

Connecticut Office of Financial and Academic Affairs for Higher Education
Attn: Student Financial Aid
61 Woodland Street
Hartford, CT 06105-2326
(860) 947-1853   Toll Free: (800) 842-0229 (within CT)
Fax: (860) 947-1314   E-mail: mtip@ctdhe.org
Web: www.ctohe.org/SFA/default.htm

Summary To provide financial assistance to Asian Americans and other minority upper-division college students in Connecticut who are interested in teaching at public schools in the state.

Eligibility This program is open to juniors and seniors enrolled full time in Connecticut college and university teacher preparation programs. Applicants must be members of a minority group, defined as African American, Hispanic/ Latino, Asian American, or Native American. They must be nominated by the education dean at their institution.

Financial data The maximum stipend is $5,000 per year. In addition, if recipients complete a credential and begin teaching at a public school in Connecticut within 16 months of graduation, they may receive up to $2,500 per year, for up to 4 years, to help pay off college loans.

Duration Up to 2 years.

Number awarded Varies each year.

Deadline October of each year.

[93]
CONNTESOL SCHOLARSHIPS

Connecticut Teachers of English to Speakers of Other Languages
P.O. Box 304
Norwich, CT 06360-0304
E-mail: ConnTESOL@gmail.com
Web: www.conntesol.net

Summary To provide financial assistance to Connecticut residents whose native language is not English and who are attending or planning to attend college in any state.

Eligibility This program is open to residents of Connecticut whose first language is not English. Awards are presented in 4 categories: 1) high school seniors entering a 2-year college; 2) high school seniors entering a 4-year college or university; 3) high school seniors who are presently or were previously enrolled in English Language Learning (ELL) or bilingual education classes and entering a 2- or 4-year college or univer-

sity (designated the CAPELL Scholarship for its sponsor, the Connecticut Administrators of Programs for English Language Learners); and 4) adult education students entering a college or university. Applicants must submit an essay of 250 to 500 words on how the education they are receiving in the United States is influencing their life.

Financial data The stipend is $1,000.

Duration 1 year.

Number awarded At least 4 each year (1 in each category).

Deadline April of each year.

[94]
CORA AGUDA MANAYAN FUND

Hawai'i Community Foundation
Attn: Scholarship Department
827 Fort Street Mall
Honolulu, HI 96813
(808) 566-5570   Toll Free: (888) 731-3863
Fax: (808) 521-6286
E-mail: scholarships@hcf-hawaii.org
Web: www.hawaiicommunityfoundation.org/scholarships

Summary To provide financial assistance to Hawaii residents of Filipino ancestry who are interested in attending college or graduate school to prepare for a career in the health field.

Eligibility This program is open to Hawaii residents of Filipino ancestry who are interested in enrolling full time in a health-related field (on the undergraduate or graduate school level). Applicants must be able to demonstrate academic achievement (GPA of 3.0 or higher), good moral character, and financial need. Along with their application, they must submit a short statement indicating their reasons for attending college, their planned course of study, their career goals, and what community service means to them. Preference may be given to applicants studying at a college or university in Hawaii.

Financial data The amounts of the awards depend on the availability of funds and the need of the recipient. Recently, the average value of each of the scholarships awarded by the foundation was $2,200.

Duration 1 year.

Number awarded Varies each year; recently, 10 of these scholarships were awarded.

Deadline February of each year.

[95]
CORRINE WILLIAMS SCHOLARSHIP

California Dietetic Association
Attn: CDA Foundation
7740 Manchester Avenue, Suite 102
Playa del Rey, CA 90293-8499
(310) 822-0177   Fax: (310) 823-0264
E-mail: patsmith@dietitian.org
Web: www.dietitian.org/d_cdaf/cdaf_outreach.html

Summary To provide financial assistance to residents of California (particularly Asian Americans, other minorities, men, and individuals with disabilities) who are members of the Academy of Nutrition and Dietetics (AND) and interested in participating in specified types of programs in any state.

Eligibility This program is open to California residents who are AND members and 1) entering the first or second year of an approved Dietetic Technician Program in any state; 2) entering at least the second year of an accredited Coordinated Program (CP) or Didactic Program in Dietetics (DPD) in any state; or 3) accepted to an accredited Supervised Practice Program in any state to begin within 6 months. Along with their application, they must submit a letter of application that includes a discussion of their career goals. Selection is based on that letter (15%), academic ability (25%), work or volunteer experience (15%), letters of recommendation (15%), extracurricular activities (5%), and financial need (25%). Applications are especially encouraged from ethnic minorities, men, and people with physical disabilities.

Financial data The stipend is normally $1,000.

Duration 1 year.

Additional information This program began in 2010. The California Dietetic Association is the California affiliate of the AND.

Number awarded 1 each year.

Deadline April of each year.

[96]
CRACKER BARREL-MINORITY TEACHER EDUCATION SCHOLARSHIPS

Florida Fund for Minority Teachers, Inc.
Attn: Executive Director
G415 Norman Hall
P.O. Box 117045
Gainesville, FL 32611-7045
(352) 392-9196, ext. 21   Fax: (352) 846-3011
E-mail: info@ffmt.org
Web: www.ffmt.org

Summary To provide funding to Asian American and other minority Florida residents who are preparing for a career as a teacher.

Eligibility This program is open to Florida residents who are African American/Black, Hispanic/Latino, Asian American/Pacific Islander, or American Indian/Alaskan Native. Applicants must be entering their junior year in a teacher education program at a participating college or university in Florida. Special consideration is given to community college graduates. Selection is based on writing ability, communication skills, overall academic performance, and evidence of commitment to the youth of America (preferably demonstrated through volunteer activities).

Financial data The stipend is $2,000 per year. Recipients are required to teach 1 year in a Florida public school for each year they receive the scholarship. If they fail to teach in a public school, they are required to repay the total amount of support received at an annual interest rate of 8%.

Duration Up to 2 consecutive years, provided the recipient remains enrolled full time with a GPA of 2.5 or higher.

Additional information For a list of the 16 participating public institutions and the 18 participating private institutions, contact the Florida Fund for Minority Teachers (FFMT). Recipients are also required to attend the annual FFMT recruitment and retention conference.

Number awarded Varies each year.

Deadline July of each year for fall semester; November of each year for spring semester.

[97]
CRCNA RACE RELATIONS MULTIRACIAL STUDENT SCHOLARSHIP

Christian Reformed Church
Attn: Office of Race Relations
2850 Kalamazoo Avenue, S.E.
Grand Rapids, MI 49560-0200
(616) 224-5883   Toll Free: (877) 279-9994
Fax: (616) 224-0834   E-mail: elugo@crcna.org
Web: www.crcna.org/race/scholarships

Summary To provide financial assistance to Asian American and other minority undergraduate and graduate students who are interested in attending colleges related to the Christian Reformed Church in North America (CRCNA).

Eligibility This program is open to students of color in the United States and Canada. Normally, applicants are expected to be members of CRCNA congregations who plan to pursue their educational goals at Calvin Theological Seminary or any of the colleges affiliated with the CRCNA. They must be interested in training for the ministry of racial reconciliation in church and/or in society. Students who have no prior history with the CRCNA must attend a CRCNA-related college or seminary for a full academic year before they are eligible to apply for this program. Students entering their sophomore year must have earned a GPA of 2.0 or higher as freshmen; students entering their junior year must have earned a GPA of 2.3 or higher as sophomores; students entering their senior year must have earned a GPA of 2.6 or higher as juniors.

Financial data First-year students receive $500 per semester. Other levels of students may receive up to $2,000 per academic year.

Duration 1 year.

Additional information This program was first established in 1971 and revised in 1991. Recipients are expected to train to engage actively in the ministry of racial reconciliation in church and in society. They must be able to work in the United States or Canada upon graduating and must consider working for 1 of the agencies of the CRCNA.

Number awarded Varies each year; recently, 31 students received a total of $21,000 in support.

Deadline March of each year.

[98]
CTA/MARTIN LUTHER KING, JR. MEMORIAL SCHOLARSHIP FUND

California Teachers Association
Attn: CTA Foundation for Teaching and Learning
1705 Murchison Drive
P.O. Box 921
Burlingame, CA 94011-0921
(650) 697-1400   E-mail: scholarships@cta.org
Web: www.cta.org

Summary To provide financial assistance for college or graduate school to Asian Americans and other racial and ethnic minorities who are members of the California Teachers Association (CTA), children of members, or members of the Student CTA.

Eligibility This program is open to members of racial or ethnic minority groups (African Americans, American Indians/Alaska Natives, Asians/Pacific Islanders, and Hispanics) who are 1) active CTA members; 2) dependent children of active, retired, or deceased CTA members; or 3) members of Student CTA. Applicants must be interested in preparing for a teaching career in public education or already engaged in such a career.

Financial data Stipends vary each year; recently, they ranged from $1,000 to $4,000.

Duration 1 year.

Number awarded Varies each year; recently, 25 of these scholarships were awarded: 5 to CTA members, 10 to children of CTA members, and 10 to Student CTA members.

Deadline February of each year.

[99]
DALIP SINGH SAUND SCHOLARSHIP

Federal Asian Pacific American Council
Attn: FAPAC Endowment Fund
P.O. Box 23184
Washington, DC 20026-3184
(202) 366-0626   E-mail: scholarship@fapac.org
Web: www.fapac.org

Summary To provide financial assistance for college to Asian Pacific Americans.

Eligibility This program is open to Asian Pacific Americans who are U.S. citizens. Applicants must be high school seniors or current college students and have a GPA of 3.0 or higher. Along with their application, they must submit a 2-page essay on a topic that changes annually but relates to public service; recently, students were asked to write about the contributions of Congressman Dalip Singh Saund (the first Asian Pacific American elected to Congress) and their goal in public service. Selection is based on academic achievement, commitment to public service (especially service to the Asian Pacific American community); and demonstrated leadership and potential for continued growth in leadership skills.

Financial data The stipend is $5,000.

Duration 1 year.

Additional information The sponsor is an organization of Asian Pacific Americans employed by the federal government and the District of Columbia. It renamed its scholarship program after Congressman Saund in 2013.

Number awarded 1 each year.

Deadline April of each year.

[100]
DAMON P. MOORE SCHOLARSHIP

Indiana State Teachers Association
Attn: Scholarships
150 West Market Street, Suite 900
Indianapolis, IN 46204-2875
(317) 263-3369   Toll Free: (800) 382-4037
Fax: (800) 777-6128   E-mail: mshoup@ista-in.org
Web: www.ista-in.org/dynamic.aspx?id=1212

Summary To provide financial assistance to Asian and other minority high school seniors in Indiana who are interested in studying education in college.

Eligibility This program is open to ethnic minority public high school seniors in Indiana who are interested in studying education in college. Selection is based on academic achievement, leadership ability as expressed through co-curricular activities and community involvement, recommenda-

tions, and a 300-word essay on their educational goals and how they plan to use this scholarship.

Financial data The stipend is $1,000.

Duration 1 year; may be renewed for 2 additional years if the recipient maintains at least a "C+" average.

Additional information This program began in 1987.

Number awarded 1 each year.

Deadline February of each year.

[101]
DARDEN RESTAURANTS FOUNDATION APIASF SCHOLARSHIPS

Asian & Pacific Islander American Scholarship Fund
2025 M Street, N.W., Suite 610
Washington, DC 20036-3363
(202) 986-6892   Toll Free: (877) 808-7032
Fax: (202) 530-0643   E-mail: info@apiasf.org
Web: www.apiasf.org/scholarship_apiasf.html

Summary To provide financial assistance to Asian and Pacific Islander Americans who are entering college for the first time, especially those planning to major in hospitality management or culinary arts.

Eligibility This program is open to U.S. citizens, nationals, permanent residents, and citizens of the Freely Associated States who are first-time incoming college students and of Asian or Pacific Islander heritage. Applicants must be enrolling full time at an accredited 2- or 4-year college or university in the United States. They must have a GPA of 3.0 or higher or the GED equivalent. In addition, they must complete the FAFSA and apply for federal financial aid. Special consideration is given to applicants planning to major in hospitality management or culinary arts.

Financial data The stipend is $2,500 per year.

Duration 2 years.

Additional information This program is sponsored by Darden Restaurants and administered by the Asian & Pacific Islander American Scholarship Fund (APIASF).

Number awarded Varies each year; recently, 7 of these scholarships were awarded.

Deadline January of each year.

[102]
DAVID EVANS AND ASSOCIATES SCHOLARSHIPS

David Evans and Associates, Inc.
2100 S.W. River Parkway
Portland, OR 97201
(503) 223-2701   Toll Free: (800) 721-1916
Fax: (503) 223-6663
Web: www.deainc.com/scholarships.aspx

Summary To provide financial assistance to Asian Americans, other minorities, and women who are working on an undergraduate degree in civil engineering or geomatics at colleges in designated states.

Eligibility This program is open to women and minority undergraduates majoring in civil engineering (including transportation, structural, land development, or environmental) or geomatics. Applicants must be enrolled at a college or university in Arizona, California, Colorado, Idaho, New York, Oregon, or Washington. They must have a GPA of 3.0 or higher.

Financial data The stipend is $3,000.

Duration 1 year; nonrenewable.

Number awarded 2 each year.

Deadline April of each year.

[103]
DEFENSE INTELLIGENCE AGENCY UNDERGRADUATE TRAINING ASSISTANCE PROGRAM

Defense Intelligence Agency
Attn: Human Resources, HCH-4
200 MacDill Boulevard, Building 6000
Bolling AFB, DC 20340-5100
(202) 231-2736   Fax: (202) 231-4889
TDD: (202) 231-5002   E-mail: staffing@dia.mil
Web: www.dia.mil/careers/students

Summary To provide financial aid and work experience to high school seniors and lower-division students (particularly Asian Americans, other minorities, women, and students with disabilities) who are interested in majoring in specified fields and working for the U.S. Defense Intelligence Agency (DIA).

Eligibility This program is open to graduating high school seniors and college freshmen and sophomores interested in working full time on a baccalaureate degree in 1 of the following fields in college: biology, chemistry, computer science, engineering, foreign area studies, intelligence analysis, international relations, microbiology, pharmacology, physics, political science, or toxicology. High school seniors must have a GPA of 2.75 or higher and either 1) an SAT combined critical reading and mathematics score of 1000 or higher plus 500 or higher on the writing portion or 2) an ACT score of 21 or higher. College freshmen and sophomores must have a GPA of 3.0 or higher. All applicants must be able to demonstrate financial need (household income ceiling of $70,000 for a family of 4 or $80,000 for a family of 5 or more) and leadership abilities through extracurricular activities, civic involvement, volunteer work, or part-time employment. Students and all members of their immediate family must be U.S. citizens. Minorities, women, and persons with disabilities are strongly encouraged to apply.

Financial data Students accepted into this program receive tuition (up to $18,000 per year) at an accredited college or university selected by the student and endorsed by the sponsor; reimbursement for books and needed supplies; an annual salary to cover college room and board expenses and for summer employment; and a position at the sponsoring agency after graduation. Recipients must work for DIA after college graduation for at least 1 and a half times the length of study. For participants who leave DIA earlier than scheduled, the agency arranges for payments to reimburse DIA for the total cost of education (including the employee's pay and allowances).

Duration 4 years, provided the recipient maintains a GPA of 2.75 during the freshman year and 3.0 or higher in subsequent semesters.

Additional information Recipients are provided a challenging summer internship and guaranteed a job at the agency in their field of study upon graduation.

Number awarded Only a few are awarded each year.

Deadline October of each year.

[104]
DENVER BUDDHIST TEMPLE DOJO SENSEI MEMORIAL SCHOLARSHIP

Japanese American Community Graduation Program
P.O. Box 13665
Denver, CO 80201-3665
(303) 288-6083
Web: www.jacgp.com/student-scholarships

Summary To provide financial assistance to high school seniors of Japanese descent in the Rocky Mountain region who have participated in judo or other martial art and plan to attend college in any state.

Eligibility This program is open to graduating high school seniors 1) who are residing in the Rocky Mountain region and an American citizen of Japanese ancestry or an American citizen whose legal parents are of Japanese ancestry; or 2) who are of Japanese ancestry residing in the Rocky Mountain region and have permanent residence status (green card) in the United States; or 3) who have a parent who is an active member of: Mile High Chapter of Japanese American Citizens League (JACL), Japanese Association of Colorado, Nisei Veterans' Heritage Foundation, Simpson United Method Church, Tri-State/Denver Buddhist Temples, Denver Nisei Bowling Association, Brighton Japanese American Association, Japanese Firms Association of Colorado, Longmont Buddhist Temple, or Fort Lupton JACL. Applicants must be planning to attend a college or university in any state. They must have been associated with a recognized martial arts program. Along with their application, they must submit a 1-page essay on how the philosophy taught in their martial art classes guides them in the way they intend to live their life. Selection is based on that essay; longevity of enrollment, participation, and volunteerism in a martial art; school records; and school and community activities and awards.

Financial data Stipends up to $5,000 are available.

Duration 1 year.

Additional information This program is sponsored by the Denver Buddhist Temple in honor of the Senseis who have taught or promoted the sport of judo in the community and the Rocky Mountain region.

Number awarded 1 each year.

Deadline April of each year.

[105]
DISTINGUISHED RAVEN FAC MEMORIAL SCHOLARSHIPS

Edgar Allan Poe Literary Society
Attn: Raven Scholarship
4320 Saddle Ridge Trail
Flower Mound, TX 75028
Web: www.ravens.org/scholar/scholarship.htm

Summary To provide financial assistance to descendants of Lao or Hmong individuals who served alongside Forward Air Controllers (FACs) in Laos between 1960 and 1975 and are interested in attending college.

Eligibility This program is open to high school seniors and graduates in any state who are enrolled or planning to enroll full time at an accredited college, university, or junior college and work on an associate or bachelor's degree in any field. Applicants must be descendants of Lao or Hmong individuals who lived in Laos between 1960 and 1975 and served alongside FACs who flew under the call sign "Raven" or its predecessor "Butterfly." Along with their application, they must submit transcripts (including SAT and/or ACT scores), information on their extracurricular activities (including Lao/Hmong cultural activities), and a 500-word essay describing their goals. Selection is based on that essay, academic achievement, character, and service beyond self.

Financial data Stipends range from $500 to $2,500 per year.

Duration 1 year;.

Additional information This program includes the Charles E. Engle Memorial Scholarship, the Gomer D. Reese, III Memorial Scholarship, the Henry L. Allen Memorial Scholarship, the James E. Cross Memorial Scholarship, the John A. Davidson, II Memorial Scholarship, the Joseph L. Chestnut Memorial Scholarship, the Park G. Bunker Memorial Scholarship, the Paul E. Williams Memorial Scholarship, the Richard G. Elzinga Memorial Scholarship, and the W. Grant Uhls Memorial Scholarship.

Number awarded Varies each year; recently, 10 of these scholarships were awarded: 1 at $2,500, 1 at $1,500, 4 at $1,000, and 4 at $500.

Deadline February.

[106]
DIVERSITY COMMITTEE SCHOLARSHIP

American Society of Safety Engineers
Attn: ASSE Foundation
Scholarship Award Program
1800 East Oakton Street
Des Plaines, IL 60018
(847) 699-2929   Fax: (847) 768-3434
E-mail: bzylstra@asse.org
Web: www.asse.org

Summary To provide financial assistance to Asian American and other diverse upper-division or graduate students who are working on a degree related to occupational safety.

Eligibility This program is open to students who are working on an undergraduate or graduate degree in occupational safety, health, environment, industrial hygiene, occupational health nursing, or a closely-related field (e.g., industrial or environmental engineering). Applicants must be full-time students who have completed at least 60 semester hours with a GPA of 3.0 or higher as undergraduates or at least 9 semester hours as graduate students. A goal of this program is to support individuals regardless of race, ethnicity, gender, religion, personal beliefs, age, sexual orientation, physical challenges, geographic location, university, or specific area of study. U.S. citizenship is not required. Membership in the American Society of Safety Engineers (ASSE) is not required, but preference is given to members.

Financial data The stipend is $1,000 per year.

Duration 1 year; recipients may reapply.

Number awarded 1 each year.

Deadline November of each year.

[107]
DIVERSITY IN PLANNING AWARD

American Planning Association-California Chapter
Attn: California Planning Foundation
c/o Paul Wack
California Polytechnic State University at San Luis Obispo
City and Regional Planning Department
San Luis Obispo, CA 93407-0283
(805) 756-6331   Fax: (805) 756-1340
E-mail: pwack@calpoly.edu
Web: www.californiaplanningfoundation.org

Summary To provide financial assistance to Asian American and other undergraduate and graduate students in accredited planning programs at California universities who will increase diversity in the profession.

Eligibility This program is open to students entering their final year for an undergraduate or master's degree in an accredited planning program at a university in California. Applicants must be students who will increase diversity in the planning profession. Selection is based on academic performance, professional promise, and financial need.

Financial data The stipend is $3,000. The award includes a 1-year student membership in the American Planning Association (APA) and payment of registration for the APA California Conference.

Duration 1 year.

Additional information The accredited planning programs are at 3 campuses of the California State University system (California State Polytechnic University at Pomona, California Polytechnic State University at San Luis Obispo, and San Jose State University), 3 campuses of the University of California (Berkeley, Irvine, and Los Angeles), and the University of Southern California.

Number awarded 1 each year.

Deadline March of each year.

[108]
DIVERSITY IN PSYCHOLOGY AND LAW RESEARCH AWARD

American Psychological Association
Attn: Division 41 (American Psychology-Law Society)
c/o Diane Sivasubramaniam, Minority Affairs Committee
  Chair
Swinburne University of Technology
Faculty of Life and Social Sciences
Mail H31
P.O. Box 218
Hawthorn, VIC 3122
Australia
61 3 9214 5858 E-mail: dsivasubramaniam@swin.edu.au
Web: www.ap-ls.org

Summary To provide funding to Asian American and other student members of the American Psychology-Law Society (AP-LS) who are interested in conducting a research project related to diversity.

Eligibility This program is open to undergraduate and graduate student members of AP-LS who are interested in conducting research on issues related to psychology, law, multiculturalism, and/or diversity (e.g., research pertaining to psycholegal issues on race, gender, culture, sexual orientation). Students from underrepresented groups are strongly encouraged to apply; underrepresented groups include, but are not limited to: racial and ethnic minorities; first-generation college students; lesbian, gay, bisexual, and transgender students; and physically disabled students. Applicants must submit a project description that includes a statement of the research problem, the project's likely impact on the field of psychology and law broadly, methodology, budget, and an overview of relevant literature. Selection is based on the impact of the project on diversity and multiculturalism and the expected completion within the allocated time.

Financial data   The grant is $1,000.

Duration   The project must be completed within 1 year.

Number awarded   Up to 4 each year.

Deadline   November of each year.

[109]
DON SAHLI–KATHY WOODALL MINORITY STUDENT SCHOLARSHIP

Tennessee Education Association
801 Second Avenue North
Nashville, TN 37201-1099
(615) 242-8392   Toll Free: (800) 342-8367
Fax: (615) 259-4581   E-mail: mjohnson@tea.nea.org
Web: www.teateachers.org

Summary   To provide financial assistance to Asian American and other minority high school seniors in Tennessee who are interested in majoring in education at a college or university in the state.

Eligibility   This program is open to minority high school seniors in Tennessee who are planning to attend a college or university in the state and major in education. Application must be made either by a Future Teachers of America chapter affiliated with the Tennessee Education Association (TEA) or by the student with the recommendation of an active TEA member. Selection is based on academic record, leadership ability, financial need, and demonstrated interest in becoming a teacher.

Financial data   The stipend is $1,000.

Duration   1 year.

Number awarded   1 each year.

Deadline   February of each year.

[110]
DORA AMES LEE LEADERSHIP DEVELOPMENT FUND

United Methodist Church
General Board of Global Ministries
Attn: United Methodist Committee on Relief
Health and Welfare Ministries
475 Riverside Drive, Room 330
New York, NY 10115
(212) 870-3871   Toll Free: (800) UMC-GBGM
E-mail: jyoung@gbgm-umc.org
Web: gbgm-umc.org/health/doralee.cfm

Summary   To provide financial assistance to Methodists and other Christians of Asian, Pacific Islander, or Native American descent who are preparing for a career in a health-related field.

Eligibility   This program is open to undergraduate and graduate students who are U.S. citizens of Asian American, Pacific Islander, or Native American descent. Applicants must be professed Christians, preferably United Methodists. They must be attending a college or university to enter or continue in a health-related field. Financial need is considered in the selection process.

Financial data   The stipend is $2,000.

Duration   1 year.

Additional information   This program began in 1980.

Number awarded   5 each year.

Deadline   June of each year.

[111]
DOUVAS MEMORIAL SCHOLARSHIP

Wyoming Department of Education
Attn: Consultant
2300 Capitol Avenue, Second Floor
Cheyenne, WY 82002-0050
(307) 777-3793   Fax: (307) 777-6234
E-mail: stephanie.brady@wyo.gov
Web: edu.wyoming.gov

Summary   To provide financial assistance to Asian American and other high school seniors or students in Wyoming who are first-generation Americans.

Eligibility   This program is open to first-generation youth in Wyoming who demonstrate need and are motivated to attend college. First-generation Americans are those born in the United States but whose parents were not born here. Applicants must be high school seniors or between the ages of 18 and 22. They must be Wyoming residents and be willing to use the scholarship at Wyoming's community colleges or the University of Wyoming.

Financial data   The stipend is $500, payable in 2 equal installments. Funds are paid directly to the recipient's school.

Duration   1 year.

Additional information   This program began in 1995.

Number awarded   1 each year.

Deadline   May of each year.

[112]
DR. MARTIN LUTHER KING, JR. SCHOLARSHIP

North Carolina Association of Educators, Inc.
Attn: Minority Affairs Commission
700 South Salisbury Street
P.O. Box 27347
Raleigh, NC 27611-7347
(919) 832-3000, ext. 205
Toll Free: (800) 662-7924, ext. 205
Fax: (919) 839-8229   E-mail: joy.bradford@ncae.org
Web: www.ncae.org/get-involved/awards

Summary   To provide financial assistance to minority and other high school seniors in North Carolina who plan to attend college in any state.

Eligibility   This program is open to seniors graduating from high schools in North Carolina who plan to attend a college or university in any state. They must have a GPA of 2.5 or higher. Along with their application, they must submit an essay on how the philosophies and ideals of Dr. Martin Luther King influenced their life. Applications are considered and judged by members of the association's Minority Affairs Commission. Selection is based on the essay, academic record, extracurricular activities and affiliations, accomplishments (honors and awards, leadership, and work experience), and financial need.

Financial data   A stipend is awarded (amount not specified).

Duration   1 year.

Number awarded   1 or more each year.

Deadline   March of each year.

[113]
DR. SYNGMAN RHEE SCHOLARSHIP

Dong Ji Hoi Society
Attn: Scholarship Committee
91-168 Puaina Place
Ewa Beach, HI 96706
E-mail: hawaiidjh@gmail.com

Summary   To provide financial assistance to Korean Americans in Hawaii who are interested in pursuing postsecondary education at a school in any state.

Eligibility   This program is open to graduating high school seniors in Hawaii who are of at least 50% Korean ancestry. Applicants must be planning to attend a 4-year college or university in any state. Selection is based on academic achievement, community service, extracurricular activities, and SAT scores.

Financial data   The stipend is $2,500 per year.

Duration   Up to 4 years.

Number awarded   10 to 16 each year.

Deadline   June of each year.

[114]
DR. THOMAS T. YATABE MEMORIAL SCHOLARSHIP

Japanese American Citizens League
Attn: National Scholarship Awards
1765 Sutter Street
San Francisco, CA 94115
(415) 345-1075   Fax: (415) 931-4671
E-mail: ncwnp@jacl.org
Web: www.jacl.org/edu/scholar.htm

Summary   To provide financial assistance to members of the Japanese American Citizens League (JACL) who are currently enrolled in an institution of higher learning.

Eligibility   This program is open to JACL members who are currently enrolled at a college, university, trade school, business college, or other institution of higher learning. Applicants must submit information on their involvement in JACL and a 2-page essay on a topic that changes annually but relates to Japanese Americans. Selection is based on that essay, academic history, JACL involvement, school activities, work history, scholastic honors, and community involvement.

Financial data   Stipends generally average more than $2,000.

Duration   1 year; nonrenewable.

Number awarded   At least 1 each year.

Deadline   March of each year.

[115]
DREAM SCHOLARSHIP FUND FOR ASIAN AMERICAN AND PACIFIC ISLANDER STUDENTS

National Korean American Service and Education
  Consortium
Attn: Scholarship
1701 K Street, N.W., Suite 650
Washington, DC 20006
(202) 299-9540   Fax: (202) 299-9729
E-mail: nakasec@nakasec.org
Web: nakasec.org

Summary   To provide financial assistance to Asian Americans and Pacific Islanders, especially immigrants, who are interested in attending college.

Eligibility   This program is open to Asian Americans and Pacific Islanders, especially Korean Americans, who are high school seniors or current full-time students at an accredited college or university in the United States. Applicants must be able to demonstrate financial need. The sponsor is a network of community-based organizations that advocates for immigrant rights issues for Korean Americans.

Financial data   A stipend is awarded (amount not specified).

Duration   1 year.

Number awarded   1 or more each year.

Deadline   May of each year.

[116]
DWIGHT MOSLEY SCHOLARSHIPS

United States Tennis Association
Attn: USTA Serves
70 West Red Oak Lane
White Plains, NY 10604
(914) 696-7223   E-mail: foundation@usta.com
Web: www.usta.com

Summary   To provide financial assistance to female and male high school seniors who are Asian American or from other diverse ethnic backgrounds, have participated in an organized community tennis program, and plan to attend college in any state.

Eligibility   This program is open to high school seniors from diverse ethnic backgrounds who have excelled academically, demonstrated achievements in leadership, and participated extensively in an organized community tennis program. Applicants must be planning to enroll as a full-time undergraduate student at a 4-year college or university. They must have a GPA of 3.0 or higher and be able to demonstrate financial need and sportsmanship. Along with their application, they must submit an essay of 1 to 2 pages about how their participation in a tennis and education program has influenced their life, including examples of special mentors, volunteer service, and future goals. Females and males are considered separately.

Financial data   The stipend is $2,500 per year. Funds are paid directly to the recipient's college or university.

Duration   4 years.

Number awarded   2 each year: 1 female and 1 male.

Deadline   February of each year.

[117]
EAST AMERICA CHAPTER UNDERGRADUATE SCHOLARSHIP AWARDS

Phi Tau Phi Scholastic Honor Society-East America
  Chapter
c/o Dr. Heng-Chun Li, Scholarship Selection Committee
39 Kennedy Circle
Closter, NJ 07624
(201) 767-9325   E-mail: hengshun.li@gmail.com
Web: www.phitauphi.org

Summary To provide financial assistance to college juniors and seniors of Chinese heritage at colleges and universities in eastern states.

Eligibility This program is open to juniors and seniors enrolled at an accredited institution of higher education east of a line along Ohio, Kentucky, and Alabama. Applicants must be of Chinese heritage or interested in and committed to Chinese heritage and culture, have a GPA of 3.5 or higher, and be sponsored by a member of Phi Tau Phi. Along with their application, they must submit a 1-page essay on their professional goals, achievements, financial need, and Chinese cultural interests.

Financial data The stipend is $1,000.

Duration 1 year.

Additional information Phi Tau Phi, first organized in 1921 in China and reestablished in 1964 in the United States, is a relatively small honor society of scholars, mainly of Chinese heritage, in various disciplines of science, technology, art, and humanities. Students who have difficulty in locating a sponsor should contact the Scholarship Selection Committee.

Number awarded 1 or 2 each year.

Deadline September of each year.

[118]
EASTERN REGION KOREAN AMERICAN COLLEGE/GRADUATE SCHOLARSHIPS

Korean American Scholarship Foundation
Eastern Region
1952 Gallows Road, Suite 310
Vienna, VA 22182
(703) 748-5935   Fax: (703) 748-1874
E-mail: erc.scholarship@kasf.org
Web: www.kasf.org/eastern

Summary To provide financial assistance to Korean American students from any state who are working on an undergraduate or graduate degree in any field at a school in eastern states.

Eligibility This program is open to Korean Americans who are high school seniors or full-time undergraduate or graduate students currently enrolled or planning to enroll at a college or university in an eastern state. Applicants may reside anywhere in the United States as long as they attend school in the eastern region: Delaware, District of Columbia, Kentucky, Maryland, North Carolina, Pennsylvania, Virginia, and West Virginia. They must have a GPA of 3.0 or higher. Both U.S. citizens and foreign nationals are eligible. Selection is based on academic achievement (25%), extracurricular activities (10%), an essay (10%), recommendations (10%), financial need (40%), and extra credit for having extraordinary circumstances (5%).

Financial data Stipends range up to $5,000.

Duration 1 year; renewable.

Number awarded Varies each year; recently, 31 of these scholarships were awarded.

Deadline July of each year.

[119]
ED BRADLEY SCHOLARSHIP

Radio Television Digital News Foundation
Attn: Programs, Awards, and Membership Manager
529 14th Street, N.W., Suite 425
Washington, DC 20045
(202) 725-8318   Fax: (202) 223-4007
E-mail: katies@rtdna.org
Web: www.rtdna.org/pages/education/scholarship-info.php

Summary To provide financial assistance to Asian American and other minority undergraduate students who are preparing for a career in electronic journalism.

Eligibility This program is open to sophomore or more advanced minority undergraduate students enrolled in an electronic journalism sequence at an accredited or nationally-recognized college or university. Applicants must submit 1 to 3 examples of their journalistic skills on audio CD or DVD (no more than 15 minutes total, accompanied by scripts); a description of their role on each story and a list of who worked on each story and what they did; a 1-page statement explaining why they are preparing for a career in electronic journalism with reference to their specific career preference (radio, television, online, reporting, producing, or newsroom management); a resume; and a letter of reference from their dean or faculty sponsor explaining why they are a good candidate for the award and certifying that they have at least 1 year of school remaining.

Financial data The stipend is $10,000, paid in semiannual installments of $5,000 each.

Duration 1 year.

Additional information The Radio Television Digital News Foundation (RTDNF) also provides an all-expense paid trip to the Radio Television Digital News Association (RTDNA) annual international conference. The RTDNF was formerly the Radio and Television News Directors Foundation (RTNDF). Previous winners of any RTDNF scholarship or internship are not eligible.

Number awarded 1 each year.

Deadline May of each year.

[120]
EDSA MINORITY SCHOLARSHIP

Landscape Architecture Foundation
Attn: Leadership in Landscape Scholarship Program
818 18th Street, N.W., Suite 810
Washington, DC 20006-3520
(202) 331-7070   Fax: (202) 331-7079
E-mail: scholarships@lafoundation.org
Web: www.lafoundation.org

Summary To provide financial assistance to Asian American and other minority college students who are interested in studying landscape architecture.

Eligibility This program is open to African American, Hispanic, Native American, and minority college students of other cultural and ethnic backgrounds. Applicants must be entering their final 2 years of undergraduate study in landscape architecture. Along with their application, they must submit a 500-word essay on a design or research effort they plan to pursue (explaining how it will contribute to the advancement of the profession and to their ethnic heritage), 3 work samples, and 2 letters of recommendation. Selection is based on professional experience, community involvement, extracurricular activities, and financial need.

Financial data The stipend is $5,000.

Additional information This scholarship was formerly designated the Edward D. Stone, Jr. and Associates Minority Scholarship.

Number awarded 1 each year.

Deadline February of each year.

[121]
EDUCATION ASSISTANCE PROGRAM

Accountancy Board of Ohio
77 South High Street, 18th Floor
Columbus, OH 43215-6128
(614) 466-4135   Fax: (614) 466-2628
Web: acc.ohio.gov/CPAExam/Education-Assistance.aspx

Summary To provide financial assistance to Asian American or other minority/financially disadvantaged students enrolled in an accounting education program at Ohio academic institutions approved by the Accountancy Board of Ohio.

Eligibility This program is open to minority and financially disadvantaged Ohio residents who apply as full-time juniors or seniors in an accounting program at an accredited college or university in the state. Students who remain in good standing at their institutions and who enter a qualified fifth-year program are then eligible to receive these funds. Minority is defined as people with significant ancestry from Africa (excluding the Middle East), Asia (excluding the Middle East), Central America and the Caribbean islands, South America, and the islands of the Pacific Ocean; in addition, persons with significant ancestry from the original peoples of North America who are of non-European descent. Financial disadvantage is defined according to information provided on the Free Application for Federal Student Aid (FAFSA). U.S. citizenship or permanent resident status is required.

Financial data The amount of the stipend is determined annually but does not exceed the in-state tuition at Ohio public universities (currently, $13,067).

Duration 1 year (the fifth year of an accounting program). Funds committed to students who apply as juniors must be used within 4 years and funds committed to students who apply as seniors must be used within 3 years. The award is nonrenewable and may only be used when the student enrolls in the fifth year of a program.

Number awarded Several each year.

Deadline Applications may be submitted at any time.

[122]
EDWARD S. ROTH MANUFACTURING ENGINEERING SCHOLARSHIP

Society of Manufacturing Engineers
Attn: SME Education Foundation
One SME Drive
P.O. Box 930
Dearborn, MI 48121-0930
(313) 425-3300   Toll Free: (800) 733-4763, ext. 3300
Fax: (313) 425-3411   E-mail: foundation@sme.org
Web: www.smeef.org/scholarships

Summary To provide financial assistance to Asian American and other students enrolled or planning to work on a bachelor's or master's degree in manufacturing engineering at selected universities.

Eligibility This program is open to U.S. citizens who are graduating high school seniors or currently-enrolled undergraduate or graduate students. Applicants must be enrolled or planning to enroll as a full-time student at 1 of 13 selected 4-year universities to work on a bachelor's or master's degree in manufacturing engineering. They must have a GPA of 3.0 or higher. Preference is given to 1) students demonstrating financial need; 2) minority students; and 3) students participating in a co-op program. Some preference may also be given to graduating high school seniors and graduate students. Along with their application, they must submit a 300-word essay that covers their career and educational objectives, how this scholarship will help them attain those objectives, and why they want to enter this field.

Financial data Stipend amounts vary; recently, the value of all scholarships provided by this foundation averaged approximately $2,330.

Duration 1 year; may be renewed.

Additional information The eligible institutions are California Polytechnic State University at San Luis Obispo, California State Polytechnic State University at Pomona, University of Miami (Florida), Bradley University (Illinois), Central State University (Ohio), Miami University (Ohio), Boston University, Worcester Polytechnic Institute (Massachusetts), University of Massachusetts, St. Cloud State University (Minnesota), University of Texas-Pan American, Brigham Young University (Utah), and Utah State University.

Number awarded 2 each year.

Deadline January of each year.

[123]
ELI LILLY AND COMPANY/BLACK DATA PROCESSING ASSOCIATES SCHOLARSHIP

Black Data Processing Associates
Attn: BDPA Education Technology Foundation
4423 Lehigh Road, Number 277
College Park, MD 20740
(513) 284-4968   Fax: (202) 318-2194
E-mail: scholarships@betf.org
Web: www.betf.org/scholarships/eli-lilly.shtml

Summary To provide financial assistance to Asian American and other minority high school seniors or current college students who are interested in studying information technology at a college in any state.

Eligibility This program is open to graduating high school seniors and current college undergraduates who are members of minority groups (African American, Hispanic, Asian, or Native American). Applicants must be enrolled or planning to enroll at an accredited 4-year college or university and work on a degree in information technology. They must have a GPA of 3.0 or higher. Along with their application, they must submit a 500-word essay on why information technology is important. Selection is based on that essay, academic achievement, leadership ability through academic or civic involvement, and participation in community service activities. U.S. citizenship or permanent resident status is required.

Financial data The stipend is $2,500. Funds may be used to pay for tuition, fees, books, room and board, or other college-related expenses.

Duration 1 year; nonrenewable.

Additional information The BDPA established its Education and Technology Foundation (BETF) in 1992 to advance the skill sets needed by African American and other minority adults and young people to compete in the information technology industry. This program is sponsored by Eli Lilly and Company.

Number awarded 1 or more each year.

Deadline July of each year.

[124]
EMPIRE STATE DIVERSITY HONORS SCHOLARSHIP PROGRAM

State University of New York
Attn: Office of Diversity, Equity and Inclusion
State University Plaza
353 Broadway
Albany, NY 12246
(518) 320-1189
Web: www.suny.edu/provost/odee/programs.cfm

Summary To provide financial assistance to residents of New York (particularly Asian Americans and other minorities) who are attending campuses of the State University of New York (SUNY) and will contribute to the diversity of the student body.

Eligibility This program is open to U.S. citizens and permanent residents who are New York residents and enrolled as undergraduate students at any of the participating SUNY colleges. Applicants must be able to demonstrate 1) how they will contribute to the diversity of the student body, primarily by having overcome a disadvantage or other impediment to success in higher education; and 2) high academic achievement. Economic disadvantage, although not a requirement, may be the basis for eligibility. Membership in a racial or ethnic group that is underrepresented at the applicant's school or program may serve as a plus factor in making awards, but may not form the sole basis of selection.

Financial data The maximum stipend provided by the SUNY system is half the student's cost of attendance or $3,000, whichever is less. The individual campus must match the SUNY award in an equal amount.

Duration 1 year; renewable.

Number awarded Varies each year; recently, nearly 1,000 students at 46 SUNY institutions received support from this program.

Deadline Deadline not specified.

[125]
ENCOURAGE MINORITY PARTICIPATION IN OCCUPATIONS WITH EMPHASIS ON REHABILITATION

Courage Center
Attn: EMPOWER Scholarship Program
3915 Golden Valley Road
Minneapolis, MN 55422
(763) 520-0214   Toll Free: (888) 8-INTAKE
Fax: (763) 520-0562   TDD: (763) 520-0245
E-mail: empower@couragecenter.org
Web: www.couragecenter.org

Summary To provide financial assistance to Asian Americans and other students of color from Minnesota and western Wisconsin interested in attending college in any state to prepare for a career in the medical rehabilitation field.

Eligibility This program is open to ethnically diverse students accepted at or enrolled in an institution of higher learning in any state. Applicants must be residents of Minnesota or western Wisconsin (Burnett, Pierce, Polk, and St. Croix counties). They must be able to demonstrate a career interest in the medical rehabilitation field by a record of volunteer involvement related to health care and must have a GPA of 2.0 or higher. Along with their application, they must submit a 1-page essay that covers their experiences and interactions to date with the area of volunteering, what they have accomplished and gained from those experiences, how those experiences will assist them in their future endeavors, why education is important to them, how this scholarship will help them with their financial need and their future career goals.

Financial data The stipend is $1,500.

Duration 1 year.

Additional information This program, established in 1995, is also identified by its acronym as the EMPOWER Scholarship Award.

Number awarded 2 each year.

Deadline May of each year.

[126]
ENTERTAINMENT SOFTWARE ASSOCIATION FOUNDATION SCHOLARSHIPS

Entertainment Software Association
Attn: ESA Foundation
317 Madison Avenue, 22nd Floor
New York, NY 10017
(917) 522-3250
Web: www.esafoundation.org/scholarship.asp

Summary To provide financial assistance to Asian Americans, other minorities, and women who are interested in attending college to prepare for a career in computer and video game arts.

Eligibility This program is open to women and members of minority groups who are high school seniors or undergraduates currently enrolled full time at an accredited 4-year college or university. Applicants must be interested in working on a degree leading to a career in computer and video game arts. They must be U.S. citizens and have a GPA of 2.75 or higher.

Financial data The stipend is $3,000.

Duration 1 year; nonrenewable.

Additional information This program began in 2007.

Number awarded Up to 30 each year: 15 to graduating high school seniors and 15 to current undergraduates.
Deadline May of each year.

[127]
ERNST & YOUNG ASCEND SCHOLARSHIPS

Ascend: Pan-Asian Leaders
Attn: Director of Programs
120 Wall Street, Ninth Floor
New York, NY 10005
(212) 248-4888   Fax: (212) 344-5636
E-mail: scholarships@ascendleadership.org
Web: www.ascendleadership.org

Summary To provide financial assistance to members of Ascend: Pan-Asian Leaders who are undergraduates working on a degree in accounting.

Eligibility This program is open to members of Ascend who are enrolled as full-time rising sophomores or juniors at colleges and universities in the United States. Applicants must have a GPA of 3.3 or higher and a major in accounting. Along with their application, they must submit a 500-word personal essay on how they have demonstrated leadership and teamwork in their academic studies, professional career, and/ or extracurricular activities and community volunteer work; why they believe those qualities are important to transforming themselves into a better leader; their career goals after graduation; and the role Ascend has played in the achievement of their academic and career goals. They must also answer questions about their leadership experience. Financial need is not considered in the selection process.

Financial data The stipend is $5,000.
Duration 1 year.
Additional information Ascend was formed in 2004 as the National Asian American Society of Accountants. This program is sponsored by Ernst & Young LLP.
Number awarded 5 each year.
Deadline May of each year.

[128]
EXCELLENCE IN DIVERSITY SCHOLARSHIPS

New Jersey Utilities Association
50 West State Street, Suite 1117
Trenton, NJ 08608
(609) 392-1000   Fax: (609) 396-4231
E-mail: info@njua.com
Web: www.njua.com/html/njua_eeo_scholarship.cfm

Summary To provide financial assistance to high school seniors in New Jersey who are Asian Americans, members of other minority groups, females, or individuals with disabilities and interested in attending college in any state.

Eligibility This program is open to seniors graduating from high schools in New Jersey who are women, minorities (Black or African American, Hispanic or Latino, American Indian or Alaska Native, Asian, Native Hawaiian or Pacific Islander, or 2 or more races), and persons with disabilities. Applicants must be planning to work on a bachelor's degree at a college or university in any state. Along with their application, they must submit a 500-word essay explaining their career ambition and why they have chosen that career. Children of employees of any New Jersey Utilities Association-member company are ineligible. Selection is based on overall academic excellence

and demonstrated financial need. U.S. citizenship or permanent resident status is required.

Financial data The stipend is $1,500 per year. Funds are paid to the recipient's college or university.
Duration 4 years.
Number awarded 2 each year.
Deadline March of each year.

[129]
FAACPA EDUCATIONAL FUND SCHOLARSHIPS

Filipino-American Association of Certified Public
  Accountants
Attn: FAACPA Educational Fund
P.O. Box 2035
Seattle, WA 98111
Web: www.faacpa.com

Summary To provide financial assistance to Filipino American residents of any state studying accounting at colleges and universities in Washington.

Eligibility This program is open to Filipino American and other residents of any state who have completed at least 2 quarters of study of accounting at a 2- or 4-year college or university in Washington. Applicants must submit a personal statement that includes their career goals and interests, what sparked their interest in accounting, and why they should be awarded this scholarship. They must be U.S. citizens or have applied for citizenship. Selection is based on their personal statement, academic achievement (GPA of 3.0 or higher), campus and/or community activities, work history, and financial need.

Financial data A stipend is awarded (amount not specified).
Duration 1 year; recipients may reapply.
Additional information This program is sponsored by the Educational Fund of the Filipino-American Association of Certified Public Accountants (FAACPA), an organization established by a group of Filipino Americans who were Certified Public Accountants. Its goal remains to serve the Filipino American community of Seattle and the state of Washington.
Number awarded 1 or more each year.
Deadline July of each year.

[130]
FACC PRESIDENT'S YOUTH AWARD

Filipino-American Community of Colorado
Attn: Scholarship Director
1900 Harlan Street
Edgewater, CO 80214
(303) 233-6817   E-mail: FACCScholarships@gmail.com
Web: www.coloradofilipinos.org

Summary To provide financial assistance to members of the Filipino-American Community of Colorado (FACC) who are high school seniors and planning to attend college in any state.

Eligibility This program is open to graduating high school seniors who have been junior members of FACC and active in its youth and cultural activities for at least 3 years. Applicants must be planning to attend a college or university in any state. They must be nominated by at least 3 officers of the FACC.

Financial data The stipend is $500.
Duration 1 year.

Additional information This program began in 1991.

Number awarded Up to 3 each year.

Deadline April of each year.

[131]
FACC SCHOLASTIC ACHIEVEMENT AWARD

Filipino-American Community of Colorado
Attn: Scholarship Director
1900 Harlan Street
Edgewater, CO 80214
(303) 233-6817   E-mail: FACCScholarships@gmail.com
Web: www.coloradofilipinos.org

Summary To provide financial assistance to Filipino Americans who are high school seniors in Colorado or attending college in that state.

Eligibility This program is open to Filipino Americans who are either 1) seniors graduating from high schools in Colorado and planning to attend a college or university in any state; or 2) residents of any state entering the final year of full-time undergraduate study at a college or university in Colorado. Applicants must have a GPA of 3.1 or higher. Along with their application, they must submit a description of their educational plans as those relate to their career objectives and future goals.

Financial data The stipend is $750.

Duration 1 year.

Additional information This program began in 1981.

Number awarded Up to 3 each year.

Deadline April of each year.

[132]
FACES SCHOLARSHIP

Filipino-American Communications Employees of AT&T
c/o Giancarlo Bautista
AT&T Services, Inc.
175 East Houston Street
San Antonio, TX 78205
(210) 821-4105   E-mail: gb4984@att.com
Web: www.kampsd.webs.com/scholarship.htm

Summary To provide financial assistance to high school seniors who have ties to the Filipino American community and plan to attend college in any state.

Eligibility This program is open to graduating high school seniors who plan to enroll at a 2- or 4-year college or university in the United States. Applicants must reside in an area served by AT&T in North America and have ties to the Filipino American community. They must be U.S. citizens or permanent residents. Along with their application, they must submit transcripts; copies of their SAT, PSAT, or ACT scores; a resume; and a 1,000-word essay on the impact and significance this scholarship will have for themselves and their family in their pursuit of a college education. Merit scholarships require a GPA of 3.0 or higher; opportunity scholarships require a GPA of 2.75 or higher.

Financial data Stipends for merit scholarships are $2,500, $1,500, and $1,250; stipends for opportunity scholarships are $1,250.

Duration 1 year.

Number awarded 3 merit scholarships (1 at $2,500, 1 at $1,500, and 1 at $1,250) and 2 opportunity scholarships (both at $1,250) are awarded each year.

Deadline April of each year.

[133]
FALLEN HEROES SCHOLARSHIPS

Vietnamese American Armed Forces Association
Attn: Scholarship Selection Committee
P.O. Box 8434
Fountain Valley, CA 92728-8434
(714) 386-9896   E-mail: vaafa.org@gmail.com
Web: www.vaafa.org/programs/fallen-heroes-scholarship

Summary To provide financial assistance to Vietnamese Americans who are involved in community service and are interested in attending college to major in any field.

Eligibility This program is open to students who are enrolled full time or accepted for enrollment as an undergraduate at an accredited college or university. Applicants must be of Vietnamese American or Vietnamese Amerasian descent. They must have a GPA of 2.8 or higher, be able to demonstrate financial need, and have a record of active involvement in a community service organization.

Financial data The stipend is $1,000.

Duration 1 year.

Additional information This program was established to honor Vietnamese Americans who served in the U.S. armed forces and lost their lives on active duty. Recipients of these scholarships are encouraged to learn about those Fallen Heroes and to work to promote the recognition and memory of them within their community.

Number awarded 12 each year.

Deadline May of each year.

[134]
FARM CREDIT EAST SCHOLARSHIPS

Farm Credit East
Attn: Scholarship Program
240 South Road
Enfield, CT 06082
(860) 741-4380   Toll Free: (800) 562-2235
Fax: (860) 741-4389
E-mail: specialoffers@famcrediteast.com
Web: www.farmcrediteast.com

Summary To provide financial assistance to Asian American and other residents of designated northeastern states who plan to attend school in any state to work on an undergraduate or graduate degree in a field related to agriculture, forestry, or fishing.

Eligibility This program is open to residents of Massachusetts, Connecticut, Rhode Island, New Jersey, and portions of New York and New Hampshire. Applicants must be working on or planning to work on an associate, bachelor's, or graduate degree in production agriculture, agribusiness, the forest products industry, or commercial fishing at a college or university in any state. They must submit a 200-word essay on why they wish to prepare for a career in agriculture, forestry, or fishing. Selection is based on the essay, extracurricular activities (especially farm work experience and activities indicative of an interest in preparing for a career in agriculture or agribusiness), and interest in agriculture. The program includes diversity scholarships reserved for members of minority groups (Black or African American, American Indian or Alaska Native, Asian, Native Hawaiian or other Pacific Islander, or Hispanic or Latino).

Financial data The stipend is $1,500. Funds are paid directly to the student to be used for tuition, room and board, books, and other academic charges.

Duration 1 year; nonrenewable.

Additional information Recipients are given priority for an internship with the sponsor in the summer following their junior year. Farm Credit East was formerly named First Pioneer Farm Credit.

Number awarded Up to 28 each year, including several diversity scholarships.

Deadline April of each year.

[135]
FEDEX APIASF SCHOLARSHIPS

Asian & Pacific Islander American Scholarship Fund
2025 M Street, N.W., Suite 610
Washington, DC 20036-3363
(202) 986-6892   Toll Free: (877) 808-7032
Fax: (202) 530-0643   E-mail: info@apiasf.org
Web: www.apiasf.org/scholarship_apiasf.html

Summary To provide financial assistance to Asian and Pacific Islander Americans who are entering college for the first time.

Eligibility This program is open to U.S. citizens, nationals, permanent residents, and citizens of the Freely Associated States who are first-time incoming college students and of Asian or Pacific Islander heritage. Applicants must be enrolling full time at an accredited 2- or 4-year college or university in the United States. They must have a GPA of 3.0 or higher or the GED equivalent. In addition, they must complete the FAFSA and apply for federal financial aid.

Financial data The stipend is $2,500 per year.

Duration 4 years.

Additional information This program is sponsored by FedEx and administered by the Asian & Pacific Islander American Scholarship Fund (APIASF).

Number awarded Varies each year; recently, 5 of these scholarships were awarded.

Deadline January of each year.

[136]
FILIPINO AMERICAN LEAGUE OF ENGINEERS AND ARCHITECTS SCHOLARSHIP PROGRAM

Filipino American League of Engineers and Architects
Attn: FALEA Foundation
P.O. Box 4135
Honolulu, HI 96812-4135
(808) 358-7111   E-mail: jeoffreycudiamat@gmail.com
Web: www.falea.org/scholarship.html

Summary To provide financial assistance to Hawaii residents who are of Filipino descent and are interested in attending college in any state to prepare for a career in engineering, architecture, or a related field.

Eligibility This program is open to high school seniors and currently-enrolled college students who are Hawaii residents and of Filipino descent. Applicants must be enrolled or planning to enroll full time at a college or university in any state to

work on a degree in engineering, architecture, surveying, or a related field. They must have a GPA of 3.0 or higher. Along with their application, they must submit an essay on why they are seeking the scholarship, the extracurricular activities in which they have been involved, the positions they have held in organizations or clubs, their community service, and other information they feel might be helpful.

Financial data The stipend is $1,000.

Duration 1 year.

Additional information This program began in 1994.

Number awarded Varies each year; recently, 5 of these scholarships were awarded.

Deadline October of each year.

[137]
FILIPINO CHAMBER OF COMMERCE OF HAWAII SCHOLARSHIPS

Filipino Chamber of Commerce of Hawaii
Attn: Foundation
P.O. Box 2441
Honolulu, HI 96804
(808) 445-4307   E-mail: filipinochamberhi@gmail.com
Web: www.filipinochamber.org

Summary To provide financial assistance to high school seniors in Hawaii who have an interest in business and are planning to attend college in any state.

Eligibility This program is open to seniors graduating from high schools in Hawaii who have a GPA of 3.5 or higher and have been accepted at a 4-year college or university in any state. Applicants must submit a 1-page essay describing how they expect to promote Hawaii's business community, broaden opportunities for Filipino entrepreneurs and other businesses, strengthen business links between Hawaii and the Philippines, and support the well-being of the community. Selection is based on that essay, academic record (including SAT and/or ACT scores), awards and honors, and activities.

Financial data Stipends are $4,000 or $3,000.

Duration 1 year.

Additional information The highest-ranked applicant receives the Renato and Maria A.F. Etrata Foundation/Filipino Chamber Foundation Scholarship.

Number awarded Varies each year; recently, 5 of these scholarships were awarded: 1 at $4,000 and 4 at $3,000.

Deadline March of each year.

[138]
FILIPINO NURSES' ORGANIZATION OF HAWAII SCHOLARSHIP

Hawai'i Community Foundation
Attn: Scholarship Department
827 Fort Street Mall
Honolulu, HI 96813
(808) 566-5570   Toll Free: (888) 731-3863
Fax: (808) 521-6286
E-mail: scholarships@hcf-hawaii.org
Web: www.hawaiicommunityfoundation.org/scholarships

Summary To provide financial assistance to Hawaii residents of Filipino ancestry who are interested in attending college in any state to prepare for a career as a nurse.

Eligibility This program is open to Hawaii residents of Filipino ancestry who are enrolled or planning to enroll full time

ancial data   The stipend is $4,000 per year. Recipients
required to teach 1 year in a Florida public school for each
ar they receive the scholarship. If they fail to teach in a pub-
school, they are required to repay the total amount of sup-
rt received at an annual interest rate of 8%.

ration   Up to 2 consecutive years, provided the recipient
mains enrolled full time with a GPA of 2.5 or higher.

dditional information   For a list of the 16 participating
blic institutions and the 18 participating private institutions,
ntact the Florida Fund for Minority Teachers (FFMT).
cipients are also required to attend the annual FFMT
cruitment and retention conference.

mber awarded   Varies each year.

adline   July of each year for fall semester; November of
ch year for spring semester.

43]
RUM FOR CONCERNS OF MINORITIES
SCHOLARSHIPS

American Society for Clinical Laboratory Science
Attn: Forum for Concerns of Minorities
1861 International Drive, Suite 200
McLean, VA 22102
(571) 748-3770   E-mail: ascls@ascls.org
Web: www.ascls.org

mmary   To provide financial assistance to Asian Ameri-
ns and other minority students in clinical laboratory scien-
and clinical laboratory technician programs.

gibility   This program is open to minority students who
enrolled in a program in clinical laboratory science,
luding clinical laboratory science/medical technology
LS/MT) and clinical laboratory technician/medical labora-
y technician (CLT/MLT). Applicants must be able to dem-
strate financial need. Membership in the American Society
Clinical Laboratory Science is encouraged but not
uired.

ancial data   Stipends depend on the need of the recipi-
s and the availability of funds.

ration   1 year.

mber awarded   2 each year: 1 to a CLS/MT student and
a CLT/MLT student.

adline   March of each year.

44]
URTH DISTRICT MOSAIC SCHOLARSHIP

American Advertising Federation-District 4
c/o Maria Lucas, Governor
Farah & Farah
10 West Adams Street
Jacksonville, FL 32202
(904) 807-3113   Toll Free: (800) 533-5555
Fax: (904) 355-5599 E-mail: mlucas@farahandfarah.com
Web: 4aaf.com/education/scholarships

nmary   To provide financial assistance to Asian Ameri-
and other minority undergraduate and graduate students
n any state who are enrolled at colleges and universities in
rida and interested in entering the field of advertising.

gibility   This program is open to undergraduate and
duate students from any state enrolled at accredited col-
es and universities in Florida who are U.S. citizens or per-
nent residents of African, African American, Hispanic, His-

panic American, Indian, Native American, Asian, Asian American, or Pacific Islander descent. Applicants must be working
on a bachelor's or master's degree in advertising, marketing,
communications, public relations, art, graphic arts, or a
related field. They must have an overall GPA of 3.0 or higher.
Along with their application, they must submit a 250-word
essay on why multiculturalism, diversity, and inclusion are
important in the advertising, marketing, and communications
industry today. Preference is given to members of the American Advertising Federation.

Financial data   The stipend is $1,000.

Duration   1 year.

Number awarded   1 or more each year.

Deadline   February of each year.

[145]
FRAMELINE COMPLETION FUND

Frameline
Attn: Completion Fund
145 Ninth Street, Suite 300
San Francisco, CA 94103
(415) 703-8650   Fax: (415) 861-1404
E-mail: info@frameline.org
Web: www.frameline.org/filmmaker-support

Summary   To provide funding to lesbian, gay, bisexual, and
transgender (LGBT) film/video artists (particularly Asian
Americans, other film/video artists of color, and women).

Eligibility   This program is open to LGBT artists who are in
the last stages of the production of documentary, educational,
narrative, animated, or experimental projects about or of
interest to LGBT people and their communities. Applicants
may be independent artists, students, producers, or nonprofit
corporations. They must be interested in completion work
and must have 90% of the production completed; projects in
development, script-development, pre-production, or production are not eligible. Student projects are eligible only if the
student maintains artistic and financial control of the project.
Women and people of color are especially encouraged to
apply. Selection is based on financial need, the contribution
the grant will make to completing the project, assurances that
the project will be completed, and the statement the project
makes about LGBT people and/or issues of concern to them
and their communities.

Financial data   Grants range from $1,000 to $5,000.

Duration   These are 1-time grants.

Additional information   This program began in 1990.

Number awarded   Varies each year; recently, 5 of these
grants were awarded. Since this program was established, it
has provided $389,200 in support to 118 films.

Deadline   October of each year.

[146]
FRANCES SONN NAM MEMORIAL
SCHOLARSHIP

Asian & Pacific Islander American Scholarship Fund
2025 M Street, N.W., Suite 610
Washington, DC 20036-3363
(202) 986-6892   Toll Free: (877) 808-7032
Fax: (202) 530-0643   E-mail: info@apiasf.org
Web: www.apiasf.org/scholarship_apiasf.html

at a college or university in any state and work on an undergraduate or graduate degree in nursing. Applicants must be able to demonstrate academic achievement (GPA of 2.7 or higher), good moral character, and financial need. Along with their application, they must submit a short statement indicating their reasons for attending college, their planned course of study, their career goals, and what community service means to them.

Financial data The amounts of the awards depend on the availability of funds and the need of the recipient. Recently, the average value of each of the scholarships awarded by the foundation was $2,200.

Duration 1 year.

Number awarded Varies each year; recently, 2 of these scholarships were awarded.

Deadline February of each year.

[139]
FILIPINO WOMEN'S LEAGUE COMMUNITY COLLEGE SCHOLARSHIP PROGRAM

Filipino Women's League
Attn: Community Scholarship Committee
P.O. Box 419
Pearl City, HI 96782

Summary To provide financial assistance to Hawaii high school seniors who are of Filipino descent and are interested in attending a community college in the state.

Eligibility This program is open to Hawaii residents who are graduating high school seniors, of Filipino ancestry, and enrolling full time at a community college in the state. Applicants must have a high school GPA of 3.5 or higher. Selection is based primarily on financial need; other selection criteria include scholastic achievement (measured by transcripts and SAT or ACT scores), educational goals, and extracurricular interests.

Financial data The award provides for full or partial payment of tuition (to a maximum of $1,000 per year). Payment is made directly to the financial aid office of the recipient's college.

Duration 1 year.

Number awarded 1 or more each year.

Deadline March of each year.

[140]
FILIPINO WOMEN'S LEAGUE UNIVERSITY SCHOLARSHIP PROGRAM

Filipino Women's League
Attn: Community Scholarship Committee
P.O. Box 419
Pearl City, HI 96782

Summary To provide financial assistance to Hawaii high school seniors who are of Filipino descent and are interested in attending a university in the state.

Eligibility This program is open to Hawaii residents who are graduating high school seniors, of Filipino ancestry, and enrolling full time at a 4-year college or university in the state. Applicants must have a high school GPA of 3.5 or higher. Selection is based primarily on financial need; other selection criteria include scholastic achievement (measured by transcripts and SAT or ACT scores), educational goals, and extracurricular interests.

Financial data Stipends provide full or parti tuition (to a maximum of $1,000 per year). Fr directly to the financial aid office of the recipien

Duration 1 year; nonrenewable.

Number awarded 1 or more each year.

Deadline March of each year.

[141]
FLORIDA BOARD OF ACCOUNTANCY SCHOLARSHIPS

Florida Department of Business and Profes
Regulation
Attn: Division of Certified Public Accounting
240 N.W. 76th Drive, Suite A
Gainesville, FL 32607-6656
(850) 487-1395   Fax: (
Web: www.myfloridalicense.com/dbpr/cpa

Summary To provide financial assistance to can, other minorities, and female residents of F entering the fifth year of an accounting prograi

Eligibility This program is open to Florida have completed at least 120 credit hours at a versity in the state and have a GPA of 2.5 or cants must be planning to remain in school as dent for the fifth year required to sit for the C.P./ They must be members of a minority grou include African Americans, Hispanic American icans, Native Americans, or women. Selectic scholastic ability and performance and financi

Financial data The stipend is $3,000 per s

Duration 1 semester; may be renewed 1 ad ter.

Number awarded Varies each year; a total available for this program annually.

Deadline May of each year.

[142]
FLORIDA MINORITY TEACHER EDUC SCHOLARSHIPS

Florida Fund for Minority Teachers, Inc.
Attn: Executive Director
G415 Norman Hall
P.O. Box 117045
Gainesville, FL 32611-7045
(352) 392-9196, ext. 21   Fax: (
E-mail: info@ffmt.org
Web: www.ffmt.org

Summary To provide funding to Asian / members of other minority groups in Florida v ing for a career as a teacher.

Eligibility This program is open to Florida are African American/Black, Hispanic/Latino can/Pacific Islander, or American Indian/A Applicants must be entering their junior year in cation program at a participating college or ur ida. Special consideration is given to com graduates. Selection is based on writing abili tion skills, overall academic performance, ar commitment to the youth of America (pref strated through volunteer activities).

Summary To provide financial assistance to Asian and Pacific Islander Americans who are entering their junior year of college and majoring in specified fields.

Eligibility This program is open to U.S. citizens, nationals, permanent residents, or citizens of the Freely Associated States who are of Asian or Pacific Islander heritage. Applicants must be entering their junior year of full-time study at an accredited 4-year college or university in the United States and preparing for a career in law, public service, or government affairs. They must have a GPA of 3.0 or higher. In addition, they must complete the FAFSA and apply for federal financial aid.

Financial data The stipend is $4,000 per year.

Duration 2 years.

Additional information This scholarship is sponsored by Sodexo.

Number awarded 2 each year.

Deadline January of each year.

[147]
FRANCIS M. KEVILLE MEMORIAL SCHOLARSHIP

Construction Management Association of America
Attn: CMAA Foundation
7926 Jones Branch Drive, Suite 800
McLean, VA 22101-3303
(703) 356-2622   Fax: (703) 356-6388
E-mail: foundation@cmaanet.org
Web: www.cmaafoundation.org

Summary To provide financial assistance to Asian Americans, other minorities, and female undergraduate and graduate students working on a degree in construction management.

Eligibility This program is open to women and members of minority groups who are enrolled as full-time undergraduate or graduate students. Applicants must have completed at least 1 year of study and have at least 1 full year remaining for a bachelor's or master's degree in construction management or a related field. Along with their application, they must submit essays on why they are interested in a career in construction management and why they should be awarded this scholarship. Selection is based on that essay (20%), academic performance (40%), recommendation of the faculty adviser (15%), and extracurricular activities (25%); a bonus of 5% is given to student members of the Construction Management Association of America (CMAA).

Financial data The stipend is $3,000. Funds are disbursed directly to the student's university.

Duration 1 year.

Number awarded 1 each year.

Deadline June of each year.

[148]
FRANK T. MARTIN LEADERSHIP SCHOLARSHIP

Conference of Minority Transportation Officials
Attn: National Scholarship Program
1875 I Street, N.W., Suite 500
Washington, DC 20006
(703) 234-4072   Fax: (202) 318-0364
Web: www.comto.org/?page=Scholarships

Summary To provide financial assistance to Asian American and other minority undergraduate and graduate students working on a degree in transportation or a related field.

Eligibility This program is open to full-time undergraduate and graduate students who are working on a degree in transportation, engineering, planning, or a related discipline. They must be able to demonstrate leadership and active commitment to community service. Along with their application, they must submit a cover letter with a 500-word statement of career goals. Financial need is not considered in the selection process. U.S. citizenship or legal resident status is required.

Financial data The stipend is $3,000. Funds are paid directly to the recipient's college or university.

Duration 1 year.

Additional information The Conference of Minority Transportation Officials (COMTO) was established in 1971 to promote, strengthen, and expand the roles of minorities in all aspects of transportation. This program is sponsored by Atkins North America. Recipients are expected to attend the COMTO National Scholarship Luncheon.

Number awarded 1 each year.

Deadline May of each year.

[149]
FRED G. LEE MEMORIAL SCHOLARSHIPS

Chinese American Citizens Alliance-Portland Lodge
Attn: Scholarship Committee
2309 S.W. First, Number 142
Portland, OR 97201
(503) 221-8773   E-mail: scholarship@cacaportland.org
Web: www.cacaportland.org/?page_id=97

Summary To provide financial assistance to high school seniors of Chinese descent in Oregon or in Clark County, Washington who plan to attend college in any state.

Eligibility This program is open to seniors graduating from high schools in Oregon or in Clark County, Washington and planning to attend an accredited 2- or 4-year college or university in any state (although 1 scholarship is reserved for a student planning to attend college in Oregon or Washington). Applicants must be a U.S. citizen or permanent resident, have at least 1 parent who is a member of the Portland Lodge of the Chinese American Citizens Alliance, be active in school and community affairs, and have a GPA of 3.5 or higher. Along with their application, they must submit 2 essays of approximately 250 words: the relationship of their educational plans or goals to their Chinese heritage, and their personal philosophy and how their Chinese heritage has affected their perspective. Selection is based on scholarship, leadership in school, community activities, and financial need.

Financial data The stipend is $1,000 per year.

Duration Either 4 years or 1 year.

Number awarded 3 each year: 1 for 4 years and 2 for 1 year.

Deadline March of each year.

[150]
GATES MILLENNIUM SCHOLARS PROGRAM

Bill and Melinda Gates Foundation
P.O. Box 10500
Fairfax, VA 22031-8044
Toll Free: (877) 690-GMSP   Fax: (703) 205-2079
Web: www.gmsp.org

Summary   To provide financial assistance to Asian American and other outstanding low-income minority students, particularly those interested in majoring in specific fields in college.

Eligibility   This program is open to African Americans, Alaska Natives, American Indians, Hispanic Americans, and Asian Pacific Islander Americans who are graduating high school seniors with a GPA of 3.3 or higher. Principals, teachers, guidance counselors, tribal higher education representatives, and other professional educators are invited to nominate students with outstanding academic qualifications, particularly those likely to succeed in the fields of computer science, education, engineering, library science, mathematics, public health, or science. Nominees should have significant financial need and have demonstrated leadership abilities through participation in community service, extracurricular, or other activities. U.S. citizenship, nationality, or permanent resident status is required. Nominees must be planning to enter an accredited college or university as a full-time, degree-seeking freshman in the following fall.

Financial data   The program covers the cost of tuition, fees, books, and living expenses not paid for by grants and scholarships already committed as part of the recipient's financial aid package.

Duration   4 years or the completion of the undergraduate degree, if the recipient maintains at least a 3.0 GPA.

Additional information   This program, established in 1999, is funded by the Bill and Melinda Gates Foundation and administered by the United Negro College Fund with support from the American Indian Graduate Center, the Hispanic Scholarship Fund, and the Asian & Pacific Islander American Scholarship Fund.

Number awarded   1,000 new scholarships are awarded each year.

Deadline   January of each year.

[151]
GEETA RASTOGI MEMORIAL SCHOLARSHIP

Upakar: Indian American Scholarship Foundation
9101 Friars Road
Bethesda, MD 20817
E-mail: upakarfoundation@hotmail.com
Web: www.upakarfoundation.org

Summary   To provide financial assistance to Indian American (from India) high school seniors who plan to attend a 4-year college and major in a field of the arts.

Eligibility   This program is open to graduating high school seniors who either were born or have at least 1 parent who was born in the Republic of India. Applicants must be planning to enroll at a 4-year college or university and major in fine arts (e.g., music, dance, drama). They must be U.S. citizens or permanent residents and have a GPA of 3.6 or higher. Their family income must be less than $75,000 per year.

Financial data   The stipend is $2,000 per year.

Duration   Up to 4 years, provided the recipient maintains a GPA of 3.3 or higher.

Additional information   This program began in 2011.

Number awarded   Varies each year; recently, 6 of these scholarships were awarded.

Deadline   April of each year.

[152]
GEORGE GENG ON LEE MINORITIES IN LEADERSHIP SCHOLARSHIP

Capture the Dream, Inc.
Attn: Scholarship Program
484 Lake Park Avenue, Suite 15
Oakland, CA 94610
(510) 343-3635   E-mail: info@capturethedream.org
Web: www.capturethedream.org/programs/scholarship.php

Summary   To provide financial assistance to Asian Americans and other minorities in California who can demonstrate leadership and are interested in attending college in any state.

Eligibility   This program is open to residents of California who are members of minority groups and either graduating high school seniors or current full-time undergraduates at 4-year colleges and universities in any state. Applicants must submit a 1,000-word essay on why they should be selected to receive this scholarship, using their experiences within school, work, and home to display the challenges they have faced as a minority and how they overcame adversity to assume a leadership role. They should also explain how their career goals and future aspirations will build them as a future minority leader. Selection is based on academic performance, community service, leadership history, professional recommendations, and financial need. U.S. citizenship or permanent resident status is required.

Financial data   The stipend is $1,000.

Duration   1 year.

Number awarded   1 or more each year.

Deadline   July of each year.

[153]
GO RED MULTICULTURAL SCHOLARSHIP FUND

American Heart Association
Attn: Go Red for Women
7272 Greenville Avenue
Dallas, TX 75231-4596
Toll Free: (800) AHA-USA1
E-mail: GoRedScholarship@heart.org
Web: www.goredforwomen.org/goredscholarship.aspx

Summary   To provide financial assistance to women from multicultural backgrounds who are preparing for a career in a field of health care.

Eligibility   This program is open to women who are currently enrolled at an accredited college, university, health care institution, or program and have a GPA of 3.0 or higher. Applicants must be undergraduates of Hispanic, African American, or other minority origin. They must be preparing for a career as a nurse, physician, or allied health care worker. Selection is based on community involvement, a personal letter, transcripts, and 2 letters of recommendation.

Financial data   The stipend is $2,500.

Duration   1 year.

Additional information This program, which began in 2012, is supported by Macy's.

Number awarded Varies each year; recently, 16 of these scholarships were awarded.

Deadline November of each year.

[154]
GOLDEN APPLE SCHOLARS OF ILLINOIS

Golden Apple Foundation
Attn: Scholars Program
8 South Michigan Avenue, Suite 700
Chicago, IL 60603-3463
(312) 407-0006   Fax: (312) 407-0344
E-mail: info@goldenapple.org
Web: www.goldenapple.org/golden-apple-scholars

Summary To provide funding to high school seniors in Illinois (particularly minority and bilingual students) who wish to study education at an Illinois college and teach in the state.

Eligibility This program is open to high school seniors at schools in Illinois. Students must be nominated by a teacher, principal, guidance counselor, or other non-family adult; self-nominations are also accepted. Nominees must be committed to teaching as a profession and must be interested in attending 1 of 53 designated colleges and universities in Illinois. A limited number of openings are also available to sophomores at those designated Illinois institutions. The program strongly encourages nomination of prospective teachers for which there is currently a shortage, especially minority and bilingual teachers. Selection is based on 7 essays included on the application, ACT scores and transcripts, letters of reference, and an interview.

Financial data Scholars receive a scholarship/loan of $2,500 per year for their freshman and sophomore year and $5,000 per year for their junior and senior year. They also receive a stipend of $2,000 per year for participating in a summer teaching internship. If they complete a bachelor's degree and teach for 5 years in an Illinois school of need, the loan is forgiven. Schools of need are defined as those either having Chapter I status by the U.S. Department of Education or having mediocre to poor PSAE or ISAT scores.

Duration 4 years, provided the recipient maintains a GPA of 2.0 or higher during the freshman year and 2.5 or higher in subsequent years. Students who enter the program as sophomores receive 2 years of support.

Additional information During the annual summer institutes, scholars participate in teaching internships and seminars on the art and craft of teaching. This program was established in 1988.

Number awarded Varies each year; recently, 110 of these scholarships were awarded.

Deadline Nominations must be submitted by November of each year.

[155]
GOLDEN DOOR SCHOLARS PROGRAM

Golden Door Scholars
c/o Red Ventures
1101 521 Corporate Center Drive
Fort Mill, SC 29707
E-mail: info@goldendoorscholars.org
Web: www.goldendoorscholars.org/apply-now.html

Summary To provide financial assistance for college to undocumented students, especially those from North Carolina and South Carolina.

Eligibility This program is open to undocumented students who are high school seniors or high school graduates who have not yet entered a 4-year college (including students currently attending a community college). Applicants must be planning to work on a 4-year degree. They must be eligible for Deferred Action for Childhood Arrivals (DACA). Along with their application, they must submit brief statements on their intended field of concentration, why they are choosing it, and why they should be selected as a recipient of this scholarship. Strong preference is given to applicants from North Carolina and South Carolina.

Financial data The program provides funding to cover tuition (less other scholarships), room, and board. The program cooperates with participating colleges and universities in North Carolina and South Carolina that have agreed to provide recipients with substantial scholarship support or reduced tuition.

Duration Until completion of a 4-year degree.

Additional information This program began in 2012.

Number awarded Varies each year, depending on the availability of funding and support from participating institutions.

Deadline October of each year.

[156]
GORDON STAFFORD SCHOLARSHIP IN ARCHITECTURE

Stafford King Wiese Architects
Attn: Scholarship Selection Committee
622 20th Street
Sacramento, CA 95811
(916) 930-5900   Fax: (916) 290-0100
E-mail: info@skwaia.com
Web: www.skwarchitects.com/about/scholarship

Summary To provide financial assistance to Asian Americans and members of other minority groups from California who are interested in studying architecture at a college in any state.

Eligibility This program is open to California residents currently enrolled at accredited schools of architecture in any state as first-year new or first-year transfer students and working on a bachelor's or 5-year master's degree. Applicants must be able to demonstrate minority status (defined as Black, Hispanic, Native American, Pacific Asian, or Asian Indian). They must submit a 500-word statement expressing their desire to prepare for a career in architecture. Finalists are interviewed and must travel to Sacramento, California at their own expense for the interview.

Financial data The stipend is $2,000 per year. That includes $1,000 deposited in the recipient's school account and $1,000 paid to the recipient directly.

Duration 1 year; may be renewed up to 4 additional years.

Additional information This program began in 1995.

Number awarded Up to 5 each year.

Deadline June of each year.

[157]
GROUNDBREAKER LEADERSHIP SCHOLARSHIP

Against the Grain Productions
3523 McKinney Avenue, Suite 231
Dallas, TX 75204
E-mail: outreach@againstthegrainproductions.com
Web: www.againstthegrainproductions.com/scholarship

Summary To provide financial assistance to Asian and Pacific Island college seniors and graduate students who have demonstrated outstanding leadership that sets an example for their community.

Eligibility This program is open to full-time college seniors and graduate students at accredited 4-year colleges and universities who have a GPA of 3.5 or higher. Applicants must be of at least 50% Asian and/or Pacific Islander ethnicity and U.S. citizens, nationals, or permanent residents. They must have demonstrated "exemplary leadership, vision, and passion that is blazing a trail for others to follow and changing lives in the Asian American community." Along with their application, they must submit a video that showcases their work and qualifications. Selection is based on that video, an essay, academic performance, leadership and community service, and an interview.

Financial data The stipend is $1,500. Funds are disbursed directly to the educational institution.

Duration 1 year.

Number awarded 2 each year.

Deadline April of each year.

[158]
HANA SCHOLARSHIPS

United Methodist Church
Attn: General Board of Higher Education and Ministry
Office of Loans and Scholarships
1001 19th Avenue South
P.O. Box 340007
Nashville, TN 37203-0007
(615) 340-7344   Fax: (615) 340-7367
E-mail: umscholar@gbhem.org
Web: www.gbhem.org

Summary To provide financial assistance to upper-division and graduate Methodist students who are of Asian, Hispanic, Native American, or Pacific Islander ancestry.

Eligibility This program is open to full-time juniors, seniors, and graduate students at accredited colleges and universities in the United States who have been active, full members of a United Methodist Church (UMC) for at least 1 year prior to applying. Applicants must have at least 1 parent who is Hispanic, Asian, Native American, or Pacific Islander. They must be able to demonstrate involvement in their Hispanic, Asian, or Native American (HANA) community in the UMC. Selection is based on that involvement, academic ability (GPA of at least 2.85), and financial need. U.S. citizenship or permanent resident status is required.

Financial data The maximum stipend is $3,000 for undergraduates or $5,000 for graduate students.

Duration 1 year; recipients may reapply.

Number awarded 50 each year.

Deadline February of each year.

[159]
HANAYAGI ROKUMIE MEMORIAL JAPANESE CULTURAL SCHOLARSHIP

Japanese American Citizens League
Attn: National Scholarship Awards
1765 Sutter Street
San Francisco, CA 94115
(415) 345-1075   Fax: (415) 931-4671
E-mail: ncwnp@jacl.org
Web: www.jacl.org/edu/scholar.htm

Summary To provide financial assistance for college to student members of the Japanese American Citizens League (JACL) who are high school seniors and excel in Japanese cultural activity.

Eligibility This program is open to JACL members who are high school seniors interested in attending a college, university, trade school, business college, or other institution of higher learning. Applicants must excel in Japanese cultural activity, including nihon buyo (classical dance); ikebana (flower arrangement); classical instruments (e.g., shamisen, koto, shakuhachi, taiko); martial arts (e.g., aikido, karate, judo kendo); or chado (tea ceremony). They may study any field in college. Along with their application, they must submit information on their involvement in JACL and a 2-page essay on a topic that changes annually but relates to Japanese Americans. Selection is based on that essay, academic history, JACL involvement, school activities, work history, scholastic honors, and community involvement.

Financial data Stipends generally average more than $2,000.

Duration 1 year; nonrenewable.

Additional information This program began in 2006.

Number awarded 1 each year.

Deadline February of each year.

[160]
HANNAH GRISWOLD GRANT

Delta Kappa Gamma Society International-Alpha Kappa State Organization
c/o Cynthia C. Huppert, Professional Affairs Committee Chair
63 Turn of the River Road
Stamford, CT 06905
E-mail: cchup3@sbcglobal.net
Web: www.deltakappagamma.org/CT/grants.php

Summary To provide financial assistance to Asian American and other minority high school seniors in Connecticut who are interested in working on a degree in education at a school in the state.

Eligibility This program is open to minority seniors graduating from high schools in Connecticut who plan to enroll at a college or university in the state to work on a degree in education. Applicants must be able to demonstrate qualities consistent with the promise of leadership in education, including scholarship and community service. Along with their application, they must submit a 500-word statement on their reasons for becoming a teacher. Financial need is not considered in the selection process.

Financial data The stipend is $750.

Duration 1 semester.

Number awarded 1 each year.

Deadline March of each year.

[161]
HATTIE J. HILLIARD SCHOLARSHIP

Wisconsin Women of Color Network, Inc.
Attn: Scholarship Committee
P.O. Box 2337
Madison, WI 53701-2337
E-mail: contact@womenofcolornetwork-wis.org
Web: www.womenofcolornetwork-wis.org/scholarship.html

Summary To provide financial assistance to Asian Americans and other women of color from Wisconsin who are interested in studying art at a school in any state.

Eligibility This program is open to residents of Wisconsin who are women of color enrolled or planning to enroll at a college, university, or vocational/technical school in any state. Applicants must be a member of 1 of the following groups: African American, Asian, American Indian, or Hispanic. Their field of study must be art, graphic art, commercial art, or a related area. They must be able to demonstrate financial need. Along with their application, they must submit a 1-page essay on how this scholarship will help them accomplish their educational goal. U.S. citizenship is required.

Financial data A stipend is awarded (amount not specified).

Duration 1 year.

Additional information This program began in 1995.

Number awarded 1 each year.

Deadline May of each year.

[162]
HAWAII KOREAN CHAMBER OF COMMERCE SCHOLARSHIPS

Hawaii Korean Chamber of Commerce
c/o Daniel J.Y. Pyun, Scholarship Committee
1188 Bishop Street, Suite 811
Honolulu, HI 96813
(808) 526-0999   Fax: (808) 599-8622
Web: www.hkccweb.org/en/scholarships.html

Summary To provide financial assistance to Hawaii residents who are of Korean ancestry and interested in attending college in any state.

Eligibility This program is open to residents of Hawaii who are of at least 50% Korean ancestry. Applicants must be graduating high school seniors or current undergraduates who are enrolled or planning to enroll full time at an accredited 4-year college or university in any state. Along with their application, they must submit an essay of 250 to 500 words that covers why they feel they are qualified to receive this scholarship, how they will participate in and contribute to their community after completing their program of study, whether or not their goal includes service to the Korean American community, and how their education will enable them to contribute to the Korean American community. Financial need is also considered in the selection process.

Financial data The stipend is $2,000.

Duration 1 year.

Number awarded 3 each year.

Deadline May of each year.

[163]
HEALTH RESEARCH AND EDUCATIONAL TRUST SCHOLARSHIPS

New Jersey Hospital Association
Attn: Health Research and Educational Trust
760 Alexander Road
P.O. Box 1
Princeton, NJ 08543-0001
(609) 275-4224   Fax: (609) 452-8097
Web: www.njha.com/education/scholarships

Summary To provide financial assistance to New Jersey residents (particularly Asian Americans, other minorities, and women) who are working on an undergraduate or graduate degree in a field related to health care administration at a school in any state.

Eligibility This program is open to residents of New Jersey enrolled in an upper-division or graduate program in hospital or health care administration, public administration, nursing, or other allied health profession at a school in any state. Graduate students working on an advanced degree to prepare to teach nursing are also eligible. Applicants must have a GPA of 3.0 or higher and be able to demonstrate financial need. Along with their application, they must submit a 2-page essay (on which 50% of the selection is based) describing their academic plans for the future. Minorities and women are especially encouraged to apply.

Financial data The stipend is $2,000.

Duration 1 year.

Additional information This program began in 1983.

Number awarded Varies each year; recently, 3 of these scholarships were awarded.

Deadline July of each year.

[164]
HECUA SCHOLARSHIPS FOR SOCIAL JUSTICE

Higher Education Consortium for Urban Affairs
Attn: Student Services
2233 University Avenue West, Suite 210
St. Paul, MN 55114-1698
(651) 287-3300   Toll Free: (800) 554-1089
Fax: (651) 659-9421   E-mail: hecua@hecua.org
Web: www.hecua.org/programs/scholarships

Summary To provide financial assistance to Asian Americans and other students from targeted groups who are enrolled in programs of the Higher Education Consortium for Urban Affairs (HECUA) at participating colleges and universities.

Eligibility This program is open to students at member colleges and universities who are participating in HECUA programs. Applicants must be a first-generation college student, from a low-income family, and/or a student of color. Along with their application, they must submit a reflective essay, drawing on their life experiences and their personal and academic goals, on what they believe they can contribute to the mission of HECUA to equip students with the knowledge, experiences, tools, and passion to address issues of social justice and social change. The essay should also explain how the HECUA program will benefit them and the people, issues, and communities they care about.

Financial data The stipend is $1,500. Funds are applied as a credit to the student's HECUA program fees for the semester.

Duration 1 semester.

Additional information This program began in 2006. Consortium members include Augsburg College (Minneapolis, Minnesota), Augustana College (Sioux Falls, South Dakota), Carleton College (Northfield, Minnesota), College of Saint Scholastica (Duluth, Minnesota), Colorado College (Colorado Springs, Colorado), Denison University (Granville, Ohio), Gustavus Adolphus College (St. Peter, Minnesota), Hamline University (St. Paul, Minnesota), Macalester College (St. Paul, Minnesota), Saint Mary's University (Winona, Minnesota), Saint Catherine University (St. Paul, Minnesota), Saint Olaf College (Northfield, Minnesota), Swarthmore College (Swarthmore, Pennsylvania), University of Minnesota (Twin Cities, Duluth, Morris, Crookston, Rochester), University of Saint Thomas (St. Paul, Minnesota), and Viterbo University (La Crosse, Wisconsin).

Number awarded Several each year.

Deadline April of each year for summer and fall programs; November of each year for January and spring programs.

[165]
HELEN LEE SCHOLARSHIP

Philip Jaisohn Memorial Foundation
Attn: Education and Scholarship Committee
6705 Old York Road
Philadelphia, PA 19126
(215) 224-2000   Fax: (215) 224-9164
E-mail: jaisohnhouse@gmail.com
Web: www.jaisohn.org

Summary To provide financial assistance to Korean American undergraduate and graduate students who demonstrate significant financial need.

Eligibility This program is open to Korean American undergraduate and graduate students who are currently enrolled at a college or university in the United States. Applicants must be able to demonstrate academic excellence, leadership and service to their school and community, and financial need. Along with their application, they must submit an essay on either "Who is Dr. Jaisohn to Me," or "The Significance of Dr. Jaisohn's Ideal to Korean Americans." They must also submit a brief statement on how they can contribute to and be involved in the activities of the Philip Jaisohn Memorial Foundation. Selection is based primarily on financial need.

Financial data The stipend is $1,500.

Duration 1 year.

Number awarded 2 each year.

Deadline November of each year.

[166]
HENRY AND CHIYO KUWAHARA CREATIVE ARTS AWARD

Japanese American Citizens League
Attn: National Scholarship Awards
1765 Sutter Street
San Francisco, CA 94115
(415) 345-1075   Fax: (415) 931-4671
E-mail: ncwnp@jacl.org
Web: www.jacl.org/edu/scholar.htm

Summary To provide financial assistance to undergraduate and graduate student members of the Japanese American Citizens League (JACL) interested in completing a project in the creative arts.

Eligibility This program is open to JACL members who are working on an undergraduate or graduate degree in the creative arts. Professional artists are not eligible. Applicants must submit a detailed proposal for a project they wish to create, including a time plan, anticipated date of completion, and itemized budget. They must also submit information on their involvement in JACL and a 2-page essay on a topic that changes annually but relates to Japanese Americans. Selection is based on that essay, academic history, JACL involvement, school activities, work history, scholastic honors, and community involvement. Preference is given to students who are interested in creative projects that reflect the Japanese American experience and culture.

Financial data Stipends generally average more than $2,000.

Duration 1 year; nonrenewable.

Number awarded At least 1 each year.

Deadline March of each year.

[167]
HENRY AND CHIYO KUWAHARA MEMORIAL SCHOLARSHIPS

Japanese American Citizens League
Attn: National Scholarship Awards
1765 Sutter Street
San Francisco, CA 94115
(415) 345-1075   Fax: (415) 931-4671
E-mail: ncwnp@jacl.org
Web: www.jacl.org/edu/scholar.htm

Summary To provide financial assistance for undergraduate or graduate study to members of the Japanese American Citizens League (JACL).

Eligibility This program is open to JACL members who are high school seniors, undergraduates, or graduate students. Applicants must be attending or planning to attend a college, university, trade school, or business college. They must submit information on their involvement in JACL and a 2-page essay on a topic that changes annually but relates to Japanese Americans. Selection is based on that essay, academic history, JACL involvement, school activities, work history, scholastic honors, and community involvement.

Financial data Stipends generally average more than $2,000.

Duration 1 year; nonrenewable.

Number awarded 6 each year: 2 each to entering freshmen, continuing undergraduates, and entering or currently-enrolled graduate students.

Deadline February of each year for graduating high school seniors; March of each year for current undergraduate or graduate students.

[168]
HIDEKO AND ZENZO MATSUYAMA SCHOLARSHIPS

Hawai'i Community Foundation
Attn: Scholarship Department
827 Fort Street Mall
Honolulu, HI 96813
(808) 566-5570   Toll Free: (888) 731-3863
Fax: (808) 521-6286
E-mail: scholarships@hcf-hawaii.org
Web: www.hawaiicommunityfoundation.org/scholarships

Summary To provide financial assistance to Hawaii residents of Japanese ancestry who are interested in attending college or graduate school in any state.

Eligibility This program is open to graduates of high schools or recipients of GED certificates in Hawaii who were born in the state and are of Japanese ancestry. Applicants must be enrolled or planning to enroll at an accredited college or university in any state as an undergraduate or graduate student. They must be able to demonstrate academic achievement (GPA of 3.0 or higher), good moral character, and financial need. Along with their application, they must submit a short statement indicating their reasons for attending college, their planned course of study, their career goals, and what community service means to them.

Financial data The amounts of the awards depend on the availability of funds and the need of the recipient. Recently, the average value of each of the scholarships awarded by the foundation was $2,200.

Duration 1 year.

Additional information This program began in 2006.

Number awarded Varies each year; recently, 13 of these scholarships were awarded.

Deadline February of each year.

[169]
HIGH SCHOOL SENIOR SCHOLARSHIPS OF THE JAPANESE AMERICAN CITIZENS LEAGUE

Japanese American Citizens League
Attn: National Scholarship Awards
1765 Sutter Street
San Francisco, CA 94115
(415) 345-1075   Fax: (415) 931-4671
E-mail: ncwnp@jacl.org
Web: www.jacl.org/edu/scholar.htm

Summary To provide financial assistance for college to student members of the Japanese American Citizens League (JACL) who are high school seniors.

Eligibility This program is open to JACL members who are high school seniors interested in attending a college, university, trade school, business college, or other institution of higher learning. Applicants must submit information on their involvement in JACL and a 2-page essay on a topic that changes annually but relates to Japanese Americans. Selec-

tion is based on that essay, academic history, JACL involvement, school activities, work history, scholastic honors, and community involvement.

Financial data Stipends generally average more than $2,000.

Duration 1 year; nonrenewable.

Additional information This program includes the following named awards: the Deni and June Uejima Memorial Scholarship, the Kenji Kasai Memorial Scholarship, the Mas and Majiu Uyesugi Memorial Scholarship, the Masao and Sumako Itano Memorial Scholarship, the Mitsuyuki Yonemura Memorial Scholarship, the Mr. and Mrs. Takashi Moriuchi Scholarship, the Patricia and Gail Ishimoto Memorial Scholarship, the Paul and Katherine Ohtaki Memorial Scholarship, the Sam and Florence Kuwahara Memorial Scholarship, and the Shigeki "Shake" Ushio Memorial Leadership Scholarship.

Number awarded Up to 10 each year.

Deadline February of each year.

[170]
HILTON APIASF SCHOLARSHIPS

Asian & Pacific Islander American Scholarship Fund
2025 M Street, N.W., Suite 610
Washington, DC 20036-3363
(202) 986-6892   Toll Free: (877) 808-7032
Fax: (202) 530-0643   E-mail: info@apiasf.org
Web: www.apiasf.org/scholarship_apiasf.html

Summary To provide financial assistance to Asian and Pacific Islander Americans who are entering college for the first time, especially those planning to major in designated business-related fields.

Eligibility This program is open to U.S. citizens, nationals, permanent residents, and citizens of the Freely Associated States who are first-time incoming college students and of Asian or Pacific Islander heritage. Applicants must be enrolling full time at an accredited 2- or 4-year college or university in the United States. They must have a GPA of 2.7 or higher or the GED equivalent. In addition, they must complete the FAFSA and apply for federal financial aid. Preference is given to applicants planning to major in business, finance, hospitality, hotel management, international affairs, or marketing.

Financial data The stipend is $2,500.

Duration 1 year; nonrenewable.

Additional information This program is sponsored by Hilton and administered by the Asian & Pacific Islander American Scholarship Fund (APIASF).

Number awarded Varies each year; recently, 7 of these scholarships were awarded.

Deadline January of each year.

[171]
H-MART LEADERSHIP SCHOLARSHIP

Philip Jaisohn Memorial Foundation
Attn: Education and Scholarship Committee
6705 Old York Road
Philadelphia, PA 19126
(215) 224-2000   Fax: (215) 224-9164
E-mail: jaisohnhouse@gmail.com
Web: www.jaisohn.org

Summary To provide financial assistance to Korean American undergraduate and graduate students who demonstrate involvement in extracurricular, athletic, and community activities.

Eligibility This program is open to Korean American undergraduate and graduate students who are currently enrolled at a college or university in the United States. Applicants must be able to demonstrate academic excellence, leadership and service to their school and community, and financial need. Along with their application, they must submit an essay on either "Who is Dr. Jaisohn to Me," or "The Significance of Dr. Jaisohn's Ideal to Korean Americans." They must also submit a brief statement on how they can contribute to and be involved in the activities of the Philip Jaisohn Memorial Foundation. Selection is based primarily on leadership in extracurricular activities, varsity sports, or community activities.

Financial data The stipend is $1,500.

Duration 1 year.

Additional information This program is sponsored by Han Ah Reum Asian Mart.

Number awarded 2 each year.

Deadline November of each year.

[172]
HMONG AMERICAN EDUCATION FUND SCHOLARSHIPS

Hmong American Education Fund
P.O. Box 17468
St. Paul, MN 55117
(651) 230-3634   E-mail: scholarships@thehaef.org
Web: www.thehaef.org

Summary To provide financial assistance to Hmong residents of Minnesota who are interested in attending college in any state.

Eligibility This program is open to residents of Minnesota who identify themselves as a person of Hmong descent. Applicants must be high school seniors, GED recipients, or students currently enrolled full time at a public 2- or 4-year college or university in any state. They must be U.S. citizens or permanent residents and have a GPA of 3.0 or higher. Along with their application, they must submit transcripts, ACT or SAT scores, and a 1,500-word essay on their goals, why they deserve this scholarship, their financial need, how this scholarship can help them, and their community service. Men and women are considered separately.

Financial data The stipend is $1,000.

Duration 1 year; nonrenewable.

Number awarded 2 each year: 1 to a man and 1 to a woman.

Deadline March of each year.

[173]
HMONG AMERICAN PARTNERSHIP LEADERSHIP SCHOLARSHIPS

Hmong American Partnership
Attn: Hmong National Development, Inc.
Scholarship Application Committee
1075 Arcade Street
St. Paul, MN 55106
(651) 495-9160   Fax: (651) 495-1699
E-mail: pdvang@stkate.edu

Summary To provide financial assistance for college to Hmong immigrants in the United States who are high school seniors.

Eligibility This program is open to Hmong immigrants who are seniors graduating from high school and planning to attend college. Applicants must have a GPA of 3.5 or higher. Along with their application, they must submit a 300-word personal essay discussing their leadership roles and plan for career and leadership development, a letter of reference from a teacher at their current school, and a letter of reference from an adult who has agreed to mentor the applicant during their college or professional career.

Financial data The stipend is $1,000; funds are sent directly to the recipient's school.

Duration 1 year; nonrenewable.

Number awarded The sponsor awards a total of 5 scholarships each year.

Deadline February of each year.

[174]
HMONG AMERICAN PARTNERSHIP NON-TRADITIONAL STUDENT SCHOLARSHIPS

Hmong American Partnership
Attn: Hmong National Development, Inc.
Scholarship Application Committee
1075 Arcade Street
St. Paul, MN 55106
(651) 495-9160   Fax: (651) 495-1699
E-mail: pdvang@stkate.edu

Summary To provide financial assistance for college to Hmong immigrants in the United States who are nontraditional students.

Eligibility This program is open to Hmong immigrants who are more than 22 years of age and either married or a single parent. Applicants must be attending or planning to attend college and have a GPA of 3.5 or higher. Along with their application, they must submit a 300-word personal essay discussing their plan for career and leadership development, a letter of reference from a teacher at their current school, and documentation of financial need.

Financial data The stipend is $1,000; funds are sent directly to the recipient's school.

Duration 1 year; nonrenewable.

Number awarded The sponsor awards a total of 5 scholarships each year.

Deadline February of each year.

[175]
HOLY FAMILY MEMORIAL SCHOLARSHIP PROGRAM

Holy Family Memorial
Attn: Human Resources
2300 Western Avenue
P.O. Box 1450
Manitowoc, WI 54221-1450
(920) 320-4031   Toll Free: (800) 994-3662, ext. 4031
Fax: (920) 320-8522   E-mail: recruiter@hfmhealth.org
Web: www.hfmhealth.org/scholarships

Summary To provide funding to students (particularly Asian Americans and other minorities) who are working on a degree in a health-related area and willing to work at a designated hospital in Wisconsin following completion of their degree.

Eligibility This program is open to students working on a degree in health-related areas that include, but are not limited to, nursing, pharmacy, sonography, occupational therapy, physical therapy, speech/language pathology, respiratory therapy, or radiology. Applicants must have a GPA of 3.0 or higher. Selection is based on a personal interview, likelihood for professional success, customer service orientation, work ethic, enthusiasm, and professionalism. Minorities are especially encouraged to apply.

Financial data Stipends are $800 per semester ($1,600 per year) for students at technical colleges, $2,000 per semester ($4,000 per year) for students at public universities, or $2,500 per semester ($5,000 per year) for students at private universities. Recipients must commit to working 6 months for each semester of support received at Holy Family Memorial in Manitowoc, Wisconsin following completion of their degree.

Duration 1 semester; renewable.

Number awarded Varies each year.

Deadline Deadline not specified.

[176]
IASF FINANCIAL AID SCHOLARSHIPS

India American Cultural Association
Attn: Indian American Scholarship Fund
2407 Waterford Cove
Decatur, GA 30033
E-mail: rajeshmkurup@gmail.com
Web: www.iasf.org/IASF/Scholarships.html

Summary To provide need-based financial assistance to high school seniors in Georgia who are of Indian descent and plan to attend college in any state.

Eligibility This program is open to seniors graduating from high schools in Georgia who are of Indian descent (at least 1 grandparent was born in India). Applicants must be planning to attend a 4-year college or university in any state as a full-time student. Along with their application, they must submit an official school transcript, resume, SAT or ACT score report, the best essay they submitted to a college to which they applied, and documentation of financial need. Selection is based primarily on financial need.

Financial data Stipends range from $1,000 to $2,500 per year.

Duration 1 year; may be renewed up to 3 additional years.

Additional information This program, established in 1993, includes the following named scholarships: the Darshan S. Bhatia Memorial Award, the P.V. Jagannatha Rao Memorial Award, the Raghavan Award, the Aman Daftari Memorial Award, the Boyapally Reddy Award, and the Jasumati B. Patel Award.

Number awarded Varies each year; recently, the sponsor awarded 6 of these scholarships: 4 for 4 years and 2 for 2 years.

Deadline May of each year.

[177]
ILLINOIS MINORITY REAL ESTATE SCHOLARSHIP

Illinois Association of Realtors
Attn: Illinois Real Estate Educational Foundation
522 South Fifth Street
P.O. Box 2607
Springfield, IL 62708
Toll Free: (866) 854-REEF   Fax: (217) 529-5893
E-mail: lclayton@iar.org
Web: www.ilreef.org/index.php/scholarship

Summary To provide financial assistance to Illinois residents who are 1) Asian Americans or members of other minority groups and 2) preparing for a career in real estate.

Eligibility This program is open to residents of Illinois who are African American, Hispanic or Latino, Native American, or Asian. Applicants must be interested in preparing for a career in real estate by pursuing: 1) courses to meet Illinois salesperson license requirements; 2) course work to meet Illinois broker license requirement; 3) course work required for Illinois appraisal licensing/certification; 4) professional development unrelated to obtaining license/certification; or 5) an undergraduate or graduate program of study. Along with their application, they must submit information on their employment history, transcripts, evidence of financial need, and an essay that describes their career goals and explains why they believe they should receive scholarship assistance through this program.

Financial data The maximum stipend is $500.

Duration Funds must be used within 24 months of the award date.

Number awarded 1 or more each year.

Deadline Applications may be submitted at any time, but they must be received at least 12 weeks prior to the beginning of the school term for which financial assistance is requested.

[178]
ILLINOIS NURSES FOUNDATION CENTENNIAL SCHOLARSHIP

Illinois Nurses Association
Attn: Illinois Nurses Foundation
105 West Adams Street, Suite 1420
Chicago, IL 60603
(312) 419-2900   Fax: (312) 419-2920
E-mail: inf@illinoisnurses.com
Web: www.illinoisnurses.com

Summary To provide financial assistance to nursing undergraduate and graduate students who are Asian American or members of other underrepresented groups.

Eligibility This program is open to students working on an associate, bachelor's, or master's degree at an accredited NLNAC or CCNE school of nursing. Applicants must be members of a group underrepresented in nursing (African Americans, Hispanics, American Indians, Asians, and males). Undergraduates must have earned a passing grade in all nursing courses taken to date and have a GPA of 2.85 or higher. Graduate students must have completed at least 12 semester hours of graduate work and have a GPA of 3.0 or higher. All applicants must be willing to 1) act as a spokesperson to other student groups on the value of the scholarship to continuing their nursing education; and 2) be profiled in any media or marketing materials developed by the Illinois Nurses

Foundation. Along with their application, they must submit a narrative of 250 to 500 words on how they, as nurses, plan to affect policy at either the state or national level that impacts on nursing or health care generally, or how they believe they will impact the nursing profession in general.

Financial data A stipend is awarded (amount not specified).

Duration 1 year.

Number awarded 1 or more each year.

Deadline March of each year.

[179]
INDIAN AMERICAN SCHOLARSHIP FUND MERIT SCHOLARSHIPS

India American Cultural Association
Attn: Indian American Scholarship Fund
2407 Waterford Cove
Decatur, GA 30033
E-mail: rajeshmkurup@gmail.com
Web: www.iasf.org/IASF/Scholarships.html

Summary To provide merit-based financial assistance to high school seniors in Georgia who are of Indian descent and plan to attend college in any state.

Eligibility This program is open to seniors graduating from high schools in Georgia who are of Indian descent (at least 1 grandparent was born in India). Applicants must be planning to attend a 4-year college or university in any state as a full-time student. Along with their application, they must submit an official school transcript, resume, and SAT or ACT score report. Financial need is not considered in the selection process.

Financial data Stipends range from $500 to $1,000.

Duration 1 year; nonrenewable.

Additional information This program, established in 1993, includes the following named scholarships: the Paras Shah Memorial Award, the N.M. Kelkar Memorial Award, the Sadashiv Bhargave Memorial Award the Kadaba/Sanghvi Family Award, the Navalkar Memorial Award, and the Ishwarlal Shroff Memorial Award.

Number awarded Varies each year; recently, the sponsor awarded 8 of these scholarships.

Deadline April of each year.

[180]
INDIANA INDUSTRY LIAISON GROUP SCHOLARSHIP

Indiana Industry Liaison Group
c/o Tony Pickell, Vice Chair
AAP Precision Planning, LLC
6215 Meridian Street West Drive
Indianapolis, IN 46260
(317) 590-4797   E-mail: vchair@indianailg.org
Web: www.indianailg.org/scholardetails.html

Summary To provide financial assistance to Asian American and other students from any state who are enrolled at colleges and universities in Indiana and have been involved in activities to promote diversity.

Eligibility This program is open to residents of any state currently enrolled at an accredited college or university in Indiana. Applicants must either 1) be enrolled in programs or classes related to diversity/Affirmative Action (AA)/Equal

Employment Opportunity (EEO); or 2) have work or volunteer experience with diversity/AA/EEO organizations. Along with their application, they must submit an essay of 400 to 500 words on 1 of the following topics: 1) their personal commitment to diversity/AA/EEO within their community or business; 2) a time or situation in which they were able to establish and/or sustain a commitment to diversity; 3) a time when they have taken a position in favor of affirmative action and/or diversity; or 4) activities in which they have participated within their community that demonstrate their personal commitment to moving the community's diversity agenda forward. Financial need is not considered in the selection process.

Financial data The stipend is $1,000.

Duration 1 year.

Number awarded 1 each year.

Deadline January of each year.

[181]
INTERMOUNTAIN SECTION AWWA DIVERSITY SCHOLARSHIP

American Water Works Association-Intermountain
  Section
Attn: Member Services Coordinator
3430 East Danish Road
Sandy, UT 94093
(801) 712-1619, ext. 2   Fax: (801) 487-6699
E-mail: nicoleb@ims-awwa.org
Web: ims-awwa.site-ym.com/group/StudentPO

Summary To provide financial assistance to Asian Americans, other minorities, and women who are interested in working on an undergraduate or graduate degree in the field of water quality, supply, and treatment at a university in Idaho or Utah.

Eligibility This program is open to 1) women; and 2) students who identify as Hispanic or Latino, Black or African American, Native Hawaiian or other Pacific Islander, Asian, or American Indian or Alaska Native. Applicants must be entering or enrolled in an undergraduate or graduate program at a college or university in Idaho or Utah that relates to water quality, supply, or treatment. Along with their application, they must submit a 2-page essay on their academic interests and career goals and how those relate to water quality, supply, or treatment. Selection is based on that essay, letters of recommendation, and potential to contribute to the field of water quality, supply, and treatment in the Intermountain West.

Financial data The stipend is $1,000. The winner also receives a 1-year student membership in the Intermountain Section of the American Water Works Association (AWWA) and a 1-year subscription to *Journal AWWA*.

Duration 1 year; nonrenewable.

Number awarded 1 each year.

Deadline October of each year.

[182]
INTERPUBLIC GROUP SCHOLARSHIP AND INTERNSHIP

New York Women in Communications, Inc.
Attn: NYWICI Foundation
355 Lexington Avenue, 15th Floor
New York, NY 10017-6603
(212) 297-2133   Fax: (212) 370-9047
E-mail: nywicipr@nywici.org
Web: www.nywici.org/foundation/scholarships

Summary To provide financial aid and work experience to Asian American and other minority women who are residents of designated eastern states and enrolled as juniors at a college in any state to prepare for a career in advertising or public relations.

Eligibility This program is open to female residents of New York, New Jersey, Connecticut, or Pennsylvania who are from ethnically diverse groups and currently enrolled as juniors at a college or university in any state. Also eligible are women who reside outside the 4 states but are currently enrolled at a college or university within 1 of the 5 boroughs of New York City. Applicants must be preparing for a career in advertising or public relations and have a GPA of 3.2 or higher. They must be available for a summer internship with Interpublic Group (IPG) in New York City. Along with their application, they must submit a 2-page resume; a personal essay of 300 words on an assigned topic that changes annually; 2 letters of recommendation; and an official transcript. Selection is based on academic record, need, demonstrated leadership, participation in school and community activities, honors and other awards or recognition, work experience, goals and aspirations, and unusual personal and/or family circumstances. U.S. citizenship is required.

Financial data The scholarship stipend ranges up to $10,000; the internship is salaried (amount not specified).

Duration 1 year.

Additional information This program is sponsored by IPG, a holding company for a large number of firms in the advertising industry.

Number awarded 2 each year.

Deadline January of each year.

[183]
ISBA SCHOLARSHIPS

Idaho State Broadcasters Association
1674 West Hill Road, Suite 3
Boise, ID 83702
(208) 345-3072   Fax: (208) 343-8946
E-mail: isba@qwestoffice.net
Web: bestinbroadcasting.com

Summary To provide financial assistance to students (particularly minority and other diverse students) at Idaho colleges and universities who are preparing for a career in the broadcasting field.

Eligibility This program is open to full-time students at Idaho schools who are preparing for a career in broadcasting, including business administration, sales, journalism, or engineering. Applicants must have a GPA of at least 2.0 for the first 2 years of school or 2.5 for the last 2 years. Along with their application, they must submit a letter of recommendation from the general manager of a broadcasting station that is a member of the Idaho State Broadcasters Association and a 1-page essay describing their career plans and why they want the scholarship. Applications are encouraged from a broad and diverse student population. Financial need is not considered in the selection process.

Financial data The stipend is $1,000.

Duration 1 year.

Number awarded At least 2 each year.

Deadline March of each year.

[184]
JACKIE ROBINSON SCHOLARSHIPS

Jackie Robinson Foundation
Attn: Education and Leadership Development Program
75 Varick Street, Second Floor
New York, NY 10013-1917
(212) 290-8600   Fax: (212) 290-8081
E-mail: general@jackierobinson.org
Web: www.jackierobinson.org

Summary To provide financial assistance for college to Asian American and other minority high school seniors.

Eligibility This program is open to members of an ethnic minority group who are high school seniors accepted at a 4-year college or university. Applicants must have a mathematics and critical reading SAT score of 1000 or higher or ACT score of 21 or higher. Selection is based on academic achievement, financial need, dedication towards community service, and leadership potential. U.S. citizenship is required.

Financial data The maximum stipend is $7,500 per year.

Duration 4 years.

Additional information The program also offers personal and career counseling on a year-round basis, a week of interaction with other scholarship students from around the country, and assistance in obtaining summer jobs and permanent employment after graduation. It was established in 1973 by a grant from Chesebrough-Pond.

Number awarded Varies each year; recently, 181 of these scholarships were awarded.

Deadline March of each year.

[185]
JAMES B. MORRIS SCHOLARSHIPS

James B. Morris Scholarship Fund
Attn: Scholarship Selection Committee
P.O. Box 12145
Des Moines, IA 50312
(515) 864-0922
Web: www.morrisscholarship.org

Summary To provide financial assistance to Asian American and other minority undergraduate, graduate, and law students from Iowa.

Eligibility This program is open to minority students (African Americans, Asian/Pacific Islanders, Hispanics, or Native Americans) who are interested in working on an undergraduate or graduate degree. Applicants must be either Iowa residents attending a college or university anywhere in the United States or non-Iowa residents who are attending a college or university in Iowa. Along with their application, they must submit an essay of 250 to 500 words on why they are applying for this scholarship, activities or organizations in which they are involved, and their future plans. Selection is based on the essay, academic achievement (GPA of 2.5 or higher), community service, and financial need. U.S. citizenship is required.

Financial data The stipend ranges from $1,000 to $2,500 per year.

Duration 1 year; may be renewed.

Additional information This fund was established in 1978 in honor of the J.B. Morris family, who founded the Iowa branch of the National Association for the Advancement of Colored People and published the *Iowa Bystander* newspaper. The program includes the Ann Chapman Scholarships, the Vincent Chapman, Sr. Scholarships, and the Brittany Hall Memorial Scholarships.

Number awarded Varies each year; recently, 19 of these scholarships were awarded.

Deadline March of each year.

[186]
JAMES CARLSON MEMORIAL SCHOLARSHIP

Oregon Student Access Commission
Attn: Grants and Scholarships Division
1500 Valley River Drive, Suite 100
Eugene, OR 97401-2146
(541) 687-7395   Toll Free: (800) 452-8807, ext. 7395
Fax: (541) 687-7414   TDD: (800) 735-2900
E-mail: awardinfo@osac.state.or.us
Web: www.oregonstudentaid.gov/scholarships.aspx

Summary To provide financial assistance to Oregon residents from diverse environments (including Asian Americans) who are majoring in education on the undergraduate or graduate school level at a school in any state.

Eligibility This program is open to residents of Oregon who are U.S. citizens or permanent residents and enrolled at a college or university in any state. Applicants must be either 1) college seniors or fifth-year students majoring in elementary or secondary education; or 2) graduate students working on an elementary or secondary certificate. Full-time enrollment and financial need are required. Priority is given to 1) students who come from diverse environments and submit an essay of 250 to 350 words on their experience living or working in diverse environments; 2) dependents of members of the Oregon Education Association; and 3) applicants committed to teaching autistic children.

Financial data Stipends for scholarships offered by the Oregon Student Access Commission (OSAC) range from $200 to $10,000 but recently averaged $2,300.

Duration 1 year.

Additional information This program is administered by the OSAC with funds provided by the Oregon Community Foundation.

Number awarded Varies each year; recently, 3 of these scholarships were awarded.

Deadline February of each year.

[187]
JAMES ECHOLS SCHOLARSHIP

California Association for Health, Physical Education, Recreation and Dance
Attn: Chair, Scholarship Committee
1501 El Camino Avenue, Suite 3
Sacramento, CA 95815-2748
(916) 922-3596   Toll Free: (800) 499-3596 (within CA)
Fax: (916) 922-0133   E-mail: cahperd@cahperd.org
Web: www.cahperd.org/scholarships.html

Summary To provide financial assistance to Asian American and other minority student members of the California Association for Health, Physical Education, Recreation and Dance.

Eligibility This program is open to California residents who have been members of the association for at least 60 days and are attending a 2- or 4-year college or university in California. Applicants must be undergraduate or graduate students working on a degree in health, physical education, recreation, or dance and have completed at least 60 semester hours of college work. Selection is based on scholastic proficiency (a GPA of 3.0 or higher); leadership ability in school, community, and professional activities; and personal qualities of enthusiasm, cooperativeness, responsibility, initiative, and ability to work with others. This scholarship is awarded to the highest-ranked minority (Asian, African American, Latino, or Native American) applicant.

Financial data The stipend is $750.

Duration 1 year.

Number awarded 1 each year.

Deadline November of each year.

[188]
JAMES J. WYCHOR SCHOLARSHIPS

Minnesota Broadcasters Association
Attn: Scholarship Program
3033 Excelsior Boulevard, Suite 440
Minneapolis, MN 55416
(612) 926-8123   Toll Free: (800) 245-5838
Fax: (612) 926-9761
E-mail: llasere@minnesotabroadcasters.com
Web: www.minnesotabroadcasters.com/membership

Summary To provide financial assistance to minority or other Minnesota residents interested in studying broadcasting at a college in any state.

Eligibility This program is open to residents of Minnesota who are accepted or enrolled at an accredited postsecondary institution in any state offering a broadcast-related curriculum. Applicants must have a high school or college GPA of 3.0 or higher and must submit a 500-word essay on why they wish to prepare for a career in broadcasting or electronic media. Employment in the broadcasting industry is not required, but students who are employed must include a letter from their general manager describing the duties they have performed as a radio or television station employee and evaluating their potential for success in the industry. Financial need is not considered in the selection process. Some of the scholarships are awarded only to minority or women candidates.

Financial data The stipend is $1,500.

Duration 1 year; recipients who are college seniors may reapply for an additional 1-year renewal as a graduate student.

Number awarded 10 each year, distributed as follows: 3 within the 7-county metro area, 5 allocated geographically throughout the state (northeast, northwest, central, southeast, southwest), and 2 reserved specifically for women and minority applicants.

Deadline June of each year.

[189]
JAPANESE AMERICAN ASSOCIATION OF NEW YORK GENERAL SCHOLARSHIPS

Japanese American Association of New York, Inc.
Attn: Scholarship Committee
15 West 44th Street, 11th Floor
New York, NY 10036
(212) 840-6942　　　　　Fax: (212) 840-0616
E-mail: info@jaany.org
Web: www.jaany.org/general_scholarship.html

Summary To provide financial assistance to high school seniors in the New York tri-state area who are of Japanese descent and plan to attend college in any state.

Eligibility This program is open to seniors of Japanese descent graduating from high schools in the New York tri-state area who plan to attend a college or university in any state. Applicants must submit their latest transcript with a copy of SAT or ACT scores, a letter of recommendation from their school counselor or teacher, and information on any special financial circumstances. Selection is based on that information as well as a 500-word essay on a topic that changes annually but relates to Japan and/or Japanese Americans.

Financial data Stipends range from $1,000 to $6,000.

Duration 1 year.

Number awarded Varies each year; recently, 11 of these scholarships were awarded.

Deadline May of each year.

[190]
JAPANESE AMERICAN ASSOCIATION OF NEW YORK MUSIC SCHOLARSHIP AWARDS

Japanese American Association of New York, Inc.
Attn: Scholarship Committee
15 West 44th Street, 11th Floor
New York, NY 10036
(212) 840-6942　　　　　Fax: (212) 840-0616
E-mail: info@jaany.org
Web: www.jaany.org/music_scholarship.html

Summary To recognize and reward Japanese and Japanese American students who participate in a music competition.

Eligibility This music competition is open to students who are Japanese or Americans of Japanese descent. Recently, the competition was limited to ensembles from trio to quintet; applicants performed 1 piece from the Classical era and another from the Romantic era or the 20th century at the recital in New York.

Financial data Awards range from $2,000 to $5,000.

Duration The competition is held annually.

Number awarded 2 each year.

Deadline September of each year.

[191]
JAPANESE AMERICAN CITIZENS LEAGUE UNDERGRADUATE SCHOLARSHIPS

Japanese American Citizens League
Attn: National Scholarship Awards
1765 Sutter Street
San Francisco, CA 94115
(415) 345-1075　　　　　Fax: (415) 931-4671
E-mail: ncwnp@jacl.org
Web: www.jacl.org/edu/scholar.htm

Summary To provide financial assistance for college to student members of the Japanese American Citizens League (JACL).

Eligibility This program is open to JACL members who are currently enrolled at a college, university, trade school, business college, or other institution of higher learning. Applicants must submit information on their involvement in JACL and a 2-page essay on a topic that changes annually but relates to Japanese Americans. Selection is based on that essay, academic history, JACL involvement, school activities, work history, scholastic honors, and community involvement.

Financial data Stipends generally average more than $2,000.

Duration 1 year; nonrenewable.

Additional information This program includes the following named awards that impose no specialized requirements: the Dr. Thomas T. Yatabe Memorial Scholarship, the Kenji Kajiwara Memorial Scholarship, the Saburo Kido Memorial Scholarship and the Shigeru "Shig" Nakahira Memorial Scholarship.

Number awarded Up to 6 each year.

Deadline March of each year.

[192]
JAPANESE AMERICAN VETERANS ASSOCIATION MEMORIAL SCHOLARSHIPS

Japanese American Veterans Association
c/o Terry Shima, Outreach and Education Committee
　Chair
415 Russell Avenue, Number 1005
Gaithersburg, MD 20877
(301) 987-6746　　　　　E-mail: ttshima@comcast.net
Web: www.javadc.org

Summary To provide financial assistance for college or graduate school to relatives of Japanese American veterans and military personnel.

Eligibility This program is open to graduating high school seniors and students currently working on an undergraduate or graduate degree at a college, university, or school of specialized study. Applicants must be related, by blood or marriage, to 1) a person who served with the 442nd Regimental Combat Team, the 100th Infantry Battalion, or other unit associated with those; 2) a person who served in the U.S. Military Intelligence Service during or after World War II; 3) a person of Japanese ancestry who is serving or has served in the U.S. armed forces and been honorable discharged; or 4) a member of the Japanese American Veterans Association (JAVA) whose membership extends back at least 1 year.

Financial data The stipend is $1,500.

Duration 1 year; recipients may reapply.

Additional information These scholarships, first awarded in 2008, include the following named awards: the Orville C. Shirey Memorial Scholarship, the Joseph Ichiuji Memorial Scholarship, the Phil Ishio Memorial Scholarship, the Kiyoko Tsuboi Taubkin Scholarship, the Grant Hirabayashi Memorial Scholarship, the Victor and Teru Matsui Scholarship, the Betty Shima Scholarship, the Dr. Warren Tsuneishi Scholarship, the Mike and Etsu Masaoka Scholarship, and the Douglas Ishio Memorial Scholarship.

Number awarded 10 each year.

Deadline April of each year.

[193]
JAY LEE SOCIAL SERVICE SCHOLARSHIP

Philip Jaisohn Memorial Foundation
Attn: Education and Scholarship Committee
6705 Old York Road
Philadelphia, PA 19126
(215) 224-2000   Fax: (215) 224-9164
E-mail: jaisohnhouse@gmail.com
Web: www.jaisohn.org

Summary To provide financial assistance to Korean American undergraduate and graduate students who have participated in social service activities.

Eligibility This program is open to Korean American undergraduate and graduate students who are currently enrolled at a college or university in the United States. Applicants must be able to demonstrate excellence in community service activities and financial need. Along with their application, they must submit an essay on either "Who is Dr. Jaisohn to Me," or "The Significance of Dr. Jaisohn's Ideal to Korean Americans." They must also submit a brief statement on how they can contribute to and be involved in the activities of the Philip Jaisohn Memorial Foundation. Selection is based on community service and future potential.

Financial data The stipend is $1,000.

Duration 1 year.

Number awarded 1 each year.

Deadline November of each year.

[194]
JIMMY A. YOUNG MEMORIAL EDUCATION RECOGNITION AWARD

American Association for Respiratory Care
Attn: American Respiratory Care Foundation
9425 North MacArthur Boulevard, Suite 100
Irving, TX 75063-4706
(972) 243-2272   Fax: (972) 484-2720
E-mail: info@arcfoundation.org
Web: www.arcfoundation.org

Summary To provide financial assistance to college students, especially Asian Americans and other minorities, interested in becoming respiratory therapists.

Eligibility Candidates must be enrolled in an accredited respiratory therapy program, have completed at least 1 semester/quarter of the program, and have a GPA of 3.0 or higher. Preference is given to nominees of minority origin. Applications must include 6 copies of an original referenced paper on some aspect of respiratory care and letters of rec-

ommendation. The foundation prefers that the candidates be nominated by a school or program, but any student may initiate a request for sponsorship by a school (in order that a deserving candidate is not denied the opportunity to compete simply because the school does not initiate the application).

Financial data The stipend is $1,000. The award also provides airfare, 1 night's lodging, and registration for the association's international congress.

Duration 1 year.

Number awarded 1 each year.

Deadline June of each year.

[195]
JOHN AND MURIEL LANDIS SCHOLARSHIPS

American Nuclear Society
Attn: Scholarship Coordinator
555 North Kensington Avenue
La Grange Park, IL 60526-5535
(708) 352-6611   Toll Free: (800) 323-3044
Fax: (708) 352-0499   E-mail: outreach@ans.org
Web: www.new.ans.org/honors/scholarships

Summary To provide financial assistance to undergraduate or graduate students (particularly Asian Americans, other minorities, and women) who are interested in preparing for a career in nuclear-related fields and can demonstrate financial need.

Eligibility This program is open to undergraduate and graduate students at colleges or universities located in the United States who are preparing for, or planning to prepare for, a career in nuclear science, nuclear engineering, or a nuclear-related field. Qualified high school seniors are also eligible. Applicants must have greater than average financial need and have experienced circumstances that render them disadvantaged. Along with their application, they must submit an essay on their academic and professional goals, experiences that have affected those goals, etc. Selection is based on that essay, academic achievement, letters of recommendation, and financial need. Women and members of minority groups are especially urged to apply. U.S. citizenship is not required.

Financial data The stipend is $5,000, to be used to cover tuition, books, fees, room, and board.

Duration 1 year; nonrenewable.

Number awarded Up to 9 each year.

Deadline January of each year.

[196]
JOHN T. SMITH SCHOLARSHIPS

Kentucky Community and Technical College System
Attn: Financial Aid
300 North Main Street
Versailles, KY 40383
(859) 256-3100   Toll Free: (877) 528-2748 (within KY)
Web: www.kctcs.edu

Summary To provide financial assistance to Asian American and other minority students attending or planning to attend participating institutions within the Kentucky Community and Technical College System (KCTCS).

Eligibility This program is open to minority residents of Kentucky who are attending or planning to attend a participating KCTCS institution. Applicants must be enrolled or planning to enroll in a transfer program to a 4-year institution. They must be able to demonstrate unmet financial need and a GPA of 2.5 or higher. Most colleges require full-time enrollment.

Financial data Stipends vary at each participating college, but they are intended to provide full payment of tuition and required fees.

Duration 1 year; may be renewed 1 additional year.

Number awarded Varies each year.

Deadline Each college sets its own deadline.

[197]
JONATHAN T.Y. YEH MEMORIAL STUDENT PRIZE

American Folklore Society
Attn: Timothy Lloyd, Executive Director
Ohio State University
Mershon Center
1501 Neil Avenue
Columbus, OH 43201-2602
(614) 292-3375   Fax: (614) 292-2407
E-mail: lloyd.100@osu.edu
Web: www.afsnet.org/?page=SectionPrizes

Summary To recognize and reward outstanding student papers on a subject dealing with Asian and/or Asian American folklore.

Eligibility This competition is open to full-time undergraduate and graduate students under 30 years of age. Applicants must submit a 10- to 12-page research paper dealing with Asian and/or Asian American folklore studies. They must be able to demonstrate prospects for publication of their scholarly work and a dedication to research and/or teaching folklore studies.

Financial data The prize is $500.

Duration The prize is awarded annually.

Number awarded 1 each year.

Deadline June of each year.

[198]
JUSTINE E. GRANNER MEMORIAL SCHOLARSHIP

Iowa United Methodist Foundation
2301 Rittenhouse Street
Des Moines, IA 50321
(515) 974-8927
Web: www.iumf.org/generalscholarships.html

Summary To provide financial assistance to Asian Americans and other ethnic minorities in Iowa interested in majoring in a health-related field.

Eligibility This program is open to ethnic minority students preparing for a career in nursing, public health, or a related field at a college or school of nursing in Iowa. Applicants must have a GPA of 3.0 or higher. They must submit transcripts, 3 letters of recommendation, ACT and/or SAT scores, and documentation of financial need. Preference is given to graduates of Iowa high schools.

Financial data The stipend is $1,000.

Duration 1 year.

Number awarded 1 each year.

Deadline March of each year.

[199]
KANSAS ETHNIC MINORITY SCHOLARSHIP PROGRAM

Kansas Board of Regents
Attn: Student Financial Assistance
1000 S.W. Jackson Street, Suite 520
Topeka, KS 66612-1368
(785) 296-3518   Fax: (785) 296-0983
E-mail: dlindeman@ksbor.org
Web: www.kansasregents.org/scholarships_and_grants

Summary To provide financial assistance to Asian Americans and other minority students in Kansas who are interested in attending college in the state.

Eligibility Eligible to apply are Kansas residents who fall into 1 of these minority groups: American Indian, Alaskan Native, African American, Asian, Pacific Islander, or Hispanic. Applicants may be current college students (enrolled in community colleges, colleges, or universities in Kansas), but high school seniors graduating in the current year receive priority consideration. Minimum academic requirements include 1 of the following: 1) ACT score of 21 or higher or combined mathematics and critical reading SAT score of 990 or higher; 2) cumulative GPA of 3.0 or higher; 3) high school rank in upper 33%; 4) completion of the Kansas Scholars Curriculum (4 years of English, 3 years of mathematics, 3 years of science, 3 years of social studies, and 2 years of foreign language); 5) selection by the National Merit Corporation in any category; or 6) selection by the College Board as a Hispanic Scholar. Selection is based primarily on financial need.

Financial data A stipend of up to $1,850 is provided, depending on financial need and availability of state funds.

Duration 1 year; may be renewed for up to 3 additional years (4 additional years for designated 5-year programs), provided the recipient maintains a 2.0 cumulative GPA and has financial need.

Additional information There is a $12 application fee.

Number awarded Approximately 200 each year.

Deadline April of each year.

[200]
KANSAS SPJ MINORITY STUDENT SCHOLARSHIP

Society of Professional Journalists-Kansas Professional Chapter
c/o Denise Neil, Scholarship Committee
Wichita Eagle
825 East Douglas Avenue
P.O. Box 820
Wichita, KS 67201-0820
(316) 268-6327   E-mail: dneil@wichitaeagle.com

Summary To provide financial assistance to Asian American and other minority residents of any state who are enrolled at colleges and universities in Kansas and interested in a career in journalism.

Eligibility This program is open to residents of any state who are members of a racial or ethnic minority group and entering their junior or senior year at colleges and universities in Kansas. Applicants do not have to be journalism or communication majors, but they must demonstrate a strong and sincere interest in print journalism, broadcast journalism, online journalism, or photojournalism. They must have a GPA of 2.5 or higher. Along with their application, they must submit a professional resume, 4 to 6 examples of their best work (clips or stories, copies of photographs, tapes or transcripts of broadcasts, printouts of web pages) and a 1-page cover letter about themselves, how they came to be interested in journalism, their professional goals, and (if appropriate) their financial need for this scholarship.

Financial data The stipend is $1,000.

Duration 1 year.

Number awarded 1 each year.

Deadline March of each year.

[201]
KANSAS TAIWANESE AMERICAN COMMUNITY SCHOLARSHIP AWARDS

North American Taiwanese Women's Association-Kansas
  Chapter
c/o Judy Kuo, Selection Committee
12809 Grant Street
Overland Park, KS 66213
E-mail: ks-chapter@natwa.com
Web: sites.google.com/site/natwakschapter

Summary To provide financial assistance to high school seniors in Kansas and Missouri who identify with the Taiwanese American community and plan to attend college in any state.

Eligibility This program is open to seniors graduating from high schools in Kansas or Missouri who plan to enroll at a college or university in any state. All students who are U.S. citizens or permanent residents are eligible, regardless of sex, race, or religion, but the program was established to serve the Taiwanese American community. Applicants must submit an essay of 500 to 1,000 words on their experience and ideas on leadership, community service, and teamwork. Financial need is not considered in the selection process.

Financial data The stipend is $600.

Duration 1 year.

Additional information This program began in 2006.

Number awarded Varies each year; normally, the sponsor attempts to award 1 scholarship at each participating high school, increasing to 2 scholarships if a school has more than 5 qualified applicants and possibly to 3 scholarships if a school has more than 10 qualified applicants.

Deadline March of each year.

[202]
KATHY MANN MEMORIAL SCHOLARSHIP

Wisconsin Education Association Council
Attn: Scholarship Committee
33 Nob Hill Drive
P.O. Box 8003
Madison, WI 53708-8003
(608) 276-7711   Toll Free: (800) 362-8034, ext. 278
Fax: (608) 276-8203   E-mail: BrisackM@weac.org
Web: www.weac.org

Summary To provide financial assistance to Asian American and other minority high school seniors whose parent is a member of the Wisconsin Education Association Council (WEAC) and who plan to study education at a college in any state.

Eligibility This program is open to high school seniors whose parent is an active WEAC member, an active retired member, or a person who died while holding a WEAC membership. Applicants must be members of a minority group (American Indian, Eskimo or Aleut, Hispanic, Asian or Pacific Islander, or Black). They must rank in the top 25% of their graduating class or have a GPA of 3.0 or higher, plan to major or minor in education at a college in any state, and intend to teach in Wisconsin. Along with their application, they must submit a 300-word essay on why they want to enter the education profession and what they hope to accomplish. Selection is based primarily on that essay, GPA, letters of recommendation, and school and community activities. Secondary consideration may be given to other factors, including financial need.

Financial data The stipend is $1,450 per year.

Duration 4 years, provided the recipient maintains a GPA of 3.0 or higher.

Number awarded 1 each year.

Deadline February of each year.

[203]
KATU THOMAS R. DARGAN SCHOLARSHIP

KATU-TV
Attn: Human Resources
2153 N.E. Sandy Boulevard
P.O. Box 2
Portland, OR 97207-0002
(503) 231-4222
Web: www.katu.com/about/scholarship

Summary To provide financial assistance to Asian American and other minority students from Oregon and Washington who are studying broadcasting or communications in college.

Eligibility This program is open to minority (Asian, Black/African American, Hispanic or Latino, Native Hawaiian or Pacific Islander, American Indian or Alaska Native) U.S. citizens, currently enrolled as a sophomore or higher at a 4-year college or university or an accredited community college in Oregon or Washington. Residents of Oregon or Washington enrolled at a school in any state are also eligible. Applicants must be majoring in broadcasting or communications and have a GPA of 3.0 or higher. Community college students must be enrolled in a broadcast curriculum that is transferable to a 4-year accredited university. Finalists are interviewed. Selection is based on financial need, academic achievement, and an essay on personal and professional goals.

Financial data The stipend is $6,000. Funds are sent directly to the recipient's school.

Duration 1 year; recipients may reapply if they have maintained a GPA of 3.0 or higher.

Additional information Winners are also eligible for a paid internship in selected departments at Fisher Broadcasting/KATU in Portland, Oregon.

Number awarded 1 each year.

Deadline April of each year.

[204]
KENJI KAJIWARA MEMORIAL SCHOLARSHIP

Japanese American Citizens League
Attn: National Scholarship Awards
1765 Sutter Street
San Francisco, CA 94115
(415) 345-1075   Fax: (415) 931-4671
E-mail: ncwnp@jacl.org
Web: www.jacl.org/edu/scholar.htm

Summary To provide funding to student members of the Japanese American Citizens League (JACL) who are currently attending a college, university, or other type of postsecondary school.

Eligibility This program is open to JACL members who are currently enrolled at a college, university, trade school, business college, or other institution of higher learning. Applicants must submit information on their involvement in JACL and a 2-page essay on a topic that changes annually but relates to Japanese Americans. Selection is based on that essay, academic history, JACL involvement, school activities, work history, scholastic honors, and community involvement.

Financial data Stipends generally average more than $2,000.

Duration 1 year; nonrenewable.

Number awarded At least 1 each year.

Deadline March of each year.

[205]
KENTUCKY LIBRARY ASSOCIATION SCHOLARSHIP FOR MINORITY STUDENTS

Kentucky Library Association
c/o Executive Secretary
1501 Twilight Trail
Frankfort, KY 40601
(502) 223-5322   Fax: (502) 223-4937
E-mail: info@kylibasn.org
Web: www.klaonline.org/scholarships965.cfm

Summary To provide financial assistance to Asian Americans and other minorities who are residents of Kentucky or attending school there and are working on an undergraduate or graduate degree in library science.

Eligibility This program is open to members of minority groups (defined as American Indian, Alaskan Native, Black, Hispanic, Pacific Islander, or other ethnic group) who are entering or continuing at a graduate library school accredited by the American Library Association (ALA) or an undergraduate library program accredited by the National Council for Teacher Education (NCATE). Applicants must be residents of Kentucky or a student in a library program in the state. Along with their application, they must submit a statement of their career objectives, why they have chosen librarianship as a career, and their reasons for applying for this scholarship. Selection is based on that statement, cumulative undergraduate and graduate GPA (if applicable), academic merit and potential, and letters of recommendation. U.S. citizenship or permanent resident status is required.

Financial data The stipend is $1,000.

Duration 1 year; nonrenewable.

Number awarded 1 or more each year.

Deadline June of each year.

[206]
KENTUCKY MINORITY EDUCATOR RECRUITMENT AND RETENTION SCHOLARSHIPS

Kentucky Department of Education
Attn: Minority Educator Recruitment and Retention
500 Mero Street, 8th Floor
Frankfort, KY 40601
(502) 564-1479, ext. 4014   Fax: (502) 564-6952
TDD: (502) 564-4970
E-mail: monica.davis@education.ky.gov
Web: www.education.ky.gov

Summary To provide funding to Asian American and other minority undergraduate and graduate students enrolled in Kentucky public institutions who want to become teachers.

Eligibility This program is open to residents of Kentucky who are undergraduate or graduate students pursuing initial teacher certification at a public university or community college in the state. Applicants must have a GPA of 2.5 or higher and either maintain full-time enrollment or be a part-time student within 18 semester hours of receiving a teacher education degree. They must be U.S. citizens and meet the Kentucky definition of a minority student.

Financial data Stipends are $5,000 per year at the 8 state universities in Kentucky or $2,000 per year at community and technical colleges. This is a scholarship/loan program. Recipients are required to teach 1 semester in Kentucky for each semester or summer term the scholarship is received. If they fail to fulfill that requirement, the scholarship converts to a loan with severe penalties for non-payment.

Duration 1 year; may be renewed up to 3 additional years.

Additional information The Kentucky General Assembly established this program in 1992.

Number awarded Varies each year.

Deadline Each state college of teacher education sets its own deadline.

[207]
KIMBALL OFFICE SCHOLARSHIP

International Interior Design Association
Attn: IIDA Foundation
222 Merchandise Mart, Suite 567
Chicago, IL 60654
(312) 467-1950   Toll Free: (888) 799-4432
Fax: (312) 467-0779   E-mail: iidahq@iida.org
Web: www.iida.org

Summary To provide financial assistance to Asian American and other minority students enrolled in the senior year of an interior design program.

Eligibility This program is open to college seniors of African, Asian, Latino, or Native American heritage. Applicants must be working on a degree in interior design. Selection is based on excellence in academics and promising design talent.

Financial data The stipend is $4,000.

Duration 1 year.

Additional information This program began in 2006 by Kimball Office, a unit of Kimball International, Inc.

Number awarded 1 each year.

Deadline Deadline not specified.

[208]
KOREAN HONOR SCHOLARSHIP

Embassy of the Republic of Korea in the USA
2320 Massachusetts Avenue, N.W.
Washington, DC 20008
(202) 939-5679   Fax: (202) 342-1597
Web: usa.mofa.go.kr

Summary To provide financial assistance to undergraduate and graduate students of Korean or Korean American heritage.

Eligibility This program is open to students of Korean or Korean American heritage. Applicants must be entering or enrolled full time in an undergraduate or graduate degree program at a college or university in the United States or Canada. They must have a GPA of 3.5 or higher. Along with their application, they must submit a 600-word essay (in English) on a topic that changes annually but relates to their Korean heritage. Selection is based on that essay, academic achievement, awards, honors, performances, extracurricular activities, and a letter of recommendation.

Financial data The stipend is $1,000.

Duration 1 year; nonrenewable.

Additional information This program began in 1981 when the government of the Republic of Korea donated $1 million to commemorate the 100th anniversary of the establishment of diplomatic relations between Korea and the United States. Subsequent donations have added to the fund.

Number awarded Approximately 65 each year. Since the program was established, it has awarded nearly 2,800 scholarships.

Deadline June of each year.

[209]
KOREAN NURSES ASSOCIATION OF SOUTHERN CALIFORNIA REGISTERED NURSE EDUCATION SCHOLARSHIPS

Korean Nurses Association of Southern California
936 South Crenshaw Boulevard, Suite 204
Los Angeles, CA 90019
(323) 934-7073

Summary To provide financial assistance to Korean nurses in California who wish to attend college in the state to work on a bachelor's or graduate degree.

Eligibility This program is open to Korean registered nurses who are living in California and enrolled or entering a baccalaureate or higher degree nursing program in the state. Applicants must be legal residents of the United States. Along with their application, they must submit a 1-page essay on their reasons for selecting nursing as a career, including their professional goals and objectives. Selection is based on that essay, work experience in nursing and related fields, community service and volunteer work experience, cumulative GPA, and letters of recommendation. Priority consideration is given to members of the Korean Nurses Association of Southern California and their immediate family members.

Financial data A stipend is awarded (amount not specified).

Duration 1 year; may be renewed 1 additional year.

Number awarded 1 or more each year.

Deadline January of each year.

[210]
KOREAN UNIVERSITY CLUB SCHOLARSHIP

Hawai'i Community Foundation
Attn: Scholarship Department
827 Fort Street Mall
Honolulu, HI 96813
(808) 566-5570   Toll Free: (888) 731-3863
Fax: (808) 521-6286
E-mail: scholarships@hcf-hawaii.org
Web: www.hawaiicommunityfoundation.org/scholarships

Summary To provide financial assistance to residents of Hawaii who are of Korean ancestry and interested in attending college in any state.

Eligibility This program is open to residents of Hawaii who are attending or planning to attend a 2- or 4-year college or university in any state. Applicants must be of Korean ancestry. They must be able to demonstrate academic achievement (GPA of 2.7 or higher), good moral character, and financial need. Along with their application, they must submit a short statement indicating their reasons for attending college, their planned course of study, their career goals, and what community service means to them.

Financial data The amounts of the awards depend on the availability of funds and the need of the recipient. Recently, the average value of each of the scholarships awarded by the foundation was $2,200.

Duration 1 year.

Additional information The Korean University Club of Hawaii was established in 1936 and began awarding scholarships to students of Korean ancestry in 1950.

Number awarded 1 or more each year.

Deadline February of each year.

[211]
KOREAN-AMERICAN ADVENTIST SCHOLARSHIP FOUNDATION

Korean-American Adventist Scholarships
c/o Korean Adventist Press
619 South New Hampshire Avenue
Los Angeles, CA 90005
(213) 388-6100   E-mail: sdascholarship@gmail.com
Web: www.sdascholarship.org/?page_id=9

Summary To provide financial assistance to Korean American Adventists who are interested in working on an undergraduate or graduate degree in any field.

Eligibility This program is open to Korean American Adventists who are high school seniors or students currently enrolled in college or graduate school. Applicants must have a GPA of 3.0 or higher. Along with their application, they must submit a 1- to 2-page personal essay that describes their personal history, life passions, long-term goals, and financial situation. Their pastor must provide an evaluation of their spiritual dedication, motivation, citizenship, church activities, academic achievement, and financial need.

Financial data The stipend is $1,000.

Duration 1 year.

Additional information This program began in 2004.

Number awarded 20 each year.

Deadline June of each year.

[212]
KSEA UNDERGRADUATE SCHOLARSHIPS

Korean-American Scientists and Engineers Association
Attn: Scholarship Committee
1952 Gallows Drive, Suite 300
Vienna, VA 22182
(703) 748-1221   Fax: (703) 748-1331
E-mail: admin@ksea.org
Web: scholarship.ksea.org/InfoUndergraduate.aspx

Summary To provide financial assistance to undergraduate student members of the Korean-American Scientists and Engineers Association (KSEA).

Eligibility This program is open to Korean American undergraduate students who are KSEA members, have completed at least 2 semesters as a college student, and are majoring in science, engineering, or a related field. Along with their application, they must submit an essay on a topic that changes annually but relates to science or engineering. Selection is based on the essay (20%), KSEA activities and community service (30%), recommendation letters (20%), and academic performance (30%).

Financial data The stipend is $1,000.

Duration 1 year.

Additional information This program includes the following named scholarships: the Inyong Ham Scholarship, the Wan-Kyoo Cho Scholarship, the Shoon Kyung Kim Scholarship, the Nam Sook and Je Hyun Kim Scholarship, the SeAh-Haiam Scholarship, the Yohan and Rumie Cho Scholarship, the Changkiu Riew and Hyunsoo Kim Scholarship, the Woojin Scholarship, the Jae S. and Kyuho Lim Scholarship, and the Hyundai Scholarship.

Number awarded Approximately 30 each year.

Deadline March of each year.

[213]
KYUTARO AND YASUO ABIKO MEMORIAL SCHOLARSHIP

Japanese American Citizens League
Attn: National Scholarship Awards
1765 Sutter Street
San Francisco, CA 94115
(415) 345-1075   Fax: (415) 931-4671
E-mail: ncwnp@jacl.org
Web: www.jacl.org/edu/scholar.htm

Summary To provide financial assistance for college to student members of the Japanese American Citizens League (JACL), especially those majoring in journalism or agriculture.

Eligibility This program is open to JACL members who are currently enrolled at a college, university, trade school, business college, or other institution of higher learning. Applicants must submit information on their involvement in JACL and a 2-page essay on a topic that changes annually but relates to Japanese Americans. Selection is based on that essay, academic history, JACL involvement, school activities, work history, scholastic honors, and community involvement. Preference is given to students majoring in journalism or agriculture.

Financial data Stipends generally average more than $2,000.

Duration 1 year; nonrenewable.

Number awarded At least 1 each year.

Deadline March of each year.

[214]
LAGRANT FOUNDATION UNDERGRADUATE SCHOLARSHIPS

Lagrant Foundation
Attn: Senior Programs and Outreach Manager
600 Wilshire Boulevard, Suite 1520
Los Angeles, CA 90017
(323) 469-8680, ext. 223   Fax: (323) 469-8683
E-mail: erickainiguez@lagrant.com
Web: www.lagrantfoundation.org

Summary To provide financial assistance to Asian American and other minority college students who are interested in majoring in advertising, public relations, or marketing.

Eligibility This program is open to African Americans, Asian Americans/Pacific Islanders, Hispanics/Latinos, and Native Americans/American Indians who are full-time students at a 4-year accredited institution. Applicants must have a GPA of 2.75 or higher and be either majoring in advertising, marketing, or public relations or minoring in communications with plans to prepare for a career in advertising, marketing, or public relations. Along with their application, they must submit 1) a 1- to 2-page essay outlining their career goals; what steps they will take to increase ethnic representation in the fields of advertising, marketing, and public relations; and the role of an advertising, marketing, or public relations practitioner; 2) a paragraph describing the college and/or community activities in which they are involved; 3) a brief paragraph describing any honors and awards they have received; 4) a letter of reference; 5) a resume; and 6) an official transcript. U.S. citizenship or permanent resident status is required.

Financial data The stipend is $5,000.

Duration 1 year.

Number awarded Varies each year; recently, 16 of these scholarships were awarded.

Deadline February of each year.

[215]
LANDMARK SCHOLARS PROGRAM

Landmark Media Enterprises LLC
c/o Ann Morris, Managing Editor
Greensboro News & Record
200 East Market Street
Greensboro, NC 27401
(540) 981-3211   Toll Free: (800) 346-1234
E-mail: amorris@news-record.com
Web: company.news-record.com/intern.htm

Summary To provide financial aid and work experience to Asian American and other minority undergraduates who are interested in preparing for a career in journalism.

Eligibility This program is open to minority (Asian, Hispanic, African American, Native American) college sophomores, preferably those with ties to the mid-Atlantic states (Delaware, Maryland, North Carolina, South Carolina, Virginia, and Washington, D.C.). Applicants must be full-time students with a GPA of 2.5 or higher in a 4-year degree program. They must be interested in preparing for a career in print journalism and participating in an internship in news, features, sports, copy editing, photography, or graphics/illustration. U.S. citizenship or permanent resident status is required. Selection is based on grades, work samples, recommendations, targeted selection interview skills, and financial need.

Financial data The stipend is $5,000 per year. During the summers following their sophomore and junior years, recipients are provided with paid internships. Following graduation, they are offered a 1-year internship with full benefits and the possibility of continued employment.

Duration 2 years (the junior and senior years of college).

Additional information The internships are offered at the *News & Record* in Greensboro, North Carolina, the *Virginian-Pilot* in Norfolk, Virginia, or the *Roanoke Times* in Roanoke, Virginia.

Number awarded 1 or more each year.

Deadline January of each year.

[216]
LAO AMERICAN NATIONAL SCHOLARSHIPS

Jai Lao Foundation
Attn: Scholarship Committee
2491 San Ramon Valley Boulevard, Suite 1 Number 103
San Ramon, CA 94583
Web: blog.jailao.org/programs/scholarship-programs

Summary To provide financial assistance to descendants of Lao refugees who are interested in attending college and majoring in any field.

Eligibility This program is open to graduating high school seniors and current undergraduates in the United States who are descendants of refugees from Laos. Applicants must have a record of active involvement in the Lao community in their area. They must be U.S. citizens or permanent residents. Along with their application, they must submit a 500-word essay on 1 of the following topics: 1) their educational and academic goals and how they plan to utilize their education to achieve a better future for themselves, their family, and the Lao community; 2) any adversities or challenges they have had to overcome in pursuit of their educational goals and how they plan to use their educational goals and/or achievements to help their local Lao community; or 3) their future career plans or professional aspirations and the need or problems with the Lao community they hope to address with their education.

Financial data Stipends are $2,000, $1,500, or $1,000.

Duration 1 year.

Additional information This program began in 2011.

Number awarded 12 each year: 2 at $2,000, 2 at $1,500, and 8 at $1,000.

Deadline November of each year.

[217]
LAO AMERICAN NEW GENERATION ACADEMIC SCHOLARSHIP PROGRAM

Lao American New Generation, Inc.
Attn: Seng Phouthakoun
Connecticut Department of Energy and Environmental
  Protection
79 Elm Street
Hartford, CT 06106-5127
(860) 578-4898   E-mail: seng.phouthakoun@ct.gov
Web: www.laoamericanct.org/?page_id=100

Summary To provide financial assistance to Lao American students from Connecticut who are interested in attending college in any state.

Eligibility This program is open to residents of Connecticut who are of Laotian ancestry. Applicants must be attending or planning to attend college in any state.

Financial data A stipend is awarded (amount not specified).

Duration 1 year.

Additional information This program began in 2014.

Number awarded Varies each year.

Deadline Deadline not specified.

[218]
LAO AMERICAN WOMEN ASSOCIATION OF WASHINGTON D.C. METROPOLITAN AREA COLLEGE SCHOLARSHIP FUND

Lao American Women Association
Attn: Scholarship Committee
3908 Carroll Court
Chantilly, VA 20151
(703) 283-8698   E-mail: info@lawadc.org
Web: www.lawadc.org

Summary To provide financial assistance to high school seniors of Lao ancestry in the Washington, D.C. area who plan to attend college in any state.

Eligibility This program is open to seniors graduating from high schools in the Washington, D.C. metropolitan area who are of Lao parentage. Applicants must have a GPA of 3.0 or higher and be planning to attend college in any state in the following fall. Along with their application, they must submit a 150-word personal statement on their purpose or motivations for going to college. Financial need is considered in the selection process (must have family income less than $75,000 per year). U.S. citizenship or permanent resident status is required.

Financial data The stipend is $1,000.

Duration 1 year.

Additional information This program began in 2004.

Number awarded 1 or more each year.

Deadline April of each year.

[219]
LAOTIAN AMERICAN SCHOLARSHIP FOUNDATION SCHOLARSHIPS

Laotian American Scholarship Foundation, Inc.
c/o Sounthone Vattana
34 Kiwanis Road
Rochester, NY 14617
(585) 342-8239   E-mail: svattana@brockport.edu
Web: www.laoamericanscholarship.wordpress.com

Summary To provide financial assistance to Laotian American high school seniors who plan to attend college and study any field.

Eligibility This program is open to Laotian American high school seniors who plan to attend a college or university and major in any field. Applicants must submit a 500-word essay that includes what it means to be a Laotian American, how their Laotian culture has influenced their assimilation into American society, how they plan to represent their Laotian culture in the community, and their goals for the next 5 or 10 years. Selection is based on the completeness of the application, quality of the essay, and achievements in academic and extracurricular activities.

Financial data Stipends are $500 or $250.

Duration 1 year.

Number awarded Each year, 3 scholarships at $500 and a varying number at $250 are awarded.

Deadline July of each year.

[220]
LAPIZ FAMILY SCHOLARSHIP

Asian Pacific Fund
Attn: Scholarship Coordinator
465 California Street, Suite 809
San Francisco, CA 94104
(415) 395-9985 E-mail: scholarship@asianpacificfund.org
Web: www.asianpacificfund.org

Summary To provide financial assistance to Asian American and other students enrolled at campuses of the University of California (UC) who are children of farm workers.

Eligibility This program is open to residents of California who will be enrolled as a full time undergraduate at a UC campus in the following fall. Preference is given to students at UC Davis and UC Santa Cruz. Applicants may be of any ethnic or racial background but they must be a farm worker or the child of farm or migrant workers. They must have a GPA of 3.0 or higher and be able to demonstrate financial need. Along with their application, they must submit essays of 250 to 500 words each on 1) their experience as a farm worker or child of a farm worker and how that experience relates to their educational and career goals; 2) a project, experience, or person related to their academic and career goals that inspired them; and 3) any unusual family or personal circumstances that have affected their achievement in school, work, or extracurricular activities. U.S. citizenship or permanent resident status is required.

Financial data The stipend is $1,000 per year.

Duration 1 year; may be renewed up to 3 additional years.

Number awarded 2 each year.

Deadline March of each year.

[221]
LARRY W. MCCORMICK COMMUNICATIONS SCHOLARSHIP FOR UNDERREPRESENTED STUDENTS

The Lullaby Guild, Inc.
Attn: Scholarship Committee
6709 La Tijera, Suite 116
Los Angeles, CA 90045
(310) 335-5655 E-mail: mail@lullabyguild.org
Web: www.lullabyguild.org

Summary To provide financial assistance to Asian American and other minority upper-division students who are working on a degree in a field related to mass communications.

Eligibility This program is open to underrepresented (e.g., African American, Hispanic American, Native American, Alaskan American, Pacific Islander, Asian) students entering their junior or senior year at an accredited college or university. Applicants must be working on a degree in a field related to mass communications, including audiovisual and elec-

tronic and print journalism. Along with their application, they must submit a personal statement regarding their volunteer services, official transcripts, 3 letters of recommendation, 3 samples of their journalistic work, and a 500-word personal statement about their interest in journalism or mass communication. Selection is based on academic achievement, letters of recommendation, journalistic experience and/or evidence of journalistic talent, clarity of purpose in plans and goals for a future in journalism or mass communications, and involvement in volunteer community service.

Financial data The stipend is $2,500.

Duration 1 year.

Number awarded 1 each year.

Deadline February of each year.

[222]
LAURENCE R. FOSTER MEMORIAL SCHOLARSHIPS

Oregon Student Access Commission
Attn: Grants and Scholarships Division
1500 Valley River Drive, Suite 100
Eugene, OR 97401-2146
(541) 687-7395 Toll Free: (800) 452-8807, ext. 7395
Fax: (541) 687-7414 TDD: (800) 735-2900
E-mail: awardinfo@osac.state.or.us
Web: www.oregonstudentaid.gov/scholarships.aspx

Summary To provide financial assistance to Asian Americans and other residents of Oregon who come from a diverse environment and are enrolled at a college or graduate school in any state to prepare for a public health career.

Eligibility This program is open to residents of Oregon who are enrolled at least half time at a 4-year college or university in any state to prepare for a career in public health (not private practice). Preference is given first to applicants from diverse environments; second to persons employed in, or graduate students working on a degree in, public health; and third to juniors and seniors majoring in a health program (e.g., nursing, medical technology, physician assistant). Applicants must be able to demonstrate financial need. Along with their application, they must submit essays of 250 to 350 words on 1) what public health means to them; 2) the public health aspect they intend to practice and the health and population issues impacted by that aspect; and 3) their experience living or working in diverse environments.

Financial data Stipends for scholarships offered by the Oregon Student Access Commission (OSAC) range from $200 to $10,000 but recently averaged $2,300.

Duration 1 year.

Additional information This program is administered by the OSAC with funds provided by the Oregon Community Foundation.

Number awarded Varies each year; recently, 6 of these scholarships were awarded.

Deadline February of each year.

[223]
LE HOANG NGUYEN COLLEGE SCHOLARSHIP

Vietnamese American Scholarship Foundation
P.O. Box 429
Stafford, TX 77497
E-mail: scholarships@vietscholarships.org
Web: www.vietscholarships.org/scholarships.html

Summary To provide financial assistance to high school seniors of Vietnamese descent in Texas who plan to attend college in any state.

Eligibility This program is open to seniors graduating from high schools in Texas who are of Vietnamese descent. Applicants must be planning to enroll at an accredited college or university in any state. They must have a GPA of 3.0 or higher and a rank in their class in the top 10%. Along with their application, they must submit a 750-word essay on either 1) accomplishments that illustrate their aptitude for leadership; or 2) where they see themselves in 5 years. An interview may be required. Financial need is not considered in the selection process.

Financial data The stipend is $500.

Duration 1 year; nonrenewable.

Number awarded 1 each year.

Deadline May of each year.

[224]
LEADERSHIP FOR DIVERSITY SCHOLARSHIP

California School Library Association
Attn: CSL Foundation
6444 East Spring Street, Number 237
Long Beach, CA 90815-1553
Toll Free: (888) 655-8480   Fax: (888) 655-8480
E-mail: info@csla.net
Web: www.csla.net

Summary To provide financial assistance to Asian American and other students who reflect the diversity of California's population and are interested in earning a credential as a library media teacher in the state.

Eligibility This program is open to students who are members of a traditionally underrepresented group enrolled in a college or university library media teacher credential program in California. Applicants must intend to work as a library media teacher in a California school library media center for a minimum of 3 years. Along with their application, they must submit a 250-word statement on their school library media career interests and goals, why they should be considered, what they can contribute, their commitment to serving the needs of multicultural and multilingual students, and their financial situation.

Financial data The stipend is $1,500.

Duration 1 year.

Number awarded 1 each year.

Deadline May of each year.

[225]
LEGACY PARK FOUNDATION SCHOLARSHIPS

Legacy Park Foundation
Attn: Scholarship Director
5240 Tennyson Parkway, Suite 207
Plano, TX 75024
E-mail: info@legacyparkfoundation.org
Web: www.legacyparkfoundation.org

Summary To provide financial assistance to Asian American and other minority or economically disadvantaged high school seniors who plan to attend college and major in any field.

Eligibility This program is open to graduating high school seniors who qualify as members of minority or other economically disadvantaged groups. Applicants must be U.S. citizens or permanent residents planning to enroll at a college or university in any state and major in any field. They must have a GPA of 3.7 or higher and scores of at least 2000 on the SAT or 29 on the ACT. Selection is based on academic achievement, extracurricular and community participation, and financial need.

Financial data The stipend is $1,000.

Duration 1 year.

Additional information This program began in 2007.

Number awarded 5 each year.

Deadline April of each year.

[226]
LEONARD M. PERRYMAN COMMUNICATIONS SCHOLARSHIP FOR ETHNIC MINORITY STUDENTS

United Methodist Communications
Attn: Communications Resourcing Team
810 12th Avenue South
P.O. Box 320
Nashville, TN 37202-0320
(615) 742-5481   Toll Free: (888) CRT-4UMC
Fax: (615) 742-5485   E-mail: scholarships@umcom.org
Web: crt.umc.org/interior.asp?ptid=44&mid=10270

Summary To provide financial assistance to Asian American and other minority students at United Methodist colleges who are interested in careers in religious communications.

Eligibility This program is open to United Methodist ethnic minority students enrolled in accredited institutions of higher education as juniors or seniors. Applicants must be interested in preparing for a career in religious communications. For the purposes of this program, "communications" is meant to cover audiovisual, electronic, and print journalism. Selection is based on Christian commitment and involvement in the life of the United Methodist church, academic achievement, journalistic experience, clarity of purpose, and professional potential as a religion communicator.

Financial data The stipend is $2,500 per year.

Duration 1 year.

Additional information The scholarship may be used at any accredited institution of higher education.

Number awarded 1 each year.

Deadline March of each year.

[227]
LIN MEDIA MINORITY SCHOLARSHIP AND TRAINING PROGRAM

LIN Television Corporation
Attn: Vice President, Human Resources
One West Exchange Street, Suite 5A
Providence, RI 02903-1064
(401) 454-2880   Fax: (401) 454-6990
Web: www.linmedia.com

Summary To provide funding to Asian American and other minority undergraduates interested in earning a degree in a field related to broadcast journalism and working at a station owned by LIN Television Corporation.

Eligibility This program is open to U.S. citizens and permanent residents of non-white origin who are enrolled as a sophomore or higher at a college or university. Applicants must have a declared major in broadcast journalism, digital multimedia, mass/speech/digital communication, television production, or marketing and a GPA of 3.0 or higher. Along with their application, they must submit a list of organizations and activities in which they have held leadership positions, 3 references, a 50-word description of their career goals, a list of personal achievements and honors, and a 500-word essay about themselves. Financial need is not considered in the selection process.

Financial data The program pays for tuition and fees, books, and room and board, to a maximum of $10,000 per year. Recipients must sign an employment agreement that guarantees them part-time employment as an intern during school and a 2-year regular position at a television station owned by LIN Television Corporation following graduation. If they fail to honor the employment agreement, they must repay all scholarship funds received.

Duration 2 years.

Additional information LIN Television Corporation owns 28 television stations in 17 media markets in the United States. Recipients of these scholarships must work at a station selected by LIN management.

Number awarded 2 each year: 1 for a student in broadcast television and 1 for a student in digital media.

Deadline March of each year.

[228]
LOUIS B. RUSSELL, JR. MEMORIAL SCHOLARSHIP

Indiana State Teachers Association
Attn: Scholarships
150 West Market Street, Suite 900
Indianapolis, IN 46204-2875
(317) 263-3369   Toll Free: (800) 382-4037
Fax: (800) 777-6128   E-mail: mshoup@ista-in.org
Web: www.ista-in.org/dynamic.aspx?id=1038

Summary To provide financial assistance to Asian American and other minority high school seniors in Indiana who are interested in attending vocational school in any state.

Eligibility This program is open to ethnic minority high school seniors in Indiana who are interested in continuing their education in the area of industrial arts, vocational education, or technical preparation at an accredited postsecondary institution in any state. Selection is based on academic achievement, leadership ability as expressed through co-cur-

ricular activities and community involvement, recommendations, and a 300-word essay on their educational goals and how they plan to use this scholarship.

Financial data The stipend is $1,000.

Duration 1 year; may be renewed for 1 additional year, provided the recipient maintains a GPA of "C+" or higher.

Number awarded 1 each year.

Deadline February of each year.

[229]
LOUISE MORITZ MOLITORIS LEADERSHIP AWARD

Women's Transportation Seminar
Attn: WTS Foundation
1701 K Street, N.W., Suite 800
Washington, DC 20006
(202) 955-5085   Fax: (202) 955-5088
E-mail: wts@wtsinternational.org
Web: www.wtsinternational.org/education/scholarships

Summary To provide financial assistance to undergraduate women (particularly minority women) who are interested in a career in transportation.

Eligibility This program is open to women who are working on an undergraduate degree in transportation or a transportation-related field (e.g., transportation engineering, planning, finance, or logistics). Applicants must have a GPA of 3.0 or higher. Along with their application, they must submit a 500-word statement about their career goals after graduation and why they think they should receive the scholarship award; their statement should specifically address the issue of leadership. Applications must be submitted first to a local chapter; the chapters forward selected applications for consideration on the national level. Minority women are especially encouraged to apply. Selection is based on transportation involvement and goals, job skills, academic record, and leadership potential; financial need is not considered.

Financial data The stipend is $5,000.

Duration 1 year.

Additional information Local chapters may also award additional funding to winners for their area.

Number awarded 1 each year.

Deadline Applications must be submitted by November to a local WTS chapter.

[230]
LTK SCHOLARSHIP

Conference of Minority Transportation Officials
Attn: National Scholarship Program
1875 I Street, N.W., Suite 500
Washington, DC 20006
(703) 234-4072   Fax: (202) 318-0364
Web: www.comto.org/?page=Scholarships

Summary To provide financial assistance to Asian American and other minority upper-division and graduate students in engineering or other fields related to transportation.

Eligibility This program is open to full-time minority juniors, seniors, and graduate students in engineering of other technical transportation-related disciplines. Applicants must have a GPA of 3.0 or higher. Along with their application, they must submit a cover letter with a 500-word statement of career goals. Financial need is not considered in the selection process. U.S. citizenship or legal resident status is required.

Financial data The stipend is $6,000. Funds are paid directly to the recipient's college or university.

Duration 1 year.

Additional information The Conference of Minority Transportation Officials (COMTO) was established in 1971 to promote, strengthen, and expand the roles of minorities in all aspects of transportation. This program is sponsored by LTK Engineering Services. Recipients are required to become members of COMTO if they are not already members and attend the COMTO National Scholarship Luncheon.

Number awarded 1 or more each year.

Deadline May of each year.

[231]
LUBRIZOL CORPORATION SCHOLARSHIP PROGRAM

College Now Greater Cleveland, Inc.
Attn: Managed Scholarships
200 Public Square, Suite 3820
Cleveland, OH 44114
(216) 241-5587 Fax: (216) 241-6184
E-mail: info@collegenowgc.org
Web: www.collegenowgc.org

Summary To provide financial assistance to Asian Americans, other minorities, and women who are working on a degree in specified fields of science and business at college in any state.

Eligibility This program is open to members of minority ethnic groups (American Indians, African Americans, Asian Pacific Americans, and Hispanic Americans) and women. Applicants must be enrolled full time at a 4-year college or university in any state and majoring in chemistry, computer information systems, computer science, engineering (chemical, computer, or mechanical), business, marketing, accounting, or finance. They must have a GPA of 3.0 or higher and be able to demonstrate financial need. Along with their application, they must submit a 500-word essay describing their academic and career goals.

Financial data The stipend is $4,000 per year.

Duration 1 year; may be renewed, provided the recipient maintains a GPA of 3.0 or higher.

Additional information This program is sponsored by the Lubrizol Corporation.

Number awarded Varies each year.

Deadline March of each year.

[232]
MABEL SMITH MEMORIAL SCHOLARSHIP

Wisconsin Women of Color Network, Inc.
Attn: Scholarship Committee
P.O. Box 2337
Madison, WI 53701-2337
E-mail: contact@womenofcolornetwork-wis.org
Web: www.womenofcolornetwork-wis.org/scholarship.html

Summary To provide financial assistance for vocational/technical school or community college to Asian American and other minority residents of Wisconsin.

Eligibility This program is open to residents of Wisconsin who are high school or GED-equivalent graduating seniors planning to continue their education at a vocational/technical school or community college in any state. Applicants must be a member of 1 of the following groups: African American, Asian, American Indian, Latina, or biracial. They must have a GPA of 2.0 or higher and be able to demonstrate financial need. Along with their application, they must submit a 1-page essay on how this scholarship will help them accomplish their educational goal. U.S. citizenship is required.

Financial data A stipend is awarded (amount not specified).

Duration 1 year.

Additional information This program began in 1990.

Number awarded 1 each year.

Deadline May of each year.

[233]
MAINE SECTION ASCE HIGH SCHOOL SCHOLARSHIP

American Society of Civil Engineers-Maine Section
c/o Leslie L. Corrow, Scholarship Chair
Kleinschmidt Associates
75 Main Street
P.O. Box 576
Pittsfield, ME 04967
(207) 487-3328 Fax: (207) 487-3124
E-mail: scholarships@maineasce.org
Web: www.maineasce.org

Summary To provide financial assistance to high school seniors in Maine (particularly Asian Americans, other minorities, and women) who are interested in studying civil engineering in college.

Eligibility This program is open to graduating high school seniors who are Maine residents and who intend to study civil engineering in college. Women and minorities are especially encouraged to apply. Applicants must submit a 200-word statement describing why they have chosen civil engineering as a career and what they hope to accomplish by being a civil engineer. Selection is based on the statement, academic performance, extracurricular activities, and letters of recommendation.

Financial data The stipend is $2,000.

Duration 1 year; nonrenewable.

Number awarded 1 each year.

Deadline January of each year.

[234]
MARATHON OIL CORPORATION COLLEGE SCHOLARSHIP PROGRAM OF THE HISPANIC SCHOLARSHIP FUND

Hispanic Scholarship Fund
Attn: Selection Committee
1411 West 190th Street, Suite 325
Gardena, CA 90248
Toll Free: (877) HSF-INFO E-mail: scholar1@hsf.net
Web: www.hsf.net

Summary To provide financial assistance to Asian American and other minority upper-division and graduate students working on a degree in a field related to the oil and gas industry.

Eligibility This program is open to U.S. citizens and permanent residents (must have a permanent resident card or a passport stamped I-551) who are of Hispanic American, African American, Asian Pacific Islander American, or American Indian/Alaskan Native heritage. Applicants must be currently enrolled full time at an accredited 4-year college or university in the United States, Puerto Rico, Guam, or the U.S. Virgin Islands with a GPA of 3.0 or higher. They must be 1) sophomores majoring in accounting, chemical engineering, computer engineering, computer science, electrical engineering, environmental engineering, geology, geosciences, information technology/management information systems, mechanical engineering, or petroleum engineering; or 2) seniors planning to work on a master's degree in geology, geosciences, or petroleum engineering. Selection is based on academic achievement, personal strengths, interest and commitment to a career in the oil and gas industry, leadership, and financial need.

Financial data The stipend is $15,000 per year.

Duration 2 years (the junior and senior undergraduate years or the first 2 years of a master's degree program).

Additional information This program is jointly sponsored by Marathon Oil Corporation and the Hispanic Scholarship Fund (HSF). Recipients may be offered a paid 8- to 10-week summer internship at various Marathon Oil Corporation locations.

Number awarded 1 or more each year.

Deadline September of each year.

[235]
MARCIA SILVERMAN MINORITY STUDENT AWARD

Public Relations Student Society of America
Attn: Vice President of Member Services
33 Maiden Lane, 11th Floor
New York, NY 10038-5150
(212) 460-1474   Fax: (212) 995-0757
E-mail: prssa@prsa.org
Web: www.prssa.org/scholarships_competitions/individual

Summary To provide financial assistance to Asian American and other minority college seniors who are interested in preparing for a career in public relations.

Eligibility This program is open to minority (African American/Black, Hispanic/Latino, Asian, Native American, Alaskan Native, or Pacific Islander) students who are entering their senior year at an accredited 4-year college or university. Applicants must have a GPA of 3.0 or higher and be working on a degree in public relations, journalism, or other field to prepare for a career in public relations. Along with their application, they must submit an essay on their view of the public relations profession and their public relations career goals. Selection is based on academic achievement, demonstrated leadership, practical experience, commitment to public relations, writing skills, and letters of recommendation.

Financial data The stipend is $5,000.

Duration 1 year.

Additional information This program began in 2010.

Number awarded 1 each year.

Deadline June of each year.

[236]
MARJORIE BOWENS-WHEATLEY SCHOLARSHIPS

Unitarian Universalist Association
Attn: UU Women's Federation
25 Beacon Street
Boston, MA 02108-2800
(617) 948-4692   Fax: (617) 742-2402
E-mail: uuwf@uua.org
Web: www.uuwf.org

Summary To provide financial assistance to Asian American and other women of color who are working on an undergraduate or graduate degree to prepare for Unitarian Universalist ministry or service.

Eligibility This program is open to women of color who are either 1) aspirants or candidates for the Unitarian Universalist ministry; or 2) candidates in the Unitarian Universalist Association's professional religious education or music leadership credentialing programs. Applicants must submit a 1- to 2-page narrative that covers their call to UU ministry, religious education, or music leadership; their passions; how their racial/ethnic/cultural background influences their goals for their calling; and how the work of the program's namesake relates to their dreams and plans for their UU service.

Financial data Stipends from $1,500 to $2,000.

Duration 1 year.

Additional information This program began in 2009.

Number awarded Varies each year; recently, 4 of these scholarships were awarded.

Deadline March of each year.

[237]
MARY ELSTAD AND DEAN P. GAGNON ENDOWMENT SCHOLARSHIP

Wisconsin FFA Foundation
Attn: Executive Director
1241 John Q. Hammons Drive
Madison, WI 53717
(608) 831-5058, ext. 3
E-mail: mnelson@wisconsinffafoundation.org
Web: www.wisconsinffafoundation.org/pg-scholarships.php

Summary To provide financial assistance to members of FFA in Wisconsin who are Asian Americans or members of other minority groups and interested in majoring in agriculture, biology, or natural resources at a college in any state.

Eligibility This program is open to FFA members in Wisconsin who are from a minority culture (Latino, Native American, African American, Asian). Applicants must be graduating high school seniors or students already enrolled at a 2- or 4-year college or university in any state. They must be interested in majoring in agriculture, biological sciences, or natural resources. Along with their application, they must submit brief statements on any personal circumstances that warrant financial assistance, their future career plans, why they should be selected for an FFA scholarship, and the circumstances of their Supervised Agricultural Experience (SAE) program. Selection is based on academic achievement (25 points) leadership activities (25 points), SAE program participation (25 points), letters of recommendation (20 points), and financial need (5 points).

Financial data The stipend is $850.

Duration 1 year.
Number awarded 1 each year.
Deadline March of each year.

[238]
MARY MOY QUON ING MEMORIAL SCHOLARSHIP

Asian American Journalists Association
Attn: Student Programs Coordinator
5 Third Street, Suite 1108
San Francisco, CA 94103
(415) 346-2051, ext. 102   Fax: (415) 346-6343
E-mail: programs@aaja.org
Web: www.aaja.org/apply-for-a-scholarship-now

Summary To provide financial assistance to student members of the Asian American Journalists Association (AAJA) entering their sophomore year of college and interested in majoring in journalism.

Eligibility This program is open to AAJA members planning to enroll full time as college sophomores and study journalism. Applicants must submit a 500-word essay on their involvement or interest in the Asian American community and how, if they are awarded this scholarship, they would contribute to the field of journalism and/or media issues involving the Asian Pacific American and Pacific Islander community. Print applicants must submit up to 4 photocopied or printed articles; broadcast applicants must submit up to 3 stories (total length less than 10 minutes) copied onto CDs; photojournalism applicants must submit a portfolio with no more than 10 entries. Selection is based on academic achievement, commitment to journalism, sensitivity to Asian American and Pacific Islander issues, demonstrated journalistic ability, and financial need.

Financial data The stipend is $2,000.
Duration 1 year.
Number awarded 1 each year.
Deadline April of each year.

[239]
MASSMUTUAL SCHOLARS PROGRAM

Massachusetts Mutual Life Insurance Company
1295 State Street
Springfield, MA 01111-0001
Toll Free: (800) 542-6767
Web: www.act.org/massmutual

Summary To provide financial assistance to Asian American and other minority undergraduates preparing for a career in the insurance and financial services industry.

Eligibility This program is open to full-time students of African American, Asian/Pacific Islander, or Hispanic descent who are entering their sophomore, junior, senior, or fifth-year senior year at an accredited college or university in the United States, Puerto Rico, U.S. Virgin Islands, or Guam. Applicants must be U.S. citizens or permanent residents and have a GPA of 3.0 or higher. They may be majoring in any field, but preference is given to students who demonstrate 1) an interest in preparing for a career in the insurance and financial services industry; and 2) leadership and participation in extracurricular activities. Financial need is considered in the selection process.

Financial data The stipend is $5,000.

Duration 1 year.
Number awarded 30 each year.
Deadline May of each year.

[240]
MATT FONG ASIAN AMERICANS IN PUBLIC FINANCE SCHOLARSHIPS

Asian Pacific Fund
Attn: Scholarship Coordinator
465 California Street, Suite 809
San Francisco, CA 94104
(415) 395-9985 E-mail: scholarship@asianpacificfund.org
Web: www.asianpacificfund.org

Summary To provide financial assistance to Asian residents of any state working on a degree related to public finance at a college in California.

Eligibility This program is open to residents of any state who are at least 50% Asian. Applicants must be entering their sophomore, junior, or senior year at a 4-year college or university in California with a major in accounting, business administration, political science, public policy, or a related field. They must have a GPA of 3.0 or higher and be able to demonstrate financial need. Preference is given to students who can demonstrate a record of community service or volunteer work.

Financial data The stipend is $1,500.
Duration 1 year; nonrenewable.
Number awarded 2 each year.
Deadline March of each year.

[241]
MEDICAL COLLEGE OF WISCONSIN DIVERSITY SUMMER HEALTH-RELATED RESEARCH EDUCATION PROGRAM

Medical College of Wisconsin
Attn: Office of Student Diversity Affairs
8701 Watertown Plank Road
Milwaukee, WI 53226
(414) 955-8735   Fax: (414) 955-0129
E-mail: studentdiversity@mcw.edu
Web: www.mcw.edu

Summary To provide an opportunity for Asian American and other undergraduate residents of any state who come from diverse backgrounds to participate in a summer research training program at the Medical College of Wisconsin.

Eligibility This program is open to U.S. citizens and permanent residents who come from an ethnically, economically, and/or educationally disadvantaged backgrounds. The program targets African Americans, Mexican Americans, Native Americans (American Indians, Alaska Natives, and Native Hawaiians), Pacific Islanders, Hmong, mainland Puerto Ricans, and individuals with disabilities. Applicants must be interested in participating in a summer research training program at the Medical College of Wisconsin. They must have completed at least 1 year of undergraduate study at an accredited college or university (or be a community college student enrolled in at least 3 courses per academic term) and have a GPA of 3.4 or higher.

Financial data The stipend is $10 per hour for a 40-hour week. Housing is provided for students who live outside Milwaukee County and travel expenses are paid for those who live outside Wisconsin.

Duration 10 weeks during the summer.

Additional information Students are "matched" with a full-time faculty investigator to participate in a research project addressing the causes, prevention, and treatment of cardiovascular, pulmonary, or hematological diseases. This program is funded by the National Heart, Lung, and Blood Institute (NHLBI) of the National Institutes of Health (NIH). Participants are required to prepare an abstract of their research and make a brief oral presentation of their project at the conclusion of the summer.

Number awarded Approximately 12 each year.

Deadline February of each year.

[242]
MERITER MINORITY HEALTH CAREERS SCHOLARSHIP

Meriter Health Services
Attn: Human Resources
202 South Park Street
Madison, WI 53715-1596
(608) 417-6567   E-mail: rthrall@meriter.com
Web: www.meriter.com/wordpress/?p=2241

Summary To provide financial assistance to Asian Americans and members of other minority groups who are preparing for a career in a health care occupation.

Eligibility This program is open to members of minority groups (African American, Hispanic, Asian or Pacific Islander, and Native American) who are U.S. citizens or permanent residents. Applicants must have completed at least 1 semester in a college or technical school and be working on a college degree, professional degree, or certification in a health care occupation. Along with their application, they must submit a 2-page essay on their reasons for selecting a health career, any unique experiences that have prepared them for such a career, and how their contributions to the health care field can enhance the fabric of life in our community. Selection is based on demonstrated history of academic success and demonstrated commitment to community service.

Financial data The stipend is $4,000. Funds are paid directly to the student for assistance with tuition.

Duration 1 year.

Number awarded 1 or more each year.

Deadline April of each year.

[243]
MICHAEL BAKER CORPORATION SCHOLARSHIP PROGRAM FOR DIVERSITY IN ENGINEERING

Association of Independent Colleges and Universities of Pennsylvania
101 North Front Street
Harrisburg, PA 17101-1405
(717) 232-8649   Fax: (717) 233-8574
E-mail: info@aicup.org
Web: www.aicup.org/fundraising

Summary To provide financial assistance to Asian Americans, other minorities, and women from any state enrolled at member institutions of the Association of Independent Colleges and Universities of Pennsylvania (AICUP) who are majoring in designated fields of engineering.

Eligibility This program is open to full-time undergraduate students from any state enrolled at designated AICUP colleges and universities who are women and/or members of the following minority groups: American Indians, Alaska Natives, Asians, Blacks/African Americans, Hispanics/Latinos, Native Hawaiians, or Pacific Islanders. Applicants must be juniors majoring in architectural, civil, or environmental engineering with a GPA of 3.0 or higher. Along with their application, they must submit a 2-page essay on what they believe will be the greatest challenge facing the engineering profession over the next decade, and why.

Financial data The stipend is $2,500 per year.

Duration 1 year; may be renewed 1 additional year if the recipient maintains appropriate academic standards.

Additional information This program, sponsored by the Michael Baker Corporation, is available at the 83 private colleges and universities in Pennsylvania that comprise the AICUP.

Number awarded 1 each year.

Deadline April of each year.

[244]
MICHIGAN STEERING COMMITTEE MINORITY SCHOLARSHIPS

Michigan Association of Certified Public Accountants
Attn: Michigan Accountancy Foundation
5480 Corporate Drive, Suite 200
Troy, MI 48098-2642
(248) 267-3723   Toll Free: (888) 877-4CPE (within MI)
Fax: (248) 267-3737   E-mail: macpa@michcpa.org
Web: www.michcpa.org/Content/22461.aspx

Summary To provide financial assistance to Asian American and other students at Michigan colleges and universities who are working on a degree in accounting.

Eligibility This program is open to members of minority groups enrolled full time at accredited Michigan colleges and universities with a declared concentration in accounting. Applicants must be seniors planning to enter the fifth or graduate year of their school's program. They must intend to or have successfully passed the Michigan C.P.A. examination and intend to practice public accounting in the state. Along with their application, they must submit a 500-word statement about their educational and career aspirations, including internships and/or other employment, volunteer and community activities, professional affiliations, and full-time employment. Documentation of financial need may also be included. U.S. citizenship or eligibility for permanent employment in the United States is required.

Financial data The stipend is $4,000; funds are disbursed directly to the recipient's college or university.

Duration 1 year.

Number awarded Varies each year; recently, 5 of these scholarships were awarded.

Deadline January of each year.

[245]
MID-AMERICA CHAPTER SCHOLARSHIPS

Phi Tau Phi Scholastic Honor Society-Mid-America
Chapter
c/o Mann-Yi Hsieh, President
6951 Springside Avenue
Downers Grove, IL 60516
E-mail: mannyi.hsieh@gmail.com
Web: www.phitauphi.org

Summary To provide financial assistance to undergraduate and graduate students of Chinese heritage at colleges and universities in selected midwestern states.

Eligibility This program is open to undergraduate and graduate students enrolled at colleges and universities in Illinois, Indiana, Iowa, Kansas, Michigan, Minnesota, Ohio, Texas, and Wisconsin who have a GPA of 3.5 or higher. Applicants must be of Chinese descent or interested in and committed to Chinese heritage and culture. They must be entering their junior or senior year of undergraduate study or their second year or higher of graduate work. Along with their application, they must submit a 500-word essay on their professional goals and achievements.

Financial data The stipend is $1,000.

Duration 1 year.

Additional information Phi Tau Phi, first organized in 1921 in China and reestablished in 1964 in the United States, is a relatively small honor society of scholars, mainly of Chinese heritage, in various disciplines of science, technology, art, and the humanities.

Number awarded 4 each year: 2 for undergraduates and 2 for graduate students.

Deadline July of each year.

[246]
MIDEASTERN REGION KOREAN AMERICAN SCHOLARSHIPS

Korean American Scholarship Foundation
Mideastern Region
c/o Jong Dae Kim, Scholarship Committee Chair
24666 Northwestern Highway Service Drive
Southfield, MI 48075
(313) 963-3810, ext. 226   Fax: (313) 963-4680
E-mail: mideastern@kasf.org
Web: www.kasf.org/mideastern

Summary To provide financial assistance for study in Indiana, Michigan, or Ohio to Korean American students from any state who are working on an undergraduate or graduate degree in any field.

Eligibility This program is open to Korean American students who are currently enrolled in a college or university as full-time undergraduate or graduate students. Applicants may reside anywhere in the United States as long as they attend school in Indiana, Michigan, or Ohio. Selection is based on academic achievement, school activities, community service, and financial need.

Financial data Stipends range from $1,000 to $2,000.

Duration 1 year; renewable.

Number awarded Varies each year.

Deadline August of each year.

[247]
MIDWESTERN REGION KOREAN AMERICAN SCHOLARSHIPS

Korean American Scholarship Foundation
Midwestern Region
c/o Augie Lee, Scholarship Committee Chair
379 Hollow Hill Drive
Wauconda, IL 60010
(847) 721-9930   E-mail: kasfmwrc@yahoo.com
Web: www.kasf.org/midwestern

Summary To provide financial assistance to Korean American students from any state who are working on or planning to work on an undergraduate or graduate degree in any field at a school in the Midwest.

Eligibility This program is open to Korean American students who are currently enrolled or planning to enroll at a college or university in the midwestern states as full-time undergraduate or graduate students. Applicants may reside anywhere in the United States as long as they attend school in the midwestern region: Illinois, Iowa, Kansas, Minnesota, Missouri, Nebraska, North Dakota, South Dakota, and Wisconsin. They must have a GPA of 3.0 or higher. Both U.S. citizens and foreign nationals are eligible. Selection is based on academic achievement (25%), extracurricular activities (10%), an essay (10%), recommendations (10%), financial need (40%), and extra credit for having extraordinary circumstances (5%).

Financial data Stipends range from $1,000 to $2,000.

Duration 1 year; renewable.

Number awarded Varies each year; recently, 21 of these scholarships were awarded.

Deadline July of each year.

[248]
MINE AND GONSAKU ITO SCHOLARSHIP

Far West Athletic Trainers' Association
c/o Ned Bergert, Scholarship Chair
4942 Casa Oro Drive
Yorba Linda, CA 92886
(714) 501-3858   E-mail: nhbergert@gmail.com
Web: www.fwata8.org/?page_id=586

Summary To provide financial assistance to members of the National Athletic Trainers Association (NATA) from any state who are of Asian descent and working on an undergraduate or graduate degree in its District 8.

Eligibility This program is open to students of Asian descent from any state who are enrolled as undergraduate or graduate students at colleges and universities in California, Guam, Hawaii, or Nevada and preparing for a career as an athletic trainer. Applicants must be student members of NATA and a District 8 member of NATA working on a bachelor's, master's, or doctoral degree in athletic training. They must have a GPA of 3.2 or higher and a record of distinction in their athletic training program, academic major, institution, intercollegiate athletics, and higher education. Along with their application, they must submit a statement on their athletic training background, experience, philosophy, and goals. Financial need is not considered in the selection process.

Financial data The stipend is $1,500.

Duration 1 year.

Additional information FWATA serves as District 8 of NATA.

Number awarded 1 each year.

Deadline February of each year.

[249]
MINNESOTA ASSOCIATION FOR KOREAN AMERICANS SCHOLARSHIPS

Minnesota Association for Korean Americans
Attn: Scholarship Committee
P.O. Box 390553
Edina, MN 55439-0553
E-mail: jungsookw@yahoo.com
Web: www.makaweb.org

Summary To provide financial assistance to Korean American high school seniors in Minnesota who are planning to attend college in any state.

Eligibility This program is open to seniors graduating from high schools in Minnesota who are of Korean origin or heritage. Applicants must be planning to attend college in any state. They must be U.S. citizens or permanent residents and have a GPA of 2.5 or higher. Along with their application, they must submit grade transcripts, SAT and/or ACT scores, 2 letters of recommendation, and a 2- or 3-page essay on a topic that changes annually; recently, students were asked to identify a person who has had a significant influence on them and explain the impact. Selection is based on the essay, academic achievement, honors, extracurricular activities, and letters of recommendation.

Financial data Stipends range from $500 to $2,000.

Duration 1 year; nonrenewable.

Number awarded Approximately 15 to 20 each year.

Deadline September of each year.

[250]
MINNESOTA TAIWANESE AMERICAN COMMUNITY SCHOLARSHIP AWARDS

Taiwanese Association of America-Minnesota Chapter
c/o Kent Cheng
11030 Stonemill Farms Curve
Woodbury, MN 55129
E-mail: TACSA@taamn.org
Web: www.taamn.org

Summary To provide financial assistance to high school seniors in Minnesota who identify with the Taiwanese American community and plan to attend college in any state.

Eligibility This program is open to seniors graduating from high schools in Minnesota who plan to enroll at a college or university in any state. All students who are U.S. citizens or permanent residents are eligible, but the program was established to serve the Taiwanese American community. Applicants must submit transcripts, a copy of their ACT/SAT score, a 300-word autobiography that describes their extracurricular activities and community service, and a 500-word essay on their experience and ideas on leadership, community service, and teamwork. Financial need is not considered in the selection process.

Financial data The stipend is $600.

Duration 1 year.

Number awarded Varies each year; normally, the sponsor attempts to award 1 or 2 scholarships for each high school that participates in the program.

Deadline April.

[251]
MINORITIES IN GOVERNMENT FINANCE SCHOLARSHIP

Government Finance Officers Association
Attn: Scholarship Committee
203 North LaSalle Street, Suite 2700
Chicago, IL 60601-1210
(312) 977-9700   Fax: (312) 977-4806
Web: www.gfoa.org

Summary To provide financial assistance to Asian American and other minority upper-division and graduate students who are preparing for a career in state and local government finance.

Eligibility This program is open to upper-division and graduate students who are preparing for a career in public finance by working on a degree in public administration, accounting, finance, political science, economics, or business administration (with a specific focus on government or nonprofit management). Applicants must be members of a minority group, citizens or permanent residents of the United States or Canada, and able to provide a letter of recommendation from a representative of their school. Selection is based on career plans, academic record, plan of study, letters of recommendation, and GPA. Financial need is not considered.

Financial data The stipend is $5,000.

Duration 1 year.

Additional information This program defines minorities as Blacks or African Americans, American Indians or Alaskan Natives, Hispanics or Latinos, Native Hawaiians or other Pacific Islanders, or Asians.

Number awarded 1 or more each year.

Deadline February of each year.

[252]
MINORITIES IN HOSPITALITY SCHOLARS PROGRAM

International Franchise Association
Attn: IFA Educational Foundation
1501 K Street, N.W., Suite 350
Washington, DC 20005
(202) 662-0784   Fax: (202) 628-0812
E-mail: mbrewer@franchise.org
Web: www.franchise.org/Scholarships.aspx

Summary To provide financial assistance to Asian American and other minority students working on an undergraduate degree related to hospitality.

Eligibility This program is open to college sophomores, juniors, and seniors who are U.S. citizens and members of a minority group (defined as African Americans, American Indians, Hispanic Americans, and Asian Americans). Applicants must be working on a degree in a field related to the hospitality industry. Along with their application, they must submit a 500-word essay on why they should be selected to receive this scholarship. Financial need is not considered in the selection process.

Financial data The stipend is $2,000.

Duration 1 year.

Additional information This program is cosponsored by the IFA Educational Foundation and Choice Hotels International.

Number awarded 1 or more each year.

Deadline January of each year.

[253]
MINORITY LEAP SCHOLARSHIPS

Missouri Society of Certified Public Accountants
Attn: LEAP Program
540 Maryville Centre Drive, Suite 200
P.O. Box 419042
St. Louis, MO 63141-9042
(314) 997-7966, ext. 125
Toll Free: (800) 264-7966, ext. 125 (within MO)
Fax: (314) 997-2592   E-mail: lsimpson@mocpa.org
Web: www.mocpa.org/students/scholarships

Summary To provide financial assistance to Asian American and other minority residents of Missouri who are working on an undergraduate or graduate degree in accounting at a university in the state.

Eligibility This program is open to members of minority groups.

Financial data The stipend is $1,250 per year.

Duration 1 year; may be renewed.

Additional information These scholarships are offered through the sponsor's Lead and Enhance the Accounting Profession (LEAP) program, established in 2001.

Number awarded Varies each year; recently, 2 of these scholarships were awarded.

Deadline February of each year.

[254]
MINORITY NURSE MAGAZINE SCHOLARSHIP PROGRAM

Minority Nurse Magazine
c/o Alloy Education
2 LAN Drive, Suite 100
Westford, MA 01886
Toll Free: (877) ASK-ALLO
E-mail: editor@minoritynurse.com
Web: www.minoritynurse.com

Summary To provide financial assistance to Asian Americans and members of other minority groups who are working on a bachelor's or master's degree in nursing.

Eligibility This program is open to students currently enrolled in 1) the third or fourth year of an accredited B.S.N. program; 2) an accelerated program leading to a B.S.N. degree (e.g., R.N. to B.S.N., B.A. to B.S.N.); or 3) an accelerated master's entry nursing program (e.g., B.A. to M.S.N.) for students with bachelor's degrees in fields other than nursing. Graduate students who already have a bachelor's degree in nursing are not eligible. Along with their application, they must submit a 250-word essay on their academic and personal accomplishments, community service, and goals for their future nursing career. Selection is based on academic excellence (GPA of 3.0 or higher), demonstrated commitment of service to the student's minority community, and financial need. U.S. citizenship of permanent resident status is required.

Financial data The stipends are $3,000 or $1,000.

Duration 1 year.

Additional information This program began in 2000. Winners are announced in the summer issue of *Minority Nurse* magazine.

Number awarded 3 each year: 1 at $3,000 and 2 at $1,000.

Deadline January of each year.

[255]
MINORITY SCHOLARSHIP AWARD FOR ACADEMIC EXCELLENCE IN PHYSICAL THERAPY

American Physical Therapy Association
Attn: Honors and Awards Program
1111 North Fairfax Street
Alexandria, VA 22314-1488
(703) 684-APTA   Toll Free: (800) 999-APTA
Fax: (703) 684-7343   TDD: (703) 683-6748
E-mail: honorsandawards@apta.org
Web: www.apta.org

Summary To provide financial assistance to Asian American and other minority students who are interested in becoming a physical therapist or physical therapy assistant.

Eligibility This program is open to U.S. citizens and permanent residents who are members of the following minority groups: African American or Black, Asian, Native Hawaiian or other Pacific Islander, American Indian or Alaska Native, or Hispanic/Latino. Applicants must be in the final year of a professional physical therapy or physical therapy assistant education program. They must submit a personal essay outlining their professional goals and minority service. U.S. citizenship or permanent resident status is required. Selection is based on 1) demonstrated evidence of contributions in the area of minority affairs and services with an emphasis on contributions made while enrolled in a physical therapy program; 2) potential to contribute to the profession of physical therapy; and 3) scholastic achievement.

Financial data The stipend varies; recently, minimum awards were $6,000 for physical therapy students or $2,500 for physical therapy assistant students.

Duration 1 year.

Number awarded Varies each year; recently, 7 of these awards were granted.

Deadline November of each year.

[256]
MINORITY SCHOLARSHIP IN CLASSICS AND CLASSICAL ARCHAEOLOGY

American Philological Association
Attn: Executive Director
University of Pennsylvania
220 South 40th Street, Suite 201E
Philadelphia, PA 19104-3512
(215) 898-4975   Fax: (215) 573-7874
E-mail: apaclassics@sas.upenn.edu
Web: www.apaclassics.org

Summary To provide Asian American and other minority undergraduates with summer training as preparation for advanced work in the classics or classical archaeology.

Eligibility Eligible to apply are minority (African American, Hispanic American, Asian American, and Native American) undergraduate students who wish to engage in summer study as preparation for graduate work in the classics or classical archaeology. Applicants may propose participation in summer programs in Italy, Greece, Egypt, or other classical centers; language training at institutions in the United States, Canada, or Europe; or other relevant courses of study. Selection is based on academic qualifications, especially in classics; demonstrated ability in at least 1 classical language; quality of the proposal for study with respect to preparation for a career in classics; and financial need. Applications must be endorsed by a member of the American Philological Association (APA).

Financial data The maximum award is $4,000.

Duration 1 summer.

Additional information This program includes 1 scholarship supported by the Gladys Krieble Delmas Foundation.

Number awarded 2 each year.

Deadline December of each year.

[257]
MINORITY TEACHERS OF ILLINOIS SCHOLARSHIP PROGRAM

Illinois Student Assistance Commission
Attn: Scholarship and Grant Services
1755 Lake Cook Road
Deerfield, IL 60015-5209
(847) 948-8550   Toll Free: (800) 899-ISAC
Fax: (847) 831-8549   TDD: (800) 526-0844
E-mail: isac.studentservices@isac.illinois.gov
Web: www.collegeilllinois.org

Summary To provide funding to Asian American and other minority students in Illinois who plan to become teachers at the preschool, elementary, or secondary level.

Eligibility Applicants must be Illinois residents, U.S. citizens or eligible noncitizens, members of a minority group (African American/Black, Hispanic American, Asian American, or Native American), and high school graduates or holders of a General Educational Development (GED) certificate. They must be enrolled at least half time as an undergraduate or graduate student, have a GPA of 2.5 or higher, not be in default on any student loan, and be enrolled or accepted for enrollment in a teacher education program.

Financial data Grants up to $5,000 per year are awarded. This is a scholarship/loan program. Recipients must agree to teach full time 1 year for each year of support received. The teaching agreement may be fulfilled at a public, private, or parochial preschool, elementary school, or secondary school in Illinois; at least 30% of the student body at those schools must be minority. It must be fulfilled within the 5-year period following the completion of the undergraduate program for which the scholarship was awarded. The time period may be extended if the recipient serves in the U.S. armed forces, enrolls full time in a graduate program related to teaching, becomes temporarily disabled, is unable to find employment as a teacher at a qualifying school, or takes additional courses on at least a half-time basis to obtain certification as a teacher in Illinois. Recipients who fail to honor this work obligation must repay the award with 5% interest.

Duration 1 year; may be renewed for a total of 8 semesters or 12 quarters.

Number awarded Varies each year.

Deadline Priority consideration is given to applications received by February of each year.

[258]
MIRIAM WEINSTEIN PEACE AND JUSTICE EDUCATION AWARD

Philanthrofund Foundation
Attn: Scholarship Committee
1409 Willow Street, Suite 109
Minneapolis, MN 55403-2241
(612) 870-1806   Toll Free: (800) 435-1402
Fax: (612) 871-6587   E-mail: info@PfundOnline.org
Web: www.pfundonline.org/scholarships.html

Summary To provide financial assistance to Asian American and other minority students from Minnesota who have supported gay, lesbian, bisexual, and transgender (GLBT) activities and are interested in working on a degree in education.

Eligibility This program is open to residents of Minnesota and students attending a Minnesota educational institution who are members of a religious, racial, or ethnic minority. Applicants must be self-identified as GLBT or from a GLBT family and have demonstrated a commitment to peace and justice issues. They may be attending or planning to attend trade school, technical college, college, or university (as an undergraduate or graduate student). Preference is given to students who have completed at least 2 years of college and are working on a degree in education. Selection is based on the applicant's 1) affirmation of GLBT or allied identity; 2) evidence of experience and skills in service and leadership; and 3) evidence of service, leading, and working for change in GLBT communities, including serving as a role model, mentor, and/or adviser.

Financial data The stipend is $3,000. Funds must be used for tuition, books, fees, or dissertation expenses.

Duration 1 year.

Number awarded 1 each year.

Deadline January of each year.

[259]
MISSOURI MINORITY TEACHING SCHOLARSHIP PROGRAM

Missouri Department of Higher Education
Attn: Student Financial Assistance
205 Jefferson Street
P.O. Box 1469
Jefferson City, MO 65102-1469
(573) 526-7958   Toll Free: (800) 473-6757
Fax: (573) 751-6635   E-mail: info@dhe.mo.gov
Web: www.dhe.mo.gov/ppc/grants/minorityteaching.php

Summary To provide scholarships and other funding to Asian American and other minority high school seniors, high school graduates, and college students in Missouri who are interested in preparing for a teaching career in mathematics or science.

Eligibility This program is open to Missouri residents who are African American, Asian American, Hispanic American, or Native American. Applicants must be 1) high school seniors, college students, or returning adults (without a degree) who rank in the top 25% of their high school class and scored at or above the 75th percentile on the ACT or SAT examination (recently, that meant a composite score of 24 or higher on the ACT or 1340 or higher on the composite critical reading and mathematics SAT); 2) individuals who have completed 30 college hours and have a cumulative GPA of 3.0 or better; or 3) baccalaureate degree-holders who are returning to an approved mathematics or science teacher education program. They must be a U.S. citizen or permanent resident or otherwise lawfully present in the United States. All applicants must be enrolled full time in an approved teacher education program at a community college, 4-year college, or university in Missouri. Selection is based on high school class rank, ACT or SAT scores, school and community activities, career interest in teaching, leadership skills, employment experience, and recommendations.

Financial data The stipend is $3,000 per year, of which $2,000 is provided by the state as a forgivable loan and $1,000 is provided by the school as a scholarship. Recipients must commit to teaching in a Missouri public elementary or secondary school for 5 years following graduation. If they fail to fulfill that obligation, they must repay the state portion of the scholarship with interest at 9.5%.

Duration Up to 4 years.

Number awarded Up to 100 each year.

Deadline June of each year.

[260]
MONTGOMERY SUMMER RESEARCH DIVERSITY FELLOWSHIPS

American Bar Foundation
Attn: Summer Research Diversity Fellowship
750 North Lake Shore Drive
Chicago, IL 60611-4403
(312) 988-6515 Fax: (312) 988-6579
E-mail: fellowships@abfn.org
Web: www.americanbarfoundation.org

Summary To provide an opportunity for Asian American and other undergraduate students from diverse backgrounds to work on a summer research project in the field of law and social science.

Eligibility This program is open to U.S. citizens and permanent residents who are African Americans, Hispanic/Latinos, Asians, Puerto Ricans, Native Americans, or other individuals who will add diversity to the field of law and social science. Applicants must be sophomores or juniors in college, have a GPA of 3.0 or higher, be majoring in the social sciences or humanities, and be willing to consider an academic or research career. Along with their application, they must submit a 200-word essay on their future plans and why this fellowship would contribute to them, another essay on an assigned topic, official transcripts, and a letter of recommendation from a faculty member familiar with their work.

Financial data Participants receive a stipend of $3,600.

Duration 35 hours per week for 8 weeks during the summer.

Additional information Students are assigned to an American Bar Foundation Research Professor who involves the student in the design and conduct of the professor's research project and who acts as mentor during the student's tenure.

Number awarded 4 each year.

Deadline February of each year.

[261]
MOSS ADAMS FOUNDATION SCHOLARSHIP

Educational Foundation for Women in Accounting
Attn: Foundation Administrator
136 South Keowee Street
Dayton, OH 45402
(937) 424-3391 Fax: (937) 222-5749
E-mail: info@efwa.org
Web: www.efwa.org/scholarships_MossAdams.php

Summary To provide financial support to women (preference given to Asian American and other minority women) who are working on an accounting degree.

Eligibility This program is open to women who are enrolled in an accounting degree program at an accredited college or university. Applicants must meet 1 of the following criteria: 1) women pursuing a fifth-year requirement either through general studies or within a graduate program; 2) women returning to school as current or reentry juniors or seniors; or 3) minority women. Selection is based on aptitude for accounting and business, commitment to the goal of working on a degree in accounting (including evidence of continued commitment after receiving this award), clear evidence that the candidate has established goals and a plan for achieving those goals (both personal and professional), financial need, and a demonstration of how the scholarship will impact her life. U.S. citizenship is required.

Financial data The stipend is $1,000.

Duration 1 year.

Additional information This program was established by Rowling, Dold & Associates LLP, a woman-owned C.P.A. firm based in San Diego. It was renamed when that firm merged with Moss Adams LLP.

Number awarded 1 each year.

Deadline April of each year.

[262]
MUTUAL OF OMAHA ACTUARIAL SCHOLARSHIP FOR MINORITY STUDENTS

Mutual of Omaha
Attn: Strategic Staffing-Actuarial Recruitment
Mutual of Omaha Plaza
Omaha, NE 68175
(402) 351-3300 E-mail: diversity@mutualofomaha.com
Web: www.mutualofomaha.com

Summary To provide financial aid and work experience to Asian American and other minority undergraduate students who are preparing for an actuarial career.

Eligibility This program is open to members of minority groups (African American, Hispanic, Native American, Asian or Pacific Islander, or Alaskan Eskimo) who have completed at least 24 semester hours of full-time study. Applicants must be working on an actuarial or mathematics-related degree with the goal of preparing for an actuarial career. They must have a GPA of 3.0 or higher and have passed at least 1 actuarial examination. Prior to accepting the award, they must be available to complete a summer internship at the sponsor's home office in Omaha, Nebraska. Along with their application, they must submit a 1-page personal statement on why they are interested in becoming an actuary and how they are preparing themselves for an actuarial career. Status as a U.S. citizen, permanent resident, asylee, or refugee must be established.

Financial data The scholarship stipend is $5,000 per year. Funds are paid directly to the student. For the internship, students receive an hourly rate of pay, subsidized housing, and financial incentives for successful examination results received during the internship period.

Duration 1 year. Recipients may reapply if they maintain a cumulative GPA of 3.0 or higher.

Number awarded Varies each year.

Deadline October of each year.

[263]
NASA UNDERGRADUATE STUDENT RESEARCH PROGRAM

Universities Space Research Association
Attn: NASA USRP Project Administrator
2101 NASA Parkway, AE2 Education Office
Houston, TX 77058
(281) 244-2036   E-mail: garza@epo.usra.edu
Web: usrp.usra.edu

Summary To provide an opportunity for undergraduate students (particularly those who represented diversity) to participate in a research project at centers of the U.S. National Aeronautics and Space Administration (NASA).

Eligibility This program is open to sophomores, juniors, and seniors enrolled full time at accredited U.S. colleges and universities. Applicants must have a GPA of 3.0 or higher with an academic major or demonstrated course work concentration in engineering, mathematics, computer science, or physical/life sciences. They must be interested in participating in a mentored research experience at a designated NASA center. The program seeks participation from students who represent America's rich and diverse population: female and male students of all races, creeds, colors, national origins, ages, and disabilities. U.S. citizenship is required.

Financial data The stipend is $6,500 for the summer session or $9,500 for the fall or spring semester. Participants also receive round-trip airfare or ground transportation costs to and from the NASA host center.

Duration 10 weeks during the summer or 15 weeks during the fall or spring semester.

Additional information The participating NASA centers include Ames Research Center (Moffett Field, California), Dryden Flight Research Center (Edwards, California), Glenn Research Center (Cleveland, Ohio), Goddard Space Flight Center (Greenbelt, Maryland), Jet Propulsion Laboratory (Pasadena, California), Johnson Space Center (Houston, Texas), Kennedy Space Center (Florida), Langley Research Center (Hampton, Virginia), Marshall Space Flight Center (Huntsville, Alabama), Stennis Space Center (Mississippi), Wallops Flight Facility (Virginia), and White Sands Test Facility (Las Cruces, New Mexico).

Number awarded Approximately 330 each year.

Deadline Deadline not specified.

[264]
NATIONAL ASSOCIATION OF ASIAN AMERICAN PROFESSIONALS SCHOLARSHIPS

National Association of Asian American Professionals
P.O. Box 354
Uwchland, PA 19480-0354
(215) 715-3046   E-mail: scholarship@naaap.org
Web: www.naaap.org/scholarships

Summary To provide financial assistance to upper-division students, especially those of Asian American heritage majoring in specified fields related to business and engineering.

Eligibility This program is open to residents of Puerto Rico and the United States who are entering their junior or senior year at a college or university. Applicants must have a GPA of 3.0 or higher and be able to demonstrate leadership accomplishment and/or potential. Preference is given to 1) students who are at least one-quarter Asian by heritage; 2) students with disabilities; and 3) students majoring in accounting, business administration, computer electronics, computer engineering, computer information systems, computer programming, computer science, electrical engineering, finance, hospitality, human resources management, industrial engineering, information technology, management information systems, marketing, mechanical engineering, network administration, or retail management. Selection is based on personal, professional, and community leadership.

Financial data The stipend is $3,000.

Duration 1 year.

Additional information This program is sponsored by the Verizon Foundation.

Number awarded 4 each year.

Deadline December of each year.

[265]
NATIONAL ASSOCIATION OF GEOSCIENCE TEACHERS SCHOLARSHIPS FOR FIELD STUDY

National Association of Geoscience Teachers
c/o Eric Riggs
Texas A&M University
Department of Geology and Geophysics
Halbouty 310
College Station, TX 77843-3115
(979) 845-3651   Fax: (979) 845-6162
E-mail: emriggs@geos.tamu.edu
Web: www.nagt.org/nagt/programs/field_scholarships.html

Summary To provide funding to advanced Asian American and other undergraduate students interested in participating in field-based courses in geoscience.

Eligibility This program is open to upper-division students who are interested in attending a field course in an aspect of geoscience (including geophysics, soil science, and hydrology) that focuses on their practicing skills of field observation, data collection, analysis, and synthesis. Applicants must have a GPA of 3.0 or higher. Along with their application, they must submit a 250-word essay on how the field camp experience fits into their long-term academic and career goals. Selection is based on the importance of the field experience in meeting educational and career goals, quality of the field aspects of the course, and the importance of the financial award in allowing them to participate in the program. The program includes awards designed for minority students, and the

Association for Women Geoscientists supports 2 awards designated for women.

Financial data The stipend ranges up to $500.

Duration This program was previously limited to students attending a traditional summer field camp, but now supports students attending field-based courses any time of year.

Number awarded Varies each year; recently, 18 of these scholarships were awarded.

Deadline February of each year.

[266]
NATIONAL PRESS CLUB SCHOLARSHIP FOR JOURNALISM DIVERSITY

National Press Club
Attn: Executive Director's Office
529 14th Street, N.W., 13th Floor
Washington, DC 20045
(202) 662-7599
Web: www.press.org/about/students

Summary To provide funding to Latin Americans and other high school seniors who are planning to major in journalism in college and who will bring diversity to the field.

Eligibility This program is open to high school seniors who have been accepted to college and plan to prepare for a career in journalism. Applicants must submit 1) a 500-word essay explaining how they would add diversity to U.S. journalism; 2) up to 5 work samples demonstrating an ongoing interest in journalism through work on a high school newspaper or other media; 3) letters of recommendation from 3 people; 4) a copy of their high school transcript; 5) documentation of financial need; 6) a letter of acceptance from the college or university of their choice; and 7) a brief description of how they have pursued journalism in high school.

Financial data The stipend is $2,000 for the first year and $2,500 for each subsequent year. The program also provides an additional $500 book stipend, designated the Ellen Masin Persina Scholarship, for the first year.

Duration 4 years.

Additional information The program began in 1990.

Number awarded 1 each year.

Deadline February of each year.

[267]
NAVY/MARINE CORPS JROTC SCHOLARSHIP

National Naval Officers Association-Washington, D.C.
  Chapter
c/o LCDR Stephen Williams
P.O. Box 30784
Alexandria, VA 22310
(703) 566-3840   Fax: (703) 566-3813
E-mail: Stephen.Williams@navy.mil
Web: dcnnoa.memberlodge.com

Summary To provide financial assistance to Asian American and other minority high school seniors from the Washington, D.C. area who have participated in Navy or Marine Corps Junior Reserve Officers Training Corps (JROTC) and are planning to attend college in any state.

Eligibility This program is open to minority seniors graduating from high schools in the Washington, D.C. metropolitan area who have participated in Navy or Marine Corps JROTC. Applicants must be planning to enroll full time at an accred-

ited 2- or 4-year college or university in any state. They must have a GPA of 2.5 or higher. Selection is based on academic achievement, community involvement, and financial need. U.S. citizenship or permanent resident status is required.

Financial data The stipend is $1,000.

Duration 1 year; nonrenewable.

Additional information Recipients are not required to join or affiliate with the military in any way after college.

Number awarded 1 each year.

Deadline March of each year.

[268]
NBCUNIVERSAL APIASF SCHOLARSHIPS

Asian & Pacific Islander American Scholarship Fund
2025 M Street, N.W., Suite 610
Washington, DC 20036-3363
(202) 986-6892   Toll Free: (877) 808-7032
Fax: (202) 530-0643   E-mail: info@apiasf.org
Web: www.apiasf.org/scholarship_apiasf.html

Summary To provide financial assistance to Asian and Pacific Islander Americans who are upper-division students working on a degree in journalism or communications.

Eligibility This program is open to U.S. citizens, nationals, permanent residents, and citizens of the Freely Associated States who are upper-division college students and of Asian or Pacific Islander heritage. Applicants must be enrolled full time at an accredited college or university in the United States and working on a degree in journalism or communications. They must have a GPA of 2.7 or higher or the GED equivalent. In addition, they must complete the FAFSA and apply for federal aid.

Financial data The stipend is $2,500.

Duration 1 year; nonrenewable.

Additional information This program is sponsored by NBCUniversal and administered by the Asian & Pacific Islander American Scholarship Fund (APIASF).

Number awarded Varies each year; recently, 17 of these scholarships were awarded.

Deadline January of each year.

[269]
NCPACA UNDERGRADUATE SCHOLARSHIPS

National Council of Philippine American Canadian
  Accountants
c/o Ed Ortiz, Scholarship Chair
333 South Des Plaines Street, Suite 2-N
Chicago, IL 60661
(312) 876-1900   Fax: (312) 876-1911
E-mail: ecortiz@ocortiz.com
Web: www.ncpaca.org

Summary To provide financial assistance to undergraduate accounting students who will promote the goals of the National Council of Philippine American Canadian Accountants (NCPACA).

Eligibility This program is open to full-time undergraduate students who have completed at least 60 semester hours (including at least 12 semester hours in accounting) at a 4-year college or university in the United States or Canada. Applicants must be able to demonstrate how they will help achieve the goal of NCPACA: "to promote the advancement of individuals with Filipino ancestry in the field of accounting, audit, finance, tax and related areas." They must have a GPA of 3.0 or higher both cumulatively and in accounting. Selection is based primarily on academic achievement; financial need is evaluated as a secondary consideration.

Financial data   The stipend is $5,000. Payments are sent directly to the recipient's school.

Duration   1 year.

Number awarded   1 or more each year.

Deadline   July of each year.

[270]
NELLIE STONE JOHNSON SCHOLARSHIP

Nellie Stone Johnson Scholarship Program
P.O. Box 40309
St. Paul, MN 55104
(651) 738-1404   Toll Free: (866) 738-5238
E-mail: info@nelliestone.org
Web: www.nelliestone.org

Summary   To provide financial assistance to Asian American and other minority union members or their families who are interested in working on an undergraduate or graduate degree in any field at a Minnesota state college or university.

Eligibility   This program is open to students in undergraduate and graduate programs at a 2- or 4-year institution that is a component of Minnesota State Colleges and Universities (MnSCU). Applicants must be a minority (Asian, American Indian, Alaska Native, Black/African American, Hispanic/ Latino, Native Hawaiian, or Pacific Islander) union member or the child, grandchild, or spouse of a minority union member. They must submit a 2-page essay about their background, educational goals, career goals, and other activities that may impact the cause of human or civil rights. Undergraduates must have a GPA of 2.0 or higher; graduate students must have a GPA of 3.0 or higher. Preference is given to Minnesota residents. Selection is based on the essay, commitment to human or civil rights, extracurricular activities, volunteer activities, community involvement, academic standing, and financial need.

Financial data   Stipends range from $500 to $2,000 per year.

Duration   1 year; may be renewed up to 3 additional years for students working on a bachelor's degree, 1 additional year for students working on a master's degree, or 1 additional year for students in a community or technical college program.

Number awarded   Varies each year; recently, 18 of these scholarships were awarded.

Deadline   April of each year.

[271]
NEW ENGLAND COUNSELORS OF COLOR BRIDGING ACCESS TO COLLEGE BOOK SCHOLARSHIPS

New England Counselors of Color Bridging Access to College
c/o Yavuz Kiremit, Treasurer
Assumption College Office of Admission
500 Salisbury Street
Worcester, MA 01609
(508) 767-7285   Toll Free: (866) 477-7776
Fax: (508) 799-4412   E-mail: ykiremit@assumption.edu
Web: www.necbac.org/students.html

Summary   To provide funding for purchase of books to high school seniors of color in New England who plan to enroll at an institution belonging to the New England Counselors of Color Bridging Access to College (NECBAC).

Eligibility   This program is open to students of color who are graduating seniors at high schools in New England and planning to enroll full time at a NECBAC institution. Applicants must submit high school transcripts and a 500-word essay on a topic of their choice.

Financial data   Funds may be used for the purchase of books.

Duration   These are 1-time awards.

Additional information   NECBAC institutions are 4-year private colleges and universities located in New England.

Number awarded   Varies each year; recently, 8 of these scholarships were awarded.

Deadline   May of each year.

[272]
NLGJA/KAY LONGCOPE SCHOLARSHIP AWARD

National Lesbian & Gay Journalists Association
2120 L Street, N.W., Suite 850
Washington, DC 20037
(202) 588-9888   Fax: (202) 588-1818
E-mail: info@nlgfa.org
Web: www.nlgja.org/students/longcope

Summary   To provide financial assistance to Asian American and other lesbian, gay, bisexual, and transgender (LGBT) undergraduate and graduate students of color who are interested in preparing for a career in journalism.

Eligibility   This program is open to LGBT students of color who are 1) high school seniors accepted to a U.S. community college or 4-year university and planning to enroll full time; 2) full-time undergraduate students at U.S. community colleges and 4-year universities; or 3) undergraduate students who have been accepted for their first year at a U.S. graduate school. Applicants must be planning a career in journalism and be committed to furthering the sponsoring organization's mission of fair and accurate coverage of the LGBT community. They must demonstrate an awareness of the issues facing the LGBT community and the importance of fair and accurate news coverage. For undergraduates, a declared major in journalism and/or communications is desirable but not required; non-journalism majors may demonstrate their commitment to a journalism career through work samples, internships, and work on a school news publication, online news service, or broadcast affiliate. Graduate students must be enrolled in a journalism program. Along with their application, they must submit a 1-page resume, 5 work samples, official transcripts, 3 letters of recommendation, and a 750-word news story on a designated subject involving the LGBT community. U.S. citizenship or permanent resident status is required. Selection is based on journalistic and scholastic ability.

Financial data The stipend is $3,000.

Duration 1 year.

Additional information This program began in 2008.

Number awarded 1 each year.

Deadline June of each year.

[273]
NOBUKO R. KODAMA FONG MEMORIAL SCHOLARSHIP

Japanese American Citizens League
Attn: National Scholarship Awards
1765 Sutter Street
San Francisco, CA 94115
(415) 345-1075   Fax: (415) 931-4671
E-mail: ncwnp@jacl.org
Web: www.jacl.org/edu/scholar.htm

Summary To provide financial assistance for college to student members of the Japanese American Citizens League (JACL), particularly those who are in the Pacific Northwest and/or the children of single parents.

Eligibility This program is open to JACL members who are currently enrolled at a college, university, trade school, business college, or other institution of higher learning. Applicants must submit information on their involvement in JACL and a 2-page essay on a topic that changes annually but relates to Japanese Americans. Selection is based on that essay, academic history, JACL involvement, school activities, work history, scholastic honors, and community involvement. Preference is given to residents of the Pacific Northwest District and children of single parents.

Financial data Stipends generally average more than $2,000.

Duration 1 year; nonrenewable.

Number awarded 1 each year.

Deadline March of each year.

[274]
NONG KHAI JUNIOR VANG SCHOLARSHIP

Hmong American Education Fund
P.O. Box 17468
St. Paul, MN 55117
(651) 230-3634   E-mail: scholarships@thehaef.org
Web: www.thehaef.org

Summary To provide financial assistance to Hmong undergraduate and graduate students who demonstrate academic achievement.

Eligibility This program is open to students of Hmong descent who are currently enrolled as full-time undergraduate or graduate students at public 2- or 4-year colleges or universities in any state. Applicants must be U.S. citizens or permanent residents and have a GPA of 3.0 or higher. Along with their application, they must submit a 1,500-word essay on their commitment to education, their financial need, how this scholarship can help them, and their community service. Selection is based on commitment to academic achievement,

drive to achieve their goals, commitment to helping their community, and financial need.

Financial data The stipend is $500.

Duration 1 year; nonrenewable.

Number awarded 1 each year.

Deadline March of each year.

[275]
NORA STONE SMITH SCHOLARSHIP

Seattle Foundation
Attn: Scholarship Administrator
1200 Fifth Avenue, Suite 1300
Seattle, WA 98101-3151
(206) 622-2294   Fax: (206) 622-7673
E-mail: scholarships@seattlefoundation.org
Web: www.seattlefoundation.org

Summary To provide financial assistance for college to high school seniors who have been enrolled in English as a Second Language/English Language Learners (ESL/ELL) programs.

Eligibility This program is open to seniors graduating from high schools who are current or former ESL/ELL students, regardless of their citizenship status. Applicants must be planning to enroll full time at a 2- or 4-year college, university, or vocational/trade school. Along with their application, they must submit a 250-word essay about themselves, where they are from, how they came to be here, their educational achievements, and their future goals. Financial need is considered in the selection process.

Financial data The maximum stipend is $2,000 per year.

Duration 1 year; may be renewed up to 3 additional years.

Number awarded 10 each year.

Deadline February of each year.

[276]
NORTH CAROLINA CPA FOUNDATION OUTSTANDING MINORITY ACCOUNTING STUDENT SCHOLARSHIPS

North Carolina Association of Certified Public
   Accountants
Attn: North Carolina CPA Foundation, Inc.
3100 Gateway Centre Boulevard
P.O. Box 80188
Raleigh, NC 27623-0188
(919) 469-1040, ext. 130   Toll Free: (800) 722-2836
Fax: (919) 378-2000   E-mail: jtahler@ncacpa.org
Web: ncacpa.org

Summary To provide financial assistance to Asian American and other minority undergraduate and graduate students working on a degree in accounting at colleges and universities in North Carolina.

Eligibility This program is open to North Carolina residents who have completed at least 36 semester hours, including at least 4 accounting courses, at a college or university in the state. Applicants must be members of a minority group, defined as Black, Native American/Alaskan Native, Middle-Eastern, Asian or Pacific Islander, or Hispanic. They must be enrolled full time in an academic program leading to a degree in accounting or its equivalent and have a GPA of 3.0 or higher. Along with their application, they must submit a 500-word essay on 1 of the following questions: 1) what the profession can do to educate minorities about understanding the impact of and ways to survive the national financial crisis; 2) how they will impact minority communities by becoming a C.P.A.; or 3) the challenges that minority C.P.A.s face in the profession. Selection is based on GPA (30%), extracurricular activities (20%), essay content (25%), and essay grammar (25%).

Financial data Stipends are $2,000 or $1,000.

Duration 1 year; may be renewed up to 2 additional years.

Number awarded 2 each year: 1 at $2,000 and 1 at $1,000.

Deadline March of each year.

[277]
NORTHEASTERN REGION KOREAN AMERICAN SCHOLARSHIPS

Korean American Scholarship Foundation
Northeastern Region
c/o James Lee, Scholarship Committee Chair
472 11th Street, Room 202
Palisades Park, NJ 07650
E-mail: kasfjames@gmail.com
Web: www.kasf.org/northeastern

Summary To provide financial assistance to Korean American students from any state who are working on an undergraduate or graduate degree in any field at a school in northeastern states.

Eligibility This program is open to residents of any state who are 1) U.S. citizens of Korean heritage; 2) Korean citizens who have a valid visa to study in the United States; and 3) citizens of any other country who are of Korean heritage and have a valid visa to study in the United States. Applicants must be enrolled or planning to enroll as a full-time undergraduate or graduate student at a college or university in Connecticut, Maine, Massachusetts, New Hampshire, New Jersey, New York, Rhode Island, or Vermont. Selection is based on academic achievement, school and community activities, letters of recommendation, a personal essay, and financial need.

Financial data Stipends range from $1,000 to $2,000.

Duration 1 year; renewable.

Number awarded Varies each year; recently, 59 of these scholarships were awarded.

Deadline June of each year.

[278]
NORTHERN CALIFORNIA UNDERGRADUATE NURSING STUDENT SCHOLARSHIP

Philippine Nurses Association of Northern California, Inc.
c/o Teresita Baluyut, Scholarship Chair
845 Mt. Vernon Avenue
San Francisco, CA 94112
E-mail: pnanorthcal@gmail.com
Web: www.pnanorthcal.org

Summary To provide financial assistance to Filipino Americans from any state enrolled in an undergraduate nursing program at a school in northern California.

Eligibility This program is open to Filipino American residents of any state who are currently enrolled in at least the third year of an accredited undergraduate nursing program in northern California. Applicants must have a GPA of 3.0 or

higher and a record of participation in extracurricular or community activities. They must have demonstrated leadership ability or potential both within and outside the clinical setting. Along with their application, they must submit brief statements on their strengths and opportunities for improvement, their career goals, why they need a financial scholarship, and how they can contribute to the goals of the Philippine Nurses Association of Northern California (PNANC). They must also submit a 1-page essay on either 1) why they chose the field of nursing; or 2) an accomplishment or activity as a nursing student that has impacted their life or the life of another person.

Financial data The stipend is $1,000.

Duration 1 year.

Additional information The recipient must commit to serve on a committee of the PNANC for at least 2 years.

Number awarded 1 each year.

Deadline October of each year.

[279]
NORTHWEST JOURNALISTS OF COLOR SCHOLARSHIP AWARDS

Northwest Journalists of Color
c/o Caroline Li
1433 12th Avenue, Suite A1
Seattle, WA 98122
E-mail: Caroline@SoMuchGoodMusic.com
Web: www.aajaseattle.org/scholarships

Summary To provide financial assistance to Asian American and other minority students from Washington state who are interested in careers in journalism.

Eligibility This program is open to members of minority groups (Asian American, African American, Native American, and Latino) who are 1) residents of Washington attending an accredited college or university in any state; 2) residents of any state attending a Washington college or university; or 3) seniors graduating from Washington high schools and planning to attend an accredited college in any state. Applicants must be planning a career in broadcast, photo, or print journalism. Along with their application, they must submit 1) a 500-word essay about their interest in a career as a journalist; 2) a current resume; 3) up to 3 work samples; 4) reference letters; and 5) documentation of financial need.

Financial data Stipends range up to $2,500 per year.

Duration 1 year; may be renewed.

Additional information This program, established in 1986, is sponsored by the Seattle chapters of the Asian American Journalists Association, the Native American Journalists Association, the National Association of Black Journalists, and the Latino Media Association. It includes the Walt and Milly Woodward Memorial Scholarship donated by the Western Washington Chapter of the Society of Professional Journalists.

Number awarded Varies each year.

Deadline April of each year.

[280]
NOVAL LEADERSHIP SCHOLARSHIP

National Organization for Vietnamese American
 Leadership
P.O. Box 34437
Washington, DC 20043
(202) 670-5370   E-mail: info@vietfest.com
Web: www.vietfest.com/noval-dc-scholarship

Summary To provide financial assistance to Vietnamese American college students who have ties to the Washington, D.C. metropolitan area and are committed to serving the Vietnamese American community in that region.

Eligibility This program is open to Vietnamese American undergraduates who reside or attend college in the Virginia, Maryland, and Washington metropolitan area. Applicants must be able to demonstrate a commitment to serving the Vietnamese American community in that region. Along with their application, they must submit a 1,000-word essay, in English or Vietnamese, on what leadership means to them and how they plan to carry out the mission of the sponsor of promoting leadership and preserving culture. Selection is based on that essay, academic performance, and community service.

Financial data The stipend is $1,000.

Duration 1 year.

Number awarded 1 each year.

Deadline July of each year.

[281]
NSCA MINORITY SCHOLARSHIPS

National Strength and Conditioning Association
Attn: Grants and Scholarships Program
1885 Bob Johnson Drive
Colorado Springs, CO 80906-4000
(719) 632-6722, ext. 152   Toll Free: (800) 815-6826
Fax: (719) 632-6367   E-mail: foundation@nsca-lift.org
Web: www.nsca-lift.org/Foundation/grants-and-scholarships

Summary To provide financial assistance to Asian Americans and other minorities who are interested in working on an undergraduate or graduate degree in strength training and conditioning.

Eligibility This program is open to Blacks, Hispanics, Asian Americans, and Native Americans who are 17 years of age and older. Applicants must have been accepted into an accredited postsecondary institution to work on an undergraduate or graduate degree in the strength and conditioning field. Along with their application, they must submit a 500-word essay on their personal and professional goals and how receiving this scholarship will assist them in achieving those goals. Selection is based on that essay, academic achievement, strength and conditioning experience, honors and awards, community involvement, letters of recommendation, and involvement in the National Strength and Conditioning Association (NSCA).

Financial data The stipend is $1,500.

Duration 1 year.

Additional information The NSCA is a nonprofit organization of strength and conditioning professionals, including coaches, athletic trainers, physical therapists, educators, researchers, and physicians. This program was first offered in 2003.

Number awarded Varies each year; recently, 9 of these scholarships were awarded.

Deadline March of each year.

[282]
NSNA/BREAKTHROUGH TO NURSING SCHOLARSHIPS

National Student Nurses' Association
Attn: Foundation
45 Main Street, Suite 606
Brooklyn, NY 11201
(718) 210-0705   Fax: (718) 797-1186
E-mail: nsna@nsna.org
Web: www.nsna.org

Summary To provide financial assistance to Asian American and other minority undergraduate and graduate students who wish to prepare for careers in nursing.

Eligibility This program is open to students currently enrolled in state-approved schools of nursing or pre-nursing associate degree, baccalaureate, diploma, generic master's, generic doctoral, R.N. to B.S.N., R.N. to M.S.N., or L.P.N./ L.V.N. to R.N. programs. Graduating high school seniors are not eligible. Support for graduate education is provided only for a first degree in nursing. Applicants must be members of a racial or ethnic minority underrepresented among registered nurses (American Indian or Alaska Native, Hispanic or Latino, Native Hawaiian or other Pacific Islander, Black or African American, or Asian). They must be committed to providing quality health care services to underserved populations. Along with their application, they must submit a 200-word description of their professional and educational goals and how this scholarship will help them achieve those goals. Selection is based on academic achievement, financial need, and involvement in student nursing organizations and community health activities. U.S. citizenship or permanent resident status is required.

Financial data Stipends range from $1,000 to $2,500.

Duration 1 year.

Additional information Applications must be accompanied by a $10 processing fee.

Number awarded Varies each year; recently, 13 of these scholarships were awarded: 10 sponsored by the American Association of Critical-Care Nurses and 3 sponsored by the Mayo Clinic.

Deadline January of each year.

[283]
NSRCF SCHOLARSHIPS

Nisei Student Relocation Commemorative Fund, Inc.
19 Scenic Drive
Portland, CT 06480
E-mail: info@nsrcfund.org
Web: www.nsrcfund.org/scholarships.overview.php

Summary To provide financial assistance for college to high school seniors in specified geographic areas who are of southeast Asian descent.

Eligibility Each year, this program operates in a different city or state (recently, Houston and southeast Texas). Within the selected area, graduating high school seniors and recent GED recipients are eligible to apply if they are first- or second-generation students from Cambodia, Laos, or Vietnam.

Applicants must be planning to attend an accredited 2- or 4-year college or university or a vocational program in any state. Selection is based on academic achievement; educational and career goals; extracurricular activities and/or work experience; financial need; and a personal essay on educational, career, and personal goals. Finalists may be interviewed.

Financial data Stipends for named scholarships are $2,000; other stipends range up to $1,500.

Duration 1 year.

Additional information This program began in 1983. The named scholarships currently available include the American Friends Service Committee Scholarship, the Hiroko Fujita and Paul Fukami Scholarship, the Michihiko and Bernice Hayashida Scholarship, the Nobu Kumekawa Hibino Scholarship, the Tama Yoshimura Ishihara Scholarship, the Alice Abe Matsumoto Scholarship, the Hisaye Hamaoka Mochijuki Scholarship, the Koh, Mitsu, and Dr. Kotaro Murai Scholarship, the Kaizo and Shizue Naka Scholarship, the Gladys Ishida Stone Scholarship, the Michi Nishiura Weglyn Scholarship, the Kay Yamashita Scholarship, and the Lafayette and Mayme Noda Scholarship.

Number awarded Varies each year; recently, 14 named scholarships (at $2,000 each) and 18 other scholarships (at $1,500 each) were awarded. Since the program was established, it has awarded nearly $588,800 to 608 students.

Deadline March of each year.

[284]
NWA/DAVID SANKEY MINORITY SCHOLARSHIP IN METEOROLOGY

National Weather Association
Attn: Executive Director
228 West Millbrook Road
Raleigh, NC 27609-4304
(919) 845-1546   Fax: (919) 845-2956
E-mail: exdir@nwas.org
Web: www.nwas.org

Summary To provide financial assistance to Asian Americans and other members of minority groups who are working on an undergraduate or graduate degree in meteorology.

Eligibility This program is open to members of minority ethnic groups who are either entering their sophomore or higher year of undergraduate study or enrolled as graduate students. Applicants must be working on a degree in meteorology. Along with their application, they must submit a 1-page statement explaining why they are applying for this scholarship. Selection is based on that statement, academic achievement, and 2 letters of recommendation.

Financial data The stipend is $1,000.

Duration 1 year.

Additional information This program began in 2002.

Number awarded 1 each year.

Deadline April of each year.

[285]
OCA/AXA ACHIEVEMENT SCHOLARSHIPS

Organization of Chinese Americans, Inc.
1322 18th Street, N.W.
Washington, DC 20036-1803
(202) 223-5500   Fax: (202) 296-0540
E-mail: oca@ocanational.org
Web: www.ocanational.org/?page=Programs_Scholarship

Summary To provide financial assistance for college to Asian Pacific Americans who are entering their first year of college and can demonstrate academic merit.

Eligibility This program is open to graduating high school seniors of Asian and/or Pacific Islander ethnicity who are entering their first year at a college, university, or community college in the following fall. Applicants must be able to demonstrate academic achievement, leadership ability, and community service. They must have a cumulative GPA of 3.0 or higher and be a U.S. citizen, national, or permanent resident. Financial need is considered in the selection process.

Financial data The stipend is $2,000.

Duration 1 year.

Additional information This program, established in 2004, is funded by the AXA Foundation and administered by the Organization of Chinese Americans (OCA).

Number awarded 10 each year.

Deadline April of each year.

[286]
OCA-WI MERIT SCHOLARSHIPS

Organization of Chinese Americans-Wisconsin Chapter
c/o Vera Lau, Scholarship Committee
120 North 73rd Street
Milwaukee, WI 53213
E-mail: ocawischolarship@yahoo.com
Web: www.ocawi.org/www/scholarships.html

Summary To provide financial assistance to high school seniors who are children of members or business affiliates of the Wisconsin Chapter of the Organization of Chinese Americans (OCA-WI) and interested in attending college in any state.

Eligibility This program is open to graduating high school seniors whose parent has been an OCA-WI member or business affiliate for at least 2 years and who are planning to enroll full time at an accredited college or university in any state. Applicants must have a GPA of 3.0 or higher or rank in the top 20% of their class. Along with their application, they must submit a personal statement that includes information on their future college and career plans; a list of scholastic awards, honors, extracurricular activities, and honor societies and offices; and a description of their volunteer service to OCA-WI and their community. Financial need is not considered in the selection process.

Financial data A stipend is awarded (amount not specified).

Duration 1 year.

Additional information This program began in 1988. It includes the following named scholarships (awarded on a rotating basis): the Professor Kwang Yu Memorial Scholarship, the Dr. Benjamin P.C. Ho and Mrs. Lien-Haw (T'ao) Ho Memorial Scholarship, the Benjamin Tsong-Wei Wu Memorial Scholarship, the Professor Shien-Ming (Samuel) Wu

Memorial Scholarship, the Yulin and King Ying Hsi Memorial Scholarship, and the Maryanne Yu Tsao Memorial Scholarship.

Number awarded   Varies each year; recently, 4 of these scholarships were awarded.

Deadline   March of each year.

[287]
OHIO HIGH SCHOOL ATHLETIC ASSOCIATION ETHNIC MINORITY SCHOLARSHIPS

Ohio High School Athletic Association
Attn: Foundation
4080 Roselea Place
Columbus, OH 43214
(614) 267-2502   Fax: (614) 267-1677
Web: www.ohsaa.org/members/scholar/application.htm

Summary   To provide financial assistance to Asian American and other minority high school seniors in Ohio who have participated in athletics and plan to attend college in any state.

Eligibility   This program is open to minority seniors graduating from high schools in Ohio that are members of the Ohio High School Athletic Association (OHSAA). Applicants must have received at least 3 varsity letters in 1 sport or 4 letters in 2 sports and have a GPA of 3.25 or higher. They must be planning to attend a college or university in any state. Along with their application, they must submit a 1-page essay on the role that interscholastic athletics has played in their life and how such participation will benefit them in the future. Selection is based on that essay, GPA, ACT and SAT scores, varsity letters earned, and athletic honors.

Financial data   The stipend is $1,000.

Duration   1 year.

Additional information   Recipients of athletic scholarships in NCAA Division I or II institutions or appointees to military academies are not eligible to apply for this scholarship.

Number awarded   6 each year: 1 in each OHSSA District.

Deadline   March of each year.

[288]
OHIO NEWSPAPERS FOUNDATION MINORITY SCHOLARSHIPS

Ohio Newspapers Foundation
Attn: Foundation
1335 Dublin Road, Suite 216-B
Columbus, OH 43215-7038
(614) 486-6677, ext. 1010   Fax: (614) 486-4940
E-mail: ariggs@ohionews.org
Web: www.ohionews.org/foundation/scholarships

Summary   To provide financial assistance to Asian American and other minority high school seniors in Ohio planning to attend college in the state to prepare for a career in journalism.

Eligibility   This program is open to high school seniors in Ohio who are members of minority groups (African American, Hispanic, Asian American, or American Indian) and planning to prepare for a career in newspaper journalism. Applicants must have a high school GPA of 2.5 or higher and demonstrate writing ability in an autobiography of 750 to 1,000 words that describes their academic and career interests, awards, extracurricular activities, and journalism-related

activities. They must be planning to attend a college or university in Ohio.

Financial data   The stipend is $1,500.

Duration   1 year; nonrenewable.

Additional information   This program began in 1990.

Number awarded   1 each year.

Deadline   March of each year.

[289]
OPERATION JUMP START III SCHOLARSHIPS

American Association of Advertising Agencies
Attn: AAAA Foundation
1065 Avenue of the Americas, 16th Floor
New York, NY 10018
(212) 262-2500   E-mail: ameadows@aaaa.org
Web: www.aaaa.org

Summary   To provide financial assistance to Asian American and other multicultural art directors and copywriters interested in working on an undergraduate or graduate degree in advertising.

Eligibility   This program is open to African Americans, Asian Americans, Hispanic Americans, and Native Americans who are U.S. citizens or permanent residents. Applicants must be incoming graduate students at 1 of 6 designated portfolio schools or full-time juniors at 1 of 2 designated colleges. They must be able to demonstrate extreme financial need, creative talent, and promise. Along with their application, they must submit 10 samples of creative work in their respective field of expertise.

Financial data   The stipend is $5,000 per year.

Duration   Most awards are for 2 years.

Additional information   Operation Jump Start began in 1997 and was followed by Operation Jump Start II in 2002. The current program began in 2006. The 6 designated portfolio schools are the AdCenter at Virginia Commonwealth University, the Creative Circus in Atlanta, the Portfolio Center in Atlanta, the Miami Ad School, the University of Texas at Austin, and Pratt Institute. The 2 designated colleges are the Minneapolis College of Art and Design and the Art Center College of Design at Pasadena, California.

Number awarded   20 each year.

Deadline   Deadline not specified.

[290]
OREGON-IDAHO CONFERENCE UMC ETHNIC MINORITY LEADERSHIP AWARDS

United Methodist Church-Oregon-Idaho Conference
Attn: Campus Ministries and Higher Education Ministry
    Team
1505 S.W. 18th Avenue
Portland, OR 97201-2524
(503) 226-7031   Toll Free: (800) J-WESLEY
Web: www.umoi.org/pages/detail/45

Summary   To provide financial assistance to Asian American and other ethnic minority Methodists from Oregon and Idaho who are interested in attending a college or graduate school in any state.

Eligibility   This program is open to members of ethnic minority groups (African American, Native American, Asian, Pacific Islander, or Hispanic) who have belonged to a congregation affiliated with the Oregon-Idaho Conference of the

United Methodist Church (UMC) for at least 1 year. Applicants must be enrolled or planning to enroll full time as an undergraduate or graduate student at a 2- or 4-year college or university in any state. Along with their application, they must submit personal statements on 1) their faith development; and 2) where they sense God is calling the church in the present and future. Selection is based primarily on demonstrated leadership excellence and/or the potential for leadership excellence in the UMC and in community projects or activities, but other factors, including financial need, are also considered.

Financial data The stipend is $750.

Duration 1 year.

Number awarded 1 each year.

Deadline April of each year.

[291]
PAGE EDUCATION FOUNDATION GRANTS

Page Education Foundation
P.O. Box 581254
Minneapolis, MN 55458-1254
(612) 332-0406   E-mail: info@page-ed.org
Web: www.page-ed.org

Summary To provide funding to Asian Americans and other high school seniors of color in Minnesota who plan to attend college in the state.

Eligibility This program is open to students of color who are graduating from high schools in Minnesota and planning to enroll full time at a postsecondary school in the state. Applicants must submit a 500-word essay that deals with why they believe education is important, their plans for the future, and the service-to-children project they would like to complete in the coming school year. Selection is based on the essay, 3 letters of recommendation, and financial need.

Financial data Stipends range from $1,000 to $2,500 per year.

Duration 1 year; may be renewed up to 3 additional years.

Additional information This program was founded in 1988 by Alan Page, a former football player for the Minnesota Vikings. While attending college, the Page Scholars fulfill a 50-hour service-to-children contract that brings them into contact with K-8 students of color.

Number awarded Varies each year; recently, 503 Page Scholars (210 new recipients and 293 renewals) were enrolled, of whom 260 were African American, 141 Asian American, 70 Chicano/Latino, 13 American Indian, and 19 biracial or multiracial.

Deadline April of each year.

[292]
PANYHA FOUNDATION STUDENT SCHOLARSHIP PROGRAM

Panyha Foundation
Attn: Student Scholarships
4994 Park Boulevard North
Pinellas Park, FL 33781
(727) 289-7293   Fax: (727) 290-9884
E-mail: info@panyhafoundation.org
Web: www.panyhafoundation.org/scholarship-program.html

Summary To provide financial assistance to Laotian Americans who are interested in attending college in Florida.

Eligibility This program is open to Laotian American youth who are incoming freshmen at accredited 4-year colleges and universities in Florida, current full-time undergraduates at such institutions, and full-time students at Florida community colleges planning to transfer to a 4-year college or university in the state. Applicants must be U.S. citizens or permanent residents and have a GPA of 3.0 or higher. Along with their application, they must submit a resume, transcripts, a copy of their SAT and/or ACT scores (high school seniors only), a 1,000-word personal statement on their future educational and career goals, and a 250-word essay on what they value most about being Laotian American and what "Panyha" means to them.

Financial data Stipends range up to $2,500 per year.

Duration Up to 4 years, provided the recipient remains enrolled full time, maintains a GPA of 3.0 or higher, and provides documentation of community service.

Number awarded Varies each year.

Deadline May of each year.

[293]
PARSONS BRINCKERHOFF ENGINEERING SCHOLARSHIP

Conference of Minority Transportation Officials
Attn: National Scholarship Program
1875 I Street, N.W., Suite 500
Washington, DC 20006
(703) 234-4072   Fax: (202) 318-0364
Web: www.comto.org/?page=Scholarships

Summary To provide financial assistance to Asian Americans and other members of the Conference of Minority Transportation Officials (COMTO) who are working on an undergraduate degree in engineering.

Eligibility This program is open to undergraduate students who have been members of COMTO for at least 1 year. Applicants must be working on a degree in engineering with a GPA of 3.0 or higher. Along with their application, they must submit a cover letter with a 500-word statement of career goals. Financial need is not considered in the selection process. U.S. citizenship or legal resident status is required.

Financial data The stipend is $2,500. Funds are paid directly to the recipient's college or university.

Duration 1 year.

Additional information COMTO was established in 1971 to promote, strengthen, and expand the roles of minorities in all aspects of transportation. This program is sponsored by Parsons Brinckerhoff, Inc. Recipients are expected to attend the COMTO National Scholarship Luncheon.

Number awarded 2 each year.

Deadline May of each year.

[294]
PARSONS BRINCKERHOFF GOLDEN APPLE SCHOLARSHIP

Conference of Minority Transportation Officials
Attn: National Scholarship Program
1875 I Street, N.W., Suite 500
Washington, DC 20006
(703) 234-4072   Fax: (202) 318-0364
Web: www.comto.org/?page=Scholarships

Summary To provide financial assistance to Asian American and other members of the Conference of Minority Transportation Officials (COMTO) and their children who are high school seniors planning to attend college to prepare for a career in the business aspects of the transportation industry.

Eligibility This program is open to graduating high school seniors who are members of COMTO or whose parents are members. Applicants must be planning to attend an accredited college, university, or vocational/technical institution to prepare for a career in transportation in the fields of communications, finance, or marketing. They must have a GPA of 2.0 or higher. Along with their application, they must submit a cover letter with a 500-word statement of career goals. Financial need is not considered in the selection process. U.S. citizenship or legal resident status is required.

Financial data The stipend is $2,500. Funds are paid directly to the recipient's college or university.

Duration 1 year.

Additional information COMTO was established in 1971 to promote, strengthen, and expand the roles of minorities in all aspects of transportation. This program is sponsored by Parsons Brinckerhoff, Inc. Recipients are expected to attend the COMTO National Scholarship Luncheon.

Number awarded 1 each year.

Deadline May of each year.

[295]
PAUL STEPHEN LIM ASIAN-AMERICAN PLAYWRITING AWARD

John F. Kennedy Center for the Performing Arts
Education Department
Attn: Kennedy Center American College Theater Festival
2700 F Street, N.W.
Washington, DC 20566
(202) 416-8857   Fax: (202) 416-8860
E-mail: KCACTF@kennedy-center.org
Web: www.kcactf.org

Summary To recognize and reward outstanding Asian America student playwrights.

Eligibility Students at any accredited junior or senior college in the United States are eligible to compete, provided their college agrees to participate in the Kennedy Center American College Theater Festival (KCACTF). Undergraduate students must be carrying at least 6 semester hours, graduate students must be enrolled in at least 3 semester hours, and continuing part-time students must be enrolled in a regular degree or certificate program. This award is presented to the author of the best play on any subject who is of Asian heritage.

Financial data The winning playwright receives a cash award of $1,000 for a full-length play or $500 for a 1-act play. The award includes an all-expense paid professional development opportunity.

Duration The award is presented annually.

Additional information This program is part of the Michael Kanin Playwriting Awards Program. The sponsoring college or university must pay a registration fee of $275 for each production.

Number awarded 2 students and 2 sponsoring institutions receive awards each year.

Deadline November of each year.

[296]
PDA FOUNDATION DIVERSITY SCHOLARSHIP

Pennsylvania Dietetic Association
Attn: Foundation
96 Northwoods Boulevard, Suite B2
Columbus, OH 43235
(614) 436-6136   Fax: (614) 436-6181
E-mail: padafoundation@eatrightpa.org
Web: www.eatrightpa.org/scholarshipapp.cfm

Summary To provide financial assistance to Asian American and other minority members of the Pennsylvania Dietetic Association (PDA) who are working on an associate or bachelor's degree in dietetics.

Eligibility This program is open to PDA members who are Black, Hispanic, Asian or Pacific Islander, or Native American (Alaskan Native, American Indian, or Hawaiian Native). Applicants must be 1) enrolled in the first year of study in an accredited dietetic technology program; or 2) enrolled in the third year of study in an accredited undergraduate or coordinated program in dietetics. They must have a GPA of 2.5 or higher. Along with their application, they must submit a letter indicating their intent and the reason they are applying for the scholarship, including a description of their personal financial situation. Selection is based on academic achievement (20%), commitment to the dietetic profession (30%), leadership ability (30%), and financial need (20%).

Financial data The stipend is $1,000.

Duration 1 year.

Additional information The Pennsylvania Dietetic Association is the Pennsylvania affiliate of the Academy of Nutrition and Dietetics.

Number awarded 1 or more each year.

Deadline March of each year.

[297]
PDEF MICKEY WILLIAMS MINORITY STUDENT SCHOLARSHIPS

Society of Nuclear Medicine and Molecular Imaging
Attn: Grants and Awards
1850 Samuel Morse Drive
Reston, VA 20190-5316
(703) 708-9000, ext. 1253   Fax: (703) 708-9015
E-mail: kpadleyh@snmmi.org
Web: www.snm.org/index.cfm?pageid=1083

Summary To provide financial support to Asian American and other minority students working on an associate or bachelor's degree in nuclear medicine technology.

Eligibility This program is open to students accepted or enrolled in a baccalaureate or associate degree program in nuclear medicine technology. Applicants must be members of a minority group: African American, Native American (including American Indian, Eskimo, Hawaiian, and Samoan), Hispanic American, Asian American, or Pacific Islander. They must have a cumulative GPA of 2.5 or higher and be able to demonstrate financial need. Along with their application, they must submit an essay on their reasons for entering the nuclear medicine technology field, their career goals, and their financial need. U.S. citizenship or permanent resident status is required.

Financial data The stipend is $2,500.

Duration 1 year; may be renewed for 1 additional year.

Additional information This program is supported by corporate sponsors of the Professional Development and Education Fund (PDEF) of the Society of Nuclear Medicine and Molecular Imaging Technologist Section (SNMMITS).

Number awarded Varies each year; recently, 2 of these scholarships were awarded.

Deadline April of each year.

[298]
PDK/DR. JO ANN OTA FUJIOKA SCHOLARSHIP

Phi Delta Kappa International
Attn: PDK Educational Foundation
320 West Eighth Street, Suite 216
P.O. Box 7888
Bloomington, IN 47407-7888
(812) 339-1156   Toll Free: (800) 766-1156
Fax: (812) 339-0018   E-mail: scholarships@pdkintl.org
Web: pdkintl.org

Summary To provide financial assistance to Asian American and other high school seniors of color who plan to study education at a college in any state and have a connection to Phi Delta Kappa (PDK).

Eligibility This program is open to high school seniors of color who are planning to major in education and can meet 1 of the following criteria: 1) is a member of a Future Educators Association (FEA) chapter; 2) is the child or grandchild of a PDK member; 3) has a reference letter written by a PDK member; or 4) is selected to represent the local PDK chapter. Applicants must submit a 500-word essay on a topic related to education that changes annually; recently, they were invited to explain what caused them to choose a career in education, what they hope to accomplish during their career as an educator, and how they will measure their success. Selection is based on the essay, academic standing, letters of recommendation, service activities, educational activities, and leadership activities; financial need is not considered.

Financial data The stipend depends on the availability of funds; recently, it was $2,000.

Duration 1 year.

Additional information This program began in 2006.

Number awarded 1 each year.

Deadline March of each year.

[299]
PFATS-NFL CHARITIES MINORITY SCHOLARSHIPS

Professional Football Athletic Trainers Society
c/o Britt Brown, ATC, Associate Athletic Trainer
Dallas Cowboys
One Cowboys Parkway
Irving, TX 75063
(972) 497-4992   E-mail: bbrown@dallascowboys.net
Web: www.pfats.com/about/scholarships

Summary To provide financial assistance to Asian American and other minority undergraduate and graduate students working on a degree in athletic training.

Eligibility This program is open to ethnic minority students who are working on an undergraduate or graduate degree in athletic training. Applicants must have a GPA of 2.5 or higher. Along with their application, they must submit a cover letter, a curriculum vitae, and a letter of recommendation from their supervising athletic trainer.

Financial data A stipend is awarded (amount not specified).

Duration 1 year.

Additional information Recipients also have an opportunity to work at summer training camp of a National Football League (NFL) team. Support for this program, which began in 1993, is provided by NFL Charities.

Number awarded 1 or more each year.

Deadline March of each year.

[300]
PHILIP JAISOHN MEMORIAL FOUNDATION JOURNALISM SCHOLARSHIP

Philip Jaisohn Memorial Foundation
Attn: Education and Scholarship Committee
6705 Old York Road
Philadelphia, PA 19126
(215) 224-2000   Fax: (215) 224-9164
E-mail: jaisohnhouse@gmail.com
Web: www.jaisohn.org

Summary To provide financial assistance to Korean American undergraduate and graduate students who are working on a degree in journalism.

Eligibility This program is open to Korean American undergraduate and graduate students who are currently enrolled at a college or university in the United States. Applicants must be working on a degree in journalism. They must be able to demonstrate academic excellence, leadership and service to their school and community, and financial need. Along with their application, they must submit an essay on either "Who is Dr. Jaisohn to Me," or "The Significance of Dr. Jaisohn's Ideal to Korean Americans." They must also submit a brief statement on how they can contribute to and be involved in the activities of the Philip Jaisohn Memorial Foundation.

Financial data The stipend is $1,000.

Duration 1 year.

Number awarded 1 each year.

Deadline November of each year.

[301]
PHOENIX CHAPTER NAAAP SCHOLARSHIPS

National Association of Asian American Professionals-
  Phoenix Chapter
Attn: Scholarship Committee
P.O. Box 25527
Tempe, AZ 85285-5527
(480) 907-4471   E-mail: info@naaapphoenix.org
Web: www.naaapphoenix.org

Summary To provide financial assistance to Asian American residents of Arizona interested in attending college in the state.

Eligibility This program is open to graduating high school seniors and current college students who are of Asian American descent and Arizona residents. Applicants must be enrolled or planning to enroll full time at a 2- or 4-year public college or university in the state. They must be U.S. citizens or permanent residents. Along with their application, they must submit a 500-word essay about themselves, their intended or current field of study, and their interests, expectations, and goals. Financial need is not considered in the selection process. Preference is given to students majoring in fields other than those of science, technology, engineering, or mathematics (STEM).

Financial data Stipends range from $500 to $1,000.

Duration 1 year; recipients may reapply.

Number awarded 1 or more each year.

Deadline May of each year.

[302]
PHYLLIS G. MEEKINS SCHOLARSHIP

Ladies Professional Golf Association
Attn: LPGA Foundation
100 International Golf Drive
Daytona Beach, FL 32124-1082
(386) 274-6200   Fax: (386) 274-1099
E-mail: foundation.scholarships@lpga.com
Web: www.lpgafoundation.org/scholarships?

Summary To provide financial assistance to Asian American and other minority female graduating high school seniors who played golf in high school and plan to continue to play in college.

Eligibility This program is open to female high school seniors who are members of a recognized minority group. Applicants must have a GPA of 3.0 or higher and a background in golf. They must be planning to enroll full time at a college or university in the United States and play competitive golf. Along with their application, they must submit a letter that describes how golf has been an integral part of their lives and includes their personal, academic, and professional goals; their chosen discipline of study; and how this scholarship will be of assistance. Financial need is considered in the selection process. U.S. citizenship or legal resident status is required.

Financial data The stipend is $1,250.

Duration 1 year.

Additional information This program began in 2006.

Number awarded 1 each year.

Deadline May of each year.

[303]
PNAO SCHOLARSHIP AWARD

Philippine Nurses Association of Ohio
c/o Erlinda Gonzalez, Foundation President
ManorCare Health Services
37603 Euclid Avenue
Willoughby, OH 44094
(440) 951-5551   Fax: (440) 951-1914
Web: www.pnao.org/?page_id=218

Summary To provide financial assistance to members of the Philippine Nurses Association of Ohio (PNAO) who are working on an undergraduate or graduate degree at a school of nursing in any state.

Eligibility This program is open to residents of Ohio or the Philippines who are of at least 50% Filipino ethnicity and an associate member of PNAO. Applicants must be enrolled in an undergraduate or graduate nursing program at a school in any state. They must have a GPA of 3.0 or higher and be able to demonstrate financial need. Along with their application, they must submit a 1-page essay on their vision of nursing.

Financial data The stipend is $500.

Duration 1 year.

Number awarded 2 each year.

Deadline July of each year.

[304]
PROFESSIONAL GOLF MANAGEMENT DIVERSITY SCHOLARSHIP

Professional Golfers' Association of America
Attn: PGA Foundation
100 Avenue of the Champions
Palm Beach Gardens, FL 33418
Toll Free: (888) 532-6661
Web: www.pgafoundation.com

Summary To provide financial assistance to Asian Americans, other minorities, and women who are interested in attending a designated college or university to prepare for a career as a golf professional.

Eligibility This program is open to women and minorities interested in becoming a licensed PGA Professional. Applicants must be interested in attending 1 of 20 colleges and universities that offer the Professional Golf Management (PGM) curriculum sanctioned by the PGA.

Financial data The stipend is $3,000 per year.

Duration 1 year; may be renewed.

Additional information This program began in 1993. Programs are offered at 20 designated universities; for a list, contact the PGA.

Number awarded Varies each year; recently, 20 of these scholarships were awarded.

Deadline Deadline not specified.

[305]
PROFESSOR CHEN WEN-CHEN SCHOLARSHIPS

Professor Chen Wen-Chen Memorial Foundation
Attn: Scholarship Committee
P.O. Box 136
Kingston, NJ 08528
(609) 936-1352   E-mail: cwcmfusa@gmail.com
Web: www.cwcmf.net/html/cwcmf_about.html

Summary To provide financial assistance to students at North American colleges and universities who have been involved in the Taiwanese community.

Eligibility This program is open to students who have participated in Taiwanese social-political movements or have made significant contributions to the Taiwanese community in North America. Applicants must be currently enrolled at a college or university in North America. Along with their application, they must submit a 2-page essay on what they, as a younger generation Taiwanese or Taiwanese American, can do to promote the sovereignty and democracy of Taiwan. Selection is based on character, academic ability, financial need, and participation in Taiwanese American community affairs.

Financial data The stipend ranges from $1,000 to $1,500.

Duration 1 year.

Number awarded 4 to 6 each year.

Deadline May of each year.

[306]
PUBLIC RELATIONS SOCIETY OF AMERICA DIVERSITY MULTICULTURAL SCHOLARSHIPS

Public Relations Student Society of America
Attn: Vice President of Member Services
33 Maiden Lane, 11th Floor
New York, NY 10038-5150
(212) 460-1474   Fax: (212) 995-0757
E-mail: prssa@prsa.org
Web: www.prssa.org/scholarships_competitions/individual

Summary To provide financial assistance to Asian American and other minority college students who are interested in preparing for a career in public relations.

Eligibility This program is open to minority (African American/Black, Hispanic/Latino, Asian, Native American, Alaskan Native, or Pacific Islander) students who are at least juniors at an accredited 4-year college or university. Applicants must be enrolled full time, be able to demonstrate financial need, and have a GPA of 3.0 or higher. Membership in the Public Relations Student Society of America is preferred but not required. A major or minor in public relations is preferred; students who attend a school that does not offer a public relations degree or program must be enrolled in a communications degree program (e.g., journalism, mass communications).

Financial data The stipend is $1,500.

Duration 1 year.

Additional information This program began in 1989.

Number awarded 2 each year.

Deadline May of each year.

[307]
PUGET SOUND CHAPTER/HORACE AND SUSIE REVELS CAYTON SCHOLARSHIP

Public Relations Society of America-Puget Sound
  Chapter
c/o Amy Turner
EnviroIssues
101 Stewart Street, Suite 1200
Seattle, WA 98101
(206) 269-5041   Fax: (206) 269-5046
E-mail: prsascholarship@asi-seattle.net
Web: www.prsapugetsound.org/Page.aspx?cid=127

Summary To provide financial assistance to Asian American and other minority upperclassmen from Washington who are interested in preparing for a career in public relations.

Eligibility This program is open to U.S. citizens who are members of minority groups, defined as African Americans, Asian Americans, Hispanic/Latino Americans, Native Americans, and Pacific Islanders. Applicants must be full-time juniors or seniors attending a college in Washington or Washington students (who graduated from a Washington high school or whose parents live in the state year-round) attending college elsewhere. They must be able to demonstrate aptitude in public relations and related courses, activities, and/or internships.

Financial data The stipend is $2,500.

Duration 1 year.

Additional information This program began in 1992.

Number awarded 1 each year.

Deadline April of each year.

[308]
PUGET SOUND CHAPTER SHARON D. BANKS MEMORIAL UNDERGRADUATE SCHOLARSHIP

Women's Transportation Seminar-Puget Sound Chapter
c/o Jennifer Barnes, Scholarship Co-Chair
Heffron Transportation, Inc.
532 27th Avenue
Seattle, WA 98122
(206) 324-3623   Fax: (877) 314-9959
E-mail: jennifer@hefftrans.com
Web: www.wtsinternational.org

Summary To provide financial assistance to women (especially Asian American and other minority women) who are undergraduate students from Washington working on a degree related to transportation.

Eligibility This program is open to women who are residents of Washington, studying at a college in the state, or working as an intern in the state. Applicants must be currently enrolled in an undergraduate degree program in a transportation-related field, such as engineering, planning, finance, or logistics. They must have a GPA of 3.0 or higher and plans to prepare for a career in a transportation-related field. Minority women are especially encouraged to apply. Along with their application, they must submit a 500-word statement about their career goals after graduation and why they think they should receive this scholarship award. Selection is based on that statement, academic record, and transportation-related activities or job skills. Financial need is not considered.

Financial data The stipend is $4,000.

Duration 1 year.

Additional information The winner is also nominated for scholarships offered by the national organization of the Women's Transportation Seminar.

Number awarded 1 each year.

Deadline November of each year.

[309]
PWC ASCEND SCHOLARSHIPS

Ascend: Pan-Asian Leaders
Attn: Director of Programs
120 Wall Street, Ninth Floor
New York, NY 10005
(212) 248-4888   Fax: (212) 344-5636
E-mail: scholarships@ascendleadership.org
Web: www.ascendleadership.org

Summary To provide financial assistance to members of Ascend: Pan-Asian Leaders who are college undergraduates with a career interest in accounting.

Eligibility This program is open to members of Ascend who are enrolled as freshmen, sophomores, or juniors (in 5-year programs) at colleges and universities in the United States. Applicants must have a GPA of 3.5 or higher and a major in accounting. Along with their application, they must submit a 500-word personal essay on how they have demonstrated leadership and teamwork in their academic studies, professional career, and/or extracurricular activities and community volunteer work; why they believe those qualities are important to transforming themselves into a better leader; their career goals after graduation; and the role Ascend has played in the achievement of their academic and career goals. They must also answer questions on whether they are authorized to work in the United States without employer sponsorship, if they are willing to be interviewed for an internship with PricewaterhouseCoopers (PwC), if they have worked for other Big 4 accounting firms, and if they completed a PwC talent profile at the firm's web site. Financial need is not considered in the selection process.

Financial data The stipend is $1,000.

Duration 1 year.

Additional information Ascend was formed in 2004 as the National Asian American Society of Accountants. This program, sponsored by PwC, began in 2008.

Number awarded 3 each year.

Deadline May of each year.

[310]
RAMA SCHOLARSHIP FOR THE AMERICAN DREAM

American Hotel & Lodging Educational Foundation
Attn: Manager of Foundation Programs
1201 New York Avenue, N.W., Suite 600
Washington, DC 20005-3931
(202) 289-3100   Fax: (202) 289-3199
E-mail: scholarships@ahlef.org
Web: www.ahlef.org/content.aspx?id=19468

Summary To provide financial assistance to Asian Indian and other undergraduate and graduate students working on a degree in hotel management at designated schools.

Eligibility This program is open to U.S. citizens and permanent residents enrolled as full-time undergraduate or graduate students with a GPA of 2.5 or higher. Applicants must be attending 1 of 13 designated hospitality management schools, which select the recipients. Preference is given to students of Asian-Indian descent and other minority groups and to JHM Hotel employees and their dependents.

Financial data The stipend varies at each of the participating schools, but ranges from $1,000 to $3,000.

Duration 1 year.

Additional information This program was established by JHM Hotels, Inc. in 1998. The participating institutions are Bethune-Cookman University, California State Polytechnic University at Pomona, Cornell University, Florida International University, Georgia State University, Greenville Technical College, Howard University, Johnson & Wales University (Providence, Rhode Island), New York University, University of Central Florida, University of Houston, University of South Carolina, and Virginia Polytechnic Institute and State University.

Number awarded Varies each year; recently, 20 of these scholarships were awarded. Since the program was established, it has awarded more than $491,000 to 287 recipients.

Deadline April of each year.

[311]
RCA ETHNIC SCHOLARSHIP FUND

Reformed Church in America
Attn: New York Office Administrator
475 Riverside Drive, 18th Floor
New York, NY 10115
(212) 870-3071   Toll Free: (800) 722-9977, ext. 3017
Fax: (212) 870-2499   E-mail: mrich@rca.org
Web: www.rca.org/ethnicscholarship

Summary To provide assistance to Asian American and other minority student members of the Reformed Church in America (RCA) who are interested in working on an undergraduate degree.

Eligibility This program is open to members of minority groups (Native American/First Nations, African American/Caribbean American, Hispanic, or Pacific/Asian American) who are attending or planning to attend a college or other institution of higher learning. Applicants must be a member of an RCA congregation or attending an RCA institution. Priority is given to applicants who will be entering undergraduate colleges or universities and students currently enrolled in occupational training programs. Selection is based primarily on financial need.

Financial data Stipends range up to $500. Funds are paid directly to the institution.

Duration 1 academic year; may be renewed until completion of an academic program.

Number awarded Several each year.

Deadline July of each year.

[312]
RDW GROUP, INC. MINORITY SCHOLARSHIP FOR COMMUNICATIONS

Rhode Island Foundation
Attn: Funds Administrator
One Union Station
Providence, RI 02903
(401) 427-4017   Fax: (401) 331-8085
E-mail: lmonahan@rifoundation.org
Web: www.rifoundation.org

Summary To provide financial assistance to Asian Americans and other residents of color from Rhode Island who are working on a undergraduate or graduate degree in communications in any state.

Eligibility This program is open to undergraduate and graduate students at colleges and universities in any state who are Rhode Island residents of color. Applicants must intend to work on a degree in communications (including computer graphics, art, cinematography, or other fields that would prepare them for a career in advertising). They must be able to demonstrate financial need and a commitment to a career in communications. Along with their application, they must submit an essay (up to 300 words) on the impact they would like to have on the communications field.

Financial data The stipend is approximately $2,000 per year.

Duration 1 year; recipients may reapply.

Additional information This program is sponsored by the RDW Group, Inc.

Number awarded 1 each year.

Deadline April of each year.

[313]
RHODE ISLAND ASSOCIATION OF CHINESE AMERICANS SCHOLARSHIPS

Rhode Island Association of Chinese Americans
48 Blackstone Avenue
Pawtucket, RI 02860
(401) 965-1140   E-mail: scholarship@riaca.us
Web: www.riaca.us/RIACA_Scholarship.html

Summary To provide financial assistance to high school seniors who are members of the Rhode Island Association of Chinese Americans (RIACA) and interested in attending college in any state.

Eligibility This program is open to ethnic Chinese seniors graduating from high schools in Rhode Island who are members of RIACA and planning to attend college in any state. Applicants must be U.S. citizens or permanent residents. Along with their application, they must submit transcripts, SAT/ACT scores, an endorsement from a member of RIACA, and an essay (in English or Chinese) of 300 to 500 words on their motivation to apply for this scholarship and why they deserve it. Selection is based on that essay; academic excellence; extracurricular activities and leadership skills; community service; participation in RIACA social activities; participation in Chinese language school, Chinese culture club, or similar activities; special talents, awards, or recognitions; and an interview.

Financial data The stipend is $3,000.

Duration 1 year.

Number awarded Varies each year; recently, 8 of these scholarships were awarded.

Deadline November of each year.

[314]
RICHARD S. SMITH SCHOLARSHIP

United Methodist Church
Attn: General Board of Discipleship
Young People's Ministries
P.O. Box 340003
Nashville, TN 37203-0003
(615) 340-7184   Toll Free: (877) 899-2780, ext. 7184
Fax: (615) 340-7063   E-mail: ypm@gbod.org
Web: globalyoungpeople.org

Summary To provide financial assistance to Asian American and other minority high school seniors who wish to prepare for a Methodist church-related career.

Eligibility This program is open to graduating high school seniors who are members of racial/ethnic minority groups and have been active members of a United Methodist Church for at least 1 year. Applicants must have been admitted to an accredited college or university to prepare for a church-related career. They must have maintained at least a "C" average throughout high school and be able to demonstrate financial need. Along with their application, they must submit brief essays on their participation in church projects and activities, a leadership experience, the role their faith plays in their life, the church-related vocation to which God is calling them, and their extracurricular interests and activities. U.S. citizenship or permanent resident status is required.

Financial data The stipend is $1,000.

Duration 1 year; nonrenewable.

Additional information This program began in 1997. Recipients must enroll full time in their first year of undergraduate study.

Number awarded 2 each year.

Deadline May of each year.

[315]
ROBERT HALF INTERNATIONAL ASCEND SCHOLARSHIPS

Ascend: Pan-Asian Leaders
Attn: Director of Programs
120 Wall Street, Ninth Floor
New York, NY 10005
(212) 248-4888   Fax: (212) 344-5636
E-mail: scholarships@ascendleadership.org
Web: www.ascendleadership.org

Summary To provide financial assistance to members of Ascend: Pan-Asian Leaders who are upper-division students working on a degree in accounting or finance.

Eligibility This program is open to members of Ascend who are enrolled as juniors or seniors at colleges and universities in the United States. Applicants must have a GPA of 3.5 or higher and a major in accounting or finance. Along with their application, they must submit a 500-word personal essay on how they have demonstrated leadership and teamwork in their academic studies, professional career, and/or extracurricular activities and community volunteer work; why they believe those qualities are important to transforming themselves into a better leader; their career goals after graduation; and the role Ascend has played in the achievement of their academic and career goals. Financial need is not considered in the selection process.

Financial data The stipend is $2,500.

Duration 1 year.

Additional information Ascend was formed in 2004 as the National Asian American Society of Accountants. This program is sponsored by Robert Half International Inc.

Number awarded 2 each year.

Deadline July of each year.

[316]
ROSA L. PARKS SCHOLARSHIPS

Conference of Minority Transportation Officials
Attn: National Scholarship Program
1875 I Street, N.W., Suite 500
Washington, DC 20006
(703) 234-4072   Fax: (202) 318-0364
Web: www.comto.org/?page=Scholarships

Summary To provide financial assistance for college to children of members of the Conference of Minority Transportation Officials (COMTO) and to other students interested in working on a bachelor's or master's degree in transportation.

Eligibility This program is open to 1) college-bound high school seniors whose parent has been a COMTO member for at least 1 year; 2) undergraduates who have completed at least 60 semester credit hours in a transportation discipline; and 3) students working on a master's degree in transportation who have completed at least 15 credits. Applicants must have a GPA of 3.0 or higher. Along with their application, they must submit a cover letter with a 500-word statement of career goals. Financial need is not considered in the selection process. U.S. citizenship or legal resident status is required.

Financial data The stipend is $4,500. Funds are paid directly to the recipient's college or university.

Duration 1 year.

Additional information COMTO was established in 1971 to promote, strengthen, and expand the roles of minorities in all aspects of transportation. Recipients are expected to attend the COMTO National Scholarship Luncheon.

Number awarded 1 each year.

Deadline May of each year.

[317]
ROYCE OSBORN MINORITY STUDENT SCHOLARSHIPS

American Society of Radiologic Technologists
Attn: ASRT Education and Research Foundation
15000 Central Avenue, S.E.
Albuquerque, NM 87123-3909
(505) 298-4500, ext. 2541
Toll Free: (800) 444-2778, ext. 2541
Fax: (505) 298-5063   E-mail: foundation@asrt.org
Web: www.asrtfoundation.org

Summary To provide financial assistance to Asian American and other minority students enrolled in entry-level radiologic sciences programs.

Eligibility This program is open to Blacks or African Americans, American Indians or Alaska Natives, Hispanics or Latinos, Asians, and Native Hawaiians or other Pacific Islanders who are enrolled in an accredited entry-level program in radiography, sonography, magnetic resonance, or nuclear medicine. Applicants must be able to finish their degree or certificate in the year for which they are applying. They must be U.S. citizens, nationals, or permanent residents have a GPA of 3.0 or higher. Along with their application, they must submit 9 essays of 200 words each on assigned topics related to their personal situation and interest in a career in radiologic science. Selection is based on those essays, academic and professional achievements, recommendations, and financial need.

Financial data The stipend is $4,000. Funds are paid directly to the recipient's institution.

Duration 1 year.

Number awarded 5 each year.

Deadline January of each year.

[318]
RTDNF/CAROLE SIMPSON SCHOLARSHIP

Radio Television Digital News Foundation
Attn: Programs, Awards, and Membership Manager
529 14th Street, N.W., Suite 425
Washington, DC 20045
(202) 725-8318   Fax: (202) 223-4007
E-mail: katies@rtdna.org
Web: www.rtdna.org/pages/education/scholarship-info.php

Summary To provide financial assistance to Asian American and other minority undergraduate students who are interested in preparing for a career in electronic journalism.

Eligibility This program is open to sophomore or more advanced minority undergraduate students enrolled in an electronic journalism sequence at an accredited or nationally-recognized college or university. Applicants must submit 1 to 3 examples of their journalistic skills on audio CD or DVD (no more than 15 minutes total, accompanied by scripts); a description of their role on each story and a list of who worked on each story and what they did; a 1-page statement explain-

ing why they are preparing for a career in electronic journalism with reference to their specific career preference (radio, television, online, reporting, producing, or newsroom management); a resume; and a letter of reference from their dean or faculty sponsor explaining why they are a good candidate for the award and certifying that they have at least 1 year of school remaining.

Financial data The stipend is $2,000, paid in semiannual installments of $1,000 each.

Duration 1 year.

Additional information The Radio Television Digital News Foundation (RTDNF) also provides an all-expense paid trip to the Radio Television Digital News Association (RTDNA) annual international conference. The RTDNF was formerly the Radio and Television News Directors Foundation (RTNDF). Previous winners of any RTDNF scholarship or internship are not eligible.

Number awarded 1 each year.

Deadline May of each year.

[319]
RYU FAMILY FOUNDATION SCHOLARSHIP GRANTS

Ryu Family Foundation, Inc.
Attn: Jenny Kang
186 Parish Drive
Wayne, NJ 07470
(973) 692-9696, ext. 20   Fax: (973) 692-0999
Web: www.seolbong.org

Summary To provide financial assistance to Korean and Korean American students in the Northeast who are working on an undergraduate or graduate degree in any field.

Eligibility This program is open to Korean Americans (U.S. citizens) and Koreans (with or without permanent resident status). Applicants must be enrolled full time and working on an undergraduate or graduate degree; have a GPA of 3.5 or higher; be able to document financial need; and be either residing or attending college in 1 of the following 10 northeastern states: Connecticut, Delaware, Maine, Massachusetts, New Hampshire, New Jersey, New York, Pennsylvania, Rhode Island, or Vermont. Along with their application, they must submit a 500-word essay on a subject that changes annually; recently, students were asked to write on either 1) the importance of religion in the minds of the Korean people; or 2) the patriotism of Korean Admiral Soon Shin Lee.

Financial data A stipend is awarded (amount not specified). Checks are made out jointly to the recipient and the recipient's school.

Duration 1 year; may be renewed.

Number awarded 1 or more each year.

Deadline June of each year.

[320]
SABURO KIDO MEMORIAL SCHOLARSHIP

Japanese American Citizens League
Attn: National Scholarship Awards
1765 Sutter Street
San Francisco, CA 94115
(415) 345-1075   Fax: (415) 931-4671
E-mail: ncwnp@jacl.org
Web: www.jacl.org/edu/scholar.htm

Summary To provide money for any type of college to student members of the Japanese American Citizens League (JACL).

Eligibility This program is open to JACL members who are currently enrolled at a college, university, trade school, business college, or other institution of higher learning. Applicants must submit information on their involvement in JACL and a 2-page essay on a topic that changes annually but relates to Japanese Americans. Selection is based on that essay, academic history, JACL involvement, school activities, work history, scholastic honors, and community involvement.

Financial data Stipends generally average more than $2,000.

Duration 1 year; nonrenewable.

Number awarded At least 1 each year.

Deadline March of each year.

[321]
SAJA SCHOLARSHIPS

South Asian Journalists Association
c/o Shefali Kulkarni, Secretary
Kaiser Health News
1330 G Street, N.W.
Washington, DC 20005
E-mail: shefali.kulkarni24@gmail.com
Web: www.saja.org/scholarships

Summary To provide financial assistance for undergraduate and graduate study to journalism students of south Asian descent.

Eligibility This program is open to students of south Asian descent (including Bangladesh, Bhutan, India, Maldives, Nepal, Pakistan, and Sri Lanka; Indo-Caribbeans are also eligible). Applicants must be serious about preparing for a journalism career and must provide evidence they plan to do so through courses, internships, or freelancing. They may be 1) high school seniors about to enroll in an accredited college or university; 2) current students in an accredited college or university in the United States or Canada; or 3) students enrolled or about to enter a graduate program in the United States or Canada. Applicants with financial hardship are given special consideration. Selection is based on interest in journalism, writing skills, participation in the sponsoring organization, reasons for entering journalism, and financial need.

Financial data The stipends are $2,500 for high school seniors, $3,000 for undergraduates, or $5,000 for graduate students.

Duration 1 year.

Additional information Recipients are expected to give back to the South Asian Journalists Association (SAJA) by volunteering at the annual convention or at other events during the year.

Number awarded Varies each year; recently, 14 of these scholarships were awarded: 2 to high school seniors, 6 to undergraduates, and 6 to graduate students.

Deadline March of each year.

[322]
SAKAE TAKAHASHI SCHOLARSHIP

100th Infantry Battalion Legacy Organization
Attn: Scholarship Committee
520 Kamoku Street
Honolulu, HI 96826-5120
(808) 637-5324   E-mail: hondan001@hawaii.rr.com
Web: www.100thlegacy.org

Summary To provide financial assistance to Japanese American and other high school seniors in Hawaii who plan to attend college in any state.

Eligibility This program is open to seniors graduating from high schools in Hawaii and planning to attend an institution of higher in any state. Applicants must submit an essay about the challenges faced by veterans of the 100th Infantry Battalion after World War II, how they were influenced by the cultural values they learned from their Issei parents, and the 4 most significant Issei values that contributed to the accomplishments of Sakae Takahashi. Selection is based on that essay (50%), academics (20%), community service (15%), and leadership (15%).

Financial data The stipend is $3,000.

Duration 1 year; nonrenewable.

Number awarded 1 each year.

Deadline March of each year.

[323]
SANDRA R. SPAULDING MEMORIAL SCHOLARSHIPS

California Nurses Association
Attn: California Nurses Foundation
2030 Franklin Street, Suite 610
Oakland, CA 94612
(510) 622-8311   Fax: (510) 663-4825
E-mail: info@calnursesfoundation.org
Web: www.nationalnursesunited.org/pages/1074

Summary To provide financial assistance to Asian Americans and other students from diverse ethnic backgrounds who are enrolled in an associate degree in nursing (A.D.N.) program in California.

Eligibility This program is open to students who have been admitted to a second-year accredited A.D.N. program in California and plan to complete the degree within 2 years. Along with their application, they must submit a 1-page essay describing their personal and professional goals. Selection is based on that essay, commitment and active participation in nursing and health-related organizations, professional vision and direction, and financial need. A goal of this scholarship program is to encourage ethnic and socioeconomic diversity in nursing.

Financial data A stipend is awarded (amount not specified).

Duration 1 year; nonrenewable.

Additional information This program began in 1985.

Number awarded 1 or more each year.

Deadline July of each year.

[324]
SARA LEE FOUNDATION APIASF SCHOLARSHIP

Asian & Pacific Islander American Scholarship Fund
2025 M Street, N.W., Suite 610
Washington, DC 20036-3363
(202) 986-6892   Toll Free: (877) 808-7032
Fax: (202) 530-0643   E-mail: info@apiasf.org
Web: www.apiasf.org/scholarship_apiasf.html

Summary To provide financial assistance to female Asian and Pacific Islander Americans who are entering college for the first time.

Eligibility This program is open to women who are U.S. citizens, nationals, permanent residents, or citizens of the Freely Associated States and of Asian or Pacific Islander heritage. Applicants must be enrolling full time at an accredited 2- or 4-year college or university in the United States as a first-year student. They must have a GPA of 2.7 or higher or the GED equivalent. In addition, they must complete the FAFSA and apply for federal financial aid.

Financial data The stipend is $2,500.

Duration 1 year; nonrenewable.

Additional information This scholarship is sponsored by the Sara Lee Foundation and administered by the Asian & Pacific Islander American Scholarship Fund (APIASF).

Number awarded Varies each year; recently, 4 of these scholarships were awarded.

Deadline January of each year.

[325]
SCHOLARSHIP AMERICA'S DREAM AWARD SCHOLARSHIPS FOR CHINESE-AMERICAN STUDENTS

Scholarship America
Attn: Scholarship Management Services
One Scholarship Way
P.O. Box 297
St. Peter, MN 56082
(952) 830-7300
Web: www.scholarshipamerica.org/dream_about.php

Summary To provide financial assistance to Chinese American college students who are working on a degree in any field and demonstrate financial need.

Eligibility This program is open to Chinese American students currently enrolled full time in at least the first year at an accredited 2- or 4-year college, university, or vocational/technical school in any state. Applicants must have a GPA of 3.0 or higher and be able to demonstrate financial need. They must be U.S. citizens or permanent residents or have been granted deferred action status under the Deferred Action for Childhood Arrivals (DACA) Program. Community service, volunteerism, and overcoming barriers to school success are also considered in the selection process.

Financial data Stipends range from $5,000 to $15,000 for the first year, increasing by $1,000 per year in each subsequent year.

Duration 1 year; may be renewed until graduation (including the fifth year of a 5-year program).

Additional information This program began in 2013.

Number awarded Varies each year.

Deadline Deadline not specified.

[326]
SCHOLARSHIP FUND OF THE 100TH INFANTRY BATTALION MEMORIAL

Hawai'i Community Foundation
Attn: Scholarship Department
827 Fort Street Mall
Honolulu, HI 96813
(808) 566-5570   Toll Free: (888) 731-3863
Fax: (808) 521-6286
E-mail: scholarships@hcf-hawaii.org
Web: www.hawaiicommunityfoundation.org/scholarships

Summary To provide financial assistance for college or graduate school to descendants of 100th Infantry Battalion World War II veterans (primarily of Americans of Japanese descent).

Eligibility This program is open to entering and continuing full-time undergraduate and graduate students at 2- and 4-year colleges and universities. Applicants must be a direct descendant of a World War II veteran of the 100th Infantry Battalion (which was comprised of Americans of Japanese descent). They must be able to demonstrate academic achievement (GPA of 3.5 or higher), an active record of extracurricular activities and community service, a willingness to promote the legacy of the 100th Infantry Battalion of World War II, and financial need. Along with their application, they must submit a short statement indicating their reasons for attending college, their planned course of study, their career goals, and what community service means to them. They must also submit a separate essay on the legacy of the 100th Infantry Battalion and how they will contribute to forwarding that legacy. Current residency in Hawaii is not required.

Financial data The amounts of the awards depend on the availability of funds and the need of the recipient. Recently, the average value of each of the scholarships awarded by the foundation was $2,200.

Duration 1 year.

Number awarded Varies each year; recently, 2 of these scholarships were awarded.

Deadline February of each year.

[327]
SCHOLARSHIPS FOR MINORITY ACCOUNTING STUDENTS

American Institute of Certified Public Accountants
Attn: Academic and Career Development Division
220 Leigh Farm Road
Durham, NC 27707-8110
(919) 402-4931   Fax: (919) 419-4705
E-mail: scholarships@aicpa.org
Web: www.aicpa.org

Summary To provide financial assistance to Asian Americans and other minorities interested in studying accounting at the undergraduate or graduate school level.

Eligibility This program is open to minority undergraduate and graduate students, enrolled full time, who have a GPA of 3.3 or higher (both cumulatively and in their major) and intend to pursue a C.P.A. credential. The program defines minority students as those whose heritage is Black or African American, Hispanic or Latino, Native American, or Asian American. Undergraduates must have completed at least 30 semester hours, including at least 6 semester hours of a major in accounting. Graduate students must be working on a master's degree in accounting, finance, taxation, or a related program. Applicants must be U.S. citizens or permanent residents and student affiliate members of the American Institute of Certified Public Accountants (AICPA). Along with their application, they must submit 500-word essays on 1) why they want to become a C.P.A. and how attaining that licensure will contribute to their goals; and 2) how they would spread the message about accounting and the C.P.A. profession in their community and school. In the selection process, some consideration is given to financial need.

Financial data Stipends range from $1,500 to $3,000 per year. Funds are disbursed directly to the recipient's school.

Duration 1 year; may be renewed up to 3 additional years or until completion of a bachelor's or master's degree, whichever is earlier.

Additional information This program began in 1969.

Number awarded Varies each year; recently, 78 students received funding through this program.

Deadline March of each year.

[328]
SCHOLARSHIPS FOR RACIAL JUSTICE

Higher Education Consortium for Urban Affairs
Attn: Student Services
2233 University Avenue West, Suite 210
St. Paul, MN 55114-1698
(651) 287-3300   Toll Free: (800) 554-1089
Fax: (651) 659-9421   E-mail: hecua@hecua.org
Web: www.hecua.org/programs/scholarships

Summary To provide financial assistance to Asian American and other students of color who are enrolled in programs of the Higher Education Consortium for Urban Affairs (HECUA) at participating colleges and universities and are committed to undoing institutionalized racism.

Eligibility This program is open to students at member colleges and universities who are participating in HECUA programs. Applicants must be a student of color who can demonstrate a commitment to undoing institutionalized racism. Along with their application, they must submit a reflective essay on the personal, social, or political influences in their lifetime that have motivated them to work on racial justice issues.

Financial data The stipend is $4,000. Funds are applied as a credit to the student's HECUA program fees for the semester.

Duration 1 semester.

Additional information This program began in 2006. Consortium members include Augsburg College (Minneapolis, Minnesota), Augustana College (Sioux Falls, South Dakota), Carleton College (Northfield, Minnesota), College of Saint Scholastica (Duluth, Minnesota), Colorado College (Colorado Springs, Colorado), Denison University (Granville, Ohio), Gustavus Adolphus College (St. Peter, Minnesota), Hamline University (St. Paul, Minnesota), Macalester College (St. Paul, Minnesota), Saint Mary's University (Winona, Minnesota), Saint Catherine University (St. Paul, Minnesota), Saint Olaf College (Northfield, Minnesota), Swarthmore College (Swarthmore, Pennsylvania), University of Minnesota (Twin Cities, Duluth, Morris, Crookston, Rochester), University of Saint Thomas (St. Paul, Minnesota), and Viterbo University (La Crosse, Wisconsin).

Number awarded Several each year.

Deadline April of each year for summer and fall programs; November of each year for January and spring programs.

[329]
SCHOLARSHIPS SUPPORTING POST-SECONDARY EDUCATION FOR A CAREER IN THE AUDIOVISUAL INDUSTRY

InfoComm International
International Communications Industries Foundation
11242 Waples Mill Road, Suite 200
Fairfax, VA 22030
(703) 273-7200   Toll Free: (800) 659-7469
Fax: (703) 278-8082   E-mail: jhardwick@infocomm.org
Web: www.infocomm.org

Summary To provide financial assistance to undergraduate and graduate students (particularly Asian Americans, other minorities, and women) who are interested in preparing for a career in the audiovisual (AV) industry.

Eligibility This program is open to second-year students at 2-year colleges, juniors and seniors at 4-year institutions, and graduate students. Applicants must have a GPA of 2.75 or higher and be majoring or planning to major in audiovisual subjects or related fields, including audio, video, audiovisual, radio/television/film, or other field related to a career in the audiovisual industry. Students in other programs, such as journalism, may be eligible if they can demonstrate a relationship to career goals in the AV industry. Along with their application, they must submit 1) an essay of 150 to 200 words on the career path they plan to pursue in the audiovisual industry in the next 5 years; and 2) an essay of 250 to 300 words on the experience or person influencing them the most in selecting the audiovisual industry as their career of choice. Minority and women candidates are especially encouraged to apply. Selection is based on the essays, presentation of the application, GPA, AV-related experience, work experience, and letters of recommendation.

Financial data The stipend is $4,000. Funds are sent directly to the school.

Duration 1 year.

Additional information InfoComm International, formerly the International Communications Industries Association, established the International Communications Industries Foundation (ICIF) to manage its charitable and educational activities.

Number awarded Varies each year.

Deadline April of each year.

[330]
SEED FOUNDATION SCHOLARSHIPS

SEED Foundation
Attn: Scholarship Director
1325 Lance Lane
Carol Stream, IL 60188
E-mail: info@seedfoundation.org
Web: www.seedfoundation.org/scholarship.html

Summary To provide financial assistance to high school seniors who are of Asian-Indian heritage and interested in attending college and majoring in any field.

Eligibility This program is open to graduating high school seniors who are of Asian-Indian heritage with at least 1 parent of Indian ancestry. Applicants must be planning to enroll full time at a college or university in the United States. They must have a GPA of 3.0 or higher and be U.S. citizens or permanent residents.

Financial data Stipends range up to $10,000.

Duration 1 year.

Additional information This program began in 1998.

Number awarded Varies each year; recently, 3 of these scholarships were awarded. Since the program began, it has awarded $243,000 in scholarships to 41 students.

Deadline April of each year.

[331]
SHARON D. BANKS MEMORIAL UNDERGRADUATE SCHOLARSHIP

Women's Transportation Seminar
Attn: WTS Foundation
1701 K Street, N.W., Suite 800
Washington, DC 20006
(202) 955-5085   Fax: (202) 955-5088
E-mail: wts@wtsinternational.org
Web: www.wtsinternational.org/education/scholarships

Summary To provide financial assistance to undergraduate women (particularly Asian Americans and other minorities) who are interested in a career in transportation.

Eligibility This program is open to women who are working on an undergraduate degree in transportation or a transportation-related field (e.g., transportation engineering, planning, finance, or logistics). Applicants must have a GPA of 3.0 or higher and be interested in a career in transportation. Along with their application, they must submit a 500-word statement about their career goals after graduation and why they think they should receive the scholarship award. Applications must be submitted first to a local chapter; the chapters forward selected applications for consideration on the national level. Minority women are especially encouraged to apply. Selection is based on transportation involvement and goals, job skills, and academic record; financial need is not considered.

Financial data The stipend is $5,000.

Duration 1 year.

Additional information This program began in 1992. Local chapters may also award additional funding to winners in their area.

Number awarded 1 each year.

Deadline Applications must be submitted by November to a local WTS chapter.

[332]
SHIGERU "SHIG" NAKAHIRA MEMORIAL SCHOLARSHIP

Japanese American Citizens League
Attn: National Scholarship Awards
1765 Sutter Street
San Francisco, CA 94115
(415) 345-1075   Fax: (415) 931-4671
E-mail: ncwnp@jacl.org
Web: www.jacl.org/edu/scholar.htm

Summary To provide financial assistance to Japanese American Citizens League (JACL) student members who are currently attending college.

Eligibility This program is open to JACL members who are currently enrolled at a college, university, trade school, business college, or other institution of higher learning. Applicants must submit information on their involvement in JACL and a 2-page essay on a topic that changes annually but relates to Japanese Americans. Selection is based on that essay, academic history, JACL involvement, school activities, work history, scholastic honors, and community involvement.

Financial data Stipends generally average more than $2,000.

Duration 1 year; nonrenewable.

Additional information This program began in 2009.

Number awarded At least 1 each year.

Deadline March of each year.

[333]
SHUI KUEN AND ALLEN CHIN SCHOLARSHIP

Asian Pacific Fund
Attn: Scholarship Coordinator
465 California Street, Suite 809
San Francisco, CA 94104
(415) 395-9985 E-mail: scholarship@asianpacificfund.org
Web: www.asianpacificfund.org

Summary To provide financial assistance for college to students who have worked or whose parent has worked in an Asian restaurant.

Eligibility This program is open to students who are entering or currently enrolled full time in an undergraduate degree program at an accredited college or university in any state. Applicants or their parents must have worked at an Asian restaurant (Asian-owned or Asian cuisine). They must have a GPA of 3.0 or higher and be able to demonstrate financial need. Along with their application, they must submit essays of 250 to 500 words each on 1) their experience as a restaurant worker or child of a restaurant worker and how that experience has affected their values, ethics, or worldview; 2) any community service or school studies or projects that have shaped their ideas about Asian Americans and the Asian American community; and 3) any unusual family or personal circumstances that have affected their achievement in school, work, or extracurricular activities. Preference is given to students who have been involved in community advocacy and social justice work on behalf of Asian American, immigrant, gay and lesbian, or other progressive causes. U.S. citizenship or permanent resident status is required.

Financial data The stipend is $1,000 per year.

Duration 1 year; recipients may reapply.

Additional information This program began in 2007.

Number awarded Up to 2 each year.

Deadline March of each year.

[334]
SMITHSONIAN MINORITY AWARDS PROGRAM

Smithsonian Institution
Attn: Office of Fellowships and Internships
470 L'Enfant Plaza, Suite 7102
P.O. Box 37012, MRC 902
Washington, DC 20013-7012
(202) 633-7070   Fax: (202) 633-7069
E-mail: siofi@si.edu
Web: www.smithsonianofi.com

Summary To provide funding to Asian American and other minority undergraduate and graduate students interested in conducting research at the Smithsonian Institution.

Eligibility This program is open to members of U.S. minority groups underrepresented in the Smithsonian's scholarly programs. Applicants must be undergraduates or beginning graduate students interested in conducting research in the Institution's disciplines and in the museum field. They must be U.S. citizens or permanent residents and have a GPA of 3.0 or higher.

Financial data Students receive a grant of $600 per week.

Duration Up to 10 weeks.

Additional information Recipients must carry out independent research projects in association with the Smithsonian's research staff. Eligible fields of study currently include animal behavior, ecology, and environmental science (including an emphasis on the tropics); anthropology (including archaeology); astrophysics and astronomy; earth sciences and paleobiology; evolutionary and systematic biology; history of science and technology; history of art (especially American, contemporary, African, Asian, and 20th-century art); American crafts and decorative arts; social and cultural history of the United States; and folklife. Students are required to be in residence at the Smithsonian for the duration of the fellowship.

Number awarded Varies each year; recently, 25 of these awards were granted: 2 for fall, 19 for summer, and 4 for spring.

Deadline January of each year for summer and fall residency; September of each year for spring residency.

[335]
SODEXO FOUNDATION APIASF SCHOLARSHIP

Asian & Pacific Islander American Scholarship Fund
2025 M Street, N.W., Suite 610
Washington, DC 20036-3363
(202) 986-6892   Toll Free: (877) 808-7032
Fax: (202) 530-0643   E-mail: info@apiasf.org
Web: www.apiasf.org/scholarship_apiasf.html

Summary To provide financial assistance to Asian and Pacific Islander Americans who have a record of service related to hunger and poverty and are entering their junior year of college.

Eligibility This program is open to U.S. citizens, nationals, permanent residents, or citizens of the Freely Associated States who are of Asian or Pacific Islander heritage. Applicants must be entering their junior year of full-time study at an accredited 4-year college or university in the United States and have a record of participation in community service programs dealing specifically with hunger and poverty in the United States. They must have a GPA of 3.0 or higher and a family income less than 60% of the median household income for the area in which they live.

Financial data The stipend is $2,500 per year.

Duration 2 years.

Additional information This scholarship is sponsored by Sodexo and administered by the Asian & Pacific Islander American Scholarship Fund (APIASF).

Number awarded 1 or more each year.

Deadline January of each year.

[336]
SOO YUEN BENEVOLENT ASSOCIATION SCHOLARSHIPS

Soo Yuen Benevolent Association
806 Clay Street
San Francisco, CA 94108
(415) 421-0602   Fax: (415) 421-0606
Web: www.sooyuen.org/node/44

Summary To provide financial assistance for college to children of members of the Soo Yuen Benevolent Association.

Eligibility This program is open to high school seniors whose parents have been members of the association for at least 1 year. Membership in the association is limited to members of the following clans: Louie (including Loui, Lui, Lei), Fong (including Fang), and Kwong (including Kwang, Kuang, and Kong). Applicants must have a GPA of 3.0 or higher and be planning to attend college in any state. As part of the selection process, a personal interview may be required.

Financial data A stipend is awarded (amount not specified).

Duration 1 year.

Number awarded 1 or more each year.

Deadline January of each year.

[337]
SOUTH ASIAN JOURNALISTS ASSOCIATION STUDENT JOURNALISM AWARDS

South Asian Journalists Association
c/o Shefali Kulkarni, Secretary
Kaiser Health News
1330 G Street, N.W.
Washington, DC 20005
E-mail: shefali.kulkarni24@gmail.com
Web: www.saja.org/awards

Summary To recognize and reward outstanding reporting on any subject by undergraduate and graduate students of south Asian origin.

Eligibility Eligible to be considered for these awards are print, broadcast, new media, and photographic works submitted by south Asian undergraduate and graduate students in the United States or Canada (on any subject). Entries must have been completed as part of a class assignment.

Financial data Prizes are $500 for the winner and $250 for the finalists.

Duration The competition is held annually.

Number awarded 3 each year.

Deadline March of each year.

[338]
SOUTHERN REGION KOREAN AMERICAN SCHOLARSHIPS

Korean American Scholarship Foundation
Southern Region
c/o Dr. Sam Sook Chung, Scholarship Committee Chair
8679 Spivey Village Trail
Jonesboro, GA 30236
E-mail: samsookchung2@gmail.com
Web: www.kasf.org/southern

Summary To provide financial assistance to Korean American students from any state who are working on or planning to work on an undergraduate or graduate degree in any field at a school in southern states.

Eligibility This program is open to Korean American students who are currently enrolled in a college or university in the southern states as full-time undergraduate or graduate students. Applicants may reside anywhere in the United States as long as they attend school in the southern region: Alabama, Florida, Georgia, South Carolina, and Tennessee. Both U.S. citizens and foreign nationals are eligible. Selection is based on academic achievement, school activities, community service, and financial need.

Financial data Stipends are $1,000 for undergraduate, graduate, or professional students or $500 for high school students.

Duration 1 year; renewable.

Number awarded Varies each year; recently, 39 of these scholarships were awarded.

Deadline May of each year.

[339]
SOUTHWESTERN REGION KOREAN AMERICAN SCHOLARSHIPS

Korean American Scholarship Foundation
Southern Region
c/o Scholarship Committee Chair
14759 Kellywood Lane
Houston, TX 77079
E-mail: kasfsw@gmail.com
Web: www.kasf.org/southwestern

Summary To provide financial assistance to Korean American students from any state who are working on or planning to work on an undergraduate or graduate degree in any field at a school in southwestern states.

Eligibility This program is open to residents of any state who are 1) U.S. citizens of Korean heritage; 2) Korean citizens who have a valid visa to study in the United States; and 3) citizens of any other country who are of Korean heritage and have a valid visa to study in the United States. Applicants must be enrolled or planning to enroll as a full-time undergraduate or graduate student at a college or university in Arkansas, Louisiana, Mississippi, Oklahoma, or Texas. Selection is based on academic performance, extracurricular activities, community service, letters of recommendation, an essay, character and integrity, and financial need.

Financial data Stipends range from $1,000 to $2,000.

Duration 1 year; nonrenewable.

Number awarded Varies each year; recently, 15 of these scholarships were awarded.

Deadline June of each year.

[340]
SPIE SCHOLARSHIP PROGRAM

SPIE-The International Society for Optical Engineering
Attn: Scholarship Committee
1000 20th Street
P.O. Box 10
Bellingham, WA 98227-0010
(360) 676-3290   Toll Free: (888) 504-8171
Fax: (360) 647-1445   E-mail: scholarships@spie.org
Web: spie.org/x7236.xml

Summary To provide financial assistance to entering or continuing undergraduate and graduate student members of SPIE-The International Society for Optical Engineering (particularly Asian Americans, other minorities, women, and veterans) who are preparing for a career in optical science or engineering.

Eligibility This program is open to high school seniors planning to attend college, current undergraduate students, and current graduate students. Applicants must be society members majoring or planning to enroll full or part time and major in optics, optoelectronics, photonics, imaging, or a related discipline (e.g., physics, electrical engineering) at a college or university anywhere in the world. Along with their application, they must submit a 500-word essay on their academic work, career objectives, how this scholarship would help them attain their goals, and what they have achieved and learned through their studies and activities. Financial need is not considered in the selection process. Women, minorities, and veterans are encouraged to apply.

Financial data Stipends range from $2,000 to $11,000. Special awards include the D.J. Lovell Scholarship at $11,000; the John Kiel Scholarship at $10,000; the Laser Technology, Engineering, and Applications Scholarship at $5,000; the Optical Design and Engineering Scholarship at $5,000, and the BACUS Scholarship at $5,000.

Duration 1 year.

Additional information The International Society for Optical Engineering was founded in 1955 as the Society of Photo-Optical Instrumentation Engineers (SPIE). This program includes the following special named scholarships: the D.J. Lovell Scholarship, sponsored by SPIE (the most prestigious of the scholarships); the John Kiel Scholarship, awarded for a student's potential for long-term contribution to the field of optics and optical engineering; the Optical Design and Engineering Scholarship in Optical Engineering, established to honor Bill Price and Warren Smith and awarded to a full-time graduate or undergraduate student in the field of optical design and engineering; the Laser Technology, Engineering, and Applications Scholarship (formerly the F-MADE Scholarship), sponsored by the Forum for Military Applications of Directed Energy (F-MADE) in recognition of a student's scholarly achievement in laser technology, engineering, or applications; and the BACUS Scholarship, awarded to a full-time undergraduate or graduate student in the field of microlithography with an emphasis on optical tooling and/or semiconductor manufacturing technologies, sponsored by BACUS (SPIE's photomask international technical group).

Number awarded Varies each year; recently, this program awarded 140 scholarships with a value of $353,000. Since the program was established, it has awarded more than $3.8 million to nearly 2,000 students in 86 countries.

Deadline February of each year.

[341]
STAN BECK FELLOWSHIP

Entomological Society of America
Attn: Entomological Foundation
9332 Annapolis Road, Suite 210
Lanham, MD 20706-3150
(301) 459-9082   Fax: (301) 459-9084
E-mail: melodie@entfdn.org
Web: www.entfdn.org/awards_education.php

Summary To assist "needy" students working on an undergraduate or graduate degree in entomology who are nominated by members of the Entomological Society of America (ESA).

Eligibility This program is open to students working on an undergraduate or graduate degree in entomology at a college or university in Canada, Mexico, or the United States. Candidates must be nominated by members of the society. They must be "needy" students; for the purposes of this program, need may be based on physical limitations, or economic, minority, or environmental conditions.

Financial data The stipend is $2,000 per year.

Duration 1 year; may be renewed up to 3 additional years.

Additional information This fellowship was first awarded in 1996. Recipients are expected to be present at the society's annual meeting, where the award will be presented.

Number awarded 1 each year.

Deadline June of each year.

[342]
STANFORD CHEN INTERNSHIP GRANTS

Asian American Journalists Association
Attn: Student Programs Coordinator
5 Third Street, Suite 1108
San Francisco, CA 94103
(415) 346-2051, ext. 102   Fax: (415) 346-6343
E-mail: programs@aaja.org
Web: www.aaja.org/stanford-chen-internship-grant

Summary To offer scholars in the humanities (particularly Asian Americans and other underrepresented minorities) an opportunity to conduct research and teach at Stanford University.

Eligibility This program is open to AAJA members who are college juniors, seniors, or graduate students with a serious intent to prepare for a career in journalism (print, online, broadcast, or photography). Applicants must have already secured an internship with a print company (daily circulation less than 100,000) or broadcast company (market smaller than the top 50). Along with their application, they must submit a 200-word essay on the kind of experience they expect as an intern at a small to medium-size media company, their career goals, and why AAJA's mission is important to them; a resume; verification of the internship; a letter of recommendation; and a statement of financial need.

Financial data The grant is $1,750. Funds are to be used for living expenses or transportation.

Duration Summer months.

Additional information This program began in 1998.

Number awarded 1 or 2 each year.

Deadline April of each year.

[343]
STATE COUNCIL ON ADAPTED PHYSICAL EDUCATION CULTURAL DIVERSITY STUDENT SCHOLARSHIP

California Association for Health, Physical Education, Recreation and Dance
Attn: State Council on Adapted Physical Education
1501 El Camino Avenue, Suite 3
Sacramento, CA 95815-2748
(916) 922-3596   Toll Free: (800) 499-3596 (within CA)
Fax: (916) 922-0133   E-mail: cahperd@cahperd.org
Web: www.napeconference.org/Awards.htm

Summary To provide financial assistance to Asian American and other culturally diverse members of the California Association for Health, Physical Education, Recreation and Dance (CAHPERD) who are preparing to become a student teacher in the field of adapted physical education.

Eligibility This program is open to CAHPERD members who are attending a California college or university and specializing in the field of adapted physical education. Applicants must be members of an ethnic or cultural minority group (e.g., African American, American Indian/Native American, Asian American, Filipino, Mexican American, other Latino, Pacific Islander). They must be planning to become a student teacher during the following academic year. Along with their application, they must submit a 300-word statement of their professional goals and philosophy of physical education for individuals with disabilities. Selection is based on academic proficiency; leadership ability; personal qualities; school, community, and professional activities; and experience and interest in working with individuals with disabilities.

Financial data The stipend is $500.

Duration 1 year.

Number awarded 1 each year.

Deadline January of each year.

[344]
STRATTON/TIPTON SCHOLARSHIPS

Kentucky Association of Vocational Education Special Needs Personnel
c/o Eric Keeling, President
Kentucky Tech-Russellville ATC
1103 West Ninth Street
Russellville, KY 42276
(270) 726-8432   E-mail: eric.keeling@ky.gov
Web: www.kacte-snponline.org

Summary To provide financial assistance to Asian American and other residents of Kentucky who have special needs and are interested in a program of technical education in the state.

Eligibility This program is open to minority and other residents of Kentucky who are either 1) high school seniors planning to enroll in a program of career or technical education in the state; or 2) postsecondary students already enrolled in such a program. Applicants must meet the definition of a special needs student: persons with disabilities, educationally and economically disadvantaged people, foster children, individuals preparing for nontraditional employment, single parents (including single pregnant women), displaced homemakers, individuals with limited English language proficiency, individuals in a correctional institution, and individuals with other barriers to educational achievement. Selection is based on academic achievement, letters of reference, and career potential.

Financial data The stipend is $500.

Duration 1 year; the high school senior recipient may apply for a postsecondary award the following year and the postsecondary recipient may apply for a 1-year renewal.

Number awarded 2 each year: 1 to a high school senior and 1 to a current postsecondary student.

Deadline April of each year.

[345]
STUDENT OPPORTUNITY SCHOLARSHIPS OF THE PRESBYTERIAN CHURCH (USA)

Presbyterian Church (USA)
Attn: Office of Financial Aid for Studies
100 Witherspoon Street, Room M-052
Louisville, KY 40202-1396
(502) 569-5224   Toll Free: (800) 728-7228, ext. 5224
Fax: (502) 569-8766   TDD: (800) 833-5955
E-mail: finaid@pcusa.org
Web: gamc.pcusa.org

Summary To provide financial assistance to Presbyterian college students, especially Asian Americans and other racial/ethnic minorities.

Eligibility This program is open to active members of the Presbyterian Church (USA) who are entering their sophomore, junior, or senior year of college as full-time students. Preference is given to applicants who are members of racial/ethnic minority groups (Asian American, African American, Hispanic American, Native American, Alaska Native). Applicants must have a GPA of 2.5 or higher and be able to demonstrate financial need.

Financial data Stipends range up to $2,000 per year, depending upon the financial need of the recipient.

Duration 1 year; may be renewed for up to 3 additional years if the recipient continues to need financial assistance and demonstrates satisfactory academic progress.

Number awarded Varies each year.

Deadline May of each year.

[346]
SUMMER RESEARCH OPPORTUNITIES PROGRAM (SROP)

Committee on Institutional Cooperation
Attn: Academic and International Programs
1819 South Neil Street, Suite D
Champaign, IL 61820-7271
(217) 333-8475   Fax: (217) 244-7127
E-mail: cic@staff.cic.net
Web: www.cic.net/Home/Students/SROP/Home.aspx

Summary To provide an opportunity for Asian Americans and other undergraduates from diverse backgrounds to gain research experience at member institutions of the Committee on Institutional Cooperation (CIC) during the summer.

Eligibility This program is open to students currently enrolled in a degree-granting program at a college or university who have a GPA of 3.0 or higher and an interest in continuing on to graduate school. Applicants must be interested in conducting a summer research project under the supervision of a faculty mentor at a CIC member institution. The pro-

gram is designed to increase educational access for students from diverse backgrounds; members of racial and ethnic minority groups and low-income first-generation students are especially encouraged to apply. U.S. citizenship or permanent resident status is required.

Financial data Participants are paid a stipend that depends on the participating CIC member institution, but ranges from $3,000 to $6,000. Faculty mentors receive a $500 research allowance for the cost of materials.

Duration 8 to 10 weeks during the summer.

Additional information Participants work directly with faculty mentors at the institution of their choice and also engage in other enrichment activities, such as workshops and social gatherings. In July, all participants come together at 1 of the CIC campuses for the annual SROP conference. The participating CIC member institutions are University of Illinois at Urbana-Champaign, University of Iowa, University of Michigan, University of Minnesota, University of Nebraska at Lincoln, University of Wisconsin at Madison, Michigan State University, Northwestern University, Ohio State University, Pennsylvania State University, and Purdue University. Students are required to write a paper and an abstract describing their projects and to present the results of their work at a campus symposium.

Number awarded Varies each year.

Deadline February of each year.

[347]
SUMMER UNDERGRADUATE RESEARCH FELLOWSHIPS IN ORGANIC CHEMISTRY

American Chemical Society
Division of Organic Chemistry
1155 16th Street, N.W.
Washington, DC 20036
(202) 872-4401   Toll Free: (800) 227-5558, ext. 4401
E-mail: division@acs.org
Web: www.organicdivision.org/?nd=p_surf_program

Summary To provide an opportunity for college juniors (particularly Asian Americans and other minorities) to work on a research project in organic chemistry during the summer.

Eligibility This program is open to students who are currently enrolled as juniors at a college or university in the United States and are nominated by their school. Nominees must be interested in conducting a research project in organic chemistry at the home institution during the following summer. The project must be mentored by a member of the Organic Division of the American Chemical Society. Along with their application, students must submit brief statements on the project they propose to undertake, their background that has prepared them to do this work, their proposed methodology, and how a summer research project fits into their long-range plans. U.S. citizenship or permanent resident status is required. Selection is based on demonstrated interest and talent in organic chemistry, merit and feasibility of the research project, commitment of a faculty mentor to support the student, academic record (particularly in organic chemistry and related sciences), and importance of the award in facilitating the personal and career plans of the student. Applications from minorities are especially encouraged.

Financial data Grants range up to $5,000. The program also covers the costs of a trip by all participants to an industrial campus in the fall for a dinner, award session, scientific talks, a tour of the campus, and a poster session where the results of the summer research investigations are presented.

Duration Summer months.

Additional information Current corporate sponsors of this program include Pfizer, Merck, and Genentech.

Number awarded 12 each year.

Deadline February of each year.

[348]
SURETY AND FIDELITY INDUSTRY SCHOLARSHIP PROGRAM

The Surety Foundation
Attn: Scholarship Program for Minority Students
1101 Connecticut Avenue, N.W., Suite 800
Washington, DC 20036
(202) 463-0600   Fax: (202) 463-0606
E-mail: scarradine@surety.org
Web: www.thesuretyfoundation.org

Summary To provide financial assistance to Asian American and other minority undergraduates working on a degree in a field related to insurance.

Eligibility This program is open to full-time undergraduates who are U.S. citizens and members of a minority group (Black, Native American/Alaskan Native, Asian/Pacific Islander, Hispanic). Applicants must have completed at least 30 semester hours of study at an accredited 4-year college or university and have a declared major in insurance/risk management, accounting, business, or finance. They must have a GPA of 3.0 or higher and be able to demonstrate financial need. Along with their application, they must submit an essay of 500 to 1,000 words on the role of surety bonding and the surety industry in public sector construction.

Financial data The stipend is $2,500 per year.

Duration 1 year; recipients may reapply.

Additional information This program, established in 2003 by The Surety & Fidelity Association of America, includes the Adrienne Alexander Scholarship and the George W. McClellan Scholarship.

Number awarded Varies each year.

Deadline April of each year.

[349]
SYNOD OF LAKES AND PRAIRIES RACIAL ETHNIC SCHOLARSHIPS

Synod of Lakes and Prairies
Attn: Committee on Racial Ethnic Ministry
2115 Cliff Drive
Eagen, MN 55122-3327
(651) 357-1140   Toll Free: (800) 328-1880, ext. 202
Fax: (651) 357-1141 E-mail: mkes@lakesandprairies.org
Web: www.lakesandprairies.org

Summary To provide financial assistance to Asian American and other minority residents of the Presbyterian Church (USA) Synod of Lakes and Prairies who are working on an undergraduate or graduate degree at a college or seminary in any state in preparation for service to the church.

Eligibility This program is open to members of Presbyterian churches who reside within the Synod of Lakes and Prairies (Iowa, Minnesota, Nebraska, North Dakota, South Dakota, and Wisconsin). Applicants must be members of eth-

nic minority groups studying at least half time for service in the Presbyterian Church (USA) as a teaching elder, ordained minister, commissioned ruling elder, lay professional, or volunteer. They must be in good academic standing, making progress toward an undergraduate or graduate degree, and able to demonstrate financial need. Along with their application, they must submit essays of 200 to 500 words on 1) what the church needs to do to be faithful to its mission in the world today; and 2) the people, practices, or events that influence their commitment to Christ in ways that renew their fair and strengthen their service.

Financial data Stipends range from $850 to $3,500.

Duration 1 year.

Number awarded Varies each year; recently, 9 of these scholarships were awarded.

Deadline September of each year.

[350]
SYNOD OF THE COVENANT ETHNIC STUDENT SCHOLARSHIPS

Synod of the Covenant
Attn: Ministries in Higher Education Committee
1911 Indianwood Circle, Suite B
Maumee, OH 43537-4063
(419) 754-4050
Toll Free: (800) 848-1030 (within MI and OH)
Fax: (419) 754-4051
E-mail: SOC@synodofthecovenant.org
Web: www.synodofthecovenant.org

Summary To provide financial assistance to Asian American and other ethnic students working on an undergraduate degree at an academic institution in any state (with priority given to Presbyterian applicants from Ohio and Michigan).

Eligibility This program is open to ethnic minority students working full or part time on a baccalaureate degree or certification at a college, university, or vocational school in any state. Applicants must have a GPA of 3.0 or higher and be able to demonstrate participation in a Presbyterian church. Priority is given to Presbyterian applicants from the states of Michigan and Ohio. Financial need is considered in the selection process.

Financial data The maximum amount allowed within a calendar year is $600 (for full-time students in their first year), $800 (for renewals to full-time students), or $400 (for part-time students). Funds are made payable to the session for distribution.

Duration Students are eligible to receive scholarships 1 time per year, up to a maximum of 5 years. Renewals are granted, provided 1) the completed application is received before the deadline date; 2) the recipient earned at least a 2.0 GPA last year; and 3) the application contains evidence of Presbyterian church participation and continued spiritual development.

Number awarded Varies each year.

Deadline August of each year.

[351]
SYNOD OF THE TRINITY RACIAL ETHNIC EDUCATIONAL SCHOLARSHIPS

Synod of the Trinity
Attn: Scholarships
3040 Market Street
Camp Hill, PA 17011-4599
(717) 737-0421, ext. 233
Toll Free: (800) 242-0534, ext. 233
Fax: (717) 737-8211   E-mail: mhumer@syntrinity.org
Web: www.syntrinity.org

Summary   To provide financial assistance to Asian American and other ethnic minority students in Pennsylvania, West Virginia, and designated counties in Ohio who are interested in attending college in any state. Ohio who are interested in attending college in any state.

Eligibility   This program is open to members of a racial minority group (African American, Asian, Hispanic, Latino, Middle Eastern, or Native American) who are enrolled or planning to enroll full time at an accredited college or vocational school in any state. Applicants may be of any religious denomination, but they must be residents of the area covered by the Presbyterian Church (USA) Synod of the Trinity, which covers all of Pennsylvania; West Virginia except for the counties of Berkeley, Grant, Hampshire, Hardy, Jefferson, Mineral, Morgan, and Pendleton; and the Ohio counties of Belmont, Columbiana, Harrison, Jefferson, and Monroe. They must have total income of less than $85,000 for a family of 4. U.S. citizenship or permanent resident status is required.

Financial data   Awards range from $100 to $1,000 per year, depending on the need of the recipient.

Duration   1 year; recipients may reapply.

Number awarded   Varies each year.

Deadline   April of each year.

[352]
TARGET APIASF SCHOLARSHIPS

Asian & Pacific Islander American Scholarship Fund
2025 M Street, N.W., Suite 610
Washington, DC 20036-3363
(202) 986-6892   Toll Free: (877) 808-7032
Fax: (202) 530-0643   E-mail: info@apiasf.org
Web: www.apiasf.org/scholarship_apiasf.html

Summary   To provide financial assistance to Asian and Pacific Islander Americans who are upper-division students, especially those preparing for a career in pharmacy.

Eligibility   This program is open to U.S. citizens, nationals, permanent residents, and citizens of the Freely Associated States who are upper-division college students and of Asian or Pacific Islander heritage. Applicants must be enrolled full time at an accredited college or university in the United States. They must have a GPA of 2.7 or higher or the GED equivalent. In addition, they must complete the FAFSA and apply for federal financial aid. Preference is given to applicants who are preparing for a career in pharmacy.

Financial data   The stipend is $2,500.

Duration   1 year; nonrenewable.

Additional information   This program is sponsored by Target Stores and administered by the Asian & Pacific Islander American Scholarship Fund (APIASF).

Number awarded   Varies each year; recently, 7 of these scholarships were awarded.

Deadline   January of each year.

[353]
TENNESSEE MINORITY TEACHING FELLOWS PROGRAM

Tennessee Student Assistance Corporation
Parkway Towers
404 James Robertson Parkway, Suite 1510
Nashville, TN 37243-0820
(615) 741-1346   Toll Free: (800) 342-1663
Fax: (615) 741-6101   E-mail: TSAC.Aidinfo@tn.gov
Web: www.tn.gov

Summary   To provide funding to Asian American and other minority residents of Tennessee who wish to attend college in the state to prepare for a career in the teaching field.

Eligibility   This program is open to minority residents of Tennessee who are either high school seniors planning to enroll full time at a college or university in the state or continuing college students at a Tennessee college or university. High school seniors must have a GPA of 2.75 or higher and an ACT score of at least 18 or a combined mathematics and critical reading SAT score of at least 860. Continuing college students must have a college GPA of 2.5 or higher. All applicants must agree to teach at the K-12 level in a Tennessee public school following graduation from college. Along with their application, they must submit a 250-word essay on why they chose teaching as a profession. U.S. citizenship is required.

Financial data   The scholarship/loan is $5,000 per year. Recipients incur an obligation to teach at the preK-12 level in a Tennessee public school 1 year for each year the award is received.

Duration   1 year; may be renewed for up to 3 additional years, provided the recipient maintains full-time enrollment and a cumulative GPA of 2.5 or higher.

Additional information   This program began in 1989.

Number awarded   20 new awards are granted each year.

Deadline   April of each year.

[354]
TEXAS CHAPTER AAJA SCHOLARSHIPS

Asian American Journalists Association-Texas Chapter
c/o Scott Nishimura, Scholarship Committee Chair
Fort Worth Star-Telegram
P.O. Box 1870
Fort Worth, TX 76101
(817) 390-7808   E-mail: snishimura@star-telegram.com
Web: www.aajatexas.org/programs/student-programs

Summary   To provide financial assistance to students from designated southwestern states who are working on an undergraduate or graduate degree in journalism and can demonstrate an awareness of Asian American issues.

Eligibility   This program is open to graduating high school seniors, undergraduates, and graduate students who are either 1) residents of Arkansas, Louisiana, New Mexico, Oklahoma, or Texas; or 2) attending or planning to attend an accredited college or university in those states. Applicants are not required to be members of the Asian American Journalists Association (AAJA). Along with their application, they must submit a 250-word autobiography that explains why they are interested in a career in journalism, a 500-word essay on the role of ethnic diversity in news coverage (both for the subjects of the news events and also the journalists involved), their most recent official transcript, 2 letters of recommendation, and a resume. Work samples to be submitted are 3 legible clips from print journalism students; 3 to 5 prints or slides with captions or descriptions from print photojournalism students; 3 to 5 samples of work from design journalism students; 2 taped VHS or DVD excerpts with corresponding scripts from television broadcast students; 2 edited VHS or DVD excepts from television photojournalism students; 3 taped cassette excerpts with corresponding scripts from radio broadcast students; or 3 legible online articles from web journalism students. Selection is based on commitment to journalism, awareness of Asian American issues, journalistic ability, and scholastic ability.

Financial data The stipend is $1,000.

Duration 1 year.

Additional information Scholarship winners are also given a 1-year free membership in the AAJA Texas chapter.

Number awarded 2 each year.

Deadline May of each year.

[355]
THAI-AMERICAN ASSOCIATION OF ILLINOIS SCHOLARSHIP FUND

Thai-American Association of Illinois
2115 Warwick Lane
Glenview, IL 60026
(847) 899-0313   E-mail: apply@taaischolarshipfund.org
Web: www.taaischolarshipfund.org

Summary To provide financial assistance to high school seniors in Illinois who are of Thai descent and planning to attend college in any state.

Eligibility This program is open to seniors graduating from high schools in Illinois who are of Thai descent. Applicants must be planning to enroll at a college or university in any state. They must have a GPA of 2.75 or higher and be able to demonstrate financial need. Along with their application, they must submit an essay about their current situation, aspirations, and/or life goals.

Financial data The stipend is $1,000.

Duration 1 year.

Additional information This program began in 2011.

Number awarded 2 each year.

Deadline October of each year.

[356]
THE LUCKY FEW SCHOLARSHIP CONTEST

Federal Asian Pacific American Council Southwest
P.O. Box 710843
San Diego, CA 92171
E-mail: theluckyfew.mayman@gmail.com

Summary To recognize and reward, with college scholarships, middle school, high school, and college students who submit outstanding essays on the fall of the Republic of Vietnam and its relationship to their families.

Eligibility This competition is open to 3 categories of students: grades 7-9, grades 10-12, and college (19 to 23 years of age). Applicants must submit an essay (1,000 words for middle school students, 1,500 words for high school and college students) that covers the following themes: the historical context of the fall of the Republic of Vietnam, the humanitarian role played by elements of the U.S. Departments of Defense and State, the evolution of the Vietnamese American community, and their family history, including their extended family's story of escape from Vietnam and resettlement in America.

Financial data Awards are presented in the form of college scholarships (value not specified).

Duration The competition is held annually.

Number awarded 15 each year: 5 in each of the categories.

Deadline Applications must be submitted by February of each year.

[357]
THE REV. J.K. FUKUSHIMA SCHOLARSHIP

Montebello Plymouth Congregational Church
144 South Greenwood Avenue
Montebello, CA 90640
(323) 721-5568   Fax: (323) 721-7955
E-mail: mpccucc@yahoo.com
Web: www.montebelloucc.org

Summary To provide financial assistance to undergraduate and graduate students who are preparing for a career in Christian ministry and can demonstrate a commitment to the Asian American community.

Eligibility This program is open to 1) third- or fourth-year college students; and 2) graduate and professional students who have not completed a bachelor's or master's degree in theological studies. Applicants must be enrolled or have been accepted at an accredited school of theology. They must be working on a degree that will provide them with the skills and understanding necessary to further the development of Christian ministries. Along with their application, they must submit an essay on their commitment to the Asian American community.

Financial data The stipend is $500.

Duration 1 year.

Number awarded 1 or more each year.

Deadline May of each year.

[358]
THOMAS G. NEUSOM SCHOLARSHIPS

Conference of Minority Transportation Officials
Attn: National Scholarship Program
1875 I Street, N.W., Suite 500
Washington, DC 20006
(703) 234-4072   Fax: (202) 318-0364
Web: www.comto.org/?page=Scholarships

Summary To provide financial assistance for college or graduate school to Asian American and other members of the Conference of Minority Transportation Officials (COMTO).

Eligibility This program is open to undergraduate and graduate students who have been members of COMTO for at least 1 year. Applicants must be working (either full or part time) on a degree in a field related to transportation and have a GPA of 2.5 or higher. Along with their application, they must submit a cover letter with a 500-word statement of career goals. Financial need is not considered in the selection process. U.S. citizenship or legal resident status is required.

Financial data The stipend is $5,500. Funds are paid directly to the recipient's college or university.

Duration 1 year.

Additional information COMTO was established in 1971 to promote, strengthen, and expand the roles of minorities in all aspects of transportation. Recipients are expected to attend the COMTO National Scholarship Luncheon.

Number awarded 1 each year.

Deadline May of each year.

[359]
THZ FO FARM SCHOLARSHIP

Hawai'i Community Foundation
Attn: Scholarship Department
827 Fort Street Mall
Honolulu, HI 96813
(808) 566-5570   Toll Free: (888) 731-3863
Fax: (808) 521-6286
E-mail: scholarships@hcf-hawaii.org
Web: www.hawaiicommunityfoundation.org/scholarships

Summary To provide financial assistance to Hawaii residents of Chinese descent who are interested in working on an undergraduate or graduate degree in any field at a school in any state.

Eligibility This program is open to high school seniors, high school graduates, and college students in Hawaii who are of Chinese ancestry and interested in studying any field as full-time undergraduate or graduate students at a college or university in any state. Applicants must be able to demonstrate academic achievement (GPA of 2.7 or higher), good moral character, and financial need. Along with their application, they must submit a short statement indicating their reasons for attending college, their planned course of study, their career goals, and what community service means to them.

Financial data The amounts of the awards depend on the availability of funds and the need of the recipient. Recently, the average value of each of the scholarships awarded by the foundation was $2,200.

Duration 1 year.

Number awarded Varies each year; recently, 6 of these scholarships were awarded.

Deadline February of each year.

[360]
TONGAN CULTURAL SOCIETY SCHOLARSHIPS

Hawai'i Community Foundation
Attn: Scholarship Department
827 Fort Street Mall
Honolulu, HI 96813
(808) 566-5570   Toll Free: (888) 731-3863
Fax: (808) 521-6286
E-mail: scholarships@hcf-hawaii.org
Web: www.hawaiicommunityfoundation.org/scholarships

Summary To provide financial assistance to Hawaii residents of Tongan ancestry who are interested in attending college or graduate school in the state.

Eligibility This program is open to Hawaii residents of Tongan ancestry who are enrolled in or planning to enroll in an accredited college or university in Hawaii. Applicants must be

full-time undergraduate or graduate students and able to demonstrate academic achievement (GPA of 2.7 or higher), good moral character, and financial need. Along with their application, they must submit a short statement indicating their reasons for attending college, their planned course of study, their career goals, and what community service means to them.

Financial data The amounts of the awards depend on the availability of funds and the need of the recipient. Recently, the average value of each of the scholarships awarded by the foundation was $2,200.

Duration 1 year.

Number awarded Varies each year; recently, 3 of these scholarships were awarded.

Deadline February of each year.

[361]
TRAILBLAZER SCHOLARSHIP

Conference of Minority Transportation Officials
Attn: National Scholarship Program
1875 I Street, N.W., Suite 500
Washington, DC 20006
(703) 234-4072   Fax: (202) 318-0364
Web: www.comto.org/?page=Scholarships

Summary To provide financial assistance to Asian American and other minority undergraduate and graduate students working on a degree in a field related to transportation.

Eligibility This program is open to minority undergraduate and graduate students who are working (either full or part time) on a degree in a field related to transportation and have a GPA of 2.5 or higher. Along with their application, they must submit a cover letter with a 500-word statement of career goals. Financial need is not considered in the selection process. U.S. citizenship or legal resident status is required.

Financial data The stipend is $2,500. Funds are paid directly to the recipient's college or university.

Duration 1 year.

Additional information The Conference of Minority Transportation Officials (COMTO) was established in 1971 to promote, strengthen, and expand the roles of minorities in all aspects of transportation. Recipients are expected to attend the COMTO National Scholarship Luncheon.

Number awarded 1 each year.

Deadline May of each year.

[362]
TYLER J. VINEY MEMORIAL SCHOLARSHIP

Texas Society of Architects
Attn: Texas Architectural Foundation
500 Chicon Street
Austin, TX 78702
(512) 478-7386   Fax: (512) 478-0528
E-mail: jallison@texasarchitect.org
Web: texasarchitects.org/v/scholarships

Summary To provide financial assistance to residents of any state (particularly Asian Americans, other minorities, and women) who are entering their fourth or fifth year of study at a school of architecture in Texas.

Eligibility This program is open to residents of any state who are entering their fourth or fifth year of study at 1 of the 8 schools of architecture in Texas. Applicants must submit their application to the office of the dean of their school. Selection is based on potential architectural talent, demonstrated interest in photography, and financial need. Priority is given to female and minority students.

Financial data   The stipend is $700.

Duration   1 year.

Number awarded   1 each year.

Deadline   Deadline not specified.

[363]
UNITED HEALTH FOUNDATION APIASF SCHOLARSHIP

Asian & Pacific Islander American Scholarship Fund
2025 M Street, N.W., Suite 610
Washington, DC 20036-3363
(202) 986-6892   Toll Free: (877) 808-7032
Fax: (202) 530-0643   E-mail: info@apiasf.org
Web: www.apiasf.org/scholarship_apiasf.html

Summary   To provide financial assistance to Asian and Pacific Islander Americans who are entering college for the first time to prepare for a career in the health field.

Eligibility   This program is open to U.S. citizens, nationals, permanent residents, or citizens of the Freely Associated States who are of Asian or Pacific Islander heritage. Applicants must be enrolling full time at an accredited 2- or 4-year college or university in the United States as a first-year student; preference is given to students entering a 2-year institution and planning to transfer to a 4-year school. They must have a GPA of 2.7 or higher or the GED equivalent and be preparing for a career in the health field. In addition, they must complete the FAFSA and apply for federal financial aid. Preference is given to students who 1) demonstrate the intent to work in an underserved community; 2) are fluent in an Asian or Pacific Islander language; or 3) reside in or attend college in the sponsor's priority states of California, Illinois, New Jersey, New York, or Texas.

Financial data   The stipend is $5,000 per year.

Duration   3 years.

Additional information   This scholarship is sponsored by the United Health Foundation and administered by the Asian & Pacific Islander American Scholarship Fund (APIASF).

Number awarded   Varies each year; recently, 25 of these scholarships were awarded.

Deadline   January of each year.

[364]
UNITED METHODIST DOLLARS FOR SCHOLARS PROGRAM

United Methodist Higher Education Foundation
Attn: Scholarships Administrator
60 Music Square East, Suite 350
P.O. Box 340005
Nashville, TN 37203-0005
(615) 649-3990   Toll Free: (800) 811-8110
Fax: (615) 649-3980
E-mail: umhefscholarships@umhef.org
Web: www.umhef.org/UMDFSapp.php

Summary   To provide financial assistance to Asian American and other students at Methodist colleges, universities, and seminaries whose home churches agree to contribute to their support.

Eligibility   The Double Your Dollars for Scholars program is open to students attending or planning to attend a United Methodist-related college, university, or seminary as a full-time student. Applicants must have been an active, full member of a United Methodist Church for at least 1 year prior to applying. Their home church must nominate them and agree to contribute to their support. Many of the United Methodist colleges and universities have also agreed to contribute matching funds for a Triple Your Dollars for Scholars Program, and a few United Methodist conference foundations have agreed to contribute additional matching funds for a Quadruple Your Dollars for Scholars Program. Awards are granted on a first-come, first-served basis. Some of the awards are designated for Hispanic, Asian, and Native American (HANA) students funded by the General Board of Higher Education and Ministry.

Financial data   The sponsoring church contributes $1,000 and the United Methodist Higher Education Foundation (UMHEF) contributes a matching $1,000. Students who attend a participating United Methodist college or university receive an additional $1,000 for the Triple Your Dollars for Scholars Program, and those from a participating conference receive a fourth $1,000 increment for the Quadruple Your Dollars for Scholars Program.

Duration   1 year; may be renewed as long as the recipients maintain satisfactory academic progress as defined by their institution.

Additional information   Currently, participants in the Double Your Dollars for Scholars program include 1 United Methodist seminary and theological school, 1 professional school, 19 senior colleges and universities, and 1 2-year college. The Triple Your Dollars for Scholars program includes an additional 12 United Methodist seminaries and theological schools, 72 senior colleges and universities, and 4 2-year colleges (for a complete list, consult the UMHEF). The conference foundations participating in the Quadruple Your Dollars for Scholars Program are limited to the Alabama-West Florida United Methodist Foundation, the East Ohio United Methodist Foundation, the Kentucky United Methodist Foundation, the Missouri United Methodist Foundation (for students at Saint Paul School of Theology or Central Methodist University), the Nashville Area United Methodist Foundation, the North Carolina United Methodist Foundation (for students at Louisburg College, Methodist University, or North Carolina Wesleyan College), the Georgia United Methodist Foundation, the Oklahoma United Methodist Foundation (for students at Oklahoma City University), the United Methodist Foundation of Arkansas, and the United Methodist Foundation of Western North Carolina.

Number awarded   350 each year, including 25 designated for HANA students.

Deadline   Local churches must submit applications in February of each year for senior colleges, universities, and seminaries or May of each year for 2-year colleges.

[365]
UNITED METHODIST ETHNIC MINORITY SCHOLARSHIPS

United Methodist Church
Attn: General Board of Higher Education and Ministry
Office of Loans and Scholarships
1001 19th Avenue South
P.O. Box 340007
Nashville, TN 37203-0007
(615) 340-7344   Fax: (615) 340-7367
E-mail: umscholar@gbhem.org
Web: www.gbhem.org

Summary To provide financial assistance to Asian Americans and other undergraduate Methodist students of ethnic minority ancestry.

Eligibility This program is open to full-time undergraduate students at accredited colleges and universities in the United States who have been active, full members of a United Methodist Church for at least 1 year prior to applying. Applicants must have at least 1 parent who is African American, Hispanic, Asian, Native American, or Pacific Islander. They must have a GPA of 2.5 or higher and be able to demonstrate financial need. U.S. citizenship, permanent resident status, or membership in a central conference of the United Methodist Church is required. Selection is based on church membership, involvement in church and community activities, GPA, and financial need.

Financial data Stipends range from $500 to $1,000.

Duration 1 year; recipients may reapply.

Number awarded Varies each year.

Deadline February of each year.

[366]
UNITED PARCEL SERVICE SCHOLARSHIP FOR MINORITY STUDENTS

Institute of Industrial Engineers
Attn: Scholarship Coordinator
3577 Parkway Lane, Suite 200
Norcross, GA 30092
(770) 449-0461, ext. 105   Toll Free: (800) 494-0460
Fax: (770) 441-3295   E-mail: bcameron@iienet.org
Web: www.iienet2.org/Details.aspx?id=857

Summary To provide financial assistance to Asian American and other minority undergraduates who are studying industrial engineering at a school in the United States, Canada, or Mexico.

Eligibility Eligible to be nominated are minority undergraduate students enrolled at any school in the United States or its territories, Canada, or Mexico, provided the school's engineering program is accredited by an agency recognized by the Institute of Industrial Engineers (IIE) and the student is pursuing a full-time course of study in industrial engineering with a GPA of at least 3.4. Nominees must have at least 5 full quarters or 3 full semesters remaining until graduation. Students may not apply directly for these awards; they must be nominated by the head of their industrial engineering department. Nominees must be IIE members. Selection is based on scholastic ability, character, leadership, and potential service to the industrial engineering profession.

Financial data The stipend is $4,000.

Duration 1 year.

Additional information Funding for this program is provided by the UPS Foundation.

Number awarded 1 each year.

Deadline Schools must submit nominations by November of each year.

[367]
UPAKAR COMMUNITY COLLEGE SCHOLARSHIPS

Upakar: Indian American Scholarship Foundation
9101 Friars Road
Bethesda, MD 20817
E-mail: upakarfoundation@hotmail.com
Web: www.upakarfoundation.org

Summary To provide financial assistance to Indian American (from India) high school seniors who plan to attend a community college and major in any field.

Eligibility This program is open to graduating high school seniors who either were born or have at least 1 parent who was born in the Republic of India. Applicants must be planning to enroll at a community college and then transfer to a 4-year institution. They must be U.S. citizens or permanent residents and have a GPA of 3.6 or higher. Their family income must be less than $75,000 per year.

Financial data The stipend is $500 per year for the first 2 years and $2,000 per year for the remaining 2 years.

Duration Up to 4 years, provided the recipient maintains a GPA of 3.3 or higher.

Additional information This program began in 2013.

Number awarded Varies each year.

Deadline April of each year.

[368]
UPAKAR SCHOLARSHIPS

Upakar: Indian American Scholarship Foundation
9101 Friars Road
Bethesda, MD 20817
E-mail: upakarfoundation@hotmail.com
Web: www.upakarfoundation.org

Summary To provide financial assistance to Indian (from India) high school seniors who plan to attend a 4-year college and major in any field.

Eligibility This program is open to graduating high school seniors who either were born or have at least 1 parent who was born in the Republic of India. Applicants must be planning to enroll at a 4-year college or university and major in any field. They must be U.S. citizens or permanent residents and have a GPA of 3.6 or higher. Their family income must be less than $75,000 per year.

Financial data The stipend is $2,000 per year.

Duration Up to 4 years, provided the recipient maintains a GPA of 3.3 or higher.

Number awarded Varies each year; recently, 6 of these scholarships were awarded.

Deadline April of each year.

[369]
UPS GOLD MOUNTAIN SCHOLARSHIP

Organization of Chinese Americans, Inc.
1322 18th Street, N.W.
Washington, DC 20036-1803
(202) 223-5500   Fax: (202) 296-0540
E-mail: oca@ocanational.org
Web: www.ocanational.org/?page=Programs_Scholarship

Summary To provide financial assistance for college to Asian Pacific Americans who are the first person in their family to attend an institution of higher education.

Eligibility This program is open to graduating high school seniors of Asian and/or Pacific Islander ethnicity who are entering their first year at a college, university, or community college in the following fall. Applicants must be the first person in their immediate family to attend college, have a cumulative GPA of 3.0 or higher, be able to demonstrate financial need, and be a U.S. citizen, national, or permanent resident.

Financial data The stipend is $2,000.

Duration 1 year.

Additional information This program, established in 1999, is funded by the UPS Foundation and administered by the Organization of Chinese Americans (OCA).

Number awarded 15 each year.

Deadline April of each year.

[370]
US PAN ASIAN AMERICAN CHAMBER OF COMMERCE SCHOLARSHIPS

US Pan Asian American Chamber of Commerce
Attn: Scholarship Coordinator
1329 18th Street, N.W.
Washington, DC 20036
(202) 296-5221   Toll Free: (800) 696-7818
Fax: (202) 296-5225   E-mail: info@uspaacc.com
Web: www.uspaacc.com/programs/college-scholarships

Summary To provide financial assistance for college to Asian Pacific American high school seniors who demonstrate financial need.

Eligibility This program is open to high school seniors of Asian or Pacific Islander heritage who are U.S. citizens or permanent residents. Applicants must be planning to enroll full time at an accredited postsecondary educational institution in the United States. Along with their application, they must submit a 500-word essay on their background, achievements, and personal goals. Selection is based on academic excellence (GPA of 3.3 or higher), leadership in extracurricular activities, community service involvement, and financial need.

Financial data Stipends range from $2,500 to $5,000. Funds are paid directly to the recipient's college or university.

Duration 1 year.

Additional information This program includes awards named after sponsoring corporations; recently, those included AT&T, D&D Unlimited, Enterprise Holdings, ExxonMobil Corporation, National Capitol Contracting, PepsiCo, PEMCO Foundation, Southern California Edison, Target, TEOCO Corporation, and UPS Foundation. Funding is not provided for correspondence courses, Internet courses, or study in a country other than the United States.

Number awarded Varies each year; recently, 16 of these scholarships were awarded.

Deadline March of each year.

[371]
VANG PAO SCHOLARSHIP

Hmong American Education Fund
P.O. Box 17468
St. Paul, MN 55117
(651) 230-3634   E-mail: scholarships@thehaef.org
Web: www.thehaef.org

Summary To provide financial assistance to Hmong undergraduate and graduate students who demonstrate leadership.

Eligibility This program is open to students of Hmong descent who are currently enrolled as full-time undergraduate or graduate students at public 2- or 4-year colleges or universities in any state. Applicants must be U.S. citizens or permanent residents and have a GPA of 3.0 or higher. Along with their application, they must submit a 1,500-word essay on their commitment to education, their leadership qualities, their financial need, how this scholarship can help them, and their community service. Selection is based on academic excellence, leadership qualities, commitment to helping their community, and financial need.

Financial data The stipend is $2,500.

Duration 1 year; nonrenewable.

Number awarded 1 each year.

Deadline March of each year.

[372]
VANGUARD MINORITY SCHOLARSHIP PROGRAM

Scholarship America
Attn: Scholarship Management Services
One Scholarship Way
P.O. Box 297
St. Peter, MN 56082
(507) 931-1682   Toll Free: (800) 537-4180
Fax: (507) 931-9168
Web: sms.scholarshipamerica.org/vanguard/index.html

Summary To provide financial assistance to Asian American and other minority students working on an undergraduate degree in specified fields.

Eligibility This program is open to U.S. citizens and permanent residents who are members of racial or ethnic minorities. Applicants must be entering their junior or senior year as a full-time student at an accredited 4-year college or university in the United States and have a GPA of 3.0 or higher. They must be working on a degree in accounting, business, economics, or finance. Selection is based on academic record, demonstrated leadership and participation in school and community activities, honors, work experience, a statement of goals and aspirations, unusual personal or family circumstances, recommendations, and a resume; financial need is not considered. Students who attended a 2-year college while working on a bachelor's degree are not eligible.

Financial data The stipend ranges up to $10,000.

Duration 1 year; nonrenewable.

Additional information This program, established in 2004, is sponsored by Vanguard Group, Inc.

Number awarded   Up to 10 each year.

Deadline   November of each year.

[373]
VERIZON APIASF SCHOLARSHIP

Asian & Pacific Islander American Scholarship Fund
2025 M Street, N.W., Suite 610
Washington, DC 20036-3363
(202) 986-6892   Toll Free: (877) 808-7032
Fax: (202) 530-0643   E-mail: info@apiasf.org
Web: www.apiasf.org/scholarship_apiasf.html

Summary   To provide financial assistance to Asian and Pacific Islander Americans who are enrolled at or entering college.

Eligibility   This program is open to U.S. citizens, nationals, permanent residents, or citizens of the Freely Associated States who are of Asian or Pacific Islander heritage. Applicants must be enrolling full time at an accredited 2- or 4-year college or university in the United States; preference is given to students entering their sophomore, junior, or senior year, but incoming freshmen are also eligible. They must have a GPA of 3.0 or higher or the GED equivalent. In addition, they must complete the FAFSA and apply for federal financial aid. Preference is given to residents of Maine, New Hampshire, New Jersey, Washington, and Washington, D.C. and of selected cities and counties within California, Florida, Massachusetts, New York, Pennsylvania, Texas, and Virginia.

Financial data   The stipend is $3,000.

Duration   1 year.

Additional information   This scholarship is sponsored by Verizon and administered by the Asian & Pacific Islander American Scholarship Fund (APIASF).

Number awarded   Varies each year; recently, 3 of these scholarships were awarded.

Deadline   January of each year.

[374]
VIETNAMESE AMERICAN ASSOCIATION OF MAINE SCHOLARSHIPS

Vietnamese American Association of Maine
P.O. Box 513
Saco, ME 04072
E-mail: admin@vaaminfo.org
Web: www.vaaminfo.org/?p=874

Summary   To provide financial assistance to Vietnamese American residents of Maine who are interested in attending college in any state.

Eligibility   This program is open to Vietnamese American residents of Maine who are enrolled or planning to enroll at a college or university in any state. Applicants must use their choice of medium (e.g., poetry, drawing, painting, photography, videography, essay) to express their view of the Vietnamese American community in Maine (1 sheet, 1 minute, or 150 words). Selection is based on that submission, academic achievement, community involvement, and financial need.

Financial data   The stipend is $500.

Duration   1 year.

Number awarded   4 each year.

Deadline   March of each year.

[375]
VIETNAMESE AMERICAN DREAMS SCHOLARSHIP

New England Intercollegiate Vietnamese Student
   Association
c/o Jenny Le
223 Eliot Mail Center
101 Dunster Street
Cambridge, MA 02138
(781) 891-2000   E-mail: jennyle@college.harvard.edu
Web: ivsamass.weebly.com/scholarship.html

Summary   To provide financial assistance to New England high school seniors of Vietnamese descent who plan to attend college in any state.

Eligibility   This program is open to seniors graduating from high schools in New England who are of Vietnamese descent. Applicants must be planning to enroll at a college or university in any state. Along with their application, they must submit 500-word essays on 1 of the following topics: 1) an experience the encountered as a Vietnamese American that shaped the way they think about being Vietnamese American; or 2) how their Vietnamese heritage has influenced their dreams and aspirations. They must also submit a 500-word essay on a main issue that the Vietnamese or Vietnamese American community faces and what they recommend to do about it. Selection is based on academics, community involvement, and character. Finalists are contacted for interviews.

Financial data   The stipend is $1,000 or $500.

Duration   1 year.

Additional information   This program began in 2001.

Number awarded   2 each year: 1 at $1,000 and 1 at $500.

Deadline   March of each year.

[376]
VIETNAMESE AMERICAN SCHOLARSHIP FOUNDATION ELEVATE SCHOLARSHIP

Vietnamese American Scholarship Foundation
P.O. Box 429
Stafford, TX 77497
E-mail: scholarships@vietscholarships.org
Web: www.vietscholarships.org/scholarships.html

Summary   To provide financial assistance to residents of any state who are of Vietnamese descent and interested in attending college.

Eligibility   This program is open to residents of any state who are of Vietnamese descent and either seniors graduating from high school or students already enrolled at an accredited 4-year college or university. Applicants must have a GPA of 3.5 or higher and be able to demonstrate financial need. Along with their application, they must submit a 1,000-word essay on a project, experience, or person related to their academic and/or career goals that inspired them. They must have a record of academic excellence, community service, and leadership.

Financial data   The stipend is $2,000.

Duration   1 year; nonrenewable.

Number awarded   1 each year.

Deadline   May of each year.

[377]
VINCENT CHIN MEMORIAL SCHOLARSHIP

Asian American Journalists Association
Attn: Student Programs Coordinator
5 Third Street, Suite 1108
San Francisco, CA 94103
(415) 346-2051, ext. 102   Fax: (415) 346-6343
E-mail: programs@aaja.org
Web: www.aaja.org/vincent-chin-scholarship

Summary To provide financial assistance to student members of the Asian American Journalists Association (AAJA) who are high school seniors, undergraduates, or graduate students and interested in preparing for a career in journalism.

Eligibility This program is open to AAJA members who are working or planning to work full time on an undergraduate or graduate degree in journalism. Applicants must submit a brief essay on their choice of 4 topics: 1) could the attack that killed Vincent Chin happen again; 2) how Asian Americans are a single people; 3) should Asian Americans protest or conform in the face of incidents such as the murder of Vincent Chin; or 4) who was Lily Chin. Selection is based on academic achievement, commitment to journalism, sensitivity to Asian American and Pacific Islander issues, demonstrated journalistic ability, and financial need.

Financial data The stipend is $500.

Duration 1 year.

Number awarded 1 each year.

Deadline May of each year.

[378]
VIRGINIA ASIAN CHAMBER OF COMMERCE STUDENT SCHOLARSHIPS

Virginia Asian Chamber of Commerce
Attn: My Lan Tran, Executive Director
P.O. Box 2640
Glen Allen, VA 23058
(804) 798-3975   E-mail: aabac@aabac.org
Web: www.aabac.org/vacc-gala-event/scholarship-awards

Summary To provide financial assistance to Asian American students from Virginia interested in working on an undergraduate or graduate degree in any field.

Eligibility This program is open to seniors graduating from high schools in Virginia and students currently enrolled in an undergraduate or graduate program at a college or university in the state. Applicants must be interested in fulfilling the sponsor's goal of promoting the "entrepreneurial spirit in Asian and other students within the context of global business opportunities and challenges." They must have a GPA of 3.0 or higher and be working on a degree in a business-related or any other academic area. Along with their application, they must submit a statement of their interest in a business, entrepreneurship, or related field.

Financial data Stipends are $1,000 or $500.

Duration 1 year.

Number awarded Varies each year; recently, 4 of these scholarships were awarded: 3 at $1,000 and 1 at $500.

Deadline October of each year.

[379]
VIRGINIA NURSE PRACTITIONER/NURSE MIDWIFE SCHOLARSHIP PROGRAM

Virginia Department of Health
Attn: Office of Minority Health and Public Health Policy
109 Governor Street, Suite 1016 East
Richmond, VA 23219
(804) 864-7435   Fax: (804) 864-7440
E-mail: IncentivePrograms@vdh.virginia.gov
Web: www.vdh.virginia.gov

Summary To provide funding to nursing students in Virginia (particularly Asian Americans and other minorities) who are willing to work as nurse practitioners and/or midwives in the state following graduation.

Eligibility This program is open to residents of Virginia who are enrolled or accepted for enrollment full or part time at a nurse practitioner program in the state or a nurse midwifery program in Virginia or a nearby state. Applicants must have a cumulative GPA of at least 3.0 in undergraduate and/or graduate courses. Preference is given to 1) residents of designated medically underserved areas of Virginia; 2) students enrolled in family practice, obstetrics and gynecology, pediatric, adult health, and geriatric nurse practitioner programs; and 3) minority students. Selection is based on scholastic achievement, character, and stated commitment to postgraduate employment in a medically underserved area of Virginia.

Financial data The stipend is $5,000 per year. Recipients must agree to serve in a designated medically underserved area of Virginia for a period of years equal to the number of years of scholarship support received. The required service must begin within 2 years of the recipient's graduation and must be in a facility that provides services to persons who are unable to pay for the service and that participates in all government-sponsored insurance programs designed to assure full access to medical care service for covered persons. If the recipient fails to complete the course of study, or pass the licensing examination, or provide the required service, all scholarship funds received must be repaid with interest and a penalty.

Duration 1 year; may be renewed for 1 additional year.

Number awarded Up to 5 each year.

Deadline June of each year.

[380]
VOCATIONAL TRAINING/GED SCHOLARSHIP FUND

Lao American Women Association
Attn: Scholarship Committee
3908 Carroll Court
Chantilly, VA 20151
(703) 283-8698   E-mail: info@lawadc.org
Web: www.lawadc.org

Summary To provide financial assistance to women of Lao ancestry in the Washington, D.C. area who need additional training to find a job.

Eligibility This program is open to women in the Washington, D.C. metropolitan area who are of Lao parentage. Applicants must be in need of additional training to find a job, to obtain work at a higher level, or to complete a GED certificate. They must provide information on their personal situation, proposed training program, work experience, family and community activities, and financial situation. They must also submit a 150-word personal statement on their family and community activities. Financial need is considered in the selection process (must have family income less than $75,000 per year).

Financial data The stipend is $1,000 for vocational training or $500 for GED completion.

Duration 1 year.

Number awarded Either 1 scholarship for vocational training or 2 for GED completion are awarded each year.

Deadline April of each year.

[381]
VSCPA MINORITY ACCOUNTING SCHOLARSHIPS

Virginia Society of Certified Public Accountants
Attn: Educational Foundation
4309 Cox Road
Glen Allen, VA 23060
(804) 612-9427   Toll Free: (800) 733-8272
Fax: (804) 273-1741   E-mail: info@vscpafoundation.com
Web: www.vscpa.com

Summary To provide financial assistance to Asian American and other minority students enrolled in an undergraduate accounting program in Virginia.

Eligibility Applicants must be minority students (African American or Black, Hispanic or Latino, American Indian or Native Alaskan, Asian, Native Hawaiian or other Pacific Islander) currently enrolled in a Virginia college or university undergraduate accounting program. They must be U.S. citizens, be majoring in accounting, have completed at least 3 hours of accounting, be currently registered for 3 more credit hours of accounting and have a GPA of 3.0 or higher. Along with their application, they must submit a 500-word essay on assigned topics. Selection is based on the essay, their most recent transcript, a current resume, a faculty letter of recommendation, and financial need.

Financial data The stipend is $1,000.

Duration 1 year.

Number awarded Varies each year; recently, 2 of these scholarships were awarded.

Deadline March of each year.

[382]
WAKE FOREST UNIVERSITY SCHOOL OF MEDICINE EXCELLENCE IN CARDIOVASCULAR SCIENCES SUMMER RESEARCH PROGRAM

Wake Forest University School of Medicine
Attn: Hypertension and Vascular Research Center
Medical Center Boulevard
Winston-Salem, NC 27157-1032
(336) 716-1080   Fax: (336) 716-2456
E-mail: nsarver@wakehealth.edu
Web: www.wakehealth.edu

Summary To provide Asian American and other underrepresented or disadvantaged students with an opportunity to engage in a summer research project in cardiovascular science at Wake Forest University in Winston-Salem, North Carolina.

Eligibility This program is open to undergraduates and master's degree students who are members of underrepresented minority groups (African Americans, Alaskan Natives, Asian Americans, Native Americans, Pacific Islanders, and Hispanics) or who come from disadvantaged backgrounds (e.g., rural areas, first-generation college students). Applicants must be interested in participating in a program of summer research in the cardiovascular sciences that includes "hands-on" laboratory research, a lecture series by faculty and guest speakers, and a research symposium at which students present their research findings. U.S. citizenship or permanent resident status is required.

Financial data The stipend is $1,731 per month, housing in a university dormitory, and round-trip transportation expense.

Duration 2 months during the summer.

Additional information This program is sponsored by the National Heart, Lung, and Blood Institute (NHLBI) of the National Institutes of Health (NIH).

Number awarded Approximately 12 each year.

Deadline February of each year.

[383]
WALTER U. LUM HIGH SCHOOL SCHOLARSHIPS

Chinese American Citizens Alliance
1044 Stockton Street
San Francisco, CA 94108
(415) 434-2222   E-mail: info@cacanational.org
Web: www.cacanational.org/purpose

Summary To provide financial assistance for college to Chinese American high school students.

Eligibility This program is open to students of Chinese descent who are high school seniors or recent graduates planning to attend college. Preference is given to U.S. citizens. Applicants must submit a copy of their high school transcripts, starting with grades 9 or 10; an essay (up to 500 words) that describes their community activities, college scholastic goals, career goals, and personal outlook; and 2 reference letters. Selection is based on academic achievement, campus and community extracurricular activities, career goals and personal outlook, and the quality of the essay.

Financial data The stipend is $500.

Duration 1 year; nonrenewable.

Additional information Students must submit their applications and supporting information to their local lodge of the Chinese American Citizens Alliance; applications directly submitted by students are not accepted.

Number awarded 2 each odd-numbered year.

Deadline April of each odd-numbered year.

[384]
WALTER U. LUM UNDERGRADUATE SCHOLARSHIP

Chinese American Citizens Alliance
1044 Stockton Street
San Francisco, CA 94108
(415) 434-2222   E-mail: info@cacanational.org
Web: www.cacanational.org/purpose

Summary To provide financial assistance to Chinese American undergraduate students.

Eligibility This program is open to students of Chinese descent who have completed the sophomore year of college. Preference is given to U.S. citizens. Applicants must submit a copy of their college transcripts; copies of their and their parents' latest income tax returns; copies of successful applications for financial aid; an essay (up to 500 words) that describes their community activities, career goals, and personal outlook; and 2 reference letters. Selection is based on academic achievement, campus and community extracurricular activities, career goals and personal outlook, quality of the essay, and financial need.

Financial data The stipend is $2,000.

Duration 1 year; nonrenewable.

Additional information Students must submit their applications and supporting information to their local lodge of the Chinese American Citizens Alliance; applications directly submitted by students are not accepted.

Number awarded 2 each odd-numbered year.

Deadline April of each odd-numbered year.

[385]
WARNER NORCROSS & JUDD PARALEGAL ASSISTANT SCHOLARSHIP

Grand Rapids Community Foundation
Attn: Education Program Officer
185 Oakes Street S.W.
Grand Rapids, MI 49503-4008
(616) 454-1751, ext. 103   Fax: (616) 454-6455
E-mail: rbishop@grfoundation.org
Web: www.grfoundation.org/scholarshipslist

Summary To provide financial assistance to Asian and other minority residents of Michigan who are interested in working on a paralegal studies degree at an institution in the state.

Eligibility This program is open to residents of Michigan who are students of color attending or planning to attend an accredited public or private 2- or 4-year college or university in the state. Applicants must have a declared major in paralegal/legal assistant studies. They must be U.S. citizens or permanent residents and have a GPA of 2.5 or higher. Financial need is considered in the selection process.

Financial data The stipend is $2,000. Funds are paid directly to the recipient's institution.

Duration 1 year.

Additional information Funding for this program is provided by the law firm Warner Norcross & Judd LLP.

Number awarded 1 each year.

Deadline March of each year.

[386]
WASA/PEMCO 21ST CENTURY EDUCATOR SCHOLARSHIP

Washington Association of School Administrators
825 Fifth Avenue, S.E.
Olympia, WA 98501
(360) 943-5717   Toll Free: (800) 859-9272
Fax: (360) 352-2043   E-mail: admin@wasa-oly.org
Web: www.wasa-oly.org

Summary To provide financial assistance to minority and other high school seniors in the state of Washington who are interested in majoring in education in college.

Eligibility This program is open to high school seniors who are enrolled in a Washington public or accredited private school, have a GPA of 3.0 or higher, and intend to major and

prepare for a career in K-12 education. Applicants must submit a completed application form, a criteria essay, a goals essay, 3 reference letters, and an official grades transcript. They compete in 3 applicant pools: eastern Washington, western Washington, and minority. Along with their application, they must submit a 1-page essay on why they have chosen K-12 education as their future profession. Selection is based on that essay, leadership, community service, honors and awards, and student activities.

Financial data The stipend is $1,000 per year.

Duration 4 years.

Additional information This program is sponsored jointly by the Washington Association of School Administrators (WASA) and the PEMCO Foundation.

Number awarded 3 each year: 1 to a student from eastern Washington, 1 to a student from western Washington, and 1 to a minority student.

Deadline March of each year.

[387]
WASHINGTON ADMIRAL'S FUND SCHOLARSHIP

National Naval Officers Association-Washington, D.C. Chapter
c/o LCDR Stephen Williams
P.O. Box 30784
Alexandria, VA 22310
(703) 566-3840   Fax: (703) 566-3813
E-mail: Stephen.Williams@navy.mil
Web: dcnnoa.memberlodge.com

Summary To provide financial assistance to Asian American and other minority high school seniors from the Washington, D.C. area who are interested in attending a college or university in any state and enrolling in the Navy Reserve Officers Training Corps (NROTC) program.

Eligibility This program is open to minority seniors graduating from high schools in the Washington, D.C. metropolitan area who plan to enroll full time at an accredited 2- or 4-year college or university in any state. Applicants must be planning to enroll in the NROTC program. They must have a GPA of 2.5 or higher and be U.S. citizens or permanent residents. Selection is based on academic achievement, community involvement, and financial need.

Financial data The stipend is $1,000.

Duration 1 year; nonrenewable.

Additional information If the recipient fails to enroll in the NROTC unit, all scholarship funds must be returned.

Number awarded 1 each year.

Deadline March of each year.

[388]
WASHINGTON DC AREA SUPPLY OFFICERS SCHOLARSHIP

National Naval Officers Association-Washington, D.C. Chapter
c/o LCDR Stephen Williams
P.O. Box 30784
Alexandria, VA 22310
(703) 566-3840   Fax: (703) 566-3813
E-mail: Stephen.Williams@navy.mil
Web: dcnnoa.memberlodge.com

Summary   To provide financial assistance to Asian American and other minority high school seniors from the Washington, D.C. area who are interested in attending college in any state.
Eligibility   This program is open to minority seniors graduating from high schools in the Washington, D.C. metropolitan area who plan to enroll full time at an accredited 2- or 4-year college or university in any state. Applicants must have a GPA of 3.0 or higher and be U.S. citizens or permanent residents. Selection is based on academic achievement, community involvement, and financial need.
Financial data   The stipend is $3,000.
Duration   1 year; nonrenewable.
Number awarded   1 each year.
Deadline   March of each year.

[389]
WASHINGTON, D.C. TAIWANESE AMERICAN COMMUNITY SCHOLARSHIP AWARD

Taiwan Culture Center
Attn: Taiwanese American Community Scholarship Award
P.O. Box 1838
Bethesda, MD 20817
E-mail: tacsa@TaiwanCultureCtr.org
Web: www.taiwanculturectr.org/new/scholarship

Summary   To provide financial assistance to high school seniors in the Washington, D.C. metropolitan area, especially Taiwanese Americans, who plan to attend college in any state.
Eligibility   This program is open to seniors graduating from high schools in the Washington, D.C. metropolitan area, defined to include the District of Columbia; the Maryland counties of Frederick, Howard, Montgomery, and Prince George's; and Alexandria, Virginia and the counties of Arlington, Fairfax, Loudoun, and Prince William. All qualified students from all ethnic groups are eligible if they are U.S. citizens or permanent residents, but a Taiwanese American Community Category is reserved for students who originated from Taiwan and whose parents, grandparents, or themselves have participated in Taiwanese American community activities. Applicants must submit a 250-word autobiography, a copy of their SAT/ACT score, their resume, transcripts, and a 500-word essay on their most rewarding experience from participation in community services. Selection is based on that essay (10%), academic achievement (30%), leadership (30%), community activities and services (20%), and extra-curricular activities (10%).
Financial data   The stipend is $600.
Duration   1 year.
Number awarded   Varies each year; recently, 20 of these scholarships were awarded.
Deadline   April of each year.

[390]
WATSON MIDWIVES OF COLOR SCHOLARSHIP

American College of Nurse-Midwives
Attn: ACNM Foundation, Inc.
8403 Colesville Road, Suite 1550
Silver Spring, MD 20910-6374
(240) 485-1850   Fax: (240) 485-1818
E-mail: fdn@acnm.org
Web: www.midwife.org

Summary   To provide financial assistance for midwifery education to Asian Americans and other students of color who belong to the American College of Nurse-Midwives (ACNM).
Eligibility   This program is open to ACNM members of color who are currently enrolled in an accredited basic midwife education program and have successfully completed 1 academic or clinical semester/quarter or clinical module. Applicants must submit a 150-word essay on their 5-year midwifery career plans and a 100-word essay on their intended future participation in the local, regional, and/or national activities of the ACNM. Selection is based on leadership potential, financial need, academic history, and potential for future professional contribution to the organization.
Financial data   The stipend is $3,000.
Duration   1 year.
Number awarded   Varies each year; recently, 3 of these scholarships were awarded.
Deadline   March of each year.

[391]
WAYNE D. CORNILS SCHOLARSHIP

Idaho State Broadcasters Association
1674 West Hill Road, Suite 3
Boise, ID 83702
(208) 345-3072   Fax: (208) 343-8946
E-mail: isba@qwestoffice.net
Web: bestinbroadcasting.com

Summary   To provide financial assistance to Asian Americans and other less advantaged students at Idaho colleges and universities who are preparing for a career in the broadcasting field.
Eligibility   This program is open to full-time students at Idaho schools who are preparing for a career in broadcasting, including business administration, sales, journalism, or engineering. Applicants must have a GPA of at least 2.0 for the first 2 years of school or 2.5 for the last 2 years. Along with their application, they must submit a letter of recommendation from the general manager of a broadcasting station that is a member of the Idaho State Broadcasters Association and a 1-page essay describing their career plans and why they want the scholarship. Applications are encouraged from a broad and diverse student population. This scholarship is reserved for a less advantaged applicant.
Financial data   The stipend depends on the need of the recipient.
Duration   1 year.
Number awarded   1 each year.
Deadline   March of each year.

[392]
WEISMAN SCHOLARSHIPS

Connecticut Office of Financial and Academic Affairs for
  Higher Education
Attn: Student Financial Aid
61 Woodland Street
Hartford, CT 06105-2326
(860) 947-1853   Toll Free: (800) 842-0229 (within CT)
Fax: (860) 947-1314   E-mail: mtip@ctdhe.org
Web: www.ctohe.org/SFA/default.htm

Summary To provide financial assistance to Asian Americans and other minority upper-division college students from any state who are enrolled at a college in Connecticut and interested in teaching mathematics or science at public middle and high schools in the state.

Eligibility This program is open to residents of any state who are enrolled full time as juniors or seniors at Connecticut colleges and universities and preparing to become a mathematics or science teacher at the middle or high school level. Applicants must be members of a minority group, defined as African American, Hispanic/Latino, Asian American, or Native American. They must be nominated by the education dean at their institution.

Financial data The maximum stipend is $5,000 per year. In addition, if recipients complete a credential and begin teaching mathematics or science at a public school in Connecticut within 16 months of graduation, they may receive up to $2,500 per year, for up to 4 years, to help pay off college loans.

Number awarded Varies each year.

Deadline October of each year.

[393]
WELLS FARGO APIASF SCHOLARSHIPS

Asian & Pacific Islander American Scholarship Fund
2025 M Street, N.W., Suite 610
Washington, DC 20036-3363
(202) 986-6892   Toll Free: (877) 808-7032
Fax: (202) 530-0643   E-mail: info@apiasf.org
Web: www.apiasf.org/scholarship_apiasf.html

Summary To provide financial assistance to Asian and Pacific Islander Americans who are entering college for the first time.

Eligibility This program is open to U.S. citizens, nationals, permanent residents, and citizens of the Freely Associated States who are first-time incoming college students and of Asian or Pacific Islander heritage. Applicants must be enrolling full time at an accredited 2- or 4-year college or university in the United States. They must have a GPA of 2.7 or higher or the GED equivalent. In addition, they must complete the FAFSA and apply for federal financial aid.

Financial data The stipend is $2,500.

Duration 1 year; nonrenewable.

Additional information This program is sponsored by Wells Fargo Bank and administered by the Asian & Pacific Islander American Scholarship Fund (APIASF).

Number awarded Varies each year; recently, 100 of these scholarships were awarded.

Deadline January of each year.

[394]
WEST AMERICA CHAPTER SCHOLARSHIP AWARDS

Phi Tau Phi Scholastic Honor Society-West America
  Chapter
c/o Thomas Y. Hou, President
California Institute of Technology
Applied and Computational Mathematics
Mail Code 9-94
1200 East California Boulevard
Pasadena, CA 91125
(626) 395-4546   Fax: (626) 578-0124
E-mail: hou@acm.caltech.edu
Web: www.phitauphi.org

Summary To provide financial assistance to upper-division and graduate students of Chinese heritage from any state at colleges and universities in southern California.

Eligibility This program is open to juniors, seniors, and graduate students from any state enrolled at accredited institutions of higher education in southern California. Applicants must be of Chinese heritage or have a demonstrated interest in Chinese and culture. They must have a GPA of 3.4 or higher. Along with their application, they must submit a 1-page essay on their professional goals, achievements, and interest in Chinese culture. Financial need is not considered in the selection process.

Financial data The stipend is $1,000.

Duration 1 year.

Additional information Phi Tau Phi, first organized in 1921 in China and reestablished in 1964 in the United States, is a relatively small honor society of scholars, mainly of Chinese heritage, in various disciplines of science, technology, art, and the humanities.

Number awarded Varies each year; recently, 4 of these scholarships were awarded: 2 to undergraduates and 2 to graduate students.

Deadline August of each year.

[395]
WESTERN REGION KOREAN AMERICAN SCHOLARSHIPS

Korean American Scholarship Foundation
Western Region
Attn: Scholarship Committee
3540 Wilshire Boulevard, Suite 920
Los Angeles, CA 90010
(213) 380-KASF   Fax: (631) 380-5274
E-mail: western@kasf.org
Web: www.kasf.org/westerrn

Summary To provide financial assistance to Korean American students from any state who are working on or planning to work on an undergraduate or graduate degree in any field at a school in western states.

Eligibility <EG>This program is open to residents of any state who are 1) U.S. citizens of Korean heritage; 2) Korean citizens who have a valid visa to study in the United States; and 3) citizens of any other country who are of Korean heritage and have a valid visa to study in the United States. Applicants must be enrolled or planning to enroll as a full-time undergraduate or graduate student at a college or university in Alaska, Arizona, California, Colorado, Hawaii, Idaho, Montana, Nevada, New Mexico, Oregon, Utah, Washington, or Wyoming. They must have a GPA of 3.0 or higher. Selection is based on academic achievement (25%), extracurricular activities (10%), an essay (10%), recommendations (10%), financial need (40%), and extra credit for having extraordinary circumstances (5%).

Financial data Stipends are at least $2,000.

Duration 1 year; renewable.

Number awarded Varies each year; recently, 48 of these scholarships were awarded.

Deadline July of each year.

[396]
WESTERN UNION FOUNDATION FAMILY SCHOLARSHIP PROGRAM

Western Union Foundation
c/o Institute of International Education
1400 K Street, N.W., Suite 700
Washington, DC 20005
(202) 326-7861   Fax: (202) 326-7696
E-mail: wufoundaton@iie.org
Web: foundation.westernunion.com

Summary To provide financial assistance to pairs of students from the same family of immigrants in designated cities, both of whom wish to attend college in any state.

Eligibility Applications to this program must be submitted jointly by 2 students who are members of the same family (parent and child, siblings). Both applicants must be 18 years of age or older, have been born outside of the United States, have been in this country for 7 years or less, and be planning to attend an accredited institution of higher education or non-profit training institute in any state. They must be residents of Chicago, Denver, Los Angeles, Miami, New York, San Francisco, or Washington, D.C. Funding is available for college or university tuition, language acquisition classes, technical or skill training, and/or financial literacy; graduate study is not supported.

Financial data Stipends range from $1,000 to $5,000 per family. Funds are paid directly to the educational institution.

Duration 1 year.

Additional information This program began in 2009.

Number awarded Varies each year.

Deadline October of each year.

[397]
WHAN SOON CHUNG SCHOLARSHIP

Philip Jaisohn Memorial Foundation
Attn: Education and Scholarship Committee
6705 Old York Road
Philadelphia, PA 19126
(215) 224-2000   Fax: (215) 224-9164
E-mail: jaisohnhouse@gmail.com
Web: www.jaisohn.org

Summary To provide financial assistance to Korean American undergraduate and graduate students who are studying health care or medicine.

Eligibility This program is open to Korean American undergraduate and graduate students who are currently enrolled at a college or university in the United States and working on a degree in health care or a field of medicine. Applicants must be able to demonstrate excellence in com-

munity activities and financial need. Along with their application, they must submit an essay on either "Who is Dr. Jaisohn to Me," or "The Significance of Dr. Jaisohn's Ideal to Korean Americans." They must also submit a brief statement on how they can contribute to and be involved in the activities of the Philip Jaisohn Memorial Foundation. Selection is based on the applicant's desire to take Dr. Jaisohn as a role model to learn and spread his legacy.

Financial data The stipend is $1,500.

Duration 1 year.

Number awarded 1 each year.

Deadline November of each year.

[398]
WILLIAM K. SCHUBERT M.D. MINORITY NURSING SCHOLARSHIP PROGRAM

Cincinnati Children's Hospital Medical Center
Attn: Office of Diversity and Inclusion, MLC 9008
3333 Burnet Avenue
Cincinnati, OH 45229-3039
(513) 803-6416   Toll Free: (800) 344-2462
Fax: (513) 636-5643   TDD: (513) 636-4900
E-mail: diversity@cchmc.org
Web: www.cincinnatichildrens.org

Summary To provide financial assistance to Asian Americans and members of other underrepresented groups who are interested in working on a bachelor's or master's degree in nursing to prepare for licensure in Ohio.

Eligibility This program is open to members of groups underrepresented in the nursing profession (males, American Indians or Alaska Natives, Blacks or African Americans, Hawaiian Natives or other Pacific Islanders, Hispanics or Latinos, or Asians). Applicants must be enrolled or accepted in a professional bachelor's or master's registered nurse program at an accredited school of nursing to prepare for initial licensure in Ohio. They must have a GPA of 2.75 or higher. Along with their application, they must submit a 750-word essay that covers 1) their long-range personal, educational, and professional goals; 2) why they chose nursing as a profession; 3) how their experience as a member of an underrepresented group has influenced a major professional and/or personal decision in their life; 4) any unique qualifications, experiences, or special talents that demonstrate their creativity; and 5) how their work experience has contributed to their personal development.

Financial data The stipend is $2,750 per year.

Duration 1 year. May be renewed up to 3 additional years for students working on a bachelor's degree or 1 additional year for students working on a master's degree; renewal requires that students maintain a GPA of 2.75 or higher.

Number awarded 1 or more each year.

Deadline April of each year.

[399]
WILLIAM ORR DINGWALL FOUNDATION KOREAN ANCESTRY GRANTS

William Orr Dingwall Foundation
P.O. Box 57088
Washington, DC 20037
E-mail: kag@dingwallfoundation.org
Web: www.dingwallfoundation.org/kag/index.html

Summary To provide financial assistance to undergraduates of Asian (preferably Korean) ancestry.

Eligibility This program is open to graduating high school seniors and undergraduates currently enrolled at a college or university in the United States. Applicants must be of at least 25% Asian ancestry; preference is given to students of Korean heritage. They must have a GPA of 3.5 or higher but may be majoring in any field. Selection is based on academic record, written statements, and letters of recommendation.

Financial data The stipend is $20,000 per year.

Duration 1 year; may be renewed up to 3 additional years, provided the recipient maintains a GPA of 3.5 or higher.

Number awarded Varies each year; recently, 32 of these grants were awarded.

Deadline February of each year.

[400]
WILLIAM RUCKER GREENWOOD SCHOLARSHIP

Association for Women Geoscientists
Attn: AWG Foundation
12000 North Washington Street, Suite 285
Thornton, CO 80241
(303) 412-6219   Fax: (303) 253-9220
E-mail: office@awg.org
Web: www.awg.org/members/po_scholarships.htm

Summary To provide financial assistance to Asian and other minority women from any state working on an undergraduate or graduate degree in the geosciences at a college in the Potomac Bay region.

Eligibility This program is open to minority women who are residents of any state and currently enrolled as full-time undergraduate or graduate geoscience majors at an accredited, degree-granting college or university in Delaware, the District of Columbia, Maryland, Virginia, or West Virginia. Selection is based on the applicant's 1) participation in geoscience or earth science educational activities; and 2) potential for leadership as a future geoscience professional.

Financial data The stipend is $1,000. The recipient also is granted a 1-year membership in the Association for Women Geoscientists (AWG).

Duration 1 year.

Additional information This program is sponsored by the AWG Potomac Area Chapter.

Number awarded 1 each year.

Deadline April of each year.

[401]
WISCONSIN MINORITY TEACHER LOANS

Wisconsin Higher Educational Aids Board
131 West Wilson Street, Suite 902
P.O. Box 7885
Madison, WI 53707-7885
(608) 267-2212   Fax: (608) 267-2808
E-mail: deanna.schulz@wisconsin.gov
Web: heab.state.wi.us/programs.html

Summary To provide funding to Asian Americans and other minorities in Wisconsin who are interested in teaching in Wisconsin school districts with large minority enrollments.

Eligibility This program is open to residents of Wisconsin who are African Americans, Hispanic Americans, American Indians, or southeast Asians (students who were admitted to the United States after December 31, 1975 and who are a former citizen of Laos, Vietnam, or Cambodia or whose ancestor was a citizen of 1 of those countries). Applicants must be enrolled at least half time as juniors, seniors, or graduate students at an independent or public institution in the state in a program leading to teaching licensure and have a GPA of 2.5 or higher. They must agree to teach in a Wisconsin school district in which minority students constitute at least 29% of total enrollment or in a school district participating in the interdistrict pupil transfer program. Financial need is not considered in the selection process.

Financial data Loans are provided up to $2,500 per year. For each year the student teaches in an eligible school district, 25% of the loan is forgiven; if the student does not teach in an eligible district, the loan must be repaid at an interest rate of 5%.

Duration 1 year; may be renewed 1 additional year.

Additional information Eligible students should apply through their school's financial aid office.

Number awarded Varies each year.

Deadline Deadline dates vary by institution; check with your school's financial aid office.

[402]
WISCONSIN MINORITY UNDERGRADUATE RETENTION GRANTS

Wisconsin Higher Educational Aids Board
131 West Wilson Street, Suite 902
P.O. Box 7885
Madison, WI 53707-7885
(608) 267-2212   Fax: (608) 267-2808
E-mail: deanna.schulz@wisconsin.gov
Web: heab.state.wi.us/programs.html

Summary To provide financial assistance to Asian Americans and other minorities in Wisconsin who are currently enrolled at a college in the state.

Eligibility This program is open to residents of Wisconsin who are African Americans, Hispanic Americans, American Indians, or southeast Asians (students who were admitted to the United States after December 31, 1975 and who are a former citizen of Laos, Vietnam, or Cambodia or whose ancestor was a citizen of 1 of those countries). Applicants must be enrolled at least half time as sophomores, juniors, seniors, or fifth-year undergraduates at a Wisconsin technical college, tribal college, or independent college or university in the state. They must be nominated by their institution and be able to demonstrate financial need.

Financial data Stipends range from $250 to $2,500 per year, depending on the need of the recipient.

Duration Up to 4 years.

Additional information The Wisconsin Higher Educational Aids Board administers this program for students at private nonprofit institutions, technical colleges, and tribal colleges. The University of Wisconsin has a similar program for students attending any of the branches of that system. Eligible students should apply through their school's financial aid office.

Number awarded Varies each year.

Deadline Deadline dates vary by institution; check with your school's financial aid office.

[403]
WISCONSIN TALENT INCENTIVE PROGRAM (TIP) GRANTS

Wisconsin Higher Educational Aids Board
131 West Wilson Street, Suite 902
P.O. Box 7885
Madison, WI 53707-7885
(608) 266-1665   Fax: (608) 267-2808
E-mail: colettem1.brown@wi.gov
Web: heab.state.wi.us/programs.html

Summary To provide financial assistance for college to Asian Americans and other needy and educationally disadvantaged students in Wisconsin.

Eligibility This program is open to residents of Wisconsin entering a college or university in the state who meet the requirements of both financial need and educational disadvantage. Financial need qualifications include 1) family contribution (a dependent student whose expected parent contribution is $200 or less or an independent student whose maximum academic year contribution is $200 or less); 2) Temporary Assistance to Needy Families (TANF) or Wisconsin Works (W2) benefits (a dependent student whose family is receiving TANF or W2 benefits or an independent student who is receiving TANF or W2 benefits); or 3) unemployment (a dependent student whose parents are ineligible for unemployment compensation and have no current income from employment, or an independent student and spouse, if married, who are ineligible for unemployment compensation and have no current income from employment). Educational disadvantage qualifications include students who are 1) minorities (African American, Native American, Hispanic, or southeast Asian); 2) enrolled in a special academic support program due to insufficient academic preparation; 3) a first-generation college student (neither parent graduated from a 4-year college or university); 4) disabled according to the Department of Workforce Development, the Division of Vocational Rehabilitation, or a Wisconsin college or university that uses the Americans with Disabilities Act definition; 5) currently or formerly incarcerated in a correctional institution; or 6) from an environmental and academic background that deters the pursuit of educational plans. Students already in college are not eligible.

Financial data Stipends range up to $1,800 per year.

Duration 1 year; may be renewed up to 4 additional years, provided the recipient continues to be a Wisconsin resident enrolled at least half time in a degree or certificate program, makes satisfactory academic progress, demonstrates financial need, and remains enrolled continuously from semester to semester and from year to year. If recipients withdraw from school or cease to attend classes for any reason (other than medical necessity), they may not reapply.

Number awarded Varies each year.

Deadline Deadline not specified.

[404]
WISCONSIN UNITED METHODIST FOUNDATION HMONG SCHOLARSHIP

Wisconsin United Methodist Foundation
750 Windsor Street, Suite 305
P.O. Box 620
Sun Prairie, WI 53590-0620
(608) 837-9582   Toll Free: (888) 903-9863
Fax: (608) 837-2492   E-mail: wumf@wumf.org
Web: www.wumf.org/grantsScholars.html

Summary To provide financial assistance to Methodists from Wisconsin who are of Hmong heritage and interested in attending college in any state.

Eligibility This program is open to Hmong members of United Methodist Churches affiliated with the Wisconsin Conference who are enrolled or planning to enroll at a college or vocational school in any state. Applicants must submit an essay that describes their personal situation and vocational goals, church-related activities and involvement, school and community involvement, and financial plan for funding their education, including any special financial needs.

Financial data Stipends range from $500 to $1,000.

Duration 1 year.

Number awarded 1 or more each year.

Deadline March of each year.

[405]
WOMEN'S TRANSPORTATION SEMINAR JUNIOR COLLEGE SCHOLARSHIP

Women's Transportation Seminar
Attn: WTS Foundation
1701 K Street, N.W., Suite 800
Washington, DC 20006
(202) 955-5085   Fax: (202) 955-5088
E-mail: wts@wtsinternational.org
Web: www.wtsinternational.org/education/scholarships

Summary To provide financial assistance to women (particularly minority women) who are enrolled at a community college or trade school to prepare for a career in transportation.

Eligibility This program is open to women who are working on an associate or technical degree in transportation or a transportation-related field (e.g., transportation engineering, planning, finance, or logistics). Applicants must have a GPA of 3.0 or higher. Along with their application, they must submit a 500-word statement about their career goals after graduation and why they think they should receive the scholarship award. Applications must be submitted first to a local chapter; the chapters forward selected applications for consideration on the national level. Minority women are especially encouraged to apply. Selection is based on transportation involvement and goals, job skills, academic record, and leadership potential; financial need is not considered.

Financial data The stipend is $1,000.

Duration 1 year.

Additional information Local chapters may also award additional funding to winners for their area.

Number awarded 1 each year.

Deadline Applications must be submitted by November to a local WTS chapter.

[406]
WOODS HOLE OCEANOGRAPHIC INSTITUTION MINORITY FELLOWSHIPS

Woods Hole Oceanographic Institution
Attn: Academic Programs Office
Clark Laboratory 223, MS 31
360 Woods Hole Road
Woods Hole, MA 02543-1541
(508) 289-2219   Fax: (508) 457-2188
E-mail: education@whoi.edu
Web: www.whoi.edu/minorityfellow

Summary To provide work experience to minority group members who are interested in preparing for careers in the marine sciences, oceanographic engineering, or marine policy.

Eligibility This program is open to ethnic minority undergraduates enrolled in U.S. colleges or universities who have completed at least 1 year of study and who are interested in the physical or natural sciences, mathematics, engineering, or marine policy. Applicants must be U.S. citizens or permanent residents and African American or Black; Asian American; Chicano, Mexican American, Puerto Rican or other Hispanic; or Native American, Alaska Native, or Native Hawaiian. They must be interested in participating in a program of study and research at Woods Hole Oceanographic Institution.

Financial data The stipend is $500 per week; trainees may also receive additional support for travel to Woods Hole.

Duration 10 to 12 weeks during the summer or 1 semester during the academic year; renewable.

Additional information Trainees are assigned advisers who supervise their research programs and supplementary study activities. Some traineeships involve field work or research cruises. This program is conducted as part of the Research Experiences for Undergraduates (REU) Program of the National Science Foundation.

Number awarded 4 to 5 each year.

Deadline February of each year.

[407]
XEROX TECHNICAL MINORITY SCHOLARSHIP PROGRAM

Xerox Corporation
Attn: Technical Minority Scholarship Program
150 State Street, Fourth Floor
Rochester, NY 14614
(585) 422-7689   E-mail: GlobalCareers@xerox.com
Web: www.xerox.com/jobs/minority-scholarships/enus.html

Summary To provide financial assistance to Asian Americans and other minorities interested in undergraduate or graduate education in the sciences and/or engineering.

Eligibility This program is open to minorities (people of African American, Asian, Pacific Islander, Native American, Native Alaskan, or Hispanic descent) working full time on a bachelor's, master's, or doctoral degree in chemistry, computing and software systems, engineering (chemical, computer, electrical, imaging, manufacturing, mechanical, optical, or software), information management, laser optics, materials science, physics, or printing management science. Applicants must be U.S. citizens or permanent residents with a GPA of 3.0 or higher and attending a 4-year college or university.

Financial data Stipends range from $1,000 to $10,000.

Duration 1 year.

Number awarded Varies each year, recently, 130 of these scholarships were awarded.

Deadline September of each year.

[408]
XIA THAO SCHOLARSHIP

Hmong American Education Fund
P.O. Box 17468
St. Paul, MN 55117
(651) 230-3634   E-mail: scholarships@thehaef.org
Web: www.thehaef.org

Summary To provide financial assistance to Hmong undergraduate and graduate students who demonstrate leadership.

Eligibility This program is open to students of Hmong descent who are currently enrolled as full-time undergraduate or graduate students at public 2- or 4-year colleges or universities in any state. Applicants must be U.S. citizens or permanent residents and have a GPA of 3.0 or higher. Along with their application, they must submit a 1,500-word essay on their commitment to education, their leadership qualities, their financial need, how this scholarship can help them, and their community service. Selection is based on academic excellence, leadership qualities, commitment to helping their community, and financial need.

Financial data The stipend is $2,000.

Duration 1 year; nonrenewable.

Number awarded 1 each year.

Deadline March of each year.

Graduate Students

Listed alphabetically by program title and described in detail here are 396 fellowships, grants, awards, and other sources of "free money" set aside for incoming, continuing, or returning graduate students of Asian origins (including those of subcontinent Asian and Pacific Islander descent) who are working on a master's, doctoral, or professional degree. This funding is available to support study, training, research, and/or creative activities in the United States.

[409]
AAJUW SCHOLARSHIP PROGRAM

American Association of Japanese University Women
Attn: Scholarship Committee
3543 West Boulevard
Los Angeles, CA 90016
E-mail: scholarship@aajuw.org
Web: www.aajuw.org/scholarship.php

Summary To provide financial assistance to Japanese American and other female students currently enrolled in upper-division or graduate classes in California.

Eligibility This program is open to women enrolled at accredited colleges or universities in California as juniors, seniors, or graduate students. Applicants must be involved in U.S.-Japan relations, cultural exchanges, and leadership development in the areas of their designated field of study. Along with their application, they must submit a current resume, an official transcript of the past 2 years of college work, 2 letters of recommendation, and an essay (up to 2 pages in English or 1,200 characters in Japanese) on what they hope to accomplish in their field of study and how that will contribute to better U.S.-Japan relations.

Financial data The stipend is $2,000.

Duration 1 year.

Additional information The association was founded in 1970 to promote the education of women as well as to contribute to U.S.-Japan relations, cultural exchanges, and leadership development.

Number awarded 1 to 3 each year. Since this program was established, it has awarded more than $100,000 worth of scholarships to nearly 100 women.

Deadline October of each year.

[410]
AAPI NATIONAL RESEARCH COMPETITION

American Association of Physicians of Indian Origin
Attn: Medical Students, Residents and Fellows Section
600 Enterprise Drive, Suite 108
Oak Brook, IL 60523
(630) 990-2277   Fax: (630) 990-2281
E-mail: preselect@aapimsr.org
Web: www.aapimsr.org/index.cfm/convention

Summary To recognize and reward members of the American Association of Physicians of Indian Origin (AAPI) who submit outstanding research abstracts for presentation at the annual conference.

Eligibility This competition is open to members of the Medical Students, Residents and Fellows (MSRF) section and the Young Physician's Section (YPS) of the AAPI. Applicants must submit abstracts of research for presentation at the AAPI annual conference. Abstracts are accepted in 4 categories: clinical sciences and patient-based research, basic science/translational research, south Asian studies, or AAPI Charitable Foundation studies. Applicants must attend the conference where finalists are chosen for a poster and an 8-minute oral presentation.

Financial data Cash prizes are awarded (amount not specified).

Duration The competition is held annually.

Number awarded Up to 4 each year (1 in each category).

Deadline April of each year.

[411]
ABA LEGAL OPPORTUNITY SCHOLARSHIP

American Bar Association
Attn: Fund for Justice and Education
321 North Clark Street, 21st Floor
Chicago, IL 60654-7598
(312) 988-5927   Fax: (312) 988-6392
E-mail: legalosf@staff.abanet.org
Web: www.americanbar.org

Summary To provide financial assistance to Asian Americans and other racial and ethnic minority students who are interested in attending law school.

Eligibility This program is open to racial and ethnic minority college graduates who are interested in attending an ABA-accredited law school. Only students beginning law school may apply; students who have completed 1 or more semesters of law school are not eligible. Applicants must have a cumulative GPA of 2.5 or higher and be citizens or permanent residents of the United States. Along with their application, they must submit a 1,000-word statement describing their personal and family background, community service activities, and other connections to their racial and ethnic minority community. Financial need is also considered in the selection process.

Financial data The stipend is $5,000 per year.

Duration 1 year; may be renewed for 2 additional years if satisfactory performance in law school has been achieved.

Additional information This program began in the 2000-01 academic year.

Number awarded Approximately 20 each year.

Deadline February of each year.

[412]
ABE AND ESTHER HAGIWARA STUDENT AID AWARD

Japanese American Citizens League
Attn: National Scholarship Awards
1765 Sutter Street
San Francisco, CA 94115
(415) 345-1075   Fax: (415) 931-4671
E-mail: ncwnp@jacl.org
Web: www.jacl.org/edu/scholar.htm

Summary To provide financial assistance for college or graduate school to student members of the Japanese American Citizens League (JACL) who can demonstrate severe financial need.

Eligibility This program is open to JACL members who are enrolled or planning to enroll at a college, university, trade school, or business college. Applicants must be undergraduate or graduate students who are able to demonstrate that, without this aid, they will have to delay or terminate their education. They must submit information on their involvement in JACL and a 2-page essay on a topic that changes annually but relates to Japanese Americans. Selection is based on that essay, financial need, academic history, JACL involvement, school activities, work history, scholastic honors, and community involvement.

Financial data Stipends generally average more than $2,000.

Duration 1 year; nonrenewable.

Number awarded At least 1 each year.
Deadline March of each year.

[413]
ACA/MARTIN LUTHER KING JR. SCHOLARSHIP AWARDS

American Correctional Association
Attn: Scholarship Award Committee
206 North Washington Street, Suite 200
Alexandria, VA 22314
(703) 224-0000   Toll Free: (800) ACA-JOIN
Fax: (703) 224-0179   E-mail: jenniferb@aca.org
Web: www.aca.org/pastpresentfuture/awards.asp

Summary To provide financial assistance for undergraduate or graduate study to Asian Americans and other minorities interested in a career in the criminal justice field.

Eligibility Members of the American Correctional Association (ACA) may nominate a minority person for these awards. Nominees do not need to be ACA members, but they must have been accepted to or be enrolled in an undergraduate or graduate program in criminal justice at a 4-year college or university. Along with the nomination package, they must submit a 250-word essay describing their reflections on the ideals and philosophies of Dr. Martin Luther King and how they have attempted to emulate those qualities in their lives. They must provide documentation of financial need, academic achievement, and commitment to the principles of Dr. King.

Financial data A stipend is awarded (amount not specified). Funds are paid directly to the recipient's college or university.

Number awarded 1 each year.
Deadline May of each year.

[414]
ACS/ORGANIC CHEMISTRY GRADUATE STUDENT FELLOWSHIPS

American Chemical Society
Division of Organic Chemistry
1155 16th Street, N.W.
Washington, DC 20036
(202) 872-4401   Toll Free: (800) 227-5558, ext. 4401
E-mail: division@acs.org
Web: www.organicdivision.org/?nd=graduate_fellowship

Summary To provide funding for research to members (particularly minority and female members) of the Division of Organic Chemistry of the American Chemical Society (ACS) who are working on a doctoral degree in organic chemistry.

Eligibility This program is open to members of the division who are entering the third or fourth year of a Ph.D. program in organic chemistry. Applicants must submit 3 letters of recommendation, a resume, and a short essay on a research area of their choice. U.S. citizenship or permanent resident status is required. Selection is based primarily on evidence of research accomplishment. Applications from women and minorities are especially encouraged.

Financial data The stipend is $26,000; that includes $750 for travel support to present a poster of their work at the National Organic Symposium.

Duration 1 year.

Additional information This program began in 1982. It includes the Emmanuil Troyansky Fellowship. Current corporate sponsors include Genentech, Organic Syntheses, Boehringer Ingelheim, and Amgen.

Number awarded Varies each year; recently, 8 of these fellowships were awarded.
Deadline May of each year.

[415]
ADDIE B. MORRIS SCHOLARSHIP

American Association of Railroad Superintendents
P.O. Box 200
La Fox, IL 60147
(630) 762-0754   E-mail: aars@supt.org
Web: www.railroadsuperintendents.org/Scholarships

Summary To provide financial assistance to undergraduate and graduate students, with preference given to Asian Americans and other minorities working on a degree in transportation.

Eligibility This program is open to full-time undergraduate and graduate students enrolled at accredited colleges and universities in Canada or the United States. Applicants must have completed enough credits to have standing as a sophomore and must have a GPA of 2.75 or higher. Preference is given to minority students enrolled in the transportation field who can demonstrate financial need.

Financial data The stipend is $1,000. Funds are sent directly to the recipient's institution.

Duration 1 year.

Number awarded 1 or more each year.

Deadline May of each year.

[416]
ADLER POLLOCK & SHEEHAN DIVERSITY SCHOLARSHIP

Adler Pollock & Sheehan P.C.
Attn: Diversity Committee Chair
175 Federal Street
Boston, MA 02110-2210
(617) 482-0600   Fax: (617) 482-0604
E-mail: Diversitycomm@apslaw.com
Web: www.apslaw.com/firm-diversity.html

Summary To provide financial assistance to Asian Americans and other residents of Massachusetts and Rhode Island who are members of diverse groups and plan to attend law school in any state.

Eligibility This program is open to residents of Massachusetts and Rhode Island who are members of a diverse group, including African American, American Indian, Hispanic, Asian/Pacific Islander, gay/lesbian, or other minority group. Applicants must be entering their first year at an ABA-accredited law school in the United States. They must be able to demonstrate academic achievement, a desire to work and reside in Massachusetts or Rhode Island after graduation, a demonstrated commitment to the community, a vision of contributions to the profession and community after graduation, and financial need.

Financial data The stipend is $10,000.

Duration 1 year.

Number awarded 1 each year.

Deadline May of each year.

[417]
ADRIENNE M. AND CHARLES SHELBY ROOKS FELLOWSHIP FOR RACIAL AND ETHNIC THEOLOGICAL STUDENTS

United Church of Christ
Attn: Local Church Ministries
700 Prospect Avenue East
Cleveland, OH 44115-1100
(216) 736-3865   Toll Free: (866) 822-8224, ext. 3865
Fax: (216) 736-3783   E-mail: lcm@ucc.org
Web: www.ucc.org/seminarians/ucc-scholarships-for.html

Summary To provide financial assistance to Asian American and other minority students who are either enrolled at an accredited seminary preparing for a career of service in the United Church of Christ (UCC) or working on a doctoral degree in the field of religion.

Eligibility This program is open to members of underrepresented ethnic groups (African American, Hispanic American, Asian American, Native American Indian, or Pacific Islander) who have been a member of a UCC congregation for at least 1 year. Applicants must be either 1) enrolled in an accredited school of theology in the United States or Canada and working on an M.Div. degree with the intent of becoming a pastor or teacher within the UCC; or 2) doctoral (Ph.D., Th.D., or Ed.D.) students within a field related to religious studies. Seminary students must have a GPA in all postsecondary work of 3.0 or higher and must have begun the in-care process; preference is given to students who have demonstrated leadership (through a history of service to the church) and scholarship (through exceptional academic performance). For doctoral students, preference is given to applicants who have demonstrated academic excellence, teaching effectiveness, and commitment to the UCC and who intend to become professors in colleges, seminaries, or graduate schools.

Financial data Grants range from $500 to $5,000 per year.

Duration 1 year; may be renewed.

Number awarded Varies each year; recently, 16 of these scholarships, including 10 for M.Div. students and 6 for doctoral students, were awarded.

Deadline February of each year.

[418]
AETNA FOUNDATION-NMF HEALTHCARE LEADERSHIP PROGRAM

National Medical Fellowships, Inc.
Attn: Scholarship Program
347 Fifth Avenue, Suite 510
New York, NY 10016
(212) 483-8880, ext. 304   Toll Free: (877) NMF-1DOC
Fax: (212) 483-8897   E-mail: mbrito@nmfonline.org
Web: www.nmfonline.org/programs/aetna-foundation

Summary To provide financial assistance to Asian Americans and other minorities who are medical students at schools in selected states.

Eligibility This program is open to members minority groups (African American, Hispanic/Latino, American Indian, Native Hawaiian, Alaska Native, Vietnamese, Cambodian, or Native Pacific Islander) who are currently enrolled in their second or third year of medical school. U.S. citizenship is required. Applicants must be attending medical school in southern California (particularly Los Angeles), Connecticut, Illinois (particularly Chicago), New Jersey, New York City, or Philadelphia. Along with their application, they must submit an essay of 500 to 1,000 words on what leadership means for physicians. Selection is based on that essay, letters of recommendation, community service and leadership activities, and financial need.

Financial data The stipend is $5,000.

Duration 1 year.

Additional information Funding for this program, which is administered by National Medical Fellowships (NMF), is provided by the Aetna Foundation.

Number awarded 10 each year.

Deadline February of each year for Illinois; March of each year for Connecticut, New Jersey, New York City, and Philadelphia; or April of each year for southern California.

[419]
AICPA ASCEND SCHOLARSHIP

Ascend: Pan-Asian Leaders
Attn: Director of Programs
120 Wall Street, Ninth Floor
New York, NY 10005
(212) 248-4888   Fax: (212) 344-5636
E-mail: scholarships@ascendleadership.org
Web: www.ascendleadership.org

Summary To provide financial assistance to undergraduate and graduate minority accounting students who are members of Ascend: Pan-Asian Leaders and of the American Institute of Certified Public Accountants (AICPA).

Eligibility This program is open to members of minority groups underrepresented in the accounting profession. Applicants must have completed at least 30 hours of college course work, including at least 6 hours in accounting, at a 4-year college or university in the United States or its territories as a full-time undergraduate or graduate student in an accounting-related field. They must be members of Ascend and AICPA, have a GPA of 3.0 or higher, and be U.S. citizens or permanent residents. Along with their application, they must submit a 500-word personal essay on how they have demonstrated leadership and teamwork in their academic studies, professional career, and/or extracurricular activities and community volunteer work; why they believe those qualities are important to transforming themselves into a better leader; their career goals after graduation; and the role Ascend has played in the achievement of their academic and career goals. They must also be able to demonstrate some financial need.

Financial data The stipend is $5,000. The program also provides travel and lodging for the Ascend annual national convention.

Duration 1 year.

Additional information Ascend was formed in 2004 as the National Asian American Society of Accountants. This program is sponsored by AICPA.

Number awarded 1 each year.

Deadline May of each year.

[420]
ALA SPECTRUM SCHOLARSHIP PROGRAM

American Library Association
Attn: Office for Diversity
50 East Huron Street
Chicago, IL 60611-2795
(312) 280-5048   Toll Free: (800) 545-2433, ext. 5048
Fax: (312) 280-3256   TDD: (888) 814-7692
E-mail: spectrum@ala.org
Web: www.ala.org/offices/diversity/spectrum

Summary To provide financial assistance to Asian American and other minority students interested in working on a degree in librarianship.

Eligibility This program is open to ethnic minority students (African American or Black, Asian, Native Hawaiian or other Pacific Islander, Latino or Hispanic, and American Indian or Alaska Native). Applicants must be U.S. or Canadian citizens or permanent residents who have completed no more than a third of the requirements for a master's or school library media degree. They must be enrolled full or part time at an ALA-accredited school of library and information studies or an ALA-recognized NCATE school library media program. Selection is based on academic leadership, outstanding service, commitment to a career in librarianship, statements indicating the nature of the applicant's library and other work experience, letters of reference, and personal presentation.

Financial data The stipend is $5,000.

Duration 1 year; nonrenewable.

Additional information This program began in 1998. It is administered by a joint committee of the American Library Association (ALA).

Number awarded Varies each year; recently, 69 of these scholarships were awarded.

Deadline February of each year.

[421]
ALAO DIVERSITY SCHOLARSHIP

Academic Library Association of Ohio
c/o Diane Kolosionek, Diversity Committee Chair
Cleveland State University, Michael Schwartz Library
2121 Euclid Avenue
RT 110D
Cleveland, OH 44115-2214
(216) 802-3358   E-mail: d.kolosionek44@csuohio.edu
Web: www.alaoweb.org

Summary To provide financial assistance to Asian American and other residents of Ohio who are working on a master's degree in library science at a school in any state and will contribute to diversity in the profession.

Eligibility This program is open to residents of Ohio who are enrolled or entering an ALA-accredited program for a master's degree in library science, either on campus or via distance education. Applicants must be able to demonstrate how they will contribute to diversity in the profession, including (but not limited to) race or ethnicity, sexual orientation, life experience, physical ability, and a sense of commitment to those and other diversity issues. Along with their application, they must submit 1) a list of participation in honor societies or professional organizations, awards, scholarships, prizes, honors, or class offices; 2) a list of their community, civic, organizational, or volunteer experiences; and 3) an essay on their understanding of and commitment to diversity in libraries, including how they, as library school students and future professionals, might address the issue.

Financial data The stipend is $1,500.

Duration 1 year.

Number awarded 1 each year.

Deadline March of each year.

[422]
ALBERT W. DENT STUDENT SCHOLARSHIP

American College of Healthcare Executives
Attn: Scholarship Committee
One North Franklin Street, Suite 1700
Chicago, IL 60606-3529
(312) 424-2800   Fax: (312) 424-0023
E-mail: geninfo@ache.org
Web: www.ache.org

Summary To provide financial assistance for college to Asian American and other minority graduate student members of the American College of Healthcare Executives (ACHE).

Eligibility This program is open to ACHE student associates entering their final year of classroom work in a health care management master's degree program. Applicants must be minority students, enrolled full time, able to demonstrate financial need, and U.S. or Canadian citizens. Along with their application, they must submit an 1- to 2-page essay describing their leadership abilities and experiences, their community and volunteer involvement, their goals as a health care executive, and how this scholarship can help them achieve their career goals.

Financial data The stipend is $5,000.

Duration 1 year.

Additional information The program was established and named in honor of Dr. Albert W. Dent, the foundation's first African American fellow and president emeritus of Dillard University.

Number awarded Varies each year; the sponsor awards up to 20 scholarships through this and its other scholarship program.

Deadline March of each year.

[423]
AMELIA KEMP MEMORIAL SCHOLARSHIP

Women of the Evangelical Lutheran Church in America
Attn: Scholarships
8765 West Higgins Road
Chicago, IL 60631-4101
(773) 380-2741   Toll Free: (800) 638-3522, ext. 2741
Fax: (773) 380-2419   E-mail: valora.starr@elca.org
Web: www.womenoftheelca.org

Summary To provide financial assistance to Asian American and other lay women of color who are members of Evangelical Lutheran Church of America (ELCA) congregations and wish to study on the undergraduate, graduate, professional, or vocational school level.

Eligibility This program is open to ELCA lay women of color who are at least 21 years of age and have experienced an interruption of at least 2 years in their education since high school. Applicants must have been admitted to an educational institution to prepare for a career in other than ordained ministry. U.S. citizenship is required.

Financial data The maximum stipend is $1,000.

Duration Up to 2 years.

Number awarded 1 or more each year.

Deadline February of each year.

[424]
AMERICAN ANTHROPOLOGICAL ASSOCIATION MINORITY DISSERTATION FELLOWSHIP PROGRAM

American Anthropological Association
Attn: Director of Academic Relations
2200 Wilson Boulevard, Suite 600
Arlington, VA 22201-3357
(703) 528-1902   Fax: (703) 528-3546
E-mail: academic@aaanet.org
Web: www.aaanet.org/cmtes/minority/Minfellow.cfm

Summary To provide funding to Asian Americans and other minorities who are working on a Ph.D. dissertation in anthropology.

Eligibility This program is open to Native American, African American, Latino(a), Pacific Islander, and Asian American doctoral students who have been admitted to degree candidacy in anthropology. Applicants must be U.S. citizens, enrolled in a full-time academic program leading to a doctoral degree in anthropology, and members of the American Anthropological Association. They must have a record of outstanding academic success, have had their dissertation proposal approved by their dissertation committee prior to application, be writing a dissertation in an area of anthropological research, and need funding to complete the dissertation. Along with their application, they must submit a cover letter, a research plan summary, a curriculum vitae, a statement regarding employment, a disclosure statement providing information about other sources of available and pending financial support, 3 letters of recommendation, and an official transcript from their doctoral program. Selection is based on the quality of the submitted information and the judged likelihood that the applicant will have a good chance of completing the dissertation.

Financial data The grant is $10,000. Funds are sent in 2 installments (in September and in January) directly to the recipient.

Duration 1 year; nonrenewable.

Number awarded 1 each year.

Deadline February of each year.

[425]
AMERICAN ASSOCIATION OF CHINESE IN TOXICOLOGY AND CHARLES RIVER BEST ABSTRACT AWARD

Society of Toxicology
Attn: American Association of Chinese in Toxicology
   Special Interest Group
1821 Michael Faraday Drive, Suite 300
Reston, VA 20190-5348
(703) 438-3115   Fax: (703) 438-3113
E-mail: sothq@toxicology.org
Web: www.toxicology.org/ai/af/awards.aspx

Summary To recognize and reward graduate student and postdoctoral members of the Society of Toxicology (SOT) who are of Chinese ethnic origin and present outstanding papers at the annual meeting.

Eligibility This award is available to SOT members who are graduate students or postdoctoral fellows of Chinese descent (having 1 or more parents of Chinese descent). Candidates must have an accepted abstract for the SOT annual meeting. Along with the abstract, they must submit a cover letter outlining the significance of the work to the field of toxicology.

Financial data The prizes are $500 for first, $300 for second, and $200 for third.

Duration The prizes are presented annually.

Number awarded 3 each year.

Deadline December of each year.

[426]
AMERICAN ASSOCIATION OF UNIVERSITY WOMEN CAREER DEVELOPMENT GRANTS

American Association of University Women
Attn: AAUW Educational Foundation
301 ACT Drive, Department 60
P.O. Box 4030
Iowa City, IA 52243-4030
(319) 337-1716, ext. 60   Fax: (319) 337-1204
E-mail: aauw@act.org
Web: www.aauw.org

Summary To provide financial assistance to Asian American and other women who are seeking career advancement, career change, or reentry into the workforce.

Eligibility This program is open to women who are U.S. citizens or permanent residents, have earned a bachelor's degree, received their most recent degree more than 4 years ago, and are making career changes, seeking to advance in current careers, or reentering the workforce. Applicants must be interested in working toward a master's degree, second bachelor's or associate degree, professional degree (e.g., M.D., J.D.), certification program, or technical school certificate. They must be planning to undertake course work at an accredited 2- or 4-year college or university (or a technical school that is licensed, accredited, or approved by the U.S. Department of Education). Primary consideration is given to women of color and women pursuing their first advanced degree or credentials in nontraditional fields. Support is not provided for prerequisite course work or for Ph.D. course work or dissertations. Selection is based on demonstrated commitment to education and equity for women and girls, reason for seeking higher education or technical training, degree to which study plan is consistent with career objectives, potential for success in chosen field, documentation of opportunities in chosen field, feasibility of study plans and proposed time schedule, validity of proposed budget and budget narrative (including sufficient outside support), and quality of written proposal.

Financial data Grants range from $2,000 to $12,000. Funds may be used for tuition, fees, books, supplies, local transportation, dependent child care, or purchase of a computer required for the study program.

Duration 1 year, beginning in July; nonrenewable.

Additional information The filing fee is $35.

Number awarded Varies each year; recently, 63 of these grants, with a value of $670,000, were awarded.

Deadline December of each year.

[427]
AMERICAN GEOPHYSICAL UNION GRADUATE FELLOWSHIP IN THE HISTORY OF SCIENCE

American Geophysical Union
Attn: History of Geophysics
2000 Florida Avenue, N.W.
Washington, DC 20009-1277
(202) 462-6900   Toll Free: (800) 966-2481
Fax: (202) 328-0566
E-mail: HistoryofGeophysics@agu.org
Web: www.agu.org/about/history/fellowship.shtml

Summary To provide funding to doctoral candidates (particularly Asian Americans, other minorities, women, and students with disabilities) who are conducting dissertation research in the history of geophysics. dissertation research in the history of geophysics.

Eligibility This program is open to doctoral candidates at U.S. institutions who have passed all preliminary examinations. Applicants must be completing a dissertation in the history of the geophysical sciences, including topics related to atmospheric sciences, biogeosciences, geodesy, geomagnetism and paleomagnetism, hydrology, ocean sciences, planetary sciences, seismology, space physics, aeronomy, tectonophysics, volcanology, geochemistry, and petrology. They must submit a cover letter with a vita, undergraduate and graduate transcripts, a 10-page description of the dissertation topic and proposed research plan, and 3 letters of recommendation. U.S. citizenship or permanent resident status is required. Applications are encouraged from women, minorities, and students with disabilities who are traditionally underrepresented in the geophysical sciences.

Financial data The grant is $5,000; funds are to be used to assist with the costs of travel to obtain archival or research materials.

Number awarded 1 each year.

Deadline August of each year.

[428]
AMERICAN HEALTH INFORMATION MANAGEMENT ASSOCIATION FOUNDATION DIVERSITY SCHOLARSHIPS

American Health Information Management Association
Attn: AHIMA Foundation
233 North Michigan Avenue, 21st Floor
Chicago, IL 60601-5809
(312) 233-1175   Fax: (312) 233-1475
E-mail: info@ahimafoundation.org
Web: www.ahimafoundation.org

Summary To provide financial assistance to Asian American and other members of the American Health Information Management Association (AHIMA) who are interested in working on an undergraduate or graduate degree in health information management (HIM) or health information technology (HIT) and who will contribute to diversity in the profession.

Eligibility This program is open to AHIMA members who are enrolled at least half time in a program accredited by the

Commission on Accreditation for Health Informatics and Information Management Education (CAHIM). Applicants must be working on a degree in HIM or HIT at the associate, bachelor's, post-baccalaureate, master's, or doctoral level. They must have a GPA of 3.5 or higher and at least 1 full semester remaining after the date of the award. To qualify for this support, applicants must demonstrate how they will contribute to diversity in the health information management profession; diversity is defined as differences in race, ethnicity, nationality, gender, sexual orientation, socioeconomic status, age, physical capabilities, and religious beliefs. Selection is based on GPA and academic achievement, volunteer and work experience, commitment to the HIM profession, quality and relevance of references, and completeness and clarity of thought.

Financial data Stipends are $1,000 for associate degree students, $1,500 for bachelor's degree or post-baccalaureate certificate students, $2,000 for master's degree students, or $2,500 for doctoral degree students.

Duration 1 year.

Number awarded Varies each year; recently, 9 of these scholarships were awarded: 6 to undergraduates and 3 to graduate students.

Deadline September of each year.

[429]
AMERICAN PEDIATRIC SOCIETY/SOCIETY FOR PEDIATRIC RESEARCH STUDENT RESEARCH PROGRAM

American Pediatric Society/Society for Pediatric Research
3400 Research Forest Drive, Suite B-7
The Woodlands, TX 77381
(281) 419-0052   Fax: (281) 419-0082
E-mail: student-research@aps-spr.org
Web: www.aps-spr.org/get-involved/student-research

Summary To provide financial assistance to medical students (particularly Asian Americans and members of other underrepresented groups) who are considering careers in research related to pediatrics.

Eligibility This program is open to students seeking a pediatric research opportunity at an institution (in the United States or Canada) other than their own medical school. Applicants must be enrolled in a medical school in good standing at the time of their application. If they already have a medical degree, they are ineligible. Letters of recommendation are required. Members of underrepresented groups are encouraged to apply.

Financial data The stipend is $61.20 per day, to a maximum of $5,508.

Duration 2 to 3 months.

Additional information Participants choose or are assigned to 1 of more than 300 leading research laboratories in the United States or Canada to work under the direct supervision of experienced scientists in the field of pediatrics.

Number awarded Varies each year.

Deadline January of each year.

[430]
AMERICAN POLITICAL SCIENCE ASSOCIATION MINORITY FELLOWS PROGRAM

American Political Science Association
Attn: APSA Minority Fellows Program
1527 New Hampshire Avenue, N.W.
Washington, DC 20036-1206
(202) 349-9362   Fax: (202) 483-2657
E-mail: sragland@apsanet.org
Web: www.apsanet.org/content_3284.cfm

Summary To provide financial assistance to Asian Americans and other underrepresented minorities interested in working on a doctoral degree in political science.

Eligibility This program is open to African Americans, Asian Pacific Americans, Latino(a)s, and Native Americans who are in their senior year at a college or university or currently enrolled in a master's degree program. Applicants must be planning to enroll in a doctoral program in political science to prepare for a career in teaching and research. They must be U.S. citizens and able to demonstrate financial need. Along with their application, they must submit a 500-word personal statement that includes why they are interested in attending graduate school in political science, what specific fields within the discipline they plan to study, and how they intend to contribute to research within the discipline. Selection is based on interest in teaching and potential for research in political science.

Financial data The stipend is $2,000 per year.

Duration 2 years.

Additional information In addition to the fellows who receive stipends from this program, students who are selected as fellows without stipend are recommended for admission and financial support to every doctoral political science program in the country. This program was established in 1969.

Number awarded Up to 12 fellows receive stipends each year.

Deadline October of each year.

[431]
AMERICAN PSYCHOLOGICAL ASSOCIATION PREDOCTORAL FELLOWSHIP IN MENTAL HEALTH AND SUBSTANCE ABUSE SERVICES

American Psychological Association
Attn: Minority Fellowship Program
750 First Street, N.E.
Washington, DC 20002-4242
(202) 336-6127   Fax: (202) 336-6012
TDD: (202) 336-6123   E-mail: mfp@apa.org
Web: www.apa.org

Summary To provide financial assistance to doctoral students (particularly Asian Americans and members of other ethnic minority groups) who are committed to providing mental health and substance abuse services to ethnic minority populations.

Eligibility Applicants must be U.S. citizens, nationals, or permanent residents, enrolled full time in an accredited doctoral program, and committed to a career in psychology related to ethnic minority mental health and substance abuse services. Members of ethnic minority groups (African Americans, Hispanics/Latinos, American Indians, Alaskan Natives,

Asian Americans, Native Hawaiians, and other Pacific Islanders) are especially encouraged to apply. Preference is given to students specializing in clinical, school, and counseling psychology. Selection is based on commitment to ethnic minority behavioral health services or policy, knowledge of ethnic minority behavioral health services, the fit between career goals and training environment selected, potential as a future leader in ethnic minority psychology as demonstrated through accomplishments and goals, scholarship and grades, and letters of recommendation.

Financial data The stipend varies but is based on the amount established by the National Institutes of Health for predoctoral students; recently that was $22,032 per year.

Duration 1 academic or calendar year; may be renewed for up to 2 additional years.

Additional information Funding is provided by the U.S. Substance Abuse and Mental Health Services Administration.

Number awarded Varies each year.

Deadline January of each year.

[432]
AMERICAN SOCIETY OF CRIMINOLOGY FELLOWSHIPS FOR ETHNIC MINORITIES

American Society of Criminology
Attn: Awards Committee
1314 Kinnear Road, Suite 212
Columbus, OH 43212-1156
(614) 292-9207   Fax: (614) 292-6767
E-mail: asc@asc41.com
Web: www.asc41.com/awards/GradMinorityFellowship.html

Summary To provide financial assistance to Asian American and other ethnic minority doctoral students in criminology and criminal justice.

Eligibility This program is open to students of color, especially members of ethnic groups underrepresented in the field of criminology and criminal justice, including (but not limited to) Asians, Blacks, Indigenous peoples, and Hispanics. Applicants must have been accepted into a doctoral program in the field. Along with their application, they must submit an up-to-date curriculum vitae; an indication of race or ethnicity; copies of undergraduate and graduate transcripts; a statement of need and prospects for other financial assistance; a letter describing career plans, salient experiences, and nature of interest in criminology and criminal justice; and 3 letters of reference.

Financial data The stipend is $6,000.

Duration 1 year.

Additional information This fellowship was first awarded in 1989.

Number awarded 3 each year.

Deadline February of each year.

[433]
AMERICAN SOCIETY OF ENGINEERS OF INDIAN ORIGIN GRADUATE SCHOLARSHIPS

American Society of Engineers of Indian Origin
Attn: Southern California Chapter
P.O. Box 18215
Irvine, CA 92623
E-mail: scholarships@aseisocal.net
Web: www.aseisocal.net/12.html

Summary To provide financial assistance to graduate students of Indian origin (from India) who are working on a degree in engineering, computer science, or related areas.

Eligibility This program is open to graduate students of Indian origin (by birth, ancestry, or relation). Applicants must be enrolled full time at an ABET-accredited college or university in the United States and working on a degree in engineering, computer science, or an allied science and have a GPA of 3.5 or higher. They must be members of the American Society of Engineers of Indian Origin (ASEI). Selection is based on demonstrated ability, academic achievement (including GPA, honors, and awards), career objectives, faculty recommendations, involvement in science fair and campus activities, financial hardship, industrial exposure (including part-time work and internships), and involvement in ASEI and other community activities.

Financial data Stipends range from $500 to $1,000.

Duration 1 year.

Number awarded Several each year.

Deadline August of each year.

[434]
AMERICAN SOCIETY OF INDIAN ENGINEERS SCHOLARSHIP PROGRAM

American Society of Indian Engineers
Attn: Scholarship Program
P.O. Box 741007
Houston, TX 77274
E-mail: asiehouston@gmail.com
Web: www.asiehouston.org/jobopspurtunities.php?id=13

Summary To provide financial assistance to residents of any state who are of Indian origin (from Indian) and are working on an undergraduate or graduate degree in engineering or architecture at a college in the Houston area of Texas.

Eligibility This program is open to residents of any state who are of Indian origin and currently enrolled at a college or university in the greater Houston metropolitan area. Applicants must be working full time on an associate, bachelor's, or graduate degree in engineering or architecture. Along with their application, they must submit an essay about themselves, their achievements, career goals, and activities. Selection is based on that essay (50%), GPA (25%), and financial need (25%). An interview may also be required.

Financial data The stipend is $1,000.

Duration 1 year.

Number awarded Up to 10 each year.

Deadline September of each year.

[435]
AMERICAN SOCIOLOGICAL ASSOCIATION MINORITY FELLOWSHIP PROGRAM GENERAL FELLOWSHIP

American Sociological Association
Attn: Minority Affairs Program
1430 K Street, N.W., Suite 600
Washington, DC 20005-2504
(202) 383-9005, ext. 322   Fax: (202) 638-0882
TDD: (202) 638-0981 E-mail: minority.affairs@asanet.org
Web: www.asanet.org/funding/mfp.cfm

Summary To provide financial assistance to doctoral students in sociology who are Asian American or members of other minority groups.

Eligibility This program is open to U.S. citizens, permanent residents, and noncitizen nationals who are Blacks/African Americans, Latinos (e.g., Mexican Americans, Puerto Ricans, Cubans), American Indians or Alaskan Natives, Asian Americans (e.g., southeast Asians, Japanese, Chinese, Koreans), or Pacific Islanders (e.g., Filipinos, Samoans, Hawaiians, Guamanians). Applicants must be entering or continuing students in sociology at the doctoral level. Along with their application, they must submit 3-page essays on 1) the reasons why they decided to undertake graduate study in sociology, their primary research interests, and why they hope to do with a Ph.D. in sociology; and 2) what led them to select the doctoral program they attend or hope to attend and how they see that doctoral program preparing them for a professional career in sociology. Selection is based on commitment to research, focus of research experience, academic achievement, writing ability, research potential, and financial need.

Financial data The stipend is $18,000 per year.

Duration 1 year; may be renewed up to 2 additional years.

Additional information This program, which began in 1974, is supported by individual members of the American Sociological Association (ASA) and by several affiliated organizations (Alpha Kappa Delta, Sociologists for Women in Society, the Association of Black Sociologists, the Midwest Sociological Society, and the Southwestern Sociological Association).

Number awarded Varies each year; since the program began, approximately 500 of these fellowships have been awarded.

Deadline January of each year.

[436]
AMERICAN SPEECH-LANGUAGE-HEARING FOUNDATION SCHOLARSHIP FOR MINORITY STUDENTS

American Speech-Language-Hearing Foundation
Attn: Programs Administrator
2200 Research Boulevard
Rockville, MD 20850-3289
(301) 296-8703   Fax: (301) 296-8567
E-mail: foundationprograms@asha.org
Web: www.ashfoundation.org/grants/GraduateScholarships

Summary To provide financial assistance to Asian American and other minority graduate students in communication sciences and disorders programs.

Eligibility This program is open to full-time graduate students who are enrolled in communication sciences and disorders programs, with preference given to U.S. citizens who are members of a racial or ethnic minority group. Applicants must submit an essay, up to 5 pages in length, on a topic that relates to the future of leadership in the discipline. Selection is based on academic promise and outstanding academic achievement.

Financial data The stipend is $5,000. Funds must be used for educational support (e.g., tuition, books, school living expenses), not for personal or conference travel.

Duration 1 year.

Number awarded 1 each year.

Deadline June of each year.

[437]
ANAPATA DIVERSITY SCHOLARSHIP CONTEST

Ms. JD
Attn: Chief Financial Officer
3207 Jackson Street
Houston, TX 77004
E-mail: staff@ms-jd.org
Web: ms-jd.org/anapata-student-scholarship

Summary To provide financial assistance to law students who are Asian American or members of other groups traditionally underrepresented in the legal profession.

Eligibility This program is open to students currently enrolled at ABA-approved law schools in the United States. Members of groups traditionally underrepresented in the legal profession are especially encouraged to apply. They must submit a resume, transcript, personal introduction paragraph, 2 recommendations, and a 750-word essay demonstrating their personal philosophy regarding diversity in the legal profession. Selection is based on academic achievement, leadership ability, writing and interpersonal skills, and interest in promoting diversity in the legal profession.

Financial data The stipend is $1,000.

Duration 1 year.

Additional information This program is offered by Ms. JD in partnership with Anapata, Inc.

Number awarded 1 or more each year.

Deadline February of each year.

[438]
ANHEUSER-BUSCH NAPABA LAW FOUNDATION PRESIDENTIAL SCHOLARSHIPS

National Asian Pacific American Bar Association
Attn: NAPABA Law Foundation
1612 K Street, N.W., Suite 1400
Washington, DC 20006
(202) 775-9555   Fax: (202) 775-9333
E-mail: nlfstaff@napaba.org
Web: www.napaba.org

Summary To provide financial assistance to law students interested in serving the Asian Pacific American community.

Eligibility This program is open to students at ABA-accredited law schools in the United States. Applicants must demonstrate leadership potential to serve the Asian Pacific American community upon graduation. Along with their application, they must submit a 500-word essay that covers 1) the most significant experiences in their background that have shaped and demonstrated their commitment to serving the needs of Asian Pacific Americans; and 2) how they intend to serve the needs of the Asian Pacific American community in their future legal career. Selection is based on that essay, academic achievement, leadership, and commitment to bettering the Asian Pacific American community. U.S. citizenship or permanent resident status is required.

Financial data The stipend is $7,500.

Duration 1 year.

Additional information This program is supported by Anheuser-Busch Companies, Inc.

Number awarded 2 each year.

Deadline September of each year.

[439]
APABA-SV CHARITY FOUNDATION/BALIF SCHOLARSHIP

Asian Pacific American Bar Association of the Silicon Valley
c/o Sallie Kim, Scholarship Committee Chair
GCA Law Partners LLP
2570 West El Camino Real, Suite 510
Mountain View, CA 94040
(650) 237-7221   E-mail: apabasv@gmail.com
Web: www.apabasv.org

Summary To provide financial assistance to students from any state who are enrolled at law schools in the San Francisco Bay area and have served the Asian Pacific American and LGBT communities.

Eligibility This program is open to students currently enrolled at law schools in the San Francisco Bay area who have 1) demonstrated leadership and service to the Asian Pacific American community and the LGBT community; 2) overcome personal hardships or challenges; and 3) shown excellence and achievement in law school. Applicants must submit a 2-page essay explaining how they satisfy those requirements. Finalists are interviewed.

Financial data The stipend is $1,500.

Duration 1 year.

Additional information This program began in 2013 with support from the Charity Foundation of the Asian Pacific American Bar Association of the Silicon Valley (APABA-SV) and the Bay Area Lawyers for Individual Freedom (BALIF).

Number awarded 1 each year.

Deadline September of each year.

[440]
APAGS COMMITTEE ON ETHNIC MINORITY AFFAIRS GRANT PROGRAM

American Psychological Association
Attn: American Psychological Association of Graduate Students
750 First Street, N.E.
Washington, DC 20002-4242
(202) 336-6014   Fax: (202) 336-5694
E-mail: apags@apa.org
Web: www.apa.org

Summary To provide funding to graduate students (particularly Asian Americans and other ethnic minorities) who are members of the American Psychological Association of Graduate Students (APAGS) and who wish to develop a project that increases membership and participation of ethnic minority students within the association.

Eligibility This program is open to members of APAGS who are enrolled at least half time in a master's or doctoral program at an accredited university. Applicants must be interested in developing a project to increase the membership and participation of ethnic minority graduate students within APAGS, advertise education and training opportunities for ethnic minorities, and enhance the recruitment and retention efforts for ethnic minority students in psychology. Examples include, but are not limited to, workshops, conferences, speaker series, mentorship programs, and the development of student organizations with a focus on multiculturalism or ethnic minority concerns.

Financial data The grant is $1,000.

Duration The grant is presented annually.

Additional information This grant was first awarded in 1997.

Number awarded 5 each year.

Deadline Deadline not specified.

[441]
APF/COGDOP GRADUATE RESEARCH SCHOLARSHIPS

American Psychological Foundation
750 First Street, N.E.
Washington, DC 20002-4242
(202) 336-5843   Fax: (202) 336-5812
E-mail: foundation@apa.org
Web: www.apa.org/apf/funding/cogdop.aspx

Summary To provide funding for research to graduate students (particularly Asian Americans and other diverse students) who are working on a graduate degree in psychology.

Eligibility Each department of psychology that is a member in good standing of the Council of Graduate Departments of Psychology (COGDOP) may nominate up to 3 candidates for these scholarships. Nominations must include a completed application form, a letter of nomination from the department chair or director of graduate studies, a letter of recommendation from the nominee's graduate research adviser, a transcript of all graduate course work completed by the nominee, a curriculum vitae, and a brief outline of the nominee's thesis or dissertation research project. Selection is based on the context for the research, the clarity and comprehensibility of the research question, the appropriateness of the research design, the general importance of the research, and the use of requested funds. The sponsor encourages applications from individuals who represent diversity in race, ethnicity, gender, age, disability, and sexual orientation.

Financial data Awards range from $1,000 to $5,000 per year. A total of $28,000 is available for these scholarships each year.

Duration 1 year.

Additional information The highest rated nominees receive the Harry and Miriam Levinson Scholarship of $5,000 and the William and Dorothy Bevan Scholarship of $5,000. The next highest rated nominee receives the Ruth G. and Joseph D. Matarazzo Scholarship of $3,000. The next highest rated nominee receives the Clarence Rosecrans Scholarship of $2,000. The next highest rated nominees receive the William C. Howell Scholarship and the Peter and Malina James

and Dr. Louis P. James Legacy Scholarship of $1,000 each. Another 9 scholarships of $1,000 each are also awarded.

Number awarded 15 each year: 2 at $5,000, 1 at $3,000, 1 at $2,000, and 11 at $1,000.

Deadline June of each year.

[442]
AP-GOOGLE JOURNALISM AND TECHNOLOGY SCHOLARSHIP PROGRAM

Online News Association
Attn: Scholarship Manager
P.O. Box 65741
Washington, DC 20035
(646) 290-7900   E-mail: irving@journalists.org
Web: journalists.org/next-gen/ap-google-scholarship

Summary To recognize and reward undergraduate and graduate students (especially Asian Americans and those from other diverse backgrounds) who propose outstanding projects "at the intersection of journalism and technology."

Eligibility This program is open to full-time undergraduates (at least sophomores) and graduate students at U.S. institutions who have at least 1 year of study remaining and a GPA of 3.0 or higher. Students from diverse backgrounds (defined as ethnic and racial minorities, members of the lesbian, gay, bisexual, and transgender (LGBT) community, and students with disabilities) and those attending rural area institutions are strongly encouraged to apply. Some scholarships are reserved for students who can demonstrate financial need. Applicants must develop original journalistic content with computer science elements; they should explain how their strategy moves digital journalism forward or provides valuable lessons or outcomes. Examples include data visualization, data mining, mobile devices and applications, 3-D storytelling, digital ethics, or microcomputers. In the selection process, emphasis is placed on innovation and creativity. U.S. citizenship is required.

Financial data The award is a $20,000 scholarship, of which half is paid to the winner's institution at the beginning of the first semester and half at the beginning of the second semester, provided the recipient earns a GPA of 3.0 or higher for the first semester.

Duration The competition is held annually.

Additional information This competition is supported by Google.

Number awarded 6 each year.

Deadline February of each year.

[443]
APIO SCHOLARSHIP PROGRAM

Asian Pacific Islander Organization
c/o Gina Schworm, Scholarship Committee Co-Chair
USDA Natural Resources Conservation Service
Coshocton County Service Center
724 South Seventh Street, Room 120
Coshocton, OH 43812-2391
(740) 622-8087   E-mail: gina.schworm@oh.usda.gov
Web: www.apio.org/scholarship.htm

Summary To provide financial assistance to Asian and Pacific Islanders who are studying designated fields in college or graduate school.

Eligibility This program is open to Asian and Pacific Islander students who have completed at least 15 semester hours of credit at an accredited 2- or 4-year college or university. Applicants must be working on an undergraduate or graduate degree in a field related to natural resources (e.g., agricultural business, agronomy, biology, botany, environmental science, forestry, geology, horticulture, plant science, rangeland management, soil science, or agricultural, civil, or environmental engineering). Along with their application, they must submit a 1-page personal statement on their background, personal and career goals, and extracurricular activities. Selection is based on academic achievement, personal strengths, leadership abilities, career goals, and work experience. U.S. citizenship is required.

Financial data The stipend is $1,000, $1,500, or $2,000.

Duration 1 year.

Additional information The Asian Pacific Islander Organization (APIO) was established in 1998 as a professional society of employees of the Natural Resources Conservation Service of the U.S. Department of Agriculture.

Number awarded 3 each year: 1 each at $1,000, $1,500, and $2,000.

Deadline April of each year.

[444]
ARCHIE MOTLEY MEMORIAL SCHOLARSHIP FOR MINORITY STUDENTS

Midwest Archives Conference
c/o Alison Stankrauff
Indiana University South Bend
Franklin D. Schurz Library
P.O. Box 7111
South Bend, IN 46634
(574) 520-4392   E-mail: astankra@iusb.edu
Web: www.midwestarchives.org/motley

Summary To provide financial assistance to Asian American and other minority graduate students preparing for a career in archival administration.

Eligibility This program is open to graduate students of African, American Indian, Asian, Pacific Islander, or Latino descent who are enrolled or accepted for enrollment in a graduate, multi-course program in archival administration at a college or university in any state. The graduate program must offer at least 3 courses in archival administration or be listed in the current Directory of Archival Education of the Society of American Archivists (SAA). Applicants must have a GPA of 3.0 or higher. They may be residents of any state and attending school in any state. Along with their application, they must submit a 500-word essay on their interests and future goals in archival administration.

Financial data The stipend is $750.

Duration 1 year.

Additional information This program began in 2004.

Number awarded 2 each year.

Deadline February of each year.

[445]
ARENT FOX DIVERSITY SCHOLARSHIPS

Arent Fox LLP
Attn: Attorney Recruitment and Professional Development
  Coordinator
1717 K Street, N.W.
Washington, DC 20036
(202) 857-6000   Fax: (202) 857-6395
E-mail: dcattorneyrecruit@arentfox.com
Web: www.arentfox.com

Summary To provide financial aid and work experience to Asian American and other minority law students.

Eligibility This program is open to first-year law students who are members of a diverse population that historically has been underrepresented in the legal profession. Applicants must be U.S. citizens or otherwise authorized to work in the United States. They must also be willing to work as a summer intern at the sponsoring law firm's offices in Los Angeles, New York City, or Washington, D.C. Along with their application, they must submit a resume, an undergraduate transcript and law school grades when available, a 5- to 10-page legal writing sample, 3 letters of recommendation, and an essay on how their background, skills, experience, and interest equip them to meet the sponsor's goal of commitment to diversity. Selection is based on academic performance during college and law school, oral and writing communication skills, leadership qualities, and community involvement.

Financial data The scholarship stipend is $15,000. The summer salary is $2,500 per week.

Duration 1 year.

Additional information These scholarships were first offered in 2006. Recipients are also offered summer internships with Arent Fox: 1 in Los Angeles, 1 in New York City, and 1 in Washington, D.C. Students interested in the summer program in Los Angeles should contact Attorney Recruitment Manager, 555 West Fifth Street, 48th Floor, Los Angeles, CA 90013, (213) 629-7400, Fax: (213) 629-7401, E-mail: laattorneyrecruit@arentfox.com. Students interested in the summer program in New York should contact Attorney Recruitment Coordinator, 1675 Broadway, New York, NY 10019, (212) 484-3983, Fax: (212) 484-3990, E-mail: nyattorneyrecruit@arentfox.com.

Number awarded 3 each year.

Deadline January of each year.

[446]
ASCA FOUNDATION SCHOLARSHIPS

American School Counselor Association
Attn: ASCA Foundation
1101 King Street, Suite 625
Alexandria, VA 22314
(703) 683-ASCA   Toll Free: (800) 306-4722
Fax: (703) 683-1619   E-mail: asca@schoolcounselor.org
Web: www.schoolcounselor.org/content.asp?contentid=176

Summary To provide financial assistance for graduate school to members of the American School Counselor Association (ASCA), especially Asian Americans, other minorities, and males.

Eligibility This program is open to ASCA members working full time on a master's degree in school counseling. Applicants must submit a 2-page essay on a topic that changes annually but relates to the role of counselors in schools. Males and minorities are especially encouraged to apply.

Financial data The stipend is $1,000.

Duration 1 year.

Additional information Support for this program is provided by Anheuser-Busch.

Number awarded Up to 10 each year.

Deadline October of each year.

[447]
ASIAN AMERICAN ARCHITECTS AND ENGINEERS FOUNDATION SCHOLARSHIPS

Asian American Architects/Engineers Association
Attn: Foundation
645 West Ninth Street, Unit 110-175
Los Angeles, CA 90015
(213) 896-9270   Fax: (213) 985-7404
E-mail: info@aaaesc.org
Web: www.aaaesc.org/student-scholarship-application

Summary To provide financial assistance to members of the Asian American Architects/Engineers Association (AAa/e) who are interested in working on an undergraduate or graduate degree at a school in southern California.

Eligibility This program is open to student members of AAa/e who are U.S. citizens, permanent residents, or noncitizens enrolled full time at a college or university in southern California. Applicants must be graduating seniors, undergraduates, or graduate students working on or planning to work on a degree in architecture, civil engineering (environmental, geotechnical, structural, transportation), electrical engineering, mechanical engineering, landscape architecture, planning and urban design, or construction and construction management. Along with their application, they must submit 1) a 1-page personal statement on their involvement and service to the Asian Pacific Islander community; 2) letters of recommendation from 2 faculty members or employers; and 3) a sample of their work, which may be a design or research project, a completed project, or a proposed project, including an assignment from a class, a senior project, or an assignment from work. Selection is based on the work sample (65%), personal statements (20%), and recommendations (15%).

Financial data Stipends range up to $5,000.

Duration 1 year.

Number awarded Varies each year.

Deadline May of each year.

[448]
ASIAN AMERICAN BAR ASSOCIATION LAW OF THE GREATER BAY AREA FOUNDATION SCHOLARSHIPS

Asian American Bar Association of the Greater Bay Area
Attn: Law Foundation
575 Market Street, Suite 2125
San Francisco, CA 94105
E-mail: info@aaba-bay.com
Web: www.aaba-bay.com

Summary To provide financial assistance to Asian American residents of any state who are enrolled at law schools in the San Francisco Bay area and planning to serve the Asian American community after graduation.

Eligibility This program is open to Asian American students from any state who are attending law schools in the Bay area and have demonstrated a strong commitment to serving the needs of the Asian American community. Students at other law schools may be eligible if they can demonstrate a commitment to serving the Asian American community in the Bay area. Applicants must submit a 3-page personal statement that covers 1) what they see as a pressing issue or concern facing the Asian American community and the role they see themselves playing in advocating or engaging in such an issue; 2) their experience in overcoming economic and other discriminatory barriers; and 3) who they see as a successful leader within the Asian American community. An interview may be required.

Financial data The amount awarded varies but is usually around $1,000.

Duration 1 year.

Additional information This program includes the Asian American Judges Scholarship, the Joe Morozumi Scholarship and the Raymond L. Ocampo Jr. President's Scholarship.

Number awarded Varies each year; recently, 4 of these scholarships were awarded.

Deadline January of each year.

[449]
ASIAN AMERICAN LAW FUND OF NEW YORK COMMUNITY SERVICE SCHOLARSHIPS

Asian American Bar Association of New York
Attn: Asian American Law Fund of New York, Inc.
c/o Sylvia Fung Chin
White & Case LLP
1155 Avenue of the Americas
New York, NY 10036-2787
(212) 819-8200   Fax: (212) 354-8113
E-mail: schin@whitecase.com
Web: www.aabany.org

Summary To provide an opportunity for law students from any state to conduct a service project that will help them pay for their own tuition as well as benefit the Asian American community of New York.

Eligibility This program is open to students enrolled at least half time at ABA- or AALS-accredited law schools in the United States. Applicants must be interested in conducting a community service project as a volunteer for a nonprofit organization that serves the Asian American community of New York. The project should involve legal work and have a supervising attorney. Along with their application, they must submit a 750-word essay that covers 1) the most significant experiences in their background that have shaped and demonstrated their commitment to serving the needs of Asian Pacific Americans; 2) what they hope to learn, accomplish, or change through their project; 3) how they will use the experience that they will gain from their project; and 4) how they will serve the needs of the Asian American community in their future legal career. Selection is based on commitment to and interest in pro bono and/or public interest legal work with the Asian American community, leadership potential, maturity and responsibility, and financial need. U.S. citizenship or permanent resident status is required.

Financial data The grant is $5,000. Funds are to be used to assist the students with their tuition while encouraging them to use their legal knowledge and training to benefit the Asian American community in New York.

Duration Recipients are expected to volunteer for at least 6 weeks during the summer.

Number awarded Up to 3 each year.

Deadline March of each year.

[450]
ASIAN AMERICAN LAWYERS ASSOCIATION OF MASSACHUSETTS SCHOLARSHIP

Asian American Lawyers Association of Massachusetts
c/o Peggy L. Ho, President
LPL Financial Corporation
One Beacon Street, 22nd Floor
Boston, MA 02108
(617) 897-4348　　　　　E-mail: Peggy.Ho@lpl.com
Web: www.aalam.org/membership_lawstudents.shtml

Summary To provide financial assistance to Asian American students from any state enrolled at law schools in Massachusetts.

Eligibility This program is open to students currently enrolled at law schools in Massachusetts who can demonstrate leadership potential, maturity and responsibility, and a commitment to making a contribution to the Asian Pacific American community. Applicants must submit a 500-word essay on how they, as a future Asian Pacific American lawyer, think they can best contribute to the Asian Pacific American community. Financial need is not considered in the selection process.

Financial data The stipend is $2,500.

Duration 1 year.

Number awarded 1 each year.

Deadline April of each year.

[451]
ASIAN AND PACIFIC AMERICAN LAWYERS ASSOCIATION OF NEW JERSEY SCHOLARSHIPS

Asian and Pacific American Lawyers Association of New
　Jersey
c/o Michelle Wu, Scholarship Committee Chair
Graham Curtin
4 Headquarters Plaza
P.O. Box 1991
Morristown, NJ 07962-1991
(973) 292-1700　　　　　Fax: (973) 292-1767
E-mail: mwu@grahamcurtin.com
Web: www.apalanj.org/foundation

Summary To provide financial assistance to students who are enrolled at law schools in New Jersey and have demonstrated an interest in the Asian American community.

Eligibility This program is open to students currently enrolled at a law school in New Jersey either as a full-time first- or second-year student or as a part-time first-, second-, or third-year student. Applicants must submit 400-word essays on 1) the most pressing issue or concern they believe the Asian American community is facing today and the role they see themselves playing in advocating for that issue or concern; 2) their suggestions on how Asians and Pacific Islander Americans can stand up and be counted in the legal community and the community at large; and 3) who they see as a successful leader within the Asian American community

and the characteristics that make the leader so successful. Selection is based on the essays, academic success, potential to contribute positively to the legal profession, and financial need.

Financial data The stipend is at least $1,000.

Duration 1 year.

Number awarded 3 each year: 1 at each law school in New Jersey.

Deadline April of each year.

[452]
ASIAN BAR ASSOCIATION OF WASHINGTON STUDENT SCHOLARSHIPS

Asian Bar Association of Washington
Attn: Student Scholarship Foundation
c/o Lisa Lui, Scholarship Chair
Miller Nash LLP
601 Union Street, Suite 4400
Seattle, WA 98101
(206) 622-8484　　　　　Fax: (206) 622-7485
E-mail: lisa.lui@millernash.com
Web: www.abaw.org/awards-and-scholarships.html

Summary To provide financial assistance to students from any state who are attending law school in Washington and have been involved in the Asian community.

Eligibility This program is open to students from any state currently attending law school in the state of Washington. Applicants must be a member of the Asian Pacific Islander (API) student organization at their school. Along with their application, they must submit a 1,000-word personal statement describing their contributions to the API community and their plans to contribute to that community following graduation from law school, a resume, a copy of their most recent law school transcript, and 2 letters of reference.

Financial data Stipends range from $500 to $6,000.

Duration 1 year.

Additional information This program includes the Yamashita Scholarship, the Sharon A. Sakamoto President's Scholarship, and the Northwest Minority Job Fair Scholarship.

Number awarded Varies each year; recently, 5 of these scholarships were awarded: 1 at $6,000, 1 at $4,000, 2 at $2,000, and 1 at $500.

Deadline September of each year.

[453]
ASIAN PACIFIC AMERICAN BAR ASSOCIATION OF COLORADO SCHOLARSHIPS

Asian Pacific American Bar Association of Colorado
c/o Nicoal C. Wolfe
Jones & Keller
1999 Broadway, Suite 3150
Denver, CO 80202
(303) 573-1600
E-mail: membership@apaba-colorado.org
Web: www.apaba-colorado.org/apaba-foundation

Summary To provide financial assistance to Asian American law students in Colorado.

Eligibility This program is open to students from any state currently enrolled at law schools in Colorado. Applicants must demonstrate a record of public service to the Asian community in the state.

Financial data The stipend is $1,000. The recipients' law schools must match the award, which then makes the total award $2,000.

Duration 1 year.

Additional information This program began in 1996.

Number awarded 2 each year.

Deadline Deadline not specified.

[454]
ASIAN PACIFIC AMERICAN BAR ASSOCIATION OF MARYLAND SCHOLARSHIPS

Asian Pacific American Bar Association of Maryland
c/o Scott L. Schubel, Scholarship Chair
The Law Firm of Scott L. Schubel
13212 Fountainhead Plaza
Hagerstown, MD 21742
(301) 739-5340　　　　　　　　　Fax: (301) 739-7617
E-mail: schublaw@verizon.net
Web: www.apaba-md.org

Summary To provide financial assistance to students from any state who are enrolled at law schools in Maryland and are committed to serving the needs of Asian Pacific Americans.

Eligibility This program is open to residents of any state who are currently enrolled at law schools in Maryland. Applicants must submit a 2-page essay on 1) the most significant experiences in their background that have shaped and demonstrated their commitment to serving the needs of Asian Pacific Americans; and 2) how they will best serve the needs of the Asian Pacific American community in their future legal career. Financial need is not considered in the selection process.

Financial data The stipend is $750.

Duration 1 year.

Number awarded 2 each year.

Deadline April of each year.

[455]
ASIAN PACIFIC AMERICAN BAR ASSOCIATION OF THE SILICON VALLEY ACHIEVEMENT SCHOLARSHIPS

Asian Pacific American Bar Association of the Silicon Valley
c/o Sallie Kim, Scholarship Committee Chair
GCA Law Partners LLP
2570 West El Camino Real, Suite 510
Mountain View, CA 94040
(650) 237-7221　　　　　　　E-mail: apabasv@gmail.com
Web: www.apabasv.org

Summary To provide financial assistance to students from any state who are enrolled at law schools in the San Francisco Bay area and have been involved in the Asian Pacific American community.

Eligibility This program is open to students currently enrolled at law schools in the San Francisco Bay area who have 1) demonstrated leadership and service to the Asian Pacific American community in the United States; 2) overcome personal hardships or challenges; and 3) shown excellence and achievement in law school. Applicants must submit a 2-page essay explaining how they satisfy those require-

ments. Strong preference is given to students who will be interning at a nonprofit organization that serves the Asian Pacific American community and who can demonstrate financial need. Finalists are interviewed.

Financial data The stipend is $3,000.

Duration 1 year.

Number awarded Up to 3 each year.

Deadline March of each year.

[456]
ASIAN PACIFIC AMERICAN LIBRARIANS ASSOCIATION SCHOLARSHIP

Asian Pacific American Librarians Association
Attn: Executive Director
P.O. Box 677593
Orlando, FL 32867-7593
(407) 823-5048　　　　　　　　　Fax: (407) 823-5865
E-mail: bbasco@mail.ucf.edu
Web: www.apalaweb.org/awards/apala-scholarship

Summary To provide financial assistance to students of Asian or Pacific Islander descent who are working on a graduate library degree.

Eligibility This program is open to students of Asian or Pacific Islander heritage who are enrolled or have been accepted into a master's program or doctoral degree program in library or information science at a library school accredited by the American Library Association (ALA). Applicants must be citizens or permanent residents of the United States or Canada. Along with their application, they must submit a 1-page essay on either their vision of a librarian's role in the 21st century or the contributions they can make as an Asian or Pacific Islander librarian.

Financial data The stipend is $1,000.

Duration 1 year.

Number awarded 1 each year.

Deadline April of each year.

[457]
ASIAN PACIFIC ISLANDER AMERICAN PUBLIC AFFAIRS ASSOCIATION COLLEGE SCHOLARSHIPS

Asian Pacific Islander American Public Affairs Association
Attn: Community Education Foundation
4000 Truxel Road, Suite 3
Sacramento, CA 95834
(916) 928-9988　　　　　　　　　Fax: (916) 928-9983
E-mail: info@apapa.org
Web: www.apapa.org/news/scholarship.aspx

Summary To provide financial assistance to residents of California, especially those of Asian or Pacific Islander ancestry, who are attending college or graduate school in any state.

Eligibility This program is open to residents of California who are currently enrolled as an undergraduate or graduate student at an accredited 2- or 4-year college or university in any state. All students are eligible, but applications are especially encouraged from those who have Asian or Pacific Islander ancestry. They must have a GPA of 2.75 or higher. Along with their application, they must submit a personal statement demonstrating their commitment to the Asian Pacific Islander community. Selection is based on academic achievement, abilities, career goals, civic activities, leadership skills, and demonstrated commitment to the Asian Pacific Islander community. U.S. citizenship or permanent resident status is required.

Financial data The stipend is $1,000. Funds are paid directly to the student's institution.

Duration 1 year; nonrenewable.

Number awarded Varies each year; recently, 14 of these scholarships were awarded.

Deadline February of each year.

[458]
ASME GRADUATE TEACHING FELLOWSHIP

ASME International
Attn: Centers Administrator
Two Park Avenue
New York, NY 10016-5675
(212) 591-8131   Toll Free: (800) THE-ASME
Fax: (212) 591-7143   E-mail: LefeverB@asme.org
Web: www.asme.org

Summary To provide funding to members of the American Society of Mechanical Engineers (ASME) who are working on a doctorate in mechanical engineering (particularly those who are Asian Americans, other minority group members, and female).

Eligibility This program is open to U.S. citizens or permanent residents who have an undergraduate degree from an ABET-accredited program, belong to the society as a student member, are currently employed as a teaching assistant with lecture responsibility, and are working on a Ph.D. in mechanical engineering. Along with their application, they must submit a statement about their interest in a faculty career. Applications from women and minorities are particularly encouraged.

Financial data Fellowship stipends are $5,000 per year.

Duration Up to 2 years.

Additional information Recipients must teach at least 1 lecture course.

Number awarded Up to 4 each year.

Deadline February of each year.

[459]
BAKER DONELSON DIVERSITY SCHOLARSHIPS

Baker, Donelson, Bearman, Caldwell & Berkowitz, P.C.
Attn: Director of Attorney Recruiting
3414 Peachtree Road N.E., Suite 1600
Atlanta, GA 30326
(404) 577-6000   Fax: (404) 221-6501
E-mail: lklein@bakerdonelson.com
Web: www.bakerdonelson.com

Summary To provide financial assistance to law students who are Asian American or members of other groups underrepresented at large law firms.

Eligibility This program is open to students who have completed the first year at an ABA-accredited law school. Applicants must be members of a group traditionally underrepresented at large law firms (American Indian or Alaskan Native, Native Hawaiian or Pacific Islander, Hispanic or Latino, Black, or Asian). Along with their application, they must submit a 10-page legal writing sample and a 1-page personal statement on challenges they have faced in pursuit of their legal career that have helped them to understand the value of diversity

and its inclusion in the legal profession. Finalists are interviewed.

Financial data The stipend is $10,000.

Duration 1 year.

Additional information Recipients are also offered summer internships at Baker Donelson offices in Atlanta (Georgia), Baton Rouge (Louisiana), Birmingham (Alabama), Chattanooga (Tennessee), Jackson (Mississippi), Johnson City (Tennessee), Knoxville (Tennessee), Memphis (Tennessee), Nashville (Tennessee), and New Orleans (Louisiana).

Number awarded 3 each year.

Deadline June of each year.

[460]
BAKERHOSTETLER DIVERSITY FELLOWSHIP PROGRAM

BakerHostetler LLP
Attn: Attorney Recruitment and Development Manager
PNC Center
1900 East Ninth Street, Suite 3200
Cleveland, OH 44114-3482
(216) 621-0200   Fax: (216) 696-0740
E-mail: ddriscole@bakerlaw.com
Web: www.bakerlaw.com/diversityfellowshipprogram

Summary To provide financial aid and summer work experience to Asian American and other minority law school students who are interested in employment with BakerHostetler.

Eligibility This program is open to full-time second-year students at ABA-accredited law schools who are members of underrepresented groups (Black/African American, Hispanic, Asian American/Pacific Islander, American Indian/Alaskan Native, 2 or more races, or gay, lesbian, bisexual, transgender). Applicants must be interested in a summer associate position with BakerHostetler and possible full-time employment following graduation. They must be U.S. citizens or otherwise authorized to work in the United States. Along with their application, they must submit a 500-word personal statement presenting their views of or experience with diversity, including why they are interested in Baker Hostetler and how they will be able to contribute to the diversity objectives of the firm. Selection is based on academic performance in college and law school, personal achievements, community involvement, oral and written communication skills, demonstrated leadership achievements, and a sincere interest and commitment to join BakerHostetler.

Financial data The stipend is $25,000, of which $10,000 is paid within the first 30 days of starting a summer associate position with the firm and the remaining $15,000 is contingent upon receiving and accepting a full-time offer with the firm.

Duration Summer associate positions are for 8 weeks.

Additional information Summer associate positions may be performed at any of the firm's offices in Chicago, Cincinnati, Cleveland, Columbus, Costa Mesa, Denver, Houston, Los Angeles, New York, Orlando, or Washington, D.C.

Number awarded 1 or more each year.

Deadline October of each year.

[461]
BALFOUR PHI DELTA PHI MINORITY SCHOLARSHIP PROGRAM

Phi Delta Phi International Legal Fraternity
1426 21st Street, N.W., First Floor
Washington, DC 20036
(202) 223-6801   Toll Free: (800) 368-5606
Fax: (202) 223-6808   E-mail: info@phideltaphi.org
Web: www.phideltaphi.org

Summary   To provide financial assistance to Asian Americans and other minorities who are members of Phi Delta Phi International Legal Fraternity.

Eligibility   This program is open to ethnic minority members of the legal fraternity. Applicants must affirm that they intend to practice law in inner-cities of the United States, especially in New England. They must submit a 750-word essay on why they consider themselves qualified to serve as role models for minority youth. Selection is based on participation, ethics, and scholastics.

Financial data   The stipend is $3,000.

Duration   1 year.

Additional information   This program began in 1997 with funding from the Lloyd G. Balfour Foundation.

Number awarded   1 each year.

Deadline   October of each year.

[462]
BEHAVIORAL SCIENCES STUDENT FELLOWSHIPS IN EPILEPSY

Epilepsy Foundation
Attn: Research Department
8301 Professional Place
Landover, MD 20785-2353
(301) 459-3700   Toll Free: (800) EFA-1000
Fax: (301) 577-2684   TDD: (800) 332-2070
E-mail: grants@efa.org
Web: www.epilepsyfoundation.org

Summary   To provide funding to undergraduate and graduate students (particularly Asian Americans, other minorities, women, and students with disabilities) who are interested in working on a summer research project in a behavioral science field relevant to epilepsy.

Eligibility   This program is open to undergraduate and graduate students in a behavioral science program relevant to epilepsy research or clinical care, including, but not limited to, sociology, social work, psychology, anthropology, nursing, economics, vocational rehabilitation, counseling, or political science. Applicants must be interested in working on an epilepsy research project under the supervision of a qualified mentor. Because the program is designed as a training opportunity, the quality of the training plans and environment are considered in the selection process. Other selection criteria include the quality of the proposed project, the relevance of the proposed work to epilepsy, the applicant's interest in the field of epilepsy, the applicant's qualifications, and the mentor's qualifications (including his or her commitment to the student and the project), and the quality of the training environment for research related to epilepsy. U.S. citizenship is not required, but the project must be conducted in the United States. Applications from women, members of minority groups, and people with disabilities are especially encour-

aged. The program is not intended for students working on a dissertation research project.

Financial data   The grant is $3,000.

Duration   3 months during the summer.

Additional information   This program is supported by the American Epilepsy Society, Abbott Laboratories, Ortho-McNeil Pharmaceutical Corporation, and Pfizer Inc.

Number awarded   Varies each year.

Deadline   March of each year.

[463]
BELFER CENTER FOR SCIENCE AND INTERNATIONAL AFFAIRS FELLOWSHIPS

Harvard University
John F. Kennedy School of Government
Belfer Center for Science and International Affairs
Attn: Fellowship Coordinator
79 John F. Kennedy Street, Mailbox 53
Cambridge, MA 02138
(617) 495-8806   Fax: (617) 495-8963
E-mail: bcsia_fellowships@hks.harvard.edu
Web: belfercenter.ksg.harvard.edu/fellowships

Summary   To provide funding to professionals, postdoctorates, and doctoral students (particularly Asian Americans, other minorities, and women) who are interested in conducting research in areas of concern to the Belfer Center for Science and International Affairs at Harvard University in Cambridge, Massachusetts.

Eligibility   The postdoctoral fellowship is open to recent recipients of the Ph.D. or equivalent degree, university faculty members, and employees of government, military, international, humanitarian, and private research institutions who have appropriate professional experience. Applicants for predoctoral fellowships must have passed their general examinations. Lawyers, economists, political scientists, those in the natural sciences, and others of diverse disciplinary backgrounds are also welcome to apply. The program especially encourages applications from women, minorities, and citizens of all countries. All applicants must be interested in conducting research in 1 of the 2 major program areas of the center: 1) the International Security Program (ISP), which addresses U.S. defense and foreign policy, security policy, nuclear proliferation, terrorism, internal and ethnic conflict, and related topics; and 2) the Science, Technology, and Public Policy Program (STPP), including technology and innovation, information and communications technology, water-energy nexus, managing the atom, energy technology innovation policy, China and environmental sustainability, geoengineering and climate policy, geopolitics of energy, and geospatial policy and management.

Financial data   The stipend is $34,000 for postdoctoral research fellows or $20,000 for predoctoral research fellows. Health insurance is also provided.

Duration   10 months.

Number awarded   A limited number each year.

Deadline   January of each year.

[464]
BENTON-MEIER NEUROPSYCHOLOGY SCHOLARSHIPS

American Psychological Foundation
750 First Street, N.E.
Washington, DC 20002-4242
(202) 336-5843   Fax: (202) 336-5812
E-mail: foundation@apa.org
Web: www.apa.org/apf/funding/benton-meier.aspx

Summary To provide research funding to graduate students (particularly Asian Americans and other students from diverse groups) who are completing a dissertation related to neuropsychology.

Eligibility This program is open to students who have been admitted to candidacy for a doctoral degree in the area of neuropsychology. Applicants must submit statements documenting their research competence and area commitment, a budget and justification, and how the scholarship money will be used. Selection is based on conformance with stated program goals and the applicant's demonstrated scholarship and research competence. The sponsor encourages applications from individuals who represent diversity in race, ethnicity, gender, age, disability, and sexual orientation.

Financial data The grant is $2,500.

Duration 1 year.

Additional information This program replaces the Henry Hécaen Scholarship, first awarded in 1994, and the Manfred Meier Scholarship, first awarded in 1997.

Number awarded 2 each year.

Deadline May of each year.

[465]
BETTY LEA STONE RESEARCH FELLOWSHIP

American Cancer Society-New England Division
30 Speen Street
Framingham, MA 01701
(508) 270-3109   Toll Free: (800) 952-7664, ext. 3109
Fax: (508) 270-4607   E-mail: koconnor@cancer.org
Web: www.cancer.org

Summary To provide funding for cancer research during the summer to medical students (particularly Asian American and other minority students) in New England.

Eligibility This program is open to first-year students at medical schools in New England. Applicants must be interested in working on a summer research project under the supervision of a faculty sponsor. Minority students and those with American Cancer Society volunteer experience are encouraged to apply.

Financial data The grant is $5,000.

Duration 10 weeks during the summer.

Number awarded 1 or more each year.

Deadline January of each year.

[466]
BILL BERNBACH DIVERSITY SCHOLARSHIPS

American Association of Advertising Agencies
Attn: AAAA Foundation
1065 Avenue of the Americas, 16th Floor
New York, NY 10018
(212) 262-2500   E-mail: bbscholarship@ddb.com
Web: www.aaaa.org

Summary To provide financial assistance to Asian American and other multicultural students who are interested in working on an undergraduate or graduate degree in advertising at designated schools.

Eligibility This program is open to African Americans, Asian Americans, Hispanic Americans, and Native Americans (including American Indians, Alaska Natives, Native Hawaiians, and other Pacific Islanders) who are interested in studying the advertising creative arts at designated institutions as a full-time student. Applicants must be working on or have already received an undergraduate degree and be able to demonstrate creative talent and promise. They must be U.S. citizens, nationals, or permanent residents. Along with their application, they must submit 10 samples of creative work in their respective field of expertise.

Financial data The stipend is $5,000.

Duration 1 year.

Additional information This program, which began in 1998, is currently sponsored by DDB Worldwide. The participating schools are the Art Center College of Design (Pasadena, California), Creative Circus (Atlanta, Georgia), Miami Ad School (Miami Beach, Florida), University of Texas at Austin, VCU Brandcenter (Richmond, Virginia), Savannah College of Art and Design (Savannah, Georgia), University of Oregon (Eugene), City College of New York, School of Visual Arts (New York, New York), Fashion Institute of Technology (New York, New York), and Brigham Young University (Provo, Utah).

Number awarded 3 each year.

Deadline October of each year.

[467]
BISHOP THOMAS HOYT, JR. FELLOWSHIP

St. John's University
Attn: Collegeville Institute for Ecumenical and Cultural Research
2475 Ecumenical Drive
P.O. Box 2000
Collegeville, MN 56321-2000
(320) 363-3366   Fax: (320) 363-3313
E-mail: staff@CollegevilleInstitute.org
Web: collegevilleinstitute.org

Summary To provide funding to Asian Americans and other students of color who wish to complete their doctoral dissertation while in residence at the Collegeville Institute for Ecumenical and Cultural Research of St. John's University in Collegeville, Minnesota.

Eligibility This program is open to people of color completing a doctoral dissertation in ecumenical and cultural research. Applicants must be interested in a residency at the Collegeville Institute for Ecumenical and Cultural Research of St. John's University. Along with their application, they must submit a 1,000-word description of the research project they plan to complete while in residence at the Institute.

Financial data The stipend covers the residency fee of $2,000, which includes housing and utilities.

Duration 1 year.

Additional information Residents at the Institute engage in research, publication, and education on the important intersections between faith and culture. They seek to discern and communicate the meaning of Christian identity and unity in a religiously and culturally diverse world.

Number awarded 1 each year.

Deadline October of each year.

[468]
BOB CHIN SCHOLARSHIP

National Asian Pacific American Bar Association
Attn: NAPABA Law Foundation
1612 K Street, N.W., Suite 1400
Washington, DC 20006
(202) 775-9555 Fax: (202) 775-9333
E-mail: nlfstaff@napaba.org
Web: www.napaba.org

Summary To provide financial assistance to students at law schools in the New York City tri-state area who have had a diagnosis of cancer within their family and are interested in serving the Asian Pacific American community.

Eligibility This program is open to students from any state enrolled at ABA-accredited law schools in the New York City tri-state area. Applicants must demonstrate leadership potential to serve the Asian Pacific American community upon graduation. Their lives must have been impacted by a diagnosis of cancer within their immediate family. Along with their application, they must submit a 500-word essay that covers 1) the most significant experiences in their background that have shaped and demonstrated their commitment to serving the needs of Asian Pacific Americans; and 2) how they intend to serve the needs of the Asian Pacific American community in their future legal career. Selection is based on that essay, academic achievement, leadership, commitment to bettering the Asian Pacific American community, and commitment to attend a scholarship award ceremony in the New York City tri-state area. U.S. citizenship or permanent resident status is required.

Financial data The stipend is $2,500.

Duration 1 year.

Number awarded 1 each year.

Deadline September of each year.

[469]
BONG HAK HYUN MEMORIAL SCHOLARSHIPS

Philip Jaisohn Memorial Foundation
Attn: Education and Scholarship Committee
6705 Old York Road
Philadelphia, PA 19126
(215) 224-2000 Fax: (215) 224-9164
E-mail: jaisohnhouse@gmail.com
Web: www.jaisohn.org

Summary To provide financial assistance to Korean American undergraduate and graduate students who are studying health care or medicine.

Eligibility This program is open to Korean American undergraduate and graduate students who are currently enrolled at a college or university in the United States and working on a degree in health care or a field of medicine. Applicants must be able to demonstrate excellence in community activities and financial need. Along with their application, they must submit an essay on either "Who is Dr. Jaisohn to Me," or "The Significance of Dr. Jaisohn's Ideal to Korean Americans." They must also submit a brief statement on how

they can contribute to and be involved in the activities of the Philip Jaisohn Memorial Foundation. Selection is based on potential, passion, and leadership.

Financial data The stipend is $1,500.

Duration 1 year.

Number awarded 2 each year.

Deadline November of each year.

[470]
BOR-UEI CHEN SCHOLARSHIPS

Photonics Society of Chinese-Americans
c/o Gordon Li, Scholarship Committee Chair
Mitac Information Systems Corporation
44131 Nobel Drive
Fremont, CA 94538
(510) 933-7254 E-mail: GordonLi77@yahoo.com
Web: www.eoa-psc.org

Summary To provide financial assistance to Chinese American graduate students in the field of optical communications and photonic devices.

Eligibility This program is open to Chinese American graduate students at universities in the United States who are nominated by a member of the Photonics Society of Chinese-Americans. Nominees must be working on a degree in a field related to optical communications and photonic devices. Selection is based on the merits of the candidate's research work as documented by publications in technical journals, conference presentations, and recommendations from the candidate's sponsor or adviser.

Financial data The stipend is $1,000.

Duration 1 year.

Additional information This program began in 1995.

Number awarded Varies each year; recently, 4 of these scholarships were awarded.

Deadline February of each year.

[471]
BROWN AND CALDWELL MINORITY SCHOLARSHIP

Brown and Caldwell
Attn: Scholarship Program
201 North Civic Drive, Suite 115
P.O. Box 8045
Walnut Creek, CA 94596
(925) 937-9010 Fax: (925) 937-9026
E-mail: scholarships@brwncald.com
Web: www.brownandcaldwell.com/scholarships.asp

Summary To provide financial assistance to Asian American and other minority students working on an undergraduate or graduate degree in an environmental or engineering field.

Eligibility This program is open to members of minority groups (African Americans, Hispanics, Asians, Pacific Islanders, Native Americans, or Alaska Natives) who are full-time juniors, seniors, or graduate students at an accredited 4-year college or university. Applicants must have a GPA of 3.0 or higher and a declared major in civil, chemical, or environmental engineering or an environmental science (e.g., biology, ecology, geology, hydrogeology). They must be U.S. citizens or permanent residents. Along with their application, they must submit an essay (up to 250 words) on their future career goals in environmental science. Financial need is not considered in the selection process.

Financial data   The stipend is $5,000.

Duration   1 year.

Number awarded   4 each year.

Deadline   April of each year.

[472]
BULLIVANT HOUSER BAILEY LAW STUDENT DIVERSITY FELLOWSHIP PROGRAM

Bullivant Houser Bailey PC
Attn: Manager of Professional Development, Recruitment and Diversity
888 S.W. Fifth Avenue, Suite 300
Portland, OR 97204-2017
(503) 228-6351   Toll Free: (800) 654-8972
Fax: (503) 295-0915   E-mail: jill.valentine@bullivant.com
Web: www.bullivant.com/diversity

Summary   To provide financial aid and work experience to Asian American and other law students who come from a minority or disadvantaged background.

Eligibility   This program is open to first-year law students who are members of a minority group (including any group underrepresented in the legal profession) and/or students coming from a disadvantaged educational or economic background. Applicants must have 1) a record of academic achievement and leadership in college and law school; 2) a willingness to complete a 12-week summer associateship at an office of the firm; and 3) a record of contributions to the community that promote diversity within society, the legal community, and/or law school.

Financial data   The program provides a salaried associate position at an office of the firm during the summer following the first year of law school and a stipend of $7,500 for the second year.

Duration   1 year.

Number awarded   2 each year: 1 assigned to an associateship in the Sacramento office and 1 assigned to an associateship in the Portland office.

Deadline   January of each year.

[473]
BUTLER RUBIN DIVERSITY SCHOLARSHIP

Butler Rubin Saltarelli & Boyd LLP
Attn: Diversity Partner
70 West Madison Street, Suite 1800
Chicago, IL 60602
(312) 242-4120   Fax: (312) 444-9294
E-mail: kborg@butlerrubin.com
Web: www.butlerrubin.com

Summary   To provide financial aid and summer work experience to Asian American and other diverse law students who are interested in the area of business litigation.

Eligibility   This program is open to law students of racial and ethnic backgrounds that will contribute to diversity in the legal profession. Applicants must be interested in the private practice of law in the area of business litigation and in a summer associateship in that field with Butler Rubin Saltarelli & Boyd in Chicago. Selection is based on academic performance and achievement, intention to remain in the Chicago

area following graduation, and interpersonal and communication skills.

Financial data   The stipend is $10,000 per year; funds are to be used for tuition and other expenses associated with law school. For the summer associateship, a stipend is paid.

Duration   1 year; may be renewed.

Additional information   This program began in 2006.

Number awarded   1 each year.

Deadline   Deadline not specified.

[474]
C. CLYDE FERGUSON LAW SCHOLARSHIP

New Jersey Commission on Higher Education
Attn: Educational Opportunity Fund
20 West State Street, Fourth Floor
P.O. Box 542
Trenton, NJ 08625-0542
(609) 984-2709   Fax: (609) 292-7225
E-mail: audrey.bennerson@njhe.state.nj.us
Web: www.state.nj.us/highereducation/EOF/index.html

Summary   To provide financial assistance to Asian Americans and other disadvantaged or minority students from New Jersey who want to study law in the state.

Eligibility   This program is open to students who 1) fall within specified income guidelines (currently, less than $21,660 for a family of 1 rising to $74,020 for a family of 8); 2) minority or disadvantaged students with financial need; or 3) former or current recipients of a New Jersey Educational Opportunity Fund undergraduate or graduate grant, or who would have been eligible to receive the grant as an undergraduate. Applicants must have been New Jersey residents for at least 12 months before receiving the award and must plan to enroll full time in the Minority Student Program at law schools in New Jersey (Rutgers University School of Law at Newark, Rutgers University School of Law at Camden, or Seton Hall Law School).

Financial data   Awards are based on financial need. In no case, however, can awards exceed the maximum amount of tuition, fees, room, and board charged at Rutgers University School of Law at Newark.

Duration   1 year; may be renewed.

Number awarded   1 or more each year.

Deadline   Deadline not specified.

[475]
CALIFORNIA BAR FOUNDATION DIVERSITY SCHOLARSHIPS

State Bar of California
Attn: California Bar Foundation
180 Howard Street
San Francisco, CA 94105-1639
(415) 856-0780   Fax: (415) 856-0788
E-mail: scholarships@calbarfoundation.org
Web: www.calbarfoundation.org/diversity-scholarship.html

Summary   To provide financial assistance to Asian Americans and other underrepresented minorities from any state who are entering law school in California.

Eligibility   This program to open to residents of any state who are entering their first year at a law school in California. Applicants must self-identify as being from a racial or ethnic group that historically has been underrepresented in the legal profession (Latino, African American, Asian and Pacific Islander, and Native American). They must be committed to making an impact in the community through leadership. Along with their application, they must submit a 500-word essay describing their commitment to serving the community and, if applicable, any significant obstacles or hurdles they have overcome to attend law school. Financial need is considered in the selection process.

Financial data The stipend is $7,500.

Duration 1 year.

Additional information This program began in 2008. Each year, the foundation grants awards named after sponsors that donate funding for the scholarships. Recipients are required to attend a reception in their honor in October of the year of their award and to submit a report on their progress at the end of that year.

Number awarded Varies each year; recently, 19 of these scholarships were awarded.

Deadline June of each year.

[476]
CALIFORNIA JAPANESE AMERICAN ALUMNI ASSOCIATION SCHOLARSHIP PROGRAM

California Japanese American Alumni Association
Attn: Katherine Yoshii
P.O. Box 15235
San Francisco, CA 94115-0235
(510) 559-9277   E-mail: scholarships@cjaaa.org
Web: www.cjaaa.org/scholarship.html

Summary To provide financial assistance to undergraduate or graduate students of Japanese American descent who are currently enrolled at campuses of the University of California.

Eligibility This program is open to continuing or returning undergraduate or graduate students of Japanese American descent from California who are attending 1 of the 10 UC campuses. They must be U.S. citizens and may be studying in any field or discipline. A GPA of 3.0 or higher is strongly recommended but not required. Applicants interested in participating in the University of California Education Abroad Program in Japan must have a GPA of 3.5 or higher. Selection is based on academic achievement, contribution to the community, personal attributes, and financial need (in that order).

Financial data Stipends range from $1,000 to $5,000. The Moriaki "Mo" Noguchi Memorial Scholarship of $3,000 is given to the top overall candidate. The George Kondo Award is at least $1,000 and is awarded to the applicant with the best community service record. The Yori Wada Award is $2,000 and is awarded to the applicant with the most outstanding record of public service. The stipend for a student accepted to the University of California Education Abroad Program ranges from $2,500 to $5,000.

Duration 1 year; nonrenewable.

Number awarded 8 to 10 each year.

Deadline April of each year.

[477]
CALIFORNIA STATE UNIVERSITY CHANCELLOR'S DOCTORAL INCENTIVE PROGRAM

California State University
Office of the Chancellor
Attn: Human Resources
401 Golden Shore, Fourth Floor
Long Beach, CA 90802-4210
(562) 951-4425   Fax: (562) 951-4954
E-mail: forgivableloan@calstate.edu
Web: www.calstate.edu/hr/cdip

Summary To provide funding to Asian Americans and other graduate students who can help increase the diversity of persons qualified to compete for instructional faculty positions at campuses of the California State University (CSU) system.

Eligibility This program is open to new and continuing full-time students enrolled in a doctoral program anywhere in the United States, whether affiliated with a CSU campus or not. Applicants must present a plan of support from a full-time CSU faculty sponsor who has agreed to advise and support the candidate throughout doctoral study. Selection is based on the applicant's academic record; professional qualifications; and relevant background, experience, skills, and motivation to educate a diverse student body in the CSU system. The factors considered include experience working with persons with a wide range of backgrounds and perspectives, research interests related to educating an increasingly diverse student body, and experience in a variety of cultural environments. Primary consideration is given to candidates whose proposed area of study falls where CSU campuses anticipate the greatest difficulty in filling instructional faculty positions.

Financial data Participants receive up to $10,000 per year or a maximum of $30,000 over 5 years. The loans are converted to fellowships at the rate of 20% of the total loan amount for each postdoctoral year that the program participant teaches, for up to 5 years. Thus, the entire loan will be forgiven after the recipient has taught full time for 5 years on a CSU campus. Recipients who do not teach on a CSU campus or who discontinue full-time studies will be required to repay the total loan amount within a 15-year period at the rate established for other student loans.

Duration Up to 5 years.

Additional information This program began in 1987 as the California State University Forgivable Loan Program. It has loaned $46 million to 1,965 doctoral students enrolled in universities throughout the nation and abroad. Participants included 17.6% African American, 13.3% Asian, 26.2% Hispanic, 4.1% American Indian, and 32.1% White.

Number awarded Varies each year; recently, 60 new participants were admitted to the program.

Deadline The deadline varies at different CSU campuses but typically falls in February of each year.

[478]
CANFIT PROGRAM GRADUATE SCHOLARSHIPS

Communities-Adolescents-Nutrition-Fitness
Attn: Scholarship Program
2140 Shattuck Avenue, Suite 610
Berkeley, CA 94704
(510) 644-1533   Toll Free: (800) 200-3131
Fax: (510) 644-1535   E-mail: info@canfit.org
Web: www.canfit.org/scholarships

Summary To provide financial assistance to Asian American and other minority graduate students who are working on a degree in nutrition, physical education, or public health in California.

Eligibility This program is open to American Indians, Alaska Natives, African Americans, Asian Americans, Pacific Islanders, and Latinos/Hispanics from California who are enrolled in 1) an approved master's or doctoral program in nutrition, public health, or physical education in the state; or 2) a pre-professional practice program approved by the American Dietetic Association at an accredited university in the state. Applicants must have completed 12 to 15 units of graduate course work and have a cumulative GPA of 3.0 or higher. Along with their application, they must submit 1) documentation of financial need; 2) letters of recommendation from 2 individuals; 3) a 1- to 2-page letter describing their academic goals and involvement in community nutrition and/ or physical education activities; and 4) an essay of 500 to 1,000 words on a topic related to healthy foods for youth from low-income communities of color.

Financial data A stipend is awarded (amount not specified).

Number awarded 1 or more each year.

Deadline March of each year.

[479]
CARL A. SCOTT BOOK FELLOWSHIPS

Council on Social Work Education
Attn: Chair, Carl A. Scott Memorial Fund
1701 Duke Street, Suite 200
Alexandria, VA 22314-3457
(703) 683-8080   Fax: (703) 683-8099
E-mail: info@cswe.org
Web: www.cswe.org

Summary To provide financial assistance to Asian American and other ethnic minority social work students in their last year of study for a baccalaureate or master's degree.

Eligibility This program is open to students from ethnic groups of color (African American, Asian American, Hispanic/ Latino, or American Indian) who are in the last year of study for a social work degree in an accredited baccalaureate or master's degree program. Applicants must have a cumulative GPA of 3.0 or higher and be enrolled full time. They must demonstrate a commitment to work for equity and social justice in social work.

Financial data The stipend is $500.

Duration This is a 1-time award.

Number awarded 2 each year.

Deadline May of each year.

[480]
CARMEN E. TURNER SCHOLARSHIPS

Conference of Minority Transportation Officials
Attn: National Scholarship Program
1875 I Street, N.W., Suite 500
Washington, DC 20006
(703) 234-4072   Fax: (202) 318-0364
Web: www.comto.org/?page=Scholarships

Summary To provide financial assistance for college or graduate school to Asian American and other members of the Conference of Minority Transportation Officials (COMTO).

Eligibility This program is open to undergraduate and graduate students who have been members of COMTO for at least 1 year. Applicants must be working on a degree in a field related to transportation and have a GPA of 2.5 or higher. They must be enrolled at least half time. Along with their application, they must submit a cover letter with a 500-word statement of career goals. Financial need is not considered in the selection process. U.S. citizenship or legal resident status is required.

Financial data The stipend is $3,500. Funds are paid directly to the recipient's college or university.

Duration 1 year.

Additional information COMTO was established in 1971 to promote, strengthen, and expand the roles of minorities in all aspects of transportation. Recipients are expected to attend the COMTO National Scholarship Luncheon.

Number awarded 1 each year.

Deadline May of each year.

[481]
CATHY L. BROCK MEMORIAL SCHOLARSHIP

Institute for Diversity in Health Management
Attn: Education Specialist
155 North Wacker Avenue, Suite 400
Chicago, IL 60606
(312) 422-2658   Toll Free: (800) 233-0996
Fax: (312) 895-4511   E-mail: cbiddle@aha.org
Web: www.diversityconnection.org

Summary To provide financial assistance to Asian American and other minority graduate students in health care management, especially financial operations.

Eligibility This program is open to members of ethnic minority groups who are enrolled in the first or second year of an accredited graduate program in health care administration. Applicants must have a GPA of 3.0 or higher. They must demonstrate commitment to a career in health care finance. Along with their application, they must submit 1) a personal statement of 1 to 2 pages on their interest in health care management and their career goals; 2) an essay on what they see as the most challenging issue facing America's hospitals and health systems; and 3) a 500-word essay on their interest and background in health care finance. Selection is based on academic achievement, commitment to a career in health care finance, and financial need. U.S. citizenship is required.

Financial data The stipend is $1,000.

Duration 1 year.

Number awarded 1 each year.

Deadline January of each year.

[482]
CENTRAL FLORIDA CHAPTER NBMBAA SCHOLARSHIPS

National Black MBA Association-Central Florida Chapter
Attn: Scholarship Committee Chair
P.O. Box 692696
Orlando, FL 32869-2696
(321) 578-8305   E-mail: scholarships@cflblackmba.org
Web: www.cflblackmba.org

Summary To provide financial assistance to Asian Americans or members of another minority group who are residents of any state working on a degree in business at a university in Florida.

Eligibility This program is open to members of the following groups from any state: African American/Black, American Indian/Alaska Native, Asian American/Pacific Islander, or Hispanic/Latino. Applicants must be enrolled in a business program at an AACSB-accredited college or university in Florida. They must have a GPA of 3.0 or higher. Along with their application, they must submit a 2-page essay on a topic that changes annually but relates to minorities and business. Selection is based on that essay, transcripts, a resume, and extracurricular activities. The highest-ranked applicant receives a named scholarship sponsored by Darden Restaurants.

Financial data The Darden Named Scholarship is $5,000; a total of $10,000 in scholarships is awarded each year.

Duration 1 year.

Number awarded Varies each year.

Deadline October of each year.

[483]
CH2M HILL PARTNERSHIP SCHOLARSHIP

Women's Transportation Seminar
Attn: WTS Foundation
1701 K Street, N.W., Suite 800
Washington, DC 20006
(202) 955-5085   Fax: (202) 955-5088
E-mail: wts@wtsinternational.org
Web: www.wtsinternational.org/education/scholarships

Summary To provide financial assistance to women graduate students (particularly Asian American and other minority women) who are interested in preparing for a career in transportation.

Eligibility This program is open to women who are enrolled in a graduate degree program in a transportation-related field (e.g., transportation engineering, planning, finance, or logistics). Applicants must have at least a 3.0 GPA and be interested in a career in transportation. Along with their application, they must submit a 750-word statement about their career goals after graduation and why they think they should receive the scholarship award. Applications must be submitted first to a local chapter; the chapters forward selected applications for consideration on the national level. Minority women are particularly encouraged to apply. Selection is based on transportation involvement and goals, job skills, and academic record.

Financial data The stipend is $10,000.

Duration 1 year.

Additional information This program is sponsored by CH2M Hill. Local chapters may also award additional funding to winners in their area.

Number awarded 1 each year.

Deadline Applications must be submitted by November to a local WTS chapter.

[484]
CHARLES B. RANGEL GRADUATE FELLOWSHIP PROGRAM

Howard University
Attn: Ralph J. Bunche International Affairs Center
2281 Sixth Street, N.W.
Washington, DC 20059
(202) 806-4367   Toll Free: (877) 633-0002
Fax: (202) 806-5424   E-mail: pscroggs@howard.edu
Web: www.rangelprogram.org

Summary To provide financial assistance for graduate study in a field related to the work of the Foreign Service, especially to Asian Americans and members of other underrepresented minority groups.

Eligibility This program is open to U.S. citizens who are either graduating college seniors or recipients of an undergraduate degree. Applicants must be planning to enter graduate school to work on a master's degree in international affairs or other area of interest to the Foreign Service of the U.S. Department of State (e.g., public administration, public policy, business administration, foreign languages, economics, political science, or communications). They must have a GPA of 3.2 or higher. Strong preference is given to members of minority groups historically underrepresented in the Foreign Service and those who can demonstrate financial need.

Financial data The stipend is $35,000 per year.

Duration 2 years.

Additional information This program is offered jointly by Howard University and the U.S. Department of State. Fellows are provided an internship working on international issues for members of Congress during the summer after they are selected and before they begin graduate study. They are provided a second internship at a U.S. embassy overseas during the summer before their second year of graduate study. Fellows who complete the program and Foreign Service entry requirements receive appointments as Foreign Service Officers. Each fellow who obtains a master's degree is committed to at least 3 years of service as a Foreign Service Officer. If recipients do not complete the program successfully or do not fulfill the 3-year service obligation, they may be subject to a reimbursement obligation.

Number awarded 20 each year.

Deadline January of each year.

[485]
CHINESE AMERICAN ASSOCIATION OF MINNESOTA SCHOLARSHIPS

Chinese American Association of Minnesota
Attn: Scholarship Program
P.O. Box 582584
Minneapolis, MN 55458-2584
E-mail: office@caam.org
Web: www.caam.org/?page_id=82

Summary To provide financial assistance to Minnesota residents of Chinese descent who are interested in attending college or graduate school in any state.

Eligibility This program is open to Minnesota residents of Chinese descent who are enrolled or planning to enroll full time at a postsecondary school, college, or graduate school in any state. Applicants must submit an essay on the role their Chinese heritage has played in their work, study, and accomplishments. Selection is based on academic record, leadership qualities, and community service; financial need is also considered for some awards. Membership in the Chinese American Association of Minnesota (CAAM) is not required. Priority is given to applicants who have not previously received a CAAM scholarship.

Financial data The stipend ranges from $1,500 to $2,000.

Duration 1 year.

Additional information Recipients who are not CAAM members are expected to become members for at least 2 years.

Number awarded 1 or more each year.

Deadline December of each year.

[486]
CHINESE AMERICAN LIBRARIANS ASSOCIATION SCHOLARSHIP

Chinese American Librarians Association
c/o Yongyi Song, Scholarship Committee Co-Chair
California State University at Los Angeles
Library North, Room B518
5151 State University Drive
Los Angeles, CA 90032
(323) 343-4884   Fax: (323) 343-3992
E-mail: ysong2@calstatela.edu
Web: www.cala-web.org/node/203

Summary To provide financial assistance to Chinese American students interested in working on a graduate degree in library or information science.

Eligibility This program is open to students enrolled full time in an accredited library school in North America and working on a master's or doctoral degree. Applicants must be of Chinese nationality or Chinese descent. They must submit a resume and a personal statement of 300 to 500 words on their past experiences, career interests, and commitment to library and information science.

Financial data The stipend is $1,000.

Duration 1 year.

Additional information This program began in 2004.

Number awarded 1 each year.

Deadline April of each year.

[487]
CHINESE AMERICAN MEDICAL SOCIETY SCHOLARSHIP PROGRAM

Chinese American Medical Society
Attn: Scholarship Committee
41 Elizabeth Street, Suite 600
New York, NY 10013
(212) 334-4760   Fax: (646) 304-6373
E-mail: jlove@camsociety.org
Web: www.chineseamericanmedicalsociety.cloverpad.org

Summary To provide financial assistance to Chinese and Chinese American students who are working on a degree in medicine or dentistry.

Eligibility This program is open to Chinese or Chinese American students who are currently enrolled in the first, second, or third year at an approved medical or dental school in the United States. Applicants must submit a personal statement that includes their career goals, a current vitae, 2 letters of recommendation, and documentation of financial need. Special consideration is given to applicants with research projects relating to health care of the Chinese.

Financial data The scholarships range from $1,000 to $1,500.

Duration 1 year; recipients may reapply.

Additional information This program, which began in 1973, includes the Esther Lim Memorial Scholarship established in 1989, the Ruth Liu Memorial Scholarship established in 1996, the American Center for Chinese Medical Sciences Scholarship established in 2004 upon the dissolution of that organization, and the Jeng Family Fund Scholarship, established in 2013.

Number awarded Varies each year; recently, 5 of these scholarships were awarded.

Deadline April of each year.

[488]
CHINESE AMERICAN MEDICAL SOCIETY SUMMER RESEARCH FELLOWSHIP

Chinese American Medical Society
Attn: Scholarship Committee
41 Elizabeth Street, Suite 600
New York, NY 10013
(212) 334-4760   Fax: (646) 304-6373
E-mail: jlove@camsociety.org
Web: www.chineseamericanmedicalsociety.cloverpad.org

Summary To provide funding to Chinese American medical and dental students who are interested in conducting a summer research project.

Eligibility This program is open to Chinese or Chinese Americans who are enrolled in a medical or dental school in the United States and are interested in conducting a research project. The research can be basic science or clinical. A physician or dentist must sponsor and supervise the project. Special consideration is given to proposals involving Chinese American health issues.

Financial data The stipend is $400 per week.

Duration 6 to 10 weeks during the summer.

Additional information A written report is expected at the conclusion of the project.

Number awarded Varies each year.

Deadline April of each year.

[489]
CHINESE AMERICAN PHYSICIANS SOCIETY SCHOLARSHIP PROGRAM FOR U.S. MEDICAL STUDENTS

Chinese American Physicians Society
c/o Lawrence Ng, M.D., Award Committee Chair
101 Callan Avenue, Suite 401
San Leandro, CA 94577
(510) 357-7077   Fax: (510) 357-4363
E-mail: admin@caps-ca.org
Web: www.caps-ca.org

Summary To provide financial assistance to medical students in the United States, especially those willing to serve Chinese communities after graduation.

Eligibility This program is open to students attending or planning to attend a U.S. medical school. Applicants may be from any location and of any sex, race, or color. Preference is given to those willing to serve Chinese communities after graduation. Along with their application, they must submit a 500-word essay on a topic that changes annually; recently, students who asked to write on how they use their time wisely. Selection is based on the essay, academic achievement, financial need, and community service.

Financial data Stipends range from $2,000 to $5,000 per year.

Duration 1 year; may be renewed.

Number awarded Varies each year; recently, 5 of these fellowships were awarded.

Deadline February of each year.

[490]
CHIYOKO AND THOMAS SHIMAZAKI SCHOLARSHIP

Japanese American Citizens League
Attn: National Scholarship Awards
1765 Sutter Street
San Francisco, CA 94115
(415) 345-1075   Fax: (415) 931-4671
E-mail: ncwnp@jacl.org
Web: www.jacl.org/edu/scholar.htm

Summary To provide financial assistance to student members of the Japanese American Citizens League (JACL) who are interested in preparing for a career in medicine.

Eligibility This program is open to JACL members who are interested in preparing for a career in the medical field. Applicants must submit information on their involvement in JACL and a 2-page essay on a topic that changes annually but relates to Japanese Americans. Selection is based on that essay, academic history, JACL involvement, school activities, work history, scholastic honors, and community involvement.

Financial data Stipends generally average more than $2,000.

Duration 1 year; nonrenewable.

Number awarded At least 1 each year.

Deadline March of each year.

[491]
CLA SCHOLARSHIP FOR MINORITY STUDENTS IN MEMORY OF EDNA YELLAND

California Library Association
2471 Flores Street
San Mateo, CA 94403
(650) 376-0886   Fax: (650) 539-2341
E-mail: info@cla-net.org
Web: www.cla-net.org

Summary To provide financial assistance to Asian American and other minority students in California who are attending graduate school in any state to prepare for a career in library or information science.

Eligibility This program is open to California residents who are members of ethnic minority groups (American Indian/Alaska Native, African American/Black, Latino/Hispanic, Asian American, or Pacific Islander). Applicants must have completed at least 1 course in a master's program at an accredited graduate library school in any state. Evidence of financial need and U.S. citizenship or permanent resident status must be submitted. Finalists are interviewed.

Financial data The stipend is $2,500.

Duration 1 academic year.

Additional information This fellowship is named for the executive secretary of the California Library Association from 1947 to 1963 who worked to promote the goals of the California Library Association and the profession. Until 1985, it was named the Edna Yelland Memorial Scholarship.

Number awarded 3 each year.

Deadline July of each year.

[492]
CLINICAL RESEARCH PRE-DOCTORAL FELLOWSHIP PROGRAM

American Nurses Association
Attn: SAMHSA Minority Fellowship Programs
8515 Georgia Avenue, Suite 400
Silver Spring, MD 20910-3492
(301) 628-5247   Toll Free: (800) 274-4ANA
Fax: (301) 628-5339   E-mail: janet.jackson@ana.org
Web: www.emfp.org

Summary To provide financial assistance to Asian American and other minority nurses who are doctoral candidates interested in psychiatric, mental health, and substance abuse issues that impact the lives of ethnic minority people.

Eligibility This program is open to nurses who have a master's degree and are members of an ethnic or racial minority group, including but not limited to Blacks or African Americans, Hispanics or Latinos, American Indians and Alaska Natives, Asian Americans, and Native Hawaiians and other Pacific Islanders. Applicants must be able to demonstrate a commitment to a research career in nursing and psychiatric/mental health issues affecting ethnic minority populations. They must be interested in a program of full-time doctoral study, with a research focus on such issues of concern to minority populations as child abuse, violence in intimate relationships, mental health disorders, substance abuse, mental health service utilization, and stigma as a barrier to mental health care and personal resilience. U.S. citizenship or permanent resident status and membership in the American Nurses Association are required. Selection is based on research potential, scholarship, writing ability, knowledge of broad issues in mental health nursing, and professional commitment to ethnic minority concerns.

Financial data The program provides an annual stipend of $22,032 and tuition assistance.

Duration 3 to 5 years.

Additional information Funds for this program are provided by the Substance Abuse and Mental Health Services Administration (SAMHSA).

Number awarded 1 or more each year.

Deadline February of each year.

[493]
COMMITTEE ON ETHNIC MINORITY RECRUITMENT SCHOLARSHIP

United Methodist Church-California-Pacific Annual
  Conference
Attn: Board of Ordained Ministry
1720 East Linfield Street
Glendora, CA 91740
(626) 335-6629   Fax: (626) 335-5750
E-mail: cathy.adminbom@gmail.com
Web: www.calpacordainedministry.org/523451

Summary To provide financial assistance to Asian Americans and members of other ethnic minority groups in the California-Pacific Annual Conference of the United Methodist Church (UMC) who are attending a seminary in any state to qualify for ordination as an elder or deacon.

Eligibility This program is open to members of ethnic minority groups in the UMC California-Pacific Annual Conference who are enrolled at a seminary in any state approved by the UMC University Senate. Applicants must have been approved as certified candidates by their district committee and be seeking Probationary Deacon or Elder's Orders. They may apply for 1 or more types of assistance: tuition scholarships, grants for books and school supplies (including computers), or emergency living expense grants.

Financial data Tuition stipends are $1,000 per year; books and supplies grants range up to $1,000 per year; emergency living expense grants depend on need and the availability of funds.

Duration 1 year; may be renewed up to 2 additional years.

Additional information The California-Pacific Annual Conference includes churches in southern California, Hawaii, Guam, and Saipan.

Number awarded Varies each year.

Deadline August of each year for fall term; December of each year for spring term.

[494]
CONSTANGY, BROOKS & SMITH DIVERSITY SCHOLARS AWARD

Constangy, Brooks & Smith LLC
Attn: Chair, Diversity Council
200 West Forsyth Street, Suite 1700
Jacksonville, FL 32202-4317
(904) 356-8900   Fax: (904) 356-8200
E-mail: mzabijaka@constangy.com
Web: www.constangy.com/f-4.html

Summary To provide financial assistance to Asian Americans and other diverse students who are enrolled in law schools in selected states.

Eligibility This program is open to second-year students enrolled in accredited law schools located in 1 of 3 regions: South (Alabama, Florida, Georgia, South Carolina, Tennessee), Midwest/West Coast (California, Illinois, Kansas, Missouri, Texas, Wisconsin), or East (Massachusetts, New Jersey, North Carolina, Virginia/Washington D.C.). Applicants must submit a personal statement on why diversity is important to them personally and in the legal profession. They must have a GPA of 2.7 or higher. Selection is based on academic achievement, commitment to diversity, and personal achievement in overcoming obstacles.

Financial data The stipend is $3,000.

Duration 1 year.

Number awarded 3 each year: 1 in each region.

Deadline November of each year.

[495]
COOK/RUTLEDGE FELLOWSHIP

New Jersey Department of Health
Office of Minority and Multicultural Health
Attn: Executive Director
John Fitch Plaza, Room 501
P.O. Box 360
Trenton, NJ 08625-0360
(609) 292-6962   Fax: (609) 292-8713
Web: www.nj.gov/health/omh/professions.shtml

Summary To provide financial support to Asian American and other public health, law, and medical students in New Jersey who are interested in conducting research related to health disparities issues during the summer.

Eligibility This program is open to students in medical science, law, or master's of public health programs who are 1) residents of New Jersey attending school in the state or elsewhere; or 2) residents of other states attending a college or university in New Jersey. Applicants must be interested in working on a supervised project at the New Jersey Department of Health in Trenton on current and relevant health equity/health disparity issues impacting the racial or ethnic minority populations in New Jersey. Along with their application, they must submit letters of recommendation from 1) a college instructor indicating their commitment to an understanding of the issues facing the racial or ethnic minority populations; or 2) a community-based or faith-based organization or public health organization where they volunteered, worked, or assisted with a health care initiative that directly impacted a racial or ethnic minority group.

Financial data The stipend is $6,000.

Duration 8 to 10 weeks during the summer.

Number awarded 1 each year.

Deadline March of each year.

[496]
COOLEY DIVERSITY FELLOWSHIP PROGRAM

Cooley LLP
Attn: Attorney Recruiting Manager
4401 Eastgate Mall
San Diego, CA 92121-1909
(858) 550-6474   E-mail: diversityfellowship@cooley.com
Web: www.cooley.com/diversityfellowship

Summary   To provide financial aid and work experience to Asian American and other law students who are committed to promoting diversity in their community and are interested in summer associateships and employment at an office of Cooley LLP.

Eligibility   This program is open to students enrolled full time at an ABA-accredited law school and planning to graduate 2 years after applying. Applicants must submit a 3-page personal statement describing their demonstrated commitment to promoting diversity (e.g., ethnicity, gender, physical disability, and/or sexual orientation) in their community. They must be interested in a summer associateship. Selection is based on undergraduate and law school academic performance, personal achievements, leadership abilities, community service, and demonstrated commitment to promoting diversity.

Financial data   The award includes a stipend of $10,000 after completing a summer associateship after the first year of law school, another stipend of $10,000 after completing another summer associateship after the second year of law school, and another stipend of $10,000 after graduating from law school and joining the firm as a full-time associate.

Duration   3 years.

Additional information   Summer associates may work in any of the firm's offices in California (Palo Alto, San Diego, or San Francisco), Colorado (Broomfield), Massachusetts (Boston), New York (New York), Virginia (Reston), Washington (Seattle), or Washington, D.C.

Number awarded   1 or more each year.

Deadline   June of each year.

[497]
CORA AGUDA MANAYAN FUND

Hawai'i Community Foundation
Attn: Scholarship Department
827 Fort Street Mall
Honolulu, HI 96813
(808) 566-5570   Toll Free: (888) 731-3863
Fax: (808) 521-6286
E-mail: scholarships@hcf-hawaii.org
Web: www.hawaiicommunityfoundation.org/scholarships

Summary   To provide financial assistance to Hawaii residents of Filipino ancestry who are interested in attending college or graduate school to prepare for a career in the health field.

Eligibility   This program is open to Hawaii residents of Filipino ancestry who are interested in enrolling full time in a health-related field (on the undergraduate or graduate school level). Applicants must be able to demonstrate academic achievement (GPA of 3.0 or higher), good moral character, and financial need. Along with their application, they must submit a short statement indicating their reasons for attending college, their planned course of study, their career goals,

and what community service means to them. Preference may be given to applicants studying at a college or university in Hawaii.

Financial data   The amounts of the awards depend on the availability of funds and the need of the recipient. Recently, the average value of each of the scholarships awarded by the foundation was $2,200.

Duration   1 year.

Number awarded   Varies each year; recently, 10 of these scholarships were awarded.

Deadline   February of each year.

[498]
CORRIS BOYD SCHOLARSHIP

Association of University Programs in Health
    Administration
Attn: Prizes, Fellowships and Scholarships
2000 14th Street North, Suite 780
Arlington, VA 22201
(703) 894-0940, ext. 115   Fax: (703) 894-0941
E-mail: aupha@aupha.org
Web: www.aupha.org/i4a/pages/index.cfm?pageid=3541

Summary   To provide financial assistance to Asian American and other minority students entering graduate schools affiliated with the Association of University Programs in Health Administration (AUPHA).

Eligibility   This program is open to students of color (African Americans, American Indians, Alaska Natives, Asian Americans, Hispanic Americans, Native Hawaiians, and other Pacific Islanders) who have been accepted to a master's degree program in health care management at an AUPHA member institution. Applicants must be U.S. citizens or permanent residents and have a GPA of 3.0 or higher. Along with their application, they must submit a personal statement explaining why they are choosing to prepare for a career in health administration. Selection is based on leadership qualities, academic achievement, community involvement, and commitment to health care; financial need may be considered if all other factors are equal.

Financial data   The stipend is $40,000.

Duration   1 year.

Additional information   This program began in 2006.

Number awarded   2 each year.

Deadline   May of each year.

[499]
CRCNA RACE RELATIONS MULTIRACIAL STUDENT SCHOLARSHIP

Christian Reformed Church
Attn: Office of Race Relations
2850 Kalamazoo Avenue, S.E.
Grand Rapids, MI 49560-0200
(616) 224-5883   Toll Free: (877) 279-9994
Fax: (616) 224-0834   E-mail: elugo@crcna.org
Web: www.crcna.org/race/scholarships

Summary   To provide financial assistance to Asian American and other minority undergraduate and graduate students who are interested in attending colleges related to the Christian Reformed Church in North America (CRCNA).

Eligibility   This program is open to students of color in the United States and Canada. Normally, applicants are expected to be members of CRCNA congregations who plan to pursue their educational goals at Calvin Theological Seminary or any of the colleges affiliated with the CRCNA. They must be interested in training for the ministry of racial reconciliation in church and/or in society. Students who have no prior history with the CRCNA must attend a CRCNA-related college or seminary for a full academic year before they are eligible to apply for this program. Students entering their sophomore year must have earned a GPA of 2.0 or higher as freshmen; students entering their junior year must have earned a GPA of 2.3 or higher as sophomores; students entering their senior year must have earned a GPA of 2.6 or higher as juniors.

Financial data First-year students receive $500 per semester. Other levels of students may receive up to $2,000 per academic year.

Duration 1 year.

Additional information This program was first established in 1971 and revised in 1991. Recipients are expected to train to engage actively in the ministry of racial reconciliation in church and in society. They must be able to work in the United States or Canada upon graduating and must consider working for 1 of the agencies of the CRCNA.

Number awarded Varies each year; recently, 31 students received a total of $21,000 in support.

Deadline March of each year.

[500]
CTA/MARTIN LUTHER KING, JR. MEMORIAL SCHOLARSHIP FUND

California Teachers Association
Attn: CTA Foundation for Teaching and Learning
1705 Murchison Drive
P.O. Box 921
Burlingame, CA 94011-0921
(650) 697-1400   E-mail: scholarships@cta.org
Web: www.cta.org

Summary To provide financial assistance for college or graduate school to Asian Americans and other racial and ethnic minorities who are members of the California Teachers Association (CTA), children of members, or members of the Student CTA.

Eligibility This program is open to members of racial or ethnic minority groups (African Americans, American Indians/Alaska Natives, Asians/Pacific Islanders, and Hispanics) who are 1) active CTA members; 2) dependent children of active, retired, or deceased CTA members; or 3) members of Student CTA. Applicants must be interested in preparing for a teaching career in public education or already engaged in such a career.

Financial data Stipends vary each year; recently, they ranged from $1,000 to $4,000.

Duration 1 year.

Number awarded Varies each year; recently, 25 of these scholarships were awarded: 5 to CTA members, 10 to children of CTA members, and 10 to Student CTA members.

Deadline February of each year.

[501]
DAVID HILLIARD EATON SCHOLARSHIP

Unitarian Universalist Association
Attn: Ministerial Credentialing Office
25 Beacon Street
Boston, MA 02108-2800
(617) 948-6403   Fax: (617) 742-2875
E-mail: mcoadministrator@uua.org
Web: www.uua.org

Summary To provide financial assistance to Asian American and other minority women preparing for the Unitarian Universalist (UU) ministry.

Eligibility This program is open to women from historically marginalized groups who are currently enrolled or planning to enroll full or at least half time in a UU ministerial training program with aspirant or candidate status. Applicants must be citizens of the United States or Canada. Priority is given first to those who have demonstrated outstanding ministerial ability and secondarily to students with the greatest financial need (especially persons of color).

Financial data The stipend ranges from $1,000 to $15,000 per year.

Duration 1 year.

Number awarded 1 or 2 each year.

Deadline April of each year.

[502]
DAVID POHL SCHOLARSHIP

Unitarian Universalist Association
Attn: Ministerial Credentialing Office
25 Beacon Street
Boston, MA 02108-2800
(617) 948-6403   Fax: (617) 742-2875
E-mail: mcoadministrator@uua.org
Web: www.uua.org

Summary To provide financial assistance to seminary students (particularly Asian Americans and other persons of color) who are preparing for the Unitarian Universalist (UU) ministry.

Eligibility This program is open to seminary students who are enrolled full or at least half time in a UU ministerial training program with candidate status. Applicants must be citizens of the United States or Canada. Priority is given first to those who have demonstrated outstanding ministerial ability and secondarily to students with the greatest financial need (especially persons of color).

Financial data The stipend ranges from $1,000 to $15,000 per year.

Duration 1 year.

Number awarded 1 each year.

Deadline April of each year.

[503]
DAVID TAMOTSU KAGIWADA MEMORIAL SCHOLARSHIP

Christian Church (Disciples of Christ)
Attn: Disciples Home Missions
130 East Washington Street
P.O. Box 1986
Indianapolis, IN 46206-1986
(317) 713-2652   Toll Free: (888) DHM-2631
Fax: (317) 635-4426   E-mail: mail@dhm.disciples.org
Web: www.discipleshomemissions.org

Summary   To provide financial assistance to Asians and Pacific Islanders interested in preparing for a career in the ministry of the Christian Church (Disciples of Christ).

Eligibility   This program is open to ministerial students of Asian and Pacific Islander descent who are members of a Christian Church (Disciples of Christ) congregation in the United States or Canada. Applicants must plan to prepare for the ordained ministry, be working on an M.Div. or equivalent degree, provide evidence of financial need, be enrolled full time at an accredited school or seminary, provide a transcript of academic work, and be under the care of a regional Commission on the Ministry or in the process of coming under care.

Financial data   A stipend is awarded (amount not specified).

Duration   1 year; recipients may reapply.

Number awarded   Varies each year.

Deadline   March of each year.

[504]
DAVIS WRIGHT TREMAINE 1L DIVERSITY SCHOLARSHIP PROGRAM

Davis Wright Tremaine LLP
Attn: Diversity Scholarship Program
1201 Third Avenue, Suite 2200
Seattle, WA 98101-3045
(206) 757-8761   Toll Free: (877) 398-8416
Fax: (206) 757-7700   E-mail: BrookDormaier@dwt.com
Web: www.dwt.com/1LDiversityScholarship

Summary   To provide financial aid and summer work experience to Asian American and other law students of color.

Eligibility   This program is open to first-year law students of color and others of diverse backgrounds. Applicants must have a record of academic achievement as an undergraduate and in the first year of law school that demonstrates promise for a successful career in law, a commitment to civic involvement that promotes diversity and will continue after entering the legal profession, and a commitment to practicing in the Northwest after law school. Although demonstrated need may be taken into account, applicants need not disclose their financial circumstances.

Financial data   The award consists of a $7,500 stipend for second-year tuition and expenses and a paid summer clerkship.

Duration   1 academic year and summer.

Number awarded   2 each year: 1 in the Seattle office and 1 in the Portland office.

Deadline   January of each year.

[505]
DICKSTEIN SHAPIRO DIVERSITY SCHOLARSHIP

Dickstein Shapiro LLP
Attn: Director of Professional Development and Attorney Recruiting
1825 Eye Street, N.W.
Washington, DC 20006-5403
(202) 420-4880   Fax: (202) 420-2201
E-mail: careers@dicksteinshapiro.com
Web: www.dicksteinshapiro.com/careers/diversity

Summary   To provide financial aid and summer work experience at Dickstein Shapiro in Washington, D.C. or New York City to Asian American and other diverse law students from any state.

Eligibility   This program is open to second-year diverse law students, including 1) members of the lesbian, gay, bisexual, and transgender (LGBT) community; 2) members of minority ethnic and racial groups (Blacks, Hispanics and Latinos, Asians, American Indians and Native Alaskans, and Native Hawaiians and Pacific Islanders); and 3) students with disabilities. Applicants must be interested in a summer associateship with Dickstein Shapiro in Washington, D.C. or New York City. Selection is based on academic and professional experience as well as the extent to which they reflect the core values of the firm: excellence, loyalty, respect, initiative, and integrity.

Financial data   The stipend is $25,000, including $15,000 upon completion of the summer associate program and $10,000 upon acceptance of a full-time offer of employment following graduation.

Duration   The associateship takes place during the summer following the second year of law school and the stipend covers the third year of law school.

Additional information   This program began in 2006.

Number awarded   1 or more each year.

Deadline   September of each year.

[506]
DINSMORE & SHOHL LLP DIVERSITY SCHOLARSHIP PROGRAM

Dinsmore & Shohl LLP
Attn: Manager of Legal Recruiting
255 East Fifth Street, Suite 1900
Cincinnati, OH 45202
(513) 977-8488   Fax: (513) 977-8141
E-mail: dinsmore.legalrecruiting@dinsmore.com
Web: www.dinsmorecareers.com

Summary   To provide financial aid and summer work experience to Asian American and other law students from groups traditionally underrepresented in the legal profession.

Eligibility   This program is open to first- and second-year law students who are members of groups traditionally underrepresented in the legal profession. Applicants must have a demonstrated record of academic or professional achievement and leadership qualities. They must also be interested in a summer associateship with Dinsmore & Shohl LLP. Along with their application, they must submit a 500-word personal statement explaining their interest in the scholarship program and how diversity has impacted their life.

Financial data The program provides an academic scholarship of $5,000 to $10,000 and a paid associateship at the firm.

Duration The academic scholarship is for 1 year. The summer associateship is for 12 weeks.

Additional information Associateships are available at firm offices in Charleston (West Virginia), Cincinnati (Ohio), or Morgantown (West Virginia). The program includes 1 associateship in which the student spends 6 weeks as a clerk in the legal department of the Procter & Gamble Company's worldwide headquarters in Cincinnati and 6 weeks at Dinsmore & Shohl's Cincinnati office. All associates are assigned to an attorney with the firm who serves as a mentor.

Number awarded Varies each year.

Deadline September of each year for second-year students; December of each year for first-year students.

[507]
DISSERTATION FELLOWSHIPS OF THE CONSORTIUM FOR FACULTY DIVERSITY

Consortium for Faculty Diversity at Liberal Arts Colleges
c/o Gettysburg College
Provost's Office
300 North Washington Street
Campus Box 410
Gettysburg, PA 17325
(717) 337-6796   E-mail: sgockows@gettysburg.edu
Web: www.gettysburg.edu/about/offices/provost/cfd

Summary To provide an opportunity for Asian Americans and other doctoral candidates who will promote diversity to work on their dissertation while in residence at selected liberal arts colleges.

Eligibility This program is open to U.S. citizens and permanent residents who have completed all the requirements for the Ph.D. or M.F.A. except the dissertation. Applicants must be interested in a residency at a member institution of the Consortium for Faculty Diversity at Liberal Arts Colleges during which they will complete their dissertation. They must be able to contribute to diversity at the institution.

Financial data Dissertation fellows receive a stipend based on the average salary paid to instructors at the participating college. Modest funds are made available to finance the fellow's proposed research, subject to the usual institutional procedures.

Duration 1 year.

Additional information The following schools are participating in the program: Allegheny College, Bard College, Bowdoin College, Bryn Mawr College, Carleton College, Centenary College of Louisiana, Centre College, College of Wooster, Colorado College, Denison University, DePauw University, Dickinson College, Gettysburg College, Goucher College, Grinnell College, Gustavus Adolphus College, Hamilton College, Haverford College, Hobart and William Smith Colleges, Lafayette College, Lawrence University, Luther College, Macalester College, Mount Holyoke College, Muhlenberg College, New College of Florida, Oberlin College, Pitzer College, Pomona College, Reed College, Rhodes College, University of Richmond, Ripon College, Scripps College, St. Olaf College, Skidmore College, Smith College, Southwestern University, Swarthmore College, Transylvania University, Trinity College, Vassar College, and Wellesley College. Fel-

lows are expected to teach at least 1 course, participate in departmental seminars, and interact with students.

Number awarded Varies each year.

Deadline October of each year.

[508]
DIVERSITY COMMITTEE SCHOLARSHIP

American Society of Safety Engineers
Attn: ASSE Foundation
Scholarship Award Program
1800 East Oakton Street
Des Plaines, IL 60018
(847) 699-2929   Fax: (847) 768-3434
E-mail: bzylstra@asse.org
Web: www.asse.org

Summary To provide financial assistance to Asian American and other diverse upper-division or graduate students who are working on a degree related to occupational safety.

Eligibility This program is open to students who are working on an undergraduate or graduate degree in occupational safety, health, environment, industrial hygiene, occupational health nursing, or a closely-related field (e.g., industrial or environmental engineering). Applicants must be full-time students who have completed at least 60 semester hours with a GPA of 3.0 or higher as undergraduates or at least 9 semester hours as graduate students. A goal of this program is to support individuals regardless of race, ethnicity, gender, religion, personal beliefs, age, sexual orientation, physical challenges, geographic location, university, or specific area of study. U.S. citizenship is not required. Membership in the American Society of Safety Engineers (ASSE) is not required, but preference is given to members.

Financial data The stipend is $1,000 per year.

Duration 1 year; recipients may reapply.

Number awarded 1 each year.

Deadline November of each year.

[509]
DIVERSITY IN PLANNING AWARD

American Planning Association-California Chapter
Attn: California Planning Foundation
c/o Paul Wack
California Polytechnic State University at San Luis Obispo
City and Regional Planning Department
San Luis Obispo, CA 93407-0283
(805) 756-6331   Fax: (805) 756-1340
E-mail: pwack@calpoly.edu
Web: www.californiaplanningfoundation.org

Summary To provide financial assistance to Asian American and other undergraduate and graduate students in accredited planning programs at California universities who will increase diversity in the profession.

Eligibility This program is open to students entering their final year for an undergraduate or master's degree in an accredited planning program at a university in California. Applicants must be students who will increase diversity in the planning profession. Selection is based on academic performance, professional promise, and financial need.

Financial data The stipend is $3,000. The award includes a 1-year student membership in the American Planning Association (APA) and payment of registration for the APA California Conference.

Duration   1 year.

Additional information   The accredited planning programs are at 3 campuses of the California State University system (California State Polytechnic University at Pomona, California Polytechnic State University at San Luis Obispo, and San Jose State University), 3 campuses of the University of California (Berkeley, Irvine, and Los Angeles), and the University of Southern California.

Number awarded   1 each year.

Deadline   March of each year.

[510]
DIVERSITY IN PSYCHOLOGY AND LAW RESEARCH AWARD

American Psychological Association
Attn: Division 41 (American Psychology-Law Society)
c/o Diane Sivasubramaniam, Minority Affairs Committee
  Chair
Swinburne University of Technology
Faculty of Life and Social Sciences
Mail H31
P.O. Box 218
Hawthorn, VIC 3122
Australia
61 3 9214 5858 E-mail: dsivasubramaniam@swin.edu.au
Web: www.ap-ls.org

Summary   To provide funding to Asian American and other student members of the American Psychology-Law Society (AP-LS) who are interested in conducting a research project related to diversity.

Eligibility   This program is open to undergraduate and graduate student members of AP-LS who are interested in conducting research on issues related to psychology, law, multiculturalism, and/or diversity (e.g., research pertaining to psycholegal issues on race, gender, culture, sexual orientation). Students from underrepresented groups are strongly encouraged to apply; underrepresented groups include, but are not limited to: racial and ethnic minorities; first-generation college students; lesbian, gay, bisexual, and transgender students; and physically disabled students. Applicants must submit a project description that includes a statement of the research problem, the project's likely impact on the field of psychology and law broadly, methodology, budget, and an overview of relevant literature. Selection is based on the impact of the project on diversity and multiculturalism and the expected completion within the allocated time.

Financial data   The grant is $1,000.

Duration   The project must be completed within 1 year.

Number awarded   Up to 4 each year.

Deadline   November of each year.

[511]
DOCTORAL DIVERSITY FELLOWSHIPS IN SCIENCE, TECHNOLOGY, ENGINEERING, AND MATHEMATICS

State University of New York
Attn: Office of Diversity, Equity and Inclusion
State University Plaza
353 Broadway
Albany, NY 12246
(518) 320-1189
Web: www.suny.edu/provost/odee/programs.cfm

Summary   To provide financial assistance to residents of any state (particularly Asian Americans and other underrepresented minorities) who are working on a doctoral degree in a field of science, technology, engineering, and mathematics (STEM) at campuses of the State University of New York (SUNY) and will contribute to the diversity of the student body.

Eligibility   This program is open to U.S. citizens who are residents of any state and enrolled as doctoral students at any of the participating SUNY institutions. Applicants must be working on a degree in a field of STEM. They must be able to demonstrate how they will contribute to the diversity of the student body, primarily by having overcome a disadvantage or other impediment to success in higher education. Economic disadvantage, although not a requirement, may be the basis for eligibility. Membership in a racial or ethnic group that is underrepresented at the applicant's school or program may serve as a plus factor in making awards, but may not form the sole basis of selection.

Financial data   The stipend is $20,000 per year.

Duration   3 years; may be renewed for up to 2 additional years.

Number awarded   Up to 3 each year.

Deadline   January of each year.

[512]
DOCTORAL/POST-DOCTORAL FELLOWSHIP PROGRAM IN LAW AND SOCIAL SCIENCE

American Bar Foundation
Attn: Administrative Assistant for Academic Affairs and
  Research Administration
750 North Lake Shore Drive
Chicago, IL 60611-4403
(312) 988-6517   Fax: (312) 988-6579
E-mail: aehrhardt@abfn.org
Web: www.americanbarfoundation.org

Summary   To provide research funding to scholars (particularly Asian Americans and other minorities) who are completing or have completed doctoral degrees in fields related to law, the legal profession, and legal institutions.

Eligibility   This program is open to Ph.D. candidates in the social sciences who have completed all doctoral requirements except the dissertation. Applicants who have completed the dissertation are also eligible. Doctoral and proposed research must be in the general area of sociolegal studies or in social scientific approaches to law, the legal profession, or legal institutions and legal processes. Applications must include 1) a dissertation abstract or proposal with an outline of the substance and methods of the research; 2) 2 letters of recommendation; and 3) a curriculum vitae. Minority candidates are especially encouraged to apply.

Financial data The stipend is $30,000. Fellows may request up to $1,500 to reimburse expenses associated with research, travel to meet with advisers, or travel to conferences at which papers are presented. Relocation expenses of up to $2,500 may be reimbursed on application.

Duration 12 months, beginning in September.

Additional information Fellows are offered access to the computing and word processing facilities of the American Bar Foundation and the libraries of Northwestern University and the University of Chicago. This program was established in 1996. Fellowships must be held in residence at the American Bar Foundation. Appointments to the fellowship are full time; fellows are not permitted to undertake other work.

Number awarded 1 or more each year.

Deadline December of each year.

[513]
DOLORES NYHUS GRADUATE FELLOWSHIP

California Dietetic Association
Attn: CDA Foundation
7740 Manchester Avenue, Suite 102
Playa del Rey, CA 90293-8499
(310) 822-0177 Fax: (310) 823-0264
E-mail: patsmith@dietitian.org
Web: www.dietitian.org/d_cdaf/cdaf_outreach.html

Summary To provide financial assistance to members (particularly Asian Americans or other minorities, men, and members with disabilities) of the Academy of Nutrition and Dietetics (AND) who live in California and are interested in working on a graduate degree in dietetics or a related field at a school in any state.

Eligibility This program is open to California residents who are AND members and have a bachelor's degree and 3 to 5 years of professional experience. Applicants must be a registered dietitian (R.D.), be a registered dietetic technician (D.T.R.), or have a credential earned at least 6 months previously. They must be enrolled in or admitted to a graduate school in any state in the areas of public health, gerontology, or a community-related program with the intention of practicing in the field of dietetics. Along with their application, they must submit a letter of application that includes a discussion of their career goals. Selection is based on that letter (15%), academic ability (25%), work or volunteer experience (15%), letters of recommendation (15%), extracurricular activities (5%), and financial need (25%). Applications are especially encouraged from ethnic minorities, men, and people with physical disabilities.

Financial data The stipend is normally $1,000.

Duration 1 year.

Additional information The California Dietetic Association is the California affiliate of the AND.

Number awarded 1 each year.

Deadline April of each year.

[514]
DONALD W. BANNER DIVERSITY SCHOLARSHIP

Banner & Witcoff, Ltd.
Attn: Christopher Hummel
1100 13th Street, N.W., Suite 1200
Washington, DC 20005-4051
(202) 824-3000 Fax: (202) 824-3001
E-mail: chummel@bannerwitcoff.com
Web: www.bannerwitcoff.com/about/diversity

Summary To provide financial assistance to Asian Americans and other law students who come from groups historically underrepresented in intellectual property law.

Eligibility This program is open to students enrolled in the first or second year of a J.D. program at an ABA-accredited law school in the United States. Applicants must come from a group historically underrepresented in intellectual property law; that underrepresentation may be the result of race, sex, ethnicity, sexual orientation, disability, education, culture, religion, age, or socioeconomic background. Selection is based on academic merit, commitment to the pursuit of a career in intellectual property law, written communication skills, oral communication skills (determined through an interview), leadership qualities, and community involvement.

Financial data The stipend is $5,000 per year.

Duration 1 year (the second or third year of law school); students who accept and successfully complete the firm's summer associate program may receive an additional $5,000 for a subsequent semester of law school.

Number awarded 2 each year.

Deadline October of each year.

[515]
DORA AMES LEE LEADERSHIP DEVELOPMENT FUND

United Methodist Church
General Board of Global Ministries
Attn: United Methodist Committee on Relief
Health and Welfare Ministries
475 Riverside Drive, Room 330
New York, NY 10115
(212) 870-3871 Toll Free: (800) UMC-GBGM
E-mail: jyoung@gbgm-umc.org
Web: gbgm-umc.org/health/doralee.cfm

Summary To provide financial assistance to Methodists and other Christians of Asian, Pacific Islander, or Native American descent who are preparing for a career in a health-related field.

Eligibility This program is open to undergraduate and graduate students who are U.S. citizens of Asian American, Pacific Islander, or Native American descent. Applicants must be professed Christians, preferably United Methodists. They must be attending a college or university to enter or continue in a health-related field. Financial need is considered in the selection process.

Financial data The stipend is $2,000.

Duration 1 year.

Additional information This program began in 1980.

Number awarded 5 each year.

Deadline June of each year.

[516]
DORSEY & WHITNEY DIVERSITY FELLOWSHIPS

Dorsey & Whitney LLP
Attn: Recruiting Manager
50 South Sixth Street, Suite 1500
Minneapolis, MN 55402-1498
(612) 340-2600   Toll Free: (800) 759-4929
Fax: (612) 340-2868 E-mail: forsmark.claire@dorsey.com
Web: www.dorsey.com/diversity_fellowship_12111

Summary To provide financial assistance for law school to Asian Americans and other students from diverse backgrounds who are interested in working during the summer at offices of the sponsoring law firm.

Eligibility This program is open to first-year students at ABA-accredited law schools who have accepted a summer associate position at an office of the sponsor in Denver, Minneapolis, or Seattle. Applicants must be able to demonstrate academic achievement and a commitment to promoting diversity in the legal community. Along with their application, they must submit a personal statement on the ways in which they have promoted and will continue to promote diversity in the legal community, what diversity means to them, and why they are interested in the sponsoring law firm.

Financial data Fellows receive a stipend of $7,500 for the second year of law school and, if they complete a summer associate position in the following summer, another stipend of $7,500 for the third year of law school. If they join the firm following graduation, they receive an additional $5,000.

Duration 1 year; may be renewed for 1 additional year.

Additional information This program began in 2006.

Number awarded 1 or more each year.

Deadline January of each year.

[517]
DR. HARIHARA MEHENDALE GRADUATE STUDENT BEST ABSTRACT AWARD

Society of Toxicology
Attn: Association of Scientists of Indian Origin Special
    Interest Group
1821 Michael Faraday Drive, Suite 300
Reston, VA 20190-5348
(703) 438-3115   Fax: (703) 438-3113
E-mail: sothq@toxicology.org
Web: www.toxicology.org/ai/af/awards.aspx

Summary To recognize and reward graduate student members of the Society of Toxicology (SOT) who are of Indian origin (from India) and present outstanding papers at the annual meeting.

Eligibility This award is available to graduate students of Indian origin who are members of SOT and its Association of Scientists of Indian Origin (ASIO). Candidates must have an accepted abstract of a research poster or platform presentation for the SOT annual meeting. Along with the abstract, they must submit a cover letter outlining the significance of their research to the field of toxicology and how this award will help them to further their career goals.

Financial data A plaque and a cash award (amount not specified) are presented.

Duration The award is presented annually.

Additional information This award was established in 2008.

Number awarded 1 each year.
Deadline December of each year.

[518]
DR. KIYOSHI SONODA MEMORIAL SCHOLARSHIP

Japanese American Citizens League
Attn: National Scholarship Awards
1765 Sutter Street
San Francisco, CA 94115
(415) 345-1075   Fax: (415) 931-4671
E-mail: ncwnp@jacl.org
Web: www.jacl.org/edu/scholar.htm

Summary To provide financial assistance to student members of the Japanese American Citizens League (JACL) who are interested in preparing for a career in dentistry.

Eligibility This program is open to JACL members who are enrolled or planning to enroll at a school of dentistry. Applicants must submit information on their involvement in JACL and a 2-page essay on a topic that changes annually but relates to Japanese Americans. Selection is based on that essay, academic history, JACL involvement, school activities, work history, scholastic honors, and community involvement.

Financial data Stipends generally average more than $2,000.

Duration 1 year; nonrenewable.

Number awarded At least 1 each year.

Deadline March of each year.

[519]
DR. LAXMAN DESAI GRADUATE STUDENT BEST ABSTRACT AWARD

Society of Toxicology
Attn: Association of Scientists of Indian Origin Special
    Interest Group
1821 Michael Faraday Drive, Suite 300
Reston, VA 20190-5348
(703) 438-3115   Fax: (703) 438-3113
E-mail: sothq@toxicology.org
Web: www.toxicology.org/ai/af/awards.aspx

Summary To recognize and reward graduate student members of the Society of Toxicology (SOT) who are of Indian origin (from India) and present outstanding papers at the annual meeting.

Eligibility This award is available to graduate students of Indian origin who are members of SOT and its Association of Scientists of Indian Origin (ASIO). Candidates must have an accepted abstract of a research poster or platform presentation for the SOT annual meeting. Along with the abstract, they must submit a cover letter outlining the significance of their research to the field of toxicology and how this award will help them to further their career goals.

Financial data A plaque and a cash award (amount not specified) are presented.

Duration The award is presented annually.

Additional information This award was established in 2009.

Number awarded 1 each year.

Deadline December of each year.

[520]
DR. NANCY FOSTER SCHOLARSHIP PROGRAM

National Oceanic and Atmospheric Administration
Attn: Office of Education
1315 East-West Highway
SSMC3, Room 11146
Silver Spring, MD 20910
(301) 713-9437, ext. 150   Fax: (301) 713-9465
E-mail: fosterscholars@noaa.gov
Web: fosterscholars.noaa.gov

Summary To provide financial assistance to graduate students (especially Asian Americans, other minorities, and women) who are interested in working on a degree in fields related to marine sciences.

Eligibility This program is open to U.S. citizens, particularly women and members of minority groups, currently working on or intending to work on a master's or doctoral degree in oceanography, marine biology, or maritime archaeology, including all science, engineering, and resource management of ocean and coastal areas. Applicants must submit a description of their academic, research, and career goals, and how their proposed course of study or research will help them to achieve those goals. They must be enrolled full time and have a GPA of 3.0 or higher. As part of their program, they must be interested in participating in a summer research collaboration at a facility of the National Oceanic and Atmospheric Administration (NOAA). Selection is based on academic record and the statement of career goals and objectives (25%); quality of project and applicability to program priorities (35%); recommendations and/or endorsements (15%); additional relevant experience related to diversity of education, extracurricular activities, honors and awards, written and oral communication skills, and interpersonal skills (15%); and financial need (10%).

Financial data The program provides a stipend of $30,000 per academic year, a tuition allowance of up to $12,000 per academic year, and up to $10,000 of support for a 4- to 6-week research collaboration at a NOAA facility is provided.

Duration Master's degree students may receive up to 2 years of stipend and tuition support and 1 research collaboration (for a total of $94,000). Doctoral students may receive up to 4 years of stipend and tuition support and 2 research collaborations (for a total of $188,000).

Additional information This program began in 2001.

Number awarded Varies each year; recently, 3 of these fellowships were awarded.

Deadline February of each year.

[521]
DRI LAW STUDENT DIVERSITY SCHOLARSHIP

DRI-The Voice of the Defense Bar
Attn: Deputy Executive Director
55 West Monroe Street, Suite 2000
Chicago, IL 60603
(312) 795-1101   Fax: (312) 795-0747
E-mail: dri@dri.org
Web: www.dri.org/About

Summary To provide financial assistance to Asian American, other minority, and female law students.

Eligibility This program is open to full-time students entering their second or third year of law school who are African American, Hispanic, Asian, Native American, or women. Applicants must submit an essay, up to 1,000 words, on a topic that changes annually but relates to the work of defense attorneys. Selection is based on that essay, demonstrated academic excellence, service to the profession, service to the community, and service to the cause of diversity. Students affiliated with the American Association for Justice as members, student members, or employees are not eligible. Finalists are invited to participate in personal interviews.

Financial data The stipend is $10,000.

Duration 1 year.

Additional information This program began in 2004.

Number awarded 2 each year.

Deadline May of each year.

[522]
EASTERN REGION KOREAN AMERICAN COLLEGE/GRADUATE SCHOLARSHIPS

Korean American Scholarship Foundation
Eastern Region
1952 Gallows Road, Suite 310
Vienna, VA 22182
(703) 748-5935   Fax: (703) 748-1874
E-mail: erc.scholarship@kasf.org
Web: www.kasf.org/eastern

Summary To provide financial assistance to Korean American students from any state who are working on an undergraduate or graduate degree in any field at a school in eastern states.

Eligibility This program is open to Korean Americans who are high school seniors or full-time undergraduate or graduate students currently enrolled or planning to enroll at a college or university in an eastern state. Applicants may reside anywhere in the United States as long as they attend school in the eastern region: Delaware, District of Columbia, Kentucky, Maryland, North Carolina, Pennsylvania, Virginia, and West Virginia. They must have a GPA of 3.0 or higher. Both U.S. citizens and foreign nationals are eligible. Selection is based on academic achievement (25%), extracurricular activities (10%), an essay (10%), recommendations (10%), financial need (40%), and extra credit for having extraordinary circumstances (5%).

Financial data Stipends range up to $5,000.

Duration 1 year; renewable.

Number awarded Varies each year; recently, 31 of these scholarships were awarded.

Deadline July of each year.

[523]
EDWARD S. ROTH MANUFACTURING ENGINEERING SCHOLARSHIP

Society of Manufacturing Engineers
Attn: SME Education Foundation
One SME Drive
P.O. Box 930
Dearborn, MI 48121-0930
(313) 425-3300   Toll Free: (800) 733-4763, ext. 3300
Fax: (313) 425-3411   E-mail: foundation@sme.org
Web: www.smeef.org/scholarships

Summary To provide financial assistance to Asian American and other students enrolled or planning to work on a bachelor's or master's degree in manufacturing engineering at selected universities.

Eligibility This program is open to U.S. citizens who are graduating high school seniors or currently-enrolled undergraduate or graduate students. Applicants must be enrolled or planning to enroll as a full-time student at 1 of 13 selected 4-year universities to work on a bachelor's or master's degree in manufacturing engineering. They must have a GPA of 3.0 or higher. Preference is given to 1) students demonstrating financial need; 2) minority students; and 3) students participating in a co-op program. Some preference may also be given to graduating high school seniors and graduate students. Along with their application, they must submit a 300-word essay that covers their career and educational objectives, how this scholarship will help them attain those objectives, and why they want to enter this field.

Financial data Stipend amounts vary; recently, the value of all scholarships provided by this foundation averaged approximately $2,330.

Duration 1 year; may be renewed.

Additional information The eligible institutions are California Polytechnic State University at San Luis Obispo, California State Polytechnic State University at Pomona, University of Miami (Florida), Bradley University (Illinois), Central State University (Ohio), Miami University (Ohio), Boston University, Worcester Polytechnic Institute (Massachusetts), University of Massachusetts, St. Cloud State University (Minnesota), University of Texas-Pan American, Brigham Young University (Utah), and Utah State University.

Number awarded 2 each year.

Deadline January of each year.

[524]
EIICHI MATSUSHITA MEMORIAL SCHOLARSHIP FUND

Evangelical Lutheran Church in America
Association of Asians and Pacific Islanders
8765 West Higgins Road
Chicago, IL 60631
(773) 380-2834   Toll Free: (800) 638-3522
Fax: (773) 380-2833
E-mail: Pongsak.Limthongviratn@elca.org
Web: www.asianlutherans.net/scholarship

Summary To provide financial assistance to Asian/Pacific Islanders who wish to receive seminary training to become ordained Lutheran pastors or certified lay teachers.

Eligibility This program is open to students who are of Asian or Pacific Islander background and are attending a Lutheran seminary, have been endorsed by the appropriate synodical or district commissions, have demonstrated financial need, and have received partial financial support from their home congregations. Applicants must include a 250-word statement on their commitment to Asian/Pacific Islander ministry.

Financial data The stipend is $750.

Duration 1 year; may be renewed.

Additional information The scholarship was established by Asian Lutherans in North America.

Number awarded 2 each year.

Deadline September of each year.

[525]
EIZO AND TOYO SAKUMOTO TRUST SCHOLARSHIPS

Hawai'i Community Foundation
Attn: Scholarship Department
827 Fort Street Mall
Honolulu, HI 96813
(808) 566-5570   Toll Free: (888) 731-3863
Fax: (808) 521-6286
E-mail: scholarships@hcf-hawaii.org
Web: www.hawaiicommunityfoundation.org/scholarships

Summary To provide financial assistance to Hawaii residents of Japanese ancestry who are interested in attending graduate school in the state.

Eligibility This program is open to Hawaiian residents of Japanese ancestry who are enrolled or planning to enroll at an accredited college or university in the state. Applicants must be full-time graduate students and able to demonstrate academic achievement (GPA of 3.5 or higher), good moral character, and financial need. They must have been born in Hawaii. Along with their application, they must submit a short statement indicating their reasons for attending college, their planned course of study, their career goals, and what community service means to them.

Financial data The amounts of the awards depend on the availability of funds and the need of the recipient. Recently, the average value of each of the scholarships awarded by the foundation was $2,200.

Duration 1 year.

Number awarded Varies each year; recently, 30 of these scholarships were awarded.

Deadline February of each year.

[526]
ELIZABETH MUNSTERBERG KOPPITZ CHILD PSYCHOLOGY GRADUATE FELLOWSHIPS

American Psychological Foundation
750 First Street, N.E.
Washington, DC 20002-4242
(202) 336-5843   Fax: (202) 336-5812
E-mail: foundation@apa.org
Web: www.apa.org/apf/funding/koppitz.aspx

Summary To provide funding to doctoral students (particularly Asian Americans, other minorities, women, and students with disabilities) who are interested in conducting research in child psychology.

Eligibility This program is open to graduate students who have progressed academically through the qualifying examinations, usually after the third or fourth year of doctoral study. Applicants must be interested in conducting psychological research that promotes the advancement of knowledge and learning in the field of child psychology. Selection is based on conformance with stated program goals, magnitude of incremental contribution, quality of proposed work, and applicant's demonstrated scholarship and research competence. The sponsor encourages applications from individuals who represent diversity in race, ethnicity, gender, age, disability, and sexual orientation.

Financial data The grant is $25,000 for fellows or $5,000 for runners-up.

Duration 1 year.

Additional information This fellowship was first awarded in 2003.

Number awarded Varies each year; recently, 6 fellows and 2 runners-up were selected.

Deadline November of each year.

[527]
ELLIOTT C. ROBERTS, SR. SCHOLARSHIP

Institute for Diversity in Health Management
Attn: Education Specialist
155 North Wacker Avenue, Suite 400
Chicago, IL 60606
(312) 422-2658   Toll Free: (800) 233-0996
Fax: (312) 895-4511   E-mail: cbiddle@aha.org
Web: www.diversityconnection.org

Summary To provide financial assistance to Asian American and other minority graduate students in health services management who have demonstrated outstanding community service.

Eligibility This program is open to members of ethnically diverse groups who are enrolled in the second year of a graduate program in health care administration. Applicants must have a GPA of 3.0 or higher. They must be able to demonstrate a commitment to community service. Along with their application, they must submit 1) a personal statement of 1 to 2 pages on their interest in health care management and their career goals; 2) an essay on what they see as the most challenging issue facing America's hospitals and health systems; and 3) a 500-word essay on how they currently serve their community beyond their academic career. Selection is based on academic achievement, commitment to community service, and financial need. U.S. citizenship is required.

Financial data The stipend is $1,000.

Duration 1 year.

Number awarded 1 each year.

Deadline January of each year.

[528]
ENDOWMENT FOR SOUTH ASIAN STUDENTS OF INDIAN DESCENT

Pennsylvania Medical Society
Attn: Foundation
777 East Park Drive
P.O. Box 8820
Harrisburg, PA 17105-8820
(717) 558-7854
Toll Free: (800) 228-7823, ext. 7854 (within PA)
Fax: (717) 558-7818
E-mail: studentservices-foundation@pamedsoc.org
Web: www.foundationpamedsoc.org

Summary To provide financial assistance to South Asian Indian residents of Pennsylvania who are enrolled at a medical school in the state.

Eligibility This program is open to South Asian Indians or descendants of South Asian Indian immigrants to the United States who have been Pennsylvania residents for at least 12 months. Applicants must be entering the second, third, or fourth year of full-time study at an accredited allopathic or osteopathic medical school in Pennsylvania. They must submit a 1-page essay explaining why they chose to become a physician and what contributions they expect to make to the

health profession. Financial need is considered in the selection process.

Financial data The stipend is $2,000. Funds are paid directly to the recipient's medical school through the appropriate channels.

Duration 1 year.

Additional information This program began in 2003.

Number awarded 1 each year.

Deadline September of each year.

[529]
EPISCOPAL ASIAMERICA MINISTRIES THEOLOGICAL EDUCATION SCHOLARSHIPS

Episcopal Church Center
Attn: Domestic and Foreign Missionary Society
Scholarship Committee
815 Second Avenue, Fifth Floor
New York, NY 10017-4503
(212) 716-6168   Toll Free: (800) 334-7626
Fax: (212) 867-0395 E-mail: tfoster@episcopalchurch.org
Web: www.episcopalchurch.org/scholarships

Summary To provide financial assistance to Asian and Pacific Island Americans interested in seeking ordination and serving in a ministry involving Asians and Pacific Islanders in the Episcopal Church.

Eligibility This program is open to Asian and Pacific Island students pursuing theological education, including diocesan programs as well as seminary education. Applicants must be a member of an Asian or Pacific Island constituency in the Episcopal Church and have begun the process of seeking ordination through a local Episcopal diocese. They must intend to serve in a ministry of the Episcopal Church involving Asian or Pacific Island Americans. Scholarships are presented only for full-time study.

Financial data The maximum stipend is $5,000 per year.

Duration 1 year; may be renewed up to 3 additional years.

Additional information This program receives support from several funds of the sponsoring agency: the Susan R. Bonsall Scholarship Fund (established in 1901), the William B. Foote Educational Fund (established in 1919), the Daniel Albert Pierce Fund (established in 1920), the Rev. Arthur Mann Memorial Fund (established in 1926), and the Theological Education Scholarship Fund (established in 1983).

Number awarded Varies each year; recently, 4 of these scholarships, with a value of $19,000, were awarded.

Deadline April of each year.

[530]
ESTHER KATZ ROSEN GRADUATE STUDENT FELLOWSHIPS

American Psychological Foundation
750 First Street, N.E.
Washington, DC 20002-4242
(202) 336-5843   Fax: (202) 336-5812
E-mail: foundation@apa.org
Web: www.apa.org/apf/funding/rosen.aspx

Summary To provide funding to graduate students (particularly Asian Americans, other minorities, and students with disabilities) who are interested in conducting research on psychological issues relevant to giftedness in children.

Eligibility This program is open to graduate students at universities in the United States and Canada who have advanced to candidacy. Applicants must be interested in conducting research on the psychological understanding of gifted and talented children and adolescents. Selection is based on conformance with stated program goals, magnitude of incremental contribution, quality of proposed work, and applicant's demonstrated scholarship and research competence. The sponsor encourages applications from individuals who represent diversity in race, ethnicity, gender, age, disability, and sexual orientation.

Financial data The grant is $20,000. The fellow's home institution is expected to provide a tuition waiver.

Duration 1 year.

Additional information This fund was established in 1974.

Number awarded 1 each year.

Deadline April of each year.

[531]
ESTHER NGAN-LING CHOW AND MAREYJOYCE GREEN SCHOLARSHIP

Sociologists for Women in Society
Attn: Executive Officer
Southern Connecticut State University
Department of Sociology
501 Crescent Street
New Haven, CT 06515
(203) 392-7714   Fax: (203) 392-7715
E-mail: swseo@socwomen.org
Web: www.socwomen.org/awards.html

Summary To provide funding to Asian American and other women of color who are conducting dissertation research in sociology.

Eligibility This program is open to women from a racial/ethnic group that faces discrimination in the United States. Applicants must be in the early stages of writing a doctoral dissertation in sociology on a topic relating to the concerns that women of color face domestically and/or internationally. They must be able to demonstrate financial need. Both domestic and international students are eligible to apply. Along with their application, they must submit a personal statement that details their short- and long-term career and research goals; a resume or curriculum vitae; 2 letters of recommendation; and a 5-page dissertation proposal that includes the purpose of the research, the work to be accomplished through support from this scholarship, and a time line for completion.

Financial data The stipend is $15,000. An additional grant of $500 is provided to enable the recipient to attend the winter meeting of Sociologists for Women in Society (SWS), and travel expenses to attend the summer meeting are reimbursed.

Duration 1 year.

Additional information This program began in 2007 and originally named the Women of Color Dissertation Scholarship.

Number awarded 1 each year.

Deadline March of each year.

[532]
FACS GRADUATE FELLOWSHIPS

National Association of Teacher Educators for Family and
   Consumer Sciences
c/o Lela G. Goar, Fellowship Committee Chair
225 CR 207A
Burnet, TX 78611
(512) 715-8249   Fax: (512) 585-7606
E-mail: lkgoar@wildblue.net
Web: www.natefacs.org/scholarship.html

Summary To provide financial assistance to Asian American and other graduate students in family and consumer science education.

Eligibility This program is open to graduate students working on a master's or doctoral degree in family and consumer sciences education. Applicants must submit an autobiographical sketch (up to 3 pages in length) presenting their professional goals, including information on the institution where they are studying or planning to study, areas or emphases of study, possible research topic, and other pertinent information regarding their plans. Selection is based on likelihood of completing the degree, likelihood of contribution to family and consumer sciences education, previous academic work, professional association involvement, professional experience (including scholarly work), and references. At least 1 fellowship is reserved for a minority (African American, Hispanic American, Native American, or Asian American) candidate.

Financial data Stipends range from $2,000 to $4,000.

Duration 1 year.

Additional information The sponsor is an affiliate of the Family and Consumer Sciences (FACS) Division of the Association for Career and Technical Education.

Number awarded Varies each year.

Deadline October of each year.

[533]
FAEGRE BAKER DANIELS DIVERSITY AND INCLUSION FELLOWSHIPS

Faegre Baker Daniels
Attn: Diversity and Pro Bono Coordinator
300 North Meridian Street, Suite 2700
Indianapolis, IN 46204
(317) 237-8298   Fax: (317) 237-1000
E-mail: brita.horvath@faegrebd.com
Web: www.faegrebd.com/fellowship

Summary To provide financial aid and summer work experience to Asian Americans and other students from diverse backgrounds entering the second year of law school.

Eligibility This program is open to residents of any state who are entering their second year at an accredited law school. Applicants must reflect diversity, defined to mean that they come from varied ethnic, racial, cultural, and lifestyle backgrounds, as well as those with disabilities or unique viewpoints. They must also be interested in a place in the sponsor's associate program during the summer between their second and third year of law school. Along with their application, they must submit a 2-page personal statement describing how or why they will contribute meaningfully to diversity and inclusion at the sponsoring firm and/or in the legal profession.

Financial data The stipend is $10,000.

Duration 1 year.

Additional information This law firm was formerly Baker & Daniels LLP. Recipients of these fellowships may elect to conduct their associateship at offices in Boulder, Chicago, Denver, Des Moines, Fort Wayne, Indianapolis, Minneapolis, Silicon Valley (East Palo Alto), South Bend, and Washington, D.C.

Number awarded 4 each year.

Deadline September of each year.

[534]
FARM CREDIT EAST SCHOLARSHIPS

Farm Credit East
Attn: Scholarship Program
240 South Road
Enfield, CT 06082
(860) 741-4380　　　　　Toll Free: (800) 562-2235
Fax: (860) 741-4389
E-mail: specialoffers@famcrediteast.com
Web: www.farmcrediteast.com

Summary To provide financial assistance to Asian American and other residents of designated northeastern states who plan to attend school in any state to work on an undergraduate or graduate degree in a field related to agriculture, forestry, or fishing.

Eligibility This program is open to residents of Massachusetts, Connecticut, Rhode Island, New Jersey, and portions of New York and New Hampshire. Applicants must be working on or planning to work on an associate, bachelor's, or graduate degree in production agriculture, agribusiness, the forest products industry, or commercial fishing at a college or university in any state. They must submit a 200-word essay on why they wish to prepare for a career in agriculture, forestry, or fishing. Selection is based on the essay, extracurricular activities (especially farm work experience and activities indicative of an interest in preparing for a career in agriculture or agribusiness), and interest in agriculture. The program includes diversity scholarships reserved for members of minority groups (Black or African American, American Indian or Alaska Native, Asian, Native Hawaiian or other Pacific Islander, or Hispanic or Latino).

Financial data The stipend is $1,500. Funds are paid directly to the student to be used for tuition, room and board, books, and other academic charges.

Duration 1 year; nonrenewable.

Additional information Recipients are given priority for an internship with the sponsor in the summer following their junior year. Farm Credit East was formerly named First Pioneer Farm Credit.

Number awarded Up to 28 each year, including several diversity scholarships.

Deadline April of each year.

[535]
FBANC LEGAL SCHOLARSHIP

Filipino Bar Association of Northern California
268 Bush Street, Suite 2928
San Francisco, CA 94104
E-mail: fbancinfo@gmail.com
Web: www.fbanc.org/law-students

Summary To provide financial assistance to entering or continuing law students who are interested in serving the Filipino American community.

Eligibility This program is open to currently-enrolled and entering law students who have a tie to the Filipino American community and intend to provide legal services to that community after graduation from law school. Applicants must submit a current transcript or admit letter, a resume, and a 2-page essay on a topic that changes annually but relates to Filipinos and the law. Selection is based on that essay, interest and desire to serve the Filipino American community, and persuasiveness.

Financial data The stipend is $5,000.

Duration 1 year.

Number awarded 1 each year.

Deadline April of each year.

[536]
FILIPINO NURSES' ORGANIZATION OF HAWAII SCHOLARSHIP

Hawai'i Community Foundation
Attn: Scholarship Department
827 Fort Street Mall
Honolulu, HI 96813
(808) 566-5570　　　　　Toll Free: (888) 731-3863
Fax: (808) 521-6286
E-mail: scholarships@hcf-hawaii.org
Web: www.hawaiicommunityfoundation.org/scholarships

Summary To provide financial assistance to Hawaii residents of Filipino ancestry who are interested in attending college in any state to prepare for a career as a nurse.

Eligibility This program is open to Hawaii residents of Filipino ancestry who are enrolled or planning to enroll full time at a college or university in any state and work on an undergraduate or graduate degree in nursing. Applicants must be able to demonstrate academic achievement (GPA of 2.7 or higher), good moral character, and financial need. Along with their application, they must submit a short statement indicating their reasons for attending college, their planned course of study, their career goals, and what community service means to them.

Financial data The amounts of the awards depend on the availability of funds and the need of the recipient. Recently, the average value of each of the scholarships awarded by the foundation was $2,200.

Duration 1 year.

Number awarded Varies each year; recently, 2 of these scholarships were awarded.

Deadline February of each year.

[537]
FINNEGAN HENDERSON DIVERSITY SCHOLARSHIP

Finnegan, Henderson, Farabow, Garrett & Dunner, LLP
Attn: Attorney Recruitment Manager
901 New York Avenue, N.W.
Washington, DC 20001-4413
(202) 408-4034　　　　　Fax: (202) 408-4400
E-mail: diversityscholarship@finnegan.com
Web: www.finnegan.com/careers/summerprogram/overview

Summary To provide financial aid and work experience to Asian American and other law students from diverse groups who are interested in a career in intellectual property law.

Eligibility This program is open to law students who have demonstrated a commitment to a career in intellectual property law and are currently enrolled either as a first-year full-time student or second-year part-time student. Applicants must contribute to enhancing diversity; the sponsor defines diversity broadly, and has considered members of racial, ethnic, disabled, and sexual orientation groups that have been historically underrepresented in the legal profession. They must have earned an undergraduate degree in life sciences, engineering, or computer science, or have substantial prior trademark experience. Selection is based on academic performance at the undergraduate, graduate (if applicable), and law school level; relevant work experience; community service; leadership skills; and special accomplishments.

Financial data The stipend is $15,000 per year.

Duration 1 year; may be renewed 1 additional year as long as the recipient completes a summer associateship with the sponsor and maintains of GPA of 3.0 or higher.

Additional information The sponsor, the world's largest intellectual property law firm, established this scholarship in 2003. Summer associateships are available at its offices in Washington, D.C., Atlanta, Boston, Palo Alto, or Reston.

Number awarded 1 each year.

Deadline February of each year.

[538]
FISH & RICHARDSON DIVERSITY FELLOWSHIP PROGRAM

Fish & Richardson P.C.
Recruiting Department
Attn: Manager of Diversity
12390 El Camino Real
San Diego, CA 92130
(858) 678-5070   Fax: (858) 678-5099
E-mail: diversity@fr.com
Web: www.fr.com/diversity

Summary To provide financial assistance for law school to Asian Americans and other students who will contribute to diversity in the legal profession.

Eligibility This program is open to students enrolled in the first year at a law school anywhere in the country. Applicants must be African American/Black, American Indian/Alaskan, Hispanic/Latino, Native Hawaiian/Pacific Islander, Asian, 2 or more races, disabled, or openly GLBT. Along with their application, they must submit a 500-word essay describing their background, what led them to the legal field, their interest in the sponsoring law firm, and what they could contribute to its practice and the profession. They must also indicate their first 3 choices of an office of the firm where they are interested in a summer associate clerkship.

Financial data The stipend is $5,000.

Duration 1 year: the second year of law school.

Additional information Recipients are also offered a paid associate clerkship during the summer following their first year of law school at an office of the firm in the location of their choice in Atlanta, Austin, Boston, Dallas, Delaware, Houston, New York, San Diego, Silicon Valley, Twin Cities, or Washington, D.C. This program began in 2005.

Number awarded 1 or more each year.

Deadline January of each year.

[539]
FIVE COLLEGE FELLOWSHIP PROGRAM

Five Colleges, Incorporated
Attn: Five Colleges Fellowship Program Committee
97 Spring Street
Amherst, MA 01002-2324
(413) 542-4013   E-mail: ntherien@fivecolleges.edu
Web: www.fivecolleges.edu/faculty/fellowships

Summary To provide funding to Asian American and other graduate students from underrepresented groups who have completed all the requirements for the Ph.D. except the dissertation and are interested in teaching at selected colleges in Massachusetts.

Eligibility Fellows are chosen by the host department in each of the 4 participating liberal arts colleges (Amherst, Hampshire, Mount Holyoke, and Smith). Applicants must be graduate students at an accredited school who have completed all doctoral requirements except the dissertation and are interested in devoting full time to the completion of the dissertation. The chief goal of the program is to support scholars from underrepresented groups and/or scholars "with unique interests and histories whose engagement in the Academy will enrich scholarship and teaching."

Financial data The program provides a stipend of $30,000, a research grant, health benefits, office space, library privileges, and housing assistance.

Duration 1 academic year; nonrenewable.

Additional information Although the primary goal is completion of the dissertation, each fellow also has many opportunities to experience working with students and faculty colleagues on the host campus as well as with those at the other colleges. The fellows are also given an opportunity to teach (generally as a team teacher, in a section of a core course, or in a component within a course). Fellows meet monthly with each other to share their experiences. At Smith College, this program is named Mendenhall Fellowships. The fifth institution that belongs to this organization, the University of Massachusetts at Amherst, does not participate in this program.

Number awarded 4 each year; 1 at each of the participating colleges.

Deadline January of each year.

[540]
F.J. MCGUIGAN DISSERTATION AWARD

American Psychological Foundation
750 First Street, N.E.
Washington, DC 20002-4242
(202) 336-5843   Fax: (202) 336-5812
E-mail: foundation@apa.org
Web: www.apa.org/apf/funding/mcguigan-dissertation.aspx

Summary To provide funding to doctoral candidates (particularly Asian Americans, other minorities, women, and students with disabilities) who are interested in conducting research on the materialistic understanding of the human mind.

Eligibility This program is open to graduate students enrolled full time in a psychology program at an accredited college or university in the United States or Canada. Applicants must be interested in conducting dissertation research that addresses an aspect of mental function (e.g., cognition, affect, motivation) and should utilize behavioral and/or neuro-scientific methods. Selection is based on conformance with stated program goals, quality of proposed work, and applicant's demonstrated scholarship and research competence. The sponsor encourages applications from individuals who represent diversity in race, ethnicity, gender, age, disability, and sexual orientation.

Financial data The grant is $2,000.

Duration 1 year.

Additional information This grant was first awarded in 2009.

Number awarded 1 each year.

Deadline May of each year.

[541]
FLORIDA LIBRARY ASSOCIATION MINORITY SCHOLARSHIPS

Florida Library Association
164 N.W. Madison Street, Suite 104
P.O. Box 1571
Lake City, FL 32056-1571
(386) 438-5795   Fax: (386) 438-5796
E-mail: fla.admin@comcast.net
Web: www.flalib.org/scholarships.php

Summary To provide financial assistance to Asian American and other minority students working on a graduate degree in library and information science in Florida.

Eligibility This program is open to residents of Florida who are working on a graduate degree in library and information science at schools in the state. Applicants must be members of a minority group: Black/African American, American Indian/Alaska Native, Asian/Pacific Islander, or Hispanic/Latino. They must have some experience in a Florida library, must be a member of the Florida Library Association, and must commit to working in a Florida library for at least 1 year after graduation. Along with their application, they must submit 1) a list of activities, honors, awards, and/or offices held during college and outside college; 2) an essay of 1 to 2 pages on why they are entering librarianship; and 3) an essay of 1 to 2 pages on their career goals with respect to Florida libraries. Financial need is considered in the selection process.

Financial data The stipend is $2,000.

Duration 1 year.

Number awarded 1 each year.

Deadline January of each year.

[542]
FOLEY & LARDNER DIVERSITY SCHOLARSHIP

Foley & Lardner LLP
Attn: Regional Legal Recruiting Coordinator
555 South Flower Street
Los Angeles, CA 90071-2411
(213) 972-4535   E-mail: enesbitt@foley.com
Web: www.foley.com/careers/lawstudents

Summary To provide financial aid and work experience to Asian American and other first-year law students who will contribute to diversity in the legal profession.

Eligibility This program is open to students completing the first year of full-time study at an ABA-accredited law school. Applicants must have demonstrated a commitment to promoting diversity and inclusion in the legal profession and the broader community. They must be interested in a summer associateship at an office of the sponsoring firm. Selection is based on involvement in diversity-related student organizations, involvement in community activities, undergraduate and law school academic achievement, and interest in employment with the sponsoring firm.

Financial data Upon completion of the associateship, participants receive a $20,000 fellowship.

Duration 1 summer and 1 academic year.

Additional information This program began in 1998. The sponsoring firm has offices in Boston, Chicago, Detroit, Jacksonville, Los Angeles, Madison, Miami, Milwaukee, New York, Orlando, Sacramento, San Diego, San Francisco, Silicon Valley, Tallahassee, Tampa, and Washington, D.C.

Number awarded 2 each year.

Deadline April of each year.

[543]
FOURTH DISTRICT MOSAIC SCHOLARSHIP

American Advertising Federation-District 4
c/o Maria Lucas, Governor
Farah & Farah
10 West Adams Street
Jacksonville, FL 32202
(904) 807-3113   Toll Free: (800) 533-5555
Fax: (904) 355-5599 E-mail: mlucas@farahandfarah.com
Web: 4aaf.com/education/scholarships

Summary To provide financial assistance to Asian American and other minority undergraduate and graduate students from any state who are enrolled at colleges and universities in Florida and interested in entering the field of advertising.

Eligibility This program is open to undergraduate and graduate students from any state enrolled at accredited colleges and universities in Florida who are U.S. citizens or permanent residents of African, African American, Hispanic, Hispanic American, Indian, Native American, Asian, Asian American, or Pacific Islander descent. Applicants must be working on a bachelor's or master's degree in advertising, marketing, communications, public relations, art, graphic arts, or a related field. They must have an overall GPA of 3.0 or higher. Along with their application, they must submit a 250-word essay on why multiculturalism, diversity, and inclusion are important in the advertising, marketing, and communications industry today. Preference is given to members of the American Advertising Federation.

Financial data The stipend is $1,000.

Duration 1 year.

Number awarded 1 or more each year.

Deadline February of each year.

[544]
FOWLER WHITE BOGGS DIVERSITY SCHOLARSHIP PROGRAM

Fowler White Boggs P.A.
Attn: Diversity Committee
501 East Kennedy Boulevard, Suite 1700
P.O. Box 1438
Tampa, FL 33601
(813) 228-7411   Fax: (813) 229-8313
E-mail: khaley@fowlerwhite.com
Web: www.fowlerwhite.com/diversity.html

Summary To provide financial assistance to Asian American and other law students who have demonstrated a commitment to diversity.

Eligibility This program is open to second- and third-year law students who have demonstrated a commitment to diversity. The sponsor defines diversity to include age, gender, race, ethnicity, culture, religion, sexual orientation, physical ability, marital status, economic background, and life experiences. Applicants must submit a 1,500-word personal statement that describes their leadership, relevant background and characteristics, and commitment to diversity. Although financial need is not determinative, they may also explain any financial issues they wish to have considered.

Financial data The stipend is $1,000.

Duration 1 year.

Number awarded 2 each year.

Deadline January of each year.

[545]
FRAMELINE COMPLETION FUND

Frameline
Attn: Completion Fund
145 Ninth Street, Suite 300
San Francisco, CA 94103
(415) 703-8650   Fax: (415) 861-1404
E-mail: info@frameline.org
Web: www.frameline.org/filmmaker-support

Summary To provide funding to lesbian, gay, bisexual, and transgender (LGBT) film/video artists (particularly Asian Americans, other film/video artists of color, and women).

Eligibility This program is open to LGBT artists who are in the last stages of the production of documentary, educational, narrative, animated, or experimental projects about or of interest to LGBT people and their communities. Applicants may be independent artists, students, producers, or nonprofit corporations. They must be interested in completion work and must have 90% of the production completed; projects in development, script-development, pre-production, or production are not eligible. Student projects are eligible only if the student maintains artistic and financial control of the project. Women and people of color are especially encouraged to apply. Selection is based on financial need, the contribution the grant will make to completing the project, assurances that the project will be completed, and the statement the project makes about LGBT people and/or issues of concern to them and their communities.

Financial data Grants range from $1,000 to $5,000.

Duration These are 1-time grants.

Additional information This program began in 1990.

Number awarded Varies each year; recently, 5 of these grants were awarded. Since this program was established, it has provided $389,200 in support to 118 films.

Deadline October of each year.

[546]
FRANCHISE LAW DIVERSITY SCHOLARSHIP AWARD

International Franchise Association
Attn: President, Educational Foundation
1501 K Street, N.W., Suite 350
Washington, DC 20005
(202) 662-0764   Fax: (202) 628-0812
E-mail: jreynolds@franchise.org
Web: www.franchise.org/files/Scholarships.aspx

Summary To provide financial assistance to Asian American and other law students from diverse groups who are interested in taking courses related to franchise law.

Eligibility This program is open to second- and third-year students who are enrolled at ABA-accredited law schools and a member of a diverse group (defined as African Americans, American Indians, Hispanic Americans, Asian Americans, or gays/lesbians). Applicants must be enrolled in at least 1 course oriented toward franchise law (e.g., torts, unfair trade practices, trade secrets, antitrust, trademarks, contracts, agency, or securities). Along with their application, they must submit a current transcript, an essay explaining their interest in franchise law, and 2 letters of recommendation.

Financial data The stipend is $4,000. Funds are paid to the recipient's law school and are to be used for tuition.

Duration 1 year.

Additional information This award is cosponsored by the IFA Educational Foundation and DLA Piper US LLP. It may not be used by the recipient's law school to reduce the amount of any institutionally-awarded financial aid.

Number awarded 1 or more each year.

Deadline December of each year.

[547]
FRANCIS M. KEVILLE MEMORIAL SCHOLARSHIP

Construction Management Association of America
Attn: CMAA Foundation
7926 Jones Branch Drive, Suite 800
McLean, VA 22101-3303
(703) 356-2622   Fax: (703) 356-6388
E-mail: foundation@cmaanet.org
Web: www.cmaafoundation.org

Summary To provide financial assistance to Asian Americans, other minorities, and female undergraduate and graduate students working on a degree in construction management.

Eligibility This program is open to women and members of minority groups who are enrolled as full-time undergraduate or graduate students. Applicants must have completed at least 1 year of study and have at least 1 full year remaining for a bachelor's or master's degree in construction management or a related field. Along with their application, they must submit essays on why they are interested in a career in construction management and why they should be awarded this scholarship. Selection is based on that essay (20%), academic performance (40%), recommendation of the faculty adviser (15%), and extracurricular activities (25%); a bonus of 5% is given to student members of the Construction Management Association of America (CMAA).

Financial data The stipend is $3,000. Funds are disbursed directly to the student's university.

Duration 1 year.

Number awarded 1 each year.

Deadline June of each year.

[548]
FRANK T. MARTIN LEADERSHIP SCHOLARSHIP

Conference of Minority Transportation Officials
Attn: National Scholarship Program
1875 I Street, N.W., Suite 500
Washington, DC 20006
(703) 234-4072   Fax: (202) 318-0364
Web: www.comto.org/?page=Scholarships

Summary To provide financial assistance to Asian American and other minority undergraduate and graduate students working on a degree in transportation or a related field.

Eligibility This program is open to full-time undergraduate and graduate students who are working on a degree in transportation, engineering, planning, or a related discipline. They must be able to demonstrate leadership and active commitment to community service. Along with their application, they must submit a cover letter with a 500-word statement of career goals. Financial need is not considered in the selection process. U.S. citizenship or legal resident status is required.

Financial data The stipend is $3,000. Funds are paid directly to the recipient's college or university.

Duration 1 year.

Additional information The Conference of Minority Transportation Officials (COMTO) was established in 1971 to promote, strengthen, and expand the roles of minorities in all aspects of transportation. This program is sponsored by Atkins North America. Recipients are expected to attend the COMTO National Scholarship Luncheon.

Number awarded 1 each year.

Deadline May of each year.

[549]
FREDRIKSON & BYRON FOUNDATION MINORITY SCHOLARSHIP

Fredrikson & Byron Foundation
Attn: Attorney Recruiting Administrator
200 South Sixth Street, Suite 4000
Minneapolis, MN 55402-1425
(612) 492-7141   Fax: (612) 492-7077
E-mail: glarson@fredlaw.com
Web: www.fredlaw.com/firm/scholarship.htm

Summary To provide financial aid and summer work experience to Asian American and other minority law students from any state who are interested in practicing in the Twin Cities area of Minnesota.

Eligibility This program is open to African American, Asian American, Pacific Islander, Hispanic, Native American, and Alaska Native students enrolled in their first year of law school. Applicants must be interested in practicing law in the Minneapolis-St. Paul area. Along with their application, they must submit brief statement on their expectations and objectives in applying for this scholarship; the factors they will use to measure success in their legal career; what they see as potential issues, obstacles, and opportunities facing new lawyers in a large private practice firm; and their interest in a summer associate position in private practice, including their interest in practicing law in the Minneapolis-St. Paul area. Financial need is not considered.

Financial data The fellowship stipend is $10,000. The internship portion of the program provides a $1,000 weekly stipend.

Duration 1 year.

Additional information Fellows are also eligible to participate in an internship at the firm's offices in Minneapolis.

Number awarded 1 each year.

Deadline March of each year.

[550]
GAIUS CHARLES BOLIN DISSERTATION AND POST-MFA FELLOWSHIPS

Williams College
Attn: Dean of the Faculty
880 Main Street
Hopkins Hall, Third Floor
P.O. Box 141
Williamstown, MA 01267
(413) 597-4351   Fax: (413) 597-3553
E-mail: gburda@williams.edu
Web: dean-faculty.williams.edu

Summary To provide financial assistance to Asian Americans and members of other underrepresented groups who are interested in teaching courses at Williams College while working on their doctoral dissertation or building their post-M.F.A. professional portfolio.

Eligibility This program is open to members of underrepresented groups, including ethnic minorities, first-generation college students, women in predominantly male fields, and scholars with disabilities. Applicants must be 1) doctoral candidates in any field who have completed all work for a Ph.D. except for the dissertation; or 2) artists who completed an M.F.A. degree within the past 2 years and are building their professional portfolio. They must be willing to teach a course at Williams College. Along with their application, they must submit a full curriculum vitae, a graduate school transcript, 3 letters of recommendation, a copy of their dissertation prospectus or samples of their artistic work, and a description of their teaching interests within a department or program at Williams College. U.S. citizenship or permanent resident status is required.

Financial data Fellows receive $36,000 for the academic year, plus housing assistance, office space, computer and library privileges, and a research allowance of up to $4,000.

Duration 2 years.

Additional information Bolin fellows are assigned a faculty adviser in the appropriate department. This program was established in 1985. Fellows are expected to teach a 1-semester course each year. They must be in residence at Williams College for the duration of the fellowship.

Number awarded 3 each year.

Deadline November of each year.

[551]
GEOLOGICAL SOCIETY OF AMERICA GRADUATE STUDENT RESEARCH GRANTS

Geological Society of America
Attn: Program Officer-Grants, Awards and Recognition
3300 Penrose Place
P.O. Box 9140
Boulder, CO 80301-9140
(303) 357-1028   Toll Free: (800) 472-1988, ext. 1028
Fax: (303) 357-1070   E-mail: awards@geosociety.org
Web: www.geosociety.org/grants/gradgrants.htm

Summary To provide funding to graduate student members (particularly Asian Americans, other minorities, women, and students with disabilities) of the Geological Society of America (GSA) who are interested in conducting research at universities in the United States, Canada, Mexico, or Central America.

Eligibility This program is open to GSA members working on a master's or doctoral degree at a university in the United States, Canada, Mexico, or Central America. Applicants must be interested in conducting geological research. Minorities, women, and persons with disabilities are strongly encouraged to apply. Selection is based on the scientific merits of the proposal, the capability of the investigator, and the reasonableness of the budget.

Financial data Grants range up to $4,000 and recently averaged $1,829. Funds can be used for the cost of travel, room and board in the field, services of a technician or field assistant, funding of chemical and isotope analyses, or other expenses directly related to the fulfillment of the research contract. Support is not provided for the purchase of ordinary field equipment, for maintenance of the families of the grantees and their assistants, as reimbursement for work already accomplished, for institutional overhead, for adviser participation, or for tuition costs.

Duration 1 year.

Additional information In addition to general grants, GSA awards a number of specialized grants: the Gretchen L. Blechschmidt Award for women (especially in the fields of biostratigraphy and/or paleoceanography); the John T. Dillon Alaska Research Award for earth science problems particular to Alaska; the Robert K. Fahnestock Memorial Award for the field of sediment transport or related aspects of fluvial geomorphology; the Lipman Research Award for volcanology and petrology; the Bruce L. "Biff" Reed Award for studies in the tectonic and magmatic evolution of Alaska; the Alexander Sisson Award for studies in Alaska and the Caribbean; the Harold T. Stearns Fellowship Award for work on the geology of the Pacific Islands and the circum-Pacific region; the Parke D. Snavely, Jr. Cascadia Research Fund Award for studies of the Pacific Northwest convergent margin; the Alexander and Geraldine Wanek Fund Award for studies of coal and petroleum; the Charles A. and June R.P. Ross Research Fund Award for stratigraphy; and the John Montagne Fund Award for research in the field of quaternary geology or geomorphology.

Number awarded Varies each year; recently, the society awarded more than 300 grants worth more than $550,000 through this and all of its specialized programs.

Deadline January of each year.

[552]
GEORGE A. STRAIT MINORITY SCHOLARSHIP ENDOWMENT

American Association of Law Libraries
Attn: Chair, Scholarships Committee
105 West Adams Street, Suite 3300
Chicago, IL 60603
(312) 939-4764   Fax: (312) 431-1097
E-mail: scholarships@aall.org
Web: www.aallnet.org

Summary To provide financial assistance to Asian American and other minority college seniors or college graduates who are interested in becoming law librarians.

Eligibility This program is open to college graduates with meaningful law library experience who are members of minority groups and intend to have a career in law librarianship. Applicants must be degree candidates at an ALA-accredited library school or an ABA-accredited law school. Along with their application, they must submit a personal statement that discusses their interest in law librarianship, reason for applying for this scholarship, career goals as a law librarian, and any other pertinent information.

Financial data The stipend is $3,500.

Duration 1 year.

Additional information This program, established in 1990, is currently supported by Thomson Reuters.

Number awarded Varies each year; recently, 5 of these scholarships were awarded.

Deadline March of each year.

[553]
GEORGE V. POWELL DIVERSITY SCHOLARSHIP

Lane Powell PC
Attn: Manager of Attorney Recruiting
1420 Fifth Avenue, Suite 4200
P.O. Box 91302
Seattle, WA 98111-9402
(206) 223-6123   Fax: (206) 223-7107
E-mail: rodenl@lanepowell.com
Web: www.lanepowell.com/422/diversity-scholarship

Summary To provide financial aid and work experience to Asian Americans and other law students who will contribute to the diversity of the legal community.

Eligibility This program is open to second-year students in good standing at an ABA-accredited law school. Applicants must be able to contribute meaningfully to the diversity of the legal community and have a demonstrated desire to work, live, and eventually practice law in Seattle or Portland. They must submit a cover letter that includes a statement indicating eligibility to participate in the program, a resume, a current copy of law school transcript, a legal writing sample, and a list of 2 or 3 professional or academic references. Selection is based on academic achievement and record of leadership abilities, community service, and involvement in community issues.

Financial data The program provides a stipend of $7,500 for the third year of law school and a paid summer associate clerkship.

Duration 1 year, including the summer.

Additional information This program began in 2005. Clerkships are provided at the offices of the sponsor in Seattle or Portland.

Number awarded 1 each year.

Deadline August of each year.

[554]
GORDON STAFFORD SCHOLARSHIP IN ARCHITECTURE

Stafford King Wiese Architects
Attn: Scholarship Selection Committee
622 20th Street
Sacramento, CA 95811
(916) 930-5900   Fax: (916) 290-0100
E-mail: info@skwaia.com
Web: www.skwarchitects.com/about/scholarship

Summary To provide financial assistance to Asian Americans and members of other minority groups from California who are interested in studying architecture at a college in any state.

Eligibility This program is open to California residents currently enrolled at accredited schools of architecture in any state as first-year new or first-year transfer students and working on a bachelor's or 5-year master's degree. Applicants must be able to demonstrate minority status (defined as Black, Hispanic, Native American, Pacific Asian, or Asian Indian). They must submit a 500-word statement expressing their desire to prepare for a career in architecture. Finalists are interviewed and must travel to Sacramento, California at their own expense for the interview.

Financial data The stipend is $2,000 per year. That includes $1,000 deposited in the recipient's school account and $1,000 paid to the recipient directly.

Duration 1 year; may be renewed up to 4 additional years.

Additional information This program began in 1995.

Number awarded Up to 5 each year.

Deadline June of each year.

[555]
GRADUATE STUDENTS OF ASIAN/ASIAN-AMERICAN/PACIFIC-ISLANDER/ARAB/MIDDLE EAST ASIAN DESCENT STUDENT ESSAY AWARD

National Women's Studies Association
Attn: Women of Color Caucus
11 East Mount Royal Avenue, Suite 100
Baltimore, MD 21202
(410) 528-0355   Fax: (410) 528-0357
E-mail: awards@nwsa.org
Web: www.nwsa.org/content.asp?pl=16&contentid=16

Summary To recognize and reward Asian, Asian American, and Pacific Islander graduate students and recent postdoctorates who are members of the National Women's Studies Association (NWSA) and submit outstanding essays on feminist issues.

Eligibility This competition is open to women of Asian descent (including Asian Americans, Pacific Islanders, Arabs, and Middle East Asians who are currently enrolled in a graduate or professional program. Recipients of Ph.D.s who completed their degree requirements within the past year are also eligible. Applicants must submit a scholarly essay that pro-

vides critical theoretical discussions and/or analyses of issues and experiences of women and girls of Asian, Asian American, Pacific Islander, Arab, or Middle East Asian descent in the United States and throughout the Diaspora. They must be members of the NWSA.

Financial data The award is $500.

Duration The award is presented annually.

Number awarded 1 each year.

Deadline May of each year.

[556]
GRADUATE TRAINING IN DISPARITIES RESEARCH

Susan G. Komen Breast Cancer Foundation
Attn: Grants Department
5005 LBJ Freeway, Suite 250
Dallas, TX 75244
(972) 855-1616   Toll Free: (866) 921-9678
Fax: (972) 855-1640
E-mail: helpdesk@komengrantsaccess.org
Web: ww5.komen.org

Summary To provide funding for training to minority and other graduate students interested in conducting research related to disparities in breast cancer outcomes.

Eligibility This program provides support to students enrolled in a master's, combined master's/doctoral, or doctoral degree program. Applications must be submitted by a full-time faculty member at their institution who is currently conducting research on disparities in breast cancer outcomes. Neither the students nor the faculty mentors are required to be U.S. citizens or residents. The application must describe a training program that combines didactic course work and hands-on laboratory, clinical, and/or public health research. The training program must ensure that all students at all levels will develop the analytic, research, scientific, clinical, and public health skills critical for them to effectively explore the basis for differences in breast cancer outcomes and to develop and translate research discoveries into clinical and public health practice to eliminate those disparities. Strong preference is given to involving trainees from populations adversely affected by disparities in breast cancer outcomes.

Financial data The grant is $45,000 per student per year for direct costs only.

Duration 2 years; a third year may be approved, based on an assessment of first-year progress.

Additional information This program was formerly known as the Post-Baccalaureate Training in Disparities Research Grants.

Number awarded Varies each year; recently, 5 of these grants were awarded.

Deadline Pre-applications must be submitted by early September of each year; full applications are due in October.

[557]
GREENSPOON MARDER DIVERSITY SCHOLARSHIP

Community Foundation of Sarasota County
Attn: Grants and Scholarships Coordinator
2635 Fruitville Road
P.O. Box 49587
Sarasota, FL 34230-6587
(941) 556-7114   Fax: (941) 952-7115
E-mail: eyoung@cfsarasota.org
Web: www.cfsarasota.org/Default.aspx?tabid=263

Summary To provide financial assistance to Asian American and other minority students from any state attending designated law schools (most of which are in Florida).

Eligibility This program is open to racial and ethnic minority students from any state who are members of groups traditionally underrepresented in the legal profession. Applicants must be entering their second year of full-time study at the University of Florida Levin College of Law, Florida State University College of Law, Stetson University College of Law, Nova Southeastern University Shepard Broad Law Center, St. Thomas University School of Law, Florida A&M University College of Law, Howard University College of Law, Texas Southern University Thurgood Marshall School of Law, Florida Coastal School of Law, or Florida International University College of Law. They must have a GPA of 2.6 or higher. Along with their application, they must submit a 1,000-word personal statement that describes their personal strengths, their contributions through community service, any special or unusual circumstances that may have affected their academic performance, or their personal and family history of educational or socioeconomic disadvantage; it should include aspects of their minority racial or ethnic identity that are relevant to their application. Applicants may also include information about their financial circumstances if they wish to have those considered in the selection process. U.S. citizenship or permanent resident status is required.

Financial data The stipend is $2,500 per semester.

Duration 1 semester (the spring semester of the second year of law school); may be renewed 1 additional semester (the fall semester of the third year).

Additional information This program was established by the Florida law firm Ruden McClosky, which was acquired by the firm Greenspoon Marder in 2011. It is administered by the Community Foundation of Sarasota County, but the law firm selects the recipients.

Number awarded 1 or more each year.

Deadline July of each year.

[558]
GROUNDBREAKER LEADERSHIP SCHOLARSHIP

Against the Grain Productions
3523 McKinney Avenue, Suite 231
Dallas, TX 75204
E-mail: outreach@againstthegrainproductions.com
Web: www.againstthegrainproductions.com/scholarship

Summary To provide financial assistance to Asian and Pacific Island college seniors and graduate students who have demonstrated outstanding leadership that sets an example for their community.

Eligibility This program is open to full-time college seniors and graduate students at accredited 4-year colleges and universities who have a GPA of 3.5 or higher. Applicants must be of at least 50% Asian and/or Pacific Islander ethnicity and U.S. citizens, nationals, or permanent residents. They must have demonstrated "exemplary leadership, vision, and passion that is blazing a trail for others to follow and changing lives in the Asian American community." Along with their application, they must submit a video that showcases their work and qualifications. Selection is based on that video, an essay, academic performance, leadership and community service, and an interview.

Financial data The stipend is $1,500. Funds are disbursed directly to the educational institution.

Duration 1 year.

Number awarded 2 each year.

Deadline April of each year.

[559]
HANA SCHOLARSHIPS

United Methodist Church
Attn: General Board of Higher Education and Ministry
Office of Loans and Scholarships
1001 19th Avenue South
P.O. Box 340007
Nashville, TN 37203-0007
(615) 340-7344   Fax: (615) 340-7367
E-mail: umscholar@gbhem.org
Web: www.gbhem.org

Summary To provide financial assistance to upper-division and graduate Methodist students who are of Asian, Hispanic, Native American, or Pacific Islander ancestry.

Eligibility This program is open to full-time juniors, seniors, and graduate students at accredited colleges and universities in the United States who have been active, full members of a United Methodist Church (UMC) for at least 1 year prior to applying. Applicants must have at least 1 parent who is Hispanic, Asian, Native American, or Pacific Islander. They must be able to demonstrate involvement in their Hispanic, Asian, or Native American (HANA) community in the UMC. Selection is based on that involvement, academic ability (GPA of at least 2.85), and financial need. U.S. citizenship or permanent resident status is required.

Financial data The maximum stipend is $3,000 for undergraduates or $5,000 for graduate students.

Duration 1 year; recipients may reapply.

Number awarded 50 each year.

Deadline February of each year.

[560]
HEALTH RESEARCH AND EDUCATIONAL TRUST SCHOLARSHIPS

New Jersey Hospital Association
Attn: Health Research and Educational Trust
760 Alexander Road
P.O. Box 1
Princeton, NJ 08543-0001
(609) 275-4224   Fax: (609) 452-8097
Web: www.njha.com/education/scholarships

Summary To provide financial assistance to New Jersey residents (particularly Asian Americans, other minorities, and women) who are working on an undergraduate or graduate degree in a field related to health care administration at a school in any state.

Eligibility This program is open to residents of New Jersey enrolled in an upper-division or graduate program in hospital or health care administration, public administration, nursing, or other allied health profession at a school in any state. Graduate students working on an advanced degree to prepare to teach nursing are also eligible. Applicants must have a GPA of 3.0 or higher and be able to demonstrate financial need. Along with their application, they must submit a 2-page essay (on which 50% of the selection is based) describing their academic plans for the future. Minorities and women are especially encouraged to apply.

Financial data The stipend is $2,000.

Duration 1 year.

Additional information This program began in 1983.

Number awarded Varies each year; recently, 3 of these scholarships were awarded.

Deadline July of each year.

[561]
HEALTH SCIENCES STUDENT FELLOWSHIPS IN EPILEPSY

Epilepsy Foundation
Attn: Research Department
8301 Professional Place
Landover, MD 20785-2353
(301) 459-3700   Toll Free: (800) EFA-1000
Fax: (301) 577-2684   TDD: (800) 332-2070
E-mail: grants@efa.org
Web: www.epilepsyfoundation.org

Summary To provide financial assistance to medical and health science graduate students (particularly Asian Americans, other minorities, women, and students with disabilities) who are interested in working on an epilepsy project during the summer.

Eligibility This program is open to students enrolled, or accepted for enrollment, in a medical school, a doctoral program, or other graduate program. Applicants must have a defined epilepsy-related study or research plan to be carried out under the supervision of a qualified mentor. Because the program is designed as a training opportunity, the quality of the training plans and environment are considered in the selection process. Other selection criteria include the quality of the proposed project, the relevance of the proposed work to epilepsy, the applicant's interest in the field of epilepsy, the applicant's qualifications, the mentor's qualifications (including his or her commitment to the student and the project), and the quality of the training environment for research related to epilepsy. U.S. citizenship is not required, but the project must be conducted in the United States. Applications from women, members of minority groups, and people with disabilities are especially encouraged. The program is not intended for students working on a dissertation research project.

Financial data Stipends are $3,000.

Duration 3 months during the summer.

Additional information Support for this program is provided by many individuals, families, and corporations, especially the American Epilepsy Society, Abbott Laboratories, Ortho-McNeil Pharmaceutical, and Pfizer Inc.

Number awarded Varies each year; recently, 3 of these fellowships were awarded.

Deadline March of each year.

[562]
HELEN LEE SCHOLARSHIP

Philip Jaisohn Memorial Foundation
Attn: Education and Scholarship Committee
6705 Old York Road
Philadelphia, PA 19126
(215) 224-2000   Fax: (215) 224-9164
E-mail: jaisohnhouse@gmail.com
Web: www.jaisohn.org

Summary To provide financial assistance to Korean American undergraduate and graduate students who demonstrate significant financial need.

Eligibility This program is open to Korean American undergraduate and graduate students who are currently enrolled at a college or university in the United States. Applicants must be able to demonstrate academic excellence, leadership and service to their school and community, and financial need. Along with their application, they must submit an essay on either "Who is Dr. Jaisohn to Me," or "The Significance of Dr. Jaisohn's Ideal to Korean Americans." They must also submit a brief statement on how they can contribute to and be involved in the activities of the Philip Jaisohn Memorial Foundation. Selection is based primarily on financial need.

Financial data The stipend is $1,500.

Duration 1 year.

Number awarded 2 each year.

Deadline November of each year.

[563]
HELENE M. OVERLY MEMORIAL GRADUATE SCHOLARSHIP

Women's Transportation Seminar
Attn: WTS Foundation
1701 K Street, N.W., Suite 800
Washington, DC 20006
(202) 955-5085   Fax: (202) 955-5088
E-mail: wts@wtsinternational.org
Web: www.wtsinternational.org/education/scholarships

Summary To provide financial assistance to women graduate students (particularly Asian American and other minority women) who are interested in preparing for a career in transportation.

Eligibility This program is open to women who are enrolled in a graduate degree program in a transportation-related field (e.g., transportation engineering, planning, finance, or logistics). Applicants must have at least a 3.0 GPA and be interested in a career in transportation. Along with their application, they must submit a 750-word statement about their career goals after graduation and why they think they should receive the scholarship award. Applications must be submitted first to a local chapter; the chapters forward selected applications for consideration on the national level. Minority women are particularly encouraged to apply. Selection is based on transportation involvement and goals, job skills, and academic record.

Financial data The stipend is $10,000.

Duration 1 year.

Additional information This program began in 1981. Local chapters may also award additional funding to winners in their area.

Number awarded 1 each year.

Deadline Applications must be submitted by November to a local WTS chapter.

[564]
HENRY AND CHIYO KUWAHARA CREATIVE ARTS AWARD

Japanese American Citizens League
Attn: National Scholarship Awards
1765 Sutter Street
San Francisco, CA 94115
(415) 345-1075   Fax: (415) 931-4671
E-mail: ncwnp@jacl.org
Web: www.jacl.org/edu/scholar.htm

Summary To provide financial assistance to undergraduate and graduate student members of the Japanese American Citizens League (JACL) interested in completing a project in the creative arts.

Eligibility This program is open to JACL members who are working on an undergraduate or graduate degree in the creative arts. Professional artists are not eligible. Applicants must submit a detailed proposal for a project they wish to create, including a time plan, anticipated date of completion, and itemized budget. They must also submit information on their involvement in JACL and a 2-page essay on a topic that changes annually but relates to Japanese Americans. Selection is based on that essay, academic history, JACL involvement, school activities, work history, scholastic honors, and community involvement. Preference is given to students who are interested in creative projects that reflect the Japanese American experience and culture.

Financial data Stipends generally average more than $2,000.

Duration 1 year; nonrenewable.

Number awarded At least 1 each year.

Deadline March of each year.

[565]
HENRY AND CHIYO KUWAHARA MEMORIAL SCHOLARSHIPS

Japanese American Citizens League
Attn: National Scholarship Awards
1765 Sutter Street
San Francisco, CA 94115
(415) 345-1075   Fax: (415) 931-4671
E-mail: ncwnp@jacl.org
Web: www.jacl.org/edu/scholar.htm

Summary To provide financial assistance for undergraduate or graduate study to members of the Japanese American Citizens League (JACL).

Eligibility This program is open to JACL members who are high school seniors, undergraduates, or graduate students. Applicants must be attending or planning to attend a college, university, trade school, or business college. They must submit information on their involvement in JACL and a 2-page essay on a topic that changes annually but relates to Japanese Americans. Selection is based on that essay, academic

history, JACL involvement, school activities, work history, scholastic honors, and community involvement.

Financial data Stipends generally average more than $2,000.

Duration 1 year; nonrenewable.

Number awarded 6 each year: 2 each to entering freshmen, continuing undergraduates, and entering or currently-enrolled graduate students.

Deadline February of each year for graduating high school seniors; March of each year for current undergraduate or graduate students.

[566]
HENRY DAVID RESEARCH GRANT IN HUMAN REPRODUCTIVE BEHAVIOR AND POPULATION STUDIES

American Psychological Foundation
750 First Street, N.E.
Washington, DC 20002-4242
(202) 336-5843   Fax: (202) 336-5812
E-mail: foundation@apa.org
Web: www.apa.org/apf/funding/david.aspx

Summary To provide funding to young psychologists (particularly Asian Americans, other minorities, women, and individuals with disabilities) who are interested in conducting research on reproductive behavior.

Eligibility This program is open to doctoral students in psychology working on a dissertation and young psychologists who have no more than 7 years of postgraduate experience. Applicants must be interested in conducting research on human reproductive behavior or an area related to population concerns. Along with their application, they must submit a current curriculum vitae, 2 letters of recommendation, and an essay of 1 to 2 pages on their interest in human reproductive behavior or in population studies. The sponsor encourages applications from individuals who represent diversity in race, ethnicity, gender, age, disability, and sexual orientation.

Financial data The grant is $1,500.

Duration The grant is presented annually.

Number awarded 1 each year.

Deadline February of each year.

[567]
HERBERT W. NICKENS MEDICAL STUDENT SCHOLARSHIPS

Association of American Medical Colleges
Attn: Division of Diversity Policy and Programs
2450 N Street, N.W.
Washington, DC 20037-1126
(202) 862-6203   Fax: (202) 828-1125
E-mail: nickensawards@aamc.org
Web: www.aamc.org/initiatives/awards/nickens-student

Summary To provide financial assistance to Asian American and other medical students who have demonstrated efforts to address the health-care needs of minorities.

Eligibility This program is open to U.S. citizens and permanent residents entering their third year of study at a U.S. allopathic medical school. Each medical school may nominate 1 student for these awards. The letter must describe the nominee's 1) academic achievement through the first and second year, including special awards and honors, clerkships or special research projects, and extracurricular activities in which the student has shown leadership abilities; 2) leadership efforts to eliminate inequities in medical education and health care; 3) demonstrated leadership efforts in addressing the educational, societal, and health-care needs of minorities; and 4) awards and honors, special research projects, and extracurricular activities in which the student has shown leadership abilities. Nominees must submit a curriculum vitae and a 2-page essay that discusses their leadership efforts in eliminating inequities in medical education and health care for minorities.

Financial data   The stipend is $5,000.

Duration   1 year.

Number awarded   5 each year.

Deadline   April of each year.

[568]
HIDEKO AND ZENZO MATSUYAMA SCHOLARSHIPS

Hawai'i Community Foundation
Attn: Scholarship Department
827 Fort Street Mall
Honolulu, HI 96813
(808) 566-5570   Toll Free: (888) 731-3863
Fax: (808) 521-6286
E-mail: scholarships@hcf-hawaii.org
Web: www.hawaiicommunityfoundation.org/scholarships

Summary   To provide financial assistance to Hawaii residents of Japanese ancestry who are interested in attending college or graduate school in any state.

Eligibility   This program is open to graduates of high schools or recipients of GED certificates in Hawaii who were born in the state and are of Japanese ancestry. Applicants must be enrolled or planning to enroll at an accredited college or university in any state as an undergraduate or graduate student. They must be able to demonstrate academic achievement (GPA of 3.0 or higher), good moral character, and financial need. Along with their application, they must submit a short statement indicating their reasons for attending college, their planned course of study, their career goals, and what community service means to them.

Financial data   The amounts of the awards depend on the availability of funds and the need of the recipient. Recently, the average value of each of the scholarships awarded by the foundation was $2,200.

Duration   1 year.

Additional information   This program began in 2006.

Number awarded   Varies each year; recently, 13 of these scholarships were awarded.

Deadline   February of each year.

[569]
HILLIS CLARK MARTIN & PETERSON DIVERSITY FELLOWSHIP

Hillis Clark Martin & Peterson P.S.
Attn: Recruiting Coordinator
1221 Second Avenue, Suite 500
Seattle, WA 98101-2925
(206) 470-7647   Fax: (206) 623-7789
E-mail: Brenda@hcmp.com
Web: www.hcmp.com/index.php?p=1_144

Summary   To provide financial aid and work experience to Asian American and other students whose background and life experiences will contribute to the diversity of the legal community.

Eligibility   This program is open to students enrolled in the first year at an ABA-accredited law school. Applicants must have a background and life experiences that will contribute meaningfully to the diversity of the legal community. Along with their application, they must submit a resume, transcripts, a personal statement of 1 to 2 pages describing their background and addressing the selection criteria, a legal writing sample, and a list of 3 references. Selection is based on distinction in academic performance, accomplishments and activities, commitment to community service, leadership ability, and financial need.

Financial data   The stipend is $7,500.

Duration   1 year.

Additional information   The program includes a salaried summer associate position following the first year of law school.

Number awarded   1 or more each year.

Deadline   January of each year.

[570]
H-MART LEADERSHIP SCHOLARSHIP

Philip Jaisohn Memorial Foundation
Attn: Education and Scholarship Committee
6705 Old York Road
Philadelphia, PA 19126
(215) 224-2000   Fax: (215) 224-9164
E-mail: jaisohnhouse@gmail.com
Web: www.jaisohn.org

Summary   To provide financial assistance to Korean American undergraduate and graduate students who demonstrate involvement in extracurricular, athletic, and community activities.

Eligibility   This program is open to Korean American undergraduate and graduate students who are currently enrolled at a college or university in the United States. Applicants must be able to demonstrate academic excellence, leadership and service to their school and community, and financial need. Along with their application, they must submit an essay on either "Who is Dr. Jaisohn to Me," or "The Significance of Dr. Jaisohn's Ideal to Korean Americans." They must also submit a brief statement on how they can contribute to and be involved in the activities of the Philip Jaisohn Memorial Foundation. Selection is based primarily on leadership in extracurricular activities, varsity sports, or community activities.

Financial data   The stipend is $1,500.

Duration   1 year.

Additional information   This program is sponsored by Han Ah Reum Asian Mart.

Number awarded   2 each year.

Deadline   November of each year.

[571]
HOLLY A. CORNELL SCHOLARSHIP
American Water Works Association
Attn: Scholarship Coordinator
6666 West Quincy Avenue
Denver, CO 80235-3098
(303) 794-7771   Toll Free: (800) 926-7337
Fax: (303) 347-0804   E-mail: lmoody@awwa.org
Web: www.awwa.org

Summary To provide financial assistance to outstanding minority and female students interested in working on an master's degree in the field of water supply and treatment.

Eligibility This program is open to minority and female students working on a master's degree in the field of water supply and treatment at a college or university in Canada, Guam, Mexico, Puerto Rico, or the United States. Students who have been accepted into graduate school but have not yet begun graduate study are encouraged to apply. Applicants must submit a 2-page resume, official transcripts, 3 letters of recommendation, a proposed curriculum of study, a 1-page statement of educational plans and career objectives demonstrating an interest in the drinking water field, and a 3-page proposed plan of research. Selection is based on academic record and potential to provide leadership in the field of water supply and treatment.

Financial data The stipend is $7,500.

Duration 1 year; nonrenewable.

Additional information Funding for this program comes from the consulting firm CH2M Hill.

Number awarded 1 each year.

Deadline January of each year.

[572]
HONJO SCHOLARSHIP
Japanese American Association of New York, Inc.
Attn: Scholarship Committee
15 West 44th Street, 11th Floor
New York, NY 10036
(212) 840-6942   Fax: (212) 840-0616
E-mail: info@jaany.org
Web: www.jaany.org/honjo_scholarship.html

Summary To provide financial assistance to graduate students of Japanese descent who are working on a degree at a school in the New York area in any field that will promote U.S.-Japan relations.

Eligibility This program is open to graduate students of Japanese descent enrolled full time at a college or university in the New York area. Applicants may be working on a degree in any field (except medicine, music, studio art, or performing arts) that furthers U.S.-Japan relations. Along with their application, they must submit a resume, 2 letters of recommendation, undergraduate and graduate transcripts, and an essay of 500 to 750 words on how their current course of study will help further U.S.-Japan relations.

Financial data A stipend is awarded (amount not specified).

Duration 1 year.

Additional information This program is supported by the Honjo Foundation.

Number awarded 1 each year.

Deadline February of each year.

[573]
HONORABLE THOMAS TANG INTERNATIONAL MOOT COURT COMPETITION SCHOLARSHIPS
National Asian Pacific American Bar Association
Attn: NAPABA Law Foundation
1612 K Street, N.W., Suite 1400
Washington, DC 20006
(202) 775-9555   Fax: (202) 775-9333
E-mail: thomastang@napaba.org
Web: www.napaba.org/napaba/showpage.asp?code=moot

Summary To recognize and reward law students who participate in a moot court competition sponsored by the National Asian Pacific American Bar Association (NAPABA).

Eligibility This competition is open to students at ABA-accredited law schools who have completed the first year of study. All students are eligible, but a goal of the program is to reach out to Asian Pacific American law students and provide them with an opportunity to showcase their writing and oral advocacy skills. Applicants must enter the competition as teams of 2 students each.

Financial data A total of $10,000 is awarded in prizes each year.

Duration The competition is held annually.

Additional information This competition began in 1993. The entry fee is $200 per team.

Number awarded Generally 6 each year: 2 for members of the first-place team, 2 for members of the second-place team, 1 for best brief, and 1 for best oralist.

Deadline September of each year.

[574]
HOWARD MAYER BROWN FELLOWSHIP
American Musicological Society
6010 College Station
Brunswick, ME 04011-8451
(207) 798-4243   Toll Free: (877) 679-7648
Fax: (207) 798-4254   E-mail: ams@ams-net.org
Web: www.ams-net.org/fellowships/hmb.php

Summary To provide financial assistance to Asian American and other minority students who are working on a doctoral degree in the field of musicology.

Eligibility This program is open to members of minority groups historically underrepresented in the field of musicology. In the United States, that includes African Americans, Native Americans, Hispanic Americans, and Asian Americans. In Canada, it refers to visible minorities. Applicants must have completed at least 1 year of full-time academic work at an institution with a graduate program in musicology and be planning to complete a Ph.D. degree in the field. There are no restrictions on research area, age, or sex. Candidates must submit a personal statement summarizing their musical and academic background and stating why they wish to work on an advanced degree in musicology, letters of support from 3 faculty members, a curriculum vitae, and samples of their work (such as term papers or published material). U.S. or Canadian citizenship or permanent resident status is required.

Financial data The stipend is $20,000.

Duration 1 year; nonrenewable.

Additional information This fellowship was first awarded in 1995.

Number awarded 1 each year.

Deadline November of each year.

[575]
HSIAO MEMORIAL ECONOMICS SCHOLARSHIP

Asian Pacific Fund
Attn: Scholarship Coordinator
465 California Street, Suite 809
San Francisco, CA 94104
(415) 395-9985 E-mail: scholarship@asianpacificfund.org
Web: www.asianpacificfund.org

Summary To provide financial assistance to Asian graduate students from any state who are working on a Ph.D. degree in economics.

Eligibility This program is open to graduate students at colleges and universities in the United States who are working on a Ph.D. degree in economics. Preference is given to students preparing for a career in academia. Applicants must be of at least 50% Asian heritage; preference is given to students of Chinese descent. They must have a GPA of 3.0 or higher and be able to demonstrate financial need. U.S. citizens, permanent residents, and foreign nationals are all eligible. Preference is given to applicants whose research interests would benefit Asians, Asian Americans, or persons in social or economic need.

Financial data The stipend is $1,000.

Duration 1 year; nonrenewable.

Number awarded 1 each year.

Deadline August of each year.

[576]
HUGH J. ANDERSEN MEMORIAL SCHOLARSHIPS

National Medical Fellowships, Inc.
Attn: Scholarship Program
347 Fifth Avenue, Suite 510
New York, NY 10016
(212) 483-8880   Toll Free: (877) NMF-1DOC
Fax: (212) 483-8897 E-mail: scholarships@nmfonline.org
Web: www.nmfonline.org

Summary To provide financial assistance to Asian American and other underrepresented minority medical students who reside or attend school in Minnesota.

Eligibility This program is open to African Americans, Hispanics/Latinos, Native Americans, Vietnamese, Cambodians, and Pacific Islanders who are entering the second or third year of medical school. Applicants must be Minnesota residents enrolled in an accredited U.S. medical school or residents of other states attending medical school in Minnesota. Selection is based on leadership, community service, and financial need.

Financial data The award is $2,500.

Duration 1 year.

Additional information This program began in 1982.

Number awarded Up to 5 each year.

Deadline September of each year.

[577]
IBM PHD FELLOWSHIP PROGRAM

IBM Corporation
Attn: University Relations
1133 Westchester Avenue
White Plains, NY 10604
Toll Free: (800) IBM-4YOU   TDD: (800) IBM-3383
E-mail: phdfellow@us.ibm.com
Web: www.research.ibm.com

Summary To provide funding and work experience to students (particularly minorities, women, and others who contribute to diversity) who are working on a Ph.D. in a research area of broad interest to IBM.

Eligibility Students nominated for this fellowship should be enrolled full time at an accredited college or university in any country and should have completed at least 1 year of graduate study in computer science or engineering, electrical or mechanical engineering, physical sciences (chemistry, material sciences, physics), mathematical sciences, public sector and business sciences, or service science, management, and engineering (SSME). Focus areas that receive special consideration include technology that creates new business or social value, innovative software, new types of computers, or interdisciplinary projects that create social and business value. Applicants should be planning a career in research. Nominations must be made by a faculty member and endorsed by the department head. The program values diversity, and encourages nominations of women, minorities, and others who contribute to that diversity. Selection is based on the applicants' potential for research excellence, the degree to which their technical interests align with those of IBM, and academic progress to date. Preference is given to students who have had an IBM internship or have closely collaborated with technical or services people from IBM.

Financial data Fellowships pay tuition, fees, and a stipend of $17,500 per year.

Duration 1 year; may be renewed up to 2 additional years, provided the recipient is renominated, interacts with IBM's technical community, and demonstrates continued progress and achievement.

Additional information Recipients are offered an internship at 1 of the IBM Research Division laboratories and are given an IBM computer.

Number awarded Varies each year; recently, 57 of these scholarships were awarded.

Deadline October of each year.

[578]
ILLINOIS MINORITY REAL ESTATE SCHOLARSHIP

Illinois Association of Realtors
Attn: Illinois Real Estate Educational Foundation
522 South Fifth Street
P.O. Box 2607
Springfield, IL 62708
Toll Free: (866) 854-REEF   Fax: (217) 529-5893
E-mail: lclayton@iar.org
Web: www.ilreef.org/index.php/scholarship

Summary To provide financial assistance to Illinois residents who are 1) Asian Americans or members of other minority groups and 2) preparing for a career in real estate.

Eligibility This program is open to residents of Illinois who are African American, Hispanic or Latino, Native American, or Asian. Applicants must be interested in preparing for a career in real estate by pursuing: 1) courses to meet Illinois salesperson license requirements; 2) course work to meet Illinois broker license requirement; 3) course work required for Illinois appraisal licensing/certification; 4) professional development unrelated to obtaining license/certification; or 5) an undergraduate or graduate program of study. Along with their application, they must submit information on their employment history, transcripts, evidence of financial need, and an essay that describes their career goals and explains why they believe they should receive scholarship assistance through this program.

Financial data The maximum stipend is $500.

Duration Funds must be used within 24 months of the award date.

Number awarded 1 or more each year.

Deadline Applications may be submitted at any time, but they must be received at least 12 weeks prior to the beginning of the school term for which financial assistance is requested.

[579]
ILLINOIS NURSES FOUNDATION CENTENNIAL SCHOLARSHIP

Illinois Nurses Association
Attn: Illinois Nurses Foundation
105 West Adams Street, Suite 1420
Chicago, IL 60603
(312) 419-2900   Fax: (312) 419-2920
E-mail: inf@illinoisnurses.com
Web: www.illinoisnurses.com

Summary To provide financial assistance to nursing undergraduate and graduate students who are Asian American or members of other underrepresented groups.

Eligibility This program is open to students working on an associate, bachelor's, or master's degree at an accredited NLNAC or CCNE school of nursing. Applicants must be members of a group underrepresented in nursing (African Americans, Hispanics, American Indians, Asians, and males). Undergraduates must have earned a passing grade in all nursing courses taken to date and have a GPA of 2.85 or higher. Graduate students must have completed at least 12 semester hours of graduate work and have a GPA of 3.0 or higher. All applicants must be willing to 1) act as a spokesperson to other student groups on the value of the scholarship to continuing their nursing education; and 2) be profiled in any media or marketing materials developed by the Illinois Nurses Foundation. Along with their application, they must submit a narrative of 250 to 500 words on how they, as nurses, plan to affect policy at either the state or national level that impacts on nursing or health care generally, or how they believe they will impact the nursing profession in general.

Financial data A stipend is awarded (amount not specified).

Duration 1 year.

Number awarded 1 or more each year.

Deadline March of each year.

[580]
INDIANA CLEO FELLOWSHIPS

Indiana Supreme Court
Attn: Division of State Court Administration
30 South Meridian Street, Suite 500
Indianapolis, IN 46204
(317) 234-1376   Toll Free: (800) 452-9963
Fax: (317) 233-6586
E-mail: jasmine.parsons@courts.in.gov
Web: www.in.gov/judiciary/cleo

Summary To provide financial assistance to Asian American and other disadvantaged college seniors from any state interested in attending law school in Indiana.

Eligibility This program is open to Indiana minority, low income, or educationally disadvantaged college seniors who have applied to a law school in the state. Selected applicants are invited to participate in the Indiana Conference for Legal Education Opportunity (Indiana CLEO) Summer Institute, held at a law school in the state. Admission to that program is based on GPA, LSAT scores, 3 letters of recommendation, a resume, a personal statement, and financial need. Students who successfully complete the Institute and become certified graduates of the program may be eligible to receive a fellowship.

Financial data All expenses for the Indiana CLEO Summer Institute are paid. The fellowship stipend is $6,500 per year for students who attend a public law school or $9,000 per year for students who attend a private law school.

Duration The Indiana CLEO Summer Institute lasts 6 weeks. Fellowships are for 1 year and may be renewed up to 2 additional years.

Additional information The first Summer Institute was held in 1997.

Number awarded 30 students are invited to participate in the summer institute; the number of those selected to receive a fellowship varies each year.

Deadline March of each year.

[581]
INITIATIVE TO RECRUIT A DIVERSE WORKFORCE

Association of Research Libraries
Attn: Director of Diversity Programs
21 Dupont Circle, N.W., Suite 800
Washington, DC 20036
(202) 296-2296   Fax: (202) 872-0884
E-mail: mpuente@arl.org
Web: www.arl.org/diversity/init/index.shtml

Summary To provide financial assistance to Asian Americans and other minorities who are interested in preparing for a career as an academic or research librarian.

Eligibility This program is open to members of racial and ethnic minority groups that are underrepresented as professionals in academic and research libraries (American Indian or Alaska Native, Asian, Black or African American, Native Hawaiian or other Pacific Islander, or Hispanic or Latino). Preference is given to students who have an academic background in a discipline of science, technology, engineering, or mathematics (STEM). Applicants must be interested in working on an M.L.I.S. degree at an ALA-accredited program. They must be citizens or permanent residents of the United

States (including Puerto Rico) or Canada. Along with their application, they must submit a 400-word essay on what attracts them to a career in a research library. The essays are judged on clarity and content of form, clear goals and benefits, enthusiasm, potential growth perceived, and professional goals.

Financial data The stipend is $5,000 per year.

Duration 2 years.

Additional information This program began in 2000. Funding is currently provided by the Institute of Museum and Library Services and by the contributions of 52 libraries that are members of the Association of Research Libraries (ARL). Recipients who do not have academic training in STEM disciplines must take additional course work to prepare them for a career in those fields.

Number awarded Varies each year; recently, 14 of these scholarships were awarded.

Deadline April of each year.

[582]
INSTITUTE FOR SUPPLY MANAGEMENT DOCTORAL DISSERTATION GRANT PROGRAM

Institute for Supply Management
Attn: Director, Education and Training
2055 East Centennial Circle
P.O. Box 22160
Tempe, AZ 85285-2160
(480) 752-6276, ext. 3092
Toll Free: (800) 888-6276, ext. 3092
Fax: (480) 752-7890　　　E-mail: cmendoza@ism.ws
Web: www.ism.ws

Summary To provide financial support to doctoral candidates (particularly Asian Americans, other minorities, women, and students with disabilities) who are conducting dissertation research in purchasing or related fields.

Eligibility This program is open to doctoral candidates who are working on a Ph.D. or D.B.A. in supply management, supply chain management, business, management, logistics, economics, industrial engineering, or a related field at an accredited university in the United States. International applicants are accepted. Examples of research projects that could be funded include: purchasing and supply management models, methodologies, measurement, supply networks, operations and logistics integration, produce/service innovation, supply relationships, supply's role in corporate success, or strategic development of supply. The research proposal (up to 25 pages) must discuss hypotheses, significance of the study, research methodology, and value of the research to the field of purchasing. The program encourages applications from a diverse population, regardless of gender, race, creed, age, ethnic or national origin, sexual orientation, or disability.

Financial data Grants range up to $6,000.

Duration 1 year.

Additional information The sponsoring organization was previously known as the National Association of Purchasing Management.

Number awarded Up to 4 each year.

Deadline January of each year.

[583]
INTELLECTUAL PROPERTY LAW SECTION WOMEN AND MINORITY SCHOLARSHIP

State Bar of Texas
Attn: Intellectual Property Law Section
c/o Syed K. Fareed, Scholarship Selection Committee
Vinson & Elkins LLP
2801 Via Fortuna, Suite 100
Austin, TX 78746
(512) 542-8400　　　Fax: (512) 542-8612
E-mail: sfareed@velaw.com
Web: texasbariplaw.org

Summary To provide financial assistance to Asian Americans, other minorities, and females who are enrolled at law schools in Texas and plan to practice intellectual property law.

Eligibility This program is open to women and members of minority groups (African Americans, Hispanics, Asian Americans, and Native Americans) from any state who are currently enrolled at an ABA-accredited law school in Texas. Applicants must be planning to practice intellectual property law in Texas. Along with their application, they must submit a 2-page essay explaining why they plan to prepare for a career in intellectual property law in Texas, any qualifications they believe are relevant for their consideration for this scholarship, and (optionally) any issues of financial need they wish to have considered.

Financial data The stipend is $2,500.

Duration 1 year.

Number awarded 2 each year: 1 to a women and 1 to a minority.

Deadline April of each year.

[584]
INTERFAITH SPIRITUALITY SCHOLARSHIP

Unitarian Universalist Association
Attn: Ministerial Credentialing Office
25 Beacon Street
Boston, MA 02108-2800
(617) 948-6403　　　Fax: (617) 742-2875
E-mail: mcoadministrator@uua.org
Web: www.uua.org

Summary To provide financial assistance to seminary students (particularly Asian Americans and other students of color) who are preparing for the Unitarian Universalist (UU) ministry and are interested in interfaith understanding.

Eligibility This program is open to seminary students who are enrolled full or at least half time in a UU ministerial training program with aspirant or candidate status. Applicants must have demonstrated 1) an interest in and desire to integrate interfaith understanding into their ministry; and 2) a commitment to guiding others on their own spiritual path. Priority is given first to those who have demonstrated outstanding ministerial ability and secondarily to students with the greatest financial need (especially persons of color).

Financial data The stipend ranges from $1,000 to $15,000 per year.

Duration 1 year.

Number awarded 1 each year.

Deadline April of each year.

[585]
INTERMOUNTAIN SECTION AWWA DIVERSITY SCHOLARSHIP

American Water Works Association-Intermountain
Section
Attn: Member Services Coordinator
3430 East Danish Road
Sandy, UT 94093
(801) 712-1619, ext. 2   Fax: (801) 487-6699
E-mail: nicoleb@ims-awwa.org
Web: ims-awwa.site-ym.com/group/StudentPO

Summary   To provide financial assistance to Asian Americans, other minorities, and women who are interested in working on an undergraduate or graduate degree in the field of water quality, supply, and treatment at a university in Idaho or Utah.

Eligibility   This program is open to 1) women; and 2) students who identify as Hispanic or Latino, Black or African American, Native Hawaiian or other Pacific Islander, Asian, or American Indian or Alaska Native. Applicants must be entering or enrolled in an undergraduate or graduate program at a college or university in Idaho or Utah that relates to water quality, supply, or treatment. Along with their application, they must submit a 2-page essay on their academic interests and career goals and how those relate to water quality, supply, or treatment. Selection is based on that essay, letters of recommendation, and potential to contribute to the field of water quality, supply, and treatment in the Intermountain West.

Financial data   The stipend is $1,000. The winner also receives a 1-year student membership in the Intermountain Section of the American Water Works Association (AWWA) and a 1-year subscription to *Journal AWWA.*

Duration   1 year; nonrenewable.

Number awarded   1 each year.

Deadline   October of each year.

[586]
ISAAC J. "IKE" CRUMBLY MINORITIES IN ENERGY GRANT

American Association of Petroleum Geologists
Foundation
Attn: Grants-in-Aid Program
1444 South Boulder Avenue
P.O. Box 979
Tulsa, OK 74101-0979
(918) 560-2644   Toll Free: (855) 302-2743
Fax: (918) 560-2642   E-mail: foundation@aapg.org
Web: foundation.aapg.org/gia/crumbly.cfm

Summary   To provide funding to Asian Americans, other minorities, and women who are in graduate school and interested in conducting research related to earth science aspects of the petroleum industry.

Eligibility   This program is open to women and ethnic minorities (Black, Hispanic, Asian, or Native American, including American Indian, Eskimo, Hawaiian, or Samoan) who are working on a master's or doctoral degree. Applicants must be interested in conducting research related to the search for and development of petroleum and energy-minerals resources and to related environmental geology issues. Selection is based on student's academic and employment history (10 points), scientific merit of proposal (30 points),

suitability to program objectives (30 points), financial merit of proposal (20 points), and endorsement by faculty or department adviser (10 points).

Financial data   Grants range from $500 to $3,000. Funds are to be applied to research-related expenses (e.g., a summer of field work). They may not be used to purchase capital equipment or to pay salaries, tuition, room, or board.

Duration   1 year. Doctoral candidates may receive a 1-year renewal.

Number awarded   1 each year.

Deadline   February of each year.

[587]
JAMES B. MORRIS SCHOLARSHIPS

James B. Morris Scholarship Fund
Attn: Scholarship Selection Committee
P.O. Box 12145
Des Moines, IA 50312
(515) 864-0922
Web: www.morrisscholarship.org

Summary   To provide financial assistance to Asian American and other minority undergraduate, graduate, and law students from Iowa.

Eligibility   This program is open to minority students (African Americans, Asian/Pacific Islanders, Hispanics, or Native Americans) who are interested in working on an undergraduate or graduate degree. Applicants must be either Iowa residents attending a college or university anywhere in the United States or non-Iowa residents who are attending a college or university in Iowa. Along with their application, they must submit an essay of 250 to 500 words on why they are applying for this scholarship, activities or organizations in which they are involved, and their future plans. Selection is based on the essay, academic achievement (GPA of 2.5 or higher), community service, and financial need. U.S. citizenship is required.

Financial data   The stipend ranges from $1,000 to $2,500 per year.

Duration   1 year; may be renewed.

Additional information   This fund was established in 1978 in honor of the J.B. Morris family, who founded the Iowa branch of the National Association for the Advancement of Colored People and published the *Iowa Bystander* newspaper. The program includes the Ann Chapman Scholarships, the Vincent Chapman, Sr. Scholarships, and the Brittany Hall Memorial Scholarships.

Number awarded   Varies each year; recently, 19 of these scholarships were awarded.

Deadline   March of each year.

[588]
JAMES CARLSON MEMORIAL SCHOLARSHIP

Oregon Student Access Commission
Attn: Grants and Scholarships Division
1500 Valley River Drive, Suite 100
Eugene, OR 97401-2146
(541) 687-7395   Toll Free: (800) 452-8807, ext. 7395
Fax: (541) 687-7414   TDD: (800) 735-2900
E-mail: awardinfo@osac.state.or.us
Web: www.oregonstudentaid.gov/scholarships.aspx

Summary To provide financial assistance to Oregon residents from diverse environments (including Asian Americans) who are majoring in education on the undergraduate or graduate school level at a school in any state.

Eligibility This program is open to residents of Oregon who are U.S. citizens or permanent residents and enrolled at a college or university in any state. Applicants must be either 1) college seniors or fifth-year students majoring in elementary or secondary education; or 2) graduate students working on an elementary or secondary certificate. Full-time enrollment and financial need are required. Priority is given to 1) students who come from diverse environments and submit an essay of 250 to 350 words on their experience living or working in diverse environments; 2) dependents of members of the Oregon Education Association; and 3) applicants committed to teaching autistic children.

Financial data Stipends for scholarships offered by the Oregon Student Access Commission (OSAC) range from $200 to $10,000 but recently averaged $2,300.

Duration 1 year.

Additional information This program is administered by the OSAC with funds provided by the Oregon Community Foundation.

Number awarded Varies each year; recently, 3 of these scholarships were awarded.

Deadline February of each year.

[589]
JAMES ECHOLS SCHOLARSHIP

California Association for Health, Physical Education, Recreation and Dance
Attn: Chair, Scholarship Committee
1501 El Camino Avenue, Suite 3
Sacramento, CA 95815-2748
(916) 922-3596   Toll Free: (800) 499-3596 (within CA)
Fax: (916) 922-0133   E-mail: cahperd@cahperd.org
Web: www.cahperd.org/scholarships.html

Summary To provide financial assistance to Asian American and other minority student members of the California Association for Health, Physical Education, Recreation and Dance.

Eligibility This program is open to California residents who have been members of the association for at least 60 days and are attending a 2- or 4-year college or university in California. Applicants must be undergraduate or graduate students working on a degree in health, physical education, recreation, or dance and have completed at least 60 semester hours of college work. Selection is based on scholastic proficiency (a GPA of 3.0 or higher); leadership ability in school, community, and professional activities; and personal qualities of enthusiasm, cooperativeness, responsibility, initiative, and ability to work with others. This scholarship is awarded to the highest-ranked minority (Asian, African American, Latino, or Native American) applicant.

Financial data The stipend is $750.

Duration 1 year.

Number awarded 1 each year.

Deadline November of each year.

[590]
JAPANESE AMERICAN ASSOCIATION OF NEW YORK MUSIC SCHOLARSHIP AWARDS

Japanese American Association of New York, Inc.
Attn: Scholarship Committee
15 West 44th Street, 11th Floor
New York, NY 10036
(212) 840-6942   Fax: (212) 840-0616
E-mail: info@jaany.org
Web: www.jaany.org/music_scholarship.html

Summary To recognize and reward Japanese and Japanese American students who participate in a music competition.

Eligibility This music competition is open to students who are Japanese or Americans of Japanese descent. Recently, the competition was limited to ensembles from trio to quintet; applicants performed 1 piece from the Classical era and another from the Romantic era or the 20th century at the recital in New York.

Financial data Awards range from $2,000 to $5,000.

Duration The competition is held annually.

Number awarded 2 each year.

Deadline September of each year.

[591]
JAPANESE AMERICAN BAR ASSOCIATION EDUCATIONAL FOUNDATION SCHOLARSHIPS

Japanese American Bar Association
Attn: JABA Educational Foundation
P.O. Box 86063
Los Angeles, CA 90086
(310) 785-6881   E-mail: JEFscholarship@gmail.com
Web: www.jabaonline.org/scholarships

Summary To provide financial assistance to law students who have been involved with the Asian Pacific American community.

Eligibility This program is open to students currently enrolled in law school. Applicants must demonstrate an intention to practice law in southern California. Selection is based on service to the Asian Pacific American community, academic achievement, adversities overcome, desire to practice law in the southern California area, and financial need.

Financial data The stipend is $2,000.

Duration 1 year.

Additional information This program, which began in 1984, includes the Justice John F. Aiso Scholarship, the Justice Stephen K. Tamura Scholarship, and the Lim, Ruger & Kim Foundation Scholarship (established in 2007).

Number awarded 3 each year.

Deadline January of each year.

[592]
JAPANESE AMERICAN VETERANS ASSOCIATION MEMORIAL SCHOLARSHIPS

Japanese American Veterans Association
c/o Terry Shima, Outreach and Education Committee
  Chair
415 Russell Avenue, Number 1005
Gaithersburg, MD 20877
(301) 987-6746   E-mail: ttshima@comcast.net
Web: www.javadc.org

Summary To provide financial assistance for college or graduate school to relatives of Japanese American veterans and military personnel.

Eligibility This program is open to graduating high school seniors and students currently working on an undergraduate or graduate degree at a college, university, or school of specialized study. Applicants must be related, by blood or marriage, to 1) a person who served with the 442nd Regimental Combat Team, the 100th Infantry Battalion, or other unit associated with those; 2) a person who served in the U.S. Military Intelligence Service during or after World War II; 3) a person of Japanese ancestry who is serving or has served in the U.S. armed forces and been honorable discharged; or 4) a member of the Japanese American Veterans Association (JAVA) whose membership extends back at least 1 year.

Financial data The stipend is $1,500.

Duration 1 year; recipients may reapply.

Additional information These scholarships, first awarded in 2008, include the following named awards: the Orville C. Shirey Memorial Scholarship, the Joseph Ichiuji Memorial Scholarship, the Phil Ishio Memorial Scholarship, the Kiyoko Tsuboi Taubkin Scholarship, the Grant Hirabayashi Memorial Scholarship, the Victor and Teru Matsui Scholarship, the Betty Shima Scholarship, the Dr. Warren Tsuneishi Scholarship, the Mike and Etsu Masaoka Scholarship, and the Douglas Ishio Memorial Scholarship.

Number awarded 10 each year.

Deadline April of each year.

[593]
JAPANESE MEDICAL SOCIETY OF AMERICA SCHOLARSHIPS

Japanese Medical Society of America, Inc.
100 Park Avenue, Suite 1600
New York, NY 10017
(212) 351-5038   Fax: (212) 351-5047
E-mail: info@jmsa.org
Web: www.jmsa.org/student-members/about-scholarships

Summary To provide funding to Japanese American medical school students, residents, and fellows who are interested in working on a project.

Eligibility This program is open to Japanese Americans who are currently enrolled as medical students, residents, or fellows. Applicants must be proposing to conduct a project that will benefit the Japanese Medical Society of America (JMSA) and the Japanese community. Along with their application, they must submit a 1-page essay about themselves and what they will do to contribute to the JMSA. Selection is based on academic excellence and interest in JMSA.

Financial data Stipends depend on the availability of funds, but have ranged from $2,500 to $20,000. Support is provided primarily for tuition, but a portion of the funds may be used to carry out the proposed project.

Duration 1 year.

Additional information This program receives support from a number of sponsors, including the Honjo Foundation, Nishioka Foundation, Mitsui USA, and Toyota USA. Examples of past projects include a service to connect elderly Japanese American patients with health care, a medical blog in Japanese detailing the experiences of a medical student in America, and a collaborative web site to connect Japanese and American medical students.

Number awarded Varies each year; recently, 11 of these scholarships were awarded.

Deadline December of each year.

[594]
JAY LEE SOCIAL SERVICE SCHOLARSHIP

Philip Jaisohn Memorial Foundation
Attn: Education and Scholarship Committee
6705 Old York Road
Philadelphia, PA 19126
(215) 224-2000   Fax: (215) 224-9164
E-mail: jaisohnhouse@gmail.com
Web: www.jaisohn.org

Summary To provide financial assistance to Korean American undergraduate and graduate students who have participated in social service activities.

Eligibility This program is open to Korean American undergraduate and graduate students who are currently enrolled at a college or university in the United States. Applicants must be able to demonstrate excellence in community service activities and financial need. Along with their application, they must submit an essay on either "Who is Dr. Jaisohn to Me," or "The Significance of Dr. Jaisohn's Ideal to Korean Americans." They must also submit a brief statement on how they can contribute to and be involved in the activities of the Philip Jaisohn Memorial Foundation. Selection is based on community service and future potential.

Financial data The stipend is $1,000.

Duration 1 year.

Number awarded 1 each year.

Deadline November of each year.

[595]
JEAN LU STUDENT SCHOLARSHIP AWARD

Society of Toxicology
Attn: American Association of Chinese in Toxicology
  Special Interest Group
1821 Michael Faraday Drive, Suite 300
Reston, VA 20190-5348
(703) 438-3115   Fax: (703) 438-3113
E-mail: sothq@toxicology.org
Web: www.toxicology.org/ai/af/awards.aspx

Summary To provide funding for research to graduate student members of the Society of Toxicology (SOT) who are of Chinese ethnic origin and working on a Ph.D. in the field.

Eligibility This program is open to Chinese students (born in China or, if born in the United States, having 1 or more parents of Chinese descent) who are SOT members. Applicants must be enrolled full time in a Ph.D. program in toxicology and have been advanced to candidacy. Selection is based on academic achievement, demonstration of leadership, relevance of thesis to toxicology, and letters of recommendation. Finalists are interviewed by telephone.

Financial data The stipend is $1,000. Funds may be used for payment of tuition and/or other educational and research-related expenses, including travel.

Duration 1 year.

Additional information This program began in 2008.

Number awarded 1 each year.

Deadline December of each year.

[596]
JEANNE SPURLOCK RESEARCH FELLOWSHIP IN SUBSTANCE ABUSE AND ADDICTION FOR MINORITY MEDICAL STUDENTS

American Academy of Child and Adolescent Psychiatry
Attn: Department of Research, Training, and Education
3615 Wisconsin Avenue, N.W.
Washington, DC 20016-3007
(202) 587-9663   Fax: (202) 966-5894
E-mail: training@aacap.org
Web: www.aacap.org

Summary To provide funding to Asian American and other minority medical students who are interested in working during the summer on the topics of drug abuse and addiction with a child and adolescent psychiatrist researcher-mentor.

Eligibility This program is open to African American, Asian American, Native American, Alaska Native, Mexican American, Hispanic, and Pacific Islander students in accredited U.S. medical schools. Applicants must present a plan for a program of research training in drug abuse and addiction that involves significant contact with a mentor who is an experienced child and adolescent psychiatrist researcher. The plan should include program planning discussions; instruction in research planning and implementation; regular meetings with the mentor, laboratory director, and research group; and assigned readings. The mentor must be a member of the American Academy of Child and Adolescent Psychiatry (AACAP). Research assignments may include responsibility for part of the observation or evaluation, developing specific aspects of the research mechanisms, conducting interviews or tests, using rating scales, and psychological or cognitive testing of subjects. The training plan also should include discussion of ethical issues in research, such as protocol development, informed consent, collection and storage of raw data, safeguarding data, bias in analyzing data, plagiarism, protection of patients, and ethical treatment of animals. U.S. citizenship or permanent resident status is required.

Financial data The stipend is $4,000. Fellows also receive reimbursement of travel expenses to attend the annual meeting of the American Academy of Child and Adolescent Psychiatry.

Duration 12 weeks during the summer.

Additional information Upon completion of the training program, the student is required to submit a brief paper summarizing the research experience. The fellowship pays expenses for the fellow to attend the academy's annual meeting and present this paper. This program is co-sponsored by the National Institute on Drug Abuse.

Number awarded Up to 5 each year.

Deadline February of each year.

[597]
JIM MCKAY SCHOLARSHIP PROGRAM

National Collegiate Athletic Association
Attn: Jim McKay Scholarship Program Staff Liaison
700 West Washington Street
P.O. Box 6222
Indianapolis, IN 46206-6222
(317) 917-6222   Fax: (317) 917-6888
E-mail: lthomas@ncaa.org
Web: www.ncaa.org

Summary To provide financial assistance to student-athletes (particularly Asian Americans, other minorities, and women) who are interested in attending graduate school to prepare for a career in sports communications.

Eligibility This program is open to college seniors planning to enroll full time in a graduate degree program and to students already enrolled full time in graduate study at an institution that is a member of the National Collegiate Athletic Association (NCAA). Applicants must have competed in intercollegiate athletics as a member of a varsity team at an NCAA member institution and have an overall undergraduate cumulative GPA of 3.5 or higher. They must be preparing for a career in the sports communications industry. Women and minorities are especially encouraged to apply. Neither financial need nor U.S. citizenship are required. Nominations must be submitted by the faculty athletics representative or chief academic officer at the institution in which the student is or was an undergraduate.

Financial data The stipend is $10,000.

Duration 1 year; nonrenewable.

Additional information This program began in 2008.

Number awarded 2 each year: 1 female and 1 male.

Deadline January of each year.

[598]
J.K. SASAKI MEMORIAL SCHOLARSHIPS

West Los Angeles United Methodist Church
Attn: Scholarship Committee
1913 Purdue Avenue
Los Angeles, CA 90025
(310) 479-1379   Fax: (310) 478-7756
E-mail: wlaumc@aol.com
Web: www.wlaumc.org

Summary To provide financial assistance to Japanese American and other Asian American seminary students who are preparing for ordained ministry in the United Methodist Church.

Eligibility This program is open to Japanese American and other Asian American students at Protestant seminaries in the United States. Applicants must be planning to serve a Japanese American or Asian American congregation of the United Methodist Church as an ordained minister. They must have a GPA of 2.5 or higher. Along with their application, they must submit 2 essays (of 500 words each) on 1) their motivations for preparing for a career in the United Methodist Church; and 2) their concerns for the local church and the United Methodist Church with issues related to Asian Americans and/or Pacific Islanders.

Financial data Stipends range from $250 to $1,000.

Duration 1 year; recipients may reapply.

Additional information This program began in 1972 and given its current name in 2006.

Number awarded 1 or more each year.

Deadline February of each year.

[599]
JOHN A. MAYES SCHOLARSHIP

National Athletic Trainers' Association
Attn: Ethnic Diversity Advisory Committee
2952 Stemmons Freeway, Suite 200
Dallas, TX 75247-6103
(214) 532-8802   Toll Free: (800) 879-6282
Fax: (214) 637-2206
Web: www.nata.org/edac/John-A-Mayes-Scholarship

Summary To provide financial aid to Asian American and other ethnically diverse graduate students who are preparing for a career as an athletic trainer.

Eligibility This program is open to members of ethnically diverse groups who have been accepted into an entry-level master's athletic training degree program or into a doctoral-level athletic training and/or sports medicine degree program. Applicants must be sponsored by a certified athletic trainer who is a member of the National Athletic Trainers' Association (NATA). They must have a cumulative GPA of 3.2 or higher. First priority is given to a student working on an entry-level athletic training master's degree; second priority is given to a student entering the second year of an athletic training master's degree program; third priority is given to a student working on a doctoral degree in athletic training or sports medicine. Special consideration is given to applicants who have been members of NATA for at least 2 years.

Financial data The stipend is $2,300.

Duration 1 year.

Additional information This program began in 2009.

Number awarded 1 each year.

Deadline February of each year.

[600]
JOHN AND MURIEL LANDIS SCHOLARSHIPS

American Nuclear Society
Attn: Scholarship Coordinator
555 North Kensington Avenue
La Grange Park, IL 60526-5535
(708) 352-6611   Toll Free: (800) 323-3044
Fax: (708) 352-0499   E-mail: outreach@ans.org
Web: www.new.ans.org/honors/scholarships

Summary To provide financial assistance to undergraduate or graduate students (particularly Asian Americans, other minorities, and women) who are interested in preparing for a career in nuclear-related fields and can demonstrate financial need.

Eligibility This program is open to undergraduate and graduate students at colleges or universities located in the United States who are preparing for, or planning to prepare for, a career in nuclear science, nuclear engineering, or a nuclear-related field. Qualified high school seniors are also eligible. Applicants must have greater than average financial need and have experienced circumstances that render them disadvantaged. Along with their application, they must submit an essay on their academic and professional goals, experiences that have affected those goals, etc. Selection is based

on that essay, academic achievement, letters of recommendation, and financial need. Women and members of minority groups are especially urged to apply. U.S. citizenship is not required.

Financial data The stipend is $5,000, to be used to cover tuition, books, fees, room, and board.

Duration 1 year; nonrenewable.

Number awarded Up to 9 each year.

Deadline January of each year.

[601]
JOHN MCLENDON MEMORIAL MINORITY POSTGRADUATE SCHOLARSHIP AWARD

National Association of Collegiate Directors of Athletics
Attn: NACDA Foundation
24651 Detroit Road
Westlake, OH 44145
(440) 788-7475   Fax: (440) 892-4007
E-mail: jbouyer@nacda.com
Web: www.nacda.com/mclendon/scholarship.html

Summary To provide financial assistance to Asian American and other minority college seniors who are interested in working on a graduate degree in athletics administration.

Eligibility This program is open to minority college students who are seniors, are attending school on a full-time basis, have a GPA of 3.2 or higher, intend to attend graduate school to earn a degree in athletics administration, and are involved in college or community activities. Also eligible are college graduates who have at least 2 years' experience in an athletics administration position. Candidates must be nominated by an official of a member institution of the National Association of Collegiate Directors of Athletics (NACDA) or (for college graduates) a supervisor.

Financial data The stipend is $10,000.

Duration 1 year.

Additional information Recipients must maintain full-time status during the senior year to retain their eligibility. They must attend NACDA-member institutions.

Number awarded 5 each year.

Deadline Nominations must be submitted by April of each year.

[602]
JOHN STANFORD MEMORIAL WLMA SCHOLARSHIP

Washington Library Media Association
c/o Susan Kaphammer, Scholarship Chair
521 North 24th Avenue
Yakima, WA 98902
(509) 972-5999   E-mail: kaphammers@wvsd208.org
Web: www.wlma.org/scholarships

Summary To provide financial assistance to Asian Americans and other ethnic minorities in Washington who are interested in attending a school in any state to prepare for a library media career.

Eligibility This program is open to residents of Washington who are working toward a library media endorsement or graduate degree in the field at a school in any state. Applicants must be members of an ethnic minority group. They must be working or planning to work in a school library. Along with their application, they must submit a 3-page letter that includes a description of themselves and their achievements to date, their interest and work in the library field, their personal and professional activities, their goals and plans for further education and professional development, how they expect the studies funded by this award to impact their professional practice and contributions to the Washington school library community, and their financial need.

Financial data The stipend is $1,000.

Duration 1 year.

Number awarded 1 each year.

Deadline April of each year.

[603]
JOHNSON & JOHNSON-AMERICAN ASSOCIATION OF COLLEGES OF NURSING MINORITY NURSE FACULTY SCHOLARS PROGRAM

American Association of Colleges of Nursing
One Dupont Circle, N.W., Suite 530
Washington, DC 20036
(202) 463-6930   Fax: (202) 785-8320
E-mail: scholarship@aacn.nche.edu
Web: www.aacn.nche.edu/students/scholarships

Summary To provide funding to Asian American and other minority students who are working on a graduate degree in nursing to prepare for a career as a faculty member.

Eligibility This program is open to members of racial and ethnic minority groups (Alaska Native, American Indian, Black or African American, Native Hawaiian or other, Pacific Islander, Hispanic or Latino, or Asian American) who are enrolled full time at a school of nursing. Applicants must be working on 1) a doctoral nursing degree (e.g., Ph.D., D.N.P.); or 2) a clinically-focused master's degree in nursing (e.g., M.S.N., M.S.). They must commit to 1) serve in a teaching capacity at a nursing school for a minimum of 1 year for each year of support they receive; 2) provide 6-month progress reports to the American Association of Colleges of Nursing (AACN) throughout the entire funding process and during the payback period; 3) agree to work with an assigned mentor throughout the period of the scholarship grant; and 4) attend an annual leadership training conference to connect with their mentor, fellow scholars, and colleagues. Selection is based on ability to contribute to nursing education; leadership potential; development of goals reflecting education, research, and professional involvement; ability to work with a mentor/adviser throughout the award period; proposed research and/or practice projects that are significant and show commitment to improving nursing education and clinical nursing practice in the United States; proposed research and/or clinical education professional development plan that exhibits quality, feasibility, and innovativeness; and evidence of commitment to a career in nursing education and to recruiting, mentoring, and retaining future underrepresented minority nurses. Preference is given to students enrolled in doctoral nursing programs. Applicants must be U.S. citizens, permanent residents, refugees, or qualified immigrants.

Financial data The stipend is $18,000 per year. The award includes $1,500 that is held in escrow to cover the costs for the recipient to attend the leadership training conference. Recipients are required to sign a letter of commitment that they will provide 1 year of service in a teaching capacity at a nursing school in the United States for each year of sup-

port received; if they fail to complete that service requirement, they must repay all funds received.

Duration 1 year; may be renewed 1 additional year.

Additional information This program, established in 2007, is sponsored by the Johnson & Johnson Campaign for Nursing's Future.

Number awarded 5 each year.

Deadline April of each year.

[604]
JONATHAN T.Y. YEH MEMORIAL STUDENT PRIZE

American Folklore Society
Attn: Timothy Lloyd, Executive Director
Ohio State University
Mershon Center
1501 Neil Avenue
Columbus, OH 43201-2602
(614) 292-3375   Fax: (614) 292-2407
E-mail: lloyd.100@osu.edu
Web: www.afsnet.org/?page=SectionPrizes

Summary To recognize and reward outstanding student papers on a subject dealing with Asian and/or Asian American folklore.

Eligibility This competition is open to full-time undergraduate and graduate students under 30 years of age. Applicants must submit a 10- to 12-page research paper dealing with Asian and/or Asian American folklore studies. They must be able to demonstrate prospects for publication of their scholarly work and a dedication to research and/or teaching folklore studies.

Financial data The prize is $500.

Duration The prize is awarded annually.

Number awarded 1 each year.

Deadline June of each year.

[605]
JOSEPH B. GITTLER AWARD

American Psychological Foundation
750 First Street, N.E.
Washington, DC 20002-4242
(202) 336-5843   Fax: (202) 336-5812
E-mail: foundation@apa.org
Web: www.apa.org/apf/funding/gittler.aspx

Summary To recognize and reward scholars and graduate students in psychology (particularly Asian Americans, other minorities, women, and individuals with disabilities) whose work has transformed the philosophical foundations of the discipline.

Eligibility This award is available to scholars and graduate students whose body of work or whose individual work has transformed the philosophical foundations of psychological knowledge. Self-nominations are welcome. Selection is based on conformance with stated program goals and magnitude of contributions The sponsor encourages nominations of individuals who represent diversity in race, ethnicity, gender, age, disability, and sexual orientation.

Financial data The award is $10,000.

Duration The award is presented annually.

Additional information This award was first presented in 2008.

Number awarded 1 each year.

Deadline Nominations must be submitted by May of each year.

[606]
JOSEPH L. FISHER DOCTORAL DISSERTATION FELLOWSHIPS

Resources for the Future
Attn: Coordinator for Academic Programs
1616 P Street, N.W., Suite 600
Washington, DC 20036-1400
(202) 328-5020 Fax: (202) 939-3460
E-mail: fisher-award@rff.org
Web: www.rff.org

Summary To provide funding to doctoral candidates in economics (particularly Asian Americans, other minorities, and women) who are interested in conducting dissertation research on issues related to the environment, natural resources, or energy.

Eligibility This program is open to graduate students in their final year of research on a dissertation related to the environment, natural resources, or energy. Applicants must submit a brief letter of application and a curriculum vitae, a graduate transcript, a 1-page abstract of the dissertation, a technical summary of the dissertation (up to 2,500 words), a letter from their department chair, and 2 letters of recommendation from faculty members on the student's dissertation committee. The technical summary should describe clearly the aim of the dissertation, its significance in relation to the existing literature, and the research methods to be used. Women and minority candidates are strongly encouraged to apply. Non-citizens are eligible if they have proper work and residency documentation.

Financial data The stipend is $18,000.

Duration 1 academic year.

Additional information It is expected that recipients will not hold other employment during the fellowship period. Recipients must notify Resources for the Future of any financial assistance they receive from any other source for support of doctoral work.

Number awarded 1 to 3 each year.

Deadline February of each year.

[607]
JOSEPHINE FORMAN SCHOLARSHIP

Society of American Archivists
Attn: Chair, Awards Committee
17 North State Street, Suite 1425
Chicago, IL 60602-4061
(312) 606-0722 Toll Free: (866) 722-7858
Fax: (312) 606-0728 E-mail: info@archivists.org
Web: www.archivists.org/recognition

Summary To provide financial assistance to Asian American and other minority graduate students working on a degree in archival science.

Eligibility This program is open to members of minority groups (American Indian/Alaska Native, Asian, Black/African American, Hispanic/Latino, or Native Hawaiian/other Pacific Islander) currently enrolled in or accepted to a graduate program or a multi-course program in archival administration. The program must offer at least 3 courses in archival science and students may have completed no more than half of the credit requirements toward their graduate degree. Selection is based on potential for scholastic and personal achievement and commitment both to the archives profession and to advancing diversity concerns within it. U.S. citizenship or permanent resident status is required.

Financial data The stipend is $10,000.

Duration 1 year.

Additional information Funding for this program, established in 2011, is provided by the General Commission on Archives and History of the United Methodist Church.

Number awarded 1 each year.

Deadline February of each year.

[608]
JOSIAH MACY JR. FOUNDATION SCHOLARSHIPS

National Medical Fellowships, Inc.
Attn: Scholarship Program
347 Fifth Avenue, Suite 510
New York, NY 10016
(212) 483-8880 Toll Free: (877) NMF-1DOC
Fax: (212) 483-8897 E-mail: scholarships@nmfonline.org
Web: www.nmfonline.org

Summary To provide financial assistance to Asian Americans and other minority medical students who demonstrate financial need.

Eligibility This program is open to African Americans, Hispanics/Latinos, Native Americans, Vietnamese, Cambodians, and Pacific Islanders who are entering their second or third year of medical school. Selection is based on academic achievement, leadership, community service, and financial need.

Financial data A stipend is awarded (amount not specified).

Duration 1 year.

Additional information This program is sponsored by the Josiah Macy Jr. Foundation.

Number awarded 4 each year.

Deadline September of each year.

[609]
JUDGE EDWARD Y. KAKITA SCHOLARSHIP

Japanese American Bar Association
Attn: JABA Educational Foundation
P.O. Box 86063
Los Angeles, CA 90086
(310) 785-6881 E-mail: JEFscholarship@gmail.com
Web: www.jabaonline.org/scholarships

Summary To provide financial assistance to law students who have participated in the Asian Pacific American community and are interested in international law, commercial litigation, and/or corporate law.

Eligibility This program is open to students currently enrolled in law school. Applicants must demonstrate an intention to practice law in southern California. Along with their application, they must submit a 500-word personal statement discussing their interest in international law, commercial litigation, and/or corporate law. Selection is based on service to the Asian Pacific American community; academic achievement; overcoming adversity; desire to practice law in the southern California area; desire to practice in the areas of international law, commercial litigation, and/or corporate law; and financial need.

Financial data The stipend is $2,000.

Duration 1 year.

Additional information This program began in 2006.

Number awarded 1 each year.

Deadline January of each year.

[610]
JUSTIN HARUYAMA MINISTERIAL SCHOLARSHIP

Japanese American United Church
Attn: Haruyama Scholarship Committee
255 Seventh Avenue
New York, NY 10001
(212) 242-9444   Fax: (212) 242-5274
E-mail: infojauc@gmail.com
Web: www.jauc.org/haruyama_e.html

Summary To provide financial assistance to Protestant seminary students who are interested in serving Japanese American congregations.

Eligibility This program is open to students of Japanese ancestry who are enrolled full time at an accredited Protestant seminary in the United States. Applicants must be working on a ministerial degree in order to serve Japanese American congregations. Along with their application, they must submit 2 letters of recommendation, a transcript of grades, information on their financial situation, and a brief statement of their spiritual journey.

Financial data The stipend is $500.

Duration 1 year; may be renewed.

Number awarded 1 or more each year.

Deadline May of each year.

[611]
KALA SINGH MEMORIAL SCHOLARSHIP

American Speech-Language-Hearing Foundation
Attn: Programs Administrator
2200 Research Boulevard
Rockville, MD 20850-3289
(301) 296-8703   Fax: (301) 296-8567
E-mail: foundationprograms@asha.org
Web: www.ashfoundation.org/grants/GraduateScholarships

Summary To provide financial assistance to Asian Americans, other minorities, and international students who are interested in working on a graduate degree in communication sciences and disorders.

Eligibility This program is open to full-time international and minority graduate students who are enrolled in communication sciences and disorders programs. Applicants must submit an essay, up to 5 pages in length, on a topic that relates to the future of leadership in the discipline. Selection is based on academic promise and outstanding academic achievement.

Financial data The stipend is $5,000. Funds must be used for educational support (e.g., tuition, books, school living expenses), not for personal or conference travel.

Duration The award is granted annually.

Number awarded 1 each year.

Deadline June of each year.

[612]
KALPANA CHAWLA SCHOLARSHIP AWARD

American Society of Engineers of Indian Origin
Attn: Southern California Chapter
P.O. Box 18215
Irvine, CA 92623
E-mail: scholarships@aseisocal.net
Web: www.aseisocal.net/12.html

Summary To provide financial assistance to graduate students of Indian origin (from India) who are working on a degree in aerospace engineering.

Eligibility This program is open to graduate students of Indian origin (by birth, ancestry, or relation). Applicants must be enrolled full time at an accredited college or university in the United States and working on a degree in aerospace engineering with a GPA of 3.7 or higher. They must be members of the American Society of Engineers of Indian Origin (ASEI) Selection is based on academic achievement, technical expertise, and leadership excellence.

Financial data The stipend is $2,000.

Duration 1 year.

Additional information This program began in 2003 to honor Kalpana Chawla, an astronaut who lost her life on the Columbia shuttle.

Number awarded 1 each year.

Deadline August of each year.

[613]
KATTEN MUCHIN ROSENMAN MINORITY SCHOLARSHIPS

Katten Muchin Rosenman LLP
Attn: Attorney Recruiting Manager
525 West Monroe Street
Chicago, IL 60661-3693
(312) 902-5200   Fax: (312) 902-1060
E-mail: nicole.morden@kattenlaw.com
Web: www.kattenlaw.com/minority-scholarship

Summary To provide financial aid and summer work experience in Chicago or New York City to Asian American and other minority law students from any state.

Eligibility This program is open to minority students from any state who have completed their first year of law school. Applicants must have applied for and been accepted as a summer associate at the sponsoring law firm's Chicago or New York office. Along with their application, they must submit 250-word statements on 1) their strongest qualifications for this award; 2) their reasons for preparing for law as a profession; and 3) their views on diversity and how their personal experience and philosophy will be an asset to the firm. Selection is based on academic achievement, leadership experience, and personal qualities that reflect the potential for outstanding contributions to the firm and the legal profession.

Financial data Participants receive the standard salary for the summer internship and a stipend of $15,000 for the academic year.

Duration 1 year.

Number awarded 2 each year; 1 for an internship in Chicago and 1 for an internship in New York City.
Deadline September of each year.

[614]
KEGLER, BROWN, HILL & RITTER MINORITY MERIT SCHOLARSHIP

Kegler, Brown, Hill & Ritter
Attn: Human Resources Manager
Capitol Square, Suite 1800
65 East State Street
Columbus, OH 43215
(614) 462-5467   Toll Free: (800) 860-7885
Fax: (614) 464-2634
E-mail: ctammaro@keglerbrown.com
Web: www.keglerbrown.com

Summary To provide financial aid and summer work experience at Kegler, Brown, Hill & Ritter in Columbus, Ohio to Asian American and other minority students at law schools in any state.

Eligibility This program is open to first-year students of minority descent at law schools in any state. Applicants must be interested in a summer clerkship with the firm following their first year of law school. Along with their application, they must submit brief essays on 1) a major accomplishment that has shaped their life, how it influenced their decision to prepare for a career in law, and how it prepared them for a future as a lawyer; 2) what diversity means to them; 3) why they have applied for the scholarship; and 4) any training and/or experience they believe to be relevant to the clerkship. Selection is based on academic performance, accomplishments, activities, and potential contributions to the legal community.

Financial data The program provides a $5,000 stipend for law school tuition and a paid summer clerkship position.
Duration 1 year.
Additional information This program began in 2004.
Number awarded 2 each year.
Deadline January of each year.

[615]
KENNETH B. CHANG MEMORIAL SCHOLARSHIPS

Korean American Bar Association of Southern California
c/o Joann H. Lee
Legal Aid Foundation of Los Angeles
1102 Crenshaw Boulevard
Los Angeles, CA 90019
(323) 801-7976   E-mail: jlee@lafla.org
Web: www.kabasocal.org

Summary To provide financial assistance to students from any state who are enrolled at law schools in southern California and have been active in the Asian Pacific Islander and/or Korean American community.

Eligibility This program is open to students from any state currently enrolled at law schools in southern California. Applicants must be able to demonstrate a commitment to serving the Korean American community and/or Asian Pacific Islander community through past, current, or future contributions. Students are evaluated on the basis of their written applications and an interview. Financial need may also be a factor.

Financial data Stipends range from $1,000 to $2,000.
Duration 1 year.
Number awarded Varies each year.
Deadline March of each year.

[616]
KENTUCKY LIBRARY ASSOCIATION SCHOLARSHIP FOR MINORITY STUDENTS

Kentucky Library Association
c/o Executive Secretary
1501 Twilight Trail
Frankfort, KY 40601
(502) 223-5322   Fax: (502) 223-4937
E-mail: info@kylibasn.org
Web: www.klaonline.org/scholarships965.cfm

Summary To provide financial assistance to Asian Americans and other minorities who are residents of Kentucky or attending school there and are working on an undergraduate or graduate degree in library science.

Eligibility This program is open to members of minority groups (defined as American Indian, Alaskan Native, Black, Hispanic, Pacific Islander, or other ethnic group) who are entering or continuing at a graduate library school accredited by the American Library Association (ALA) or an undergraduate library program accredited by the National Council for Teacher Education (NCATE). Applicants must be residents of Kentucky or a student in a library program in the state. Along with their application, they must submit a statement of their career objectives, why they have chosen librarianship as a career, and their reasons for applying for this scholarship. Selection is based on that statement, cumulative undergraduate and graduate GPA (if applicable), academic merit and potential, and letters of recommendation. U.S. citizenship or permanent resident status is required.

Financial data The stipend is $1,000.
Duration 1 year; nonrenewable.
Number awarded 1 or more each year.
Deadline June of each year.

[617]
KENTUCKY MINORITY EDUCATOR RECRUITMENT AND RETENTION SCHOLARSHIPS

Kentucky Department of Education
Attn: Minority Educator Recruitment and Retention
500 Mero Street, 8th Floor
Frankfort, KY 40601
(502) 564-1479, ext. 4014   Fax: (502) 564-6952
TDD: (502) 564-4970
E-mail: monica.davis@education.ky.gov
Web: www.education.ky.gov

Summary To provide funding to Asian American and other minority undergraduate and graduate students enrolled in Kentucky public institutions who want to become teachers.

Eligibility This program is open to residents of Kentucky who are undergraduate or graduate students pursuing initial teacher certification at a public university or community college in the state. Applicants must have a GPA of 2.5 or higher and either maintain full-time enrollment or be a part-time student within 18 semester hours of receiving a teacher education degree. They must be U.S. citizens and meet the Kentucky definition of a minority student.

Financial data Stipends are $5,000 per year at the 8 state universities in Kentucky or $2,000 per year at community and technical colleges. This is a scholarship/loan program. Recipients are required to teach 1 semester in Kentucky for each semester or summer term the scholarship is received. If they fail to fulfill that requirement, the scholarship converts to a loan with severe penalties for non-payment.

Duration 1 year; may be renewed up to 3 additional years.

Additional information The Kentucky General Assembly established this program in 1992.

Number awarded Varies each year.

Deadline Each state college of teacher education sets its own deadline.

[618]
KING & SPALDING DIVERSITY FELLOWSHIP PROGRAM

King & Spalding
Attn: Diversity Fellowship Program
1180 Peachtree Street
Atlanta, GA 30309
(404) 572-4643   Fax: (404) 572-5100
E-mail: fellowship@kslaw.com
Web: www.kslaw.com/careers/Law-Students

Summary To provide financial aid and summer work experience at U.S. offices of King & Spalding to Asian American and other law students who will contribute to the diversity of the legal community.

Eligibility This program is open to second-year law students who 1) come from a minority ethnic or racial group (American Indian/Alaskan Native, Asian American/Pacific Islander, Black/African American, Hispanic, or multi-racial); 2) are a member of the gay, lesbian, bisexual, or transgender (GLBT) community; or 3) have a disability. Applicants must receive an offer of a clerkship at a U.S. office of King & Spalding during their second-year summer. Along with their application, they must submit a 500-word personal statement that describes their talents, qualities, and experiences and how they would contribute to the diversity of the firm.

Financial data Fellows receive a stipend of $10,000 for their second year of law school and a paid summer associate clerkship at a U.S. office of the firm during the following summer.

Duration 1 year.

Additional information The firm's U.S. offices are located in Atlanta, Austin, Charlotte, Houston, New York, San Francisco, Silicon Valley, and Washington.

Number awarded Up to 4 each year.

Deadline August of each year.

[619]
KIRKLAND & ELLIS LLP DIVERSITY FELLOWSHIP PROGRAM

Kirkland & Ellis LLP
Attn: Attorney Recruiting Manager
333 South Hope Street
Los Angeles, CA 90071
(213) 680-8436   Fax: (213) 680-8500
E-mail: cherie.beffa@kirkland.com
Web: www.kirkland.com

Summary To provide financial assistance and summer work experience at an office of Kirkland & Ellis to Asian American and other minority law students from any state.

Eligibility This program is open to second-year students at ABA-accredited law schools who meet the racial and ethnic categories established by the Equal Employment Opportunity Commission. Applicants must have been accepted as summer associates at a domestic office of the sponsoring law firm (Chicago, Los Angeles, New York, Palo Alto, San Francisco, Washington, D.C.) and be likely to practice at 1 of those offices after graduation. Along with their application, they must submit a 1-page personal statement that describes ways in which they have promoted and will continue to promote diversity in the legal community, along with their interest in the firm. Selection is based on merit.

Financial data Fellows receive a salary during their summer associateship and a $25,000 stipend at the conclusion of the summer. Stipend funds are to be used for payment of educational expenses during the third year of law school.

Duration 1 year.

Additional information This program, which replaced the Kirkland & Ellis Minority Fellowship Program, was established at 14 law schools in 2004. In 2006, it began accepting applications from students at all ABA-accredited law schools.

Number awarded Varies each year; recently, 10 of these fellowships were awarded. Since the program began, it has awarded 121 fellowships worth more than $1.9 million.

Deadline August of each year.

[620]
KOREAN AMERICAN BAR ASSOCIATION OF WASHINGTON SCHOLARSHIP

Korean American Bar Association of Washington
c/o David Ko
Keller Rohrback L.L.P.
1201 Third Avenue, Suite 3200
Seattle, WA 98101
(206) 428-0562   Fax: (206) 623-3384
E-mail: kaba@kaba-washington.org
Web: kaba-washington.org/for-students

Summary To provide financial assistance to students from any state who are enrolled at law schools in Washington and have a record of service to the Korean community.

Eligibility This program is open to residents of any state currently enrolled at law schools in Washington. Applicants are not required to be of Korean ancestry, but they must have a demonstrated significant commitment to community service, particularly service to the Korean or Korean American community. Along with their application, they must submit a 2-page essay on what they see as a challenge facing the Korean American community and what they feel they can do to help overcome that challenge as an attorney. Selection is based on the essay, academic achievement, work experience, activities, post-law school goals, and service to the Korean or Korean American community.

Financial data The stipend is $4,000.

Duration 1 year.

Number awarded 1 each year.

Deadline January of each year.

[621]
KOREAN AMERICAN CHRISTIAN SCHOLARSHIP FOUNDATION OF GREATER WASHINGTON SCHOLARSHIPS

Korean American Christian Scholarship Foundation of
  Greater Washington
7024 Highland Meadows Court
Alexandria, VA 22315
E-mail: sangkuenpark@gmail.com
Web: www.kapastorscholarship.org/?page_id=2

Summary To provide financial assistance to theology students who plan to become pastors serving Korean Americans.

Eligibility This program is open to Christian students who are entering or attending an approved theological seminary. Applicants must have a clear purpose to serve the second and third generations of Korean Americans. They must be U.S. citizens or permanent residents living in any state. Along with their application, they must submit a letter of recommendation (in Korean or English) from their senior pastor, transcripts, a testimony of faith, and information on their financial status.

Financial data A stipend is awarded (amount not specified).

Duration 1 year.

Number awarded 10 to 12 each year.

Deadline Deadline not specified.

[622]
KOREAN AMERICAN LIBRARIANS AND INFORMATION PROFESSIONALS ASSOCIATION SCHOLARSHIP

Korean American Librarians and Information
  Professionals Association
c/o Heawon Paick, Scholarship Committee Chair
Los Angeles Public Library
Junipero Serra Branch
4607 South Main Street
Los Angeles, CA 90037
(323) 846-5382   Fax: (323) 846-5389
E-mail: hpaick@lapl.org
Web: kalipa.apanet.org/?q=node/6

Summary To provide funding to students of Korean descent who are interested in working on a graduate degree in library science.

Eligibility This program is open to students of Korean heritage who are enrolled in an ALA-accredited school of library and information science. Applicants must be working on a master's or doctoral degree. Along with their application, they must submit a 1-page essay on the contributions they can make as a Korean American librarian to the profession and

the community. U.S. citizenship or permanent resident status is required.

Financial data The stipend is $500.

Duration 1 year.

Number awarded 2 each year.

Deadline March of each year.

[623]
KOREAN AMERICAN MEDICAL ASSOCIATION SCHOLARSHIPS

Korean American Medical Association
Attn: Executive Director
200 Sylvan Avenue, Number 22
Englewood Cliffs, NJ 07632
(201) 567-1434   Fax: (201) 567-1753
E-mail: info@kamaus.org
Web: www.kamaus.org/info/index.php/medical-students

Summary To provide financial assistance to members of the Korean American Medical Students Association (KAMSA) who are attending medical school in Korea or the United States.

Eligibility This program is open to first-, second-, and third-year students at medical schools in Korea or the United States. Applicants must be members of KAMSA. Along with their application, they must submit transcripts, 2 letters of recommendation, and a 5-page essay on why they are applying for this scholarship and what is unique about them.

Financial data The stipend is $1,000.

Duration 1 year.

Additional information This program began in 1993.

Number awarded Varies each year; recently, 7 of these scholarships were awarded.

Deadline May of each year.

[624]
KOREAN HONOR SCHOLARSHIP

Embassy of the Republic of Korea in the USA
2320 Massachusetts Avenue, N.W.
Washington, DC 20008
(202) 939-5679   Fax: (202) 342-1597
Web: usa.mofa.go.kr

Summary To provide financial assistance to undergraduate and graduate students of Korean or Korean American heritage.

Eligibility This program is open to students of Korean or Korean American heritage. Applicants must be entering or enrolled full time in an undergraduate or graduate degree program at a college or university in the United States or Canada. They must have a GPA of 3.5 or higher. Along with their application, they must submit a 600-word essay (in English) on a topic that changes annually but relates to their Korean heritage. Selection is based on that essay, academic achievement, awards, honors, performances, extracurricular activities, and a letter of recommendation.

Financial data The stipend is $1,000.

Duration 1 year; nonrenewable.

Additional information This program began in 1981 when the government of the Republic of Korea donated $1 million to commemorate the 100th anniversary of the establishment of diplomatic relations between Korea and the United States. Subsequent donations have added to the fund.

Number awarded Approximately 65 each year. Since the program was established, it has awarded nearly 2,800 scholarships.

Deadline June of each year.

[625]
KOREAN NURSES ASSOCIATION OF SOUTHERN CALIFORNIA REGISTERED NURSE EDUCATION SCHOLARSHIPS

Korean Nurses Association of Southern California
936 South Crenshaw Boulevard, Suite 204
Los Angeles, CA 90019
(323) 934-7073

Summary To provide financial assistance to Korean nurses in California who wish to attend college in the state to work on a bachelor's or graduate degree.

Eligibility This program is open to Korean registered nurses who are living in California and enrolled or entering a baccalaureate or higher degree nursing program in the state. Applicants must be legal residents of the United States. Along with their application, they must submit a 1-page essay on their reasons for selecting nursing as a career, including their professional goals and objectives. Selection is based on that essay, work experience in nursing and related fields, community service and volunteer work experience, cumulative GPA, and letters of recommendation. Priority consideration is given to members of the Korean Nurses Association of Southern California and their immediate family members.

Financial data A stipend is awarded (amount not specified).

Duration 1 year; may be renewed 1 additional year.

Number awarded 1 or more each year.

Deadline January of each year.

[626]
KOREAN TOXICOLOGISTS ASSOCIATION IN AMERICA BEST PRESENTATIONS BY GRADUATE STUDENT AND POSTDOCTORAL TRAINEE AWARD

Society of Toxicology
Attn: Korean Toxicologists Association in America Special
    Interest Group
1821 Michael Faraday Drive, Suite 300
Reston, VA 20190-5348
(703) 438-3115   Fax: (703) 438-3113
E-mail: sothq@toxicology.org
Web: www.toxicology.org/ai/af/awards.aspx

Summary To recognize and reward graduate students and postdoctoral trainees who present outstanding papers at a session of the Korean Toxicologists Association in America (KTAA) at the annual meeting of the Society of Toxicology (SOT).

Eligibility This award is available to graduate students and postdoctoral trainees who have an accepted abstract of a research poster or platform presentation for a KTAA session at the SOT annual meeting. Along with the abstract, they must submit a letter of nomination from their major adviser.

Financial data A plaque and a cash award (amount not specified) are presented.

Duration The awards are presented annually.

Additional information These awards are presented jointly by KTAA and the Korean Institute of Toxicology (KIT).

Number awarded 2 each year.

Deadline January of each year.

[627]
KOREAN-AMERICAN ADVENTIST SCHOLARSHIP FOUNDATION

Korean-American Adventist Scholarships
c/o Korean Adventist Press
619 South New Hampshire Avenue
Los Angeles, CA 90005
(213) 388-6100   E-mail: sdascholarship@gmail.com
Web: www.sdascholarship.org/?page_id=9

Summary To provide financial assistance to Korean American Adventists who are interested in working on an undergraduate or graduate degree in any field.

Eligibility This program is open to Korean American Adventists who are high school seniors or students currently enrolled in college or graduate school. Applicants must have a GPA of 3.0 or higher. Along with their application, they must submit a 1- to 2-page personal essay that describes their personal history, life passions, long-term goals, and financial situation. Their pastor must provide an evaluation of their spiritual dedication, motivation, citizenship, church activities, academic achievement, and financial need.

Financial data The stipend is $1,000.

Duration 1 year.

Additional information This program began in 2004.

Number awarded 20 each year.

Deadline June of each year.

[628]
KUSCO-KSEA SCHOLARSHIPS FOR GRADUATE STUDENTS

Korean-American Scientists and Engineers Association
Attn: Scholarship Committee
1952 Gallows Drive, Suite 300
Vienna, VA 22182
(703) 748-1221   Fax: (703) 748-1331
E-mail: admin@ksea.org
Web: scholarship.ksea.org/InfoGraduate.aspx

Summary To provide financial assistance to graduate student members of the Korean-American Scientists and Engineers Association (KSEA) studying Korea-U.S. science and technology cooperation.

Eligibility This program is open to graduate students at colleges and universities in the United States who are either 1) of Korean heritage; or 2) non-ethnic Korean students working on a degree related to Korea-U.S. science and technology cooperation. Applicants must be KSEA members working on a degree in science, engineering, or a related field. Along with their application, they must submit an essay on a topic that changes annually but relates to cooperation in science. Selection is based on that essay (20%), KSEA activities and community service (30%), recommendation letters (20%), and academic performance (30%).

Financial data The stipend is $2,000.

Duration 1 year.

Additional information This program, established in 2005, is supported by the Korea-US Science Cooperation Center (KUSCO).

Number awarded Approximately 20 each year.

Deadline March of each year.

[629]
LAGRANT FOUNDATION GRADUATE SCHOLARSHIPS

Lagrant Foundation
Attn: Senior Programs and Outreach Manager
600 Wilshire Boulevard, Suite 1520
Los Angeles, CA 90017
(323) 469-8680, ext. 223   Fax: (323) 469-8683
E-mail: erickainiguez@lagrant.com
Web: www.lagrantfoundation.org

Summary To provide financial assistance to Asian American and other minority graduate students who are working on a degree in advertising, public relations, or marketing.

Eligibility This program is open to African Americans, Asian American/Pacific Islanders, Hispanics/Latinos, and Native Americans/American Indians who are full-time graduate students at an accredited institution. Applicants must have a GPA of 3.2 or higher and be working on a master's degree in advertising, marketing, or public relations. They must have at least 2 academic semesters remaining to complete their degree. Along with their application, they must submit 1) a 1- to 2-page essay outlining their career goals; why it is important to increase ethnic representation in the fields of advertising, marketing, and public relations; and the role of an advertising, marketing, or public relations practitioner; 2) a paragraph describing the graduate school and/or community activities in which they are involved; 3) a brief paragraph describing any honors and awards they have received; 4) a letter of reference; 5) a resume; and 6) an official transcript. U.S. citizenship or permanent resident status is required.

Financial data The stipend is $10,000 per year.

Duration 1 year.

Number awarded Varies each year; recently, 7 of these scholarships were awarded.

Deadline February of each year.

[630]
LATHAM & WATKINS DIVERSITY SCHOLARS PROGRAM

Latham & Watkins LLP
Attn: Diversity Committee Co-Chair
885 Third Avenue
New York, NY 10022-4834
(212) 906-1332   Fax: (212) 751-4864
E-mail: sharon.bowen@lw.com
Web: www.lw.com/AboutUs/Diversity

Summary To provide financial assistance to Asian American and other minority law students interested in working for a global law firm.

Eligibility Applicants must be second-year law students at an ABA-accredited law school and plan to practice law in a major city in the United States. Students who have received a similar scholarship from another sponsor are not eligible to apply. Applicants must submit a 500-word personal statement that describes their ability to contribute to the diversity objec-

tives of global law firms; the life experiences that have shaped their values and that provide them with a unique perspective, including any obstacles or challenges they have overcome; their academic and/or leadership achievements; and their intent to practice in a global law firm environment.

Financial data The stipend is $10,000.

Duration 1 year; nonrenewable.

Additional information This program began in 2005. Recipients are not required to work for Latham & Watkins after graduation.

Number awarded 6 each year.

Deadline September of each year.

[631]
LAURENCE R. FOSTER MEMORIAL SCHOLARSHIPS

Oregon Student Access Commission
Attn: Grants and Scholarships Division
1500 Valley River Drive, Suite 100
Eugene, OR 97401-2146
(541) 687-7395   Toll Free: (800) 452-8807, ext. 7395
Fax: (541) 687-7414   TDD: (800) 735-2900
E-mail: awardinfo@osac.state.or.us
Web: www.oregonstudentaid.gov/scholarships.aspx

Summary To provide financial assistance to Asian Americans and other residents of Oregon who come from a diverse environment and are enrolled at a college or graduate school in any state to prepare for a public health career.

Eligibility This program is open to residents of Oregon who are enrolled at least half time at a 4-year college or university in any state to prepare for a career in public health (not private practice). Preference is given first to applicants from diverse environments; second to persons employed in, or graduate students working on a degree in, public health; and third to juniors and seniors majoring in a health program (e.g., nursing, medical technology, physician assistant). Applicants must be able to demonstrate financial need. Along with their application, they must submit essays of 250 to 350 words on 1) what public health means to them; 2) the public health aspect they intend to practice and the health and population issues impacted by that aspect; and 3) their experience living or working in diverse environments.

Financial data Stipends for scholarships offered by the Oregon Student Access Commission (OSAC) range from $200 to $10,000 but recently averaged $2,300.

Duration 1 year.

Additional information This program is administered by the OSAC with funds provided by the Oregon Community Foundation.

Number awarded Varies each year; recently, 6 of these scholarships were awarded.

Deadline February of each year.

[632]
LAW SCHOLARSHIPS OF THE JAPANESE AMERICAN CITIZENS LEAGUE

Japanese American Citizens League
Attn: National Scholarship Awards
1765 Sutter Street
San Francisco, CA 94115
(415) 345-1075   Fax: (415) 931-4671
E-mail: ncwnp@jacl.org
Web: www.jacl.org/edu/scholar.htm

Summary   To provide financial assistance to student members of the Japanese American Citizens League (JACL) who are interested in preparing for a career in law.

Eligibility   This program is open to JACL members who are currently enrolled or planning to enroll at an accredited law school. Applicants must submit information on their involvement in JACL and a 2-page essay on a topic that changes annually but relates to Japanese Americans. Selection is based on that essay, academic history, JACL involvement, school activities, work history, scholastic honors, and community involvement.

Financial data   Stipends generally average more than $2,000.

Duration   1 year; nonrenewable.

Additional information   This program consists of the following named awards: the Grace Andow Memorial Scholarship, the Mary Reiko Osaka Memorial Scholarship, the Sho Sato Memorial Scholarship, and the Thomas T. Hayashi Memorial Scholarship.

Number awarded   4 each year.

Deadline   March of each year.

[633]
LEADERSHIP FOR DIVERSITY SCHOLARSHIP

California School Library Association
Attn: CSL Foundation
6444 East Spring Street, Number 237
Long Beach, CA 90815-1553
Toll Free: (888) 655-8480   Fax: (888) 655-8480
E-mail: info@csla.net
Web: www.csla.net

Summary   To provide financial assistance to Asian American and other students who reflect the diversity of California's population and are interested in earning a credential as a library media teacher in the state.

Eligibility   This program is open to students who are members of a traditionally underrepresented group enrolled in a college or university library media teacher credential program in California. Applicants must intend to work as a library media teacher in a California school library media center for a minimum of 3 years. Along with their application, they must submit a 250-word statement on their school library media career interests and goals, why they should be considered, what they can contribute, their commitment to serving the needs of multicultural and multilingual students, and their financial situation.

Financial data   The stipend is $1,500.

Duration   1 year.

Number awarded   1 each year.

Deadline   May of each year.

[634]
LEADERSHIP LEGACY SCHOLARSHIP FOR GRADUATES

Women's Transportation Seminar
Attn: WTS Foundation
1701 K Street, N.W., Suite 800
Washington, DC 20006
(202) 955-5085   Fax: (202) 955-5088
E-mail: wts@wtsinternational.org
Web: www.wtsinternational.org/education/scholarships

Summary   To provide financial assistance to graduate women (particularly Asian Americans and other minorities) who are interested in a career in transportation.

Eligibility   This program is open to women who are working on a graduate degree in transportation or a transportation-related field (e.g., transportation engineering, planning, business management, finance, or logistics). Applicants must have a GPA of 3.0 or higher and be interested in a career in transportation. Along with their application, they must submit a 1,000-word statement about their vision of how their education will give them the tools to better serve their community's needs and transportation issues. Applications must be submitted first to a local chapter; the chapters forward selected applications for consideration on the national level. Minority women are especially encouraged to apply. Selection is based on transportation involvement and goals, job skills, and academic record; financial need is not considered.

Financial data   The stipend is $5,000.

Duration   1 year.

Additional information   This program began in 2008. Each year, it focuses on women with a special interest; recently, it was reserved for women who have a specific interest in addressing the impact of transportation on sustainability, land use, environmental impact, security, and quality of life issues internationally.

Number awarded   1 each year.

Deadline   Applications must be submitted by November to a local WTS chapter.

[635]
LIBRARY AND INFORMATION TECHNOLOGY ASSOCIATION MINORITY SCHOLARSHIPS

American Library Association
Attn: Library and Information Technology Association
50 East Huron Street
Chicago, IL 60611-2795
(312) 280-4270   Toll Free: (800) 545-2433, ext. 4270
Fax: (312) 280-3257   TDD: (888) 814-7692
E-mail: lita@ala.org
Web: www.ala.org/lita/awards

Summary   To provide financial assistance to Asian American and other minority graduate students interested in preparing for a career in library automation.

Eligibility   This program is open to U.S. or Canadian citizens who are interested in working on a master's degree in library/information science and preparing for a career in the field of library and automated systems. Applicants must be a member of 1 of the following ethnic groups: American Indian, Alaskan Native, Asian, Pacific Islander, African American, or Hispanic. They may not have completed more than 12 credit hours of course work for their degree. Selection is based on academic excellence, leadership potential, evidence of a commitment to a career in library automation and information technology, and prior activity and experience in those fields. Financial need is considered when all other factors are equal.

Financial data Stipends are $3,000 or $2,500. Funds are paid directly to the recipient.

Duration 1 year.

Additional information This program includes scholarships funded by Online Computer Library Center (OCLC) and by Library Systems & Services, Inc. (LSSI).

Number awarded 2 each year: 1 at $3,000 (funded by OCLC) and 1 at $2,500 (funded by LSSI).

Deadline February of each year.

[636]
LIONEL C. BARROW MINORITY DOCTORAL STUDENT SCHOLARSHIP

Association for Education in Journalism and Mass Communication
Attn: Communication Theory and Methodology Division
234 Outlet Pointe Boulevard, Suite A
Columbia, SC 29210-5667
(803) 798-0271   Fax: (803) 772-3509
E-mail: aejmc@aejmc.org
Web: aejmc.net

Summary To provide financial assistance to Asian Americans and other minorities who are interested in working on a doctorate in mass communication.

Eligibility This program is open to minority students enrolled in a Ph.D. program in journalism and/or mass communication. Applicants must submit 2 letters of recommendation, a resume, and a brief letter outlining their research interests and career plans. Membership in the association is not required, but applicants must be U.S. citizens or permanent residents. Selection is based on the likelihood that the applicant's work will contribute to communication theory and/or methodology.

Financial data The stipend is $1,400.

Duration 1 year.

Additional information This program began in 1972.

Number awarded 1 each year.

Deadline May of each year.

[637]
LIZETTE PETERSON-HOMER INJURY PREVENTION RESEARCH GRANT

American Psychological Foundation
750 First Street, N.E.
Washington, DC 20002-4242
(202) 336-5843   Fax: (202) 336-5812
E-mail: foundation@apa.org
Web: www.apa.org/apf/funding/peterson-homer.aspx

Summary To provide funding to graduate students and faculty (particularly Asian Americans, other minorities, women, and individuals with disabilities) who are interested in conducting research related to the prevention of injuries in children.

Eligibility This program is open to graduate students and faculty interested in conducting research that focuses on the prevention of physical injury in children and young adults through accidents, violence, abuse, or suicide. Applicants

must submit a 100-word abstract, description of the project, detailed budget, curriculum vitae, and letter from the supporting faculty supervisor (if the applicant is a student). Selection is based on conformance with stated program goals, magnitude of incremental contribution, quality of proposed work, and applicant's demonstrated scholarship and research competence. The sponsor encourages applications from individuals who represent diversity in race, ethnicity, gender, age, disability, and sexual orientation.

Financial data Grants up to $5,000 are available.

Additional information This program began in 1999 as the Rebecca Routh Coon Injury Research Award. The current name was adopted in 2003. It is supported by Division 54 (Society of Pediatric Psychology) of the American Psychological Association and the American Psychological Foundation.

Number awarded 1 each year.

Deadline September of each year.

[638]
LLOYD M. JOHNSON, JR. SCHOLARSHIP PROGRAM

United Negro College Fund
Attn: Scholarships and Grants Department
8260 Willow Oaks Corporate Drive
P.O. Box 10444
Fairfax, VA 22031-8044
(703) 205-3466   Toll Free: (800) 331-2244
Fax: (703) 205-3574
Web: www.uncf.org

Summary To provide financial assistance to Asian Americans and other law students from disadvantaged backgrounds who are interested in corporate law and will contribute to diversity in the legal profession.

Eligibility Applicants must be U.S. citizens, have a strong academic record (an undergraduate GPA of 3.2 or higher), have been accepted to an ABA-accredited law school, be able to demonstrate community service and leadership qualities, have an interest in diversity, be financially disadvantaged, plan to study on a full-time basis, and have an interest in corporate law, including working in a corporate law department and/or law firm. Applicants must submit a current transcript, a resume, 2 letters of recommendation, a personal statement, and a diversity essay. All students are eligible, but the sponsor expects that most recipients will contribute to diversity in the legal profession.

Financial data The stipend is $10,000 for the first year and varying amounts for subsequent years.

Duration 1 year; may be renewed up to 2 additional years.

Additional information The Minority Corporate Counsel Association first began this program in 2005 and now cosponsors it with the United Negro College Fund. Mentoring and internship experiences are also offered to the winners.

Number awarded Approximately 10 each year.

Deadline May of each year.

[639]
LTK SCHOLARSHIP

Conference of Minority Transportation Officials
Attn: National Scholarship Program
1875 I Street, N.W., Suite 500
Washington, DC 20006
(703) 234-4072   Fax: (202) 318-0364
Web: www.comto.org/?page=Scholarships

Summary To provide financial assistance to Asian American and other minority upper-division and graduate students in engineering or other fields related to transportation.

Eligibility This program is open to full-time minority juniors, seniors, and graduate students in engineering of other technical transportation-related disciplines. Applicants must have a GPA of 3.0 or higher. Along with their application, they must submit a cover letter with a 500-word statement of career goals. Financial need is not considered in the selection process. U.S. citizenship or legal resident status is required.

Financial data The stipend is $6,000. Funds are paid directly to the recipient's college or university.

Duration 1 year.

Additional information The Conference of Minority Transportation Officials (COMTO) was established in 1971 to promote, strengthen, and expand the roles of minorities in all aspects of transportation. This program is sponsored by LTK Engineering Services. Recipients are required to become members of COMTO if they are not already members and attend the COMTO National Scholarship Luncheon.

Number awarded 1 or more each year.

Deadline May of each year.

[640]
MAGOICHI AND SHIZUKO KATO MEMORIAL SCHOLARSHIP

Japanese American Citizens League
Attn: National Scholarship Awards
1765 Sutter Street
San Francisco, CA 94115
(415) 345-1075   Fax: (415) 931-4671
E-mail: ncwnp@jacl.org
Web: www.jacl.org/edu/scholar.htm

Summary To provide financial assistance for graduate study, especially in medicine or the ministry, to members of the Japanese American Citizens League (JACL).

Eligibility This program is open to JACL members who are attending or planning to attend an accredited college or university as a graduate student. Applicants must submit information on their involvement in JACL and a 2-page essay on a topic that changes annually but relates to Japanese Americans. Selection is based on that essay, academic history, JACL involvement, school activities, work history, scholastic honors, and community involvement. Preference is given to applicants planning a career in medicine or the ministry.

Financial data Stipends generally average more than $2,000.

Duration 1 year; nonrenewable.

Number awarded 1 each year.

Deadline March of each year.

[641]
MARATHON OIL CORPORATION COLLEGE SCHOLARSHIP PROGRAM OF THE HISPANIC SCHOLARSHIP FUND

Hispanic Scholarship Fund
Attn: Selection Committee
1411 West 190th Street, Suite 325
Gardena, CA 90248
Toll Free: (877) HSF-INFO   E-mail: scholar1@hsf.net
Web: www.hsf.net

Summary To provide financial assistance to Asian American and other minority upper-division and graduate students working on a degree in a field related to the oil and gas industry.

Eligibility This program is open to U.S. citizens and permanent residents (must have a permanent resident card or a passport stamped I-551) who are of Hispanic American, African American, Asian Pacific Islander American, or American Indian/Alaskan Native heritage. Applicants must be currently enrolled full time at an accredited 4-year college or university in the United States, Puerto Rico, Guam, or the U.S. Virgin Islands with a GPA of 3.0 or higher. They must be 1) sophomores majoring in accounting, chemical engineering, computer engineering, computer science, electrical engineering, environmental engineering, geology, geosciences, information technology/management information systems, mechanical engineering, or petroleum engineering; or 2) seniors planning to work on a master's degree in geology, geosciences, or petroleum engineering. Selection is based on academic achievement, personal strengths, interest and commitment to a career in the oil and gas industry, leadership, and financial need.

Financial data The stipend is $15,000 per year.

Duration 2 years (the junior and senior undergraduate years or the first 2 years of a master's degree program).

Additional information This program is jointly sponsored by Marathon Oil Corporation and the Hispanic Scholarship Fund (HSF). Recipients may be offered a paid 8- to 10-week summer internship at various Marathon Oil Corporation locations.

Number awarded 1 or more each year.

Deadline September of each year.

[642]
MARJORIE BOWENS-WHEATLEY SCHOLARSHIPS

Unitarian Universalist Association
Attn: UU Women's Federation
25 Beacon Street
Boston, MA 02108-2800
(617) 948-4692   Fax: (617) 742-2402
E-mail: uuwf@uua.org
Web: www.uuwf.org

Summary To provide financial assistance to Asian American and other women of color who are working on an undergraduate or graduate degree to prepare for Unitarian Universalist ministry or service.

Eligibility This program is open to women of color who are either 1) aspirants or candidates for the Unitarian Universalist ministry; or 2) candidates in the Unitarian Universalist Association's professional religious education or music leadership credentialing programs. Applicants must submit a 1- to 2-page narrative that covers their call to UU ministry, religious education, or music leadership; their passions; how their racial/ethnic/cultural background influences their goals for their calling; and how the work of the program's namesake relates to their dreams and plans for their UU service.

Financial data Stipends from $1,500 to $2,000.

Duration 1 year.

Additional information This program began in 2009.

Number awarded Varies each year; recently, 4 of these scholarships were awarded.

Deadline March of each year.

[643]
MARK T. BANNER SCHOLARSHIP FOR LAW STUDENTS

Richard Linn American Inn of Court
c/o Matthew Walch, Scholarship Chair
Latham & Watkins LLP
233 South Wacker Drive, Suite 5800
Chicago, IL 60606
(312) 876-7603   E-mail: matthew.walch@lw.com
Web: www.linninn.org/marktbanner.htm

Summary To provide financial assistance to Asian American and other law students who are members of historically underrepresented groups and interested in specializing in intellectual property law.

Eligibility This program is open to students at ABA-accredited law schools in the United States who are members of groups historically underrepresented (by race, sex, ethnicity, sexual orientation, or disability) in intellectual property law. Applicants must submit a 3-page statement on how they have focused on ethics, civility, and professionalism have been their focus; how diversity has impacted them; and their commitment to a career in intellectual property law.

Financial data The stipend is $5,000.

Duration 1 year.

Number awarded 1 each year.

Deadline November of each year.

[644]
MARRIAGE AND FAMILY THERAPY MASTER'S STUDENT MINORITY SCHOLARSHIP

American Association for Marriage and Family Therapy
Attn: AAMFT Research and Education Foundation
112 South Alfred Street
Alexandria, VA 22314-3061
(703) 838-9808   Fax: (703) 838-9805
Web: www.aamft.org

Summary To provide financial assistance to Asian American and other minority students enrolled in master's and post-degree training programs in marriage and family therapy.

Eligibility This program is open to minority students (including African Americans, Hispanics, Native Americans, Asian Americans, and Pacific Islanders) enrolled in master's degree programs or post-degree institutes that provide training in marriage and family therapy. Applicants must be members of the American Association for Marriage and Family Therapy (AAMFT). They must be citizens or permanent residents of the United States or Canada and show promise in and commitment to a career in marital and family therapy

education, research, or practice. Along with their application, they must submit a personal statement explaining how their racial or ethnic background has had an impact on them and their career decision; the statement should include their professional interests, goals, and commitment to the field of marriage and family therapy.

Financial data The stipend is $2,000. Awardees also receive a plaque and funding up to $750 to attend the association's annual conference.

Duration 1 year.

Additional information This program began in 1986.

Number awarded Up to 3 each year.

Deadline January of each year.

[645]
MARTHA AND ROBERT ATHERTON MINISTERIAL SCHOLARSHIP

Unitarian Universalist Association
Attn: Ministerial Credentialing Office
25 Beacon Street
Boston, MA 02108-2800
(617) 948-6403   Fax: (617) 742-2875
E-mail: mcoadministrator@uua.org
Web: www.uua.org

Summary To provide financial assistance minority and other seminary students preparing for the Unitarian Universalist (UU) ministry.

Eligibility This program is open to second- or third-year seminary students currently enrolled full or at least half time in a UU ministerial training program with aspirant or candidate status. Applicants must respect hard work as a foundation of a full life and appreciate the freedom, political system, and philosophical underpinnings of our country. They should be citizens of the United States or Canada. Priority is given first to those who have demonstrated outstanding ministerial ability and secondarily to students with the greatest financial need (especially persons of color).

Financial data The stipend ranges from $1,000 to $15,000 per year.

Duration 1 year.

Additional information This program began in 1997.

Number awarded 1 or 2 each year.

Deadline April of each year.

[646]
MCANDREWS DIVERSITY IN PATENT LAW FELLOWSHIP

McAndrews, Held & Malloy, Ltd.
Attn: Diversity Fellowship
500 West Madison Street, Suite 3400
Chicago, IL 60661
(312) 775-8000   Fax: (312) 775-8100
E-mail: info@mcandrews-ip.com
Web: www.mcandrews-ip.com/diversity_fellowship.html

Summary To provide financial aid and work experience to Asian American and other law students who come from a diverse background and are interested in patent law.

Eligibility This program is open to first-year students at ABA-accredited law schools who come from a diverse background. Applicants must have a degree in science or engineering and be planning to practice patent law in the Chicago area. Along with their application, they must submit a 500-word personal statement on why they wish to prepare for a career in patent law, why they are interested in the sponsoring firm as a place to work, and how their background and/or life experiences would improve diversity in the field of intellectual property law. Selection is based on that statement, a resume (including their science or engineering educational credentials), a legal writing sample, undergraduate transcript, and at least 1 letter of recommendation.

Financial data The stipend is $5,000.

Duration 1 year (the second year of law school).

Additional information This fellowship was first awarded in 2008. It includes a paid clerkship position at McAndrews, Held & Malloy during the summer after the first year of law school and possibly another clerkship during the summer after the second year.

Number awarded 1 each year.

Deadline January of each year.

[647]
MCDERMOTT MINORITY SCHOLARSHIP

McDermott Will & Emery
Attn: Recruiting Coordinator
227 West Monroe Street
Chicago, IL 60606
(312) 984-6470   Fax: (312) 984-7700
E-mail: mcdermottscholarship@mwe.com
Web: www.mwe.com

Summary To provide financial aid and work experience to Asian American and other minority law students.

Eligibility This program is open to second-year minority (African American, Asian, Hispanic, Middle Eastern, Native American, LGBT) law students at ABA-accredited U.S. law schools. Applicants must be able to demonstrate leadership, community involvement, and a commitment to improving diversity in the legal community. They must be interested in participating in the sponsor's summer program and be able to meet its hiring criteria. Along with their application, they must submit an essay of 1 to 2 pages that provides ideas they have on how the number of minority students in law schools can be increased and how they have improved and intend to help improve diversity in the legal profession throughout their law school and legal career.

Financial data The stipend is $15,000.

Duration 1 year.

Additional information Recipients also participate in a summer program at the sponsor's offices in Boston, Chicago, Houston, Los Angeles, Miami, New York, Orange County, San Diego, Silicon Valley, or Washington, D.C.

Number awarded 2 each year.

Deadline October of each year.

[648]
MEDICAL LIBRARY ASSOCIATION SCHOLARSHIP FOR MINORITY STUDENT

Medical Library Association
Attn: Grants and Scholarships
65 East Wacker Place, Suite 1900
Chicago, IL 60601-7246
(312) 419-9094, ext. 15   Fax: (312) 419-8950
E-mail: grants@mlahq.org
Web: www.mlanet.org/awards/grants

Summary To assist Asian American and other minority students interested in preparing for a career in medical librarianship.

Eligibility This program is open to racial minority students (Asians, Blacks or African Americans, Hispanics or Latinos, Aboriginals, North American Indians or Alaskan Natives, or Native Hawaiians or other Pacific Islanders) who are entering an ALA-accredited graduate program in librarianship or who have completed less than half of their academic requirements for a master's degree in library science. They must be interested in preparing for a career in medical librarianship. Selection is based on academic record, letters of reference, professional potential, and the applicant's statement of career objectives. U.S. or Canadian citizenship or permanent resident status is required.

Financial data The stipend is $5,000.

Duration 1 year.

Additional information This program began in 1973.

Number awarded 1 each year.

Deadline November of each year.

[649]
MENTAL HEALTH AND SUBSTANCE ABUSE FELLOWSHIP PROGRAM

Council on Social Work Education
Attn: Minority Fellowship Program
1701 Duke Street, Suite 200
Alexandria, VA 22314-3457
(703) 683-2050   Fax: (703) 683-8099
E-mail: cbrock@cswe.org
Web: www.cswe.org

Summary To provide financial assistance to Asian Americans and other minorities who are interested in preparing for a clinical career in the mental health fields.

Eligibility This program is open to U.S. citizens, noncitizen nationals, and permanent residents who have been underrepresented in the field of social work. These include but are not limited to the following groups: American Indians/Alaskan Natives, Asian/Pacific Islanders (e.g., Chinese, East Indians, South Asians, Filipinos, Hawaiians, Japanese, Koreans, and Samoans), Blacks, and Hispanics (e.g., Mexicans/Chicanos, Puerto Ricans, Cubans, Central or South Americans). Applicants must be interested in and committed to a career in mental health and/or substance abuse with specialization in the delivery of services of ethnic and racial minority groups. They must have a master's degree in social work and be accepted to or enrolled in a full-time doctoral degree program. Selection is based on potential for assuming leadership roles; potential for success in doctoral studies; and commitment to a career providing mental health and substance abuse services to ethnic, racial, social, and cultural minority individuals and communities.

Financial data Awards provide a stipend of $22,032 per year and tuition support to a maximum of $3,000.

Duration 1 academic year; renewable for 2 additional years if funds are available and the recipient makes satisfactory progress toward the degree objectives.

Additional information This program has been funded since 1978 by the Center for Mental Health Services (CMHS), the Center for Substance Abuse Prevention (CSAP), and the Center for Substance Abuse Treatment (CSAT) in the Substance Abuse and Mental Health Services Administration.

Number awarded Varies each year; recently, 9 new fellows and 16 returning fellows were appointed.

Deadline February of each year.

[650]
MICHIGAN STEERING COMMITTEE MINORITY SCHOLARSHIPS

Michigan Association of Certified Public Accountants
Attn: Michigan Accountancy Foundation
5480 Corporate Drive, Suite 200
Troy, MI 48098-2642
(248) 267-3723   Toll Free: (888) 877-4CPE (within MI)
Fax: (248) 267-3737   E-mail: macpa@michcpa.org
Web: www.michcpa.org/Content/22461.aspx

Summary To provide financial assistance to Asian American and other students at Michigan colleges and universities who are working on a degree in accounting.

Eligibility This program is open to members of minority groups enrolled full time at accredited Michigan colleges and universities with a declared concentration in accounting. Applicants must be seniors planning to enter the fifth or graduate year of their school's program. They must intend to or have successfully passed the Michigan C.P.A. examination and intend to practice public accounting in the state. Along with their application, they must submit a 500-word statement about their educational and career aspirations, including internships and/or other employment, volunteer and community activities, professional affiliations, and full-time employment. Documentation of financial need may also be included. U.S. citizenship or eligibility for permanent employment in the United States is required.

Financial data The stipend is $4,000; funds are disbursed directly to the recipient's college or university.

Duration 1 year.

Number awarded Varies each year; recently, 5 of these scholarships were awarded.

Deadline January of each year.

[651]
MID-AMERICA CHAPTER SCHOLARSHIPS

Phi Tau Phi Scholastic Honor Society-Mid-America
    Chapter
c/o Mann-Yi Hsieh, President
6951 Springside Avenue
Downers Grove, IL 60516
E-mail: mannyi.hsieh@gmail.com
Web: www.phitauphi.org

Summary To provide financial assistance to undergraduate and graduate students of Chinese heritage at colleges and universities in selected midwestern states.

Eligibility This program is open to undergraduate and graduate students enrolled at colleges and universities in Illinois, Indiana, Iowa, Kansas, Michigan, Minnesota, Ohio, Texas, and Wisconsin who have a GPA of 3.5 or higher. Applicants must be of Chinese descent or interested in and committed to Chinese heritage and culture. They must be entering their junior or senior year of undergraduate study or their second year or higher of graduate work. Along with their application, they must submit a 500-word essay on their professional goals and achievements.

Financial data The stipend is $1,000.

Duration 1 year.

Additional information Phi Tau Phi, first organized in 1921 in China and reestablished in 1964 in the United States, is a relatively small honor society of scholars, mainly of Chinese heritage, in various disciplines of science, technology, art, and the humanities.

Number awarded 4 each year: 2 for undergraduates and 2 for graduate students.

Deadline July of each year.

[652]
MIDEASTERN REGION KOREAN AMERICAN SCHOLARSHIPS

Korean American Scholarship Foundation
Mideastern Region
c/o Jong Dae Kim, Scholarship Committee Chair
24666 Northwestern Highway Service Drive
Southfield, MI 48075
(313) 963-3810, ext. 226   Fax: (313) 963-4680
E-mail: mideastern@kasf.org
Web: www.kasf.org/mideastern

Summary To provide financial assistance for study in Indiana, Michigan, or Ohio to Korean American students from any state who are working on an undergraduate or graduate degree in any field.

Eligibility This program is open to Korean American students who are currently enrolled in a college or university as full-time undergraduate or graduate students. Applicants may reside anywhere in the United States as long as they attend school in Indiana, Michigan, or Ohio. Selection is based on academic achievement, school activities, community service, and financial need.

Financial data Stipends range from $1,000 to $2,000.

Duration 1 year; renewable.

Number awarded Varies each year.

Deadline August of each year.

[653]
MIDWESTERN REGION KOREAN AMERICAN SCHOLARSHIPS

Korean American Scholarship Foundation
Midwestern Region
c/o Augie Lee, Scholarship Committee Chair
379 Hollow Hill Drive
Wauconda, IL 60010
(847) 721-9930   E-mail: kasfmwrc@yahoo.com
Web: www.kasf.org/midwestern

Summary To provide financial assistance to Korean American students from any state who are working on or planning to work on an undergraduate or graduate degree in any field at a school in the Midwest.

Eligibility This program is open to Korean American students who are currently enrolled or planning to enroll at a college or university in the midwestern states as full-time undergraduate or graduate students. Applicants may reside anywhere in the United States as long as they attend school in the midwestern region: Illinois, Iowa, Kansas, Minnesota, Missouri, Nebraska, North Dakota, South Dakota, and Wisconsin. They must have a GPA of 3.0 or higher. Both U.S. citizens and foreign nationals are eligible. Selection is based on academic achievement (25%), extracurricular activities (10%), an essay (10%), recommendations (10%), financial need (40%), and extra credit for having extraordinary circumstances (5%).

Financial data Stipends range from $1,000 to $2,000.

Duration 1 year; renewable.

Number awarded Varies each year; recently, 21 of these scholarships were awarded.

Deadline July of each year.

[654]
MILBANK DIVERSITY SCHOLARS PROGRAM

Milbank, Tweed, Hadley & McCloy LLP
Attn: Manager, Diversity and Inclusion
One Chase Manhattan Plaza
New York, NY 10005
(212) 530-5316   Fax: (212) 530-5219
E-mail: syohn@milbank.com
Web: www.milbank.com

Summary To provide financial aid and work experience to law students, especially those who are Asian Americans or members of other groups underrepresented at large law firms.

Eligibility This program is open to students who have completed their first year of a full-time J.D. program at an ABA-accredited law school. Joint degree candidates must have successfully completed 2 years of a J.D. program. Applications are particularly encouraged from members of groups traditionally underrepresented at large law firms. Applicants must submit a 500-word essay on 1) the challenges they have faced in pursuit of a legal career that have helped them understand the value of diversity and inclusion in the legal profession; and 2) the personal contributions they would make to furthering the diversity objectives of the sponsoring law firm. Selection is based on academic achievement, demonstrated leadership ability, writing and interpersonal skills, and interest in the firm's practice.

Financial data The stipend is $25,000. A paid associate position during the summer after the second year of law school is also provided. If the student is offered and accepts a permanent position with the firm after graduation, an additional $25,000 scholarship stipend is also awarded.

Duration 1 year (the third year of law school).

Additional information Scholars may be offered a permanent position with the firm, but there is no guarantee of such an offer.

Number awarded At least 2 each year.

Deadline August of each year.

[655]
MILLER JOHNSON WEST MICHIGAN DIVERSITY LAW SCHOOL SCHOLARSHIP

Grand Rapids Community Foundation
Attn: Education Program Officer
185 Oakes Street S.W.
Grand Rapids, MI 49503-4008
(616) 454-1751, ext. 103   Fax: (616) 454-6455
E-mail: rbishop@grfoundation.org
Web: www.grfoundation.org/scholarshipslist

Summary To provide financial assistance to Asian Americans and other minorities from Michigan who are attending law school in any state.

Eligibility This program is open to U.S. citizens who are students of color (African American, Asian, Hispanic, Native American, Pacific Islander) and residents of Michigan. Applicants must be attending an accredited law school in any state. They must have a GPA of 3.0 or higher and be able to demonstrate financial need.

Financial data The stipend is $5,000. Funds are paid directly to the recipient's institution.

Duration 1 year.

Number awarded 1 each year.

Deadline March of each year.

[656]
MILLER NASH LAW STUDENT DIVERSITY FELLOWSHIP PROGRAM

Miller Nash LLP
Attn: Director of Recruiting and Professional Development
3400 U.S. Bancorp Tower
111 S.W. Fifth Avenue
Portland, OR 97204-3699
(503) 224-5858   Fax: (503) 224-0155
E-mail: MNrecruiting@millernash.com
Web: www.millernash.com

Summary To provide financial aid and work experience to Asian American and other law students who contribute to diversity and are interested in living and working in the Pacific Northwest following graduation from law school.

Eligibility This program is open to first- and second-year students at ABA-accredited law schools in any state. Applicants must be able to demonstrate academic excellence, interpersonal skills, leadership qualities, contributions to diversity, and meaningful contributions to the community. They must intend to work, live, and practice law in the Pacific Northwest. Along with their application, they must submit a personal statement of 2 to 4 pages that includes a description of organizations or projects in which they currently participate or have participated that address diversity issues or support diversity in their legal, business, or local communities.

Financial data Fellows receive a paid summer clerk position and a stipend of $7,500 for law school.

Duration 1 year (including 12 weeks for the summer clerk position); nonrenewable.

Additional information Summer clerk positions may be offered (depending on availability) at the sponsoring law firm's offices in Portland (Oregon), Seattle (Washington), or Vancouver (Washington).

Number awarded Up to 2 each year.

Deadline September of each year for second-year students; January of each year for first-year students.

[657]
MINE AND GONSAKU ITO SCHOLARSHIP

Far West Athletic Trainers' Association
c/o Ned Bergert, Scholarship Chair
4942 Casa Oro Drive
Yorba Linda, CA 92886
(714) 501-3858   E-mail: nhbergert@gmail.com
Web: www.fwatad8.org/?page_id=586

Summary To provide financial assistance to members of the National Athletic Trainers Association (NATA) from any state who are of Asian descent and working on an undergraduate or graduate degree in its District 8.

Eligibility This program is open to students of Asian descent from any state who are enrolled as undergraduate or graduate students at colleges and universities in California, Guam, Hawaii, or Nevada and preparing for a career as an athletic trainer. Applicants must be student members of NATA and a District 8 member of NATA working on a bachelor's, master's, or doctoral degree in athletic training. They must have a GPA of 3.2 or higher and a record of distinction in their athletic training program, academic major, institution, intercollegiate athletics, and higher education. Along with their application, they must submit a statement on their athletic training background, experience, philosophy, and goals. Financial need is not considered in the selection process.

Financial data The stipend is $1,500.

Duration 1 year.

Additional information FWATA serves as District 8 of NATA.

Number awarded 1 each year.

Deadline February of each year.

[658]
MINORITIES IN GOVERNMENT FINANCE SCHOLARSHIP

Government Finance Officers Association
Attn: Scholarship Committee
203 North LaSalle Street, Suite 2700
Chicago, IL 60601-1210
(312) 977-9700   Fax: (312) 977-4806
Web: www.gfoa.org

Summary To provide financial assistance to Asian American and other minority upper-division and graduate students who are preparing for a career in state and local government finance.

Eligibility This program is open to upper-division and graduate students who are preparing for a career in public finance by working on a degree in public administration, accounting, finance, political science, economics, or business administration (with a specific focus on government or nonprofit management). Applicants must be members of a minority group, citizens or permanent residents of the United States or Canada, and able to provide a letter of recommendation from a representative of their school. Selection is based on career plans, academic record, plan of study, letters of recommendation, and GPA. Financial need is not considered.

Financial data The stipend is $5,000.

Duration 1 year.

Additional information This program defines minorities as Blacks or African Americans, American Indians or Alaskan Natives, Hispanics or Latinos, Native Hawaiians or other Pacific Islanders, or Asians.

Number awarded 1 or more each year.

Deadline February of each year.

[659]
MINORITY FACULTY DEVELOPMENT SCHOLARSHIP AWARD IN PHYSICAL THERAPY

American Physical Therapy Association
Attn: Honors and Awards Program
1111 North Fairfax Street
Alexandria, VA 22314-1488
(703) 684-APTA   Toll Free: (800) 999-APTA
Fax: (703) 684-7343   TDD: (703) 683-6748
E-mail: honorsandawards@apta.org
Web: www.apta.org

Summary To provide financial assistance to Asian American and other minority faculty members in physical therapy who are interested in working on a post-professional doctoral degree.

Eligibility This program is open to U.S. citizens and permanent residents who are members of the following minority groups: African American or Black, Asian, Native Hawaiian or other Pacific Islander, American Indian or Alaska Native, or Hispanic/Latino. Applicants must be full-time faculty members, teaching in an accredited or developing professional physical therapist education program, who will have completed the equivalent of 2 full semesters of post-professional doctoral course work. They must possess a license to practice physical therapy in a U.S. jurisdiction and be enrolled as a student in an accredited post-professional doctoral program whose content has a demonstrated relationship to physical therapy. Along with their application, they must submit a personal essay on their professional goals, including their plans to contribute to the profession and minority services. Selection is based on 1) commitment to minority affairs and services; 2) commitment to further the physical therapy profession through teaching and research; and 3) scholastic achievement.

Financial data A stipend is awarded (amount not specified).

Duration 1 year.

Additional information This program began in 1999.

Number awarded 1 or more each year.

Deadline November of each year.

[660]
MINORITY FELLOWSHIPS IN EDUCATION RESEARCH

American Educational Research Association
1430 K Street, N.W., Suite 1200
Washington, DC 20005
(202) 238-3200   Fax: (202) 238-3250
E-mail: fellowships@aera.net
Web: www.aera.net

Summary To provide funding to Asian American and other minority doctoral students writing their dissertation on educational research.

Eligibility This program is open to U.S. citizens and permanent residents who have advanced to candidacy and successfully defended their Ph.D./Ed.D. dissertation research proposal. Applicants must plan to work full time on their dissertation in educational research. This program is targeted for members of groups historically underrepresented in higher education (African Americans, American Indians, Alaskan Natives, Asian Americans, Native Hawaiian or Pacific Islanders, and Hispanics or Latinos). Selection is based on scholarly achievements and publications, letters of recommendation, quality and significance of the proposed research, and commitment of the applicant's faculty mentor to the goals of the program.

Financial data The grant is $12,000. Up to $1,000 is provided to pay for travel to the sponsor's annual conference.

Duration 1 year; nonrenewable.

Additional information This program began in 1991.

Number awarded Up to 3 each year.

Deadline November of each year.

[661]
MINORITY LEAP SCHOLARSHIPS

Missouri Society of Certified Public Accountants
Attn: LEAP Program
540 Maryville Centre Drive, Suite 200
P.O. Box 419042
St. Louis, MO 63141-9042
(314) 997-7966, ext. 125
Toll Free: (800) 264-7966, ext. 125 (within MO)
Fax: (314) 997-2592   E-mail: lsimpson@mocpa.org
Web: www.mocpa.org/students/scholarships

Summary To provide financial assistance to Asian American and other minority residents of Missouri who are working on an undergraduate or graduate degree in accounting at a university in the state.

Eligibility This program is open to members of minority groups.

Financial data The stipend is $1,250 per year.

Duration 1 year; may be renewed.

Additional information These scholarships are offered through the sponsor's Lead and Enhance the Accounting Profession (LEAP) program, established in 2001.

Number awarded Varies each year; recently, 2 of these scholarships were awarded.

Deadline February of each year.

[662]
MINORITY MEDICAL STUDENT ELECTIVE IN HIV PSYCHIATRY

American Psychiatric Association
Attn: Office of HIV Psychiatry
1000 Wilson Boulevard, Suite 1825
Arlington, VA 22209-3901
(703) 907-8668   Toll Free: (888) 357-7849
Fax: (703) 907-1087   E-mail: dpennessi@psych.org
Web: www.psychiatry.org

Summary To provide an opportunity for Asian American and other minority medical students to spend an elective residency learning about HIV psychiatry.

Eligibility This program is open to medical students entering their fourth year at an accredited M.D. or D.O. degree-granting institution. Preference is given to minority candidates and those who have primary interests in services related to HIV/AIDS and substance abuse and its relationship to the mental health or the psychological well-being of ethnic minorities. Applicants should be interested in a psychiatry, internal medicine, pediatrics, or research career. They must be interested in participating in a program that includes intense training in HIV mental health (including neuropsychiatry), a clinical and/or research experience working with a mentor, and participation in the Committee on AIDS of the American Psychiatric Association (APA). U.S. citizenship is required.

Financial data A small stipend is provided (amount not specified).

Duration 1 year.

Additional information The heart of the program is in establishing a mentor relationship at 1 of 5 sites, becoming involved with a cohort of medical students interested in HIV medicine/psychiatry, participating in an interactive didactic/experimental learning program, and developing expertise in areas related to ethnic minority mental health research or psychiatric services. Students selected for the program who are not APA members automatically receive membership.

Number awarded Varies each year.

Deadline March of each year.

[663]
MINORITY MEDICAL STUDENT SUMMER EXTERNSHIP IN ADDICTION PSYCHIATRY

American Psychiatric Association
Attn: Department of Minority and National Affairs
1000 Wilson Boulevard, Suite 1825
Arlington, VA 22209-3901
(703) 907-8653   Toll Free: (888) 35-PSYCH
Fax: (703) 907-7852   E-mail: mking@psych.org
Web: www.psychiatry.org

Summary To provide funding to Asian American and other minority medical students who are interested in working on a research project during the summer with a mentor who specializes in addiction psychiatry.

Eligibility This program is open to minority medical students who have a specific interest in services related to substance abuse treatment and prevention. Minorities include American Indians, Alaska Natives, Native Hawaiians, Asian Americans, Hispanics/Latinos, and African Americans. Applicants must be interested in working with a mentor who specializes in addiction psychiatry. Work settings provide an emphasis on working clinically with or studying underserved minority populations and issues of co-occurring disorders, substance abuse treatment, and mental health disparity. Most of them are in inner-city or rural settings.

Financial data Externships provide $1,500 for travel expenses to go to the work setting of the mentor and up to another $1,500 for out-of-pocket expenses directly related to the conduct of the externship.

Duration 1 month during the summer.

Additional information Funding for this program is provided by the Substance Abuse and Mental Health Services Administration (SAMHSA).

Number awarded 10 each year.

Deadline February of each year.

[664]
MINORITY MEDICAL STUDENT SUMMER MENTORING PROGRAM

American Psychiatric Association
Attn: Department of Minority and National Affairs
1000 Wilson Boulevard, Suite 1825
Arlington, VA 22209-3901
(703) 907-8653   Toll Free: (888) 35-PSYCH
Fax: (703) 907-7852   E-mail: mking@psych.org
Web: www.psychiatry.org

Summary   To provide an opportunity for Asian American and other minority medical students to spend an elective residency learning about HIV psychiatry.

Eligibility   This program is open to minority medical students who are interested in psychiatric issues. Minorities include American Indians, Alaska Natives, Native Hawaiians, Asian Americans, Hispanic/Latinos, and African Americans. Applicants must be interested in working with a psychiatrist mentor, primarily on clinical work with underserved minority populations and mental health care disparities. Work settings may be in a research, academic, or clinical environment. Most of them are inner-city or rural and deal with psychiatric subspecialties, particularly substance abuse and geriatrics. Selection is based on interest of the medical student and specialty of the mentor, practice setting, and geographic proximity of the mentor to the student. U.S. citizenship or permanent resident status is required.

Financial data   Fellowships provide $1,500 for living and out-of-pocket expenses directly related to the conduct of the fellowship.

Duration   Summer months.

Additional information   This program is funded by the Substance Abuse and Mental Health Services Administration.

Number awarded   Varies each year.

Deadline   March of each year.

[665]
MINORITY NURSE MAGAZINE SCHOLARSHIP PROGRAM

Minority Nurse Magazine
c/o Alloy Education
2 LAN Drive, Suite 100
Westford, MA 01886
Toll Free: (877) ASK-ALLO
E-mail: editor@minoritynurse.com
Web: www.minoritynurse.com

Summary   To provide financial assistance to Asian Americans and members of other minority groups who are working on a bachelor's or master's degree in nursing.

Eligibility   This program is open to students currently enrolled in 1) the third or fourth year of an accredited B.S.N. program; 2) an accelerated program leading to a B.S.N. degree (e.g., R.N. to B.S.N., B.A. to B.S.N.); or 3) an accelerated master's entry nursing program (e.g., B.A. to M.S.N.) for students with bachelor's degrees in fields other than nursing. Graduate students who already have a bachelor's degree in nursing are not eligible. Along with their application, they must submit a 250-word essay on their academic and personal accomplishments, community service, and goals for their future nursing career. Selection is based on academic excellence (GPA of 3.0 or higher), demonstrated commitment of service to the student's minority community, and financial need. U.S. citizenship of permanent resident status is required.

Financial data   The stipends are $3,000 or $1,000.

Duration   1 year.

Additional information   This program began in 2000. Winners are announced in the summer issue of *Minority Nurse* magazine.

Number awarded   3 each year: 1 at $3,000 and 2 at $1,000.

Deadline   January of each year.

[666]
MINORITY TEACHERS OF ILLINOIS SCHOLARSHIP PROGRAM

Illinois Student Assistance Commission
Attn: Scholarship and Grant Services
1755 Lake Cook Road
Deerfield, IL 60015-5209
(847) 948-8550   Toll Free: (800) 899-ISAC
Fax: (847) 831-8549   TDD: (800) 526-0844
E-mail: isac.studentservices@isac.illinois.gov
Web: www.collegeillinois.org

Summary   To provide funding to Asian American and other minority students in Illinois who plan to become teachers at the preschool, elementary, or secondary level.

Eligibility   Applicants must be Illinois residents, U.S. citizens or eligible noncitizens, members of a minority group (African American/Black, Hispanic American, Asian American, or Native American), and high school graduates or holders of a General Educational Development (GED) certificate. They must be enrolled at least half time as an undergraduate or graduate student, have a GPA of 2.5 or higher, not be in default on any student loan, and be enrolled or accepted for enrollment in a teacher education program.

Financial data   Grants up to $5,000 per year are awarded. This is a scholarship/loan program. Recipients must agree to teach full time 1 year for each year of support received. The teaching agreement may be fulfilled at a public, private, or parochial preschool, elementary school, or secondary school in Illinois; at least 30% of the student body at those schools must be minority. It must be fulfilled within the 5-year period following the completion of the undergraduate program for which the scholarship was awarded. The time period may be extended if the recipient serves in the U.S. armed forces, enrolls full time in a graduate program related to teaching, becomes temporarily disabled, is unable to find employment as a teacher at a qualifying school, or takes additional courses on at least a half-time basis to obtain certification as a teacher in Illinois. Recipients who fail to honor this work obligation must repay the award with 5% interest.

Duration   1 year; may be renewed for a total of 8 semesters or 12 quarters.

Number awarded   Varies each year.

Deadline   Priority consideration is given to applications received by February of each year.

[667]
MINORU YASUI MEMORIAL SCHOLARSHIP

Japanese American Citizens League
Attn: National Scholarship Awards
1765 Sutter Street
San Francisco, CA 94115
(415) 345-1075   Fax: (415) 931-4671
E-mail: ncwnp@jacl.org
Web: www.jacl.org/edu/scholar.htm

Summary To provide financial assistance for graduate study in selected fields to members of the Japanese American Citizens League (JACL).

Eligibility This program is open to JACL members who are attending or planning to attend an accredited college or university as a graduate student. Applicants must submit information on their involvement in JACL and a 2-page essay on a topic that changes annually but relates to Japanese Americans. Selection is based on that essay, academic record, JACL involvement, school activities, work history, scholastic honors, and community involvement. Preference is given to applicants with a strong interest in human and civil rights; fields of study may also include sociology, law, or education.

Financial data Stipends generally average more than $2,000.

Duration 1 year; nonrenewable.

Number awarded At least 1 each year.

Deadline March of each year.

[668]
MIRIAM WEINSTEIN PEACE AND JUSTICE EDUCATION AWARD

Philanthrofund Foundation
Attn: Scholarship Committee
1409 Willow Street, Suite 109
Minneapolis, MN 55403-2241
(612) 870-1806   Toll Free: (800) 435-1402
Fax: (612) 871-6587   E-mail: info@PfundOnline.org
Web: www.pfundonline.org/scholarships.html

Summary To provide financial assistance to Asian American and other minority students from Minnesota who have supported gay, lesbian, bisexual, and transgender (GLBT) activities and are interested in working on a degree in education.

Eligibility This program is open to residents of Minnesota and students attending a Minnesota educational institution who are members of a religious, racial, or ethnic minority. Applicants must be self-identified as GLBT or from a GLBT family and have demonstrated a commitment to peace and justice issues. They may be attending or planning to attend trade school, technical college, college, or university (as an undergraduate or graduate student). Preference is given to students who have completed at least 2 years of college and are working on a degree in education. Selection is based on the applicant's 1) affirmation of GLBT or allied identity; 2) evidence of experience and skills in service and leadership; and 3) evidence of service, leading, and working for change in GLBT communities, including serving as a role model, mentor, and/or adviser.

Financial data The stipend is $3,000. Funds must be used for tuition, books, fees, or dissertation expenses.

Duration 1 year.

Number awarded 1 each year.

Deadline January of each year.

[669]
MLA/NLM SPECTRUM SCHOLARSHIPS

Medical Library Association
Attn: Grants and Scholarships
65 East Wacker Place, Suite 1900
Chicago, IL 60601-7246
(312) 419-9094, ext. 15   Fax: (312) 419-8950
E-mail: grants@mlahq.org
Web: www.mlanet.org/awards/grants

Summary To provide financial assistance to Asian Americans and other minorities who are interested in preparing for a career as a medical librarian.

Eligibility This program is open to members of minority groups (African Americans, Hispanics, Asian, Native Americans, and Pacific Islanders) who are attending library schools accredited by the American Library Association (ALA). Applicants must be interested in preparing for a career as a health sciences information professional.

Financial data The stipend is $3,250.

Duration 1 year.

Additional information This program, established in 2001, is jointly sponsored by the Medical Library Association (MLA) and the National Library of Medicine (NLM) of the U.S. National Institutes of Health (NIH). It operates as a component of the Spectrum Initiative Scholarship program of the ALA.

Number awarded 2 each year.

Deadline February of each year.

[670]
MOSAIC SCHOLARSHIPS

Society of American Archivists
Attn: Chair, Awards Committee
17 North State Street, Suite 1425
Chicago, IL 60602-4061
(312) 606-0722   Toll Free: (866) 722-7858
Fax: (312) 606-0728   E-mail: info@archivists.org
Web: www.archivists.org/recognition

Summary To provide financial assistance to Asian American and other minority students who are working on a graduate degree in archival science.

Eligibility This program is open to minority graduate students, defined as those of American Indian/Alaska Native, Asian, Black/African American, Hispanic/Latino, or Native Hawaiian/other Pacific Islander descent. Applicants must be enrolled or planning to enroll full or part time in a graduate program or a multi-course program in archival administration. They may have completed no more than half of the credit requirements for a degree. Along with their application, they must submit a 500-word essay outlining their interests and future goals in the archives profession. U.S. or Canadian citizenship or permanent resident status is required.

Financial data The stipend is $5,000.

Duration 1 year.

Additional information This program began in 2009.

Number awarded 2 each year.

Deadline February of each year.

[671]
MOSS ADAMS FOUNDATION SCHOLARSHIP

Educational Foundation for Women in Accounting
Attn: Foundation Administrator
136 South Keowee Street
Dayton, OH 45402
(937) 424-3391   Fax: (937) 222-5749
E-mail: info@efwa.org
Web: www.efwa.org/scholarships_MossAdams.php

Summary   To provide financial support to women (preference given to Asian American and other minority women) who are working on an accounting degree.

Eligibility   This program is open to women who are enrolled in an accounting degree program at an accredited college or university. Applicants must meet 1 of the following criteria: 1) women pursuing a fifth-year requirement either through general studies or within a graduate program; 2) women returning to school as current or reentry juniors or seniors; or 3) minority women. Selection is based on aptitude for accounting and business, commitment to the goal of working on a degree in accounting (including evidence of continued commitment after receiving this award), clear evidence that the candidate has established goals and a plan for achieving those goals (both personal and professional), financial need, and a demonstration of how the scholarship will impact her life. U.S. citizenship is required.

Financial data   The stipend is $1,000.

Duration   1 year.

Additional information   This program was established by Rowling, Dold & Associates LLP, a woman-owned C.P.A. firm based in San Diego. It was renamed when that firm merged with Moss Adams LLP.

Number awarded   1 each year.

Deadline   April of each year.

[672]
NAPABA LAW FOUNDATION SCHOLARSHIPS

National Asian Pacific American Bar Association
Attn: NAPABA Law Foundation
1612 K Street, N.W., Suite 1400
Washington, DC 20006
(202) 775-9555   Fax: (202) 775-9333
E-mail: nlfstaff@napaba.org
Web: www.napaba.org

Summary   To provide financial assistance to law students interested in serving the Asian Pacific American community.

Eligibility   This program is open to students at ABA-accredited law schools in the United States. Applicants must demonstrate leadership potential to serve the Asian Pacific American community upon graduation. Along with their application, they must submit a 500-word essay that covers 1) the most significant experiences in their background that have shaped and demonstrated their commitment to serving the needs of Asian Pacific Americans; and 2) how they intend to serve the needs of the Asian Pacific American community in their future legal career. Selection is based on that essay, academic achievement, leadership, and commitment to bettering the Asian Pacific American community. U.S. citizenship or permanent resident status is required.

Financial data   The stipend is $2,500 or $2,000.

Duration   1 year.

Additional information   This program began in 1995. In 2003, 1 of the scholarships was named the Chris Nakamura Scholarship in honor of a leader of the Asian Pacific American legal community in Arizona. Another scholarship was established in 2004 with support from the law firm of Lim, Ruger & Kim of Los Angeles.

Number awarded   8 to 10 each year: 2 at $2,500 (the Chris Nakamura Scholarship and the Lim, Ruger & Kim Scholarship) and the remainder at $2,000.

Deadline   September of each year.

[673]
NATIONAL ASSOCIATION OF SCHOOL PSYCHOLOGISTS MINORITY SCHOLARSHIP

National Association of School Psychologists
Attn: Education and Research Trust
4340 East-West Highway, Suite 402
Bethesda, MD 20814
(301) 657-0270   Toll Free: (866) 331-NASP
Fax: (301) 657-0275   TDD: (301) 657-4155
E-mail: kbritton@naspweb.org
Web: www.nasponline.org

Summary   To provide financial assistance to Asian American and other minority graduate students who are members of the National Association of School Psychologists (NASP) and enrolled in a school psychology program.

Eligibility   This program is open to minority students who are NASP members enrolled in a regionally-accredited school psychology program in the United States. Applicants must have a GPA of 3.0 or higher. Doctoral candidates are not eligible. Applications must be accompanied by 1) a resume that includes undergraduate and/or graduate schools attended, awards and honors, student and professional activities, work and volunteer experiences, research and publications, workshops or other presentations, and any special skills, training, or experience, such as bilingualism, teaching experience, or mental health experience; 2) a statement, up to 1,000 words, of professional goals; 3) at least 2 letters of recommendation, including at least 1 from a faculty member from their undergraduate or graduate studies (if a first-year student) or at least 1 from a faculty member of their school psychology program (if a second- or third-year student); 4) a completed financial statement; 5) an official transcript of all graduate course work (first-year students may submit an official undergraduate transcript); 6) other personal accomplishments that the applicant wishes to be considered; and 7) a letter of acceptance from a school psychology program for first-year applicants. U.S. citizenship is required.

Financial data   The stipend is $5,000 per year.

Duration   1 year; may be renewed up to 2 additional years.

Number awarded   Varies each year; recently, 4 of these scholarships were awarded.

Deadline   October of each year.

[674]
NATIONAL DEFENSE SCIENCE AND ENGINEERING GRADUATE FELLOWSHIP PROGRAM

American Society for Engineering Education
Attn: NDSEG Fellowship Program
1818 N Street, N.W., Suite 600
Washington, DC 20036-2479
(202) 649-3831   Fax: (202) 265-8504
E-mail: ndseg@asee.org
Web: ndseg.asee.org

Summary To provide financial assistance to students (particularly Asian Americans, other minorities, women, and students with disabilities) who are working on a doctoral degree in areas of science and engineering that are of potential military importance.

Eligibility This program is open to U.S. citizens and nationals entering or enrolled in the early stages of a doctoral program in aeronautical and astronautical engineering; biosciences, including toxicology; chemical engineering; chemistry; civil engineering; cognitive, neural, and behavioral sciences; computer and computational sciences; electrical engineering; geosciences, including terrain, water, and air; materials science and engineering; mathematics; mechanical engineering; naval architecture and ocean engineering; oceanography; or physics, including optics. Applicants must be enrolled or planning to enroll as full-time students. Applications are particularly encouraged from women, members of ethnic minority groups (American Indians, African Americans, Hispanics or Latinos, Native Hawaiians, Alaska Natives, Asians, and Pacific Islanders), and persons with disabilities. Selection is based on all available evidence of ability, including academic records, letters of recommendation, and GRE scores.

Financial data The annual stipend is $30,500 for the first year, $31,000 for the second year; and $31,500 for the third year; the program also pays the recipient's institution full tuition and required fees (not to include room and board). Medical insurance is covered up to $1,000 per year.

Duration 3 years, as long as satisfactory academic progress is maintained.

Additional information This program is sponsored by the High Performance Computing Modernization Program within the Department of Defense, the Army Research Office, the Air Force Office of Scientific Research, and the Office of Naval Research. Recipients do not incur any military or other service obligation.

Number awarded Approximately 200 each year.

Deadline December of each year.

[675]
NATIONAL ESTUARINE RESEARCH RESERVE SYSTEM GRADUATE FELLOWSHIPS

National Oceanic and Atmospheric Administration
Attn: Estuarine Reserves Division
1305 East-West Highway
N/ORMS, SSMC4, Station 10503
Silver Spring, MD 20910
(301) 713-3155, ext. 105   Fax: (301) 713-4367
E-mail: Alison.Krepp@noaa.gov
Web: www.nerrs.noaa.gov/Fellowship.aspx

Summary To provide funding to graduate students (particularly Asian Americans and other minorities) who are interested in conducting research within the National Estuarine Research Reserve System (NERRS).

Eligibility This program is open to students admitted to or enrolled in a full-time master's or doctoral program at U.S. accredited universities. Applicants should have completed a majority of their course work at the beginning of their fellowship and have an approved thesis research program focused on improving coastal zone management while providing hands-on training in conducting ecological monitoring. Proposed research topics must address 1 of the following topics: 1) eutrophication, effects of non-point source pollution and/or nutrient dynamics; 2) habitat conservation and/or restoration; 3) biodiversity and/or the effects of invasive species; 4) mechanisms for sustaining resources within estuarine ecosystems; or 5) economic, sociological, and/or anthropological research applicable to estuarine ecosystem management. They must be willing to conduct their research within the NERRS. Minority students are specifically encouraged to apply. Selection is based on academic record and a statement of career goals and objectives (5%), quality of proposed research and its applicability to the NERRS research focus areas (70%), the research's applicability to specific reserve research and resource management goals (20%), and recommendations and endorsements (5%).

Financial data The stipend is $28,5720 per year, of which the federal government provides $20,000 and the recipient's institution provides $8,572 as matching funds. Grants may be used for any combination of research support, salary, tuition, supplies, or other costs as needed, including overhead.

Duration 1 to 3 years.

Additional information This program began in 1997. For a list of the National Estuarine Research Reserves, with the name and address of a coordinator at each, contact NERRS. Fellows are required to work with the research coordinator or manager at the host reserve to develop a plan to participate in the reserve's research and/or monitoring program for up to 15 hours per week.

Number awarded Varies each year; recently, 9 of these fellowships were available.

Deadline October of each year.

[676]
NATIONAL MEDICAL FELLOWSHIPS EMERGENCY SCHOLARSHIP FUND

National Medical Fellowships, Inc.
Attn: Scholarship Program
347 Fifth Avenue, Suite 510
New York, NY 10016
(212) 483-8880   Toll Free: (877) NMF-1DOC
Fax: (212) 483-8897   E-mail: info@nmfonline.org
Web: www.nmfonline.org

Summary To provide financial assistance to Asian American and other minority medical students who are facing financial emergencies.

Eligibility This program is open to U.S. citizens who are enrolled in the third or fourth year of an accredited M.D. or D.O. degree-granting program in the United States and are facing extreme financial difficulties because of unforeseen training-related expenses. Applicants must be African Americans, Latinos, Native Hawaiians, Alaska Natives, American

Indians, Pacific Islanders, Vietnamese, or Cambodians who permanently reside in the United States. They must be interested in primary care practice in underserved communities.

Financial data   Assistance ranges up to $10,000.

Duration   1 year; nonrenewable.

Additional information   This program began in 2008, with support from the W.K. Kellogg Foundation.

Number awarded   Varies each year; recently, 3 of these scholarships were awarded.

Deadline   August of each year.

[677]
NATIONAL URBAN FELLOWS PROGRAM

National Urban Fellows, Inc.
Attn: Program Director
989 Avenue of the Americas, Suite 400
New York, NY 10018
(212) 730-1700   Fax: (212) 730-1823
E-mail: info@nuf.org
Web: www.nuf.org/fellows-overview

Summary   To offer financial assistance to mid-career public sector professionals (especially Asian Americans, other minorities, and women) who are interested in working on a master's degree program coupled with a mentorship.

Eligibility   This program is open to U.S. citizens who have a bachelor's degree, have at least 3 years of administrative or managerial experience, have demonstrated exceptional ability and leadership potential, meet academic admission requirements, have a high standard of integrity and work ethic, and are committed to the solution of urban problems. Applicants must a 1,000-word autobiographical statement and a 1,000-word statement on their career goals. They may be of any racial or ethnic background, but the program's goal is to increase the number of competent administrators from underrepresented ethnic and cultural groups at all levels of public and private urban management organizations. Semifinalists are interviewed.

Financial data   The stipend is $25,000. The program also provides full payment of tuition, a relocation allowance of $500, a book allowance of $500, and reimbursement for program-related travel.

Duration   14 months.

Additional information   The program begins with a summer semester of study at Bernard M. Baruch College of the City University of New York. Following this, fellows spend 9 months in mentorship assignments with a senior administrator in a government agency, a major nonprofit, or a foundation. The final summer is spent in another semester of study at Baruch College. Fellows who successfully complete all requirements are granted a master's of public administration from that college. A $75 processing fee must accompany each application.

Number awarded   Varies; approximately 40 each year.

Deadline   February of each year.

[678]
NCAA ETHNIC MINORITY ENHANCEMENT SCHOLARSHIP PROGRAM

National Collegiate Athletic Association
Attn: Office for Diversity and Inclusion
700 West Washington Street
P.O. Box 6222
Indianapolis, IN 46206-6222
(317) 917-6222   Fax: (317) 917-6888
E-mail: tstrum@ncaa.org
Web: www.ncaa.org

Summary   To provide funding to Asian American and other ethnic minority graduate students who are interested in preparing for a career in intercollegiate athletics.

Eligibility   This program is open to members of minority groups who have been accepted into a program at a National Collegiate Athletic Association (NCAA) member institution that will prepare them for a career in intercollegiate athletics (athletics administrator, coach, athletic trainer, or other career that provides a direct service to intercollegiate athletics). Applicants must be U.S. citizens, have performed with distinction as a student body member at their respective undergraduate institution, and be entering the first semester or term of full-time postgraduate study. Selection is based on the applicant's involvement in extracurricular activities, course work, commitment to preparing for a career in intercollegiate athletics, and promise for success in that career. Financial need is not considered.

Financial data   The stipend is $6,000; funds are paid to the college or university of the recipient's choice.

Duration   1 year; nonrenewable.

Number awarded   13 each year.

Deadline   November of each year.

[679]
NCPACA GRADUATE SCHOLARSHIPS

National Council of Philippine American Canadian
   Accountants
c/o Ed Ortiz, Scholarship Chair
333 South Des Plaines Street, Suite 2-N
Chicago, IL 60661
(312) 876-1900   Fax: (312) 876-1911
E-mail: ecortiz@ocortiz.com
Web: www.ncpaca.org

Summary   To provide financial assistance to graduate students working on a degree in accounting, business administration, finance, or taxation) who will promote the goals of the National Council of Philippine American Canadian Accountants (NCPACA).

Eligibility   This program is open to full-time graduate students at a 4-year college or university in the United States or Canada. Applicants must be 1) enrolled in an accounting program; 2) have been an accounting major as an undergraduate and be accepted to a master's-level accounting, business administration, finance, or taxation program; or 3) have any undergraduate major and be presently accepted to a master's-level accounting program. They must be able to demonstrate how they will help achieve the goal of NCPACA: "to promote the advancement of individuals with Filipino ancestry in the field of accounting, audit, finance, tax and related areas." Selection is based primarily on academic achievement; financial need is evaluated as a secondary consideration.

Financial data The stipend is $5,000. Payments are sent directly to the recipient's school.

Duration 1 year.

Number awarded 1 or more each year.

Deadline July of each year.

[680]
NELLIE STONE JOHNSON SCHOLARSHIP

Nellie Stone Johnson Scholarship Program
P.O. Box 40309
St. Paul, MN 55104
(651) 738-1404   Toll Free: (866) 738-5238
E-mail: info@nelliestone.org
Web: www.nelliestone.org

Summary To provide financial assistance to Asian American and other minority union members or their families who are interested in working on an undergraduate or graduate degree in any field at a Minnesota state college or university.

Eligibility This program is open to students in undergraduate and graduate programs at a 2- or 4-year institution that is a component of Minnesota State Colleges and Universities (MnSCU). Applicants must be a minority (Asian, American Indian, Alaska Native, Black/African American, Hispanic/Latino, Native Hawaiian, or Pacific Islander) union member or the child, grandchild, or spouse of a minority union member. They must submit a 2-page essay about their background, educational goals, career goals, and other activities that may impact the cause of human or civil rights. Undergraduates must have a GPA of 2.0 or higher; graduate students must have a GPA of 3.0 or higher. Preference is given to Minnesota residents. Selection is based on the essay, commitment to human or civil rights, extracurricular activities, volunteer activities, community involvement, academic standing, and financial need.

Financial data Stipends range from $500 to $2,000 per year.

Duration 1 year; may be renewed up to 3 additional years for students working on a bachelor's degree, 1 additional year for students working on a master's degree, or 1 additional year for students in a community or technical college program.

Number awarded Varies each year; recently, 18 of these scholarships were awarded.

Deadline April of each year.

[681]
NEXSEN PRUET DIVERSITY SCHOLARSHIPS

Nexsen Pruet
Attn: Diversity Scholarship
1230 Main Street, Suite 700
P.O. Drawer 2426
Columbia, SC 29202-2426
(803) 771-8900   Fax: (803) 727-1469
E-mail: diversity@nexsenpruet.com
Web: www.nexsenpruet.com/firm-diversity.html

Summary To provide financial assistance to Asian Americans and members of other minority groups attending designated law schools in North and South Carolina.

Eligibility This program is open to minority students currently enrolled in the first year at the University of North Carolina School of Law, University of South Carolina School of Law, Wake Forest University School of Law, North Carolina Central University School of Law, Charleston School of Law, or Charlotte School of Law. Applicants must be interested in practicing law in North or South Carolina after graduation. Along with their application, they must submit information on their academic achievements; their contributions to promoting diversity in their community, school, or work environment; and their ability to overcome challenges in the pursuit of their goals. They must also submit essays of 250 words each on 1) their reasons for preparing for a legal career; 2) their interest in the private practice of law in North Carolina and/or South Carolina; 3) any obstacles, including but not limited to financial obstacles, that the scholarship will help them overcome; and 4) what they see as potential obstacles, issues, and opportunities facing new minority lawyers.

Financial data The stipend is $3,000 per year.

Duration 1 year; recipients may reapply.

Additional information Recipients are considered for summer employment in an office of the firm after completion of their first year of law school.

Number awarded Varies each year; recently, 3 of these scholarships were awarded.

Deadline October of each year.

[682]
NJLA DIVERSITY SCHOLARSHIP

New Jersey Library Association
c/o Mimi Hui, Scholarship Committee Chair
Free Public Library of Hasbrouck Heights
320 Boulevard
Hasbrouck Heights, NJ 07604
(201) 288-0488   Fax: (201) 288-5467
E-mail: Hui@bccls.org
Web: www.njla.org

Summary To provide financial assistance to New Jersey residents who are members of minority groups and interested in working on a graduate or postgraduate degree in public librarianship at a school in any state.

Eligibility This program is open to residents of New Jersey and individuals who have worked in a New Jersey library for at least 12 months. Applicants must be members of a minority group (African American, Asian/Pacific Islander, Latino/Hispanic, or Native American/Native Alaskan). They must be enrolled or planning to enroll at an ALA-accredited school of library science in any state to work on a graduate or postgraduate degree in librarianship. Along with their application, they must submit an essay of 150 to 250 words explaining their choice of librarianship as a profession. An interview is required. Selection is based on academic ability and financial need.

Financial data The stipend is $800.

Duration 1 year.

Number awarded 1 each year.

Deadline March of each year.

[683]
NLGJA/KAY LONGCOPE SCHOLARSHIP AWARD

National Lesbian & Gay Journalists Association
2120 L Street, N.W., Suite 850
Washington, DC 20037
(202) 588-9888   Fax: (202) 588-1818
E-mail: info@nlgfa.org
Web: www.nlgja.org/students/longcope

Summary To provide financial assistance to Asian American and other lesbian, gay, bisexual, and transgender (LGBT) undergraduate and graduate students of color who are interested in preparing for a career in journalism.

Eligibility This program is open to LGBT students of color who are 1) high school seniors accepted to a U.S. community college or 4-year university and planning to enroll full time; 2) full-time undergraduate students at U.S. community colleges and 4-year universities; or 3) undergraduate students who have been accepted for their first year at a U.S. graduate school. Applicants must be planning a career in journalism and be committed to furthering the sponsoring organization's mission of fair and accurate coverage of the LGBT community. They must demonstrate an awareness of the issues facing the LGBT community and the importance of fair and accurate news coverage. For undergraduates, a declared major in journalism and/or communications is desirable but not required; non-journalism majors may demonstrate their commitment to a journalism career through work samples, internships, and work on a school news publication, online news service, or broadcast affiliate. Graduate students must be enrolled in a journalism program. Along with their application, they must submit a 1-page resume, 5 work samples, official transcripts, 3 letters of recommendation, and a 750-word news story on a designated subject involving the LGBT community. U.S. citizenship or permanent resident status is required. Selection is based on journalistic and scholastic ability.

Financial data The stipend is $3,000.

Duration 1 year.

Additional information This program began in 2008.

Number awarded 1 each year.

Deadline June of each year.

[684]
NONG KHAI JUNIOR VANG SCHOLARSHIP

Hmong American Education Fund
P.O. Box 17468
St. Paul, MN 55117
(651) 230-3634   E-mail: scholarships@thehaef.org
Web: www.thehaef.org

Summary To provide financial assistance to Hmong undergraduate and graduate students who demonstrate academic achievement.

Eligibility This program is open to students of Hmong descent who are currently enrolled as full-time undergraduate or graduate students at public 2- or 4-year colleges or universities in any state. Applicants must be U.S. citizens or permanent residents and have a GPA of 3.0 or higher. Along with their application, they must submit a 1,500-word essay on their commitment to education, their financial need, how this scholarship can help them, and their community service. Selection is based on commitment to academic achievement,

drive to achieve their goals, commitment to helping their community, and financial need.

Financial data The stipend is $500.

Duration 1 year; nonrenewable.

Number awarded 1 each year.

Deadline March of each year.

[685]
NORMAN'S ORCHIDS MASTERS SCHOLARSHIP

American Orchid Society
c/o Fairchild Tropical Botanic Garden
10901 Old Cutler Road
Coral Gables, FL 33156
(305) 740-2010   Fax: (305) 740-2011
E-mail: TheAOS@aos.org
Web: www.aos.org/Default.aspx?id=545

Summary To provide funding for research to students (particularly Asian Americans, other underrepresented minorities, women, and individuals with disabilities) who are working on a master's degree in a field related to orchids.

Eligibility This program is open to students working on a master's degree at an accredited institution. Applicants must have a thesis project that deals with an aspect of orchid education, applied science, or orchid biology in the disciplines of physiology, molecular biology, structure, systematics, cytology, ecology, or evolution. They must submit a current curriculum vitae, transcripts of all college course work, a synopsis of the proposed project or research, a 1-page statement of the value of their project and importance to the future of orchid education or orchidology, and a letter of recommendation from their chairperson. Women, minorities, and persons with disabilities are especially encouraged to apply.

Financial data The grant is $5,000 per year. Funds are paid through the recipient's college or university, but institutional overhead is not allowed.

Duration 2 years.

Additional information This program, established in 2005, is supported by Norman's Orchids of Montclair, California.

Number awarded 1 each year.

Deadline March of each year.

[686]
NORTH AMERICAN TAIWANESE MEDICAL ASSOCIATION SCHOLARSHIPS

North American Taiwanese Medical Association
   Foundation
Attn: Director
7923 Garden Grove Boulevard
Garden Grove, CA 92841
(714) 898-2275   E-mail: hsu0316
Web: www.natma.org/scholarshipinfo.html

Summary To provide financial assistance for additional study to Taiwanese American medical, dental, and allied health graduate students, residents, or fellows.

Eligibility This program is open to medical, dental, and allied health students, residents, or fellows who are of Taiwanese American descent. Applicants must have completed at least 1 year of graduate school study and be enrolled in a program of training at an accredited U.S. institution or program. Along with their application, they must submit a 1-page personal statement, a transcript, and 2 letters of recommendation.

Financial data The stipend is $1,000.

Duration 1 year.

Number awarded 5 each year.

Deadline April of each year.

[687]
NORTH CAROLINA CPA FOUNDATION OUTSTANDING MINORITY ACCOUNTING STUDENT SCHOLARSHIPS

North Carolina Association of Certified Public
  Accountants
Attn: North Carolina CPA Foundation, Inc.
3100 Gateway Centre Boulevard
P.O. Box 80188
Raleigh, NC 27623-0188
(919) 469-1040, ext. 130   Toll Free: (800) 722-2836
Fax: (919) 378-2000   E-mail: jtahler@ncacpa.org
Web: ncacpa.org

Summary To provide financial assistance to Asian American and other minority undergraduate and graduate students working on a degree in accounting at colleges and universities in North Carolina.

Eligibility This program is open to North Carolina residents who have completed at least 36 semester hours, including at least 4 accounting courses, at a college or university in the state. Applicants must be members of a minority group, defined as Black, Native American/Alaskan Native, Middle-Eastern, Asian or Pacific Islander, or Hispanic. They must be enrolled full time in an academic program leading to a degree in accounting or its equivalent and have a GPA of 3.0 or higher. Along with their application, they must submit a 500-word essay on 1 of the following questions: 1) what the profession can do to educate minorities about understanding the impact of and ways to survive the national financial crisis; 2) how they will impact minority communities by becoming a C.P.A.; or 3) the challenges that minority C.P.A.s face in the profession. Selection is based on GPA (30%), extracurricular activities (20%), essay content (25%), and essay grammar (25%).

Financial data Stipends are $2,000 or $1,000.

Duration 1 year; may be renewed up to 2 additional years.

Number awarded 2 each year: 1 at $2,000 and 1 at $1,000.

Deadline March of each year.

[688]
NORTHEASTERN REGION KOREAN AMERICAN SCHOLARSHIPS

Korean American Scholarship Foundation
Northeastern Region
c/o James Lee, Scholarship Committee Chair
472 11th Street, Room 202
Palisades Park, NJ 07650
E-mail: kasfjames@gmail.com
Web: www.kasf.org/northeastern

Summary To provide financial assistance to Korean American students from any state who are working on an undergraduate or graduate degree in any field at a school in northeastern states.

Eligibility This program is open to residents of any state who are 1) U.S. citizens of Korean heritage; 2) Korean citizens who have a valid visa to study in the United States; and 3) citizens of any other country who are of Korean heritage and have a valid visa to study in the United States. Applicants must be enrolled or planning to enroll as a full-time undergraduate or graduate student at a college or university in Connecticut, Maine, Massachusetts, New Hampshire, New Jersey, New York, Rhode Island, or Vermont. Selection is based on academic achievement, school and community activities, letters of recommendation, a personal essay, and financial need.

Financial data Stipends range from $1,000 to $2,000.

Duration 1 year; renewable.

Number awarded Varies each year; recently, 59 of these scholarships were awarded.

Deadline June of each year.

[689]
NORTHERN CALIFORNIA GRADUATE NURSING STUDENT SCHOLARSHIP

Philippine Nurses Association of Northern California, Inc.
c/o Teresita Baluyut, Scholarship Chair
845 Mt. Vernon Avenue
San Francisco, CA 94112
E-mail: pnanorthcal@gmail.com
Web: www.pnanorthcal.org

Summary To provide financial assistance to Filipino Americans from any state enrolled in a graduate nursing program at a school in northern California.

Eligibility This program is open to Filipino American residents of any state who are currently enrolled in at least the second year of an accredited graduate nursing program in northern California. Applicants must have a GPA of 3.5 or higher and a record of participation in extracurricular or community activities. They must have demonstrated leadership ability or potential both within and outside the clinical setting. Along with their application, they must submit brief statements on their strengths and opportunities for improvement, their career goals, why they need a financial scholarship, and how they can contribute to the goals of the Philippine Nurses Association of Northern California (PNANC). They must also submit a 200-word essay on an accomplishment or activity as a nursing student that has impacted their life or the life of another person. Preference is given to members of PNANC.

Financial data The stipend is $1,000.

Duration 1 year.

Additional information The recipient must commit to serve on a committee of the PNANC for at least 2 years.

Number awarded 1 each year.

Deadline October of each year.

[690]
NOTRE DAME INSTITUTE FOR ADVANCED STUDY GRADUATE STUDENT FELLOWSHIPS

University of Notre Dame
Institute for Advanced Study
Attn: Programs Administrator
1124 Flanner Hall
Notre Dame, IN 46556
(574) 631-6240   E-mail: csherman@nd.edu
Web: ndias.nd.edu/fellowships/graduate-student

Summary To provide funding to graduate students (particularly Asian Americans and members of other traditionally underrepresented groups) who are interested in conducting research on topics of interest to the Notre Dame Institute for Advanced Study (NDIAS) while in residence at the institute.

Eligibility This program is open to graduate students in all disciplines, including the arts, engineering, the humanities, law, and the natural, social, and physical sciences. Applicants must be interested in conducting research that furthers the work of the NDIAS, defined as cultivating "the contemplative ideal that is an essential factor in the Catholic intellectual tradition and vital for the progression of scholarship." They must be able to demonstrate excellent records of scholarly, artistic, or research accomplishment in their field; ability to interact with other fellows and to engage in collegial discussions of research presentations; a willingness to contribute to a cooperative community of scholars; and projects that touch on normative, integrative, or ultimate questions, especially as the involve the Catholic intellectual tradition. Applications are especially encouraged from traditionally underrepresented groups. There are no citizenship requirements; non-U.S. nationals are welcome to apply.

Financial data The grant is $25,000, including a $1,000 research account, office facilities, a computer and printer, access to libraries and other facilities, and weekly institute seminars and events.

Duration 1 academic year.

Number awarded 1 or more each year.

Deadline October of each year.

[691]
NSCA MINORITY SCHOLARSHIPS

National Strength and Conditioning Association
Attn: Grants and Scholarships Program
1885 Bob Johnson Drive
Colorado Springs, CO 80906-4000
(719) 632-6722, ext. 152   Toll Free: (800) 815-6826
Fax: (719) 632-6367   E-mail: foundation@nsca-lift.org
Web: www.nsca-lift.org/Foundation/grants-and-scholarships

Summary To provide financial assistance to Asian Americans and other minorities who are interested in working on an undergraduate or graduate degree in strength training and conditioning.

Eligibility This program is open to Blacks, Hispanics, Asian Americans, and Native Americans who are 17 years of age and older. Applicants must have been accepted into an accredited postsecondary institution to work on an undergraduate or graduate degree in the strength and conditioning field. Along with their application, they must submit a 500-word essay on their personal and professional goals and how receiving this scholarship will assist them in achieving those goals. Selection is based on that essay, academic achievement, strength and conditioning experience, honors and awards, community involvement, letters of recommendation, and involvement in the National Strength and Conditioning Association (NSCA).

Financial data The stipend is $1,500.

Duration 1 year.

Additional information The NSCA is a nonprofit organization of strength and conditioning professionals, including coaches, athletic trainers, physical therapists, educators, researchers, and physicians. This program was first offered in 2003.

Number awarded Varies each year; recently, 9 of these scholarships were awarded.

Deadline March of each year.

[692]
NSF GRADUATE RESEARCH FELLOWSHIP PROGRAM

National Science Foundation
Directorate for Education and Human Resources
Attn: Division of Graduate Education
4201 Wilson Boulevard, Room 875S
Arlington, VA 22230
(703) 292-8694   Toll Free: (866) NSF-GRFP
Fax: (703) 292-9048   E-mail: info@nsfgrfp.org
Web: www.nsf.gov/funding/pgm_summ.jsp?pims_id=6201

Summary To provide financial assistance to graduate students (particularly Asian Americans, other minorities, women, veterans, and students with disabilities) who are interested in working on a master's or doctoral degree in fields supported by the National Science Foundation (NSF).

Eligibility This program is open to U.S. citizens, nationals, and permanent residents who wish to work on research-based master's or doctoral degrees in a field of science, technology, engineering, or mathematics (STEM) supported by NSF (including astronomy, chemistry, computer and information sciences and engineering, geosciences, engineering, life sciences, materials research, mathematical sciences, physics, psychology, social sciences, or STEM education and learning). Other work in medical, dental, law, public health, or practice-oriented professional degree programs, or in joint science-professional degree programs, such as M.D./Ph.D. and J.D./Ph.D. programs, is not eligible. Applications normally should be submitted during the senior year in college or in the first year of graduate study; eligibility is limited to those who have completed no more than 12 months of graduate study since completion of a baccalaureate degree. Applicants who have already earned an advanced degree in science, engineering, or medicine (including an M.D., D.D.S., or D.V.M.) are ineligible. Selection is based on 1) intellectual merit of the proposed activity: strength of the academic record, proposed plan of research, previous research experience, references, appropriateness of the choice of institution; and 2) broader impacts of the proposed activity: how well does the activity advance discovery and understanding, how well does it broaden the participation of underrepresented groups (e.g., women, minorities, persons with disabilities, veterans), to what extent will it enhance the infrastructure for research and education, will the results be disseminated broadly to enhance scientific and technological understanding, what may be the benefits of the proposed activity to society).

Financial data The stipend is $30,000 per year; an additional $12,000 cost-of-education allowance is provided to the recipient's institution.

Duration Up to 3 years, usable over a 5-year period.

Number awarded Approximately 2,000 each year.

Deadline November of each year.

[693]
NSNA/BREAKTHROUGH TO NURSING SCHOLARSHIPS

National Student Nurses' Association
Attn: Foundation
45 Main Street, Suite 606
Brooklyn, NY 11201
(718) 210-0705   Fax: (718) 797-1186
E-mail: nsna@nsna.org
Web: www.nsna.org

Summary To provide financial assistance to Asian American and other minority undergraduate and graduate students who wish to prepare for careers in nursing.

Eligibility This program is open to students currently enrolled in state-approved schools of nursing or pre-nursing associate degree, baccalaureate, diploma, generic master's, generic doctoral, R.N. to B.S.N., R.N. to M.S.N., or L.P.N./L.V.N. to R.N. programs. Graduating high school seniors are not eligible. Support for graduate education is provided only for a first degree in nursing. Applicants must be members of a racial or ethnic minority underrepresented among registered nurses (American Indian or Alaska Native, Hispanic or Latino, Native Hawaiian or other Pacific Islander, Black or African American, or Asian). They must be committed to providing quality health care services to underserved populations. Along with their application, they must submit a 200-word description of their professional and educational goals and how this scholarship will help them achieve those goals. Selection is based on academic achievement, financial need, and involvement in student nursing organizations and community health activities. U.S. citizenship or permanent resident status is required.

Financial data Stipends range from $1,000 to $2,500.

Duration 1 year.

Additional information Applications must be accompanied by a $10 processing fee.

Number awarded Varies each year; recently, 13 of these scholarships were awarded: 10 sponsored by the American Association of Critical-Care Nurses and 3 sponsored by the Mayo Clinic.

Deadline January of each year.

[694]
NWA/DAVID SANKEY MINORITY SCHOLARSHIP IN METEOROLOGY

National Weather Association
Attn: Executive Director
228 West Millbrook Road
Raleigh, NC 27609-4304
(919) 845-1546   Fax: (919) 845-2956
E-mail: exdir@nwas.org
Web: www.nwas.org

Summary To provide financial assistance to Asian Americans and other members of minority groups who are working on an undergraduate or graduate degree in meteorology.

Eligibility This program is open to members of minority ethnic groups who are either entering their sophomore or higher year of undergraduate study or enrolled as graduate students. Applicants must be working on a degree in meteorology. Along with their application, they must submit a 1-page statement explaining why they are applying for this scholarship. Selection is based on that statement, academic achievement, and 2 letters of recommendation.

Financial data The stipend is $1,000.

Duration 1 year.

Additional information This program began in 2002.

Number awarded 1 each year.

Deadline April of each year.

[695]
OLIVER GOLDSMITH, M.D. SCHOLARSHIP

Kaiser Permanente Southern California
Attn: Residency Administration and Recruitment
393 East Walnut Street, Fifth Floor
Pasadena, CA 91188
Toll Free: (877) 574-0002   Fax: (626) 405-6581
E-mail: socal.residency@kp.org
Web: residency.kp.org

Summary To provide financial assistance to Asian American and other medical students who will help bring diversity to the profession.

Eligibility This program is open to students entering their third or fourth year of allopathic or osteopathic medical school. Members of all ethnic and racial groups are encouraged to apply, but applicants must have demonstrated their commitment to diversity through community service, clinical volunteering, or research. They may be attending medical school in any state, but they must intend to practice in southern California and they must be available to participate in a mentoring program and a clerkship at a Kaiser Permanente facility in that region.

Financial data The stipend is $5,000.

Duration 1 year.

Additional information This program began in 2004.

Number awarded 14 each year.

Deadline February of each year.

[696]
OLIVER W. HILL SCHOLARSHIP

LeClairRyan
Attn: Recruiting Manager
Riverfront Plaza, East Tower
951 East Byrd Street, Eighth Floor
Richmond, VA 23219
(804) 783-7597   Fax: (804) 783-2294
E-mail: droberts@leclairryan.com
Web: www.leclairryan.com

Summary To provide financial assistance to Asian Americans and other students of color at law schools in designated states.

Eligibility This program is open to students who have completed at least 1 semester at a law school in a state in which the sponsoring firm has an office (currently, California, Connecticut, Massachusetts, Michigan, New Jersey, New York, Pennsylvania, Virginia, and Washington, D.C.). Applicants must identify as a member of a minority racial ethnic group or as LGBT. They must have a GPA of 3.0 or higher. Along with their application, they must submit a 2,000-word essay presenting their ideas of pursuing social justice through the law.

Financial data The stipend is $5,000.

Duration 1 year.

Additional information This program began in 2009.

Number awarded 1 each year.

Deadline April of each year.

[697]
OLYMPIA BROWN AND MAX KAPP AWARD

Unitarian Universalist Association
Attn: Ministerial Credentialing Office
25 Beacon Street
Boston, MA 02108-2800
(617) 948-6403   Fax: (617) 742-2875
E-mail: mcoadministrator@uua.org
Web: www.uua.org

Summary To provide financial assistance to Unitarian Universalist (UU) candidates for the ministry (especially Asian Americans and other students of color) who submit a project on an aspect of Universalism.

Eligibility This program is open to students currently enrolled full or at least half time in a UU ministerial training program with candidate status. Applicants are primarily citizens of the United States or Canada. Along with their application, they may submit a paper, sermon, or a special project on an aspect of Unitarian Universalism. Priority is given first to those who have demonstrated outstanding ministerial ability and secondarily to students with the greatest financial need (especially persons of color).

Financial data The stipend is $2,500.

Duration 1 year.

Number awarded 1 each year.

Deadline April of each year.

[698]
OPERATION JUMP START III SCHOLARSHIPS

American Association of Advertising Agencies
Attn: AAAA Foundation
1065 Avenue of the Americas, 16th Floor
New York, NY 10018
(212) 262-2500   E-mail: ameadows@aaaa.org
Web: www.aaaa.org

Summary To provide financial assistance to Asian American and other multicultural art directors and copywriters interested in working on an undergraduate or graduate degree in advertising.

Eligibility This program is open to African Americans, Asian Americans, Hispanic Americans, and Native Americans who are U.S. citizens or permanent residents. Applicants must be incoming graduate students at 1 of 6 designated portfolio schools or full-time juniors at 1 of 2 designated colleges. They must be able to demonstrate extreme financial need, creative talent, and promise. Along with their application, they must submit 10 samples of creative work in their respective field of expertise.

Financial data The stipend is $5,000 per year.

Duration Most awards are for 2 years.

Additional information Operation Jump Start began in 1997 and was followed by Operation Jump Start II in 2002. The current program began in 2006. The 6 designated portfolio schools are the AdCenter at Virginia Commonwealth University, the Creative Circus in Atlanta, the Portfolio Center in Atlanta, the Miami Ad School, the University of Texas at Austin, and Pratt Institute. The 2 designated colleges are the Minneapolis College of Art and Design and the Art Center College of Design at Pasadena, California.

Number awarded 20 each year.

Deadline Deadline not specified.

[699]
OREGON STATE BAR SCHOLARSHIPS

Oregon State Bar
Attn: Diversity and Inclusion Department
16037 S.W. Upper Boones Ferry Road
P.O. Box 231935
Tigard, OR 97281-1935
(503) 431-6338
Toll Free: (800) 452-8260, ext. 338 (within OR)
Fax: (503) 598-6938   E-mail: tkelich@osbar.org
Web: www.osbar.org/diversity

Summary To provide financial assistance to entering and continuing students from any state enrolled at law schools in Oregon, especially those who will help the Oregon State Bar achieve its diversity objectives.

Eligibility This program is open to students entering or continuing at 1 of the law schools in Oregon (Willamette, University of Oregon, and Lewis and Clark). Preference is given to students who will contribute to the Oregon State Bar's diversity program to "increase the diversity of the Oregon bench and bar to reflect the diversity of the people of Oregon." Applicants must submit 1) a personal statement on their history of disadvantage or barriers to educational advancement, personal experiences of discrimination, extraordinary financial obligations, composition of immediate family, extraordinary health or medical needs, and languages in which they are fluent as well as barriers they have experienced because English is a second language; and 2) a state bar statement on why they chose to attend an Oregon law school; if they are not committed but are considering practicing in Oregon, what would help them to decide to practice in the state; and how they will improve the quality of legal service or increase access to justice in Oregon. Selection is based on financial need (30%), the personal statement (25%), the state bar statement (25%), community activities (10%), and employment history (10%).

Financial data The stipend is $2,000 per year. Funds are credited to the recipient's law school tuition account.

Duration 1 year; recipients may reapply.

Number awarded 8 each year.

Deadline March of each year.

[700]
OREGON-IDAHO CONFERENCE UMC ETHNIC MINORITY LEADERSHIP AWARDS

United Methodist Church-Oregon-Idaho Conference
Attn: Campus Ministries and Higher Education Ministry Team
1505 S.W. 18th Avenue
Portland, OR 97201-2524
(503) 226-7031   Toll Free: (800) J-WESLEY
Web: www.umoi.org/pages/detail/45

Summary To provide financial assistance to Asian American and other ethnic minority Methodists from Oregon and Idaho who are interested in attending a college or graduate school in any state.

Eligibility This program is open to members of ethnic minority groups (African American, Native American, Asian, Pacific Islander, or Hispanic) who have belonged to a congregation affiliated with the Oregon-Idaho Conference of the United Methodist Church (UMC) for at least 1 year. Applicants must be enrolled or planning to enroll full time as an undergraduate or graduate student at a 2- or 4-year college or university in any state. Along with their application, they must submit personal statements on 1) their faith development; and 2) where they sense God is calling the church in the present and future. Selection is based primarily on demonstrated leadership excellence and/or the potential for leadership excellence in the UMC and in community projects or activities, but other factors, including financial need, are also considered.

Financial data The stipend is $750.

Duration 1 year.

Number awarded 1 each year.

Deadline April of each year.

[701]
PANGARAP SCHOLARSHIP

Filipino Lawyers of Washington
c/o Abigail Daquiz
Department of Labor, Office of the Solicitor
300 Fifth Avenue, Suite 1120
Seattle, WA 98104
(206) 757-6759   E-mail: abigail.daquiz@gmail.com
Web: www.filipinolawyers.org/scholarship

Summary To provide financial assistance to students from any state who are enrolled at law schools in Washington and have a record of service to the Filipino community.

Eligibility This program is open to residents of any state currently enrolled at law schools in Washington. Applicants are not required to be of Filipino ancestry, but they must have a demonstrated significant commitment to community service, particularly service to the Filipino or Filipino American community. Along with their application, they must submit a 2-page essay on a topic that changes annually but relates to the sponsoring organization and its work. Selection is based on the essay, academic achievement, work experience, activities, post-law school goals, and service to the Filipino or Filipino American community.

Financial data The stipend is $1,500.

Duration 1 year.

Number awarded 2 each year.

Deadline October of each year.

[702]
PATRICIA G. ARCHBOLD PREDOCTORAL SCHOLAR AWARD

Gerontological Society of America
Attn: National Hartford Centers of Gerontological Nursing Excellence
1220 L Street, N.W., Suite 901
Washington, DC 20005-4001
(202) 842-1275   Fax: (202) 842-1150
E-mail: nhcgne@geron.org
Web: www.geriatricnursing.org

Summary To provide funding to Asian American and other nurses from underrepresented minority groups who are interested in working on a doctoral degree in gerontological nursing.

Eligibility This program is open to registered nurses who are members of underrepresented minority groups (American Indians, Alaska Natives, Asians, Blacks or African Americans, Hispanics or Latinos/Latinas, Native Hawaiians or other Pacific Islanders) and have been admitted to a doctoral program as a full-time student. Applicants must plan an academic research career in geriatric nursing. They must identify a mentor/adviser with whom they will work and whose program of research in geriatric nursing is a good match with their own research interest area. Selection is based on potential for substantial long-term contributions to the knowledge base in geriatric nursing; leadership potential; evidence of commitment to a career in academic geriatric nursing; and evidence of involvement in educational, research, and professional activities. U.S. citizenship or permanent resident status is required.

Financial data The stipend is $50,000 per year. An additional stipend of $5,000 is available to fellows whose research includes the study of pain in the elderly.

Duration 2 years.

Additional information This program began in 2001 with funding from the John A. Hartford Foundation. In 2004, the Mayday Fund added support to scholars who focus on the study of pain in the elderly. Until 2013 it was known as the Building Academic Geriatric Nursing Capacity Program.

Number awarded Varies each year; recently, 12 of these scholarships were awarded.

Deadline January of each year.

[703]
PATRICK D. MCJULIEN MINORITY GRADUATE SCHOLARSHIP

Association for Educational Communications and Technology
Attn: ECT Foundation
1800 North Stonelake Drive, Suite 2
P.O. Box 2447
Bloomington, IN 47402-2447
(812) 335-7675   Toll Free: (877) 677-AECT
Fax: (812) 335-7678   E-mail: aect@aect.org
Web: www.aect.org/newsite

Summary To provide financial assistance to Asian American and other minority members of the Association for Educational Communications and Technology (AECT) who are working on a graduate degree in the field of educational communications and technology.

Eligibility This program is open to AECT members who are members of minority groups. Applicants must be full-time graduate students enrolled in a degree-granting program in educational technology at the master's (M.S.), specialist (Ed.S.), or doctoral (Ph.D., Ed.D.) levels. They must have a GPA of 3.0 or higher.

Financial data A stipend is awarded (amount not specified).

Duration 1 year.

Number awarded 1 each year.

Deadline July of each year.

[704]
PAUL D. WHITE SCHOLARSHIP

BakerHostetler LLP
Attn: Attorney Recruitment and Development Manager
PNC Center
1900 East Ninth Street, Suite 3200
Cleveland, OH 44114-3482
(216) 621-0200   Fax: (216) 696-0740
E-mail: ddriscole@bakerlaw.com
Web: www.bakerlaw.com/firmdiversity/scholarship

Summary To provide financial aid and summer work experience to Asian American and other minority law school students.

Eligibility This program is open to first- and second-year law students of Black/African American, Hispanic/Latino, Asian, Native Hawaiian/Pacific Islander or American Indian/ Alaska Native descent. Selection is based on law school performance, demonstrated leadership abilities (as evidenced by community and collegiate involvement), collegiate academic record, extracurricular activities, work experience, and a written personal statement.

Financial data The program provides a stipend of $7,500 for the scholarship and a paid summer clerkship with the sponsoring firm. To date, the firm has expended more than $2.0 million in scholarships and clerkships.

Duration 1 year, including the following summer.

Additional information This program began in 1997. Clerkships may be performed at any of the firm's offices in Cincinnati, Cleveland, or Orlando.

Number awarded 1 or more each year.

Deadline January of each year.

[705]
PAUL P. VOURAS DISSERTATION RESEARCH GRANT

Association of American Geographers
Attn: Grants and Awards
1710 16th Street, N.W.
Washington, DC 20009-3198
(202) 234-1450   Fax: (202) 234-2744
E-mail: grantsawards@aag.org
Web: www.aag.org/cs/grants/dissertation

Summary To provide funding to members of the Association of American Geographers (AAG), especially Asian Americans and other minorities, who are preparing dissertations in geography.

Eligibility This program is open to doctoral students who have been AAG members for at least 1 year, have completed all Ph.D. requirements except the dissertation, and will not

have earned the doctorate by the time of the award. The applicant's dissertation supervisor must certify eligibility. Preference is given to minority applicants.

Financial data Grants are approximately $500.

Duration 1 year.

Number awarded 1 or more each year.

Deadline December of each year.

[706]
PAUL STEPHEN LIM ASIAN-AMERICAN PLAYWRITING AWARD

John F. Kennedy Center for the Performing Arts
Education Department
Attn: Kennedy Center American College Theater Festival
2700 F Street, N.W.
Washington, DC 20566
(202) 416-8857   Fax: (202) 416-8860
E-mail: KCACTF@kennedy-center.org
Web: www.kcactf.org

Summary To recognize and reward outstanding Asian America student playwrights.

Eligibility Students at any accredited junior or senior college in the United States are eligible to compete, provided their college agrees to participate in the Kennedy Center American College Theater Festival (KCACTF). Undergraduate students must be carrying at least 6 semester hours, graduate students must be enrolled in at least 3 semester hours, and continuing part-time students must be enrolled in a regular degree or certificate program. This award is presented to the author of the best play on any subject who is of Asian heritage.

Financial data The winning playwright receives a cash award of $1,000 for a full-length play or $500 for a 1-act play. The award includes an all-expense paid professional development opportunity.

Duration The award is presented annually.

Additional information This program is part of the Michael Kanin Playwriting Awards Program. The sponsoring college or university must pay a registration fee of $275 for each production.

Number awarded 2 students and 2 sponsoring institutions receive awards each year.

Deadline November of each year.

[707]
PERKINS COIE DIVERSITY STUDENT FELLOWSHIPS

Perkins Coie LLP
Attn: Chief Diversity Officer
131 South Dearborn Street, Suite 1700
Chicago, IL 60603-5559
(312) 324-8593   Fax: (312) 324-9400
E-mail: diversity@perkinscoie.com
Web: www.perkinscoie.com/diversity/Diversity.aspx

Summary To provide financial assistance to Asian American and other law students who reflect the diversity of communities in the country.

Eligibility This program is open to students enrolled in the first year of a J.D. program at an ABA-accredited law school. Applicants must contribute meaningfully to the diversity of the law school student body and the legal profession. Diversity is defined broadly to include members of racial, ethnic, disabled, and sexual orientation minority groups, as well as those who may be the first person in their family to pursue higher education. Applicants must submit a 1-page personal statement that describes their unique personal history, a legal writing sample, a current resume, and undergraduate and law school transcripts. They are not required to disclose their financial circumstances, but a demonstrated need for financial assistance may be taken into consideration.

Financial data The stipend is $7,500.

Duration 1 year.

Additional information Fellows are also offered a summer associateship at their choice of the firm's offices in Anchorage, Bellevue, Boise, Chicago, Dallas, Los Angeles, Madison, Palo Alto, Phoenix, Portland, San Diego, San Francisco, Seattle, or Washington, D.C.

Number awarded Varies each year; recently, 7 of these fellowships were awarded.

Deadline January of each year.

[708]
PFATS-NFL CHARITIES MINORITY SCHOLARSHIPS

Professional Football Athletic Trainers Society
c/o Britt Brown, ATC, Associate Athletic Trainer
Dallas Cowboys
One Cowboys Parkway
Irving, TX 75063
(972) 497-4992   E-mail: bbrown@dallascowboys.net
Web: www.pfats.com/about/scholarships

Summary To provide financial assistance to Asian American and other minority undergraduate and graduate students working on a degree in athletic training.

Eligibility This program is open to ethnic minority students who are working on an undergraduate or graduate degree in athletic training. Applicants must have a GPA of 2.5 or higher. Along with their application, they must submit a cover letter, a curriculum vitae, and a letter of recommendation from their supervising athletic trainer.

Financial data A stipend is awarded (amount not specified).

Duration 1 year.

Additional information Recipients also have an opportunity to work at summer training camp of a National Football League (NFL) team. Support for this program, which began in 1993, is provided by NFL Charities.

Number awarded 1 or more each year.

Deadline March of each year.

[709]
PHILIP JAISOHN MEMORIAL FOUNDATION JOURNALISM SCHOLARSHIP

Philip Jaisohn Memorial Foundation
Attn: Education and Scholarship Committee
6705 Old York Road
Philadelphia, PA 19126
(215) 224-2000   Fax: (215) 224-9164
E-mail: jaisohnhouse@gmail.com
Web: www.jaisohn.org

Summary To provide financial assistance to Korean American undergraduate and graduate students who are working on a degree in journalism.

Eligibility This program is open to Korean American undergraduate and graduate students who are currently enrolled at a college or university in the United States. Applicants must be working on a degree in journalism. They must be able to demonstrate academic excellence, leadership and service to their school and community, and financial need. Along with their application, they must submit an essay on either "Who is Dr. Jaisohn to Me," or "The Significance of Dr. Jaisohn's Ideal to Korean Americans." They must also submit a brief statement on how they can contribute to and be involved in the activities of the Philip Jaisohn Memorial Foundation.

Financial data The stipend is $1,000.

Duration 1 year.

Number awarded 1 each year.

Deadline November of each year.

[710]
PHILIPPINE NURSES ASSOCIATION OF AMERICA SCHOLARSHIP

Philippine Nurses Association of America
Attn: PNAA Foundation
c/o Cornelio S.J. Obordo, Scholarship Committee Chair
73 Hawkins Circle
Wheaton, IL 60187
(630) 653-0630   E-mail: icare1@sbcglobal.net
Web: www.mypnaafoundation.org/index.php/scholarships

Summary To provide financial assistance for graduate study to members of the Philippine Nurses Association of America (PNAA).

Eligibility This program is open to PNAA members who are enrolled or admitted at an accredited program for a master's degree in nursing, post-master's study, or doctoral degree. Applicants must be endorsed by their PNAA chapter president. Along with their application, they must submit a 150-word essay on how this scholarship will help them attain their goals. Selection is based on that essay (10%), academic record (10%), 3 letters of recommendation (20%), work experience (10%), education and certification (10%), publications and research papers (10%), community activities and leadership roles (10%), professional affiliation (10%), and awards and achievements (10%).

Financial data The stipend is $1,000 per year.

Duration 1 year; may be renewed, provided the recipient maintains a GPA of 3.0 or higher.

Number awarded Varies each year; recently, 6 of these scholarships were awarded.

Deadline May of each year.

[711]
PNAO SCHOLARSHIP AWARD

Philippine Nurses Association of Ohio
c/o Erlinda Gonzalez, Foundation President
ManorCare Health Services
37603 Euclid Avenue
Willoughby, OH 44094
(440) 951-5551   Fax: (440) 951-1914
Web: www.pnao.org/?page_id=218

Summary To provide financial assistance to members of the Philippine Nurses Association of Ohio (PNAO) who are working on an undergraduate or graduate degree at a school of nursing in any state.

Eligibility This program is open to residents of Ohio or the Philippines who are of at least 50% Filipino ethnicity and an associate member of PNAO. Applicants must be enrolled in an undergraduate or graduate nursing program at a school in any state. They must have a GPA of 3.0 or higher and be able to demonstrate financial need. Along with their application, they must submit a 1-page essay on their vision of nursing.

Financial data The stipend is $500.

Duration 1 year.

Number awarded 2 each year.

Deadline July of each year.

[712]
PORTER PHYSIOLOGY DEVELOPMENT AWARDS

American Physiological Society
Attn: Education Office
9650 Rockville Pike, Room 3111
Bethesda, MD 20814-3991
(301) 634-7132   Fax: (301) 634-7098
E-mail: education@the-aps.org
Web: www.the-aps.org

Summary To provide financial assistance to Asian Americans and other minorities who are members of the American Physiological Society (APS) and interested in working on a doctoral degree in physiology.

Eligibility This program is open to U.S. citizens and permanent residents who are members of racial or ethnic minority groups (Hispanic or Latino, American Indian or Alaska Native, Asian, Black or African American, or Native Hawaiian or other Pacific Islander). Applicants must be currently enrolled in or accepted to a doctoral program in physiology at a university as full-time students. They must be APS members and have actively participated in its work. Selection is based on the applicant's potential for success (academic record, statement of interest, previous awards and experiences, letters of recommendation); applicant's proposed training environment (including quality of preceptor); and applicant's research and training plan (clarity and quality).

Financial data The stipend is $23,500 per year. No provision is made for a dependency allowance or tuition and fees.

Duration 1 year; may be renewed for 1 additional year and, in exceptional cases, for a third year.

Additional information This program is supported by the William Townsend Porter Foundation (formerly the Harvard Apparatus Foundation). The first Porter Fellowship was awarded in 1920. In 1966 and 1967, the American Physiological Society established the Porter Physiology Development Committee to award fellowships to minority students engaged in graduate study in physiology. The highest ranked applicant for these fellowships is designated the Eleanor Ison Franklin Fellow.

Number awarded Varies each year; recently, 8 of these fellowships were awarded.

Deadline January of each year.

[713]
PREDOCTORAL RESEARCH TRAINING FELLOWSHIPS IN EPILEPSY

Epilepsy Foundation
Attn: Research Department
8301 Professional Place
Landover, MD 20785-2353
(301) 459-3700   Toll Free: (800) EFA-1000
Fax: (301) 577-2684   TDD: (800) 332-2070
E-mail: grants@efa.org
Web: www.epilepsyfoundation.org

Summary To provide funding to doctoral candidates (particularly Asian Americans, other minorities, women, and individuals with disabilities) who are enrolled in designated fields and interested in conducting dissertation research on a topic related to epilepsy.

Eligibility This program is open to full-time graduate students working on a Ph.D. in biochemistry, genetics, neuroscience, nursing, pharmacology, pharmacy, physiology, or psychology. Applicants must be conducting dissertation research on a topic relevant to epilepsy under the guidance of a mentor with expertise in the area of epilepsy investigation. Applications from women, members of minority groups, and people with disabilities are especially encouraged. U.S. citizenship is not required, but the project must be conducted in the United States. Selection is based on the relevance of the proposed work to epilepsy, the applicant's qualifications, the mentor's qualifications, the scientific quality of the proposed dissertation research, the quality of the training environment for research related to epilepsy, and the adequacy of the facility.

Financial data The grant is $20,000, consisting of $19,000 for a stipend and $1,000 to support travel to attend the annual meeting of the American Epilepsy Society.

Duration 1 year.

Additional information Support for this program, which began in 1998, is provided by many individuals, families, and corporations, especially the American Epilepsy Society, Abbott Laboratories, Ortho-McNeil Pharmaceutical, and Pfizer Inc.

Number awarded Varies each year.

Deadline August of each year.

[714]
PUBLIC INTEREST FELLOWSHIPS FOR LAW STUDENTS OF COLOR

Goodwin Procter LLP
Attn: Recruiting Manager
53 State Street
Boston, MA 02109
(617) 570-8156   Fax: (617) 523-1231
E-mail: fellowships@goodwinprocter.com
Web: www.goodwinprocter.com

Summary To provide financial aid and work experience to Asian American and other minority students who are interested in public interest law.

Eligibility This program is open to students of color entering their second year at a law school in any state. Applicants must actively express an interest in working in the sponsoring firm's summer program in public interest law. If they are applying for the Goodwin MassMutual Diversity Fellowship, they must express an interest in working with MassMutual's legal department in Springfield, Massachusetts for 2 weeks as part of the summer program and specializing in the investment or insurance business or in a legal focus to advance business objectives. Selection is based on academic performance, leadership abilities, involvement in minority student organizations, commitment to community service, interpersonal skills, other special achievements and honors, and interest in working with the firm during the summer.

Financial data The stipend is $7,500.

Duration 1 year; nonrenewable.

Additional information This program began in 2005. In 2007, it added the Goodwin MassMutual Diversity Fellowship, created in conjunction with its long-standing client, Massachusetts Mutual Life Insurance Company (MassMutual). Summer positions are available at the firm's offices in Boston, Los Angeles, New York, Palo Alto, San Diego, San Francisco, and Washington, D.C.

Number awarded 4 each year, including 1 Goodwin MassMutual Diversity Fellowship.

Deadline October of each year.

[715]
RACIAL ETHNIC PASTORAL LEADERSHIP PROGRAM

Synod of Southern California and Hawaii
Attn: Racial Ethnic Pastoral Leadership Work Group
3325 Wilshire Boulevard, Suite 850
Los Angeles, CA 90010-1761
(213) 483-3840, ext. 103   Fax: (213) 483-4275
E-mail: LeonFanniel@synod.org
Web: www.synod.org/repl/index.html

Summary To provide financial assistance to Asian Americans and members of other racial minority groups in the Presbyterian Church (USA) Synod of Southern California and Hawaii who are preparing for a career as a pastor or other church vocation.

Eligibility Applicants must be under care of their church's Session and enrolled with a Presbytery within the Synod of Southern California and Hawaii. They must be members of racial ethnic groups interested in becoming a Presbyterian pastor or other church worker (e.g., commissioned ruling elder, certified Christian educator) and serving in a racial ethnic ministry within the PCUSA. Racial ethnic persons who already have an M.Div. degree, are from another denomination in correspondence with the PCUSA, and are seeking to meet PCUSA requirements for ordination or transfer may also be eligible if they plan to serve in a racial ethnic congregation or an approved specialized ministry. Applicants must submit documentation of financial need, recommendations from the appropriate presbytery committee or session, a current transcript, and essays on their goals and objectives. They must be enrolled full or part time in a PCUSA seminary or other seminary approved by the Committee on Preparation for Ministry of their Presbytery.

Financial data The stipend is $2,000 per year.

Duration 1 year; may be renewed.

Additional information This program began in 1984.

Number awarded Varies each year.

Deadline April of each year.

[716]
RACIAL ETHNIC SUPPLEMENTAL GRANTS

Presbyterian Church (USA)
Attn: Office of Financial Aid for Studies
100 Witherspoon Street, Room M-052
Louisville, KY 40202-1396
(502) 569-5224   Toll Free: (800) 728-7228, ext. 5224
Fax: (502) 569-8766   TDD: (800) 833-5955
E-mail: finaid@pcusa.org
Web: gamc.pcusa.org

Summary To provide financial assistance to Asian American and other minority graduate students who are Presbyterian Church (USA) members interested in preparing for church occupations.

Eligibility This program is open to racial/ethnic graduate students (Asian American, African American, Hispanic American, Native American, or Alaska Native) who are enrolled full time at a PCUSA seminary or accredited theological institution approved by their Committee on Preparation for Ministry. Applicants must be working on 1) an M.Div. degree and enrolled as an inquirer or candidate by a PCUSA presbytery; or 2) an M.A.C.E. degree and preparing for a church occupation. They must be PCUSA members, U.S. citizens or permanent residents, able to demonstrate financial need, and recommended by the financial aid officer at their theological institution. Along with their application, they must submit a 1,000-word essay on what they believe God is calling them to do in ministry.

Financial data Stipends range from $500 to $1,000 per year. Funds are intended as supplements to students who have been awarded a Presbyterian Study Grant but still demonstrate remaining financial need.

Duration 1 year; may be renewed up to 2 additional years.

Number awarded Varies each year.

Deadline June of each year.

[717]
RAILROAD AND MINE WORKERS MEMORIAL SCHOLARSHIP

Japanese American Citizens League
Attn: National Scholarship Awards
1765 Sutter Street
San Francisco, CA 94115
(415) 345-1075   Fax: (415) 931-4671
E-mail: ncwnp@jacl.org
Web: www.jacl.org/edu/scholar.htm

Summary To provide financial assistance for graduate study in any field to members of the Japanese American Citizens League (JACL).

Eligibility This program is open to JACL members who are attending or planning to attend an accredited college or university as a graduate student. Applicants must submit information on their involvement in JACL and a 2-page essay on a topic that changes annually but relates to Japanese Americans. Selection is based on that essay, academic history, JACL involvement, school activities, work history, scholastic honors, and community involvement.

Financial data Stipends generally average more than $2,000.

Duration 1 year; nonrenewable.

Additional information This program was established to honor the Japanese American railroad and mine workers who lost their jobs during World War II.

Number awarded At least 1 each year.

Deadline March of each year.

[718]
RALPH W. SHRADER DIVERSITY SCHOLARSHIPS

Armed Forces Communications and Electronics
Association
Attn: AFCEA Educational Foundation
4400 Fair Lakes Court
Fairfax, VA 22033-3899
(703) 631-6138   Toll Free: (800) 336-4583, ext. 6138
Fax: (703) 631-4693   E-mail: scholarshipsinfo@afcea.org
Web: www.afcea.org

Summary To provide financial assistance to Asian American and other master's degree students in fields related to communications and electronics.

Eligibility This program is open to U.S. citizens working on a master's degree at an accredited college or university in the United States. Applicants must be enrolled full time and studying computer science, computer technology, engineering (chemical, electrical, electronic, communications, or systems), mathematics, physics, management information systems, or a field directly related to the support of U.S. national security or intelligence enterprises. At least 1 of these scholarships is set aside for a woman or a minority. Selection is based primarily on academic excellence.

Financial data The stipend is $3,000. Funds are paid directly to the recipient.

Duration 1 year.

Additional information This program is sponsored by Booz Allen Hamilton.

Number awarded Up to 5 each year, at least 1 of which is for a woman or minority candidate.

Deadline February of each year.

[719]
RAMA SCHOLARSHIP FOR THE AMERICAN DREAM

American Hotel & Lodging Educational Foundation
Attn: Manager of Foundation Programs
1201 New York Avenue, N.W., Suite 600
Washington, DC 20005-3931
(202) 289-3100   Fax: (202) 289-3199
E-mail: scholarships@ahlef.org
Web: www.ahlef.org/content.aspx?id=19468

Summary To provide financial assistance to Asian Indian and other undergraduate and graduate students working on a degree in hotel management at designated schools.

Eligibility This program is open to U.S. citizens and permanent residents enrolled as full-time undergraduate or graduate students with a GPA of 2.5 or higher. Applicants must be attending 1 of 13 designated hospitality management schools, which select the recipients. Preference is given to students of Asian-Indian descent and other minority groups and to JHM Hotel employees and their dependents.

Financial data The stipend varies at each of the participating schools, but ranges from $1,000 to $3,000.

Duration 1 year.

Additional information This program was established by JHM Hotels, Inc. in 1998. The participating institutions are Bethune-Cookman University, California State Polytechnic University at Pomona, Cornell University, Florida International University, Georgia State University, Greenville Technical College, Howard University, Johnson & Wales University (Providence, Rhode Island), New York University, University of Central Florida, University of Houston, University of South Carolina, and Virginia Polytechnic Institute and State University.

Number awarded Varies each year; recently, 20 of these scholarships were awarded. Since the program was established, it has awarded more than $491,000 to 287 recipients.

Deadline April of each year.

[720]
RANDY GERSON MEMORIAL GRANT

American Psychological Foundation
750 First Street, N.E.
Washington, DC 20002-4242
(202) 336-5843   Fax: (202) 336-5812
E-mail: foundation@apa.org
Web: www.apa.org/apf/funding/gerson.aspx

Summary To provide funding to graduate students (particularly Asian Americans, other minorities, women, and students with disabilities) who are interested in conducting research in the psychology of couple and/or family dynamics and/or multi-generational processes.

Eligibility This program is open to full-time graduate students in psychology. Applicants must be proposing a project that advances the systemic understanding of couple and/or family dynamics and/or multi-generational processes. Work that advances theory, assessment, or clinical practice in those areas is eligible. Preference is given to projects that use or contribute to the development of Bowen family systems. Selection is based on conformance with stated program goals, magnitude of incremental contribution, quality of proposed work, and applicant's demonstrated scholarship and research competence. The sponsor encourages applications from individuals who represent diversity in race, ethnicity, gender, age, disability, and sexual orientation.

Financial data The grant is $6,000.

Duration The grant is presented annually.

Additional information This grant was first awarded in 1998.

Number awarded 1 each year.

Deadline January of each year.

[721]
RAYMOND L. OCAMPO JR. SCHOLARSHIP

Filipino Bar Association of Northern California
268 Bush Street, Suite 2928
San Francisco, CA 94104
E-mail: fbancinfo@gmail.com
Web: www.fbanc.org/law-students

Summary To provide financial assistance to entering or continuing law students who are interested in serving the Filipino American community.

Eligibility This program is open to currently-enrolled and entering law students who have a tie to the Filipino American community and intend to provide legal services to that community after graduation from law school. Applicants must submit a current transcript or admit letter, a resume, and a 2-page essay on a topic that changes annually but relates to Filipinos and the law. Selection is based on that essay, interest and desire to serve the Filipino American community, and persuasiveness.

Financial data The stipend is $5,000.

Duration 1 year.

Additional information This program began in 2000 as a result of a gift from Raymond L. Ocampo, Jr., who founded the Filipino Bar Association of Northern California in 1980.

Number awarded 1 each year.

Deadline April of each year.

[722]
RDW GROUP, INC. MINORITY SCHOLARSHIP FOR COMMUNICATIONS

Rhode Island Foundation
Attn: Funds Administrator
One Union Station
Providence, RI 02903
(401) 427-4017　　　　　　　　Fax: (401) 331-8085
E-mail: lmonahan@rifoundation.org
Web: www.rifoundation.org

Summary To provide financial assistance to Asian Americans and other residents of color from Rhode Island who are working on a undergraduate or graduate degree in communications in any state.

Eligibility This program is open to undergraduate and graduate students at colleges and universities in any state who are Rhode Island residents of color. Applicants must intend to work on a degree in communications (including computer graphics, art, cinematography, or other fields that would prepare them for a career in advertising). They must be able to demonstrate financial need and a commitment to a career in communications. Along with their application, they must submit an essay (up to 300 words) on the impact they would like to have on the communications field.

Financial data The stipend is approximately $2,000 per year.

Duration 1 year; recipients may reapply.

Additional information This program is sponsored by the RDW Group, Inc.

Number awarded 1 each year.

Deadline April of each year.

[723]
REED SMITH DIVERSE SCHOLARS PROGRAM

Reed Smith LLP
Attn: U.S. Director of Legal Recruiting
2500 One Liberty Place
1650 Market Street
Philadelphia, PA 19103
(215) 851-8100　　　　　　E-mail: dlevin@reedsmith.com
Web: www.reedsmith.com/Diverse_Scholars_Program

Summary To provide financial aid and summer work experience to Asian American and other law students who are will contribute to diversity in the field.

Eligibility This program is open to students completing their first year of law school. Applicants must be able to dem-

onstrate a record of academic excellence and a commitment to diversity, inclusion, and community. Along with their application, they must submit a 750-word personal statement on how they believe they can contribute to the sponsoring law firm's goals of diversity and inclusion, including 1) how their life experiences have impacted their commitment to diversity; 2) their community involvement; and 3) their academic or leadership achievements.

Financial data The stipend is $15,000. Recipients are also offered a summer associate position at their choice of the firm's 9 U.S. offices after completion of their second year of law school (in Chicago, Houston, Los Angeles, New York, Philadelphia, Pittsburgh, Richmond, San Francisco, or Washington, D.C.).

Duration 1 year (the second year of law school).

Additional information The firm established this program in 2008 as part of its commitment to promote diversity in the legal profession.

Number awarded 2 each year.

Deadline August of each year.

[724]
REVEREND H. JOHN YAMASHITA MEMORIAL SCHOLARSHIP

Japanese American Citizens League
Attn: National Scholarship Awards
1765 Sutter Street
San Francisco, CA 94115
(415) 345-1075　　　　　　　　Fax: (415) 931-4671
E-mail: ncwnp@jacl.org
Web: www.jacl.org/edu/scholar.htm

Summary To provide financial assistance for graduate study in any field to members of the Japanese American Citizens League (JACL).

Eligibility This program is open to JACL members who are attending or planning to attend an accredited college or university as a graduate student. Applicants must submit information on their involvement in JACL and a 2-page essay on a topic that changes annually but relates to Japanese Americans. Selection is based on that essay, academic history, JACL involvement, school activities, work history, scholastic honors, and community involvement.

Financial data Stipends generally average more than $2,000.

Duration 1 year; nonrenewable.

Number awarded At least 1 each year.

Deadline March of each year.

[725]
RICHARD AND HELEN BROWN COREM SCHOLARSHIPS

United Church of Christ
Parish Life and Leadership Ministry Team
Attn: COREM Administrator
700 Prospect Avenue East
Cleveland, OH 44115-1100
(216) 736-2113　　　　Toll Free: (866) 822-8224, ext. 2113
Fax: (216) 736-3783
Web: www.ucc.org/seminarians/ucc-scholarships-for.html

Summary To provide financial assistance to Asian American and other minority seminary students who are interested in becoming a pastor in the United Church of Christ (UCC).

Eligibility This program is open to students at accredited seminaries who have been members of a UCC congregation for at least 1 year. Applicants must work through 1 of the member bodies of the Council for Racial and Ethnic Ministries (COREM): United Black Christians (UBC), Ministers for Racial, Social and Economic Justice (MRSEJ), Council for Hispanic Ministries (CHM), Pacific Islander and Asian American Ministries (PAAM), or Council for American Indian Ministries (CAIM). They must 1) have a GPA of 3.0 or higher; 2) be enrolled in a course of study leading to ordained ministry; 3) be in care of an association or conference at the time of application; and 4) demonstrate leadership ability through participation in their local church, association, conference, or academic environment.

Financial data Stipends are approximately $10,000 per year.

Duration 1 year.

Number awarded Varies each year; recently, 7 scholarships were awarded by UBC, 2 by MRSEJ, 1 by PAAM, and 2 by CHM.

Deadline Deadline not specified.

[726]
RICHARD D. HAILEY AAJ LAW STUDENT SCHOLARSHIPS

American Association for Justice
Attn: Scholarships
777 Sixth Street, N.W., Suite 200
Washington, DC 20001
(202) 965-3500, ext. 2834
Toll Free: (800) 424-2725, ext. 2834
Fax: (202) 965-0355
E-mail: catherine.rodman@justice.org
Web: www.justice.org/cps/rde/xchg/justice/hs.xsl/648.htm

Summary To provide financial assistance for law school to Asian American and other minority student members of the American Association for Justice (AAJ).

Eligibility This program is open to African American, Hispanic, Asian American, Native American, and biracial members of the association who are entering the first, second, or third year of law school. Applicants must submit a 500-word essay on how they meet the selection criteria: commitment to the association, involvement in student chapter and minority caucus activities, desire to represent victims, interest and proficiency of skills in trial advocacy, and financial need.

Financial data The stipend is $1,000.

Duration 1 year.

Additional information The American Association for Justice was formerly the Association of Trial Lawyers of America.

Number awarded Up to 6 each year.

Deadline May of each year.

[727]
ROBERT T. MATSUI ANNUAL WRITING COMPETITION

Asian Pacific American Bar Association Educational Fund
P.O. Box 2209
Washington, DC 20013-2209
Fax: (202) 408-4400   E-mail: aefboard@gmail.com
Web: www.aefdc.com/?page_id=93

Summary To recognize and reward law students who submit outstanding articles on topics of interest to the Asian Pacific American legal community.

Eligibility This competition is open to law students in the United States. Applicants must submit an original law review article, up to 10,000 words in length, that has not been published. The topic must relate to Asian Pacific Americans and the law.

Financial data The award is $1,500.

Duration The award is presented annually.

Additional information This competition was established in 2005. The winning entry is published by the *Asian Pacific American Law Journal* at the University of California, Los Angeles School of Law.

Number awarded 1 each year.

Deadline June of each year.

[728]
ROBERT TOIGO FOUNDATION FELLOWSHIPS

Robert Toigo Foundation
Attn: Fellowship Program Administrator
180 Grand Avenue, Suite 900
Oakland, CA 94612
(510) 763-5771   Fax: (510) 763-5778
E-mail: info@toigofoundation.org
Web: www.toigofoundation.org

Summary To provide financial assistance to Asian American and other minority students working on a master's degree in business administration or a related field.

Eligibility This program is open to members of minority groups (African American, Hispanic/Latino, Native American/Alaskan Native, South Asian American, or Asian American/Pacific Islander) who are entering or enrolled in a program for an M.B.A., J.D./M.B.A., master's in real estate, or master's in finance. Applicants must be preparing for a career in finance, including (but not limited to) investment management, investment banking, corporate finance, real estate, private equity, venture capital, business development, pension fund investment, or financial services consulting. U.S. citizenship or permanent resident status is required.

Financial data The stipend is $2,500 per year.

Duration Up to 2 years.

Additional information The application fee is $40.

Number awarded Approximately 50 to 60 each year.

Deadline March of each year.

[729]
ROSA L. PARKS SCHOLARSHIPS

Conference of Minority Transportation Officials
Attn: National Scholarship Program
1875 I Street, N.W., Suite 500
Washington, DC 20006
(703) 234-4072   Fax: (202) 318-0364
Web: www.comto.org/?page=Scholarships

Summary To provide financial assistance for college to children of members of the Conference of Minority Transportation Officials (COMTO) and to other students interested in working on a bachelor's or master's degree in transportation.

Eligibility This program is open to 1) college-bound high school seniors whose parent has been a COMTO member for at least 1 year; 2) undergraduates who have completed at least 60 semester credit hours in a transportation discipline; and 3) students working on a master's degree in transportation who have completed at least 15 credits. Applicants must have a GPA of 3.0 or higher. Along with their application, they must submit a cover letter with a 500-word statement of career goals. Financial need is not considered in the selection process. U.S. citizenship or legal resident status is required.

Financial data The stipend is $4,500. Funds are paid directly to the recipient's college or university.

Duration 1 year.

Additional information COMTO was established in 1971 to promote, strengthen, and expand the roles of minorities in all aspects of transportation. Recipients are expected to attend the COMTO National Scholarship Luncheon.

Number awarded 1 each year.

Deadline May of each year.

[730]
ROY H. POLLACK SCHOLARSHIP

Unitarian Universalist Association
Attn: Ministerial Credentialing Office
25 Beacon Street
Boston, MA 02108-2800
(617) 948-6403   Fax: (617) 742-2875
E-mail: mcoadministrator@uua.org
Web: www.uua.org

Summary To provide financial assistance to seminary students (especially Asian Americans and other students of color) preparing for the Unitarian Universalist (UU) ministry.

Eligibility This program is open to seminary students who are enrolled full or at least half time in their second or third year in a UU ministerial training program with candidate status. Applicants must be citizens of the United States or Canada. Priority is given first to those who have demonstrated outstanding ministerial ability and secondarily to students with the greatest financial need (especially persons of color).

Financial data The stipend ranges from $1,000 to $15,000 per year.

Duration 1 year.

Number awarded Varies each year; recently, 2 of these scholarships were awarded.

Deadline April of each year.

[731]
ROY SCRIVNER MEMORIAL RESEARCH GRANTS

American Psychological Foundation
750 First Street, N.E.
Washington, DC 20002-4242
(202) 336-5843   Fax: (202) 336-5812
E-mail: foundation@apa.org
Web: www.apa.org/apf/funding/scrivner.aspx

Summary To provide funding to graduate students (particularly Asian Americans and other students from diverse backgrounds) who are interested in conducting dissertation research on lesbian, gay, bisexual, and transgender (LGBT) family psychology and therapy.

Eligibility This program is open to doctoral candidates who are interested in conducting empirical research in all fields of the behavioral and social sciences that focus on LGBT family psychology and LGBT family therapy. Proposals are especially encouraged for empirical studies that address the following: problems faced by LGBT families such as those associated with cultural, racial, socioeconomic, and family structure diversity; successful coping mechanisms such as sources of support and resilience for family members; and clinical issues and interventions in the domain of LGBT. Selection is based on conformance with stated program goals, magnitude of incremental contribution, quality of proposed work, and applicant's demonstrated scholarship and research competence. The sponsor encourages applications from individuals who represent diversity in race, ethnicity, gender, age, disability, and sexual orientation.

Financial data The grant is $12,000.

Duration 1 year.

Number awarded 1 each year.

Deadline October of each year.

[732]
R.P. AND J.L. CARR SOCIAL JUSTICE SCHOLARSHIP

Organization of Chinese Americans-Wisconsin Chapter
c/o Vera Lau, Scholarship Committee
120 North 73rd Street
Milwaukee, WI 53213
E-mail: ocawischolarship@yahoo.com
Web: www.ocawi.org/www/scholarships.html

Summary To provide financial assistance to members of the Wisconsin Chapter of the Organization of Chinese Americans (OCA-WI) who are interested in working on a graduate degree in a field related to peace and social justice.

Eligibility This program is open to OCA-WI members who are enrolled or planning to enroll full time in a graduate program at an accredited college or university in any state. Applicants must be interested in working on a degree in a field related to peace and social justice (e.g., law, public policy, political science, community development). Along with their application, they must submit a 2-page personal statement that describes themselves, their field of study, pertinent personal history, and professional plans. U.S. citizenship or permanent resident status is required.

Financial data The stipend is $2,000.

Duration 1 year.

Additional information This program began in 2008.

Number awarded 1 each year.

Deadline April of each year.

[733]
RYU FAMILY FOUNDATION SCHOLARSHIP GRANTS

Ryu Family Foundation, Inc.
Attn: Jenny Kang
186 Parish Drive
Wayne, NJ 07470
(973) 692-9696, ext. 20   Fax: (973) 692-0999
Web: www.seolbong.org

Summary To provide financial assistance to Korean and Korean American students in the Northeast who are working on an undergraduate or graduate degree in any field.

Eligibility This program is open to Korean Americans (U.S. citizens) and Koreans (with or without permanent resident status). Applicants must be enrolled full time and working on an undergraduate or graduate degree; have a GPA of 3.5 or higher; be able to document financial need; and be either residing or attending college in 1 of the following 10 northeastern states: Connecticut, Delaware, Maine, Massachusetts, New Hampshire, New Jersey, New York, Pennsylvania, Rhode Island, or Vermont. Along with their application, they must submit a 500-word essay on a subject that changes annually; recently, students were asked to write on either 1) the importance of religion in the minds of the Korean people; or 2) the patriotism of Korean Admiral Soon Shin Lee.

Financial data A stipend is awarded (amount not specified). Checks are made out jointly to the recipient and the recipient's school.

Duration 1 year; may be renewed.

Number awarded 1 or more each year.

Deadline June of each year.

[734]
SAJA SCHOLARSHIPS

South Asian Journalists Association
c/o Shefali Kulkarni, Secretary
Kaiser Health News
1330 G Street, N.W.
Washington, DC 20005
E-mail: shefali.kulkarni24@gmail.com
Web: www.saja.org/scholarships

Summary To provide financial assistance for undergraduate and graduate study to journalism students of south Asian descent.

Eligibility This program is open to students of south Asian descent (including Bangladesh, Bhutan, India, Maldives, Nepal, Pakistan, and Sri Lanka; Indo-Caribbeans are also eligible). Applicants must be serious about preparing for a journalism career and must provide evidence they plan to do so through courses, internships, or freelancing. They may be 1) high school seniors about to enroll in an accredited college or university; 2) current students in an accredited college or university in the United States or Canada; or 3) students enrolled or about to enter a graduate program in the United States or Canada. Applicants with financial hardship are given special consideration. Selection is based on interest in journalism, writing skills, participation in the sponsoring organization, reasons for entering journalism, and financial need.

Financial data The stipends are $2,500 for high school seniors, $3,000 for undergraduates, or $5,000 for graduate students.

Duration 1 year.

Additional information Recipients are expected to give back to the South Asian Journalists Association (SAJA) by volunteering at the annual convention or at other events during the year.

Number awarded Varies each year; recently, 14 of these scholarships were awarded: 2 to high school seniors, 6 to undergraduates, and 6 to graduate students.

Deadline March of each year.

[735]
SBE DOCTORAL DISSERTATION RESEARCH IMPROVEMENT GRANTS

National Science Foundation
Attn: Directorate for Social, Behavioral, and Economic Sciences
4201 Wilson Boulevard, Room 905N
Arlington, VA 22230
(703) 292-8700   Fax: (703) 292-9083
TDD: (800) 281-8749
Web: www.nsf.gov/funding/pgm_summ.jsp?pims_id=13453

Summary To provide partial support to doctoral candidates (particularly Asian Americans, other minorities, women, and students with disabilities) who are conducting dissertation research in areas of interest to the Directorate for Social, Behavioral, and Economic Sciences (SBE) of the National Science Foundation (NSF).

Eligibility Applications may be submitted through regular university channels by dissertation advisers on behalf of graduate students who have advanced to candidacy and have begun or are about to begin dissertation research. Students must be enrolled at U.S. institutions, but they need not be U.S. citizens. The proposed research must relate to SBE's Division of Behavioral and Cognitive Sciences (archaeology, cultural anthropology, documenting endangered languages, geography and spatial sciences, linguistics, or biological anthropology); Division of Social and Economic Sciences (decision, risk, and management science; economics; law and social science; methodology, measurement, and statistics; political science; sociology; or science, technology, and society); National Center for Science and Engineering Statistics (science and technology surveys and statistics); or Office of Multidisciplinary Activities (science and innovation policy). Women, minorities, and persons with disabilities are strongly encouraged to apply.

Financial data Grants have the limited purpose of providing funds to enhance the quality of dissertation research. They are to be used exclusively for necessary expenses incurred in the actual conduct of the dissertation research, including (but not limited to) conducting field research in settings away from campus that would not otherwise be possible, data collection and sample survey costs, payments to subjects or informants, specialized research equipment, analysis and services not otherwise available, supplies, travel to archives, travel to specialized facilities or field research locations, and partial living expenses for conducting necessary research away from the student's U.S. academic institution. Funding is not provided for stipends, tuition, textbooks, journals, allowances for dependents, travel to scientific meetings, publication costs, dissertation preparation or reproduction, or indirect costs.

Duration Up to 2 years.

Number awarded 200 to 300 each year. Approximately $2.5 million is available for this program annually.

Deadline Deadline dates for the submission of dissertation improvement grant proposals differ by program within the divisions of the SBE Directorate; applicants should obtain information regarding target dates for proposals from the relevant program.

[736]
SCHOLARSHIP FUND OF THE 100TH INFANTRY BATTALION MEMORIAL

Hawai'i Community Foundation
Attn: Scholarship Department
827 Fort Street Mall
Honolulu, HI 96813
(808) 566-5570   Toll Free: (888) 731-3863
Fax: (808) 521-6286
E-mail: scholarships@hcf-hawaii.org
Web: www.hawaiicommunityfoundation.org/scholarships

Summary To provide financial assistance for college or graduate school to descendants of 100th Infantry Battalion World War II veterans (primarily of Americans of Japanese descent).

Eligibility This program is open to entering and continuing full-time undergraduate and graduate students at 2- and 4-year colleges and universities. Applicants must be a direct descendant of a World War II veteran of the 100th Infantry Battalion (which was comprised of Americans of Japanese descent). They must be able to demonstrate academic achievement (GPA of 3.5 or higher), an active record of extra-curricular activities and community service, a willingness to promote the legacy of the 100th Infantry Battalion of World War II, and financial need. Along with their application, they must submit a short statement indicating their reasons for attending college, their planned course of study, their career goals, and what community service means to them. They must also submit a separate essay on the legacy of the 100th Infantry Battalion and how they will contribute to forwarding that legacy. Current residency in Hawaii is not required.

Financial data The amounts of the awards depend on the availability of funds and the need of the recipient. Recently, the average value of each of the scholarships awarded by the foundation was $2,200.

Duration 1 year.

Number awarded Varies each year; recently, 2 of these scholarships were awarded.

Deadline February of each year.

[737]
SCHOLARSHIPS FOR MINORITY ACCOUNTING STUDENTS

American Institute of Certified Public Accountants
Attn: Academic and Career Development Division
220 Leigh Farm Road
Durham, NC 27707-8110
(919) 402-4931   Fax: (919) 419-4705
E-mail: scholarships@aicpa.org
Web: www.aicpa.org

Summary To provide financial assistance to Asian Americans and other minorities interested in studying accounting at the undergraduate or graduate school level.

Eligibility This program is open to minority undergraduate and graduate students, enrolled full time, who have a GPA of 3.3 or higher (both cumulatively and in their major) and intend to pursue a C.P.A. credential. The program defines minority students as those whose heritage is Black or African American, Hispanic or Latino, Native American, or Asian American. Undergraduates must have completed at least 30 semester hours, including at least 6 semester hours of a major in accounting. Graduate students must be working on a master's degree in accounting, finance, taxation, or a related program. Applicants must be U.S. citizens or permanent residents and student affiliate members of the American Institute of Certified Public Accountants (AICPA). Along with their application, they must submit 500-word essays on 1) why they want to become a C.P.A. and how attaining that licensure will contribute to their goals; and 2) how they would spread the message about accounting and the C.P.A. profession in their community and school. In the selection process, some consideration is given to financial need.

Financial data Stipends range from $1,500 to $3,000 per year. Funds are disbursed directly to the recipient's school.

Duration 1 year; may be renewed up to 3 additional years or until completion of a bachelor's or master's degree, whichever is earlier.

Additional information This program began in 1969.

Number awarded Varies each year; recently, 78 students received funding through this program.

Deadline March of each year.

[738]
SCHOLARSHIPS SUPPORTING POST-SECONDARY EDUCATION FOR A CAREER IN THE AUDIOVISUAL INDUSTRY

InfoComm International
International Communications Industries Foundation
11242 Waples Mill Road, Suite 200
Fairfax, VA 22030
(703) 273-7200   Toll Free: (800) 659-7469
Fax: (703) 278-8082   E-mail: jhardwick@infocomm.org
Web: www.infocomm.org

Summary To provide financial assistance to undergraduate and graduate students (particularly Asian Americans, other minorities, and women) who are interested in preparing for a career in the audiovisual (AV) industry.

Eligibility This program is open to second-year students at 2-year colleges, juniors and seniors at 4-year institutions, and graduate students. Applicants must have a GPA of 2.75 or higher and be majoring or planning to major in audiovisual subjects or related fields, including audio, video, audiovisual, radio/television/film, or other field related to a career in the audiovisual industry. Students in other programs, such as journalism, may be eligible if they can demonstrate a relationship to career goals in the AV industry. Along with their application, they must submit 1) an essay of 150 to 200 words on the career path they plan to pursue in the audiovisual industry in the next 5 years; and 2) an essay of 250 to 300 words on the experience or person influencing them the most in selecting the audiovisual industry as their career of choice. Minority and women candidates are especially encouraged to apply.

Selection is based on the essays, presentation of the application, GPA, AV-related experience, work experience, and letters of recommendation.

Financial data The stipend is $4,000. Funds are sent directly to the school.

Duration 1 year.

Additional information InfoComm International, formerly the International Communications Industries Association, established the International Communications Industries Foundation (ICIF) to manage its charitable and educational activities.

Number awarded Varies each year.

Deadline April of each year.

[739]
SCHWABE, WILLIAMSON & WYATT SUMMER ASSOCIATE DIVERSITY SCHOLARSHIP

Schwabe, Williamson & Wyatt, Attorneys at Law
Attn: Attorney Recruiting Administrator
1211 S.W. Fifth Avenue, Suite 1500-2000
Portland, OR 97204
(503) 796-2889   Fax: (503) 796-2900
E-mail: dcphillips@schwabe.com
Web: www.schwabe.com/recruitdiversity.aspx

Summary To provide financial aid and summer work experience in Portland, Oregon or Seattle, Washington to Asian American and other law students who will contribute to the diversity of the legal profession.

Eligibility This program is open to first-year students working on a J.D. degree at an ABA-accredited law school. Applicants must 1) contribute to the diversity of the law school student body and the legal community; 2) possess a record of academic achievement, capacity, and leadership as an undergraduate and in law school that indicates promise for a successful career in the legal profession; and 3) demonstrate a commitment to practice law in the Pacific Northwest upon completion of law school. They must be interested in a paid summer associateship at the sponsoring law firm's office in Portland, Oregon or Seattle, Washington. Along with their application, they must submit a resume, undergraduate and law school transcripts, a legal writing sample, and a 1- to 2-page personal statement explaining their interest in the scholarship and how they will contribute to diversity in the legal community.

Financial data The program provides a paid summer associateship during the summer following completion of the first year of law school and an academic scholarship of $7,500 to help pay tuition and other expenses during the recipient's second year of law school.

Duration 1 year.

Number awarded 1 each year.

Deadline January of each year.

[740]
SCOTT AND PAUL PEARSALL SCHOLARSHIP

American Psychological Foundation
750 First Street, N.E.
Washington, DC 20002-4242
(202) 336-5843   Fax: (202) 336-5812
E-mail: foundation@apa.org
Web: www.apa.org/apf/funding/pearsall.aspx

Summary To provide funding to graduate students (particularly Asian Americans, other minorities, and students with disabilities) who are interested in conducting research on the psychological effect of stigma on people with disabilities.

Eligibility This program is open to full-time graduate students at accredited universities in the United States and Canada. Applicants must be interested in conducting research that seeks to increase the public's understanding of the psychological pain and stigma experiences by adults living with physical disabilities, such as cerebral palsy. Selection is based on conformance with stated program goals and the quality of proposed work. The sponsor encourages applications from individuals who represent diversity in race, ethnicity, gender, age, disability, and sexual orientation.

Financial data The grant is $10,000.

Duration 1 year.

Additional information This program began in 2013.

Number awarded 1 each year.

Deadline September of each year.

[741]
SEATTLE CHAPTER NAAAP CONTINUING EDUCATION SCHOLARSHIP

National Association of Asian American Professionals-
Seattle Chapter
c/o Louisa Lambert, Scholarship Chair
Washington State Attorney General's Office
800 Fifth Avenue, Suite 2000
Seattle, WA 98104-3188
(206) 464-7744   E-mail: naaap.scholarship@gmail.com
Web: seattle.naaap.org/Scholarship.aspx

Summary To provide financial assistance to Asian American and Pacific Islander college students from any state planning to enter graduate school in the Greater Seattle area of Washington.

Eligibility This program is open to students currently enrolled at a college or university in any state who are of Asian or Pacific Islander ethnicity. Applicants must be planning to enroll in a graduate program at a college or university in the Greater Seattle area of Washington. They must have a GPA of 3.0 or higher. Selection is based on academic achievement, leadership skills, community involvement, and financial need.

Financial data The stipend ranges up to $3,000.

Duration 1 year.

Number awarded 1 each year.

Deadline May of each year.

[742]
SELECTED PROFESSIONS FELLOWSHIPS FOR WOMEN OF COLOR

American Association of University Women
Attn: AAUW Educational Foundation
301 ACT Drive, Department 60
P.O. Box 4030
Iowa City, IA 52243-4030
(319) 337-1716, ext. 60   Fax: (319) 337-1204
E-mail: aauw@act.org
Web: www.aauw.org

Summary To provide financial assistance to Asian American and other women of color who are in their final year of graduate training in the fields of business administration, law, or medicine.

Eligibility This program is open to women who are working full time on a degree in fields in which women of color have been historically underrepresented: business administration (M.B.A.), law (J.D.), or medicine (M.D., D.O.). They must be African Americans, Mexican Americans, Puerto Ricans and other Hispanics, Native Americans, Alaska Natives, Asian Americans, or Pacific Islanders. U.S. citizenship or permanent resident status is required. Applicants in business administration must be entering their second year of study; applicants in law must be entering their third year of study; applicants in medicine may be entering their third or fourth year of study. Special consideration is given to applicants who 1) demonstrate their intent to enter professional practice in disciplines in which women are underrepresented, to serve underserved populations and communities, or to pursue public interest areas; and 2) are nontraditional students. Selection is based on professional promise and personal attributes (50%), academic excellence and related academic success indicators (40%), and financial need (10%).

Financial data Stipends range from $5,000 to $18,000.

Duration 1 academic year, beginning in September.

Additional information The filing fee is $35.

Number awarded Varies each year; recently, a total of 25 Selected Professions Fellowships were awarded.

Deadline January of each year.

[743]
SHEILA SUEN LAI SCHOLARSHIP OF LIBRARY AND INFORMATION SCIENCE

Chinese American Librarians Association
c/o Yongyi Song, Scholarship Committee Co-Chair
California State University at Los Angeles
Library North, Room B518
5151 State University Drive
Los Angeles, CA 90032
(323) 343-4884   Fax: (323) 343-3992
E-mail: ysong2@calstatela.edu
Web: www.cala-web.org/node/203

Summary To provide financial assistance to Chinese American students interested in working on a graduate degree in library or information science.

Eligibility This program is open to students enrolled full time in an accredited library school in North America and working on a master's or doctoral degree. Applicants must be of Chinese nationality or Chinese descent. They must submit verification of admission to an accredited graduate program as a full-time student and/or proof of current full-time enrollment status, a curriculum vitae, a personal statement, an official transcript, and 3 letters of recommendation.

Financial data The stipend is $500.

Duration 1 year.

Additional information The program was established in 1989.

Number awarded 1 each year.

Deadline April of each year.

[744]
SHRI RAM ARORA AWARD

The Minerals, Metals & Materials Society
Attn: TMS Foundation
184 Thorn Hill Road
Warrendale, PA 15086-7514
(724) 776-9000, ext. 221   Toll Free: (800) 759-4867
Fax: (724) 776-3770   E-mail: foundation@tms.org
Web: www.tms.org/Foundation/tfactivities.aspx

Summary To provide funding to graduate students and postdoctoral scholars of Indian origin who are interested in educational activities in materials science and engineering.

Eligibility This program is open to graduate students working on a degree in materials science or a related field and postdoctoral scholars actively involved in materials research. First priority is given to applicants living in India; if there are no qualified candidates from India, applicants of Indian heritage currently residing in other countries are considered. Applicants must be younger than 30 years of age. Along with their application, they must submit a statement that describes the purpose for which the award is being sought, including details on how this activity will contribute to their career plans and their aspiration to a leadership role in the materials science and engineering profession.

Financial data The award is $2,500, including a cash grant of $1,000 to be used at the recipient's discretion and $1,500 for travel, accommodation, and registration expenses to attend the annual meeting of The Minerals, Metals & Materials Society (TMS).

Duration The award is presented annually.

Additional information This award was first presented in 2000.

Number awarded 1 each year.

Deadline June of each year.

[745]
SIDLEY DIVERSITY AND INCLUSION SCHOLARSHIP

Sidley Austin LLP
Attn: Scholarships
One South Dearborn Street
Chicago, IL 60603
(312) 853-7000   Fax: (312) 853-7036
E-mail: scholarship@sidley.com
Web: www.sidley.com

Summary To provide financial aid and work experience to Asian American and other law students who come from a diverse background.

Eligibility The program is open to students entering their second year of law school; preference is given to students at schools where the sponsor conducts on-campus interviews or participates in a resume collection. Applicants must have a demonstrated ability to contribute meaningfully to the diversity of the law school and/or legal profession. Along with their application, they must submit a 500-word essay that includes their thoughts on and efforts to improve diversity, how they might contribute to the sponsor's commitment to improving diversity, and their interest in practicing law at a global firm (specifically the sponsor). Selection is based on academic achievement and leadership qualities.

Financial data The stipend is $15,000.

Duration 1 year.

Additional information These scholarships were first offered in 2011. Recipients are expected to participate in the sponsor's summer associate program following their second year of law school. They must apply separately for the associate position. The firm has offices in Chicago, Dallas, Los Angeles, New York, Palo Alto, San Francisco, and Washington, D.C.

Number awarded A limited number are awarded each year.

Deadline August of each year.

[746]
SMITHSONIAN MINORITY AWARDS PROGRAM

Smithsonian Institution
Attn: Office of Fellowships and Internships
470 L'Enfant Plaza, Suite 7102
P.O. Box 37012, MRC 902
Washington, DC 20013-7012
(202) 633-7070   Fax: (202) 633-7069
E-mail: siofi@si.edu
Web: www.smithsonianofi.com

Summary To provide funding to Asian American and other minority undergraduate and graduate students interested in conducting research at the Smithsonian Institution.

Eligibility This program is open to members of U.S. minority groups underrepresented in the Smithsonian's scholarly programs. Applicants must be undergraduates or beginning graduate students interested in conducting research in the Institution's disciplines and in the museum field. They must be U.S. citizens or permanent residents and have a GPA of 3.0 or higher.

Financial data Students receive a grant of $600 per week.

Duration Up to 10 weeks.

Additional information Recipients must carry out independent research projects in association with the Smithsonian's research staff. Eligible fields of study currently include animal behavior, ecology, and environmental science (including an emphasis on the tropics); anthropology (including archaeology); astrophysics and astronomy; earth sciences and paleobiology; evolutionary and systematic biology; history of science and technology; history of art (especially American, contemporary, African, Asian, and 20th-century art); American crafts and decorative arts; social and cultural history of the United States; and folklife. Students are required to be in residence at the Smithsonian for the duration of the fellowship.

Number awarded Varies each year; recently, 25 of these awards were granted: 2 for fall, 19 for summer, and 4 for spring.

Deadline January of each year for summer and fall residency; September of each year for spring residency.

[747]
SOCIETY OF PEDIATRIC PSYCHOLOGY DIVERSITY RESEARCH GRANT

American Psychological Association
Attn: Division 54 (Society of Pediatric Psychology)
c/o Anna Maria Patino-Fernandez
University of Miami School of Medicine
Mailman Center for Child Development
Division of Clinical Psychology
1601 N.W. 12th Avenue, 4018B
Miami, FL 33136-1005
(305) 243-6837   Fax: (305) 243-8470
E-mail: Apatino-fernandez@med.miami.edu
Web: www.apadivisions.org

Summary To provide funding to graduate student and post-doctoral members of the Society of Pediatric Psychology (particularly Asian Americans and others who come from diverse backgrounds) who are interested in conducting research on diversity aspects of pediatric psychology.

Eligibility This program is open to current members of the society who are graduate students, fellows, or early-career (within 3 years of appointment) faculty. Applicants must be interested in conducting pediatric psychology research that features diversity-related variables, such as race or ethnicity, gender, culture, sexual orientation, language differences, socioeconomic status, and/or religiosity. Along with their application, they must submit a 2,000-word description of the project, including its purpose, methodology, predictions, and implications; a detailed budget; a current curriculum vitae, and (for students) a curriculum vitae of the faculty research mentor and a letter of support from that mentor. Selection is based on relevance to diversity in child health (5 points), significance of the study (5 points), study methods and procedures (10 points), and investigator qualifications (10 points).

Financial data Grants up to $1,000 are available. Funds may not be used for convention or meeting travel, indirect costs, stipends of principal investigators, or costs associated with manuscript preparation.

Duration The grant is presented annually.

Additional information The Society of Pediatric Psychology is Division 54 of the American Psychological Association (APA). This grant was first presented in 2008.

Number awarded 1 each year.

Deadline September of each year.

[748]
SOONGOOK CHOI SCHOLARSHIPS

Christian Church (Disciples of Christ)
Attn: Disciples Home Missions
130 East Washington Street
P.O. Box 1986
Indianapolis, IN 46206-1986
(317) 713-2652   Toll Free: (888) DHM-2631
Fax: (317) 635-4426   E-mail: mail@dhm.disciples.org
Web: www.discipleshomemissions.org

Summary To provide financial assistance to Asians and Pacific Islanders interested in preparing for a career in the ministry of the Christian Church (Disciples of Christ).

Eligibility This program is open to ministerial students of Asian and Pacific Islander descent who are members of a Christian Church (Disciples of Christ) congregation in the United States or Canada. Applicants must plan to prepare for the ordained ministry in a multiracial community, be working on an M.Div. or equivalent degree, provide evidence of financial need, be enrolled full time in an accredited school or seminary, provide a transcript of academic work, and be under the care of a regional Commission on the Ministry or in the process of coming under care.

Financial data A stipend is awarded (amount not specified).

Duration 1 year; may be renewed.

Additional information This program began in 2004.

Number awarded 1 each year.

Deadline March of each year.

[749]
SOUTH ASIAN JOURNALISTS ASSOCIATION STUDENT JOURNALISM AWARDS

South Asian Journalists Association
c/o Shefali Kulkarni, Secretary
Kaiser Health News
1330 G Street, N.W.
Washington, DC 20005
E-mail: shefali.kulkarni24@gmail.com
Web: www.saja.org/awards

Summary To recognize and reward outstanding reporting on any subject by undergraduate and graduate students of south Asian origin.

Eligibility Eligible to be considered for these awards are print, broadcast, new media, and photographic works submitted by south Asian undergraduate and graduate students in the United States or Canada (on any subject). Entries must have been completed as part of a class assignment.

Financial data Prizes are $500 for the winner and $250 for the finalists.

Duration The competition is held annually.

Number awarded 3 each year.

Deadline March of each year.

[750]
SOUTHERN CALIFORNIA CHINESE LAWYERS ASSOCIATION SCHOLARSHIPS

Southern California Chinese Lawyers Association
c/o Faith Santoso
Asian Pacific American Legal Center
1145 Wilshire Boulevard, Second Floor
Los Angeles, CA 90017
(213) 977-7500   E-mail: fsantoso@apalc.org
Web: www.sccla.org

Summary To provide financial assistance to Asian Pacific American students from any state enrolled at law schools in southern California.

Eligibility This program is open to Asian Pacific American students at law schools in southern California. Applicants may be in any year of law school, including entering first-year students and fourth-year evening students. Selection is based on academic accomplishment, financial need, and/or potential contribution to the Chinese American community.

Financial data The stipend is $1,000.

Duration 1 year.

Additional information This program includes the following named scholarships: the Ming Y. Moy Memorial Scholar-

ship, the Justice Elwood Lui Scholarship, the Lee Gum Low Presidential Scholarship, the Judge Jack B. Tso Scholarship, the George S. Lee Scholarship, and the Margaret and Ned Good Scholarships.

Number awarded Several each year.

Deadline March of each year.

[751]
SOUTHERN REGION KOREAN AMERICAN SCHOLARSHIPS

Korean American Scholarship Foundation
Southern Region
c/o Dr. Sam Sook Chung, Scholarship Committee Chair
8679 Spivey Village Trail
Jonesboro, GA 30236
E-mail: samsookchung2@gmail.com
Web: www.kasf.org/southern

Summary To provide financial assistance to Korean American students from any state who are working on or planning to work on an undergraduate or graduate degree in any field at a school in southern states.

Eligibility This program is open to Korean American students who are currently enrolled in a college or university in the southern states as full-time undergraduate or graduate students. Applicants may reside anywhere in the United States as long as they attend school in the southern region: Alabama, Florida, Georgia, South Carolina, and Tennessee. Both U.S. citizens and foreign nationals are eligible. Selection is based on academic achievement, school activities, community service, and financial need.

Financial data Stipends are $1,000 for undergraduate, graduate, or professional students or $500 for high school students.

Duration 1 year; renewable.

Number awarded Varies each year; recently, 39 of these scholarships were awarded.

Deadline May of each year.

[752]
SOUTHERN REGIONAL EDUCATION BOARD DISSERTATION AWARDS

Southern Regional Education Board
Attn: Coordinator, Program and Scholar Services
592 Tenth Street N.W.
Atlanta, GA 30318-5776
(404) 879-5569   Fax: (404) 872-1477
E-mail: doctoral.scholars@sreb.org
Web: www.sreb.org/page/1113/types_of_awards.html

Summary To provide funding to Asian American and other minority students who wish to complete a Ph.D. dissertation, especially in the fields of science, technology, engineering, or mathematics (STEM), while in residence at a university in the southern states.

Eligibility This program is open to U.S. citizens and permanent residents who are members of racial/ethnic minority groups (Native Americans, Hispanic Americans, Asian Americans, and African Americans) and have completed all requirements for a Ph.D. except the dissertation. Applicants must be enrolled at a designated college or university in the following 10 states: Alabama, Arkansas, Georgia, Kentucky, Louisiana, Mississippi, South Carolina, Tennessee, Virginia,

West Virginia. Enrollment at a graduate school in 5 of those states (Georgia, Mississippi, South Carolina, Tennessee, and Virginia) is available only to residents of those states. Residents of any state in the country may attend a university in the other 5 states. Preference is given to students in STEM disciplines with particularly low minority representation, although all academic fields are eligible. Applicants must be in a position to write full time and must expect to complete their dissertation within the year of the fellowship. Eligibility is limited to individuals who plan to become full-time faculty members at a college or university upon completion of their doctoral degree. The program is not open to students working on other doctoral degrees (e.g., M.D., D.B.A., D.D.S., J.D., D.V.M., Ed.D., Pharm.D., D.N.P., D.P.T.).

Financial data Fellows receive waiver of tuition and fees (in or out of state), a stipend of $20,000, a $500 research allowance, and reimbursement of expenses for attending the Compact for Faculty Diversity's annual Institute on Teaching and Mentoring.

Duration 1 year; nonrenewable.

Additional information This program began in 1993 as part of the Compact for Faculty Diversity, supported by the Pew Charitable Trusts and the Ford Foundation. It currently operates at universities in 10 of the member states of the Southern Regional Education Board (SREB): Alabama, Arkansas, Georgia, Kentucky, Louisiana, Mississippi, South Carolina, Tennessee, Virginia, and West Virginia; the other 6 member states (Delaware, Florida, Maryland, North Carolina, Oklahoma, and Texas) do not participate.

Number awarded Varies each year.

Deadline March of each year.

[753]
SOUTHWESTERN REGION KOREAN AMERICAN SCHOLARSHIPS

Korean American Scholarship Foundation
Southern Region
c/o Scholarship Committee Chair
14759 Kellywood Lane
Houston, TX 77079
E-mail: kasfsw@gmail.com
Web: www.kasf.org/southwestern

Summary To provide financial assistance to Korean American students from any state who are working on or planning to work on an undergraduate or graduate degree in any field at a school in southwestern states.

Eligibility This program is open to residents of any state who are 1) U.S. citizens of Korean heritage; 2) Korean citizens who have a valid visa to study in the United States; and 3) citizens of any other country who are of Korean heritage and have a valid visa to study in the United States. Applicants must be enrolled or planning to enroll as a full-time undergraduate or graduate student at a college or university in Arkansas, Louisiana, Mississippi, Oklahoma, or Texas. Selection is based on academic performance, extracurricular activities, community service, letters of recommendation, an essay, character and integrity, and financial need.

Financial data Stipends range from $1,000 to $2,000.

Duration 1 year; nonrenewable.

Number awarded Varies each year; recently, 15 of these scholarships were awarded.

Deadline June of each year.

[754]
SPIE SCHOLARSHIP PROGRAM

SPIE-The International Society for Optical Engineering
Attn: Scholarship Committee
1000 20th Street
P.O. Box 10
Bellingham, WA 98227-0010
(360) 676-3290   Toll Free: (888) 504-8171
Fax: (360) 647-1445   E-mail: scholarships@spie.org
Web: spie.org/x7236.xml

Summary To provide financial assistance to entering or continuing undergraduate and graduate student members of SPIE-The International Society for Optical Engineering (particularly Asian Americans, other minorities, women, and veterans) who are preparing for a career in optical science or engineering.

Eligibility This program is open to high school seniors planning to attend college, current undergraduate students, and current graduate students. Applicants must be society members majoring or planning to enroll full or part time and major in optics, optoelectronics, photonics, imaging, or a related discipline (e.g., physics, electrical engineering) at a college or university anywhere in the world. Along with their application, they must submit a 500-word essay on their academic work, career objectives, how this scholarship would help them attain their goals, and what they have achieved and learned through their studies and activities. Financial need is not considered in the selection process. Women, minorities, and veterans are encouraged to apply.

Financial data Stipends range from $2,000 to $11,000. Special awards include the D.J. Lovell Scholarship at $11,000; the John Kiel Scholarship at $10,000; the Laser Technology, Engineering, and Applications Scholarship at $5,000; the Optical Design and Engineering Scholarship at $5,000, and the BACUS Scholarship at $5,000.

Duration 1 year.

Additional information The International Society for Optical Engineering was founded in 1955 as the Society of Photo-Optical Instrumentation Engineers (SPIE). This program includes the following special named scholarships: the D.J. Lovell Scholarship, sponsored by SPIE (the most prestigious of the scholarships); the John Kiel Scholarship, awarded for a student's potential for long-term contribution to the field of optics and optical engineering; the Optical Design and Engineering Scholarship in Optical Engineering, established to honor Bill Price and Warren Smith and awarded to a full-time graduate or undergraduate student in the field of optical design and engineering; the Laser Technology, Engineering, and Applications Scholarship (formerly the F-MADE Scholarship), sponsored by the Forum for Military Applications of Directed Energy (F-MADE) in recognition of a student's scholarly achievement in laser technology, engineering, or applications; and the BACUS Scholarship, awarded to a full-time undergraduate or graduate student in the field of microlithography with an emphasis on optical tooling and/or semiconductor manufacturing technologies, sponsored by BACUS (SPIE's photomask international technical group).

Number awarded Varies each year; recently, this program awarded 140 scholarships with a value of $353,000. Since the program was established, it has awarded more than $3.8 million to nearly 2,000 students in 86 countries.

Deadline February of each year.

[755]
SREB DOCTORAL AWARDS

Southern Regional Education Board
Attn: Coordinator, Program and Scholar Services
592 Tenth Street N.W.
Atlanta, GA 30318-5776
(404) 879-5569 Fax: (404) 872-1477
E-mail: doctoral.scholars@sreb.org
Web: www.sreb.org/page/1113/types_of_awards.html

Summary To provide financial assistance to Asian American and other minority students who wish to work on a doctoral degree, especially in fields of science, technology, engineering, or mathematics (STEM), at designated universities in the southern states.

Eligibility This program is open to U.S. citizens and permanent residents who are members of racial/ethnic minority groups (Native Americans, Hispanic Americans, Asian Americans, and African Americans) and have or will receive a bachelor's or master's degree. Applicants must be entering or enrolled in the first year of a Ph.D. program at a designated college or university in the following 10 states: Alabama, Arkansas, Georgia, Kentucky, Louisiana, Mississippi, South Carolina, Tennessee, Virginia, West Virginia. Enrollment at a graduate school in 5 of those states (Georgia, Mississippi, South Carolina, Tennessee, and Virginia) is available only to residents of those states. Residents of any state in the country may attend a university in the other 5 states. Applicants must indicate an interest in becoming a full-time college or university professor. The program does not support students working on other doctoral degrees (e.g., M.D., D.B.A., D.D.S., J.D., D.V.M., Ed.D., Pharm.D., D.N.P., D.P.T.). Preference is given to applicants in STEM disciplines with particularly low minority representation, although all academic fields are eligible.

Financial data Scholars receive a waiver of tuition and fees (in or out of state) for up to 5 years, an annual stipend of $20,000 for 3 years, an annual allowance of $500 for research and professional development activities, and reimbursement of travel expenses to attend the Compact for Faculty Diversity's annual Institute on Teaching and Mentoring.

Duration Up to 5 years.

Additional information This program began in 1993 as part of the Compact for Faculty Diversity, supported by the Pew Charitable Trusts and the Ford Foundation.

Number awarded Varies each year; recently, the program was supporting more than 300 scholars.

Deadline March year.

[756]
SSSP RACIAL/ETHNIC MINORITY GRADUATE SCHOLARSHIP

Society for the Study of Social Problems
Attn: Executive Officer
University of Tennessee
901 McClung Tower
Knoxville, TN 37996-0490
(865) 689-1531 Fax: (865) 689-1534
E-mail: sssp@utk.edu
Web: www.sssp1.org

Summary To provide funding to Asian American and other minority members of the Society for the Study of Social Problems (SSSP) who are interested in conducting research for their doctoral dissertation.

Eligibility This program is open to SSSP members who are Black or African American, Hispanic or Latino, Asian or Asian American, Native Hawaiian or other Pacific Islander, or American Indian or Alaska Native. Applicants must have completed all requirements for a Ph.D. (course work, examinations, and approval of a dissertation prospectus) except the dissertation. They must have a GPA of 3.25 or higher and be able to demonstrate financial need. Their field of study may be any of the social and/or behavioral sciences that will enable them to expand their perspectives in the investigation into social problems. U.S. citizenship or permanent resident status is required.

Financial data The stipend is $12,000. Additional grants provide $500 for the recipient to 1) attend the SSSP annual meeting prior to the year of the work to receive the award; and 2) attend the meeting after the year of the award to present a report on the work completed.

Duration 1 year.

Number awarded 1 each year.

Deadline January of each year.

[757]
STAN BECK FELLOWSHIP

Entomological Society of America
Attn: Entomological Foundation
9332 Annapolis Road, Suite 210
Lanham, MD 20706-3150
(301) 459-9082 Fax: (301) 459-9084
E-mail: melodie@entfdn.org
Web: www.entfdn.org/awards_education.php

Summary To assist "needy" students working on an undergraduate or graduate degree in entomology who are nominated by members of the Entomological Society of America (ESA).

Eligibility This program is open to students working on an undergraduate or graduate degree in entomology at a college or university in Canada, Mexico, or the United States. Candidates must be nominated by members of the society. They must be "needy" students; for the purposes of this program, need may be based on physical limitations, or economic, minority, or environmental conditions.

Financial data The stipend is $2,000 per year.

Duration 1 year; may be renewed up to 3 additional years.

Additional information This fellowship was first awarded in 1996. Recipients are expected to be present at the society's annual meeting, where the award will be presented.

Number awarded 1 each year.

Deadline June of each year.

[758]
STANFORD CHEN INTERNSHIP GRANTS

Asian American Journalists Association
Attn: Student Programs Coordinator
5 Third Street, Suite 1108
San Francisco, CA 94103
(415) 346-2051, ext. 102   Fax: (415) 346-6343
E-mail: programs@aaja.org
Web: www.aaja.org/stanford-chen-internship-grant

Summary To offer scholars in the humanities (particularly Asian Americans and other underrepresented minorities) an opportunity to conduct research and teach at Stanford University.

Eligibility This program is open to AAJA members who are college juniors, seniors, or graduate students with a serious intent to prepare for a career in journalism (print, online, broadcast, or photography). Applicants must have already secured an internship with a print company (daily circulation less than 100,000) or broadcast company (market smaller than the top 50). Along with their application, they must submit a 200-word essay on the kind of experience they expect as an intern at a small to medium-size media company, their career goals, and why AAJA's mission is important to them; a resume; verification of the internship; a letter of recommendation; and a statement of financial need.

Financial data The grant is $1,750. Funds are to be used for living expenses or transportation.

Duration Summer months.

Additional information This program began in 1998.

Number awarded 1 or 2 each year.

Deadline April of each year.

[759]
STAR FELLOWSHIPS FOR GRADUATE ENVIRONMENTAL STUDY

Environmental Protection Agency
Attn: National Center for Environmental Research
Ariel Rios Building
1200 Pennsylvania Avenue, N.W.
Washington, DC 20460
(202) 343-9850   Toll Free: (800) 490-9194
E-mail: jones.brandon@epa.gov
Web: www.epa.gov/careers/fellowships

Summary To provide financial support to graduate students (particularly Asian Americans, other minorities, women, and students with disabilities) who are planning to obtain advanced degrees and prepare for a career in environmentally-related fields.

Eligibility Applicants must be U.S. citizens or permanent residents enrolled or accepted for enrollment at an accredited U.S. college or university. They must be interested in working on a master's or doctoral degree, in the United States or abroad, in an environmentally-related field of specialization. Relevant fields of study include ecology, economics, engineering, modeling, the health sciences, physical sciences, earth sciences, exposure sciences, social sciences, informational sciences, mathematical and computer sciences, and environmental sciences; applications are also welcome from students who have not participated in traditional environmental conversations or research, especially those that attend Minority Academic Institutions. Selection is based on demonstrated commitment to an environmental career, potential for success in the proposed area of inquiry, and potential for their proposal to have broader societal impacts. The program strongly encourages women, minorities, and persons with disabilities to apply. At least 10% of the awards are reserved for students at Minority Academic Institutions, defined as Historically Black Colleges and Universities, Tribal Colleges and Universities, Hispanic Serving Institutions, and Asian American and Native Pacific Islander-Serving Institutions.

Financial data The total award is $42,000 per year, including a student stipend of $25,000 (paid at the rate of $2,083 per month for 12 months), an expense allowance of $5,000, and an allowance of up to $12,000 for tuition and fees paid directly to the institution.

Duration Up to 2 years for master's students; up to 3 years for doctoral students, usable over a period of 5 years.

Additional information This program, which began in 1995, is the graduate student component of the Science to Achieve Results (STAR) program of the Environmental Protection Agency. Fellows may conduct research outside the United States, but no additional funding is provided for foreign travel or other expenses.

Number awarded Approximately 80 each year, of which 8 are reserved for students at Minority Academic Institutions.

Deadline November of each year.

[760]
STOEL RIVES FIRST-YEAR DIVERSITY FELLOWSHIPS

Stoel Rives LLP
Attn: Lawyer Recruiting Manager
900 S.W. Fifth Avenue, Suite 2600
Portland, OR 97204
(503) 224-3380   Fax: (503) 220-2480
E-mail: portlandfellowship@stoel.com
Web: www.stoel.com/diversity.aspx?Show=2805

Summary To provide financial aid for law school and work experience to law students who bring diversity to the profession and are interested in a summer associate position with Stoel Rives.

Eligibility This program is open to first-year law students who contribute to the diversity of the student body at their law school and who will contribute to the diversity of the legal community. Diverse students include those who are American Indian or Alaskan Native, Asian, Black or African American, Hispanic or Latino, Native Hawaiian or other Pacific Islander, disabled, or LGBT. Applicants must be willing to accept a summer associate position at Stoel Rives offices in designated communities. Selection is based on academic excellence, leadership, community service, interest in practicing in the Pacific Northwest, and financial need.

Financial data The program provides a stipend of $7,500 to help defray expenses of law school and a salaried summer associate position.

Duration 1 year.

Additional information This program began in 2004. The firm has offices in Anchorage, Boise, Lake Tahoe, Minneapolis, Portland, Sacramento, Salt Lake City, San Diego, San Francisco, Seattle, and Vancouver.

Number awarded At least 2 each year.

Deadline January of each year.

[761]
STUDENT AFFILIATES IN SCHOOL PSYCHOLOGY DIVERSITY SCHOLARSHIPS

American Psychological Association
Attn: Division 16 (School Psychology)
750 First Street, N.E.
Washington, DC 20002-4242
(202) 336-6165   Fax: (202) 218-3599
TDD: (202) 336-6123   E-mail: cchambers@apa.org
Web: www.apadivisions.org/division-16/awards/index.aspx

Summary To provide financial assistance to graduate student members of the Student Affiliates in School Psychology (SASP) of Division 16 (School Psychology) of the American Psychological Association (APA) who are Asian Americans or from other underrepresented cultural backgrounds.

Eligibility This program is open to SASP members who come from underrepresented cultural backgrounds. Applicants must be working on a graduate degree to prepare for a career as a school psychologist. Awards are available to both incoming students (entering their first or second year of graduate study) and advanced students (entering their third, fourth, or fifth year of graduate study).

Financial data The stipend is $1,000.

Duration 1 year; nonrenewable.

Number awarded 2 each year: 1 to an incoming student and 1 to an advanced student.

Deadline Deadline not specified.

[762]
SUNY GRADUATE DIVERSITY FELLOWSHIP PROGRAM

State University of New York
Attn: Office of Diversity, Equity and Inclusion
State University Plaza
353 Broadway
Albany, NY 12246
(518) 320-1189
Web: www.suny.edu/provost/odee/programs.cfm

Summary To provide financial assistance to Asian Americans and other graduate students at campuses of the State University of New York (SUNY) who will contribute to the diversity of the student body.

Eligibility This program is open to U.S. citizens and permanent residents who are entering or enrolled full-time graduate or professional students at any of the participating SUNY colleges. Applicants must be able to demonstrate how they will contribute to the diversity of the student body for the program for which they are applying, including having overcome a disadvantage or other impediment to success in higher education. Economic disadvantage, although not a requirement, may be the basis for eligibility. Membership in a racial or ethnic group that is underrepresented in the graduate or professional program involved may serve as a plus factor in making awards, but may not form the sole basis of selection. Awards are granted in the following priority order: 1) new graduate students who are being recruited but have

not yet accepted admission to a graduate program; 2) Graduate Opportunity Waiver Program students who can be awarded a stipend to supplement their waiver to tuition; 3) currently-enrolled doctoral candidates who have completed all degree requirements except the dissertation; and 4) graduate assistants and teaching assistants who can receive a supplement to their current stipends to enhance their retention in graduate studies.

Financial data Stipends range from $7,500 to $10,000.

Duration 1 year; renewable.

Number awarded Varies each year; recently, this program awarded nearly $6 million in fellowships to 551 graduate students on 24 SUNY campuses. Of the recipients 38% were Latinos, 35% African Americans, 12% Whites, 6% Asians, and 6% Native Americans.

Deadline Deadline not specified.

[763]
SUSAN M. JACKSON MINISTERIAL SCHOLARS FUND

Unitarian Universalist Association
Attn: Ministerial Credentialing Office
25 Beacon Street
Boston, MA 02108-2800
(617) 948-6403   Fax: (617) 742-2875
E-mail: mcoadministrator@uua.org
Web: www.uua.org

Summary To provide financial assistance to seminary students (particularly Asian Americans and other students of color) who are preparing for the Unitarian Universalist (UU) ministry and demonstrate enthusiasm about their faith.

Eligibility This program is open to seminary students who are enrolled full or at least half time in a UU ministerial training program with candidate status. Applicants must be citizens of the United States or Canada. They must be able to demonstrate their enthusiasm about Unitarian Universalist ideas and conclusions, drawn from their faith, that influence their lives. Priority is given first to those who have demonstrated outstanding ministerial ability and secondarily to students with the greatest financial need (especially persons of color).

Financial data The stipend ranges from $1,000 to $15,000 per year.

Duration 1 year.

Number awarded 1 each year.

Deadline April of each year.

[764]
SYNOD OF LAKES AND PRAIRIES RACIAL ETHNIC SCHOLARSHIPS

Synod of Lakes and Prairies
Attn: Committee on Racial Ethnic Ministry
2115 Cliff Drive
Eagen, MN 55122-3327
(651) 357-1140   Toll Free: (800) 328-1880, ext. 202
Fax: (651) 357-1141 E-mail: mkes@lakesandprairies.org
Web: www.lakesandprairies.org

Summary To provide financial assistance to Asian American and other minority residents of the Presbyterian Church (USA) Synod of Lakes and Prairies who are working on an undergraduate or graduate degree at a college or seminary in any state in preparation for service to the church.

Eligibility This program is open to members of Presbyterian churches who reside within the Synod of Lakes and Prairies (Iowa, Minnesota, Nebraska, North Dakota, South Dakota, and Wisconsin). Applicants must be members of ethnic minority groups studying at least half time for service in the Presbyterian Church (USA) as a teaching elder, ordained minister, commissioned ruling elder, lay professional, or volunteer. They must be in good academic standing, making progress toward an undergraduate or graduate degree, and able to demonstrate financial need. Along with their application, they must submit essays of 200 to 500 words on 1) what the church needs to do to be faithful to its mission in the world today; and 2) the people, practices, or events that influence their commitment to Christ in ways that renew their fair and strengthen their service.

Financial data Stipends range from $850 to $3,500.

Duration 1 year.

Number awarded Varies each year; recently, 9 of these scholarships were awarded.

Deadline September of each year.

[765]
SYNOD OF THE COVENANT ETHNIC THEOLOGICAL SCHOLARSHIPS

Synod of the Covenant
Attn: Ministries in Higher Education
1911 Indianwood Circle, Suite B
Maumee, OH 43537-4063
(419) 754-4050
Toll Free: (800) 848-1030 (within MI and OH)
Fax: (419) 754-4051
E-mail: SOC@synodofthecovenant.org
Web: www.synodofthecovenant.org

Summary To provide financial assistance to Asian American and other ethnic students working on a master's degree at an approved Presbyterian theological institution (with priority given to Presbyterian applicants from Ohio and Michigan).

Eligibility This program is open to ethnic individuals enrolled full time in church vocations programs at approved Presbyterian theological institutions. Priority is given to Presbyterian applicants from the states of Michigan and Ohio. Financial need is considered in the selection process.

Financial data Students may be awarded a maximum of $1,500 on initial application. They may receive up to $2,000 on subsequent applications, with evidence of continuing progress. Funds are made payable to the session for distribution.

Duration Students are eligible to receive scholarships 1 time per year, up to a maximum of 5 years.

Number awarded Varies each year.

Deadline August of each year.

[766]
TEXAS CHAPTER AAJA SCHOLARSHIPS

Asian American Journalists Association-Texas Chapter
c/o Scott Nishimura, Scholarship Committee Chair
Fort Worth Star-Telegram
P.O. Box 1870
Fort Worth, TX 76101
(817) 390-7808   E-mail: snishimura@star-telegram.com
Web: www.aajatexas.org/programs/student-programs

Summary To provide financial assistance to students from designated southwestern states who are working on an undergraduate or graduate degree in journalism and can demonstrate an awareness of Asian American issues.

Eligibility This program is open to graduating high school seniors, undergraduates, and graduate students who are either 1) residents of Arkansas, Louisiana, New Mexico, Oklahoma, or Texas; or 2) attending or planning to attend an accredited college or university in those states. Applicants are not required to be members of the Asian American Journalists Association (AAJA). Along with their application, they must submit a 250-word autobiography that explains why they are interested in a career in journalism, a 500-word essay on the role of ethnic diversity in news coverage (both for the subjects of the news events and also the journalists involved), their most recent official transcript, 2 letters of recommendation, and a resume. Work samples to be submitted are 3 legible clips from print journalism students; 3 to 5 prints or slides with captions or descriptions from print photojournalism students; 3 to 5 samples of work from design journalism students; 2 taped VHS or DVD excerpts with corresponding scripts from television broadcast students; 2 edited VHS or DVD excepts from television photojournalism students; 3 taped cassette excerpts with corresponding scripts from radio broadcast students; or 3 legible online articles from web journalism students. Selection is based on commitment to journalism, awareness of Asian American issues, journalistic ability, and scholastic ability.

Financial data The stipend is $1,000.

Duration 1 year.

Additional information Scholarship winners are also given a 1-year free membership in the AAJA Texas chapter.

Number awarded 2 each year.

Deadline May of each year.

[767]
TEXAS YOUNG LAWYERS ASSOCIATION MINORITY SCHOLARSHIP PROGRAM

Texas Young Lawyers Association
Attn: Minority Involvement Committee
1414 Colorado, Suite 502
P.O. Box 12487
Austin, TX 78711-2487
(512) 427-1529   Toll Free: (800) 204-2222, ext. 1529
Fax: (512) 427-4117   E-mail: btrevino@texasbar.com
Web: www.tyla.org

Summary To provide financial assistance to Asian Americans, other minorities, and women from any state who are attending law school in Texas.

Eligibility This program is open to members of recognized minority groups, including students of varying gender, national origin, racial and ethnic backgrounds, sexual orientation and gender identity, and of disability status. Applicants must be attending an ABA-accredited law school in Texas. Along with their application, they must submit a 2-page essay on either 1) the role the minority attorney should play in the community and profession; or 2) how attorneys, specifically minority attorneys, can improve the image of the legal profession. Selection is based on academic performance, merit, participation in extracurricular activities inside and outside law school, and financial need.

Financial data The stipend is $1,000.

Duration 1 year.

Number awarded 9 each year: 1 at each accredited law school in Texas.

Deadline October of each year.

[768]
THE REV. J.K. FUKUSHIMA SCHOLARSHIP

Montebello Plymouth Congregational Church
144 South Greenwood Avenue
Montebello, CA 90640
(323) 721-5568   Fax: (323) 721-7955
E-mail: mpccucc@yahoo.com
Web: www.montebelloucc.org

Summary To provide financial assistance to undergraduate and graduate students who are preparing for a career in Christian ministry and can demonstrate a commitment to the Asian American community.

Eligibility This program is open to 1) third- or fourth-year college students; and 2) graduate and professional students who have not completed a bachelor's or master's degree in theological studies. Applicants must be enrolled or have been accepted at an accredited school of theology. They must be working on a degree that will provide them with the skills and understanding necessary to further the development of Christian ministries. Along with their application, they must submit an essay on their commitment to the Asian American community.

Financial data The stipend is $500.

Duration 1 year.

Number awarded 1 or more each year.

Deadline May of each year.

[769]
THOMAS G. NEUSOM SCHOLARSHIPS

Conference of Minority Transportation Officials
Attn: National Scholarship Program
1875 I Street, N.W., Suite 500
Washington, DC 20006
(703) 234-4072   Fax: (202) 318-0364
Web: www.comto.org/?page=Scholarships

Summary To provide financial assistance for college or graduate school to Asian American and other members of the Conference of Minority Transportation Officials (COMTO).

Eligibility This program is open to undergraduate and graduate students who have been members of COMTO for at least 1 year. Applicants must be working (either full or part time) on a degree in a field related to transportation and have a GPA of 2.5 or higher. Along with their application, they must submit a cover letter with a 500-word statement of career goals. Financial need is not considered in the selection process. U.S. citizenship or legal resident status is required.

Financial data The stipend is $5,500. Funds are paid directly to the recipient's college or university.

Duration 1 year.

Additional information COMTO was established in 1971 to promote, strengthen, and expand the roles of minorities in all aspects of transportation. Recipients are expected to attend the COMTO National Scholarship Luncheon.

Number awarded 1 each year.

Deadline May of each year.

[770]
THZ FO FARM SCHOLARSHIP

Hawai'i Community Foundation
Attn: Scholarship Department
827 Fort Street Mall
Honolulu, HI 96813
(808) 566-5570   Toll Free: (888) 731-3863
Fax: (808) 521-6286
E-mail: scholarships@hcf-hawaii.org
Web: www.hawaiicommunityfoundation.org/scholarships

Summary To provide financial assistance to Hawaii residents of Chinese descent who are interested in working on an undergraduate or graduate degree in any field at a school in any state.

Eligibility This program is open to high school seniors, high school graduates, and college students in Hawaii who are of Chinese ancestry and interested in studying any field as full-time undergraduate or graduate students at a college or university in any state. Applicants must be able to demonstrate academic achievement (GPA of 2.7 or higher), good moral character, and financial need. Along with their application, they must submit a short statement indicating their reasons for attending college, their planned course of study, their career goals, and what community service means to them.

Financial data The amounts of the awards depend on the availability of funds and the need of the recipient. Recently, the average value of each of the scholarships awarded by the foundation was $2,200.

Duration 1 year.

Number awarded Varies each year; recently, 6 of these scholarships were awarded.

Deadline February of each year.

[771]
TONGAN CULTURAL SOCIETY SCHOLARSHIPS

Hawai'i Community Foundation
Attn: Scholarship Department
827 Fort Street Mall
Honolulu, HI 96813
(808) 566-5570   Toll Free: (888) 731-3863
Fax: (808) 521-6286
E-mail: scholarships@hcf-hawaii.org
Web: www.hawaiicommunityfoundation.org/scholarships

Summary To provide financial assistance to Hawaii residents of Tongan ancestry who are interested in attending college or graduate school in the state.

Eligibility This program is open to Hawaii residents of Tongan ancestry who are enrolled in or planning to enroll in an accredited college or university in Hawaii. Applicants must be full-time undergraduate or graduate students and able to demonstrate academic achievement (GPA of 2.7 or higher), good moral character, and financial need. Along with their application, they must submit a short statement indicating their reasons for attending college, their planned course of study, their career goals, and what community service means to them.

Financial data The amounts of the awards depend on the availability of funds and the need of the recipient. Recently, the average value of each of the scholarships awarded by the foundation was $2,200.

Duration 1 year.

Number awarded Varies each year; recently, 3 of these scholarships were awarded.

Deadline February of each year.

[772]
TRAILBLAZER SCHOLARSHIP

Conference of Minority Transportation Officials
Attn: National Scholarship Program
1875 I Street, N.W., Suite 500
Washington, DC 20006
(703) 234-4072   Fax: (202) 318-0364
Web: www.comto.org/?page=Scholarships

Summary To provide financial assistance to Asian American and other minority undergraduate and graduate students working on a degree in a field related to transportation.

Eligibility This program is open to minority undergraduate and graduate students who are working (either full or part time) on a degree in a field related to transportation and have a GPA of 2.5 or higher. Along with their application, they must submit a cover letter with a 500-word statement of career goals. Financial need is not considered in the selection process. U.S. citizenship or legal resident status is required.

Financial data The stipend is $2,500. Funds are paid directly to the recipient's college or university.

Duration 1 year.

Additional information The Conference of Minority Transportation Officials (COMTO) was established in 1971 to promote, strengthen, and expand the roles of minorities in all aspects of transportation. Recipients are expected to attend the COMTO National Scholarship Luncheon.

Number awarded 1 each year.

Deadline May of each year.

[773]
UNITED HEALTH FOUNDATION/NMF DIVERSE MEDICAL SCHOLARS PROGRAM

National Medical Fellowships, Inc.
Attn: Scholarship Program
347 Fifth Avenue, Suite 510
New York, NY 10016
(212) 483-8880   Toll Free: (877) NMF-1DOC
Fax: (212) 483-8897 E-mail: scholarships@nmfonline.org
Web: www.nmfonline.org/uhf

Summary To provide financial assistance to Asian American and other underrepresented minority students at medical schools in designated areas who are interested in conducting a community health project.

Eligibility This program is open to African Americans, Hispanics/Latinos, Native Americans, Vietnamese, Cambodians, and Pacific Islanders who are currently enrolled at an accredited medical school in the greater New York City metropolitan

area (including Connecticut, New Jersey, New York, and Pennsylvania), Florida (greater Miami area), Louisiana (Baton Rouge, New Orleans, or Shreveport), or Georgia (Atlanta). Applicants must have demonstrated leadership and a commitment to serving medically underserved communities. They must be interested in conducting a self-directed health project of 200 hours at a site of choice in an underserved community in the same area as their medical school. U.S. citizenship is required.

Financial data The grant is $7,000.

Duration 1 year; recipients may apply for a second year of funding.

Additional information This program, sponsored by United Health Foundation, began in 2007.

Number awarded 22 each year.

Deadline October of each year.

[774]
UNITED METHODIST DOLLARS FOR SCHOLARS PROGRAM

United Methodist Higher Education Foundation
Attn: Scholarships Administrator
60 Music Square East, Suite 350
P.O. Box 340005
Nashville, TN 37203-0005
(615) 649-3990   Toll Free: (800) 811-8110
Fax: (615) 649-3980
E-mail: umhefscholarships@umhef.org
Web: www.umhef.org/UMDFSapp.php

Summary To provide financial assistance to Asian American and other students at Methodist colleges, universities, and seminaries whose home churches agree to contribute to their support.

Eligibility The Double Your Dollars for Scholars program is open to students attending or planning to attend a United Methodist-related college, university, or seminary as a full-time student. Applicants must have been an active, full member of a United Methodist Church for at least 1 year prior to applying. Their home church must nominate them and agree to contribute to their support. Many of the United Methodist colleges and universities have also agreed to contribute matching funds for a Triple Your Dollars for Scholars Program, and a few United Methodist conference foundations have agreed to contribute additional matching funds for a Quadruple Your Dollars for Scholars Program. Awards are granted on a first-come, first-served basis. Some of the awards are designated for Hispanic, Asian, and Native American (HANA) students funded by the General Board of Higher Education and Ministry.

Financial data The sponsoring church contributes $1,000 and the United Methodist Higher Education Foundation (UMHEF) contributes a matching $1,000. Students who attend a participating United Methodist college or university receive an additional $1,000 for the Triple Your Dollars for Scholars Program, and those from a participating conference receive a fourth $1,000 increment for the Quadruple Your Dollars for Scholars Program.

Duration 1 year; may be renewed as long as the recipients maintain satisfactory academic progress as defined by their institution.

Additional information Currently, participants in the Double Your Dollars for Scholars program include 1 United Methodist seminary and theological school, 1 professional school, 19 senior colleges and universities, and 1 2-year college. The Triple Your Dollars for Scholars program includes an additional 12 United Methodist seminaries and theological schools, 72 senior colleges and universities, and 4 2-year colleges (for a complete list, consult the UMHEF). The conference foundations participating in the Quadruple Your Dollars for Scholars Program are limited to the Alabama-West Florida United Methodist Foundation, the East Ohio United Methodist Foundation, the Kentucky United Methodist Foundation, the Missouri United Methodist Foundation (for students at Saint Paul School of Theology or Central Methodist University), the Nashville Area United Methodist Foundation, the North Carolina United Methodist Foundation (for students at Louisburg College, Methodist University, or North Carolina Wesleyan College), the Georgia United Methodist Foundation, the Oklahoma United Methodist Foundation (for students at Oklahoma City University), the United Methodist Foundation of Arkansas, and the United Methodist Foundation of Western North Carolina.

Number awarded 350 each year, including 25 designated for HANA students.

Deadline Local churches must submit applications in February of each year for senior colleges, universities, and seminaries or May of each year for 2-year colleges.

[775]
UNITED METHODIST WOMEN OF COLOR SCHOLARS PROGRAM

United Methodist Church
Attn: General Board of Higher Education and Ministry
Office of Loans and Scholarships
1001 19th Avenue South
P.O. Box 340007
Nashville, TN 37203-0007
(615) 340-7344   Fax: (615) 340-7367
E-mail: umscholar@gbhem.org
Web: www.gbhem.org

Summary To provide financial assistance to Asian American and other Methodist women of color who are working on a doctoral degree to prepare for a career as an educator at a United Methodist seminary.

Eligibility This program is open to women of color (have at least 1 parent who is African American, African, Hispanic, Asian, Native American, Alaska Native, or Pacific Islander) who have an M.Div. degree. Applicants must have been active, full members of a United Methodist Church for at least 3 years prior to applying. They must be enrolled full time in a degree program at the Ph.D. or Th.D. level to prepare for a career teaching at a United Methodist seminary.

Financial data The maximum stipend is $10,000 per year.

Duration 1 year; may be renewed up to 3 additional years.

Number awarded Varies each year; recently, 10 of these scholarships were awarded.

Deadline January of each year.

[776]
UPS/NAPABA LAW FOUNDATION GOLD MOUNTAIN SCHOLARSHIPS

National Asian Pacific American Bar Association
Attn: NAPABA Law Foundation
1612 K Street, N.W., Suite 1400
Washington, DC 20006
(202) 775-9555   Fax: (202) 775-9333
E-mail: nlfstaff@napaba.org
Web: www.napaba.org

Summary To provide financial assistance to law students who are the first in their family to attend law school and interested in serving the Asian Pacific American community.

Eligibility This program is open to students at ABA-accredited law schools in the United States who are the first in their family to attend law school. Applicants must demonstrate leadership potential to serve the Asian Pacific American community upon graduation. Along with their application, they must submit a 500-word essay that covers 1) the most significant experiences in their background that have shaped and demonstrated their commitment to serving the needs of Asian Pacific Americans; and 2) how they intend to serve the needs of the Asian Pacific American community in their future legal career. Selection is based on that essay, academic achievement, leadership, and commitment to bettering the Asian Pacific American community. U.S. citizenship or permanent resident status is required.

Financial data The stipend is $2,500.

Duration 1 year.

Additional information This program is supported by the UPS Foundation.

Number awarded 2 each year.

Deadline September of each year.

[777]
VAMA SCHOLARSHIP PROGRAM

Vietnamese American Medical Association
Attn: Scholarship Committee
4108 Surfside Court
Arlington, TX 76016
(682) 667-1016   Fax: (817) 468-1852
E-mail: scholarship@vamausa.org
Web: www.vamausa.org/a3/index.php/scholarship

Summary To provide financial assistance to medical students who are interested in serving the Vietnamese American community.

Eligibility This program is open to students enrolled in their third year at an accredited medical school in the United States. Applicants must be able to demonstrate a strong interest in serving the Vietnamese American community when they complete their training. Along with their application, they must submit a letter from the financial aid office of their medical school verifying the amount of other assistance they are receiving, a letter of recommendation, their medical school transcript, and a 600-word essay describing the reason why they wish to serve Vietnamese community in the United States, including the specific location where they plan to practice. Preference is given to applicants who demonstrate the greatest financial need.

Financial data The stipend is $1,000.

Duration 1 year.

Number awarded Varies each year.

Deadline June of each year.

[778]
VANG PAO SCHOLARSHIP

Hmong American Education Fund
P.O. Box 17468
St. Paul, MN 55117
(651) 230-3634 E-mail: scholarships@thehaef.org
Web: www.thehaef.org

Summary To provide financial assistance to Hmong undergraduate and graduate students who demonstrate leadership.

Eligibility This program is open to students of Hmong descent who are currently enrolled as full-time undergraduate or graduate students at public 2- or 4-year colleges or universities in any state. Applicants must be U.S. citizens or permanent residents and have a GPA of 3.0 or higher. Along with their application, they must submit a 1,500-word essay on their commitment to education, their leadership qualities, their financial need, how this scholarship can help them, and their community service. Selection is based on academic excellence, leadership qualities, commitment to helping their community, and financial need.

Financial data The stipend is $2,500.

Duration 1 year; nonrenewable.

Number awarded 1 each year.

Deadline March of each year.

[779]
VARNUM DIVERSITY AND INCLUSION FELLOWSHIPS

Varnum LLP
Attn: Human Resources
333 Bridge Street N.W.
P.O. Box 352
Grand Rapids, MI 49501-0352
(616) 336-6620 Fax: (616) 336-7000
E-mail: 2Lfellowship@varnumlaw.com
Web: www.varnumlaw.com

Summary To provide financial assistance for law school to Asian Americans and other law students who will contribute to diversity in the legal profession and are interested in a summer associateship in Grand Rapids, Michigan.

Eligibility This program is open to students currently enrolled at an accredited law school in any state who have a GPA of 3.3 or higher. Applicants must be members of an ethnic or racial minority or demonstrate a significant commitment to issues of diversity and inclusion. They must have a GPA of 3.0 or higher and have accepted an offer to participate in the sponsoring firm's summer associate program. Along with their application, they must submit a 750-word statement on their efforts to promote greater ethnic or racial diversity and inclusion within the legal profession and/or their community.

Financial data The stipend is $7,500.

Duration 1 year.

Number awarded 2 each year.

Deadline October of each year.

[780]
VIETNAMESE AMERICAN BAR ASSOCIATION OF NORTHERN CALIFORNIA SCHOLARSHIPS

Vietnamese American Bar Association of Northern
California
Attn: Scholarships
1570 The Alameda
San Jose, CA 95126
(408) 512-3818 E-mail: scholarship@vabanc.org
Web: www.vabanc.org/events/scholarship-dinner

Summary To provide financial assistance to Vietnamese law students, especially those who are committed to serving the Vietnamese American community in northern California.

Eligibility This program is open to Vietnamese law students from any state. Priority is given to those who can demonstrate either 1) a commitment to serving the Vietnamese American community in northern California; or 2) a desire to engage in public interest or social justice work through postgraduate work or a summer position. Applicants must submit an 800-word personal statement on 1) what they see as a pressing concern facing the Vietnamese American community and how they see themselves contributing to or engaging in such an issue; and/or 2) their contributions to or activism within the Vietnamese American community; and/or 3) their experiences in overcoming socioeconomic and/or other barriers.

Financial data The stipend is $1,000.

Duration 1 year.

Additional information This program began in 2002. Recipients are required to attend the sponsor's annual scholarship dinner. No support is provided for transportation or lodging expenses to attend the dinner.

Number awarded 2 each year.

Deadline June of each year.

[781]
VIETNAMESE AMERICAN BAR ASSOCIATION OF THE GREATER WASHINGTON DC AREA SCHOLARSHIP

Vietnamese American Bar Association of the Greater
Washington DC Area
33 Eighth Street, N.E.
Washington, DC 20002
E-mail: vabadc@gmail.com
Web: www.vabadc.com

Summary To provide financial assistance to students at law schools in the greater Washington, D.C. area who are committed to serving the Vietnamese American community.

Eligibility This program is open to residents of any state who are currently enrolled at a law school in the greater Washington, D.C. area. Applicants must be able to demonstrate a commitment to serving the Vietnamese American community. Along with their application, they must submit a 750-word essay on either of the following topics: 1) how they plan to serve the needs of Vietnamese Americans in their legal career; or 2) how they have overcome barriers to achieve their academic and/or career goals. Selection is based on the essay, academic performance, and community service.

Financial data The stipend is $1,500.

Duration 1 year.

Additional information This program began in 2009.

Number awarded 2 each year.

Deadline February of each year.

[782]
VINCENT CHIN MEMORIAL SCHOLARSHIP

Asian American Journalists Association
Attn: Student Programs Coordinator
5 Third Street, Suite 1108
San Francisco, CA 94103
(415) 346-2051, ext. 102   Fax: (415) 346-6343
E-mail: programs@aaja.org
Web: www.aaja.org/vincent-chin-scholarship

Summary To provide financial assistance to student members of the Asian American Journalists Association (AAJA) who are high school seniors, undergraduates, or graduate students and interested in preparing for a career in journalism.

Eligibility This program is open to AAJA members who are working or planning to work full time on an undergraduate or graduate degree in journalism. Applicants must submit a brief essay on their choice of 4 topics: 1) could the attack that killed Vincent Chin happen again; 2) how Asian Americans are a single people; 3) should Asian Americans protest or conform in the face of incidents such as the murder of Vincent Chin; or 4) who was Lily Chin. Selection is based on academic achievement, commitment to journalism, sensitivity to Asian American and Pacific Islander issues, demonstrated journalistic ability, and financial need.

Financial data The stipend is $500.

Duration 1 year.

Number awarded 1 each year.

Deadline May of each year.

[783]
VINSON & ELKINS DIVERSITY FELLOWSHIPS

Vinson & Elkins L.L.P.
Attn: Talent Management
1001 Fannin Street, Suite 2500
Houston, TX 77002-6760
(713) 758-2222   Fax: (713) 758-2346
Web: www.velaw.com/careers/law_students.aspx?id=602

Summary To provide financial assistance to Asian American and other minority law students who are interested in working in a law firm setting.

Eligibility This program is open to students who are entering the second year at an ABA-accredited law school and are members of a racial or ethnic group that has been historically underrepresented in the legal profession (Asian, American Indian/Alaskan Native, Black/African American, Hispanic/Latino, multiracial, or Native Hawaiian or other Pacific Islander). Applicants must be able to demonstrate a strong undergraduate and law school record, excellent writing skills, and an interest in working in a law firm setting.

Financial data The stipend is $3,500 per year.

Duration 2 years (the second and third year of law school).

Additional information Fellows are also considered for summer associate positions at the sponsor's offices in Austin, Dallas, or Houston following their first year of law school.

Number awarded 4 each year.

Deadline January of each year.

[784]
VIOLET AND CYRIL FRANKS SCHOLARSHIP

American Psychological Foundation
750 First Street, N.E.
Washington, DC 20002-4242
(202) 336-5843   Fax: (202) 336-5812
E-mail: foundation@apa.org
Web: www.apa.org/apf/funding/franks.aspx

Summary To provide funding to doctoral students (particularly Asian Americans and others from diverse backgrounds) who are interested in conducting research related to mental illness.

Eligibility This program is open to full-time graduate students who are interested in conducting a research project that uses a psychological perspective to help understand and reduce stigma associated with mental illness. Applicants must identify the project's goal, the prior research that has been conducted in the area, whom the project will serve, the in intended outcomes and how the project will achieve those, and the total cost of the project. Selection is based on conformance with stated program goals and quality of proposed work. The sponsor encourages applications from individuals who represent diversity in race, ethnicity, gender, age, disability, and sexual orientation.

Financial data The grant is $5,000.

Duration 1 year.

Additional information This grant was first awarded in 2007.

Number awarded 1 each year.

Deadline May of each year.

[785]
VIRGINIA ASIAN CHAMBER OF COMMERCE STUDENT SCHOLARSHIPS

Virginia Asian Chamber of Commerce
Attn: My Lan Tran, Executive Director
P.O. Box 2640
Glen Allen, VA 23058
(804) 798-3975   E-mail: aabac@aabac.org
Web: www.aabac.org/vacc-gala-event/scholarship-awards

Summary To provide financial assistance to Asian American students from Virginia interested in working on an undergraduate or graduate degree in any field.

Eligibility This program is open to seniors graduating from high schools in Virginia and students currently enrolled in an undergraduate or graduate program at a college or university in the state. Applicants must be interested in fulfilling the sponsor's goal of promoting the "entrepreneurial spirit in Asian and other students within the context of global business opportunities and challenges." They must have a GPA of 3.0 or higher and be working on a degree in a business-related or any other academic area. Along with their application, they must submit a statement of their interest in a business, entrepreneurship, or related field.

Financial data Stipends are $1,000 or $500.

Duration 1 year.

Number awarded Varies each year; recently, 4 of these scholarships were awarded: 3 at $1,000 and 1 at $500.

Deadline October of each year.

[786]
VIRGINIA NURSE PRACTITIONER/NURSE MIDWIFE SCHOLARSHIP PROGRAM

Virginia Department of Health
Attn: Office of Minority Health and Public Health Policy
109 Governor Street, Suite 1016 East
Richmond, VA 23219
(804) 864-7435   Fax: (804) 864-7440
E-mail: IncentivePrograms@vdh.virginia.gov
Web: www.vdh.virginia.gov

Summary To provide funding to nursing students in Virginia (particularly Asian Americans and other minorities) who are willing to work as nurse practitioners and/or midwives in the state following graduation.

Eligibility This program is open to residents of Virginia who are enrolled or accepted for enrollment full or part time at a nurse practitioner program in the state or a nurse midwifery program in Virginia or a nearby state. Applicants must have a cumulative GPA of at least 3.0 in undergraduate and/or graduate courses. Preference is given to 1) residents of designated medically underserved areas of Virginia; 2) students enrolled in family practice, obstetrics and gynecology, pediatric, adult health, and geriatric nurse practitioner programs; and 3) minority students. Selection is based on scholastic achievement, character, and stated commitment to postgraduate employment in a medically underserved area of Virginia.

Financial data The stipend is $5,000 per year. Recipients must agree to serve in a designated medically underserved area of Virginia for a period of years equal to the number of years of scholarship support received. The required service must begin within 2 years of the recipient's graduation and must be in a facility that provides services to persons who are unable to pay for the service and that participates in all government-sponsored insurance programs designed to assure full access to medical care service for covered persons. If the recipient fails to complete the course of study, or pass the licensing examination, or provide the required service, all scholarship funds received must be repaid with interest and a penalty.

Duration 1 year; may be renewed for 1 additional year.

Number awarded Up to 5 each year.

Deadline June of each year.

[787]
WAKE FOREST UNIVERSITY SCHOOL OF MEDICINE EXCELLENCE IN CARDIOVASCULAR SCIENCES SUMMER RESEARCH PROGRAM

Wake Forest University School of Medicine
Attn: Hypertension and Vascular Research Center
Medical Center Boulevard
Winston-Salem, NC 27157-1032
(336) 716-1080   Fax: (336) 716-2456
E-mail: nsarver@wakehealth.edu
Web: www.wakehealth.edu

Summary To provide Asian American and other underrepresented or disadvantaged students with an opportunity to engage in a summer research project in cardiovascular science at Wake Forest University in Winston-Salem, North Carolina.

Eligibility This program is open to undergraduates and master's degree students who are members of underrepresented minority groups (African Americans, Alaskan Natives,

Asian Americans, Native Americans, Pacific Islanders, and Hispanics) or who come from disadvantaged backgrounds (e.g., rural areas, first-generation college students). Applicants must be interested in participating in a program of summer research in the cardiovascular sciences that includes "hands-on" laboratory research, a lecture series by faculty and guest speakers, and a research symposium at which students present their research findings. U.S. citizenship or permanent resident status is required.

Financial data The stipend is $1,731 per month, housing in a university dormitory, and round-trip transportation expense.

Duration 2 months during the summer.

Additional information This program is sponsored by the National Heart, Lung, and Blood Institute (NHLBI) of the National Institutes of Health (NIH).

Number awarded Approximately 12 each year.

Deadline February of each year.

[788]
WARNER NORCROSS & JUDD LAW SCHOOL SCHOLARSHIP

Grand Rapids Community Foundation
Attn: Education Program Officer
185 Oakes Street S.W.
Grand Rapids, MI 49503-4008
(616) 454-1751, ext. 103   Fax: (616) 454-6455
E-mail: rbishop@grfoundation.org
Web: www.grfoundation.org/scholarshipslist

Summary To provide financial assistance to Asian Americans and other minorities from Michigan who are attending law school.

Eligibility This program is open to students of color who are attending or planning to attend an accredited law school. Applicants must be residents of Michigan or attending law school in the state. They must be U.S. citizens or permanent residents and have a GPA of 2.5 or higher. Financial need is considered in the selection process.

Financial data The stipend is $5,000. Funds are paid directly to the recipient's institution.

Duration 1 year.

Additional information Funding for this program is provided by the law firm Warner Norcross & Judd LLP.

Number awarded 1 each year.

Deadline March of each year.

[789]
WATSON MIDWIVES OF COLOR SCHOLARSHIP

American College of Nurse-Midwives
Attn: ACNM Foundation, Inc.
8403 Colesville Road, Suite 1550
Silver Spring, MD 20910-6374
(240) 485-1850   Fax: (240) 485-1818
E-mail: fdn@acnm.org
Web: www.midwife.org

Summary To provide financial assistance for midwifery education to Asian Americans and other students of color who belong to the American College of Nurse-Midwives (ACNM).

Eligibility This program is open to ACNM members of color who are currently enrolled in an accredited basic midwife education program and have successfully completed 1 academic or clinical semester/quarter or clinical module. Applicants must submit a 150-word essay on their 5-year midwifery career plans and a 100-word essay on their intended future participation in the local, regional, and/or national activities of the ACNM. Selection is based on leadership potential, financial need, academic history, and potential for future professional contribution to the organization.

Financial data The stipend is $3,000.

Duration 1 year.

Number awarded Varies each year; recently, 3 of these scholarships were awarded.

Deadline March of each year.

[790]
WAYNE F. PLACEK GRANTS

American Psychological Foundation
750 First Street, N.E.
Washington, DC 20002-4242
(202) 336-5843   Fax: (202) 336-5812
E-mail: foundation@apa.org
Web: www.apa.org/apf/funding/placek.aspx

Summary To provide funding to pre- and postdoctoral scholars (particularly Asian Americans, other minorities, women, and individuals with disabilities) who are interested in conducting research that will increase the general public's understanding of homosexuality and alleviate the stress experienced by gay men and lesbians.

Eligibility This program is open to scholars who have a doctoral degree (e.g., Ph.D., Psy.D., M.D.) and to graduate students in all fields of the behavioral and social sciences. Applicants must be interested in conducting empirical studies that address the following topics: prejudice, discrimination, and violence based on sexual orientation, including heterosexuals' attitudes and behaviors toward lesbian, gay, bisexual, and transgender (LGBT) people; family and workplace issues relevant to LGBT people; and subgroups of the LGBT population that have been historically underrepresented in scientific research. Selection is based on conformance with stated program goals, magnitude of incremental contribution, quality of proposed work, and applicant's demonstrated scholarship and research competence. The sponsor encourages applications from individuals who represent diversity in race, ethnicity, gender, age, disability, and sexual orientation.

Financial data The grant is $15,000.

Duration 1 year.

Additional information This program began in 1995.

Number awarded 1 or 2 each year.

Deadline February of each year.

[791]
WEST AMERICA CHAPTER SCHOLARSHIP AWARDS

Phi Tau Phi Scholastic Honor Society-West America Chapter
c/o Thomas Y. Hou, President
California Institute of Technology
Applied and Computational Mathematics
Mail Code 9-94
1200 East California Boulevard
Pasadena, CA 91125
(626) 395-4546   Fax: (626) 578-0124
E-mail: hou@acm.caltech.edu
Web: www.phitauphi.org

Summary To provide financial assistance to upper-division and graduate students of Chinese heritage from any state at colleges and universities in southern California.

Eligibility This program is open to juniors, seniors, and graduate students from any state enrolled at accredited institutions of higher education in southern California. Applicants must be of Chinese heritage or have a demonstrated interest in Chinese and culture. They must have a GPA of 3.4 or higher. Along with their application, they must submit a 1-page essay on their professional goals, achievements, and interest in Chinese culture. Financial need is not considered in the selection process.

Financial data The stipend is $1,000.

Duration 1 year.

Additional information Phi Tau Phi, first organized in 1921 in China and reestablished in 1964 in the United States, is a relatively small honor society of scholars, mainly of Chinese heritage, in various disciplines of science, technology, art, and the humanities.

Number awarded Varies each year; recently, 4 of these scholarships were awarded: 2 to undergraduates and 2 to graduate students.

Deadline August of each year.

[792]
WESTERN REGION KOREAN AMERICAN SCHOLARSHIPS

Korean American Scholarship Foundation
Western Region
Attn: Scholarship Committee
3540 Wilshire Boulevard, Suite 920
Los Angeles, CA 90010
(213) 380-KASF   Fax: (631) 380-5274
E-mail: western@kasf.org
Web: www.kasf.org/westerrn

Summary To provide financial assistance to Korean American students from any state who are working on or planning to work on an undergraduate or graduate degree in any field at a school in western states.

Eligibility <EG>This program is open to residents of any state who are 1) U.S. citizens of Korean heritage; 2) Korean citizens who have a valid visa to study in the United States; and 3) citizens of any other country who are of Korean heritage and have a valid visa to study in the United States. Applicants must be enrolled or planning to enroll as a full-time undergraduate or graduate student at a college or university in Alaska, Arizona, California, Colorado, Hawaii, Idaho, Montana, Nevada, New Mexico, Oregon, Utah, Washington, or Wyoming. They must have a GPA of 3.0 or higher. Selection is based on academic achievement (25%), extracurricular activities (10%), an essay (10%), recommendations (10%), financial need (40%), and extra credit for having extraordinary circumstances (5%).

Financial data Stipends are at least $2,000.

Duration 1 year; renewable.

Number awarded Varies each year; recently, 48 of these scholarships were awarded.

Deadline July of each year.

[793]
WHAN SOON CHUNG SCHOLARSHIP

Philip Jaisohn Memorial Foundation
Attn: Education and Scholarship Committee
6705 Old York Road
Philadelphia, PA 19126
(215) 224-2000   Fax: (215) 224-9164
E-mail: jaisohnhouse@gmail.com
Web: www.jaisohn.org

Summary To provide financial assistance to Korean American undergraduate and graduate students who are studying health care or medicine.

Eligibility This program is open to Korean American undergraduate and graduate students who are currently enrolled at a college or university in the United States and working on a degree in health care or a field of medicine. Applicants must be able to demonstrate excellence in community activities and financial need. Along with their application, they must submit an essay on either "Who is Dr. Jaisohn to Me," or "The Significance of Dr. Jaisohn's Ideal to Korean Americans." They must also submit a brief statement on how they can contribute to and be involved in the activities of the Philip Jaisohn Memorial Foundation. Selection is based on the applicant's desire to take Dr. Jaisohn as a role model to learn and spread his legacy.

Financial data The stipend is $1,500.

Duration 1 year.

Number awarded 1 each year.

Deadline November of each year.

[794]
WILLIAM G. ANDERSON, D.O. MINORITY SCHOLARSHIP

American Osteopathic Foundation
Attn: Director of Programs
142 East Ontario Street
Chicago, IL 60611-2864
(312) 202-8232   Toll Free: (866) 455-9383
Fax: (312) 202-8216   E-mail: vheck@aof-foundation.org
Web: www.aof-foundation.org

Summary To provide financial assistance to Asian American and other minority students enrolled in colleges of osteopathic medicine.

Eligibility This program is open to minority (African American, Native American, Asian American, Pacific Islander, or Hispanic) students entering their second, third, or fourth year at an accredited college of osteopathic medicine. Applicants must demonstrate 1) interest in osteopathic medicine, its philosophy, and its principles; 2) academic achievement; 3) lead-

ership efforts in addressing the educational, societal, and health needs of minorities; 4) leadership efforts in addressing inequities in medical education and health care; 5) accomplishments, awards and honors, clerkships or special projects; and extracurricular activities in which the student has shown leadership abilities; and 6) financial need.

Financial data The stipend is $5,000.

Duration 1 year.

Additional information This program began in 1998.

Number awarded 1 each year.

Deadline April of each year.

[795]
WILLIAM K. SCHUBERT M.D. MINORITY NURSING SCHOLARSHIP PROGRAM

Cincinnati Children's Hospital Medical Center
Attn: Office of Diversity and Inclusion, MLC 9008
3333 Burnet Avenue
Cincinnati, OH 45229-3039
(513) 803-6416   Toll Free: (800) 344-2462
Fax: (513) 636-5643   TDD: (513) 636-4900
E-mail: diversity@cchmc.org
Web: www.cincinnatichildrens.org

Summary To provide financial assistance to Asian Americans and members of other underrepresented groups who are interested in working on a bachelor's or master's degree in nursing to prepare for licensure in Ohio.

Eligibility This program is open to members of groups underrepresented in the nursing profession (males, American Indians or Alaska Natives, Blacks or African Americans, Hawaiian Natives or other Pacific Islanders, Hispanics or Latinos, or Asians). Applicants must be enrolled or accepted in a professional bachelor's or master's registered nurse program at an accredited school of nursing to prepare for initial licensure in Ohio. They must have a GPA of 2.75 or higher. Along with their application, they must submit a 750-word essay that covers 1) their long-range personal, educational, and professional goals; 2) why they chose nursing as a profession; 3) how their experience as a member of an underrepresented group has influenced a major professional and/or personal decision in their life; 4) any unique qualifications, experiences, or special talents that demonstrate their creativity; and 5) how their work experience has contributed to their personal development.

Financial data The stipend is $2,750 per year.

Duration 1 year. May be renewed up to 3 additional years for students working on a bachelor's degree or 1 additional year for students working on a master's degree; renewal requires that students maintain a GPA of 2.75 or higher.

Number awarded 1 or more each year.

Deadline April of each year.

[796]
WILLIAM RUCKER GREENWOOD SCHOLARSHIP

Association for Women Geoscientists
Attn: AWG Foundation
12000 North Washington Street, Suite 285
Thornton, CO 80241
(303) 412-6219   Fax: (303) 253-9220
E-mail: office@awg.org
Web: www.awg.org/members/po_scholarships.htm

Summary To provide financial assistance to Asian and other minority women from any state working on an undergraduate or graduate degree in the geosciences at a college in the Potomac Bay region.
Eligibility This program is open to minority women who are residents of any state and currently enrolled as full-time undergraduate or graduate geoscience majors at an accredited, degree-granting college or university in Delaware, the District of Columbia, Maryland, Virginia, or West Virginia. Selection is based on the applicant's 1) participation in geoscience or earth science educational activities; and 2) potential for leadership as a future geoscience professional.
Financial data The stipend is $1,000. The recipient also is granted a 1-year membership in the Association for Women Geoscientists (AWG).
Duration 1 year.
Additional information This program is sponsored by the AWG Potomac Area Chapter.
Number awarded 1 each year.
Deadline April of each year.

[797]
WINSTON & STRAWN DIVERSITY SCHOLARSHIP PROGRAM

Winston & Strawn LLP
Attn: Amanda Sommerfeld
333 South Grand Avenue
Los Angeles, CA 90071-1543
(213) 615-1724   Fax: (213) 615-1750
E-mail: asommerfeld@winston.com
Web: www.winston.com

Summary To provide financial assistance to Hispanic American and other diverse law students who are interested in practicing in a city in which Winston & Strawn LLP has an office.
Eligibility This program is open to second-year law students who self-identify as a member of 1 of the following groups: American Indian or Alaska Native, Asian or Pacific Islander, Black or African American, or Hispanic or Latino. Applicants must submit a resume, law school transcript, and 500-word personal statement. Selection is based on 1) interest in practicing law after graduation in a large law firm in a city in which Winston & Strawn has an office (currently, Charlotte, Chicago, Houston, Los Angeles, New York, San Francisco, and Washington, D.C.); 2) law school and undergraduate record, including academic achievements and involvement in extracurricular activities; 3) demonstrated leadership skills; 4) and interpersonal skills.
Financial data The stipend is $10,000.
Duration 1 year (the third year of law school).
Additional information This program began in 2004.
Number awarded 3 each year.
Deadline September of each year.

[798]
WISCONSIN LIBRARY ASSOCIATION DIVERSITY SCHOLARSHIP

Wisconsin Library Association
Attn: Scholarship Committee
4610 South Biltmore Lane, Suite 100
Madison, WI 53718-2153
(608) 245-3640   Fax: (608) 245-3646
E-mail: wla@wisconsinlibraries.org
Web: wla.wisconsinlibraries.org

Summary To provide financial assistance to Asian American and other minority residents of Wisconsin who are working on a master's degree in library and information science or library media at a school in the state.
Eligibility This program is open to members of racial and ethnic minority groups (African Americans, Latinos or Hispanics, Asians and Pacific Islanders, or Native Americans and Alaskan Natives) who are residents of Wisconsin. Applicants must have been admitted to a master's degree program in library and information science or in library media as a full- or part-time student at a college or university in the state. Along with their application, they must submit a 500-word essay describing 1) their background, experience, and career plans in the library profession; and 2) what this scholarship will mean to them. Selection is based on past academic performance, experience and background in library and library-related work, career plans in the library profession, and need and desire for the scholarship.
Financial data The stipend is $750.
Duration 1 year.
Number awarded 1 each year.
Deadline June of each year.

[799]
WISCONSIN MINORITY TEACHER LOANS

Wisconsin Higher Educational Aids Board
131 West Wilson Street, Suite 902
P.O. Box 7885
Madison, WI 53707-7885
(608) 267-2212   Fax: (608) 267-2808
E-mail: deanna.schulz@wisconsin.gov
Web: heab.state.wi.us/programs.html

Summary To provide funding to Asian Americans and other minorities in Wisconsin who are interested in teaching in Wisconsin school districts with large minority enrollments.
Eligibility This program is open to residents of Wisconsin who are African Americans, Hispanic Americans, American Indians, or southeast Asians (students who were admitted to the United States after December 31, 1975 and who are a former citizen of Laos, Vietnam, or Cambodia or whose ancestor was a citizen of 1 of those countries). Applicants must be enrolled at least half time as juniors, seniors, or graduate students at an independent or public institution in the state in a program leading to teaching licensure and have a GPA of 2.5 or higher. They must agree to teach in a Wisconsin school district in which minority students constitute at least 29% of total enrollment or in a school district participating in the interdistrict pupil transfer program. Financial need is not considered in the selection process.
Financial data Loans are provided up to $2,500 per year. For each year the student teaches in an eligible school dis-

trict, 25% of the loan is forgiven; if the student does not teach in an eligible district, the loan must be repaid at an interest rate of 5%.

Duration 1 year; may be renewed 1 additional year.

Additional information Eligible students should apply through their school's financial aid office.

Number awarded Varies each year.

Deadline Deadline dates vary by institution; check with your school's financial aid office.

[800]
WOMBLE CARLYLE SCHOLARS PROGRAM

Womble Carlyle Sandridge & Rice, PLLC
Attn: Director of Entry-Level Recruiting and Development
301 South College Street, Suite 3500
Charlotte, NC 28202-6037
(704) 331-4900   Fax: (704) 331-4955
E-mail: wcsrscholars@wcsr.com
Web: www.wcsr.com

Summary To provide financial aid and summer work experience to Asian Americans and other diverse students at designated law schools.

Eligibility This program is open to students at designated law schools who are members of underrepresented groups. Applicants must be able to demonstrate solid academic credentials, personal or professional achievement outside the classroom, and significant participation in community service. Along with their application, they must submit a 300-word essay on their choice of 2 topics that change annually but relate to the legal profession. They must also submit a brief statement explaining how they would contribute to the goal of creating a more diverse legal community.

Financial data The stipend is $4,000 per year. Recipients are also offered summer employment at 1 of the 14 offices of the sponsoring law firm. Salaries are the same as the firm's other summer associates in each office.

Duration 1 year (the second year of law school); may be renewed 1 additional year.

Additional information This program began in 2004. The eligible law schools are North Carolina Central University School of Law (Durham, North Carolina), University of North Carolina at Chapel Hill School of Law (Chapel Hill, North Carolina), Duke University School of Law (Durham, North Carolina), Wake Forest University School of Law (Winston-Salem, North Carolina), University of South Carolina School of Law (Columbia, South Carolina), Howard University School of Law (Washington, D.C.), University of Virginia School of Law (Charlottesville, Virginia), University of Georgia School of Law (Athens, Georgia), Georgia Washington University Law School (Washington, D.C.), Emory University School of Law (Atlanta, Georgia), and University of Maryland School of Law (Baltimore, Maryland). The sponsoring law firm has offices in Atlanta (Georgia), Baltimore (Maryland), Charleston (South Carolina), Charlotte (North Carolina), Columbia (South Carolina), Greensboro (North Carolina), Greenville (South Carolina), Raleigh (North Carolina), Research Triangle Park (North Carolina), Silicon Valley (Cupertino, California), Tysons Corner (Virginia), Washington (D.C.), Wilmington (Delaware), and Winston-Salem (North Carolina).

Number awarded Varies each year; recently, 9 of these scholarships were awarded.

Deadline May of each year.

[801]
WORLD COMMUNION NATIONAL SCHOLARSHIPS

United Methodist Church
General Board of Global Ministries
Attn: Scholarship/Leadership Development Office
475 Riverside Drive, Room 333
New York, NY 10115
(212) 870-3787   Toll Free: (800) UMC-GBGM
E-mail: scholars@umcmission.org
Web: www.umcmission.org/Explore-Our-Work/Scholarships

Summary To provide financial assistance to Asian Americans and other students of color who are interested in attending graduate school to prepare for leadership in promoting the mission goals of the United Methodist Church.

Eligibility This program is open to U.S. citizens and permanent residents who are members of a community of color. Applicants must have applied to or been admitted to a master's, doctoral, or professional program at an institution of higher education in the United States. They must indicate a willingness to provide 5 years of Christian service after graduation in the areas of elimination of poverty, expansion of global health, leadership development, or congregational development. High priority is given to members of the United Methodist Church. Financial need is considered in the selection process.

Financial data The stipend ranges from $1,000 to $12,500, depending on the recipient's related needs and school expenses.

Duration 1 year.

Additional information These awards are funded by the World Communion Offering received in United Methodist Churches on the first Sunday in October.

Number awarded 5 to 10 each year.

Deadline November of each year.

[802]
XEROX TECHNICAL MINORITY SCHOLARSHIP PROGRAM

Xerox Corporation
Attn: Technical Minority Scholarship Program
150 State Street, Fourth Floor
Rochester, NY 14614
(585) 422-7689   E-mail: GlobalCareers@xerox.com
Web: www.xerox.com/jobs/minority-scholarships/enus.html

Summary To provide financial assistance to Asian Americans and other minorities interested in undergraduate or graduate education in the sciences and/or engineering.

Eligibility This program is open to minorities (people of African American, Asian, Pacific Islander, Native American, Native Alaskan, or Hispanic descent) working full time on a bachelor's, master's, or doctoral degree in chemistry, computing and software systems, engineering (chemical, computer, electrical, imaging, manufacturing, mechanical, optical, or software), information management, laser optics, materials science, physics, or printing management science. Applicants must be U.S. citizens or permanent residents with a

GPA of 3.0 or higher and attending a 4-year college or university.

Financial data Stipends range from $1,000 to $10,000.

Duration 1 year.

Number awarded Varies each year, recently, 130 of these scholarships were awarded.

Deadline September of each year.

[803]
XIA THAO SCHOLARSHIP

Hmong American Education Fund
P.O. Box 17468
St. Paul, MN 55117
(651) 230-3634   E-mail: scholarships@thehaef.org
Web: www.thehaef.org

Summary To provide financial assistance to Hmong undergraduate and graduate students who demonstrate leadership.

Eligibility This program is open to students of Hmong descent who are currently enrolled as full-time undergraduate or graduate students at public 2- or 4-year colleges or universities in any state. Applicants must be U.S. citizens or permanent residents and have a GPA of 3.0 or higher. Along with their application, they must submit a 1,500-word essay on their commitment to education, their leadership qualities, their financial need, how this scholarship can help them, and their community service. Selection is based on academic excellence, leadership qualities, commitment to helping their community, and financial need.

Financial data The stipend is $2,000.

Duration 1 year; nonrenewable.

Number awarded 1 each year.

Deadline March of each year.

[804]
YOUNG SOO CHOI STUDENT SCHOLARSHIP AWARD

Society of Toxicology
Attn: Korean Toxicologists Association in America Special
   Interest Group
1821 Michael Faraday Drive, Suite 300
Reston, VA 20190-5348
(703) 438-3115   Fax: (703) 438-3113
E-mail: sothq@toxicology.org
Web: www.toxicology.org/ai/af/awards.aspx

Summary To provide financial assistance to Korean students who are working on a graduate degree in toxicology.

Eligibility This program is open to Korean students (having been born in Korea or, if born in the United States, having 1 or more parents of Korean descent) who are enrolled or planning to enroll in a graduate program in toxicology or in a field of biomedical science related to toxicology. Applicants must submit a description of their graduate program (including any research conducted or planned), copies of any abstracts prepared for presentations at professional meetings, a brief statement indicating how the scholarship will assist in their graduate training, and a letter of recommendation from their mentor. Selection is based on merit and financial need.

Financial data A stipend is awarded (amount not specified).

Duration 1 year.

Additional information This program began in 2008.

Number awarded 1 each year.

Deadline January of each year.

Professionals/
Postdoctorates

Listed alphabetically by program title and described in detail here are 143 grants, awards, educational support programs, residencies, and other sources of "free money" available to professionals and postdoctorates of Asian origins (including those of subcontinent Asian and Pacific Islander descent). This funding can be used to support research, creative activities, formal academic classes, training courses, and/or residencies in the United States.

[805]
AAOGF FOUNDATION SCHOLARSHIPS

American Association of Obstetricians and Gynecologists
Foundation
2105 Laurel Bush Road, Suite 201
Bel Air, MD 21015
(443) 640-1051   Fax: (443) 640-1031
E-mail: info@aaogf.org
Web: www.aaogf.org/scholarship.asp

Summary To provide funding to physicians (particularly Asian Americans, other minorities, and women) who are interested in a program of research training in obstetrics and gynecology.

Eligibility Applicants must have an M.D. degree and be eligible for the certification process of the American Board of Obstetrics and Gynecology (ABOG). They must be interested in participating in research training conducted by 1 or more faculty mentors at an academic department of obstetrics and gynecology in the United States or Canada. The research training may be either laboratory-based or clinical, and should focus on fundamental biology, disease mechanisms, interventions or diagnostics, epidemiology, or translational research. Applicants for the scholarship co-sponsored by the Society for Maternal-Fetal Medicine (SMFM) must also be members or associate members of the SMFM. Women and minority candidates are strongly encouraged to apply. Selection is based on the scholarly, clinical, and research qualifications of the candidate; evidence of the candidate's commitment to an investigative career in academic obstetrics and gynecology in the United States or Canada; qualifications of the sponsoring department and mentor; overall quality of the mentoring plan; and quality of the research project.

Financial data The grant is $120,000 per year. Sufficient funds to support travel to the annual fellows' retreat must be set aside. The balance of the funds may be used for salary, technical support, and supplies.

Duration 1 year; may be renewed for 2 additional years, based on satisfactory progress of the scholar.

Additional information Scholars must devote at least 75% of their effort to the program of research training.

Number awarded 2 each year: 1 co-sponsored by ABOG and 1 co-sponsored by SMFM.

Deadline June of each year.

[806]
AAPA-APF OKURA MENTAL HEALTH
LEADERSHIP FOUNDATION FELLOWSHIP

American Psychological Foundation
750 First Street, N.E.
Washington, DC 20002-4242
(202) 336-5843   Fax: (202) 336-5812
E-mail: foundation@apa.org
Web: www.apa.org/apf/funding/okura-fellow.aspx

Summary To provide funding to members of the Asian American Psychological Association (AAPA) who are interested in conducting projects related to the Asian American and Pacific Islander (AAPI) community.

Eligibility This program is open to AAPA members who are interested in conducting psychological projects that will benefit the AAPI community. The emphasis of the program rotates among support for research (2015), support for training initia-

tives (2016), and support for service and practice initiatives (2017). Applicants must be within 10 years of completing their doctoral degree and be affiliated with a nonprofit organization. Selection is based on conformance with stated program goals and requirements; innovative and potential impact qualities; competence and capability of project leaders; and quality, viability, and promise of the proposed work.

Financial data The grant is $20,000.

Duration The grant is presented annually.

Additional information This program, established in 2009, is administered on behalf of AAPA by the American Psychological Foundation (APF), with funding provided by the Okura Mental Health Leadership Foundation.

Number awarded 1 each year.

Deadline September of each year.

[807]
AAPI NATIONAL RESEARCH COMPETITION

American Association of Physicians of Indian Origin
Attn: Medical Students, Residents and Fellows Section
600 Enterprise Drive, Suite 108
Oak Brook, IL 60523
(630) 990-2277   Fax: (630) 990-2281
E-mail: preselect@aapimsr.org
Web: www.aapimsr.org/index.cfm/convention

Summary To recognize and reward members of the American Association of Physicians of Indian Origin (AAPI) who submit outstanding research abstracts for presentation at the annual conference.

Eligibility This competition is open to members of the Medical Students, Residents and Fellows (MSRF) section and the Young Physician's Section (YPS) of the AAPI. Applicants must submit abstracts of research for presentation at the AAPI annual conference. Abstracts are accepted in 4 categories: clinical sciences and patient-based research, basic science/translational research, south Asian studies, or AAPI Charitable Foundation studies. Applicants must attend the conference where finalists are chosen for a poster and an 8-minute oral presentation.

Financial data Cash prizes are awarded (amount not specified).

Duration The competition is held annually.

Number awarded Up to 4 each year (1 in each category).

Deadline April of each year.

[808]
AERA-AIR FELLOWS PROGRAM

American Educational Research Association
1430 K Street, N.W., Suite 1200
Washington, DC 20005
(202) 238-3200   Fax: (202) 238-3250
E-mail: fellowships@aera.net
Web: www.aera.net

Summary To provide an opportunity for junior scholars in the field of education (particularly Asian Americans and other underrepresented minorities) to engage in a program of research and advanced training while in residence in Washington, D.C.

Eligibility This program is open to early scholars who received a Ph.D. or Ed.D. degree within the past 3 years in a field related to education and educational processes. Applicants must be proposing a program of intensive research and training in Washington, D.C. Selection is based on past academic record, writing sample, goal statement, range and quality of research experiences, other relevant work or professional experiences, potential contributions to education research, and references. A particular goal of the program is to increase the number of underrepresented minority professionals conducting advanced research or providing technical assistance. U.S. citizenship or permanent resident status is required.

Financial data Stipends range from $55,000 to $65,000 per year.

Duration Up to 2 years.

Additional information This program, jointly sponsored by the American Educational Research Association (AERA) and the American Institutes for Research (AIR), was first offered for 2006. Fellows rotate between the 2 organizations and receive mentoring from recognized researchers and practitioners in a variety of substantive areas in education.

Number awarded Up to 3 each year.

Deadline November of each year.

[809]
AGA RESEARCH SCHOLAR AWARDS

American Gastroenterological Association
Attn: AGA Research Foundation
Research Awards Manager
4930 Del Ray Avenue
Bethesda, MD 20814-2512
(301) 222-4012   Fax: (301) 654-5920
E-mail: awards@gastro.org
Web: www.gastro.org/aga-foundation/grants

Summary To provide research funding to young investigators (particularly Asian Americans, other minorities, and women) who are developing an independent career in an area of gastroenterology, hepatology, or related fields.

Eligibility Applicants must hold full-time faculty positions at North American universities or professional institutes at the time of application. They should be early in their careers (fellows and established investigators are not appropriate candidates). Candidates with an M.D. degree must have completed clinical training within the past 5 years and those with a Ph.D. must have completed their degree within the past 5 years. Membership in the American Gastroenterological Association (AGA) is required. Selection is based on significance, investigator, innovation, approach, environment, relevance to AGA mission, and evidence of institutional commitment. Women, minorities, and physician/scientist investigators are strongly encouraged to apply.

Financial data The grant is $90,000 per year. Funds are to be used for project costs, including salary, supplies, and equipment but excluding travel. Indirect costs are not allowed.

Duration 2 years.

Additional information At least 70% of the recipient's research effort should relate to the gastrointestinal tract or liver.

Number awarded 4 each year.

Deadline October of each year.

[810]
ALEXANDER GRALNICK RESEARCH INVESTIGATOR PRIZE

American Psychological Foundation
750 First Street, N.E.
Washington, DC 20002-4242
(202) 336-5843   Fax: (202) 336-5812
E-mail: foundation@apa.org
Web: www.apa.org/apf/funding/gralnick.aspx

Summary To recognize and reward psychologists (particularly Asian Americans and members of other groups representing diversity) who have conducted exceptional research on serious mental illness.

Eligibility This program is open to psychologists who have a doctoral degree, have a record of significant research productivity, and are able to demonstrate evidence on continuing creativity in the area of research on serious mental illness (including, but not limited to, schizophrenia, bipolar disorder, and paranoia). Nominees must also have significant involvement in training and development of younger investigators. They must have an affiliation with an accredited college, university, or other treatment or research institution. The sponsor encourages nominations of individuals who represent diversity in race, ethnicity, gender, age, disability, and sexual orientation.

Financial data The award is $20,000.

Duration The award is presented biennially, in even-numbered years.

Additional information This award was first presented in 2002.

Number awarded 1 each even-numbered year.

Deadline April of each even-numbered year.

[811]
AMERICAN ASSOCIATION FOR THE ADVANCEMENT OF SCIENCE CONGRESSIONAL FELLOWSHIPS

American Association for the Advancement of Science
Attn: Science and Technology Policy Fellowships
1200 New York Avenue, N.W.
Washington, DC 20005-3920
(202) 326-6700   Fax: (202) 289-4950
E-mail: fellowships@aaas.org
Web: www.fellowships.aaas.org

Summary To provide a fellowship to postdoctoral scientists and engineers (particularly Asian Americans, other minorities, and individuals with disabilities) so they can work as special legislative assistants on the staffs of members of Congress or Congressional committees.

Eligibility This program is open to doctoral-level scientists (Ph.D., M.D., D.V.M., D.Sc., and other terminal degrees) in any field of science (behavioral, biological, computational, earth, health, medical, physical, or social), engineering, or mathematics. Engineers with a master's degree and at least 3 years of professional experience are also eligible. Applicants must demonstrate solid scientific and technical credentials; a commitment to serve society; good communication skills; the ability to engage with non-scientific audiences; and an interest in working as special legislative assistants for Congress. U.S. citizenship is required; federal employees are not eligible. The sponsor seeks candidates from a broad array of backgrounds and a diversity of geographic, disciplinary, gender, and ethnic perspectives, as well as disability status.

Financial data The stipend is $74,872. Also provided are a $4,000 relocation allowance for fellows from outside the Washington, D.C. area, reimbursement for health insurance, and a $4,000 travel allowance.

Duration 1 year, beginning in September.

Additional information The program includes an orientation on Congressional and executive branch operations and a year-long seminar program on issues involving science and public policy. Approximately 30 other national science and engineering societies sponsor fellows in collaboration with this program; for a list of all of those, contact the sponsor.

Number awarded 2 each year.

Deadline October of each year.

[812]
AMERICAN ASSOCIATION OF CHINESE IN TOXICOLOGY AND CHARLES RIVER BEST ABSTRACT AWARD

Society of Toxicology
Attn: American Association of Chinese in Toxicology
 Special Interest Group
1821 Michael Faraday Drive, Suite 300
Reston, VA 20190-5348
(703) 438-3115   Fax: (703) 438-3113
E-mail: sothq@toxicology.org
Web: www.toxicology.org/ai/af/awards.aspx

Summary To recognize and reward graduate student and postdoctoral members of the Society of Toxicology (SOT) who are of Chinese ethnic origin and present outstanding papers at the annual meeting.

Eligibility This award is available to SOT members who are graduate students or postdoctoral fellows of Chinese descent (having 1 or more parents of Chinese descent). Candidates must have an accepted abstract for the SOT annual meeting. Along with the abstract, they must submit a cover letter outlining the significance of the work to the field of toxicology.

Financial data The prizes are $500 for first, $300 for second, and $200 for third.

Duration The prizes are presented annually.

Number awarded 3 each year.

Deadline December of each year.

[813]
AMERICAN ASSOCIATION OF UNIVERSITY WOMEN CAREER DEVELOPMENT GRANTS

American Association of University Women
Attn: AAUW Educational Foundation
301 ACT Drive, Department 60
P.O. Box 4030
Iowa City, IA 52243-4030
(319) 337-1716, ext. 60   Fax: (319) 337-1204
E-mail: aauw@act.org
Web: www.aauw.org

Summary To provide financial assistance to Asian American and other women who are seeking career advancement, career change, or reentry into the workforce.

Eligibility This program is open to women who are U.S. citizens or permanent residents, have earned a bachelor's degree, received their most recent degree more than 4 years ago, and are making career changes, seeking to advance in current careers, or reentering the workforce. Applicants must be interested in working toward a master's degree, second bachelor's or associate degree, professional degree (e.g., M.D., J.D.), certification program, or technical school certificate. They must be planning to undertake course work at an accredited 2- or 4-year college or university (or a technical school that is licensed, accredited, or approved by the U.S. Department of Education). Primary consideration is given to women of color and women pursuing their first advanced degree or credentials in nontraditional fields. Support is not provided for prerequisite course work or for Ph.D. course work or dissertations. Selection is based on demonstrated commitment to education and equity for women and girls, reason for seeking higher education or technical training, degree to which study plan is consistent with career objectives, potential for success in chosen field, documentation of opportunities in chosen field, feasibility of study plans and proposed time schedule, validity of proposed budget and budget narrative (including sufficient outside support), and quality of written proposal.

Financial data Grants range from $2,000 to $12,000. Funds may be used for tuition, fees, books, supplies, local transportation, dependent child care, or purchase of a computer required for the study program.

Duration 1 year, beginning in July; nonrenewable.

Additional information The filing fee is $35.

Number awarded Varies each year; recently, 63 of these grants, with a value of $670,000, were awarded.

Deadline December of each year.

[814]
ANISFIELD-WOLF BOOK AWARDS

Cleveland Foundation
1422 Euclid Avenue, Suite 1300
Cleveland, OH 44115-2001
(216) 861-3810   Fax: (216) 861-1729
E-mail: Hello@anisfield-wolf.org
Web: www.anisfield-wolf.org

Summary To recognize and reward recent books that have contributed to an understanding of racism or appreciation of the rich diversity of human cultures.

Eligibility Works published in English during the preceding year that "contribute to our understanding of racism or our appreciation of the rich diversity of human cultures" are eligible to be considered. Entries may be either scholarly or imaginative (fiction, poetry, memoir). Plays and screenplays are not eligible, nor are works in progress. Manuscripts and self-published works are not eligible, and no grants are made for completing or publishing manuscripts.

Financial data The prize is $10,000. If more than 1 author is chosen in a given year, the prize is divided equally among the winning books.

Duration The award is presented annually.

Additional information This program began in 1936.

Number awarded 5 each year: 2 for fiction, 1 for poetry, 1 for nonfiction, and 1 for lifetime achievement.

Deadline December of each year.

[815]
APA/SAMHSA MINORITY FELLOWSHIP PROGRAM

American Psychiatric Association
Attn: Department of Minority and National Affairs
1000 Wilson Boulevard, Suite 1825
Arlington, VA 22209-3901
(703) 907-8653   Toll Free: (888) 35-PSYCH
Fax: (703) 907-7852   E-mail: mking@psych.org
Web: www.psychiatry.org

Summary To provide educational enrichment to psychiatrists-in-training (particularly Asian Americans and other minorities) who are interested in providing quality and effective services to minorities and the underserved.

Eligibility This program is open to residents who are in at least their second year of psychiatric training, members of the American Psychiatric Association (APA), and U.S. citizens or permanent residents. A goal of the program is to develop leadership to improve the quality of mental health care for members of ethnic minority groups (American Indians, Native Alaskans, Asian Americans, Native Hawaiians, Native Pacific Islanders, African Americans, and Hispanics/Latinos). Applicants must be interested in working with a component of the APA that is of interest to them and relevant to their career goals. Along with their application, they must submit a 2-page essay on how the fellowship would be utilized to alter their present training and ultimately assist them in achieving their career goals. Selection is based on commitment to serve ethnic minority populations, demonstrated leadership abilities, awareness of the importance of culture in mental health, and interest in the interrelationship between mental health/illness and transcultural factors.

Financial data Fellows receive a monthly stipend (amount not specified) and reimbursement of transportation, lodging, meals, and incidentals in connection with attendance at program-related activities. They are expected to use the funds to enhance their own professional development, improve training in cultural competence at their training institution, improve awareness of culturally relevant issues in psychiatry at their institution, expand research in areas relevant to minorities and underserved populations, enhance the current treatment modalities for minority patients and underserved individuals at their institution, and improve awareness in the surrounding community about mental health issues (particularly with regard to minority populations).

Duration 1 year; may be renewed 1 additional year.

Additional information Funding for this program is provided by the Substance Abuse and Mental Health Services Administration (SAMHSA). As part of their assignment to an APA component, fellows must attend the fall component meetings in September and the APA annual meeting in May. At those meeting, they can share their experiences as residents and minorities and discuss issues that impact on minority populations. This program is an outgrowth of the fellowships that were established in 1974 under a grant from the National Institute of Mental Health in answer to concerns about the underrepresentation of minorities in psychiatry.

Number awarded Varies each year; recently, 21 of these fellowships were awarded.

Deadline January of each year.

[816]
APA SUBSTANCE ABUSE FELLOWSHIP PROGRAM

American Psychiatric Association
Attn: Department of Minority and National Affairs
1000 Wilson Boulevard, Suite 1825
Arlington, VA 22209-3901
(703) 907-8653   Toll Free: (888) 35-PSYCH
Fax: (703) 907-7852   E-mail: mking@psych.org
Web: www.psychiatry.org

Summary To provide educational enrichment to Asian American and other minority psychiatrists-in-training and stimulate their interest in providing quality and effective services related to substance abuse to minorities and the underserved.

Eligibility This program is open to psychiatric residents who are members of the American Psychiatric Association (APA) and U.S. citizens or permanent residents. A goal of the program is to develop leadership to improve the quality of mental health care for members of ethnic minority groups (American Indians, Native Alaskans, Asian Americans, Native Hawaiians, Native Pacific Islanders, African Americans, and Hispanics/Latinos). Applicants must be in at least their fifth year of a substance abuse training program approved by an affiliated medical school or agency where a significant number of substance abuse patients are from minority and underserved groups. They must also be interested in working with a component of the APA that is of interest to them and relevant to their career goals. Along with their application, they must submit a 2-page essay on how the fellowship would be utilized to alter their present training and ultimately assist them in achieving their career goals. Selection is based on commitment to serve ethnic minority populations, demonstrated leadership abilities, awareness of the importance of culture in mental health, and interest in the interrelationship between mental health/illness and transcultural factors.

Financial data Fellows receive a monthly stipend (amount not specified) and reimbursement of transportation, lodging, meals, and incidentals in connection with attendance at program-related activities. They are expected to use the funds to enhance their own professional development, improve training in cultural competence at their training institution, improve awareness of culturally relevant issues in psychiatry at their institution, expand research in areas relevant to minorities and underserved populations, enhance the current treatment modalities for minority patients and underserved individuals at their institution, and improve awareness in the surrounding community about mental health issues (particularly with regard to minority populations).

Duration 1 year; may be renewed 1 additional year.

Additional information Funding for this program is provided by the Substance Abuse and Mental Health Services Administration (SAMHSA). As part of their assignment to an APA component, fellows must attend the fall component meetings in September and the APA annual meeting in May. At those meeting, they can share their experiences as residents and minorities and discuss issues that impact minority populations. This program is an outgrowth of the fellowships that were established in 1974 under a grant from the National Institute of Mental Health in answer to concerns about the underrepresentation of minorities in psychiatry.

Number awarded Varies each year; recently, 3 of these fellowships were awarded.

Deadline January of each year.

[817]
ASIAN AMERICAN STUDIES VISITING SCHOLAR AND VISITING RESEARCHER PROGRAM

University of California at Los Angeles
Institute of American Cultures
Asian American Studies Center
3230 Campbell Hall
P.O. Box 951546
Los Angeles, CA 90095-1546
(310) 825-2974   Fax: (310) 206-9844
E-mail: melanyd@ucla.edu
Web: www.iac.ucla.edu/fellowships_visitingscholar.html

Summary To provide funding to scholars interested in conducting research in Asian American studies at UCLA's Asian American Studies Center.

Eligibility Applicants must have completed a doctoral degree in Asian American or related studies. They must be interested in teaching or conducting research at UCLA's Asian American Studies Center. Visiting Scholar appointments are available to people who currently hold permanent academic appointments; Visiting Researcher appointments are available to postdoctorates who recently received their degree. UCLA faculty, students, and staff are not eligible. U.S. citizenship or permanent resident status is required.

Financial data Fellows receive a stipend of $32,000 to $35,000 (depending on rank, experience, and date of completion of the Ph.D.), health benefits, and up to $4,000 in research support. Visiting Scholars are paid through their home institution; Visiting Researchers receive their funds directly from UCLA.

Duration 9 months, beginning in October.

Additional information Fellows must teach or do research in the programs of the center. The award is offered in conjunction with UCLA's Institute of American Cultures (IAC).

Number awarded 1 each year.

Deadline February of each year.

[818]
BEHAVIORAL SCIENCES POSTDOCTORAL FELLOWSHIPS IN EPILEPSY

Epilepsy Foundation
Attn: Research Department
8301 Professional Place
Landover, MD 20785-2353
(301) 459-3700   Toll Free: (800) EFA-1000
Fax: (301) 577-2684   TDD: (800) 332-2070
E-mail: grants@efa.org
Web: www.epilepsyfoundation.org

Summary To provide funding to postdoctorates in the behavioral sciences (particularly Asian Americans, other minorities, women, and individuals with disabilities) who wish to pursue research training in an area related to epilepsy.

Eligibility Applicants must have received a Ph.D. or equivalent degree in a field of social science, including (but not limited to) sociology, social work, anthropology, nursing, or economics. They must be interested in receiving additional research training to prepare for a career in clinical behavioral aspects of epilepsy. Academic faculty holding the rank of instructor or above are not eligible, nor are graduate or medical students, medical residents, permanent government employees, or employees in private industry. Because these fellowships are designed as training opportunities, the quality of the training plans and environment are considered in the selection process. Other selection criteria include the scientific quality of the proposed research, a statement regarding the relevance of the research to epilepsy, the applicant's qualifications, the preceptor's qualifications, adequacy of the facility, and related epilepsy programs at the institution. Applications from women, members of minority groups, and people with disabilities are especially encouraged. U.S. citizenship is not required, but the research must be conducted in the United States.

Financial data Grants up to $40,000 are available.

Duration 1 year.

Number awarded Varies each year.

Deadline March of each year.

[819]
BELFER CENTER FOR SCIENCE AND INTERNATIONAL AFFAIRS FELLOWSHIPS

Harvard University
John F. Kennedy School of Government
Belfer Center for Science and International Affairs
Attn: Fellowship Coordinator
79 John F. Kennedy Street, Mailbox 53
Cambridge, MA 02138
(617) 495-8806   Fax: (617) 495-8963
E-mail: bcsia_fellowships@hks.harvard.edu
Web: belfercenter.ksg.harvard.edu/fellowships

Summary To provide funding to professionals, postdoctorates, and doctoral students (particularly Asian Americans, other minorities, and women) who are interested in conducting research in areas of concern to the Belfer Center for Science and International Affairs at Harvard University in Cambridge, Massachusetts.

Eligibility The postdoctoral fellowship is open to recent recipients of the Ph.D. or equivalent degree, university faculty members, and employees of government, military, international, humanitarian, and private research institutions who have appropriate professional experience. Applicants for predoctoral fellowships must have passed their general examinations. Lawyers, economists, political scientists, those in the natural sciences, and others of diverse disciplinary backgrounds are also welcome to apply. The program especially encourages applications from women, minorities, and citizens of all countries. All applicants must be interested in conducting research in 1 of the 2 major program areas of the center: 1) the International Security Program (ISP), which addresses U.S. defense and foreign policy, security policy, nuclear proliferation, terrorism, internal and ethnic conflict, and related topics; and 2) the Science, Technology, and Public Policy Program (STPP), including technology and innovation, information and communications technology, water-energy nexus, managing the atom, energy technology innovation policy, China and environmental sustainability, geoengineering and climate policy, geopolitics of energy, and geospatial policy and management.

Financial data The stipend is $34,000 for postdoctoral research fellows or $20,000 for predoctoral research fellows. Health insurance is also provided.

Duration 10 months.

Number awarded A limited number each year.

Deadline January of each year.

[820]
BIG DATA AND ANALYTICS FELLOWSHIPS OF THE AMERICAN ASSOCIATION FOR THE ADVANCEMENT OF SCIENCE

American Association for the Advancement of Science
Attn: Science and Technology Policy Fellowships
1200 New York Avenue, N.W.
Washington, DC 20005-3920
(202) 326-6700   Fax: (202) 289-4950
E-mail: fellowships@aaas.org
Web: www.fellowships.aaas.org

Summary To provide postdoctoral scientists and engineers (particularly Asian Americans, other minorities, women, and individuals with disabilities) at all career stages with an opportunity to work at a federal agency on data and trend analysis issues.

Eligibility This program is open to doctoral-level scientists (Ph.D., M.D., D.V.M., D.Sc., and other terminal degrees) in any field of science (behavioral, biological, computational, earth, health, medical, physical, or social), engineering, or mathematics. Engineers with a master's degree and at least 3 years of professional experience are also eligible. Applicants should be able to apply their analytical skills to data and trend analysis issues from infrastructure, technology, quality control, and presentation to security, integrity, and ethics. They must demonstrate solid scientific and technical credentials; a commitment to serve society; good communication skills; the ability to engage with non-scientific audiences; and an interest in working as special assistants for any federal agency in Washington, D.C. that partners with the sponsoring organization. U.S. citizenship is required; federal employees are not eligible. The sponsor seeks candidates from a broad array of backgrounds and a diversity of geographic, disciplinary, gender, and ethnic perspectives, as well as disability status.

Financial data The stipend for fellows with 0 to 7 years of postdoctoral experience is $74,872 in the first year and $77,368 in the second year. For fellows with 7 to 15 years of experience, the stipend is $84,855 in the first year and $87,350 in the second year. Fellows who have 15 or more years of postdoctoral experience receive $97,333 in the first year and $99,829 in the second year. Also provided are a $4,000 relocation allowance for fellows from outside the Washington, D.C. area, reimbursement for health insurance, and a $4,000 travel allowance.

Duration 1 year, beginning in September; may be renewed for 1 additional year.

Additional information This program began in 2014.

Number awarded 5 to 15 each year.

Deadline October of each year.

[821]
BYRD FELLOWSHIP PROGRAM

Ohio State University
Byrd Polar Research Center
Attn: Fellowship Committee
Scott Hall Room 108
1090 Carmack Road
Columbus, OH 43210-1002
(614) 292-6531   Fax: (614) 292-4697
Web: bprc.osu.edu/byrdfellow

Summary To provide funding to postdoctorates (particularly Asian Americans, other minorities, women, individuals with disabilities, and those with ties to the military) who are interested in conducting research on the Arctic or Antarctic areas at Ohio State University.

Eligibility This program is open to postdoctorates of superior academic background who are interested in conducting advanced research on either Arctic or Antarctic problems at the Byrd Polar Research Center at Ohio State University. Applicants must have received their doctorates within the past 5 years. Along with their application, they must submit a description of the specific research to be conducted during the fellowship and a curriculum vitae. Women, minorities, Vietnam-era veterans, disabled veterans, and individuals with disabilities are particularly encouraged to apply.

Financial data The stipend is $42,000 per year; an allowance of $5,000 for research and travel is also provided.

Duration 18 months.

Additional information This program was established by a major gift from the Byrd Foundation in memory of Rear Admiral Richard Evelyn Byrd and Marie Ames Byrd, his wife. Except for field work or other research activities requiring absence from campus, fellows are expected to be in residence at the university for the duration of the program.

Deadline March of each year.

[822]
CAROLINE CRAIG AUGUSTYN AND DAMIAN AUGUSTYN AWARD IN DIGESTIVE CANCER

American Gastroenterological Association
Attn: AGA Research Foundation
Research Awards Manager
4930 Del Ray Avenue
Bethesda, MD 20814-2512
(301) 222-4012   Fax: (301) 654-5920
E-mail: awards@gastro.org
Web: www.gastro.org/aga-foundation/grants

Summary To provide funding to junior investigators (particularly Asian Americans, other minorities, and individuals with disabilities) who are interested in conducting research related to digestive cancer.

Eligibility Applicants must have an M.D., Ph.D., or equivalent degree and a full-time faculty position at an accredited North American institution. They must have received an NIH K series or other federal or non-federal career development award of at least 4 years duration, but may not have received an R01 or equivalent award. For M.D. applicants, no more than 7 years may have elapsed following the completion of clinical training, and for Ph.D. applicants no more than 7 years may have elapsed since the completion of their degree. Individual membership in the American Gastroenterology

Association (AGA) is required. The proposal must relate to the pathogenesis, prevention, diagnosis, or treatment of digestive cancer. Women and minority investigators are strongly encouraged to apply. Selection is based on the qualifications of the candidate and the novelty, feasibility, and significance of their research.

Financial data The grant is $40,000. Funds may be used for salary, supplies, or equipment. Indirect costs are not allowed.

Duration 1 year.

Number awarded 1 each year.

Deadline January of each year.

[823]
CENTER FOR ADVANCED STUDY IN THE BEHAVIORAL SCIENCES RESIDENTIAL POSTDOCTORAL FELLOWSHIPS

Center for Advanced Study in the Behavioral Sciences
Attn: Secretary and Program Coordinator
75 Alta Road
Stanford, CA 94305-8090
(650) 736-0100   Fax: (650) 736-0221
E-mail: casbs-secretary@casbs.org
Web: www.casbs.org

Summary To provide funding to behavioral scientists (particularly Asian Americans, other minorities, women, and younger scholars) who are interested in conducting research at the Center for Advanced Study in the Behavioral Sciences in Stanford, California.

Eligibility Eligible to be nominated for this fellowship are scientists and scholars from this country or abroad who show exceptional accomplishment or promise in the core social and behavioral disciplines: anthropology, economics, political science, psychology, or sociology; applications are also accepted from scholars in a wide range of humanistic disciplines, education, linguistics, and the biological sciences. Selection is based on standing in the field rather than on the merit of a particular project under way at a given time. A special effort is made to promote diversity among the scholars by encouraging participation from groups that often have been overlooked in academia: younger scholars, women, minorities, international scholars, and scholars whose home universities are not research-oriented.

Financial data The stipend is based on the fellow's regular salary for the preceding year, with a cap of $65,000. In most cases, the fellow contributes to the cost of the stipend with support from sabbatical or other funding source.

Duration From 9 to 11 months.

Additional information Fellows must be in residence in a community within 10 miles of the center for the duration of the program (that requirement excludes San Francisco, Berkeley, and San Jose, for example).

Number awarded Approximately 45 each year.

Deadline September of each year.

[824]
CENTER FOR ASIAN AMERICAN MEDIA DOCUMENTARY FUND

Center for Asian American Media
Attn: Media Fund Director
145 Ninth Street, Suite 350
San Francisco, CA 94103-2641
(415) 863-0814   Fax: (415) 863-7428
E-mail: mediafund@caamedia.org
Web: www.caamedia.org/filmmaker-support/funding

Summary To provide funding to producers of public television documentaries that relate to the Asian American experience.

Eligibility This program is open to independent producers who are interested in developing and finishing public television documentaries on Asian American issues. Applicants must have previous film or television experience as demonstrated by a sample tape and must have artistic, budgetary, and editorial control. They must be 18 years of age or older and citizens or legal residents of the United States. All programs must be standard broadcast length and in accordance with PBS broadcast specifications. Ineligible projects include those for which the exclusive domestic television broadcast rights are not available; in the script development stage; intended solely for theatrical release or commercial in nature; in which the applicant is commissioned, employed, or hired by a commercial or public television station; that are thesis projects or student films co- or solely owned or copyrighted, or editorially or fiscally controlled by the school; that are foreign-based, owned, or controlled; or that are industrial or promotional projects. In the selection process, the following questions are considered: is the project a good match for American public television and its national audience; is the story idea compelling, engaging, original, and well-conceived; is the visual/stylistic treatment effective and distinctive; can the project be completed with a realistic timeline; will the project appeal not only to Asian American viewers, but also to a broader television audience; and does the sample tape show the skills and/or potential of the applicant to complete the proposed project.

Financial data Grants range from $15,000 to $50,000. Funding may be used either for production or completion activities.

Additional information This program was formerly known as the National Asian American Telecommunications Association Media Fund Grants. Funding is provided by the Corporation for Public Broadcasting.

Number awarded 5 to 10 grants are awarded each year.

Deadline April or November of each year.

[825]
CHANG-LIN TIEN EDUCATION LEADERSHIP AWARDS

Asian Pacific Fund
465 California Street, Suite 809
San Francisco, CA 94104
(415) 395-9985   E-mail: info@asianpacificfund.org
Web: www.asianpacificfund.org

Summary To recognize and reward Asian American administrators at colleges and universities who demonstrate outstanding leadership in higher education.

Eligibility This award is available to Asian Americans who are currently serving at the level of dean (or a position of comparable responsibility) or higher at a 4-year public or private college or university in the United States. Nominees should have demonstrated scholarly achievement, administrative experience, pride in their Asian and American heritage, dedication to excellence, and commitment to providing access to academic institutions for a diverse population of students. Self-nominations are not accepted.

Financial data Awards consist of an unrestricted grant of $10,000.

Duration The awards are presented annually.

Additional information These awards were first presented in 2007 to honor Dr. Chang-Lin Tien, the first Asian American to head a major research university as chancellor of UC Berkeley from 1990 to 1997.

Number awarded 2 each year.

Deadline Nominations must be submitted by April of each year.

[826]
CHARLES L. BREWER DISTINGUISHED TEACHING OF PSYCHOLOGY AWARD

American Psychological Foundation
750 First Street, N.E.
Washington, DC 20002-4242
(202) 336-5843   Fax: (202) 336-5812
E-mail: foundation@apa.org
Web: www.apa.org/apf/funding/brewer.aspx

Summary To recognize and reward the distinguished career contributions of outstanding psychology professors, particularly those who are Asian Americans, other minorities, women, or individuals with disabilities.

Eligibility This award is available to psychologists who demonstrate outstanding teaching. Selection is based on evidence of influence as a teacher of students who become psychologists, research on teaching, development of effective teaching methods and/or materials, development of innovation curricula and courses, performance as a classroom teacher, demonstrated training of teachers of psychology, teaching of advanced research methods and practice in psychology, and/or administrative facilitation of teaching. Nominators must complete an application form, write a letter of support, and submit the nominee's current vitae and bibliography. The sponsor encourages nominations of individuals who represent diversity in race, ethnicity, gender, age, disability, and sexual orientation.

Financial data Awardees receive a plaque, a $2,000 honorarium, and an all-expense paid trip to the annual convention where the award is presented.

Duration The award is presented annually.

Additional information This award, originally named the Distinguished Teaching in Psychology Award, was first presented in 1970.

Number awarded 1 each year.

Deadline Nominations must be submitted by November of each year.

[827]
CLINICAL RESEARCH POST-DOCTORAL FELLOWSHIP PROGRAM

American Nurses Association
Attn: SAMHSA Minority Fellowship Programs
8515 Georgia Avenue, Suite 400
Silver Spring, MD 20910-3492
(301) 628-5247   Toll Free: (800) 274-4ANA
Fax: (301) 628-5339   E-mail: janet.jackson@ana.org
Web: www.emfp.org

Summary To provide funding to Asian American and other minority postdoctoral nurses who are interested in a program of research and study on psychiatric, mental health, and substance abuse issues that impact the lives of ethnic minority people.

Eligibility This program is open to doctoral-prepared nurses who are members of an ethnic or racial minority group, including but not limited to Blacks or African Americans, Hispanics or Latinos, American Indians and Alaska Natives, Asian Americans, and Native Hawaiians and other Pacific Islanders. Applicants must be able to demonstrate a commitment to a research career in nursing and psychiatric/mental health issues affecting ethnic minority populations. They must be interested in a program of full-time postdoctoral study, with a research focus on such issues of concern to minority populations as substance abuse treatment capacity, mental health system transformation, prevention, co-occurring disorders, seclusion and restraint, children and families, disaster readiness and response, homelessness, older adults, HIV/AIDS and hepatitis, and criminal and juvenile justice. U.S. citizenship or permanent resident status and membership in the American Nurses Association are required.

Financial data The stipend depends on the number of years of postdoctoral experience, ranging from $39,264 for less than 1 year to $54,180 for 7 or more years.

Duration 1 to 2 years.

Additional information Funds for this program are provided by the Substance Abuse and Mental Health Services Administration (SAMHSA).

Number awarded 1 or more each year.

Deadline February of each year.

[828]
CLINICAL RESEARCH PRE-DOCTORAL FELLOWSHIP PROGRAM

American Nurses Association
Attn: SAMHSA Minority Fellowship Programs
8515 Georgia Avenue, Suite 400
Silver Spring, MD 20910-3492
(301) 628-5247   Toll Free: (800) 274-4ANA
Fax: (301) 628-5339   E-mail: janet.jackson@ana.org
Web: www.emfp.org

Summary To provide financial assistance to Asian American and other minority nurses who are doctoral candidates interested in psychiatric, mental health, and substance abuse issues that impact the lives of ethnic minority people.

Eligibility This program is open to nurses who have a master's degree and are members of an ethnic or racial minority group, including but not limited to Blacks or African Americans, Hispanics or Latinos, American Indians and Alaska Natives, Asian Americans, and Native Hawaiians and other

Pacific Islanders. Applicants must be able to demonstrate a commitment to a research career in nursing and psychiatric/mental health issues affecting ethnic minority populations. They must be interested in a program of full-time doctoral study, with a research focus on such issues of concern to minority populations as child abuse, violence in intimate relationships, mental health disorders, substance abuse, mental health service utilization, and stigma as a barrier to mental health care and personal resilience. U.S. citizenship or permanent resident status and membership in the American Nurses Association are required. Selection is based on research potential, scholarship, writing ability, knowledge of broad issues in mental health nursing, and professional commitment to ethnic minority concerns.

Financial data The program provides an annual stipend of $22,032 and tuition assistance.

Duration 3 to 5 years.

Additional information Funds for this program are provided by the Substance Abuse and Mental Health Services Administration (SAMHSA).

Number awarded 1 or more each year.

Deadline February of each year.

[829]
CTA/MARTIN LUTHER KING, JR. MEMORIAL SCHOLARSHIP FUND

California Teachers Association
Attn: CTA Foundation for Teaching and Learning
1705 Murchison Drive
P.O. Box 921
Burlingame, CA 94011-0921
(650) 697-1400   E-mail: scholarships@cta.org
Web: www.cta.org

Summary To provide financial assistance for college or graduate school to Asian Americans and other racial and ethnic minorities who are members of the California Teachers Association (CTA), children of members, or members of the Student CTA.

Eligibility This program is open to members of racial or ethnic minority groups (African Americans, American Indians/Alaska Natives, Asians/Pacific Islanders, and Hispanics) who are 1) active CTA members; 2) dependent children of active, retired, or deceased CTA members; or 3) members of Student CTA. Applicants must be interested in preparing for a teaching career in public education or already engaged in such a career.

Financial data Stipends vary each year; recently, they ranged from $1,000 to $4,000.

Duration 1 year.

Number awarded Varies each year; recently, 25 of these scholarships were awarded: 5 to CTA members, 10 to children of CTA members, and 10 to Student CTA members.

Deadline February of each year.

[830]
DANIEL H. EFRON RESEARCH AWARD

American College of Neuropsychopharmacology
Attn: Executive Office
5034-A Thoroughbred Lane
Brentwood, TN 37027
(615) 324-2360   Fax: (615) 523-1715
E-mail: acnp@acnp.org
Web: www.acnp.org/programs/awards.aspx

Summary To recognize and reward young scientists (particularly Asian Americans, other minorities, and women) who have completed outstanding basic or translational research to neuropsychopharmacology.

Eligibility This award is available to scientists who are younger than 50 years of age. Nominees must have made an outstanding basic or translational contribution to neuropsychopharmacology. The contribution may be preclinical or work that emphasizes the relationship between basic and clinical research. Selection is based on the quality of the contribution and its impact on advancing neuropsychopharmacology. Membership in the American College of Neuropsychopharmacology (ACNP) is not required. Nomination of women and minorities is highly encouraged.

Financial data The award consists of an expense-paid trip to the ACNP annual meeting, a monetary honorarium, and a plaque.

Duration The award is presented annually.

Additional information This award was first presented in 1974.

Number awarded 1 each year.

Deadline Nominations must be submitted by June of each year.

[831]
DEPARTMENT OF DEFENSE SMALL BUSINESS INNOVATION RESEARCH GRANTS

Department of Defense
Attn: Office of Small Business Programs
4800 Mark Center Drive, Suite 15G13
Alexandria, VA 22530
Toll Free: (866) SBIR-HLP
E-mail: administrator.dodsbir@osd.mil
Web: www.acq.osd.mil/osbp/sbir

Summary To support small businesses (especially those owned by Asian Americans, other minorities, or women) that have the technological expertise to contribute to the research and development mission of various agencies within the Department of Defense.

Eligibility For the purposes of this program, a "small business" is defined as a firm that is organized for profit with a location in the United States; is in the legal form of an individual proprietorship, partnership, limited liability company, corporation, joint venture, association, trust, or cooperative; is at least 51% owned and controlled by 1 or more individuals who are citizens or permanent residents of the United States; and has (including its affiliates) fewer than 500 employees. The primary employment of the principal investigator must be with the firm at the time of award and during the conduct of the proposed project. Applications are encouraged from 1) women-owned small business concerns, defined as those that are at least 51% owned by a woman or women who also control and operate them; and 2) socially and economically disadvantaged small business concerns that are at least 51% owned by an Indian tribe, a Native Hawaiian organization, or 1 or more socially and economically disadvantaged individuals (African Americans, Hispanic Americans, Native Americans, Asian Pacific Americans, or subcontinent Asian Americans). Agencies that offer Department of Defense Small Business Innovation Research (SBIR) programs are the Department of the Army, Department of the Navy, Department of the Air Force, Defense Advanced Research Projects Agency (DARPA), Defense Threat Reduction Agency (DTRA), Chemical and Biological Defense (CBD), Defense Health Program (DHP), Defense Logistics Agency (DLA), Special Operations Command (SOCOM), Missile Defense Agency (MDA), National Geospatial-Intelligence Agency (NGA), Defense Microelectronics Activity (DMEA), and Office of Secretary of Defense (OSD). Selection is based on the soundness, technical merit, and innovation of the proposed approach and its incremental progress toward topic or subtopic solution; the qualifications of the principal investigator, supporting staff, and consultants; and the potential for commercial application and the benefits expected to accrue from this commercialization.

Financial data Grants are offered in 2 phases. In phase 1, awards normally range from $70,000 to $150,000 (for both direct and indirect costs); in phase 2, awards normally range from $500,000 to $1,000,000 (including both direct and indirect costs).

Duration Phase 1 awards may extend up to 6 months; phase 2 awards may extend up to 2 years.

Number awarded Varies each year; recently, 1,816 Phase 1 awards were granted: 582 for Department of the Navy, 295 for Department of the Army, 480 for Department of the Air Force, 68 for DARPA, 17 for DTRA, 16 for CBD, 16 for SOCOM, 122 for MDA, 7 for DLA, 40 for DHP, 4 for NGA, and 160 for OSD. The number of Phase 2 awards was 938, including 321 for Department of the Navy, 190 for Department of the Army, 207 for Department of the Air Force, 60 for DARPA, 4 for DTRA, 12 for CBD, 8 for SOCOM, 67 for MDA, 2 for DLA, 1 for DMEA, 27 for DHP, and 39 for OSD. Total funding was approximately $1.04 billion.

Deadline September of each year.

[832]
DEPARTMENT OF DEFENSE SMALL BUSINESS TECHNOLOGY TRANSFER GRANTS

Department of Defense
Attn: Office of Small Business Programs
4800 Mark Center Drive, Suite 15G13
Alexandria, VA 22530
Toll Free: (866) SBIR-HLP
E-mail: administrator.dodsbir@osd.mil
Web: www.acq.osd.mil/osbp/sbir

Summary To provide financial support to cooperative research and development projects carried out between small business concerns (particularly those owned by Asian Americans, other minorities, or women) and research institutions in areas of interest to various agencies within the Department of Defense.

Eligibility For the purposes of this program, a "small business" is defined as a firm that is organized for profit with a location in the United States; is in the legal form of an individ-

ual proprietorship, partnership, limited liability company, corporation, joint venture, association, trust, or cooperative; is at least 51% owned and controlled by 1 or more individuals who are citizens or permanent residents of the United States; and has (including its affiliates) fewer than 500 employees. Unlike the Department of Defense Small Business Innovation Research Grants, the primary employment of the principal investigator does not need to be with the business concern. This program, however, requires that the small business apply in collaboration with a nonprofit research institution for conduct of a project that has potential for commercialization. At least 40% of the work must be performed by the small business and at least 30% of the work must be performed by the research institution. Principal investigators from the nonprofit research institution must commit at least 10% of their effort to the project. Applications are encouraged from 1) women-owned small business concerns, defined as those that are at least 51% owned by a woman or women who also control and operate them; and 2) socially and economically disadvantaged small business concerns that are at least 51% owned by an Indian tribe, a Native Hawaiian organization, or 1 or more socially and economically disadvantaged individuals (African Americans, Hispanic Americans, Native Americans, Asian Pacific Americans, or subcontinent Asian Americans). Partnerships between small businesses and Historically Black Colleges and Universities (HBCUs) and Minority Institutions (MIs) are especially encouraged. Agencies of the Department of Defense currently participating in this program are the Department of the Army, Department of the Navy, Department of the Air Force, Defense Advanced Research Projects Agency (DARPA), Missile Defense Agency (MDA), and Office of Secretary of Defense (OSD). Selection is based on the soundness, technical merit, and innovation of the proposed approach and its incremental progress toward topic or subtopic solution; the qualifications of the proposed principal investigators, supporting staff, and consultants; and the potential for commercial application and the benefits expected to accrue from this commercialization.

Financial data In the first phase, annual awards range from $70,000 to $150,000 for direct costs, indirect costs, and negotiated fixed fees. In the second phase, awards from $500,000 to $1,000,000 for the full period are available.

Duration Generally 1 year for the first phase and 2 years for the second phase.

Additional information Grants in the first phase are to determine the scientific, technical, and commercial merit and feasibility of the proposed cooperative effort and the quality of performance of the small business concern. In the second phase, the research and development efforts continue, depending on the results of the first phase.

Number awarded Varies each year; recently, 309 Phase 1 awards were granted: 63 for Department of the Army, 117 for Department of the Navy, 87 for Department of the Air Force, 23 for OSD, and 19 for MDA. The number of Phase 2 awards was 127, including 31 for Department of the Army, 54 for Department of the Navy, 28 for Department of the Air Force, 5 for DARPA, 3 for OSD, and 6 for MDA. Total funding was approximately $117 million.

Deadline April of each year.

[833]
DEPARTMENT OF EDUCATION SMALL BUSINESS INNOVATION RESEARCH GRANTS

Department of Education
Attn: Institute of Education Sciences
555 New Jersey Avenue, N.W., Room 608D
Washington, DC 20208-5544
(202) 208-1983 Fax: (202) 219-2030
E-mail: Edward.metz@ed.gov
Web: www2.ed.gov/programs/sbir/index.html

Summary To support small businesses (especially those owned by Asian Americans, other minorities, or women) that have the technological expertise to contribute to the research and development mission of the Department of Education.

Eligibility For the purposes of this program, a "small business" is defined as a firm that is organized for profit with a location in the United States; is in the legal form of an individual proprietorship, partnership, limited liability company, corporation, joint venture, association, trust, or cooperative; is at least 51% owned and controlled by 1 or more individuals who are citizens or permanent residents of the United States; and has (including its affiliates) fewer than 500 employees. The primary employment of the principal investigator must be with the firm at the time of award and during the conduct of the proposed project. Applications are encouraged from 1) women-owned small business concerns, defined as those that are at least 51% owned by a woman or women who also control and operate them; and 2) socially and economically disadvantaged small business concerns that are at least 51% owned by an Indian tribe, a Native Hawaiian organization, or 1 or more socially and economically disadvantaged individuals (African Americans, Hispanic Americans, Native Americans, Asian Pacific Americans, or subcontinent Asian Americans). Firms with strong research capabilities in science, engineering, or educational technology in any of the topic areas are encouraged to participate. Recently, the program operated in 2 branches of the Department of Education: 1) the National Institute on Disability and Rehabilitations Research (NIDRR) within the Office of Special Education and Rehabilitative Services (OSERS); and 2) the Institute of Education Sciences (IES), formerly the Office of Educational Research and Improvement (OERI). Selection is based on quality of project design (45 points), significance (25 points), quality of project personnel (20 points), and adequacy of resources (10 points).

Financial data Grants are offered in 2 phases. Phase 1 awards normally do not exceed $150,000; phase 2 awards normally do not exceed $750,000 for IES programs or $500,000 for OSERS/NIDRR programs.

Duration Phase 1 awards may extend up to 6 months; phase 2 awards may extend up to 2 years.

Additional information Information on the NIDRR program is available from the Office of Special Education and Rehabilitative Services, Potomac Center Plaza, 550 12th Street, Room 5140, Washington, DC 20202-2700, (202) 245-7338, E-mail: Lynn.Medley@ed.gov.

Number awarded Varies each year; recently, 25 Phase 1 awards (9 for IES and 16 for NIDRR) and 21 Phase 1 awards (16 for IES and 5 for NIDRR) were granted.

Deadline February of each year for IES proposals; June of each year for NIDRR proposals.

[834]
DEPARTMENT OF HOMELAND SECURITY SMALL BUSINESS INNOVATION RESEARCH GRANTS

Department of Homeland Security
Homeland Security Advanced Research Projects Agency
Attn: SBIR Program Manager
Washington, DC 20528
(202) 254-6768 Toll Free: (800) 754-3043
Fax: (202) 254-7170 E-mail: elissa.sobolewski@dhs.gov
Web: www.dhs.gov/files/grants/gc_1247254058883.shtm

Summary To support small businesses (especially those owned by Asian Americans, other minorities, disabled veterans, or women) that have the technological expertise to contribute to the research and development mission of the Department of Homeland Security (DHS).

Eligibility For the purposes of this program, a "small business" is defined as a firm that is organized for profit with a location in the United States; is in the legal form of an individual proprietorship, partnership, limited liability company, corporation, joint venture, association, trust, or cooperative; is at least 51% owned and controlled by 1 or more individuals who are citizens or permanent residents of the United States; and has (including its affiliates) fewer than 500 employees. The primary employment of the principal investigator must be with the firm at the time of award and during the conduct of the proposed project. Applications are encouraged from 1) women-owned small business concerns, defined as those that are at least 51% owned by a woman or women who also control and operate them; 2) socially and economically disadvantaged small business concerns that are at least 51% owned by an Indian tribe, a Native Hawaiian organization, or 1 or more socially and economically disadvantaged individuals (African Americans, Hispanic Americans, Native Americans, Asian Pacific Americans, or subcontinent Asian Americans); and 3) service-disabled veteran small business concerns that are at least 51% owned by a service-disabled veteran and controlled by such a veteran or (for veterans with permanent and severe disability) the spouse or permanent caregiver of such a veteran. Each year, DHS identifies specialized topics for investigation. Selection is based on the soundness, technical merit, and innovation of the proposed approach and its incremental progress toward topic or subtopic solution; the qualifications of the proposed principal investigators, supporting staff, and consultants; the potential for commercial application and the benefits expected to accrue from this commercialization; and the realism and reasonableness of the cost proposal.

Financial data Grants are offered in 2 phases. In phase 1, awards normally range up to $100,000; in phase 2, awards normally range up to $750,000.

Duration Phase 1 awards may extend up to 6 months; phase 2 awards may extend up to 2 years.

Number awarded Varies each year; recently, 61 Phase 1 awards were granted.

Deadline January and July of each year.

[835]
DIANE J. WILLIS EARLY CAREER AWARD

American Psychological Foundation
750 First Street, N.E.
Washington, DC 20002-4242
(202) 336-5843   Fax: (202) 336-5812
E-mail: foundation@apa.org
Web: www.apa.org/apf/funding/div-37-willis.aspx

Summary   To provide funding to young psychologists (particularly Asian Americans, other underrepresented minorities, women, and individuals with disabilities) who are interested in conducting research or other projects related to children and families.

Eligibility   This program is open to young psychologists who completed a doctoral degree (Ed.D., Psy.D., Ph.D.) within the past 7 years. Applicants must be interested in conducting research or other projects that inform, advocate for, and improve the mental health and well-being of children and families, particularly through public policy. The sponsor encourages applications from individuals who represent diversity in race, ethnicity, gender, age, disability, and sexual orientation.

Financial data   The grant is $2,000.

Duration   1 year.

Additional information   This program, sponsored by Division 37 (Child and Family Policy and Practice) of the American Psychological Association (APA), began in 2013.

Number awarded   1 each year.

Deadline   January of each year.

[836]
DIPLOMACY, SECURITY, AND DEVELOPMENT FELLOWSHIPS OF THE AMERICAN ASSOCIATION FOR THE ADVANCEMENT OF SCIENCE

American Association for the Advancement of Science
Attn: Science and Technology Policy Fellowships
1200 New York Avenue, N.W.
Washington, DC 20005-3920
(202) 326-6700   Fax: (202) 289-4950
E-mail: fellowships@aaas.org
Web: www.fellowships.aaas.org

Summary   To provide postdoctoral scientists and engineers (particularly Asian Americans, other minorities, women, and individuals with disabilities) with an opportunity to work at designated federal agencies on scientific and engineering issues related to diplomacy, security, and development.

Eligibility   This program is open to doctoral-level scientists (Ph.D., M.D., D.V.M., D.Sc., and other terminal degrees) in any field of science (behavioral, biological, computational, earth, health, medical, physical, or social), engineering, or mathematics. Engineers with a master's degree and at least 3 years of professional experience are also eligible. Applicants should be able to contribute scientific and technical expertise into policy development, program planning, implementation, and evaluation in the areas of 1) foreign policy, international trade, treaty engagement, and multilateral cooperation; 2) disaster preparedness and response; 3) infrastructure, environmental, cyber and health security; terrorism and warfare prevention; and non-proliferation; or 4) international aid, capacity building, and development assistance. They must

demonstrate solid scientific and technical credentials; a commitment to serve society; good communication skills; the ability to engage with non-scientific audiences; and an interest in working as special assistants for designated federal agencies (Department of Homeland Security (DHS), Agency for International Development (AID), Fogarty International Center of the National Institutes of Health (NIH), Foreign Agriculture Service of the U.S. Department of Agriculture (USDA), Department of Defense, or Department of State). U.S. citizenship is required; federal employees are not eligible. The sponsor seeks candidates from a broad array of backgrounds and a diversity of geographic, disciplinary, gender, and ethnic perspectives, as well as disability status.

Financial data   The stipend for fellows with 0 to 7 years of postdoctoral experience is $74,872 in the first year and $77,368 in the second year. For fellows with 7 to 15 years of experience, the stipend is $84,855 in the first year and $87,350 in the second year. Fellows who have 15 or more years of postdoctoral experience receive $97,333 in the first year and $99,829 in the second year. Also provided are a $4,000 relocation allowance for fellows from outside the Washington, D.C. area, reimbursement for health insurance, and a $4,000 travel allowance.

Duration   1 year, beginning in September; may be renewed for 1 additional year.

Number awarded   35 to 45 each year.

Deadline   October of each year.

[837]
DISTINGUISHED CHINESE TOXICOLOGIST LECTURESHIP AWARD

Society of Toxicology
Attn: American Association of Chinese in Toxicology
 Special Interest Group
1821 Michael Faraday Drive, Suite 300
Reston, VA 20190-5348
(703) 438-3115   Fax: (703) 438-3113
E-mail: sothq@toxicology.org
Web: www.toxicology.org/ai/af/awards.aspx

Summary   To recognize and reward members of the Society of Toxicology (SOT) who are of Chinese ethnic origin and have made outstanding contributions to the field.

Eligibility   This award is available to SOT members who are of Chinese ethnic origin. Nominees should have contributed significantly to the science of toxicology and have an exemplary professional life. Nominations must be submitted by at least 2 members of the American Association of Chinese in Toxicology Special Interest Group (AACT-SIG) of SOT.

Financial data   The award consists of a plaque and a $500 honorarium.

Duration   The award is presented annually.

Additional information   The winner delivers an award lecture at an AACT-SIG session of the SOT annual meeting.

Number awarded   1 each year.

Deadline   Nominations must be submitted by October of each year.

[838]
DIVISION 17 COUNSELING PSYCHOLOGY GRANTS

American Psychological Foundation
750 First Street, N.E.
Washington, DC 20002-4242
(202) 336-5843   Fax: (202) 336-5812
E-mail: foundation@apa.org
Web: www.apa.org/apf/funding/counseling.aspx

Summary To provide funding to psychologists (particularly Asian Americans, other minorities, women, and individuals with disabilities) who wish to conduct a project related to counseling psychology.

Eligibility This program is open to psychologists who wish to conduct a project to enhance the science and practice of counseling psychology, including basic and applied research, literary, and educational activities. Applicants must be members of Division 17 (Society of Counseling Psychotherapy) of the American Psychological Association, members of an educational institution or nonprofit organization, or affiliate of an educational institution or nonprofit organization. Selection is based on conformance with stated program goals, magnitude of incremental contribution in specified activity area, quality of proposed work, and applicant's demonstrated competence and capability to execute the proposed work. The sponsor encourages applications from individuals who represent diversity in race, ethnicity, gender, age, disability, and sexual orientation.

Financial data Grants range up to $5,000.

Duration 1 year.

Additional information These grants were first awarded in 2007.

Number awarded Varies each year; recently, 2 of these grants were awarded.

Deadline March of each year.

[839]
DIVISION 29 EARLY CAREER AWARD

American Psychological Foundation
750 First Street, N.E.
Washington, DC 20002-4242
(202) 336-5843   Fax: (202) 336-5812
E-mail: foundation@apa.org
Web: www.apa.org/apf/funding/div-29.aspx

Summary To recognize and reward young psychologists (particularly Asian Americans, other underrepresented minorities, women, and individuals with disabilities) who have made outstanding contributions to psychotherapy.

Eligibility This award is available to psychologists who are no more than 7 years past completion of their doctoral degree. Nominees must have demonstrated promising professional achievement related to psychotherapy theory, practice, research, or training. They must be members of Division 29 (Psychotherapy) of the American Psychological Association. Self-nominations are not accepted. Selection is based on conformance with stated program goals and qualifications and applicant's demonstrated accomplishments and promise. The sponsor encourages nominations of individuals who represent diversity in race, ethnicity, gender, age, disability, and sexual orientation.

Financial data The award is $2,500.

Duration The award is presented annually.

Additional information This award was established in 1981 and named the Jack D. Krasner Memorial Award. It was renamed in 2007.

Number awarded 1 each year.

Deadline Nominations must be submitted by December of each year.

[840]
DOCTORAL/POST-DOCTORAL FELLOWSHIP PROGRAM IN LAW AND SOCIAL SCIENCE

American Bar Foundation
Attn: Administrative Assistant for Academic Affairs and
  Research Administration
750 North Lake Shore Drive
Chicago, IL 60611-4403
(312) 988-6517   Fax: (312) 988-6579
E-mail: aehrhardt@abfn.org
Web: www.americanbarfoundation.org

Summary To provide research funding to scholars (particularly Asian Americans and other minorities) who are completing or have completed doctoral degrees in fields related to law, the legal profession, and legal institutions.

Eligibility This program is open to Ph.D. candidates in the social sciences who have completed all doctoral requirements except the dissertation. Applicants who have completed the dissertation are also eligible. Doctoral and proposed research must be in the general area of sociolegal studies or in social scientific approaches to law, the legal profession, or legal institutions and legal processes. Applications must include 1) a dissertation abstract or proposal with an outline of the substance and methods of the research; 2) 2 letters of recommendation; and 3) a curriculum vitae. Minority candidates are especially encouraged to apply.

Financial data The stipend is $30,000. Fellows may request up to $1,500 to reimburse expenses associated with research, travel to meet with advisers, or travel to conferences at which papers are presented. Relocation expenses of up to $2,500 may be reimbursed on application.

Duration 12 months, beginning in September.

Additional information Fellows are offered access to the computing and word processing facilities of the American Bar Foundation and the libraries of Northwestern University and the University of Chicago. This program was established in 1996. Fellowships must be held in residence at the American Bar Foundation. Appointments to the fellowship are full time; fellows are not permitted to undertake other work.

Number awarded 1 or more each year.

Deadline December of each year.

[841]
DOE SMALL BUSINESS INNOVATION RESEARCH GRANTS

Department of Energy
Attn: SBIR/STTR Program, SC-29
Germantown Building
1000 Independence Avenue, S.W.
Washington, DC 20585-1290
(301) 903-5707   Fax: (301) 903-5488
E-mail: sbir-sttr@science.doe.gov
Web: science.energy.gov/sbir

Summary To support small businesses (especially those owned by Asian Americans, other minorities, or women) that have the technological expertise to contribute to the research and development mission of the Department of Energy (DOE).

Eligibility For the purposes of this program, a "small business" is defined as a firm that is organized for profit with a location in the United States; is in the legal form of an individual proprietorship, partnership, limited liability company, corporation, joint venture, association, trust, or cooperative; is at least 51% owned and controlled by 1 or more individuals who are citizens or permanent residents of the United States; and has (including its affiliates) fewer than 500 employees. The primary employment of the principal investigator must be with the firm at the time of award and during the conduct of the proposed project. Applications are encouraged from 1) women-owned small business concerns, defined as those that are at least 51% owned by a woman or women who also control and operate them; and 2) socially and economically disadvantaged small business concerns that are at least 51% owned by an Indian tribe, a Native Hawaiian organization, or 1 or more socially and economically disadvantaged individuals (African Americans, Hispanic Americans, Native Americans, Asian Pacific Americans, or subcontinent Asian Americans). Each office within DOE defines technical topics eligible for research.

Financial data Support is offered in 2 phases: in phase 1, awards normally do not exceed $150,000 (for both direct and indirect costs); in phase 2, awards normally do not exceed $1,000,000 (including both direct and indirect costs).

Duration Phase 1: up to 9 months; phase 2: up to 2 years.

Additional information The objectives of this program include increasing private sector commercialization of technology developed through research and development supported by the Department of Energy, stimulating technological innovation in the private sector, strengthening the role of small business in meeting federal research and development needs, and improving the return on investment from federally-funded research for economic and social benefits to the nation.

Number awarded Varies each year; recently 279 Phase 1 and 113 Phase 2 grants were awarded.

Deadline November of each year.

[842]
DOE SMALL BUSINESS TECHNOLOGY TRANSFER GRANTS

Department of Energy
Attn: SBIR/STTR Program, SC-29
Germantown Building
1000 Independence Avenue, S.W.
Washington, DC 20585-1290
(301) 903-5707 Fax: (301) 903-5488
E-mail: sbir-sttr@science.doe.gov
Web: science.energy.gov/sbir

Summary To provide financial support to cooperative research and development projects carried out between small business concerns (particularly those owned by Asian Americans, other minorities, or women) and research institutions in areas of interest to the Department of Energy (DOE).

Eligibility For the purposes of this program, a "small business" is defined as a firm that is organized for profit with a

location in the United States; is in the legal form of an individual proprietorship, partnership, limited liability company, corporation, joint venture, association, trust, or cooperative; is at least 51% owned and controlled by 1 or more individuals who are citizens or permanent residents of the United States; and has (including its affiliates) fewer than 500 employees. Unlike the Department of Energy Small Business Innovation Research Grants, the primary employment of the principal investigator does not need to be with the business concern. This program, however, requires that the small business apply in collaboration with a nonprofit research institution for conduct of a project that has potential for commercialization. At least 40% of the work must be performed by the small business and at least 30% of the work must be performed by the research institution. Principal investigators from the nonprofit research institution must commit at least 10% of their effort to the project. Applications are encouraged from 1) women-owned small business concerns, defined as those that are at least 51% owned by a woman or women who also control and operate them; and 2) socially and economically disadvantaged small business concerns that are at least 51% owned by an Indian tribe, a Native Hawaiian organization, or 1 or more socially and economically disadvantaged individuals (African Americans, Hispanic Americans, Native Americans, Asian Pacific Americans, or subcontinent Asian Americans). Each office within DOE defines technical topics eligible for research.

Financial data In the first phase, annual awards do not exceed $150,000 for direct costs, indirect costs, and negotiated fixed fees. In the second phase, awards up to $1,000,000 are available.

Duration Generally 9 months for the first phase and 2 years for the second phase.

Additional information Grants in the first phase are to determine the scientific, technical, and commercial merit and feasibility of the proposed cooperative effort and the quality of performance of the small business concern. In the second phase, the research and development efforts continue, depending on the results of the first phase.

Number awarded Varies each year; recently 39 Phase 1 and 15 Phase 2 grants were awarded.

Deadline January of each year.

[843]
DOLORES NYHUS GRADUATE FELLOWSHIP

California Dietetic Association
Attn: CDA Foundation
7740 Manchester Avenue, Suite 102
Playa del Rey, CA 90293-8499
(310) 822-0177 Fax: (310) 823-0264
E-mail: patsmith@dietitian.org
Web: www.dietitian.org/d_cdaf/cdaf_outreach.html

Summary To provide financial assistance to members (particularly Asian Americans or other minorities, men, and members with disabilities) of the Academy of Nutrition and Dietetics (AND) who live in California and are interested in working on a graduate degree in dietetics or a related field at a school in any state.

Eligibility This program is open to California residents who are AND members and have a bachelor's degree and 3 to 5 years of professional experience. Applicants must be a registered dietitian (R.D.), be a registered dietetic technician

(D.T.R.), or have a credential earned at least 6 months previously. They must be enrolled in or admitted to a graduate school in any state in the areas of public health, gerontology, or a community-related program with the intention of practicing in the field of dietetics. Along with their application, they must submit a letter of application that includes a discussion of their career goals. Selection is based on that letter (15%), academic ability (25%), work or volunteer experience (15%), letters of recommendation (15%), extracurricular activities (5%), and financial need (25%). Applications are especially encouraged from ethnic minorities, men, and people with physical disabilities.

Financial data The stipend is normally $1,000.

Duration 1 year.

Additional information The California Dietetic Association is the California affiliate of the AND.

Number awarded 1 each year.

Deadline April of each year.

[844]
DORA AMES LEE LEADERSHIP DEVELOPMENT FUND

United Methodist Church
General Board of Global Ministries
Attn: United Methodist Committee on Relief
Health and Welfare Ministries
475 Riverside Drive, Room 330
New York, NY 10115
(212) 870-3871   Toll Free: (800) UMC-GBGM
E-mail: jyoung@gbgm-umc.org
Web: gbgm-umc.org/health/doralee.cfm

Summary To provide financial assistance to Methodists and other Christians of Asian, Pacific Islander, or Native American descent who are preparing for a career in a health-related field.

Eligibility This program is open to undergraduate and graduate students who are U.S. citizens of Asian American, Pacific Islander, or Native American descent. Applicants must be professed Christians, preferably United Methodists. They must be attending a college or university to enter or continue in a health-related field. Financial need is considered in the selection process.

Financial data The stipend is $2,000.

Duration 1 year.

Additional information This program began in 1980.

Number awarded 5 each year.

Deadline June of each year.

[845]
DR. DHARM SINGH POSTDOCTORAL FELLOW/ YOUNG INVESTIGATOR BEST ABSTRACT AWARD

Society of Toxicology
Attn: Association of Scientists of Indian Origin Special
    Interest Group
1821 Michael Faraday Drive, Suite 300
Reston, VA 20190-5348
(703) 438-3115   Fax: (703) 438-3113
E-mail: sothq@toxicology.org
Web: www.toxicology.org/ai/af/awards.aspx

Summary To recognize and reward postdoctoral members of the Society of Toxicology (SOT) who are of Indian origin (from India) and present outstanding papers at the annual meeting.

Eligibility This award is available to postdoctoral fellows of Indian origin who are members of SOT and its Association of Scientists of Indian Origin (ASIO). Candidates must have an accepted abstract of a research poster or platform presentation for the SOT annual meeting. Along with the abstract, they must submit a cover letter outlining the significance of their research to the field of toxicology and how this award will help them to further their career goals.

Financial data A plaque and a cash award (amount not specified) are presented.

Duration The award is presented annually.

Additional information This award was established in 2008.

Number awarded 1 each year.

Deadline December of each year.

[846]
DR. SUZANNE AHN AWARD FOR CIVIL RIGHTS AND SOCIAL JUSTICE FOR ASIAN AMERICANS

Asian American Journalists Association
Attn: Professional Programs Coordinator
5 Third Street, Suite 1108
San Francisco, CA 94103
(415) 346-2051, ext. 107   Fax: (415) 346-6343
E-mail: MarciaS@aaja.org
Web: www.aaja.org/programs/awards

Summary To recognize and reward journalists who have published or broadcast outstanding coverage of Asian American Pacific Islander civil rights and social justice issues.

Eligibility This award is presented to journalists for excellence in coverage of civil rights of Asian American Pacific Islanders and/or issues of social justice. Nominees do not need to be Asians or members of the Asian American Journalists Association (AAJA). Their work must have been published (in newspapers, news services, web sites, magazines, books) or broadcast (on radio or TV). Book entries and documentaries must include a synopsis of the work, explaining how it specifically impacts social justice or civil rights in the Asian American Pacific Islander community. Submissions in other languages must come with an English translation.

Financial data The award consists of $5,000 and a plaque.

Duration The award is presented annually.

Additional information This award, first presented in 2003, is named for a Korean American physician, neurologist, and inventor. Nominations by non-members of AAJA must be accompanied by a $25 entry fee.

Number awarded 1 each year.

Deadline March of each year.

[847]
DRS. ROSALEE G. AND RAYMOND A. WEISS RESEARCH AND PROGRAM INNOVATION GRANT

American Psychological Foundation
750 First Street, N.E.
Washington, DC 20002-4242
(202) 336-5843   Fax: (202) 336-5812
E-mail: foundation@apa.org
Web: www.apa.org/apf/funding/vision-weiss.aspx

Summary To provide funding to professionals (particularly Asian Americans, other minorities, women, and individuals with disabilities) who are interested in conducting projects that use psychology to solve social problems related to the priorities of the American Psychological Foundation (APF).

Eligibility This program is open to professionals at non-profit organizations engaged in research, education, and intervention projects and programs. Applicants must be interested in conducting an activity that uses psychology to solve social problems in the following priority areas: understanding and fostering the connection between mental and physical health; reducing stigma and prejudice; understanding and preventing violence to create a safer, more humane world; or addressing the long-term psychological needs of individuals and communities in the aftermath of disaster. Selection is based on the criticality of the proposed funding for the proposed work; conformance with stated program goals and requirements; innovative and potential impact qualities; quality, viability, and promise of proposed work, and competence and capability of project leaders. The sponsor encourages applications from individuals who represent diversity in race, ethnicity, gender, age, disability, and sexual orientation.

Financial data The grant is $2,500.

Duration 1 year; nonrenewable.

Additional information This program began in 2003.

Number awarded 1 each year.

Deadline March of each year.

[848]
E.E. JUST ENDOWED RESEARCH FELLOWSHIP FUND

Marine Biological Laboratory
Attn: Chief Academic and Scientific Officer
7 MBL Street
Woods Hole, MA 02543-1015
(508) 289-7173   Fax: (508) 457-1924
E-mail: casoofice@mbl.edu
Web: hermes.mbl.edu

Summary To provide funding to Asian American and other minority scientists who wish to conduct summer research at the Marine Biological Laboratory (MBL) in Woods Hole, Massachusetts.

Eligibility This program is open to minority faculty members who are interested in conducting summer research at the MBL. Applicants must submit a statement of the potential impact of this award on their career development. Fields of study include, but are not limited to, cell biology, developmental biology, ecology, evolution, microbiology, neurobiology, physiology, regenerative biology, and tissue engineering.

Financial data Grants range from $5,000 to $25,000, typically to cover laboratory rental and/or housing costs. Award-ees are responsible for other costs, such as supplies, shared resource usage, affiliated staff who accompany them, or travel.

Duration 8 to 10 weeks during the summer.

Number awarded 1 each year.

Deadline December of each year.

[849]
EINSTEIN POSTDOCTORAL FELLOWSHIP PROGRAM

Smithsonian Astrophysical Observatory
Attn: Chandra X-Ray Center
Einstein Fellowship Program Office
60 Garden Street, MS4
Cambridge, MA 02138
(617) 496-7941   Fax: (617) 495-7356
E-mail: fellows@head.cfa.harvard.edu
Web: cxc.harvard.edu/fellows

Summary To provide funding to recent postdoctoral scientists (particularly Asian Americans, other minorities, and women) who are interested in conducting research related to high energy astrophysics missions of the National Aeronautics and Space Administration (NASA).

Eligibility This program is open to postdoctoral scientists who completed their Ph.D., Sc.D., or equivalent doctoral degree within the past 3 years in astronomy, physics, or related disciplines. Applicants must be interested in conducting research related to NASA Physics of the Cosmos program missions: Chandra, Fermi, XMM-Newton and International X-Ray Observatory, cosmological investigations relevant to the Planck and JDEM missions, and gravitational astrophysics relevant to the LISA mission. They must be citizens of the United States or English-speaking citizens of other countries who have valid visas. Women and minorities are strongly encouraged to apply.

Financial data Stipends are approximately $66,500 per year. Fellows may also receive health insurance, relocation costs, and moderate support (up to $16,000 per year) for research-related travel, computing services, publications, and other direct costs.

Duration 3 years (depending on a review of scientific activity).

Additional information This program, which began in 2009 with funding from NASA, incorporates the former Chandra and GLAST Fellowship programs.

Number awarded Up to 10 each year.

Deadline November of each year.

[850]
ELSEVIER GUT MICROBIOME PILOT RESEARCH AWARD

American Gastroenterological Association
Attn: AGA Research Foundation
Research Awards Manager
4930 Del Ray Avenue
Bethesda, MD 20814-2512
(301) 222-4012   Fax: (301) 654-5920
E-mail: awards@gastro.org
Web: www.gastro.org/aga-foundation/grants

Summary To provide funding to Asian American and other new or established gastroenterologists for pilot research projects in areas related to the gut microbiome.

Eligibility Applicants must have an M.D., Ph.D., or equivalent degree and a full-time faculty position at an accredited North American institution. They may not hold grants for projects on a similar topic from other agencies. Individual membership in the American Gastroenterology Association (AGA) is required. The proposal must enable investigators to obtain new data on the relationships of the gut microbiota to digestive health and disease that can ultimately lead to subsequent grant applications for more substantial funding and duration. Women and minority investigators are strongly encouraged to apply. Selection is based on novelty, importance, feasibility, environment, commitment of the institution, and overall likelihood that the project will lead to more substantial grants in gut microbiome research.

Financial data The grant is $25,000. Funds may be used for salary, supplies, or equipment. Indirect costs are not allowed.

Duration 1 year.

Additional information This award is sponsored by Elsevier Science.

Number awarded 1 each year.

Deadline January of each year.

[851]
ELSEVIER PILOT RESEARCH AWARDS

American Gastroenterological Association
Attn: AGA Research Foundation
Research Awards Manager
4930 Del Ray Avenue
Bethesda, MD 20814-2512
(301) 222-4012   Fax: (301) 654-5920
E-mail: awards@gastro.org
Web: www.gastro.org/aga-foundation/grants

Summary To provide funding to new or established investigators (particularly Asian Americans, other minorities, and women) for pilot research projects in areas related to gastroenterology or hepatology.

Eligibility Applicants must have an M.D., Ph.D., or equivalent degree and a full-time faculty position at an accredited North American institution. They may not hold grants for projects on a similar topic from other agencies. Individual membership in the American Gastroenterology Association (AGA) is required. The proposal must involve obtaining new data that can ultimately provide the basis for subsequent grant applications for more substantial funding and duration in gastroenterology- or hepatology-related areas. Women and minority investigators are strongly encouraged to apply. Selection is based on novelty, importance, feasibility, environment, commitment of the institution, and overall likelihood that the project will lead to more substantial grant applications.

Financial data The grant is $25,000. Funds may be used for salary, supplies, or equipment. Indirect costs are not allowed.

Duration 1 year.

Additional information This award is sponsored by Elsevier Science.

Number awarded 3 each year.

Deadline January of each year.

[852]
ENERGY, ENVIRONMENT, AND AGRICULTURE FELLOWSHIPS OF THE AMERICAN ASSOCIATION FOR THE ADVANCEMENT OF SCIENCE

American Association for the Advancement of Science
Attn: Science and Technology Policy Fellowships
1200 New York Avenue, N.W.
Washington, DC 20005-3920
(202) 326-6700   Fax: (202) 289-4950
E-mail: fellowships@aaas.org
Web: www.fellowships.aaas.org

Summary To provide a fellowship to postdoctoral scientists and engineers (particularly Asian Americans, other minorities, women, and individuals with disabilities) who are interested in participating on projects relating to energy, environment, or agriculture at specified federal agencies.

Eligibility This program is open to doctoral-level scientists (Ph.D., M.D., D.V.M., D.Sc., and other terminal degrees) in any field of science (behavioral, biological, computational, earth, health, medical, physical, or social), engineering, or mathematics. Engineers with a master's degree and at least 3 years of professional experience are also eligible. Applicants should be able to engage in projects, policies, risk assessment, evaluation, and outreach initiatives to 1) protect animal, plant, and environmental health; 2) address ecosystem degradation, pollution, and biological threats; 3) tackle challenges and opportunities in agriculture, fisheries, climate change, and energy; or 4) safeguard air, water, land, wildlife, and natural resources. They must demonstrate solid scientific and technical credentials; a commitment to serve society; good communication skills; the ability to engage with non-scientific audiences; and an interest in working as special assistants for designated federal agencies (the U.S. Department of Agriculture (USDA), the Department of Energy (DOE), the National Oceanic and Atmospheric Administration (NOAA), the National Science Foundation (NSF), the Environmental Protection Agency (EPA), the National Aeronautics and Space Administration (NASA), the U.S. Geological Survey (USGS), or the Forest Service). U.S. citizenship is required; federal employees are not eligible. The sponsor seeks candidates from a broad array of backgrounds and a diversity of geographic, disciplinary, gender, and ethnic perspectives, as well as disability status.

Financial data The stipend for fellows with 0 to 7 years of postdoctoral experience is $74,872 in the first year and $77,368 in the second year. For fellows with 7 to 15 years of experience, the stipend is $84,855 in the first year and $87,350 in the second year. Fellows who have 15 or more years of postdoctoral experience receive $97,333 in the first year and $99,420 in the second year. Also provided are a $4,000 relocation allowance for fellows from outside the Washington, D.C. area, reimbursement for health insurance, and a $4,000 travel allowance.

Duration 1 year, beginning in September; may be renewed 1 additional year.

Number awarded 35 to 45 each year.

Deadline October of each year.

[853]
EPILEPSY FOUNDATION RESEARCH GRANTS PROGRAM

Epilepsy Foundation
Attn: Research Department
8301 Professional Place
Landover, MD 20785-2353
(301) 459-3700   Toll Free: (800) EFA-1000
Fax: (301) 577-2684   TDD: (800) 332-2070
E-mail: grants@efa.org
Web: www.epilepsyfoundation.org

Summary To provide funding to junior investigators (particularly Asian Americans, other minorities, women, and individuals with disabilities) who are interested in conducting research that will advance the understanding, treatment, and prevention of epilepsy.

Eligibility Applicants must have a doctoral degree and an academic appointment at the level of assistant professor in a university or medical school (or equivalent standing at a research institution or medical center). They must be interested in conducting basic or clinical research to advance understanding of the behavioral and psychosocial aspects of having epilepsy. Faculty with appointments at the level of associate professor or higher are not eligible. Applications from women, members of minority groups, and people with disabilities are especially encouraged. U.S. citizenship is not required, but the research must be conducted in the United States. Selection is based on the scientific quality of the research plan, the relevance of the proposed research to epilepsy, the applicant's qualifications, and the adequacy of the institution and facility where research will be conducted.

Financial data The grant is $50,000 per year.

Duration 1 year; recipients may reapply for 1 additional year of funding.

Additional information Support for this program is provided by many individuals, families, and corporations, especially the American Epilepsy Society, Abbott Laboratories, Ortho-McNeil Pharmaceutical, and Pfizer Inc.

Number awarded Varies each year.

Deadline August of each year.

[854]
EPILEPSY RESEARCH RECOGNITION AWARDS PROGRAM

American Epilepsy Society
342 North Main Street
West Hartford, CT 06117-2507
(860) 586-7505   Fax: (860) 586-7550
E-mail: ctubby@aesnet.org
Web: www.aesnet.org/research/research-awards

Summary To provide funding to investigators (particularly Asian Americans, other minorities, and women) who are interested in conducting research related to epilepsy.

Eligibility This program is open to active scientists and clinicians working in any aspect of epilepsy. Candidates must be nominated by their home institution and be at the level of associate professor or professor. There are no geographic restrictions; nominations from outside the United States and North America are welcome. Nominations of women and members of minority groups are especially encouraged. Selection is based on pioneering research, originality of

research, quality of publications, research productivity, relationship of the candidate's work to problems in epilepsy, training activities, other contributions in epilepsy, and productivity over the next decade; all criteria are weighted equally.

Financial data The grant is $10,000. No institutional overhead is allowed.

Additional information This program began in 1991.

Number awarded 2 each year.

Deadline August of each year.

[855]
EVA KING KILLAM RESEARCH AWARD

American College of Neuropsychopharmacology
Attn: Executive Office
5034-A Thoroughbred Lane
Brentwood, TN 37027
(615) 324-2360   Fax: (615) 523-1715
E-mail: acnp@acnp.org
Web: www.acnp.org/programs/awards.aspx

Summary To recognize and reward young scientists (particularly Asian Americans, other minorities, and individuals with disabilities) who have made outstanding translational research contributions to neuropsychopharmacology.

Eligibility This award is available to scientists who are younger than 50 years of age. Nominees must have made an outstanding translational research contribution to neuropsychopharmacology. The contributions should focus on translating advances from basic science to human investigations. Selection is based on the quality of the contribution and its impact in advancing neuropsychopharmacology. Neither membership in the American College of Neuropsychopharmacology (ACNP) nor U.S. citizenship are required. Nomination of women and minorities is highly encouraged.

Financial data The award consists of an expense-paid trip to the ACNP annual meeting, a monetary honorarium, and a plaque.

Duration The award is presented annually.

Additional information This award was first presented in 2011.

Number awarded 1 each year.

Deadline Nominations must be submitted by June of each year.

[856]
FELLOWSHIP PROGRAM IN MEASUREMENT

American Educational Research Association
1430 K Street, N.W., Suite 1200
Washington, DC 20005
(202) 238-3200   Fax: (202) 238-3250
E-mail: fellowships@aera.net
Web: www.aera.net

Summary To provide an opportunity for junior scholars in the field of education (particularly Asian Americans, other minorities, and women) to engage in a program of research and advanced training while in residence at Educational Testing Service (ETS) in Princeton, New Jersey.

Eligibility This program is open to junior scholars and early career research scientists in fields and disciplines related to education research. Applicants must have completed their Ph.D. or Ed.D. degree within the past 3 years. They must be proposing a program of intensive research and training at the

ETS campus in Princeton, New Jersey in such areas as educational measurement, assessment design, psychometrics, statistical analyses, large-scale evaluations, and other studies directed to explaining student progress and achievement. A particular goal of the program is to increase the involvement of women and minority professionals in measurement, psychometrics, assessment, and related fields. U.S. citizenship or permanent resident status is required.

Financial data The stipend is $55,000 per year. Fellows also receive relocation expenses and ETS employee benefits.

Duration Up to 2 years.

Additional information This program is jointly sponsored by the American Educational Research Association (AERA) and ETS.

Number awarded Up to 2 each year.

Deadline November of each year.

[857]
FIRST BOOK GRANT PROGRAM FOR MINORITY SCHOLARS

Louisville Institute
Attn: Executive Director
1044 Alta Vista Road
Louisville, KY 40205-1798
(502) 992-5432   Fax: (502) 894-2286
E-mail: info@louisville-institute.org
Web: www.louisville-institute.org/Grants/programs.aspx

Summary To provide funding to Asian Americans and other scholars of color who are interested in completing a major research and book project that focuses on an aspect of Christianity in North America.

Eligibility This program is open to members of racial/ethnic minority groups (African Americans, Hispanics, Native Americans, Asian Americans, Arab Americans, and Pacific Islanders) who have an earned doctoral degree (normally the Ph.D. or Th.D.). Applicants must be a pre-tenured faculty member in a full-time, tenure-track position at an accredited institution of higher education (college, university, or seminary) in North America. They must be able to negotiate a full academic year free from teaching and committee responsibilities in order to engage in a scholarly research project leading to the publication of their first (or second) book focusing on an aspect of Christianity in North America. Selection is based on the intellectual quality of the research and writing project, its potential to contribute to scholarship in religion, and the potential contribution of the research to the vitality of North American Christianity.

Financial data The grant is $40,000. Awards are intended to make possible a full academic year of sabbatical research and writing by providing up to half of the grantee's salary and benefits for that year. Funds are paid directly to the grantee's institution, but no indirect costs are allowed.

Duration 1 academic year; nonrenewable.

Additional information The Louisville Institute is located at Louisville Presbyterian Theological Seminary and is supported by the Lilly Endowment. These grants were first awarded in 2003. Grantees may not accept other awards that provide a stipend during the tenure of this award, and they must be released from all teaching and committee responsibilities during the award year.

Number awarded Varies each year; recently, 2 of these grants were awarded.

Deadline January of each year.

[858]
F.J. MCGUIGAN EARLY CAREER INVESTIGATOR RESEARCH PRIZE

American Psychological Foundation
750 First Street, N.E.
Washington, DC 20002-4242
(202) 336-5843   Fax: (202) 336-5812
E-mail: foundation@apa.org
Web: www.apa.org/apf/funding/mcguigan-prize.aspx

Summary To provide funding to young psychologists (particularly Asian Americans, other minorities, women, and individuals with disabilities) who are interested in conducting research related to the human mind.

Eligibility This program is open to investigators who have earned a doctoral degree in psychology or in a related field within the past 9 years. Nominees must have an affiliation with an accredited college, university, or other research institution. They must be engaged in research that seeks to explicate the concept of the human mind. The approach must be materialistic and should be primarily psychophysiological, but physiological and behavioral research may also qualify. Self-nominations are not accepted; candidates must be nominated by a senior colleague. The sponsor encourages nominations of individuals who represent diversity in race, ethnicity, gender, age, disability, and sexual orientation.

Financial data The grant is $25,000.

Duration These grants are awarded biennially, in even-numbered years.

Additional information The first grant under this program was awarded in 2002.

Number awarded 1 every other year.

Deadline February of even-numbered years.

[859]
FRAMELINE COMPLETION FUND

Frameline
Attn: Completion Fund
145 Ninth Street, Suite 300
San Francisco, CA 94103
(415) 703-8650   Fax: (415) 861-1404
E-mail: info@frameline.org
Web: www.frameline.org/filmmaker-support

Summary To provide funding to lesbian, gay, bisexual, and transgender (LGBT) film/video artists (particularly Asian Americans, other film/video artists of color, and women).

Eligibility This program is open to LGBT artists who are in the last stages of the production of documentary, educational, narrative, animated, or experimental projects about or of interest to LGBT people and their communities. Applicants may be independent artists, students, producers, or nonprofit corporations. They must be interested in completion work and must have 90% of the production completed; projects in development, script-development, pre-production, or production are not eligible. Student projects are eligible only if the student maintains artistic and financial control of the project. Women and people of color are especially encouraged to apply. Selection is based on financial need, the contribution the grant will make to completing the project, assurances that the project will be completed, and the statement the project makes about LGBT people and/or issues of concern to them and their communities.

Financial data Grants range from $1,000 to $5,000.

Duration These are 1-time grants.

Additional information This program began in 1990.

Number awarded Varies each year; recently, 5 of these grants were awarded. Since this program was established, it has provided $389,200 in support to 118 films.

Deadline October of each year.

[860]
GAIUS CHARLES BOLIN DISSERTATION AND POST-MFA FELLOWSHIPS

Williams College
Attn: Dean of the Faculty
880 Main Street
Hopkins Hall, Third Floor
P.O. Box 141
Williamstown, MA 01267
(413) 597-4351   Fax: (413) 597-3553
E-mail: gburda@williams.edu
Web: dean-faculty.williams.edu

Summary To provide financial assistance to Asian Americans and members of other underrepresented groups who are interested in teaching courses at Williams College while working on their doctoral dissertation or building their post-M.F.A. professional portfolio.

Eligibility This program is open to members of underrepresented groups, including ethnic minorities, first-generation college students, women in predominantly male fields, and scholars with disabilities. Applicants must be 1) doctoral candidates in any field who have completed all work for a Ph.D. except for the dissertation; or 2) artists who completed an M.F.A. degree within the past 2 years and are building their professional portfolio. They must be willing to teach a course at Williams College. Along with their application, they must submit a full curriculum vitae, a graduate school transcript, 3 letters of recommendation, a copy of their dissertation prospectus or samples of their artistic work, and a description of their teaching interests within a department or program at Williams College. U.S. citizenship or permanent resident status is required.

Financial data Fellows receive $36,000 for the academic year, plus housing assistance, office space, computer and library privileges, and a research allowance of up to $4,000.

Duration 2 years.

Additional information Bolin fellows are assigned a faculty adviser in the appropriate department. This program was established in 1985. Fellows are expected to teach a 1-semester course each year. They must be in residence at Williams College for the duration of the fellowship.

Number awarded 3 each year.

Deadline November of each year.

[861]
GANNETT AWARD FOR INNOVATION IN WATCHDOG JOURNALISM

Asian American Journalists Association
Attn: Professional Programs Coordinator
5 Third Street, Suite 1108
San Francisco, CA 94103
(415) 346-2051, ext. 107   Fax: (415) 346-6343
E-mail: MarciaS@aaja.org
Web: www.aaja.org

Summary To recognize and reward members of the Asian American Journalism Association (AAJA) who have used digital tools in their role as a community watchdog.

Eligibility This award is available to full members of AAJA who have used digital tools to complete spot news, editorials, news analysis, columns, or features. Submitted work must have involved innovation that has contributed to the journalist's role as a community watchdog; special consideration is given to journalism that helps a community understand and address important issues. Criteria for evaluating innovation include interactivity, creation of new tools, innovative adaptation of existing tools, and creative use of a digital medium. Submission of work by a team of reporters is also acceptable.

Financial data The award is $5,000.

Duration The award is presented annually.

Additional information This award is sponsored by the Gannett Foundation.

Number awarded 1 each year.

Deadline March of each year.

[862]
GEORGE A. STRAIT MINORITY SCHOLARSHIP ENDOWMENT

American Association of Law Libraries
Attn: Chair, Scholarships Committee
105 West Adams Street, Suite 3300
Chicago, IL 60603
(312) 939-4764   Fax: (312) 431-1097
E-mail: scholarships@aall.org
Web: www.aallnet.org

Summary To provide financial assistance to Asian American and other minority college seniors or college graduates who are interested in becoming law librarians.

Eligibility This program is open to college graduates with meaningful law library experience who are members of minority groups and intend to have a career in law librarianship. Applicants must be degree candidates at an ALA-accredited library school or an ABA-accredited law school. Along with their application, they must submit a personal statement that discusses their interest in law librarianship, reason for applying for this scholarship, career goals as a law librarian, and any other pertinent information.

Financial data The stipend is $3,500.

Duration 1 year.

Additional information This program, established in 1990, is currently supported by Thomson Reuters.

Number awarded Varies each year; recently, 5 of these scholarships were awarded.

Deadline March of each year.

[863]
GERALD OSHITA MEMORIAL FELLOWSHIP

Djerassi Resident Artists Program
Attn: Admissions
2325 Bear Gulch Road
Woodside, CA 94062-4405
(650) 747-1250   Fax: (650) 747-0105
E-mail: drap@djerassi.org
Web: www.djerassi.org/artistresidencies.html

Summary To provide an opportunity for Asian Americans and other composers of color to participate in the Djerassi Resident Artists Program.

Eligibility This program is open to composers of Asian, African, Latino, or Native American ethnic background. Applicants must be interested in utilizing a residency to compose, study, rehearse, and otherwise advance their own creative projects.

Financial data The fellow is offered housing, meals, studio space, and a stipend of $2,500.

Duration 1 month, from late March through mid-November.

Additional information This fellowship was established in 1994. The program is located in northern California, 45 miles south of San Francisco, on 600 acres of rangeland, redwood forests, and hiking trails. There is a $45 non-refundable application fee.

Number awarded 1 each year.

Deadline February of each year.

[864]
GERTRUDE AND MAURICE GOLDHABER DISTINGUISHED FELLOWSHIPS

Brookhaven National Laboratory
Attn: Bill Bookless
Building 460
40 Brookhaven Avenue
Upton, NY 11973
(631) 344-5734   E-mail: wbookless@bnl.gov
Web: www.bnl.gov/hr/goldhaber.asp

Summary To provide funding to postdoctoral scientists (particularly Asian Americans, other minorities, and women) who are interested in conducting research at Brookhaven National Laboratory (BNL).

Eligibility This program is open to scholars who are no more than 3 years past receipt of the Ph.D. and are interested in working at BNL. Candidates must be interested in working in close collaboration with a member of the BNL scientific staff and qualifying for a scientific staff position at BNL upon completion of the appointment. The sponsoring scientist must have an opening and be able to support the candidate at the standard starting salary for postdoctoral research associates. The program especially encourages applications from minorities and women.

Financial data The program provides additional funds to bring the salary to $75,000 per year.

Duration 3 years.

Additional information This program is funded by Battelle Memorial Institute and the State University of New York at Stony Brook.

Number awarded Up to 2 each year.

Deadline June of each year.

[865]
GILBERT F. WHITE POSTDOCTORAL FELLOWSHIP PROGRAM

Resources for the Future
Attn: Coordinator for Academic Programs
1616 P Street, N.W., Suite 600
Washington, DC 20036-1400
(202) 328-5020   Fax: (202) 939-3460
E-mail: white-award@rff.org
Web: www.rff.org

Summary To provide funding to postdoctoral researchers (particularly Asian Americans, other minorities, and women) who wish to devote a year to scholarly work at Resources for the Future (RFF) in Washington, D.C.

Eligibility This program is open to individuals in any discipline who have completed their doctoral requirements and are interested in conducting scholarly research at RFF in social or policy science areas that relate to natural resources, energy, or the environment. Teaching and/or research experience at the postdoctoral level is preferred but not essential. Individuals holding positions in government as well as at academic institutions are eligible. Women and minority candidates are strongly encouraged to apply. Non-citizens are eligible if they have proper work and residency documentation.

Financial data Fellows receive an annual stipend (based on their academic salary) plus research support, office facilities at RFF, and an allowance of up to $1,000 for moving or living expenses. Fellowships do not provide medical insurance or other RFF fringe benefits.

Duration 11 months.

Additional information Fellows are assigned to an RFF research division: the Energy and Natural Resources division, the Quality of the Environment division, or the Center for Risk, Resource, and Environmental Management. Fellows are expected to be in residence at Resources for the Future for the duration of the program.

Number awarded 1 each year.

Deadline February of each year.

[866]
GLORIA E. ANZALDUA BOOK PRIZE

National Women's Studies Association
Attn: Book Prizes
11 East Mount Royal Avenue, Suite 100
Baltimore, MD 21202
(410) 528-0355   Fax: (410) 528-0357
E-mail: awards@nwsa.org
Web: www.nwsa.org/content.asp?pl=16&contentid=16

Summary To recognize and reward members of the National Women's Studies Association (NWSA) who have written outstanding books on women of color and transnational issues.

Eligibility This award is available to NWSA members who submit a book that was published during the preceding year. Entries must present groundbreaking scholarship in women's studies and make a significant multicultural feminist contribution to women of color and/or transnational studies.

Financial data The award provides an honorarium of $1,000 and lifetime membership in NWSA.

Duration The award is presented annually.

Additional information This award was first presented in 2008.

Number awarded 1 each year.

Deadline April of each year.

[867]
GRADUATE STUDENTS OF ASIAN/ASIAN-AMERICAN/PACIFIC-ISLANDER/ARAB/MIDDLE EAST ASIAN DESCENT STUDENT ESSAY AWARD

National Women's Studies Association
Attn: Women of Color Caucus
11 East Mount Royal Avenue, Suite 100
Baltimore, MD 21202
(410) 528-0355   Fax: (410) 528-0357
E-mail: awards@nwsa.org
Web: www.nwsa.org/content.asp?pl=16&contentid=16

Summary To recognize and reward Asian, Asian American, and Pacific Islander graduate students and recent post-doctorates who are members of the National Women's Studies Association (NWSA) and submit outstanding essays on feminist issues.

Eligibility This competition is open to women of Asian descent (including Asian Americans, Pacific Islanders, Arabs, and Middle East Asians who are currently enrolled in a graduate or professional program. Recipients of Ph.D.s who completed their degree requirements within the past year are also eligible. Applicants must submit a scholarly essay that provides critical theoretical discussions and/or analyses of issues and experiences of women and girls of Asian, Asian American, Pacific Islander, Arab, or Middle East Asian descent in the United States and throughout the Diaspora. They must be members of the NWSA.

Financial data The award is $500.

Duration The award is presented annually.

Number awarded 1 each year.

Deadline May of each year.

[868]
HARRY AND MIRIAM LEVINSON AWARD FOR EXCEPTIONAL CONTRIBUTIONS TO CONSULTING ORGANIZATIONAL PSYCHOLOGY

American Psychological Association
Attn: Office of Division Services
750 First Street, N.E.
Washington, DC 20002-4242
(202) 336-6022   E-mail: divisions@apa.org
Web: www.apa.org/about/awards/div-13-levinson.aspx

Summary To provide an opportunity for postdoctoral scholars (particularly Asian Americans or other minorities) with an advanced degree in the social and basic sciences who are interested in a postdoctoral fellowship to obtain research training at Harvard Medical School.

Eligibility This award is presented to a member of the American Psychological Association (APA) who is a consulting psychologist. Nominees must have shown evidence of ability to convert psychological theory and concepts into applications through which managers and leaders can create effective, healthy, and humane organizations. The sponsor encourages nominations of individuals who represent diver-

sity in race, ethnicity, gender, age, disability, and sexual orientation.

Financial data The award is $5,000.

Duration The award is presented annually.

Additional information This award, first presented in 1992, is sponsored by Division 13 (Consulting Psychology) in conjunction with Division 12 (Society of Clinical Psychology), Division 14 (Industrial/Organizational Psychology), and Division 39 (Psychoanalysis) of the APA.

Number awarded 1 each year.

Deadline Nominations must be submitted by March of each year.

[869]
HARVARD MEDICAL SCHOOL DEAN'S POSTDOCTORAL FELLOWSHIP

Harvard Medical School
Office for Diversity Inclusion and Community Partnership
Attn: Program Manager, Dean's Postdoctoral Fellowship
164 Longwood Avenue, Second Floor
Boston, MA 02115-5818
(617) 432-1083   Fax: (617) 432-3834
E-mail: brian_anderson@hms.harvard.edu
Web: www.hms.harvard.edu/dcp/deanspdfellowship

Summary To provide an opportunity for postdoctoral scholars in the social and basic sciences (particularly Asian Americans, other minorities, and individuals from disadvantaged backgrounds) to obtain research training at Harvard Medical School.

Eligibility This program is open to U.S. citizens and permanent residents who have completed an M.D., Ph.D., Sc.D., or equivalent degree in the basic or social sciences and have less than 5 years of relevant postdoctoral research experience. Applicants must be interested in a program of research training under the mentorship of a professor in 1 of the departments of Harvard Medical School: biological chemistry and molecular pharmacology, cell biology, genetics, global health and social medicine, health care policy, microbiology and immunobiology, neurobiology, stem cell and regenerative biology, or systems biology. Scientists from minority and disadvantaged backgrounds are especially encouraged to apply. Selection is based on academic achievement, scholarly promise, potential to add to the diversity of the Harvard Medical School community, and the likelihood that the application will become an independent scientist and societal leader.

Financial data Fellows receive a professional development allowance of $1,250 per year and a stipend that depends on the years of postdoctoral experience, ranging from $40,992 for zero to $47,820 for 4 years.

Duration 2 years.

Number awarded 2 each year.

Deadline Applications may be submitted at any time.

[870] HARVARD–NEWCOMEN POSTDOCTORAL FELLOWSHIP IN BUSINESS HISTORY

Harvard Business School
Attn: Fellowships
Rock Center 104
Boston, MA 02163
(617) 495-1003   Fax: (617) 495-0594
E-mail: wfriedman@hbs.edu
Web: www.hbs.edu/businesshistory/fellowships.html

Summary To provide residencies for study and research at Harvard Business School to scholars (particularly Asian Americans, other minorities, and women) in the fields of history, economics, or a related field.

Eligibility This program is open to scholars who, within the last 10 years, have received a Ph.D. degree in history, economics, or a related field. Applicants must be proposing to engage in research that would benefit from the resources at the Harvard Business School and the larger Boston scholarly community. In addition, they must be interested in participating in the school's business history courses, seminars, and case development activities. Along with their application, they must submit concise statements and descriptions of academic research undertaken in the past and a detailed description of the research they wish to undertake at Harvard. Women and minorities are especially encouraged to apply.

Financial data The stipend is $46,000. In addition, a travel fund, a book fund, and administrative support are provided.

Duration 12 months, beginning in July.

Additional information This program began in 1949. Fellows spend approximately two-thirds of their time conducting research of their own choosing. The remainder of their time is devoted to participating in activities of the school, including attendance at the business history seminar and working with faculty teaching the business history courses offered in the M.B.A. program. Fellows are strongly encouraged to submit an article to *Business History Review* during their year at the school. Support for this fellowship is provided by the Newcomen Society of the United States.

Deadline October of each year.

[871] HEALTH AND AGING POLICY FELLOWSHIPS

Columbia University College of Physicians and Surgeons
Attn: Department of Psychiatry
Director, Health and Aging Policy Fellows
1051 Riverside Drive, Unit 9
New York, NY 10032
(212) 543-5401   Fax: (212) 543-6063
E-mail: pincush@nyspi.columbia.edu
Web: www.healthandagingpolicy.org

Summary To provide an opportunity for health professionals (particularly Asian Americans and members of other underrepresented groups) who have an interest in aging and policy issues to work as legislative assistants in Congress or at other sites.

Eligibility This program is open to physicians, nurses, and social workers who have a demonstrated commitment to health and aging issues and a desire to be involved in health policy at the federal, state, or local levels. Other professionals with clinical backgrounds (e.g., dentists, dieticians, econo-

mists, epidemiologists, health care administrators, psychologists) working in the field of health and aging are also eligible. Preference is given to professionals early or midway through their careers. Applicants must be interested serving as residential fellows by participating in the policymaking process on either the federal or state level as legislative assistants in Congress or as professional staff members in executive agencies or policy organizations. A non-residential track is also available to applicants who wish to work on a policy project throughout the year at relevant sites. Candidates from underrepresented groups are strongly encouraged to apply. Selection is based on commitment to health and aging issues and improving the health and well-being of older Americans, potential for leadership in health policy, professional qualifications and achievements, impact of the fellowship experience on the applicant's career, and interpersonal and communication skills. U.S. citizenship or permanent resident status is required.

Financial data For residential fellows, the stipend depends on their current base salary, to a maximum of $120,000 per year; other benefits include a travel allowance for pre-fellowship arrangements and to fellowship-related meetings, a relocation grant of up to $3,500, and up to $400 per month for health insurance. For non-residential fellows, grants provide up to $30,000 to cover related fellowship and travel costs.

Duration 9 to 12 months; fellows may apply for a second year of participation.

Additional information This program, which began in 2009, operates in collaboration with the American Political Science Association Congressional Fellowship Program. Funding is provided by The Atlantic Philanthropies. The John Heinz/Health and Aging Policy Fellowship, an activity of the Teresa and H. John Heinz III Foundation, supports 1 fellow to work in the Senate. Support is also provided by the Centers for Disease Control and Prevention, the John A. Hartford Foundation, and the Gerontological Society of America.

Number awarded Varies each year; recently, 4 residential and 6 non-residential fellowships were awarded.

Deadline May of each year.

[872] HEALTH, EDUCATION, AND HUMAN SERVICES FELLOWSHIPS OF THE AMERICAN ASSOCIATION FOR THE ADVANCEMENT OF SCIENCE

American Association for the Advancement of Science
Attn: Science and Technology Policy Fellowships
1200 New York Avenue, N.W.
Washington, DC 20005-3920
(202) 326-6700   Fax: (202) 289-4950
E-mail: fellowships@aaas.org
Web: www.fellowships.aaas.org

Summary To provide postdoctoral scientists and engineers (particularly Asian Americans, other minorities, and individuals with disabilities) with an opportunity to work at designated federal agencies on issues of health, education, and human services.

Eligibility This program is open to doctoral-level scientists (Ph.D., M.D., D.V.M., D.Sc., and other terminal degrees) in any field of science (behavioral, biological, computational, earth, health, medical, physical, or social), engineering, or mathematics. Engineers with a master's degree and at least 3 years of professional experience are also eligible. Applicants should be able to support improved programs, policies, planning, risk analysis, regulation, monitoring, and evaluation for a broad range of initiatives in 1) preventive and community health, disease identification and response, and medical research; 2) individual, family, and community social services, systems, and support; 3) food processing and distribution safety; and 4) science education, research, and innovation. They must demonstrate solid scientific and technical credentials; a commitment to serve society; good communication skills; the ability to engage with non-scientific audiences; and an interest in working as special assistants for designated federal agencies (the Food Safety Inspection Service (FSIS) of the U.S. Department of Agriculture (USDA), National Science Foundation (NSF), National Institutes of Health (NIH), Department of Health and Human Services (DHHS), or Department of Veterans Affairs). U.S. citizenship is required; federal employees are not eligible. The sponsor seeks candidates from a broad array of backgrounds and a diversity of geographic, disciplinary, gender, and ethnic perspectives, as well as disability status.

Financial data The stipend for fellows with 0 to 7 years of postdoctoral experience is $74,872 in the first year and $77,368 in the second year. For fellows with 7 to 15 years of experience, the stipend is $84,855 in the first year and $87,350 in the second year. Fellows who have 15 or more years of postdoctoral experience receive $97,333 in the first year and $99,420 in the second year. Also provided are a $4,000 relocation allowance for fellows from outside the Washington, D.C. area, reimbursement for health insurance, and a $4,000 travel allowance.

Duration 1 year, beginning in September.

Number awarded 30 to 40 each year.

Deadline October of each year.

[873]
HENRY DAVID RESEARCH GRANT IN HUMAN REPRODUCTIVE BEHAVIOR AND POPULATION STUDIES

American Psychological Foundation
750 First Street, N.E.
Washington, DC 20002-4242
(202) 336-5843　　　　　　　　Fax: (202) 336-5812
E-mail: foundation@apa.org
Web: www.apa.org/apf/funding/david.aspx

Summary To provide funding to young psychologists (particularly Asian Americans, other minorities, women, and individuals with disabilities) who are interested in conducting research on reproductive behavior.

Eligibility This program is open to doctoral students in psychology working on a dissertation and young psychologists who have no more than 7 years of postgraduate experience. Applicants must be interested in conducting research on human reproductive behavior or an area related to population concerns. Along with their application, they must submit a current curriculum vitae, 2 letters of recommendation, and an essay of 1 to 2 pages on their interest in human reproductive behavior or in population studies. The sponsor encourages applications from individuals who represent diversity in race, ethnicity, gender, age, disability, and sexual orientation.

Financial data The grant is $1,500.

Duration The grant is presented annually.

Number awarded 1 each year.

Deadline February of each year.

[874]
HUBBLE FELLOWSHIPS

Space Telescope Science Institute
Attn: Hubble Fellowship Program Office
3700 San Martin Drive
Baltimore, MD 21218
(410) 338-5079　　　　　　　　Fax: (410) 338-4211
E-mail: hfinquiry@stsci.edu
Web: www.stsci.edu/institute/smo/fellowships/hubble

Summary To provide funding to recent postdoctoral scientists (particularly Asian Americans, other minorities, and women) who are interested in conducting research related to the Hubble Space Telescope or related missions of the National Aeronautics and Space Administration (NASA).

Eligibility This program is open to postdoctoral scientists who completed their doctoral degree within the past 3 years in astronomy, physics, or related disciplines. Applicants must be interested in conducting research related to NASA Cosmic Origins missions: the Hubble Space Telescope, Herschel Space Observatory, James Webb Space Telescope, Stratospheric Observatory for Infrared Astronomy, or the Spitzer Space Telescope. They may U.S. citizens or English-speaking citizens of other countries with valid visas. Research may be theoretical, observational, or instrumental. Women and members of minority groups are strongly encouraged to apply.

Financial data Stipends are approximately $66,500 per year. Other benefits may include health insurance, relocation costs, and support for travel, equipment, and other direct costs of research.

Duration 3 years: an initial 1-year appointment and 2 annual renewals, contingent on satisfactory performance and availability of funds.

Additional information This program, funded by NASA, began in 1990 and was limited to work with the Hubble Space Telescope. A parallel program, called the Spitzer Fellowship, began in 2002 and was limited to work with the Spitzer Space Telescope. In 2009, those programs were combined into this single program, which was also broadened to include the other NASA Cosmic Origins missions. Fellows are required to be in residence at their host institution engaged in full-time research for the duration of the grant.

Number awarded Varies each year; recently, 17 of these fellowships were awarded.

Deadline October of each year.

[875]
ILLINOIS MINORITY REAL ESTATE SCHOLARSHIP

Illinois Association of Realtors
Attn: Illinois Real Estate Educational Foundation
522 South Fifth Street
P.O. Box 2607
Springfield, IL 62708
Toll Free: (866) 854-REEF　　　　Fax: (217) 529-5893
E-mail: lclayton@iar.org
Web: www.ilreef.org/index.php/scholarship

Summary To provide financial assistance to Illinois residents who are 1) Asian Americans or members of other minority groups and 2) preparing for a career in real estate.

Eligibility This program is open to residents of Illinois who are African American, Hispanic or Latino, Native American, or Asian. Applicants must be interested in preparing for a career in real estate by pursuing: 1) courses to meet Illinois salesperson license requirements; 2) course work to meet Illinois broker license requirement; 3) course work required for Illinois appraisal licensing/certification; 4) professional development unrelated to obtaining license/certification; or 5) an undergraduate or graduate program of study. Along with their application, they must submit information on their employment history, transcripts, evidence of financial need, and an essay that describes their career goals and explains why they believe they should receive scholarship assistance through this program.

Financial data The maximum stipend is $500.

Duration Funds must be used within 24 months of the award date.

Number awarded 1 or more each year.

Deadline Applications may be submitted at any time, but they must be received at least 12 weeks prior to the beginning of the school term for which financial assistance is requested.

[876]
INVESTIGATOR AWARDS IN HEALTH POLICY RESEARCH

Robert Wood Johnson Foundation
College Road East and U.S. Route 1
P.O. Box 2316
Princeton, NJ 08543-2316
(609) 932-8701   Toll Free: (877) 843-RWJF
E-mail: mail@rwjf.org
Web: www.rwjf.org

Summary To provide funding to Asian Americans and other investigators from diverse fields who are interested in conducting research on health policy.

Eligibility This program is open to investigators in the health, social, and behavioral sciences. Members of minority groups, researchers early in their careers, and individuals in non-academic settings, such as research firms and policy organizations, are especially encouraged to apply. The proposed research should help develop, interpret, or substantially advance ideas or knowledge that can improve health or health care policy in the United States. Selection is based on the relevance of the research to national policy and its potential to inform and improve policy-making; the contribution and potential significance of the project to the theoretical underpinnings and knowledge base of health care, health policy, or other disciplines; the extent to which the work represents an innovative perspective on health, health care, or health policy; the soundness of the project's conceptual framework and methodology; the feasibility of the work; the likelihood that the findings can be useful to policy-makers and other leaders; capability of the investigator to undertake and complete the project on schedule; and investigator's research record.

Financial data Grants up to $335,000 are provided. Funds are to be used primarily for project salary support for the principal investigator(s) and for indirect costs at a rate of up to 12%.

Duration 24 to 36 months.

Number awarded Approximately 8 each year.

Deadline Letters of intent must be submitted by January of each year. Completed applications are due in June.

[877]
JAMES A. RAWLEY PRIZE

Organization of American Historians
Attn: Award and Committee Coordinator
112 North Bryan Street
Bloomington, IN 47408-4141
(812) 855-7311   Fax: (812) 855-0696
E-mail: khamm@oah.org
Web: www.oah.org/awards/awards.rawley.index.html

Summary To recognize and reward authors of outstanding books dealing with race relations in the United States.

Eligibility This award is presented to the author of the outstanding book on the history of race relations in America. Entries must have been published during the current calendar year.

Financial data The award is $1,000 and a certificate.

Duration The award is presented annually.

Additional information This award was established in 1990.

Number awarded 1 each year.

Deadline September of each year.

[878]
JAPANESE MEDICAL SOCIETY OF AMERICA SCHOLARSHIPS

Japanese Medical Society of America, Inc.
100 Park Avenue, Suite 1600
New York, NY 10017
(212) 351-5038   Fax: (212) 351-5047
E-mail: info@jmsa.org
Web: www.jmsa.org/student-members/about-scholarships

Summary To provide funding to Japanese American medical school students, residents, and fellows who are interested in working on a project.

Eligibility This program is open to Japanese Americans who are currently enrolled as medical students, residents, or fellows. Applicants must be proposing to conduct a project that will benefit the Japanese Medical Society of America (JMSA) and the Japanese community. Along with their application, they must submit a 1-page essay about themselves and what they will do to contribute to the JMSA. Selection is based on academic excellence and interest in JMSA.

Financial data Stipends depend on the availability of funds, but have ranged from $2,500 to $20,000. Support is provided primarily for tuition, but a portion of the funds may be used to carry out the proposed project.

Duration 1 year.

Additional information This program receives support from a number of sponsors, including the Honjo Foundation, Nishioka Foundation, Mitsui USA, and Toyota USA. Examples of past projects include a service to connect elderly Japanese American patients with health care, a medical blog in Japanese detailing the experiences of a medical student in America, and a collaborative web site to connect Japanese and American medical students.

Number awarded Varies each year; recently, 11 of these scholarships were awarded.

Deadline December of each year.

[879]
JOEL ELKES RESEARCH AWARD

American College of Neuropsychopharmacology
Attn: Executive Office
5034-A Thoroughbred Lane
Brentwood, TN 37027
(615) 324-2360 Fax: (615) 523-1715
E-mail: acnp@acnp.org
Web: www.acnp.org/programs/awards.aspx

Summary To recognize and reward young scientists (particularly Asian Americans, other minorities, and women) who have contributed outstanding clinical or translational research to neuropsychopharmacology.

Eligibility This award is available to scientists who are younger than 50 years of age. Nominees must have made an outstanding clinical or translational contribution to neuropsychopharmacology. The contribution may be based on a single discovery or a cumulative body of work. Emphasis is placed on contributions that further understanding of self-regulatory processes as they affect mental function and behavior in disease and well-being. Membership in the American College of Neuropsychopharmacology (ACNP) is not required. Nomination of women and minorities is highly encouraged.

Financial data The award consists of an expense-paid trip to the ACNP annual meeting, a monetary honorarium, and a plaque.

Duration The award is presented annually.

Additional information This award was first presented in 1986.

Number awarded 1 each year.

Deadline Nominations must be submitted by June of each year.

[880]
JOHN AND POLLY SPARKS EARLY CAREER GRANT

American Psychological Foundation
750 First Street, N.E.
Washington, DC 20002-4242
(202) 336-5843 Fax: (202) 336-5812
E-mail: foundation@apa.org
Web: www.apa.org/apf/funding/sparks-early-career.aspx

Summary To provide funding to young psychologists (particularly Asian Americans, other minorities, women, and individuals with disabilities) who are interested in conducting research on serious emotional disturbance in children.

Eligibility This program is open to young psychologists who completed a doctoral degree (Ed.D., Psy.D., Ph.D.) within the past 7 years. Applicants must be interested in conducting research in the area of early intervention and treatment for serious emotional disturbance in children. The sponsor encourages applications from individuals who represent diversity in race, ethnicity, gender, age, disability, and sexual orientation.

Financial data The grant is $10,000.

Duration 1 year.

Additional information This program began in 2013.

Number awarded 1 each year.

Deadline May of each year.

[881]
JOHN MCLENDON MEMORIAL MINORITY POSTGRADUATE SCHOLARSHIP AWARD

National Association of Collegiate Directors of Athletics
Attn: NACDA Foundation
24651 Detroit Road
Westlake, OH 44145
(440) 788-7475 Fax: (440) 892-4007
E-mail: jbouyer@nacda.com
Web: www.nacda.com/mclendon/scholarship.html

Summary To provide financial assistance to Asian American and other minority college seniors who are interested in working on a graduate degree in athletics administration.

Eligibility This program is open to minority college students who are seniors, are attending school on a full-time basis, have a GPA of 3.2 or higher, intend to attend graduate school to earn a degree in athletics administration, and are involved in college or community activities. Also eligible are college graduates who have at least 2 years' experience in an athletics administration position. Candidates must be nominated by an official of a member institution of the National Association of Collegiate Directors of Athletics (NACDA) or (for college graduates) a supervisor.

Financial data The stipend is $10,000.

Duration 1 year.

Additional information Recipients must maintain full-time status during the senior year to retain their eligibility. They must attend NACDA-member institutions.

Number awarded 5 each year.

Deadline Nominations must be submitted by April of each year.

[882]
JOHN V. KRUTILLA RESEARCH STIPEND

Resources for the Future
Attn: Coordinator for Academic Programs
1616 P Street, N.W., Suite 600
Washington, DC 20036-1400
(202) 328-5020 Fax: (202) 939-3460
E-mail: krutilla-award@rff.org
Web: www.rff.org

Summary To provide funding for research related to environmental and resource economics to young scholars (particularly Asian Americans, other minorities, and women).

Eligibility This program is open to scholars who received their doctoral degree within the past 5 years. Applicants must be interested in conducting research related to environmental and resource economics. They must submit a short description of the proposed research, a curriculum vitae, and a letter of recommendation. Women and minority candidates are strongly encouraged to apply. Non-citizens are eligible if they have proper work and residency documentation.

Financial data The grant is $5,500.

Duration 1 year.

Additional information This award was first presented in 2006.

Number awarded 1 each year.

Deadline February of each year.

[883]
JOSEPH B. GITTLER AWARD

American Psychological Foundation
750 First Street, N.E.
Washington, DC 20002-4242
(202) 336-5843   Fax: (202) 336-5812
E-mail: foundation@apa.org
Web: www.apa.org/apf/funding/gittler.aspx

Summary To recognize and reward scholars and graduate students in psychology (particularly Asian Americans, other minorities, women, and individuals with disabilities) whose work has transformed the philosophical foundations of the discipline.

Eligibility This award is available to scholars and graduate students whose body of work or whose individual work has transformed the philosophical foundations of psychological knowledge. Self-nominations are welcome. Selection is based on conformance with stated program goals and magnitude of contributions The sponsor encourages nominations of individuals who represent diversity in race, ethnicity, gender, age, disability, and sexual orientation.

Financial data The award is $10,000.

Duration The award is presented annually.

Additional information This award was first presented in 2008.

Number awarded 1 each year.

Deadline Nominations must be submitted by May of each year.

[884]
JUDICIAL BRANCH FELLOWSHIPS

American Association for the Advancement of Science
Attn: Science and Technology Policy Fellowships
1200 New York Avenue, N.W.
Washington, DC 20005-3920
(202) 326-6700   Fax: (202) 289-4950
E-mail: fellowships@aaas.org
Web: www.fellowships.aaas.org

Summary To provide postdoctoral scientists and engineers (particularly Asian Americans, other minorities, women, and individuals with disabilities) with an opportunity to work with the federal judiciary.

Eligibility This program is open to doctoral-level scientists (Ph.D., M.D., D.V.M., D.Sc., and other terminal degrees) in any field of science (behavioral, biological, computational, earth, health, medical, physical, or social), engineering, or mathematics who have at least 3 years of professional post-doctoral experience. Preference is given to scientists and engineers who also have a J.D. degree or legal experience. Applicants should be able to contribute scientific and technical expertise to judicial administration, operations, education programs, protocol and discovery, or courtroom technology while learning first-hand about contemporary policy issues facing the judiciary. They must demonstrate solid scientific and technical credentials; a commitment to serve society; good communication skills; the ability to engage with non-scientific audiences; and an interest in working as special assistants for the Federal Judicial Center or the Federal Judicial Court of Washington, D.C. U.S. citizenship is required; federal employees are not eligible. The sponsor seeks candidates from a broad array of backgrounds and a diversity of geo-graphic, disciplinary, gender, and ethnic perspectives, as well as disability status.

Financial data The stipend for fellows with 0 to 7 years of postdoctoral experience is $74,872 in the first year and $77,368 in the second year. For fellows with 7 to 15 years of experience, the stipend is $84,855 in the first year and $87,350 in the second year. Fellows who have 15 or more years of postdoctoral experience receive $97,333 in the first year and $99,829 in the second year. Also provided are a $4,000 relocation allowance for fellows from outside the Washington, D.C. area, reimbursement for health insurance, and a $4,000 travel allowance.

Duration 1 year, beginning in September; may be renewed for 1 additional year.

Additional information This program began in 2014.

Number awarded 5 to 15 each year.

Deadline October of each year.

[885]
JUDITH L. WEIDMAN RACIAL ETHNIC MINORITY FELLOWSHIP

United Methodist Communications
Attn: Communications Resourcing Team
810 12th Avenue South
P.O. Box 320
Nashville, TN 37202-0320
(615) 742-5481   Toll Free: (888) CRT-4UMC
Fax: (615) 742-5485   E-mail: scholarships@umcom.org
Web: crt.umc.org/interior.asp?ptid=1&mid=6891

Summary To provide an opportunity to work on professional development to Asian American and other Methodists who are interested in a communications career.

Eligibility This program is open to United Methodists of racial ethnic minority heritage who are interested in preparing for a career in communications with the United Methodist Church. Applicants must be recent college or seminary graduates who have broad communications training, including work in journalism, mass communications, marketing, public relations, and electronic media. They must be able to understand and speak English proficiently and to relocate for a year. Selection is based on Christian commitment and involvement in the life of the United Methodist Church; achievement as revealed by transcripts, GPA, letters of reference, and work samples; study, experience, and evidence of talent in the field of communications; clarity of purpose and goals for the future; desire to learn how to be a successful United Methodist conference communicator; and potential leadership ability as a professional religion communicator for the United Methodist Church.

Financial data The stipend is $30,000 per year. Benefits and expenses for moving and professional travel are also provided.

Duration 1 year, starting in July.

Additional information This program began in 1998. Recipients are assigned to 1 of the 63 United Methodist Annual Conferences, the headquarters of local churches within a geographic area. At the Annual Conference, the fellow will be assigned an experienced communicator as a mentor and will work closely with that mentor and with United Methodist Communications in Nashville, Tennessee. Following the successful completion of the fellowship, United Methodist Communications and the participating Annual Conference will assist in a search for permanent employment within the United Methodist Church but cannot guarantee a position.

Number awarded   1 each year.

Deadline   March of each year.

[886]
JULIUS AXELROD MENTORSHIP AWARD

American College of Neuropsychopharmacology
Attn: Executive Office
5034-A Thoroughbred Lane
Brentwood, TN 37027
(615) 324-2360   Fax: (615) 523-1715
E-mail: acnp@acnp.org
Web: www.acnp.org/programs/awards.aspx

Summary   To recognize and reward professionals and postdoctorates (particularly Asian Americans, other minorities, and women) who are members of the American College of Neuropsychopharmacology (ACNP) and have demonstrated outstanding mentoring of young scientists.

Eligibility   This award is available to ACNP members who have made an outstanding contribution to neuropsychopharmacology by mentoring and developing young scientists into leaders in the field. Nominations must be accompanied by letters of support from up to 3 people who have been mentored by the candidate. Nomination of women and minorities is highly encouraged.

Financial data   The award consists of a monetary honorarium and a plaque.

Duration   The award is presented annually.

Additional information   This award was first presented in 2004.

Number awarded   1 each year.

Deadline   Nominations must be submitted by June of each year.

[887]
KOREAN NURSES ASSOCIATION OF SOUTHERN CALIFORNIA REGISTERED NURSE EDUCATION SCHOLARSHIPS

Korean Nurses Association of Southern California
936 South Crenshaw Boulevard, Suite 204
Los Angeles, CA 90019
(323) 934-7073

Summary   To provide financial assistance to Korean nurses in California who wish to attend college in the state to work on a bachelor's or graduate degree.

Eligibility   This program is open to Korean registered nurses who are living in California and enrolled or entering a baccalaureate or higher degree nursing program in the state. Applicants must be legal residents of the United States. Along with their application, they must submit a 1-page essay on their reasons for selecting nursing as a career, including their professional goals and objectives. Selection is based on that essay, work experience in nursing and related fields, community service and volunteer work experience, cumulative GPA, and letters of recommendation. Priority consideration is given to members of the Korean Nurses Association of Southern California and their immediate family members.

Financial data   A stipend is awarded (amount not specified).

Duration   1 year; may be renewed 1 additional year.

Number awarded   1 or more each year.

Deadline   January of each year.

[888]
KOREAN TOXICOLOGISTS ASSOCIATION IN AMERICA BEST PRESENTATIONS BY GRADUATE STUDENT AND POSTDOCTORAL TRAINEE AWARD

Society of Toxicology
Attn: Korean Toxicologists Association in America Special Interest Group
1821 Michael Faraday Drive, Suite 300
Reston, VA 20190-5348
(703) 438-3115   Fax: (703) 438-3113
E-mail: sothq@toxicology.org
Web: www.toxicology.org/ai/af/awards.aspx

Summary   To recognize and reward graduate students and postdoctoral trainees who present outstanding papers at a session of the Korean Toxicologists Association in America (KTAA) at the annual meeting of the Society of Toxicology (SOT).

Eligibility   This award is available to graduate students and postdoctoral trainees who have an accepted abstract of a research poster or platform presentation for a KTAA session at the SOT annual meeting. Along with the abstract, they must submit a letter of nomination from their major adviser.

Financial data   A plaque and a cash award (amount not specified) are presented.

Duration   The awards are presented annually.

Additional information   These awards are presented jointly by KTAA and the Korean Institute of Toxicology (KIT).

Number awarded   2 each year.

Deadline   January of each year.

[889]
KUNDIMAN POETRY PRIZE

Alice James Books
Attn: Director
238 Main Street
Farmington, ME 04938
(207) 778-7071   Fax: (207) 778-7766
E-mail: ajb@alicejamesbooks.org
Web: www.alicejamesbooks.org/pages/kundiman_prize.php

Summary   To recognize and reward outstanding unpublished poetry by Asian Americans.

Eligibility   This competition is open to emerging and established Asian American poets. They must submit a manuscript of 50 to 70 pages. Individual poems from the manuscript may have been previously published in magazines, anthologies, or chapbooks of less than 25 pages, but the collection as a whole must be unpublished. Translations and self-published books are not eligible.

Financial data   The prize is $1,000 and publication of the winning manuscript by Alice James Books.

Duration   The competition is held annually.

Additional information   There is a $28 entry fee.

Number awarded   1 each year.

Deadline   March of each year.

[890]
LAURENCE R. FOSTER MEMORIAL SCHOLARSHIPS

Oregon Student Access Commission
Attn: Grants and Scholarships Division
1500 Valley River Drive, Suite 100
Eugene, OR 97401-2146
(541) 687-7395   Toll Free: (800) 452-8807, ext. 7395
Fax: (541) 687-7414   TDD: (800) 735-2900
E-mail: awardinfo@osac.state.or.us
Web: www.oregonstudentaid.gov/scholarships.aspx

Summary To provide financial assistance to Asian Americans and other residents of Oregon who come from a diverse environment and are enrolled at a college or graduate school in any state to prepare for a public health career.

Eligibility This program is open to residents of Oregon who are enrolled at least half time at a 4-year college or university in any state to prepare for a career in public health (not private practice). Preference is given first to applicants from diverse environments; second to persons employed in, or graduate students working on a degree in, public health; and third to juniors and seniors majoring in a health program (e.g., nursing, medical technology, physician assistant). Applicants must be able to demonstrate financial need. Along with their application, they must submit essays of 250 to 350 words on 1) what public health means to them; 2) the public health aspect they intend to practice and the health and population issues impacted by that aspect; and 3) their experience living or working in diverse environments.

Financial data Stipends for scholarships offered by the Oregon Student Access Commission (OSAC) range from $200 to $10,000 but recently averaged $2,300.

Duration 1 year.

Additional information This program is administered by the OSAC with funds provided by the Oregon Community Foundation.

Number awarded Varies each year; recently, 6 of these scholarships were awarded.

Deadline February of each year.

[891]
LIZETTE PETERSON-HOMER INJURY PREVENTION RESEARCH GRANT

American Psychological Foundation
750 First Street, N.E.
Washington, DC 20002-4242
(202) 336-5843   Fax: (202) 336-5812
E-mail: foundation@apa.org
Web: www.apa.org/apf/funding/peterson-homer.aspx

Summary To provide funding to graduate students and faculty (particularly Asian Americans, other minorities, women, and individuals with disabilities) who are interested in conducting research related to the prevention of injuries in children.

Eligibility This program is open to graduate students and faculty interested in conducting research that focuses on the prevention of physical injury in children and young adults through accidents, violence, abuse, or suicide. Applicants must submit a 100-word abstract, description of the project, detailed budget, curriculum vitae, and letter from the supporting faculty supervisor (if the applicant is a student). Selection

is based on conformance with stated program goals, magnitude of incremental contribution, quality of proposed work, and applicant's demonstrated scholarship and research competence. The sponsor encourages applications from individuals who represent diversity in race, ethnicity, gender, age, disability, and sexual orientation.

Financial data Grants up to $5,000 are available.

Additional information This program began in 1999 as the Rebecca Routh Coon Injury Research Award. The current name was adopted in 2003. It is supported by Division 54 (Society of Pediatric Psychology) of the American Psychological Association and the American Psychological Foundation.

Number awarded 1 each year.

Deadline September of each year.

[892]
LONI DING AWARD FOR SOCIAL ISSUE DOCUMENTARY SHORT

Center for Asian American Media
Attn: James T. Yee Talent Development Program
145 Ninth Street, Suite 350
San Francisco, CA 94103-2641
(415) 863-0814   Fax: (415) 863-7428
E-mail: mediafund@caamedia.org
Web: www.caamedia.org

Summary To recognize and reward Asian American filmmakers who produce short features that relate to the experiences of underrepresented communities.

Eligibility This award is available to Asian American filmmakers whose work includes a short documentary that illuminates the experiences of Asian American and other underrepresented communities.

Financial data The award is $1,000.

Number awarded 1 each year.

Deadline Deadline not specified.

[893]
LYMAN T. JOHNSON POSTDOCTORAL FELLOWSHIP

University of Kentucky
Attn: Vice President for Research
311 Main Building
Lexington, KY 40506-0032
(859) 257-5090   Fax: (859) 323-2800
E-mail: vprgrants@uky.edu
Web: www.research.uky.edu

Summary To provide an opportunity for recent postdoctorates, especially Asian Americans and other minorities, to conduct research at the University of Kentucky (U.K.).

Eligibility This program is open to U.S. citizens and permanent residents who have completed a doctoral degree within the past 2 years. Applicants must be interested in conducting an individualized research program under the mentorship of a U.K. professor. They should indicate, in their letter of application, how their participation in this program would contribute to the compelling interest of diversity at U.K. Race, ethnicity, and national origin are among the factors that contribute to diversity. Selection is based on evidence of scholarship with competitive potential for a tenure-track faculty appointment at a research university, compatibility of specific research interests with those in doctorate-granting units at

U.K., quality of the research proposal, support from mentor and references, and effect of the appointment on the educational benefit of diversity within the research or professional area.

Financial data The fellowship provides a stipend of $35,000 plus $5,000 for support of research activities.

Duration Up to 2 years.

Additional information In addition to conducting an individualized research program under the mentorship of a U.K. professor, fellows actively participate in research, teaching, and service to the university, their profession, and the community. This program began in 1992.

Number awarded 2 each year.

Deadline October of each year.

[894]
MANY VOICES FELLOWSHIPS

Playwrights' Center
2301 Franklin Avenue East
Minneapolis, MN 55406-1099
(612) 332-7481   Fax: (612) 332-6037
E-mail: info@pwcenter.org
Web: www.pwcenter.org/fellows_voices.php

Summary To provide funding to Asian Americans and other playwrights of color so they can spend a year in residence at the Playwrights' Center in Minneapolis.

Eligibility This program is open to playwrights of color who are citizens or permanent residents of the United States; both residents of Minnesota and of any state are eligible. Applicants must be interested in playwriting and creating theater in a supportive artist community at the Playwrights' Center.

Financial data Fellows receive a $10,000 stipend, $2,500 for living expenses, and $1,500 in play development funds.

Duration 9 months, beginning in October.

Additional information This program, which began in 1994, is funded by the Jerome Foundation. Fellows must be in residence at the Playwrights' Center for the duration of the program.

Number awarded 2 each year: 1 to a resident of Minnesota and 1 to a resident of any state.

Deadline February of each year.

[895]
MARRIAGE AND FAMILY THERAPY MASTER'S STUDENT MINORITY SCHOLARSHIP

American Association for Marriage and Family Therapy
Attn: AAMFT Research and Education Foundation
112 South Alfred Street
Alexandria, VA 22314-3061
(703) 838-9808   Fax: (703) 838-9805
Web: www.aamft.org

Summary To provide financial assistance to Asian American and other minority students enrolled in master's and post-degree training programs in marriage and family therapy.

Eligibility This program is open to minority students (including African Americans, Hispanics, Native Americans, Asian Americans, and Pacific Islanders) enrolled in master's degree programs or post-degree institutes that provide training in marriage and family therapy. Applicants must be members of the American Association for Marriage and Family Therapy (AAMFT). They must be citizens or permanent resi-

dents of the United States or Canada and show promise in and commitment to a career in marital and family therapy education, research, or practice. Along with their application, they must submit a personal statement explaining how their racial or ethnic background has had an impact on them and their career decision; the statement should include their professional interests, goals, and commitment to the field of marriage and family therapy.

Financial data The stipend is $2,000. Awardees also receive a plaque and funding up to $750 to attend the association's annual conference.

Duration 1 year.

Additional information This program began in 1986.

Number awarded Up to 3 each year.

Deadline January of each year.

[896]
MINORITIES IN CANCER RESEARCH JANE COOK WRIGHT LECTURESHIP

American Association for Cancer Research
Attn: Scientific Awards
615 Chestnut Street, 17th Floor
Philadelphia, PA 19106-4404
(215) 440-9300   Toll Free: (866) 423-3965
Fax: (215) 440-9372   E-mail: awards@aacr.org
Web: www.aacr.org

Summary To recognize and reward investigators who, through leadership or by example, have furthered the advancement of minorities in cancer research.

Eligibility This award is available to investigators affiliated with institutions in any country involved in cancer research, cancer medicine, or cancer-related biomedical science. Nominees must have made meritorious contributions to the field of cancer research and, through leadership or by example, have furthered the advancement of minority investigators in cancer research. Selection is based on the nominee's contributions to cancer research and to the advancement of minorities; no consideration is given to age, race, gender, nationality, geographic location, or religious or political views.

Financial data The award consists of an honorarium (amount not specified), a commemorative item, and support for the winner and a guest to attend the sponsor's annual meeting where the winner delivers a major lecture.

Duration The award is presented annually.

Additional information This award was established in 2006.

Number awarded 1 each year.

Deadline October of each year.

[897]
MINORITY FACULTY DEVELOPMENT SCHOLARSHIP AWARD IN PHYSICAL THERAPY

American Physical Therapy Association
Attn: Honors and Awards Program
1111 North Fairfax Street
Alexandria, VA 22314-1488
(703) 684-APTA   Toll Free: (800) 999-APTA
Fax: (703) 684-7343   TDD: (703) 683-6748
E-mail: honorsandawards@apta.org
Web: www.apta.org

Summary To provide financial assistance to Asian American and other minority faculty members in physical therapy who are interested in working on a post-professional doctoral degree.

Eligibility This program is open to U.S. citizens and permanent residents who are members of the following minority groups: African American or Black, Asian, Native Hawaiian or other Pacific Islander, American Indian or Alaska Native, or Hispanic/Latino. Applicants must be full-time faculty members, teaching in an accredited or developing professional physical therapist education program, who will have completed the equivalent of 2 full semesters of post-professional doctoral course work. They must possess a license to practice physical therapy in a U.S. jurisdiction and be enrolled as a student in an accredited post-professional doctoral program whose content has a demonstrated relationship to physical therapy. Along with their application, they must submit a personal essay on their professional goals, including their plans to contribute to the profession and minority services. Selection is based on 1) commitment to minority affairs and services; 2) commitment to further the physical therapy profession through teaching and research; and 3) scholastic achievement.

Financial data A stipend is awarded (amount not specified).

Duration 1 year.

Additional information This program began in 1999.

Number awarded 1 or more each year.

Deadline November of each year.

[898]
NASA ASTROBIOLOGY PROGRAM MINORITY INSTITUTION RESEARCH SUPPORT

United Negro College Fund Special Programs
  Corporation
Attn: NASA Astrobiology Program
6402 Arlington Boulevard, Suite 600
Falls Church, VA 22042
(703) 205-6581   Toll Free: (800) 530-6232
Fax: (703) 205-7645   E-mail: malik.hopkins@uncfsp.org
Web: www.uncfsp.org

Summary To provide an opportunity for faculty at Minority Serving Institutions (MSIs) to work on a summer research project in partnership with an established astrobiology investigator.

Eligibility This program is open to full-time tenured or tenure-track faculty members at MSIs who have a Ph.D., Sc.D., or equivalent degree in a field of STEM (science, technology, engineering, or mathematics). Applicants must be interested in conducting a summer research project on a topic related to astrobiology. They must identify an established investigator of the National Aeronautics and Space Administration (NASA) Astrobiology Program who has agreed to serve as host researcher. Eligible fields of study include biology, microbiology, astronomy, planetary science, astrochemistry, astrophysics, geology, geochemistry, or geobiochemistry. U.S. citizenship or permanent resident status is required.

Financial data Fellows receive a stipend of $10,000 and an additional grant of $5,000 to cover travel, lodging, and living expenses.

Duration 10 weeks during the summer.

Additional information This program is funded by the NASA Astrobiology Institute and administered by the United Negro College Fund Special Programs Corporation.

Number awarded Varies each year.

Deadline March of each year.

[899]
NATIONAL ALUMNI CHAPTER GRANTS

Kappa Omicron Nu
Attn: Awards Committee
4990 Northwind Drive, Suite 140
East Lansing, MI 48823-5031
(517) 351-8335   Fax: (517) 351-8336
E-mail: info@kon.org
Web: www.kon.org/awards/grants.html

Summary To provide financial assistance to members of Kappa Omicron Nu, an honor society in family and consumer sciences, who are interested in conducting research (especially those who are Asian, Hispanic, and Native American).

Eligibility This program is open to 1) individual scholars who are members of the society; and 2) research teams where the leader is a member of the society. Applicants must be interested in conducting research in family and consumer sciences or any of its related specializations. The research approach should be integrative in nature and shall make connections across specializations to pursue problems or questions. Special consideration is given to research that studies the cultural and religious differences affecting leadership, especially Hispanic, Asian, and Native American. Another topic of interest is the exploration of how minority students "strike out on their own" in career development.

Financial data The grant is $1,000.

Duration 1 year; multi-year funding may be accomplished by including a multi-year management plan in the initial proposal and reporting successful accomplishment of previous objectives annually.

Additional information Funding for these grants is provided by the National Alumni Chapter of Kappa Omicron Nu.

Number awarded 1 or more each year.

Deadline February of each year.

[900]
NATIONAL CENTER FOR ATMOSPHERIC RESEARCH POSTDOCTORAL APPOINTMENTS

National Center for Atmospheric Research
Attn: Advanced Study Program
3090 Center Green Drive
P.O. Box 3000
Boulder, CO 80307-3000
(303) 497-1601   Fax: (303) 497-1646
E-mail: apply@asp.ucar.edu
Web: www.asp.ucar.edu/pdfp/pd_announcement.jsp

Summary To provide funding to recent Ph.D.s (particularly Asian Americans, other minorities, and women) who wish to conduct research at the National Center for Atmospheric Research (NCAR) in Boulder, Colorado.

Eligibility This program is open to recent Ph.D.s and Sc.D.s in applied mathematics, chemistry, engineering, and physics as well as specialists in atmospheric sciences from such disciplines as biology, economics, geography, geology, and science education. Applicants must be interested in conducting research at the center in atmospheric sciences and global change. Selection is based on the applicant's scientific capability and potential, originality and independence, and the match between their interests and the research opportunities at the center. Applications from women and minorities are encouraged.

Financial data The stipend is $57,500 in the first year and $60,000 in the second year. Fellows also receive life and health insurance, a relocation allowance (up to $1,000 for travel within the United States or up to $2,500 for travel from abroad), an allowance of $750 for moving and storing personal belongings, and At least $3,500 per year for scientific travel and registration fees.

Duration 2 years.

Additional information NCAR is operated by the University Corporation for Atmospheric Research (a consortium of 70 universities and research institutes) and sponsored by the National Science Foundation.

Number awarded Varies; currently, up to 9 each year.

Deadline January of each year.

[901]
NATIONAL URBAN FELLOWS PROGRAM

National Urban Fellows, Inc.
Attn: Program Director
989 Avenue of the Americas, Suite 400
New York, NY 10018
(212) 730-1700   Fax: (212) 730-1823
E-mail: info@nuf.org
Web: www.nuf.org/fellows-overview

Summary To offer financial assistance to mid-career public sector professionals (especially Asian Americans, other minorities, and women) who are interested in working on a master's degree program coupled with a mentorship.

Eligibility This program is open to U.S. citizens who have a bachelor's degree, have at least 3 years of administrative or managerial experience, have demonstrated exceptional ability and leadership potential, meet academic admission requirements, have a high standard of integrity and work ethic, and are committed to the solution of urban problems. Applicants must a 1,000-word autobiographical statement and a 1,000-word statement on their career goals. They may be of any racial or ethnic background, but the program's goal is to increase the number of competent administrators from underrepresented ethnic and cultural groups at all levels of public and private urban management organizations. Semifinalists are interviewed.

Financial data The stipend is $25,000. The program also provides full payment of tuition, a relocation allowance of $500, a book allowance of $500, and reimbursement for program-related travel.

Duration 14 months.

Additional information The program begins with a summer semester of study at Bernard M. Baruch College of the City University of New York. Following this, fellows spend 9 months in mentorship assignments with a senior administrator in a government agency, a major nonprofit, or a foundation. The final summer is spent in another semester of study at Baruch College. Fellows who successfully complete all requirements are granted a master's of public administration from that college. A $75 processing fee must accompany each application.

Number awarded Varies; approximately 40 each year.

Deadline February of each year.

[902]
NEW INITIATIVES GRANTS

Kappa Omicron Nu
Attn: Awards Committee
4990 Northwind Drive, Suite 140
East Lansing, MI 48823-5031
(517) 351-8335   Fax: (517) 351-8336
E-mail: info@kon.org
Web: www.kon.org/awards/grants.html

Summary To provide financial assistance to members of Kappa Omicron Nu, an honor society in home economics, who are interested in conducting research (especially those who are Asian, Hispanic, and Native American).

Eligibility This program is open to 1) individual members of the society; and 2) research teams where the leader is a member of the society. Applicants must be interested in conducting research in family and consumer sciences or any of its related specializations. The research approach should be integrative in nature and must make connections across specializations to pursue problems or questions. Special consideration is given to research that studies the cultural and religious differences that affect leadership, especially Hispanic, Asian, and Native American. Another topic of interest is the exploration of how minority students "strike out on their own" in career development.

Financial data The maximum grant is $3,000.

Duration 1 year; multi-year funding may be accomplished by including a multi-year management plan in the initial proposal and reporting successful accomplishment of previous objectives annually.

Additional information Funding for these grants is provided by the New Initiatives Fund of Kappa Omicron Nu.

Number awarded 1 or more each year.

Deadline February of each year.

[903]
NEW VISIONS AWARD

Lee & Low Books
95 Madison Avenue, Suite 1205
New York, NY 10016
(212) 779-4400   Fax: (212) 683-1894
E-mail: general@leeandlow.com
Web: www.leeandlow.com/p/new_visions_award.mhtml

Summary To recognize and reward outstanding unpublished fantasy or mystery books for young readers by Asian Americans and other writers of color.

Eligibility The contest is open to writers of color who are residents of the United States. Applicants must submit a manuscript of a fantasy, science fiction, or mystery book directed to readers at the middle grade or young adult level.

Financial data The award is a $1,000 cash grant plus the standard publication contract, including the standard advance and royalties. The Honor Award winner receives a cash grant of $500.

Duration The competition is held annually.

Additional information This program began in 2012. Manuscripts may not be sent to any other publishers while under consideration for this award.

Number awarded 2 each year.
Deadline October of each year.

[904]
NEW VOICES AWARD

Lee & Low Books
95 Madison Avenue, Suite 1205
New York, NY 10016
(212) 779-4400   Fax: (212) 683-1894
E-mail: general@leeandlow.com
Web: www.leeandlow.com/p/new_voices_award.mhtml

Summary To recognize and reward outstanding unpublished children's picture books by Asian Americans and other writers of color.

Eligibility The contest is open to writers of color who are residents of the United States and who have not previously published a children's picture book. Writers who have published in other venues, (e.g., children's magazines, young adult fiction and nonfiction) are eligible. Manuscripts previously submitted to the sponsor are not eligible. Submissions should be no more than 1,500 words and must address the needs of children of color by providing stories with which they can identify and relate and that promote a greater understanding of each other. Submissions may be fiction or nonfiction for children between the ages of 5 and 12. Folklore and animal stories are not considered. Up to 2 submissions may be submitted per entrant.

Financial data The award is a $1,000 cash grant plus the standard publication contract, including the standard advance and royalties. The Honor Award winner receives a cash grant of $500.

Duration The competition is held annually.

Additional information This program began in 2000. Manuscripts may not be sent to any other publishers while under consideration for this award.

Number awarded 2 each year.
Deadline October of each year.

[905]
NJLA DIVERSITY SCHOLARSHIP

New Jersey Library Association
c/o Mimi Hui, Scholarship Committee Chair
Free Public Library of Hasbrouck Heights
320 Boulevard
Hasbrouck Heights, NJ 07604
(201) 288-0488   Fax: (201) 288-5467
E-mail: Hui@bccls.org
Web: www.njla.org

Summary To provide financial assistance to New Jersey residents who are members of minority groups and interested in working on a graduate or postgraduate degree in public librarianship at a school in any state.

Eligibility This program is open to residents of New Jersey and individuals who have worked in a New Jersey library for at least 12 months. Applicants must be members of a minority group (African American, Asian/Pacific Islander, Latino/Hispanic, or Native American/Native Alaskan). They must be enrolled or planning to enroll at an ALA-accredited school of library science in any state to work on a graduate or postgraduate degree in librarianship. Along with their application, they must submit an essay of 150 to 250 words explaining their

choice of librarianship as a profession. An interview is required. Selection is based on academic ability and financial need.

Financial data The stipend is $800.
Duration 1 year.
Number awarded 1 each year.
Deadline March of each year.

[906]
NOAA SMALL BUSINESS INNOVATION RESEARCH GRANTS

National Oceanic and Atmospheric Administration
Office of Research and Technology Applications
Attn: SBIR Program Manager
1335 East-West Highway, SSMC1, Room 106
Silver Spring, MD 20910-3284
(301) 713-3565   Fax: (301) 713-4100
E-mail: Kelly.Wright@noaa.gov
Web: www.oar.noaa.gov/orta

Summary To support small businesses (especially those owned by Asian Americans, other minorities, or women) that have the technological experience to contribute to the research and development mission of the National Oceanic and Atmospheric Administration (NOAA).

Eligibility For the purposes of this program, a "small business" is defined as a firm that is organized for profit with a location in the United States; is in the legal form of an individual proprietorship, partnership, limited liability company, corporation, joint venture, association, trust, or cooperative; is at least 51% owned and controlled by 1 or more individuals who are citizens or permanent residents of the United States; and has (including its affiliates) fewer than 500 employees. The primary employment of the principal investigator must be with the firm at the time of award and during the conduct of the proposed project. Applications are encouraged rom 1) women-owned small business concerns, defined as those that are at least 51% owned by a woman or women who also control and operate them; and 2) socially and economically disadvantaged small business concerns that are at least 51% owned by an Indian tribe, a Native Hawaiian organization, or 1 or more socially and economically disadvantaged individuals (African Americans, Hispanic Americans, Native Americans, Asian Pacific Americans, or subcontinent Asian Americans). Current priority areas of research include: 1) resilient coastal communities and economics; 2) healthy oceans; 3) climate adaptation and mitigation; or 4) weather-ready nation. Selection is based on the technical approach and anticipated agency and commercial benefits that may be derived from the research (25 points); the adequacy of the proposed effort and its relationship to the fulfillment of the requirements of the research topic (20 points); the soundness and technical merit of the proposed approach and its incremental progress towards topic solution (20 points); qualifications of the principal investigators, supporting staff, and consultants (15 points); and the proposal's commercial potential (20 points).

Financial data Grants are offered in 2 phases. In phase 1, awards normally do not exceed $95,000 (for both direct and indirect costs); in phase 2, awards normally do not exceed $400,000 (including both direct and indirect costs).

Duration Phase 1 awards may extend up to 6 months; phase 2 awards may extend up to 2 years.

Number awarded Varies each year; recently, NOAA planned to award 15 Phase 1 contracts. Approximately half of Phase 1 awardees receive Phase 2 awards.

Deadline January of each year.

[907]
NORTH AMERICAN TAIWANESE MEDICAL ASSOCIATION SCHOLARSHIPS

North American Taiwanese Medical Association
  Foundation
Attn: Director
7923 Garden Grove Boulevard
Garden Grove, CA 92841
(714) 898-2275   E-mail: hsu0316
Web: www.natma.org/scholarshipinfo.html

Summary To provide financial assistance for additional study to Taiwanese American medical, dental, and allied health graduate students, residents, or fellows.

Eligibility This program is open to medical, dental, and allied health students, residents, or fellows who are of Taiwanese American descent. Applicants must have completed at least 1 year of graduate school study and be enrolled in a program of training at an accredited U.S. institution or program. Along with their application, they must submit a 1-page personal statement, a transcript, and 2 letters of recommendation.

Financial data The stipend is $1,000.

Duration 1 year.

Number awarded 5 each year.

Deadline April of each year.

[908]
NOTRE DAME INSTITUTE FOR ADVANCED STUDY RESIDENTIAL FELLOWSHIPS

University of Notre Dame
Institute for Advanced Study
Attn: Programs Administrator
1124 Flanner Hall
Notre Dame, IN 46556
(574) 631-6240   E-mail: csherman@nd.edu
Web: ndias.nd.edu/fellowships/residential

Summary To provide funding to scholars (particularly Asian Americans and members of other traditionally underrepresented groups) who are interested in conducting research on topics of interest to the Notre Dame Institute for Advanced Study (NDIAS) while in residence at the institute.

Eligibility This program is open to faculty, scholars, public intellectuals, fellows from other institutes, and professional researchers in all disciplines, including the arts, engineering, the humanities, law, and the natural, social, and physical sciences. Applicants must be interested in conducting research that aligns with the intellectual orientation of the NDIAS, which asks scholars "to include questions of values in their analyses, to integrate diverse disciplines, and to ask how their findings advance civilization." They must be able to demonstrate excellent records of scholarly, artistic, or research accomplishment in their field; ability to interact with other fellows and to engage in collegial discussions of research presentations; a willingness to contribute to a cooperative community of scholars; and projects that touch on normative, integrative, or ultimate questions, especially as the involve the Catholic intellectual tradition. Applications are especially encouraged from traditionally underrepresented groups. There are no citizenship requirements; non-U.S. nationals are welcome to apply.

Financial data The grant is $60,000 for a full academic year or pro-rated amounts for shorter periods. Other benefits include subsidized visiting faculty housing, research support up to $1,000, a private office at the institute, a computer and printer, access to university libraries and other facilities, and weekly institute seminars and events.

Duration Up to 1 academic year.

Number awarded 1 or more each year.

Deadline October of each year.

[909]
NSF SMALL BUSINESS INNOVATION RESEARCH GRANTS

National Science Foundation
Directorate for Engineering
Attn: Division of Industrial Innovation and Partnerships
4201 Wilson Boulevard, Room 590 N
Arlington, VA 22230
(703) 292-8050   Fax: (703) 292-9057
TDD: (800) 281-8749
Web: www.nsf.gov/eng/iip/spir

Summary To provide funding to small and creative engineering, science, education, and technology-related firms (particularly those owned by Asian Americans, other minorities, or women) to conduct innovative, high-risk research on scientific and technical problems.

Eligibility For the purposes of this program, a "small business" is defined as a firm that is organized for profit with a location in the United States; is in the legal form of an individual proprietorship, partnership, limited liability company, corporation, joint venture, association, trust, or cooperative; is at least 51% owned and controlled by 1 or more individuals who are citizens or permanent residents of the United States; and has (including its affiliates) fewer than 500 employees. The primary employment of the principal investigator must be with the firm at the time of award and during the conduct of the proposed project. Applications are encouraged from 1) women-owned small business concerns, defined as those that are at least 51% owned by a woman or women who also control and operate them; and 2) socially and economically disadvantaged small business concerns that are at least 51% owned by an Indian tribe, a Native Hawaiian organization, or 1 or more socially and economically disadvantaged individuals (African Americans, Hispanic Americans, Native Americans, Asian Pacific Americans, or subcontinent Asian Americans). Current priorities for critical technology areas of national importance include 1) biological and chemical technologies; 2) education applications; 3) electronics, information and communication technologies; and 4) nanotechnology, advanced materials, and manufacturing. Selection is based on the intellectual merit and the broader impacts of the proposed activity.

Financial data Support is offered in 2 phases. In phase 1, awards normally may not exceed $150,000 (for both direct and indirect costs); in phase 2, awards normally may not exceed $500,000 (including both direct and indirect costs).

Duration Phase 1 awards may extend up to 6 months; phase 2 awards may extend up to 2 years.

Number awarded Depends on the availability of funds; the National Science Foundation (NSF) plans to award approximately 100 phase 1 grants each year; recently, $15 million was budgeted for this program.

Deadline June of each year.

[910]
NSF SMALL BUSINESS TECHNOLOGY TRANSFER GRANTS

National Science Foundation
Directorate for Engineering
Attn: Division of Industrial Innovation and Partnerships
4201 Wilson Boulevard, Room 590 N
Arlington, VA 22230
(703) 292-8050   Fax: (703) 292-9057
TDD: (800) 281-8749
Web: www.nsf.gov/eng/iip/spir

Summary To provide financial support for cooperative research and development projects carried out between small business concerns and research institutions ((particularly those owned by Asian Americans, other minorities, or women) in areas of concern to the National Science Foundation (NSF).

Eligibility For the purposes of this program, a "small business" is defined as a firm that is organized for profit with a location in the United States; is in the legal form of an individual proprietorship, partnership, limited liability company, corporation, joint venture, association, trust, or cooperative; is at least 51% owned and controlled by 1 or more individuals who are citizens or permanent residents of the United States; and has (including its affiliates) fewer than 500 employees. Unlike the NSF Small Business Innovation Research Grants, the primary employment of the principal investigator does not need to be with the business concern. This program, however, requires that the small business apply in collaboration with a nonprofit research institution for conduct of a project that has potential for commercialization. Principal investigators from the nonprofit research institution must commit at least 10% of their effort to the project. At least 40% of the work must be performed by the small business and at least 30% of the work must be performed by the research institution. Applications are encouraged from 1) women-owned small business concerns, defined as those that are at least 51% owned by a woman or women who also control and operate them; and 2) socially and economically disadvantaged small business concerns that are at least 51% owned by an Indian tribe, a Native Hawaiian organization, or 1 or more socially and economically disadvantaged individuals (African Americans, Hispanic Americans, Native Americans, Asian Pacific Americans, or subcontinent Asian Americans). Recently, the program was accepting applications only for the topic area of enhancing access to the radio spectrum; previous topics have included 1) advanced materials, chemical technology and manufacturing; 2) biotechnology; 3) electronics; 4) information technology; and 5) emerging opportunities (projects with a focus on near-term commercialization). Selection is based on the intellectual merit and the broader impacts of the proposed activity.

Financial data In the first phase, annual awards may not exceed $150,000 for direct costs, indirect costs, and negotiated fixed fees. In the second phase, awards up to $500,000 are available.

Duration Normally, 12 months for phase 1 and 2 years for phase 2.

Additional information Grants in the first phase are to determine the scientific, technical, and commercial merit and feasibility of the proposed cooperative effort and the quality of performance of the small business concern. In the second phase, the research and development efforts continue, depending on the results of the first phase.

Number awarded 35 phase 1 grants are awarded each year. Approximately one-third of phase 1 awardees receive phase 2 grants. Approximately $5,250,000 is budgeted for this program each year.

Deadline December of each year.

[911]
ONLINE BIBLIOGRAPHIC SERVICES/ TECHNICAL SERVICES JOINT RESEARCH GRANT

American Association of Law Libraries
Attn: Online Bibliographic Services Special Interest Section
105 West Adams Street, Suite 3300
Chicago, IL 60603
(312) 939-4764   Fax: (312) 431-1097
E-mail: aallhq@aall.org
Web: www.aallnet.org/sis/obssis/research/funding.htm

Summary To provide funding to members of the American Association of Law Libraries (AALL), particularly minorities and women, who are interested in conducting a research project related to technical services.

Eligibility This program is open to AALL members who are technical services law librarians. Preference is given to members of the Online Bibliographic Services and Technical Services Special Interest Sections, although members of other special interest sections are eligible if their work relates to technical services law librarianship. Applicants must be interested in conducting research that will enhance technical services law librarianship. Women and minorities are especially encouraged to apply. Preference is given to projects that can be completed in the United States or Canada, although foreign research projects are given consideration.

Financial data Grants range up to $1,000.

Duration 1 year.

Number awarded 1 or more each year.

Deadline March or September of each year.

[912]
OPEN BOOK AWARD

PEN American Center
Attn: Literary Awards Associate
588 Broadway, Suite 303
New York, NY 10012
(212) 334-1660, ext. 126   Fax: (212) 334-2181
E-mail: awards@pen.org
Web: www.pen.org/page.php/prmID/280

Summary To recognize and reward Asian Americans and other outstanding authors of color from any country.

Eligibility This award is presented to an author of color (African, Arab, Asian, Caribbean, Latino, and Native American) whose book-length writings were published in the United States during the current calendar year. Works of fiction, literary nonfiction, biography/memoir, poetry, and other works of literary character are strongly preferred. U.S. citizenship or residency is not required. Nominations must be submitted by publishers or agents.

Financial data The prize is $5,000.

Duration The prizes are awarded annually.

Additional information This prize was formerly known as the Beyond Margins Award. The entry fee is $50.

Number awarded 5 each year.

Deadline January of each year.

[913]
PAUL HOCH DISTINGUISHED SERVICE AWARD

American College of Neuropsychopharmacology
Attn: Executive Office
5034-A Thoroughbred Lane
Brentwood, TN 37027
(615) 324-2360   Fax: (615) 523-1715
E-mail: acnp@acnp.org
Web: www.acnp.org/programs/awards.aspx

Summary To recognize and reward members (particularly Asian Americans, other minorities, and women) who belong to the American College of Neuropsychopharmacology (ACNP) and have contributed outstanding service to the organization.

Eligibility This award is available to ACNP members who have made unusually significant contributions to the College. The emphasis of the award is on service to the organization, not on teaching, clinical, or research accomplishments. Any member or fellow of ACNP may nominate another member. Nomination of women and minorities is highly encouraged.

Financial data The award consists of an expense-paid trip to the ACNP annual meeting, a monetary honorarium, and a plaque.

Duration The award is presented annually.

Additional information This award was first presented in 1965.

Number awarded 1 each year.

Deadline Nominations must be submitted by June of each year.

[914]
PAUL TOBENKIN MEMORIAL AWARD

Columbia University
Attn: Graduate School of Journalism
Mail Code 3809
2950 Broadway
New York, NY 10027-7004
(212) 854-7696   Fax: (212) 854-3939
E-mail: lt2026@columbia.edu
Web: www.journalism.columbia.edu

Summary To recognize and reward outstanding newspaper writing that reflects the spirit of Paul Tobenkin, who fought all his life against racial and religious hatred, bigotry, bias, intolerance, and discrimination.

Eligibility Materials reflecting the spirit of Paul Tobenkin may be submitted by newspaper reporters in the United States, editors of their publications, or interested third parties. The items submitted must have been published during the previous calendar year in a weekly or daily newspaper.

Financial data The award is $1,500 plus a plaque.

Duration The award is presented annually.

Additional information This award was first presented in 1961,.

Number awarded 1 or more each year.

Deadline March of each year.

[915]
PEARSON EARLY CAREER GRANT

American Psychological Foundation
750 First Street, N.E.
Washington, DC 20002-4242
(202) 336-5843   Fax: (202) 336-5812
E-mail: foundation@apa.org
Web: www.apa.org/apf/funding/pearson.aspx

Summary To provide funding to early career psychologists (particularly Asian Americans, other minorities, and individuals with disabilities) who are interested in conducting a project in an area of critical society need.

Eligibility This program is open to psychologists who have an Ed.D., Psy.D., or Ph.D. from an accredited experience and no more than 7 years of postdoctoral experience. Applicants must be interested in conducting a project to improve areas of critical need in society, including (but not limited to) innovative scientifically-based clinical work with serious mental illness, serious emotional disturbance, incarcerated or homeless individuals, children with serious emotional disturbance (SED), or adults with serious mental illness (SMI). The sponsor encourages applications from individuals who represent diversity in race, ethnicity, gender, age, disability, and sexual orientation.

Financial data The grant is $12,000.

Duration 1 year.

Additional information This grant was first awarded in 2010.

Number awarded 1 each year.

Deadline December of each year.

[916]
POSTDOCTORAL FELLOWSHIP IN MENTAL HEALTH AND SUBSTANCE ABUSE SERVICES

American Psychological Association
Attn: Minority Fellowship Program
750 First Street, N.E.
Washington, DC 20002-4242
(202) 336-6127   Fax: (202) 336-6012
TDD: (202) 336-6123   E-mail: mfp@apa.org
Web: www.apa.org/pi/mfp/psychology/postdoc/index.aspx

Summary To provide financial assistance to postdoctoral scholars (particularly Asian Americans and members of other ethnic minority groups) who are interested in a program of research training related to providing mental health and substance abuse services to ethnic minority populations.

Eligibility This program is open to U.S. citizens, nationals, and permanent residents who received a doctoral degree in psychology in the last 5 years. Applicants must be interested in participating in a program of training under a qualified sponsor for research and have a strong commitment to a career in ethnic minority behavioral health services or policy. Members of ethnic minority groups (African Americans, Hispanics/Latinos, American Indians, Alaskan Natives, Asian Americans, Native Hawaiians, and other Pacific Islanders) are especially encouraged to apply. Selection is based on commitment to a career in ethnic minority mental health service delivery or public policy; qualifications of the sponsor; the fit between career goals and training environment selected; merit of the training proposal; potential as a future leader in ethnic minority psychology, demonstrated through accomplishments and goals; consistency between the applicant's work and the goals of the program; and letters of recommendation.

Financial data The stipend depends on the number of years of research experience and is equivalent to the standard postdoctoral stipend level of the National Institutes of Health (recently ranging from $39,264 for no years of experience to $54,180 for 7 or more years of experience).

Duration 1 academic or calendar year; may be renewed for 1 additional year.

Additional information Funding is provided by the U.S. Substance Abuse and Mental Health Services Administration.

Number awarded Varies each year.

Deadline January of each year.

[917]
POSTDOCTORAL FELLOWSHIP IN THE HISTORY OF MODERN SCIENCE AND TECHNOLOGY IN EAST ASIA

Harvard University
Attn: Department of East Asian Languages and
  Civilizations
2 Divinity Avenue
Cambridge, MA 02138
(617) 495-2754   Fax: (617) 496-6040
E-mail: ealc@fas.harvard.edu
Web: harvardealc.org/postdoc.html

Summary To provide funding to postdoctoral scholars (particularly Asian Americans, other minorities, and women) who wish to conduct research at Harvard University on a topic related to the history of science and technology in east Asia.

Eligibility This program is open to junior scholars who completed a Ph.D. within the past 5 years. Applicants must be interested in conducting research in residence at Harvard University to revise their dissertation and prepare it for publication. Preference is given to research projects exploring the understudied histories of modern science and technology in Korea and Japan, but all proposals concerning the development of science and technology in post-19th century east Asia are eligible. Applicants from women and minority candidates are strongly encouraged.

Financial data The stipend is $43,000.

Duration 1 academic year.

Additional information Fellows are provided with office space and access to the libraries and resources of Harvard University. They are invited to participate in the academic life of the Departments of East Asian Languages and Civilizations and the History of Science. Fellows are expected to reside in the Cambridge/Boston area during the term of the fellowship; work on revising their dissertation for publication; teach or collaborate on a course related to the history of modern science and/or technology in east Asia; and give at least 1 presentation of research to faculty and graduate students in East Asian Languages and Civilizations and the History of Science.

Number awarded 1 each year.

Deadline February of each year.

[918]
POSTDOCTORAL FELLOWSHIPS OF THE CONSORTIUM FOR FACULTY DIVERSITY

Consortium for Faculty Diversity at Liberal Arts Colleges
c/o Gettysburg College
Provost's Office
300 North Washington Street
Campus Box 410
Gettysburg, PA 17325
(717) 337-6796   E-mail: sgockows@gettysburg.edu
Web: www.gettysburg.edu/about/offices/provost/cfd

Summary To make available the facilities of liberal arts colleges to scholars, particularly Asian Americans and others who will enhance diversity at their college and who recently received their doctoral/advanced degree.

Eligibility This program is open to scholars in the liberal arts and engineering who are U.S. citizens or permanent residents and received the Ph.D. or M.F.A. degree within the past 5 years. Applicants must be interested in a residency at a participating institution that is part of the Consortium for a Strong Minority Presence at Liberal Arts Colleges. They must be able to enhance diversity at the institution.

Financial data Fellows receive a stipend equivalent to the average salary paid by the host college to beginning assistant professors. Modest funds are made available to finance the fellow's proposed research, subject to the usual institutional procedures.

Duration 1 year.

Additional information The following schools are participating in the program: Allegheny College, Bard College, Bowdoin College, Bryn Mawr College, Carleton College, Centenary College of Louisiana, Centre College, College of Wooster, Colorado College, Denison University, DePauw University, Dickinson College, Gettysburg College, Goucher College, Grinnell College, Gustavus Adolphus College, Hamilton College, Haverford College, Hobart and William Smith Colleges, Lafayette College, Lawrence University, Luther College, Macalester College, Mount Holyoke College, Muhlenberg College, New College of Florida, Oberlin College, Pitzer College, Pomona College, Reed College, Rhodes College, University of Richmond, Ripon College, Scripps College, St. Olaf College, Skidmore College, Smith College, Southwestern University, Swarthmore College, Transylvania University, Trinity College, Vassar College, and Wellesley College. Fellows are expected to teach at least 1 course in each academic term of residency, participate in departmental seminars, and interact with students.

Number awarded Varies each year.

Deadline October of each year.

[919]
POSTDOCTORAL RESEARCH TRAINING FELLOWSHIPS IN EPILEPSY

Epilepsy Foundation
Attn: Research Department
8301 Professional Place
Landover, MD 20785-2353
(301) 459-3700   Toll Free: (800) EFA-1000
Fax: (301) 577-2684   TDD: (800) 332-2070
E-mail: grants@efa.org
Web: www.epilepsyfoundation.org

Summary To provide funding for a program of postdoctoral training to academic physicians and scientists (particularly Asian Americans, other minorities, women, and individuals with disabilities) who are committed to epilepsy research.

Eligibility Applicants must have a doctoral degree (M.D., Sc.D., Ph.D., or equivalent) and be a clinical or postdoctoral fellow at a university, medical school, research institution, or medical center. They must be interested in participating in a training experience and research project that has potential significance for understanding the causes, treatment, or consequences of epilepsy. The program is geared toward applicants who will be trained in research in epilepsy rather than those who use epilepsy as a tool for research in other fields. Equal consideration is given to applicants interested in acquiring experience either in basic laboratory research or in the conduct of human clinical studies. Academic faculty holding the rank of instructor or higher are not eligible, nor are graduate or medical students, medical residents, permanent government employees, or employees of private industry. Applications from women, members of minority groups, and people with disabilities are especially encouraged. U.S. citizenship is not required, but the project must be conducted in the United States. Selection is based on scientific quality of the proposed research, a statement regarding its relevance to epilepsy, the applicant's qualifications, the preceptor's qualifications, and the adequacy of facility and related epilepsy programs at the institution.

Financial data The grant is $45,000. No indirect costs are covered.

Duration 1 year.

Additional information Support for this program is provided by many individuals, families, and corporations, especially the American Epilepsy Society, Abbott Laboratories, Ortho-McNeil Pharmaceutical, and Pfizer Inc. The fellowship must be carried out at a facility in the United States where there is an ongoing epilepsy research program.

Number awarded Varies each year.

Deadline August of each year.

[920]
R. ROBERT & SALLY D. FUNDERBURG RESEARCH AWARD IN GASTRIC CANCER

American Gastroenterological Association
Attn: AGA Research Foundation
Research Awards Manager
4930 Del Ray Avenue
Bethesda, MD 20814-2512
(301) 222-4012   Fax: (301) 654-5920
E-mail: awards@gastro.org
Web: www.gastro.org/aga-foundation/grants

Summary To provide funding to established investigators (particularly Asian Americans, other minorities, and women) who are working on research that enhances fundamental understanding of gastric cancer pathobiology.

Eligibility This program is open to faculty at accredited North American institutions who have established themselves as independent investigators in the field of gastric biology, pursuing novel approaches to gastric mucosal cell biology, including the fields of gastric mucosal cell biology, regeneration and regulation of cell growth, inflammation as precancerous lesions, genetics of gastric carcinoma, oncogenes in gastric epithelial malignancies, epidemiology of gastric cancer, etiology of gastric epithelial malignancies, or clinical research in diagnosis or treatment of gastric carcinoma. Applicants must be individual members of the American Gastroenterological Association (AGA). Women and minority investigators are strongly encouraged to apply. Selection is based on the novelty, feasibility, and significance of the proposal. Preference is given to novel approaches.

Financial data The grant is $50,000 per year. Funds are to be used for the salary of the investigator. Indirect costs are not allowed.

Duration 2 years.

Number awarded 1 each year.

Deadline August of each year.

[921]
RALPH J. BUNCHE AWARD

American Political Science Association
1527 New Hampshire Avenue, N.W.
Washington, DC 20036-1206
(202) 483-2512   Fax: (202) 483-2657
E-mail: apsa@apsanet.org
Web: www.apsanet.org/content_4129.cfm?navID=756

Summary To recognize and reward outstanding scholarly books on ethnic/cultural pluralism.

Eligibility Eligible to be nominated (by publishers or individuals) are scholarly political science books issued the previous year that explore issues of ethnic and/or cultural pluralism.

Financial data The award is $1,000.

Duration The award is presented annually.

Additional information This award was first presented in 1978.

Number awarded 1 each year.

Deadline January of each year for nominations from individuals; February of each year for nominations from publishers.

[922]
READY, SET, PITCH CAMPAIGN AWARD

Center for Asian American Media
Attn: CAAMFEST
145 Ninth Street, Suite 350
San Francisco, CA 94103-2641
(415) 863-0814   Fax: (415) 863-7428
E-mail: mediafund@caamedia.org
Web: www.caamedia.org

Summary To recognize and reward Asian American media producers who make outstanding fundraising presentations at a festival organized by the Center for Asian American Media (CAAM).

Eligibility This award is available to Asian American media producers and directors who participate in the annual CAAM-FEST. Candidates participate in the festival's fundraising event at which they pitch their proposed projects. Their project may be in any genre (e.g., documentary, narrative, multimedia) but it should incorporate as central themes innovation, engagement, and community. CAAM is seeking projects that are timely and compelling, incorporate a well thought out audience engagement strategy, and explore topics that are of interest to a wide audience including the Asian American community. Each pitch should last between 5 and 10 minutes and include 2 to 3 minutes of a trailer or sample media. The jury selects 10 finalists and the audience votes to elect the winner.

Financial data The award is $5,000. Funds are to be used for research and development.

Number awarded 1 each year.

Deadline February of each year.

[923]
REGINALD F. LEWIS FELLOWSHIP FOR LAW TEACHING

Harvard Law School
Attn: Lewis Committee
Griswold Two South
1525 Massachusetts Avenue
Cambridge, MA 02138
(617) 495-3109   E-mail: oaa@law.harvard.edu
Web: www.law.harvard.edu

Summary To provide funding to law school graduates, especially those of color, who are preparing for a career in law teaching and are interested in a program of research and training at Harvard Law School.

Eligibility This program is open to recent graduates of law school who have demonstrated an interest in law scholarship and teaching. Applicants must be interested in spending time in residence at Harvard Law School where they will audit courses, attend workshops, and follow a schedule of research under the sponsorship of the committee. The program encourages the training of prospective law teachers who will enhance the diversity of the profession and especially encourages applications from candidates of color.

Financial data The stipend is $50,000 per year.

Duration 2 years.

Number awarded 1 each year.

Deadline February of each year.

[924]
RESEARCH AND TRAINING FELLOWSHIPS IN EPILEPSY FOR CLINICIANS

Epilepsy Foundation
Attn: Research Department
8301 Professional Place
Landover, MD 20785-2353
(301) 459-3700   Toll Free: (800) EFA-1000
Fax: (301) 577-2684   TDD: (800) 332-2070
E-mail: grants@efa.org
Web: www.epilepsyfoundation.org

Summary To provide funding to clinically-trained professionals (particularly Asian Americans, other minorities, women, and individuals with disabilities) who are interested in gaining additional training in order to develop an epilepsy research program.

Eligibility Applicants must have an M.D., D.O., Ph.D., D.Sc., or equivalent degree and be a clinical or postdoctoral fellow at a university, medical school, or other appropriate research institution. Holders of other doctoral-level degrees (e.g., Pharm.D., D.S.N.) may also be eligible. Candidates must be interested in a program of research training that may include mechanisms of epilepsy, novel therapeutic approaches, clinical trials, development of new technologies, or behavioral and psychosocial impact of epilepsy. The training program may consist of both didactic training and a supervised research experience that is designed to develop the necessary knowledge and skills in the chosen area of research and foster the career goals of the candidate. Academic faculty holding the rank of instructor or higher are not eligible, nor are graduate or medical students, medical residents, permanent government employees, or employees of private industry. Applications from women, members of minority groups, and people with disabilities are especially encouraged. U.S. citizenship is not required, but the project must be conducted in the United States. Selection is based on the quality of the proposed research training program, the applicant's qualifications, the preceptor's qualifications, and the adequacy of clinical training, research facilities, and other epilepsy-related programs at the institution.

Financial data The grant is $50,000 per year. No indirect costs are provided.

Duration Up to 2 years.

Additional information Support for this program is provided by many individuals, families, and corporations, especially the American Epilepsy Society, Abbott Laboratories, Ortho-McNeil Pharmaceutical, and Pfizer Inc. Grantees are expected to dedicate at least 50% of their time to research training and conducting research.

Number awarded Varies each year.

Deadline September of each year.

[925]
ROBERT L. FANTZ MEMORIAL AWARD

American Psychological Foundation
750 First Street, N.E.
Washington, DC 20002-4242
(202) 336-5843   Fax: (202) 336-5812
E-mail: foundation@apa.org
Web: www.apa.org/apf/funding/fantz.aspx

Summary To provide funding to promising young investigators in psychology (particularly Asian Americans and individuals from other diverse groups).

Eligibility This program is open to young investigators in psychology or related disciplines. Candidates must show 1) evidence of basic scientific research or scholarly writing in perceptual-cognitive development and the development of selection attention; and 2) research and writing on the development of individuality, creativity, and free-choice of behavior. The sponsor encourages applications from individuals who represent diversity in race, ethnicity, gender, age, disability, and sexual orientation.

Financial data The award is $2,000. Funds are paid directly to the recipient's institution for equipment purchases, travel, computer resources, or other expenses related to the work recognized by the award.

Duration The award is presented annually.

Additional information This award was first presented in 1992.

Number awarded 1 each year.

Deadline Deadline not specified.

[926]
ROBERT WOOD JOHNSON CLINICAL SCHOLARS PROGRAM

Robert Wood Johnson Foundation
c/o University of North Carolina at Chapel Hill
Department of Social Medicine
333 MacNider Hall
Chapel Hill, NC 27599-7105
(919) 843-1351   Fax: (919) 843-2666
E-mail: rwjcsp_admin@med.unc.edu
Web: rwjcsp.unc.edu

Summary To provide financial support to young physicians (particularly Asian Americans, other minorities, and women) who wish to conduct additional research and training in areas of importance to health care policy.

Eligibility This program is open to U.S. citizens and permanent residents who have completed residency requirements for an M.D. or D.O. degree. Applicants must be committed to a career in academic medicine, public health, health policy, or other career related to developing physician leaders and skilled researchers. They must be interested in participating in a research and training program at 1 of 4 designated universities. The program embraces racial, ethnic, and gender diversity and encourages applications from candidates with diverse backgrounds and clinical disciplines.

Financial data The stipend is $67,000 for the first year and greater for the second year. Additional support is provided for research projects and professional travel.

Duration 2 years. Interested scholars may be considered for a third year.

Additional information Currently, the participating institutions are schools of medicine at the University of California at Los Angeles, the University of Michigan, the University of Pennsylvania, and Yale University. Each institution offers a program of study with generous protected time for research.

Number awarded Up to 20 each year, including 10 supported by the Robert Wood Johnson Foundation and 10 by the U.S. Department of Veterans Affairs through VA medical centers affiliated with the participating universities.

Deadline February of each year.

[927]
ROBERT WOOD JOHNSON FOUNDATION HEALTH AND SOCIETY SCHOLARS PROGRAM

Robert Wood Johnson Foundation
c/o New York Academy of Medicine
1216 Fifth Avenue
New York, NY 10029-5202
(212) 419-3566   Fax: (212) 419-3569
E-mail: hss@nyam.org
Web: www.healthandsocietyscholars.org

Summary To provide support to scholars (particularly Asian Americans and other scholars from diverse backgrounds) who from a variety of disciplines and wish to become leaders in health policy.

Eligibility This program is open to scholars who have a doctoral degree in fields that include (but are not limited to) behavioral and social sciences, biological and natural sciences, health professions, public policy, public health, history, demography, environmental sciences, urban planning, or engineering. Applicants must be U.S. citizens or permanent residents who have significant research experience. They must be interested in participating in a program at 1 of 4 universities that includes intensive seminars, mentored research, and focused training in the skills necessary for effective leadership, program implementation, and policy change. The sponsor is committed to a program that embraces diversity and inclusion across multiple dimensions of race, ethnicity, gender, age, socioeconomic background, and academic discipline; it encourages applications from candidates who will help it include diverse perspectives and experiences.

Financial data The stipend is $80,000 per year. Additional support is available for research-related expenses, training workshops, and travel to professional meetings.

Duration 2 years.

Additional information Fellows train at 1 of 4 nationally prominent universities: University of California at Berkeley (in collaboration with the University of California at San Francisco), Harvard University, Columbia University, or University of Wisconsin at Madison.

Number awarded Up to 12 each year.

Deadline September of each year.

[928]
ROBERT WOOD JOHNSON HEALTH POLICY FELLOWSHIPS

Institute of Medicine
Attn: Health Policy Fellowships Program
500 Fifth Street, N.W.
Washington, DC 20001
(202) 334-1506   Fax: (202) 334-3862
E-mail: info@healthpolicyfellows.org
Web: www.healthpolicyfellows.org/fellowship.php

Summary To provide an opportunity for health professionals or behavioral and social scientists (particularly minorities and others with diverse backgrounds) who have an interest in health to participate in the formulation of national health policies while in residence at the Institute of Medicine (IOM) in Washington, D.C.

Eligibility This program is open to mid-career professionals from academic faculties and nonprofit health care organizations who are interested in experiencing health policy processes at the federal level. Applicants must have a background in allied health professions, biomedical sciences, dentistry, economics or other social sciences, health services organization and administration, medicine, nursing, public health, or social and behavioral health or health law. They must be sponsored by the chief executive officer of an eligible nonprofit health care organization or academic institution. Selection is based on potential for leadership in health policy, potential for future growth and career advancement, professional achievements, interpersonal and communication skills, and individual plans for incorporating the fellowship experience into specific career goals. U.S. citizenship or permanent resident status is required. Applications are especially encouraged from candidates with diverse backgrounds of race, ethnicity, gender, age, disadvantaged socioeconomic status, and discipline.

Financial data Total support for the Washington stay and continuing activities may not exceed $165,000. Grant funds may cover salary support at a level of up to $94,000 plus fringe benefits. Fellows are reimbursed for relocation expenses to and from Washington, D.C. No indirect costs are paid.

Duration The program lasts 1 year and includes an orientation in September and October; meetings in November and December with members of Congress, journalists, policy analysts, and other experts on the national political and governmental process; and working assignments from January through August. Fellows then return to their home institutions, but they receive up to 2 years of continued support for further development of health policy leadership skills.

Additional information This program, initiated in 1973, is funded by the Robert Wood Johnson Foundation.

Number awarded Up to 6 each year.

Deadline November of each year.

[929]
RUBY YOSHINO SCHAAR PLAYWRIGHT AWARD

Japanese American Citizens League-New York Chapter
75 Grove Street, Number 2
Bloomfield, NJ 07003
(973) 680-1441 Fax: (973) 680-1441
E-mail: lckimura@worldnet.att.net
Web: www.jacl.org/edu/yosh-award.htm

Summary To recognize and reward outstanding Japanese American playwrights.

Eligibility This award is available to U.S. or Canadian citizens of Japanese descent who are playwrights and sponsored by a member or chapter of the Japanese American Citizens League. Applicants must have had at least 1 of their plays presented in a public forum, such as an established theater, workshop, or formal reading. They must submit a manuscript for a play that has not been theatrically produced. Selection is based on dramatic excellence and insight into the Japanese American or Canadian experience.

Financial data The award is $3,000.

Duration 1 every other year, in even-numbered years.

Additional information This award, established in 1984, is named in memory of a former Japanese American Citizens League chapter president and executive director.

Number awarded 1 every even-numbered year.

Deadline May of even-numbered years.

[930]
SALLY C. TSENG PROFESSIONAL DEVELOPMENT GRANT

Chinese American Librarians Association
c/o Ying Xu, Professional Development Grant Committee
California State University at Los Angeles
University Library, Room LN 2020A
5151 State University Drive
Los Angeles, CA 90032
(323) 343-3959 E-mail: yxu1@calstatela.edu
Web: www.cala-web.org/node/203

Summary To provide funding to members of the Chinese American Librarians Association (CALA) who are interested in conducting a research project.

Eligibility This program is open to full-time librarians of Chinese descent who have been CALA members for at least 2 years. Applicants must be interested in conducting a research project in library and information science for which they are qualified and which will result in the advancement of their professional status. Preference is given to members with 15 or fewer years of professional library experience.

Financial data The grant is $1,000.

Duration 1 year.

Number awarded 1 or 2 each year.

Deadline March of each year.

[931]
SAN FRANCISCO INTERNATIONAL LGBT FILM FESTIVAL PRIZES

Frameline
Attn: Festival
145 Ninth Street, Suite 300
San Francisco, CA 94103
(415) 703-8650 Fax: (415) 861-1404
E-mail: info@frameline.org
Web: www.frameline.org

Summary To recognize and reward outstanding films of interest to the lesbian, gay, bisexual, and transgender (LGBT) audience, particularly those produced by people of color or women.

Eligibility This competition is open to directors of films by, about, and of interest to LGBT people. Applicants must submit previews of their work on DVD or VHS in the following categories: narrative feature films (40 minutes and longer), documentary feature films (40 minutes and longer), and shorts (all films less than 40 minutes in length). The program actively seeks out work by women and people of color. Recently, awards have been presented for best feature film, best documentary film, and best short film.

Financial data Awards are $2,000 for best feature and best documentary and $1,000 for best short film.

Duration The awards are presented annually.

Additional information No fees are charged for the early deadline. Standard fees are $35 for the regular deadline, $50 for the late deadline, or $55 for the extended deadline. Student fees are $15 for regular, late, and extended deadlines. Fees are waived for youth up to 18 years of age.

Number awarded 3 each year.

Deadline December of each year for the early deadline; January of each year for the regular deadline; mid-February for the late deadline; and the end of February for the extended deadline.

[932]
SARA WHALEY BOOK PRIZE

National Women's Studies Association
Attn: Book Prizes
11 East Mount Royal Avenue, Suite 100
Baltimore, MD 21202
(410) 528-0355   Fax: (410) 528-0357
E-mail: awards@nwsa.org
Web: www.nwsa.org/content.asp?pl=16&contentid=16

Summary To recognize and reward members of the National Women's Studies Association (NWSA), particularly Asian Americans and other women of color, who have written outstanding books on topics related to women and labor.

Eligibility This award is available to NWSA members who submit a book manuscript that relates to women and labor, including migration and women's paid jobs, illegal immigration and women's work, impact of AIDS on women's employment, trafficking of women and women's employment, women and domestic work, or impact of race on women's work. Both senior scholars (who have issued at least 2 books and published the entry within the past year) and junior scholars (who have a publication contract or a book in production) are eligible. Women of color of U.S. or international origin are encouraged to apply.

Financial data The award is $2,000.

Duration The awards are presented annually.

Additional information This award was first presented in 2008.

Number awarded 2 each year: 1 to a senior scholar and 1 to a junior scholar.

Deadline April of each year.

[933]
SCHOLARS IN HEALTH POLICY RESEARCH PROGRAM

Robert Wood Johnson Foundation
c/o Boston University Health Policy Institute
53 Bay State Road
Boston, MA 02215-2197
(617) 353-9220   Fax: (617) 353-9227
E-mail: rwjf@bu.edu
Web: www.healthpolicyscholars.org

Summary To provide support for postdoctoral training in health policy to scholars (particularly Asian Americans, other underrepresented minorities, and women) in economics, political science, and sociology.

Eligibility This program is open to scholars who have a doctoral degree in economics, political science, or sociology. Applicants must have earned their degree during the past 5 years and be U.S. citizens or permanent residents. Preference is given to applicants who have not worked previously in the areas of health or health policy research. Selection is based on the applicant's commitment to a health policy career, quality of the past research, capability to undertake this challenging program, recommendations, and potential to contribute creatively to future U.S. health policies. The program embraces racial, ethnic, and gender diversity and encourages applications from candidates from groups that

historically have been underrepresented in the 3 disciplines of interest.

Financial data The stipend is $89,000 per year.

Duration 2 years.

Additional information Fellows train at 1 of 3 nationally prominent academic institutions: University of California at Berkeley (in collaboration with the University of California at San Francisco), Harvard University, or the University of Michigan. There, they have the opportunity to work closely with faculty from the social sciences, as well as from medicine, public health, and public policy. Specific activities vary by institution but generally include seminars, workshops, tutorials, independent research projects, and policy placements in local or state government.

Number awarded Up to 9 each year.

Deadline October of each year.

[934]
SHEILA SUEN LAI RESEARCH GRANT

Asian Pacific American Librarians Association
Attn: Executive Director
P.O. Box 677593
Orlando, FL 32867-7593
(407) 823-5048   Fax: (407) 823-5865
E-mail: bbasco@mail.ucf.edu
Web: www.apalaweb.org

Summary To provide research funding to members of the Asian Pacific American Librarians Association (APALA).

Eligibility Eligible to apply are APALA members in good standing who have been members for at least 1 year prior to applying. Applicants must have an M.L.S. or M.L.I.S. degree and currently be employed in a professional position in library science or a related field. They must be seeking funding to conduct research projects, attend research-related conferences and workshops, conduct research workshops and programs, or assist in research writing; attendance at professional association conferences is not supported. Current recipients of other APALA grants or scholarships are not eligible for this award. U.S. citizenship or permanent resident status is required.

Financial data Grants range up to $1,000.

Duration Grants are awarded annually.

Number awarded 1 or more each year.

Deadline February of each year.

[935]
SHRI RAM ARORA AWARD

The Minerals, Metals & Materials Society
Attn: TMS Foundation
184 Thorn Hill Road
Warrendale, PA 15086-7514
(724) 776-9000, ext. 221   Toll Free: (800) 759-4867
Fax: (724) 776-3770   E-mail: foundation@tms.org
Web: www.tms.org/Foundation/tfactivities.aspx

Summary To provide funding to graduate students and postdoctoral scholars of Indian origin who are interested in educational activities in materials science and engineering.

Eligibility This program is open to graduate students working on a degree in materials science or a related field and postdoctoral scholars actively involved in materials research. First priority is given to applicants living in India; if there are no qualified candidates from India, applicants of Indian heritage currently residing in other countries are considered. Applicants must be younger than 30 years of age. Along with their application, they must submit a statement that describes the purpose for which the award is being sought, including details on how this activity will contribute to their career plans and their aspiration to a leadership role in the materials science and engineering profession.

Financial data The award is $2,500, including a cash grant of $1,000 to be used at the recipient's discretion and $1,500 for travel, accommodation, and registration expenses to attend the annual meeting of The Minerals, Metals & Materials Society (TMS).

Duration The award is presented annually.

Additional information This award was first presented in 2000.

Number awarded 1 each year.

Deadline June of each year.

[936]
SOCIETY OF PEDIATRIC PSYCHOLOGY DIVERSITY RESEARCH GRANT

American Psychological Association
Attn: Division 54 (Society of Pediatric Psychology)
c/o Anna Maria Patino-Fernandez
University of Miami School of Medicine
Mailman Center for Child Development
Division of Clinical Psychology
1601 N.W. 12th Avenue, 4018B
Miami, FL 33136-1005
(305) 243-6837   Fax: (305) 243-8470
E-mail: Apatino-fernandez@med.miami.edu
Web: www.apadivisions.org

Summary To provide funding to graduate student and post-doctoral members of the Society of Pediatric Psychology (particularly Asian Americans and others who come from diverse backgrounds) who are interested in conducting research on diversity aspects of pediatric psychology.

Eligibility This program is open to current members of the society who are graduate students, fellows, or early-career (within 3 years of appointment) faculty. Applicants must be interested in conducting pediatric psychology research that features diversity-related variables, such as race or ethnicity, gender, culture, sexual orientation, language differences, socioeconomic status, and/or religiosity. Along with their application, they must submit a 2,000-word description of the project, including its purpose, methodology, predictions, and implications; a detailed budget; a current curriculum vitae, and (for students) a curriculum vitae of the faculty research mentor and a letter of support from that mentor. Selection is based on relevance to diversity in child health (5 points), significance of the study (5 points), study methods and procedures (10 points), and investigator qualifications (10 points).

Financial data Grants up to $1,000 are available. Funds may not be used for convention or meeting travel, indirect costs, stipends of principal investigators, or costs associated with manuscript preparation.

Duration The grant is presented annually.

Additional information The Society of Pediatric Psychology is Division 54 of the American Psychological Association (APA). This grant was first presented in 2008.

Number awarded 1 each year.

Deadline September of each year.

[937]
THEODORE BLAU EARLY CAREER AWARD FOR OUTSTANDING CONTRIBUTION TO PROFESSIONAL CLINICAL PSYCHOLOGY

American Psychological Foundation
750 First Street, N.E.
Washington, DC 20002-4242
(202) 336-5843   Fax: (202) 336-5812
E-mail: foundation@apa.org
Web: www.apa.org/apf/funding/blau.aspx

Summary To recognize and reward young clinical psychologists (particularly Asian Americans, other minorities, women, and individuals with disabilities) who have a record of outstanding professional accomplishments.

Eligibility This award is available to clinical psychologists who are no more than 7 years past completion of their doctoral degree. Nominees must have a record of accomplishments that may include promoting the practice of clinical psychology through professional service; innovation in service delivery; novel application of applied research methodologies to professional practice; positive impact on health delivery systems; development of creative educational programs for practice; or other novel or creative activities advancing the service of the profession. Self-nominations are accepted. The sponsor encourages nominations of individuals who represent diversity in race, ethnicity, gender, age, disability, and sexual orientation.

Financial data The award is $4,000.

Duration The award is presented annually.

Additional information This award, first presented in 1998, is sponsored by Division 12 (Society of Clinical Psychology) of the American Psychological Association.

Number awarded 1 each year.

Deadline Nominations must be submitted by October of each year.

[938]
THEODORE MILLON AWARD IN PERSONALITY PSYCHOLOGY

American Psychological Foundation
750 First Street, N.E.
Washington, DC 20002-4242
(202) 336-5843   Fax: (202) 336-5812
E-mail: foundation@apa.org
Web: www.apa.org/apf/funding/millon.aspx

Summary To recognize and reward psychologists (particularly Asian Americans, other minorities, women, and individuals with disabilities) who have a record of outstanding contributions to the science of personality psychology.

Eligibility This award is available to psychologists engaged in advancing the science of personality psychology, including the areas of personology, personality theory, personality disorders, and personality measurement. Nominees should be between 8 and 20 years past completion of their doctoral degree. The sponsor encourages nominations of individuals who represent diversity in race, ethnicity, gender, age, disability, and sexual orientation.

Financial data The award is $1,000.

Duration The award is presented annually.

Additional information This award, established in 2004, is sponsored by Division 12 (Society of Clinical Psychology) of the American Psychological Association.

Number awarded 1 each year.

Deadline Nominations must be submitted by October of each year.

[939]
TIMOTHY JEFFREY MEMORIAL AWARD IN CLINICAL HEALTH PSYCHOLOGY

American Psychological Foundation
750 First Street, N.E.
Washington, DC 20002-4242
(202) 336-5843   Fax: (202) 336-5812
E-mail: foundation@apa.org
Web: www.apa.org/apf/funding/jeffrey.aspx

Summary To recognize and reward psychologists (particularly Asian Americans, other minorities, women, and individuals with disabilities) who have made outstanding contributions to clinical health psychology.

Eligibility This award is available to full-time providers of direct clinical services who demonstrate an outstanding commitment to clinical health psychology. Nominees must be members of Division 38 (Health Psychology) of the American Psychological Association. They must have a full and unrestricted license to practice psychology and typically spend 15 to 20 hours per week in direct patient care. Letters of nomination should be accompanied by a curriculum vitae, at least 1 letter of support from a non-psychologist professional colleague, and another letter of support from a psychologist colleague. The sponsor encourages nominations of individuals who represent diversity in race, ethnicity, gender, age, disability, and sexual orientation.

Financial data The award is $3,000.

Duration The award is presented annually.

Additional information This award is sponsored by Division 38.

Number awarded 1 each year.

Deadline April of each year.

[940]
TRAINEESHIPS IN AIDS PREVENTION STUDIES (TAPS)

University of California at San Francisco
Attn: Center for AIDS Prevention Studies
50 Beale Street, Suite 1300
San Francisco, CA 94105
(415) 597-9260   Fax: (415) 597-9213
E-mail: Rochelle.Blanco@ucsf.edu
Web: www.caps.ucsf.edu/training/taps

Summary To provide funding to scientists (particularly Asian American and other minority scientists) who are interested in conducting HIV prevention research at the Center for AIDS Prevention Studies (CAPS) of the University of California at San Francisco (UCSF).

Eligibility This program is open to U.S. citizens, nationals, and permanent residents who have a Ph.D., M.D., or equivalent degree. Applicants must be interested in a program of research training at CAPS in the following areas of special emphasis in AIDS research: epidemiological research, stud-

ies of AIDS risk behaviors, substance abuse and HIV, primary prevention interventions, research addressing minority populations, studies of HIV-positive individuals, policy and ethics, international research, and other public health and clinical aspects of AIDS. Recent postdoctorates who have just completed their training as well as those who are already faculty members in academic or clinical departments are eligible. Members of minority ethnic groups are strongly encouraged to apply.

Financial data Stipends depend on years of relevant postdoctoral experience, based on the NIH stipend scale for Institutional Research Training Grants (currently ranging from $39,264 for fellows with no relevant postdoctoral experience to $54,180 for those with 7 or more years of experience). Other benefits include a computer, travel to at least 1 annual professional meeting, health insurance, and other required support. The costs of the M.P.H. degree, if required, are covered.

Duration 2 or 3 years.

Additional information The TAPS program is designed to ensure that at the end of the training each fellow will have: 1) completed the M.P.H. degree or its equivalent; 2) taken advanced courses in research methods, statistics, and other topics relevant to a major field of interest; 3) participated in and led numerous seminars on research topics within CAPS, as well as in the formal teaching programs of the university; 4) designed several research protocols and completed at least 1 significant research project under the direction of a faculty mentor; and 5) made presentations at national or international meetings and submitted several papers for publication.

Number awarded Varies each year.

Deadline November of each year.

[941]
TRAINING PROGRAM FOR SCIENTISTS CONDUCTING RESEARCH TO REDUCE HIV/STI HEALTH DISPARITIES

University of California at San Francisco
Attn: Center for AIDS Prevention Studies
50 Beale Street, Suite 1300
San Francisco, CA 94105
(415) 597-9139   Fax: (415) 597-9213
E-mail: dale.danley@ucsf.edu
Web: www.caps.ucsf.edu

Summary To provide funding to scientists (particularly Asian Americans and other minorities) who are interested in obtaining additional training at the University of California at San Francisco (UCSF) Center for AIDS Prevention Studies (CAPS) for HIV prevention research in minority communities.

Eligibility This program is open to scientists in tenure-track positions or investigators in research institutes who have not yet obtained research funding from the U.S. National Institutes of Health (NIH) or equivalent. Applicants must be interested in a program of activity at CAPS to improve their programs of HIV-prevention research targeting vulnerable ethnic minority populations. They must be eligible to serve as principal investigators at their home institutions. Selection is based on commitment to HIV social and behavioral research, prior HIV prevention research with communities and community-based organizations targeting communities with high levels of health disparities (e.g., communities with a high proportion of disadvantaged or disabled persons, racial and ethnic minority communities), creativity and innovativeness for a pilot research project to serve as a preliminary study for a subsequent larger R01 grant proposal to NIH or other suitable funding agency, past experience conducting research and writing papers, quality of letters of recommendation from colleagues and mentors, and support from the home institution (e.g., time off for research, seed money). A goal of the program is to increase the number of minority group members among principal investigators funded by NIH and other agencies. U.S. citizenship or permanent resident status is required.

Financial data Participants receive 1) a monthly stipend for living expenses and round-trip airfare to San Francisco for each summer; and 2) a grant of $25,000 to conduct preliminary research before the second summer to strengthen their R01 application.

Duration 6 weeks during each of 3 consecutive summers.

Additional information This program is funded by the NIH National Institute of Child Health and Human Development (NICHHD) and National Institute on Drug Abuse (NIDA).

Number awarded Approximately 4 each year.

Deadline January of each year.

[942]
UNIVERSITY OF ILLINOIS AT CHICAGO ACADEMIC RESIDENT LIBRARIAN PROGRAM

University of Illinois at Chicago
Attn: Library Human Resources
801 South Morgan
MC 234
Chicago, IL 60607
(312) 996-7353
Web: library.uic.edu/about/employment

Summary To provide a residency at the University of Illinois at Chicago (UIC) to librarians (particularly Asian Americans, other underrepresented minorities, and individuals with disabilities) who are interested in preparing for a career in academic librarianship.

Eligibility This program is open to librarians who graduated within the past year with a master's degree from an ALA-accredited program. Applicants must be interested in preparing for a career as an academic librarian through a residency at (UIC). Preference is given to applicants who can demonstrate an interest in 1 or more of the following areas: 1) technical services, with an emphasis on development and assessment of library discovery tools; 2) outreach, with an emphasis on initiatives to rural and underserved users; 3) reference and instruction, with an emphasis on instructional technical design and the development of multimedia learning objects; 4) E-science, with an emphasis on data curation in support of university-wide data management and preservation initiatives; 5) digital preservation, with an emphasis on preservation architectures, standards, and workflows; or 7) digital image collections, with an emphasis on mapping using GIS technologies. A goal of the program is to increase diversity within the profession of academic librarianship; applications are especially welcome from women, underrepresented minority group members, persons with disabilities, members of sexual minority groups, and others whose background, education, experience, and academic interests would enrich the diversity of the profession.

Financial data The stipend is at least $42,000.

Duration 1 year; may be renewed 1 additional year.

Number awarded 2 or more each year.

Deadline June of each year.

[943]
USDA SMALL BUSINESS INNOVATION RESEARCH PROGRAM

Department of Agriculture
National Institute of Food and Agriculture
Attn: Director, SBIR Program
1400 Independence Avenue, S.W.
Stop 2201
Washington, DC 20250-2201
(202) 401-4002   Fax: (202) 401-6070
E-mail: sbir@nifa.usda.gov
Web: www.csrees.usda.gov/funding/sbir/sbir.html

Summary To stimulate technological innovation related to agriculture in the private sector by small business firms, especially those owned by Asian Americans, members of other socially and economically disadvantaged groups, and women.

Eligibility For the purposes of this program, a "small business" is defined as a firm that is organized for profit with a location in the United States; is in the legal form of an individual proprietorship, partnership, limited liability company, corporation, joint venture, association, trust, or cooperative; is at least 51% owned and controlled by 1 or more individuals who are citizens or permanent residents of the United States; and has (including its affiliates) fewer than 500 employees. The primary employment of the principal investigator must be with the firm at the time of award and during the conduct of the proposed project. Applications are encouraged from 1) women-owned small business concerns, defined as those that are at least 51% owned by a woman or women who also control and operate them; and 2) socially and economically disadvantaged small business concerns that are at least 51% owned by an Indian tribe, a Native Hawaiian organization, or 1 or more socially and economically disadvantaged individuals (African Americans, Hispanic Americans, Native Americans, Asian Pacific Americans, or subcontinent Asian Americans). Proposals are accepted in 10 topic areas: forests and related resources; plant production and protection (biology); animal production and protection; air, water, and soils; food science and nutrition; rural development; aquaculture; biofuels and biobased products; small and mid-sized farms; and plant production and protection (engineering). Selection is based on scientific and technical feasibility of the project, importance of the problem, qualifications of the investigator and research facilities, appropriateness of the budget, and extent of duplication of the project with other ongoing or previous research.

Financial data Support is offered in 2 phases. In phase 1, awards normally do not exceed $100,000 (for both direct and indirect costs); in phase 2, awards normally do not exceed $450,000 (including both direct and indirect costs).

Duration Phase 1 awards may extend up to 8 months; phase 2 awards may extend up to 2 years.

Additional information Phase 1 is to determine the scientific or technical feasibility of ideas submitted by the applicants on research topic areas. Phase 2 awards are made to firms with approaches that appear sufficiently promising as a result of phase 1 studies.

Number awarded Recently, the department granted 80 phase 1 awards and 32 phase 2 awards. Total program funding was approximately $19 million.

Deadline September of each year for phase 1 awards; February of each year for phase 2 awards.

[944]
VISIONARY GRANTS

American Psychological Foundation
750 First Street, N.E.
Washington, DC 20002-4242
(202) 336-5843   Fax: (202) 336-5812
E-mail: foundation@apa.org
Web: www.apa.org/apf/funding/vision-weiss.aspx

Summary To provide funding to professionals (particularly Asian Americans and those from other diverse backgrounds) who are interested in conducting projects that use psychology to solve social problems related to the priorities of the American Psychological Foundation (APF).

Eligibility This program is open to professionals at non-profit organizations engaged in research, education, and intervention projects and programs. Applicants must be interested in conducting an activity that uses psychology to solve social problems in the following priority areas: understanding and fostering the connection between mental and physical health; reducing stigma and prejudice; understanding and preventing all forms of violence; or addressing the long-term psychological needs of individuals and communities in the aftermath of disaster. Selection is based on the criticality of the proposed funding for the proposed work; conformance with stated program goals and requirements; innovative and potential impact qualities; quality, viability, and promise of proposed work, and competence and capability of project leaders. The sponsor encourages applications from individuals who represent diversity in race, ethnicity, gender, age, disability, and sexual orientation.

Financial data Grants range from $2,500 to $20,000.

Duration 1 year; nonrenewable.

Additional information This program began in 2003.

Number awarded 1 or more each year.

Deadline March of each year.

[945]
WAYNE F. PLACEK GRANTS

American Psychological Foundation
750 First Street, N.E.
Washington, DC 20002-4242
(202) 336-5843   Fax: (202) 336-5812
E-mail: foundation@apa.org
Web: www.apa.org/apf/funding/placek.aspx

Summary To provide funding to pre- and postdoctoral scholars (particularly Asian Americans, other minorities, women, and individuals with disabilities) who are interested in conducting research that will increase the general public's understanding of homosexuality and alleviate the stress experienced by gay men and lesbians.

Eligibility This program is open to scholars who have a doctoral degree (e.g., Ph.D., Psy.D., M.D.) and to graduate students in all fields of the behavioral and social sciences. Applicants must be interested in conducting empirical studies that address the following topics: prejudice, discrimination,

and violence based on sexual orientation, including heterosexuals' attitudes and behaviors toward lesbian, gay, bisexual, and transgender (LGBT) people; family and workplace issues relevant to LGBT people; and subgroups of the LGBT population that have been historically underrepresented in scientific research. Selection is based on conformance with stated program goals, magnitude of incremental contribution, quality of proposed work, and applicant's demonstrated scholarship and research competence. The sponsor encourages applications from individuals who represent diversity in race, ethnicity, gender, age, disability, and sexual orientation.

Financial data The grant is $15,000.

Duration 1 year.

Additional information This program began in 1995.

Number awarded 1 or 2 each year.

Deadline February of each year.

[946]
W.E.B. DUBOIS FELLOWSHIP PROGRAM

Department of Justice
National Institute of Justice
Attn: W.E.B. DuBois Fellowship Program
810 Seventh Street, N.W.
Washington, DC 20531
(202) 514-6205   E-mail: Marilyn.Moses@usdoj.gov
Web: www.nij.gov

Summary To provide funding to junior investigators (particularly Asian Americans and other minorities) who are interested in conducting research on "crime, violence and the administration of justice in diverse cultural contexts."

Eligibility This program is open to investigators who have a Ph.D. or other doctoral-level degree (including a legal degree of J.D. or higher). Applicants should be early in their careers and not have been awarded tenure. They must be interested in conducting research that relates to specific areas that change annually but relate to criminal justice policy and practice in the United States. The sponsor strongly encourages applications from diverse racial and ethnic backgrounds. Selection is based on quality and technical merit; impact of the proposed project; capabilities, demonstrated productivity, and experience of the applicant; budget; dissemination strategy; and relevance of the project for policy and practice.

Financial data Grants range up to $100,000. Funds may be used for salary, fringe benefits, reasonable costs of relocation, travel essential to the project, and office expenses not provided by the sponsor. Indirect costs are limited to 20%.

Duration 6 to 12 months; fellows are required to be in residence at the National Institute of Justice (NIJ) for the first 2 months and may elect to spend all or part of the remainder of the fellowship period either in residence at NIJ or at their home institution.

Number awarded 1 each year.

Deadline January of each year.

[947]
WILLIAM L. FISHER CONGRESSIONAL GEOSCIENCE FELLOWSHIP

American Geological Institute
Attn: Government Affairs Program
4220 King Street
Alexandria, VA 22302-1502
(703) 379-2480, ext. 212   Fax: (703) 379-7563
E-mail: govt@agiweb.org
Web: www.agiweb.org/gap/csf/index.html

Summary   To provide members of an American Geological Institute (AGI) component society (particularly Asian Americans, other minorities, and women) with an opportunity to gain professional experience in the office of a member of Congress or a Congressional committee.

Eligibility   This program is open to members of 1 of AGI's 49 member societies who have a master's degree and at least 3 years of post-degree work experience or a Ph.D. Applicants should have a broad geoscience background and excellent written and oral communications skills. They must be interested in working with Congress. Although prior experience in public policy is not required, a demonstrated interest in applying science to the solution of public problems is desirable. Applications from women and minorities are especially encouraged. U.S. citizenship or permanent resident status is required.

Financial data   Fellows receive a stipend of up to $65,000 plus allowances for health insurance, relocation, and travel.

Duration   12 months, beginning in September.

Additional information   This program is 1 of more than 20 Congressional Science Fellowships operating in affiliation with the American Association for the Advancement of Science (AAAS), which provides a 2-week orientation on Congressional and executive branch operations.

Number awarded   1 each year.

Deadline   January of each year.

Indexes

- Program Title Index •
- Sponsoring Organization Index •
- Residency Index •
- Tenability Index •
- Subject Index •
- Calendar Index •

Program Title Index

If you know the name of a particular funding program open to Asian Americans and want to find out where it is covered in the directory, use the Program Title Index. Here, program titles are arranged alphabetically, word by word. To assist you in your search, every program is listed by all its known names or abbreviations. In addition, we've used an alphabetical code (within parentheses) to help you determine if the program is aimed at you: U = Undergraduates; G = Graduate Students; P = Professionals/Postdoctorates. Here's how the code works: if a program is followed by (U) 241, the program is described in the Undergraduates chapter, in entry 241. If the same program title is followed by another entry number—for example, (P) 901—the program is also described in the Professionals/Postdoctorates chapter, in entry 901. Remember: the numbers cited here refer to program entry numbers, not to page numbers in the book.

A

AAF Minority/Disadvantaged Scholarship Program, (U) 1

AAFO Scholarships, (U) 2

AAJUW Scholarship Program, (U) 3, (G) 409

AAOGF Foundation Scholarships, (P) 805

AAPA-APF Okura Mental Health Leadership Foundation Fellowship, (P) 806

AAPI National Research Competition, (G) 410, (P) 807

ABA Legal Opportunity Scholarship, (G) 411

Abe and Esther Hagiwara Student Aid Award, (U) 4, (G) 412

Abiko Memorial Scholarship. See Kyutaro and Yasuo Abiko Memorial Scholarship, entry (U) 213

ACA/Martin Luther King Jr. Scholarship Awards, (U) 5, (G) 413

Academic Library Association of Ohio Diversity Scholarship. See ALAO Diversity Scholarship, entry (G) 421

Accelerator Applications Division Scholarship. See ANS/ Accelerator Applications Division Scholarship, entry (U) 27

Access Path to Psychology and Law Experience Program. See APPLE Program, entry (U) 31

ACS/Organic Chemistry Graduate Student Fellowships, (G) 414

Act Six Scholarships, (U) 6

A.D. Osherman Scholarship Fund, (U) 7

Addie B. Morris Scholarship, (U) 8, (G) 415

Adler Pollock & Sheehan Diversity Scholarship, (G) 416

Adrienne Alexander Scholarship. See Surety and Fidelity Industry Scholarship Program, entry (U) 348

Adrienne M. and Charles Shelby Rooks Fellowship for Racial and Ethnic Theological Students, (G) 417

Advisors of America Scholarship, (U) 9

AERA-AIR Fellows Program, (P) 808

Aetna Foundation-NMF Healthcare Leadership Program, (G) 418

AFPD Minority Scholarships, (U) 10

AGA Research Scholar Awards, (P) 809

Against the Grain Artistic Scholarship, (U) 11

AHLEF/Hyatt Hotels Fund for Minority Lodging Management Students, (U) 12

Ahn Award for Civil Rights and Social Justice for Asian Americans. See Dr. Suzanne Ahn Award for Civil Rights and Social Justice for Asian Americans, entry (P) 846

AICPA Ascend Scholarship, (U) 13, (G) 419

Aiko Susanna Tashiro Hiratsuka Memorial Scholarship, (U) 14

AIR Fellows Program. See AERA-AIR Fellows Program, entry (P) 808

Aiso Scholarship. See Japanese American Bar Association Educational Foundation Scholarships, entry (G) 591

ALA Spectrum Scholarship Program, (G) 420

Alabama Society of Certified Public Accountants Educational Foundation Diversity Scholarships. See ASCPA Educational Foundation Diversity Scholarships, entry (U) 36

Alan Compton and Bob Stanley Minority and International Scholarship, (U) 15

ALAO Diversity Scholarship, (G) 421

Albert W. Dent Student Scholarship, (G) 422

Alexander and Geraldine Wanek Fund Award. See Geological Society of America Graduate Student Research Grants, entry (G) 551

Alexander Gralnick Research Investigator Prize, (P) 810

Alexander Scholarship. See Surety and Fidelity Industry Scholarship Program, entry (U) 348

Alexander Sisson Award. See Geological Society of America Graduate Student Research Grants, entry (G) 551

Alice Abe Matsumoto Scholarship. See NSRCF Scholarships, entry (U) 283

Alice Yuriko Endo Memorial Scholarship, (U) 16

Allen Chin Scholarship. See Shui Kuen and Allen Chin Scholarship, entry (U) 333

Allen Memorial Scholarship. See Distinguished Raven FAC Memorial Scholarships, entry (U) 105

Allman Scholarship. See Arizona Chapter Japanese American Citizens League Scholarships, entry (U) 33

U–Undergraduates   **G–Graduate Students**   **P–Professionals/Postdoctorates**

U–Undergraduates   **G–Graduate Students**   **P–Professionals/Postdoctorates**

U–Undergraduates   **G–Graduate Students**   **P–Professionals/Postdoctorates**

U–Undergraduates   G–Graduate Students   P–Professionals/Postdoctorates

H

H. John Yamashita Memorial Scholarship. *See* Reverend H. John Yamashita Memorial Scholarship, entry (G) 724

Hagiwara Student Aid Award. *See* Abe and Esther Hagiwara Student Aid Award, entries (U) 4, (G) 412

Hailey AAJ Law Student Scholarships. *See* Richard D. Hailey AAJ Law Student Scholarships, entry (G) 726

Hall Memorial Scholarships. *See* James B. Morris Scholarships, entries (U) 185, (G) 587

Ham Scholarship. *See* KSEA Undergraduate Scholarships, entry (U) 212

HANA Scholarships, (U) 158, (G) 559

Hanayagi Rokumie Memorial Japanese Cultural Scholarship, (U) 159

Hannah Griswold Grant, (U) 160

Harihara Mehendale Graduate Student Best Abstract Award. *See* Dr. Harihara Mehendale Graduate Student Best Abstract Award, entry (G) 517

Harold T. Stearns Fellowship Award. *See* Geological Society of America Graduate Student Research Grants, entry (G) 551

Harry and Miriam Levinson Award for Exceptional Contributions to Consulting Organizational Psychology, (P) 868

Harry and Miriam Levinson Scholarship. *See* APF/COGDOP Graduate Research Scholarships, entry (G) 441

Haruyama Ministerial Scholarship. *See* Justin Haruyama Ministerial Scholarship, entry (G) 610

Harvard Medical School Dean's Postdoctoral Fellowship, (P) 869

Harvard–Newcomen Postdoctoral Fellowship in Business History, (P) 870

Hattie J. Hilliard Scholarship, (U) 161

Hawaii Korean Chamber of Commerce Scholarships, (U) 162

Hayashi Memorial Scholarship. *See* Law Scholarships of the Japanese American Citizens League, entry (G) 632

Hayashida Scholarship. *See* NSRCF Scholarships, entry (U) 283

Health and Aging Policy Fellowships, (P) 871

Health, Education, and Human Services Fellowships of the American Association for the Advancement of Science, (P) 872

Health Research and Educational Trust Scholarships, (U) 163, (G) 560

Health Sciences Student Fellowships in Epilepsy, (G) 561

Hécaen Scholarship. *See* Benton-Meier Neuropsychology Scholarships, entry (G) 464

HECUA Scholarships for Social Justice, (U) 164

Helen Brown COREM Scholarships. *See* Richard and Helen Brown COREM Scholarships, entry (G) 725

Helen Lee Scholarship, (U) 165, (G) 562

Helene M. Overly Memorial Graduate Scholarship, (G) 563

Henry and Chiyo Kuwahara Creative Arts Award, (U) 166, (G) 564

Henry and Chiyo Kuwahara Memorial Scholarships, (U) 167, (G) 565

Henry David Research Grant in Human Reproductive Behavior and Population Studies, (G) 566, (P) 873

Henry Hécaen Scholarship. *See* Benton-Meier Neuropsychology Scholarships, entry (G) 464

Henry L. Allen Memorial Scholarship. *See* Distinguished Raven FAC Memorial Scholarships, entry (U) 105

Herbert Jensen Scholarship. *See* Arizona Chapter Japanese American Citizens League Scholarships, entry (U) 33

Herbert W. Nickens Medical Student Scholarships, (G) 567

Hibino Scholarship. *See* NSRCF Scholarships, entry (U) 283

Hideko and Zenzo Matsuyama Scholarships, (U) 168, (G) 568

High School Senior Scholarships of the Japanese American Citizens League, (U) 169

Hill Scholarship. *See* Oliver W. Hill Scholarship, entry (G) 696

Hilliard Scholarship. *See* Hattie J. Hilliard Scholarship, entry (U) 161

Hillis Clark Martin & Peterson Diversity Fellowship, (G) 569

Hilton APIASF Scholarships, (U) 170

Hirabayashi Memorial Scholarship. *See* Japanese American Veterans Association Memorial Scholarships, entries (U) 192, (G) 592

Hiratsuka Memorial Scholarship. *See* Aiko Susanna Tashiro Hiratsuka Memorial Scholarship, entry (U) 14

Hiroko Fujita and Paul Fukami Scholarship. *See* NSRCF Scholarships, entry (U) 283

Hiroshi (Nick) Nakagawa Scholarship. *See* Arizona Chapter Japanese American Citizens League Scholarships, entry (U) 33

Hisaye Hamaoka Mochijuki Scholarship. *See* NSRCF Scholarships, entry (U) 283

Hispanic, Asian, Native American Scholarships. *See* HANA Scholarships, entries (U) 158, (G) 559

H-Mart Leadership Scholarship, (U) 171, (G) 570

Hmong American Education Fund Scholarships, (U) 172

Hmong American Partnership Leadership Scholarships, (U) 173

Hmong American Partnership Non-traditional Student Scholarships, (U) 174

Ho Memorial Scholarship. *See* OCA-WI Merit Scholarships, entry (U) 286

Hoch Distinguished Service Award. *See* Paul Hoch Distinguished Service Award, entry (P) 913

Holly A. Cornell Scholarship, (G) 571

Holy Family Memorial Scholarship Program, (U) 175

Hong Memorial Scholarship. *See* Chinese American Citizens Alliance Foundation Scholarships, entry (U) 81

Honjo Scholarship, (G) 572

Honorable Thomas Tang International Moot Court Competition Scholarships, (G) 573

Horace and Susie Revels Cayton Scholarship. *See* Puget Sound Chapter/Horace and Susie Revels Cayton Scholarship, entry (U) 307

Howard Mayer Brown Fellowship, (G) 574

Howell Scholarship. *See* APF/COGDOP Graduate Research Scholarships, entry (G) 441

Hoyt, Jr. Fellowship. *See* Bishop Thomas Hoyt, Jr. Fellowship, entry (G) 467

Hsi Memorial Scholarship. *See* OCA-WI Merit Scholarships, entry (U) 286

Hsiao Memorial Economics Scholarship, (G) 575

Huan Lin Cheng Memorial Scholarship. *See* Chinese American Citizens Alliance Foundation Scholarships, entry (U) 81

Hubble Fellowships, (P) 874

Hugh J. Andersen Memorial Scholarships, (G) 576

Hyatt Hotels Fund for Minority Lodging Management. *See* AHLEF/Hyatt Hotels Fund for Minority Lodging Management Students, entry (U) 12

Hyun Memorial Scholarships. *See* Bong Hak Hyun Memorial Scholarships, entries (U) 59, (G) 469

Hyundai Scholarship. *See* KSEA Undergraduate Scholarships, entry (U) 212

Hyunsoo Kim Scholarship. *See* KSEA Undergraduate Scholarships, entry (U) 212

U–Undergraduates   **G–Graduate Students**   **P–Professionals/Postdoctorates**

Masao and Sumako Itano Memorial Scholarship. *See* High School Senior Scholarships of the Japanese American Citizens League, entry (U) 169

Masaoka Scholarship. *See* Japanese American Veterans Association Memorial Scholarships, entries (U) 192, (G) 592

MassMutual Scholars Program, (U) 239

Matarazzo Scholarship. *See* APF/COGDOP Graduate Research Scholarships, entry (G) 441

Matsui Annual Writing Competition. *See* Robert T. Matsui Annual Writing Competition, entry (G) 727

Matsui Scholarship. *See* Japanese American Veterans Association Memorial Scholarships, entries (U) 192, (G) 592

Matsumoto Scholarship. *See* NSRCF Scholarships, entry (U) 283

Matsushita Memorial Scholarship Fund. *See* Eiichi Matsushita Memorial Scholarship Fund, entry (G) 524

Matsuyama Scholarships. *See* Hideko and Zenzo Matsuyama Scholarships, entries (U) 168, (G) 568

Matt Fong Asian Americans in Public Finance Scholarships, (U) 240

Maurice Goldhaber Distinguished Fellowships. *See* Gertrude and Maurice Goldhaber Distinguished Fellowships, entry (P) 864

Max Kapp Award. *See* Olympia Brown and Max Kapp Award, entry (G) 697

Mayes Scholarship. *See* John A. Mayes Scholarship, entry (G) 599

Mayme Noda Scholarship. *See* NSRCF Scholarships, entry (U) 283

McAndrews Diversity in Patent Law Fellowship, (G) 646

McClellan Scholarship. *See* Surety and Fidelity Industry Scholarship Program, entry (U) 348

McCormick Communications Scholarship for Underrepresented Students. *See* Larry W. McCormick Communications Scholarship for Underrepresented Students, entry (U) 221

McDermott Minority Scholarship, (G) 647

McGuigan Dissertation Award. *See* F.J. McGuigan Dissertation Award, entry (G) 540

McGuigan Early Career Investigator Research Prize. *See* F.J. McGuigan Early Career Investigator Research Prize, entry (P) 858

McJulien Minority Graduate Scholarship. *See* Patrick D. McJulien Minority Graduate Scholarship, entry (G) 703

McKay Scholarship Program. *See* Jim McKay Scholarship Program, entry (G) 597

McLendon Minority Postgraduate Scholarship Program. *See* John McLendon Memorial Minority Postgraduate Scholarship Award, entries (G) 601, (P) 881

Medical College of Wisconsin Diversity Summer Health-Related Research Education Program, (U) 241

Medical Library Association/National Library of Medicine Spectrum Scholarships. *See* MLA/NLM Spectrum Scholarships, entry (G) 669

Medical Library Association Scholarship for Minority Student, (G) 648

Medical Library Association Scholarship for Minority Students. *See* Medical Library Association Scholarship for Minority Student, entry (G) 648

Meekins Scholarship. *See* Phyllis G. Meekins Scholarship, entry (U) 302

Mehendale Graduate Student Best Abstract Award. *See* Dr. Harihara Mehendale Graduate Student Best Abstract Award, entry (G) 517

Meier Scholarship. *See* Benton-Meier Neuropsychology Scholarships, entry (G) 464

Mendenhall Fellowships. *See* Five College Fellowship Program, entry (G) 539

Mental Health and Substance Abuse Fellowship Program, (G) 649

Meriter Minority Health Careers Scholarship, (U) 242

Michael Baker Corporation Scholarship Program for Diversity in Engineering, (U) 243

Michi Nishiura Weglyn Scholarship. *See* NSRCF Scholarships, entry (U) 283

Michigan Steering Committee Minority Scholarships, (U) 244, (G) 650

Michihiko and Bernice Hayashida Scholarship. *See* NSRCF Scholarships, entry (U) 283

Mickey Williams Minority Student Scholarships. *See* PDEF Mickey Williams Minority Student Scholarships, entry (U) 297

Mid-America Chapter Scholarships, (U) 245, (G) 651

Mideastern Region Korean American Scholarships, (U) 246, (G) 652

Midwestern Region Korean American Scholarships, (U) 247, (G) 653

Mike and Etsu Masaoka Scholarship. *See* Japanese American Veterans Association Memorial Scholarships, entries (U) 192, (G) 592

Milbank Diversity Scholars Program, (G) 654

Miller Johnson West Michigan Diversity Law School Scholarship, (G) 655

Miller Nash Law Student Diversity Fellowship Program, (G) 656

Millon Award. *See* Theodore Millon Award in Personality Psychology, entry (P) 938

Milly Woodward Memorial Scholarship. *See* Northwest Journalists of Color Scholarship Awards, entry (U) 279

Mine and Gonsaku Ito Scholarship, (U) 248, (G) 657

Minerva Jean Falcon Hawai'i Scholarship. *See* Ambassador Minerva Jean Falcon Hawai'i Scholarship, entry (U) 20

Ming Y. Moy Memorial Scholarship. *See* Southern California Chinese Lawyers Association Scholarships, entry (G) 750

Minnesota Association for Korean Americans Scholarships, (U) 249

Minnesota Taiwanese American Community Scholarship Awards, (U) 250

Minorities in Cancer Research Jane Cook Wright Lectureship, (P) 896

Minorities in Government Finance Scholarship, (U) 251, (G) 658

Minorities in Hospitality Scholars Program, (U) 252

Minorities in Leadership Scholarship. *See* George Geng On Lee Minorities in Leadership Scholarship, entry (U) 152

Minority Faculty Development Scholarship Award in Physical Therapy, (G) 659, (P) 897

Minority Fellowships in Education Research, (G) 660

Minority LEAP Scholarships, (U) 253, (G) 661

Minority Medical Student Elective in HIV Psychiatry, (G) 662

Minority Medical Student Summer Externship in Addiction Psychiatry, (G) 663

Minority Medical Student Summer Mentoring Program, (G) 664

Minority Nurse Magazine Scholarship Program, (U) 254, (G) 665

Minority Scholarship Award for Academic Excellence in Physical Therapy, (U) 255

Minority Scholarship in Classics and Classical Archaeology, (U) 256

Minority Teachers of Illinois Scholarship Program, (U) 257, (G) 666

Minoru Yasui Memorial Scholarship, (G) 667

U–Undergraduates   G–Graduate Students   P–Professionals/Postdoctorates

U–Undergraduates   **G–Graduate Students**   **P–Professionals/Postdoctorates**

Shirey Memorial Scholarship. *See* Japanese American Veterans Association Memorial Scholarships, entries (U) 192, (G) 592

Shizue Naka Scholarship. *See* NSRCF Scholarships, entry (U) 283

Shizuko Kato Memorial Scholarship. *See* Magoichi and Shizuko Kato Memorial Scholarship, entry (G) 640

Sho Sato Memorial Scholarship. *See* Law Scholarships of the Japanese American Citizens League, entry (G) 632

Shoon Kyung Kim Scholarship. *See* KSEA Undergraduate Scholarships, entry (U) 212

Shrader Diversity Scholarships. *See* Ralph W. Shrader Diversity Scholarships, entry (G) 718

Shri Ram Arora Award, (G) 744, (P) 935

Shroff Memorial Award. *See* Indian American Scholarship Fund Merit Scholarships, entry (U) 179

Shui Kuen and Allen Chin Scholarship, (U) 333

Sidley Diversity and Inclusion Scholarship, (G) 745

Silverman Minority Student Award. *See* Marcia Silverman Minority Student Award, entry (U) 235

Simpson RTDNF Scholarship. *See* RTDNF/Carole Simpson Scholarship, entry (U) 318

Singh Memorial Scholarship. *See* Kala Singh Memorial Scholarship, entry (G) 611

Singh Postdoctoral Fellow/Young Investigator Best Abstract Award. *See* Dr. Dharm Singh Postdoctoral Fellow/Young Investigator Best Abstract Award, entry (P) 845

Sisson Award. *See* Geological Society of America Graduate Student Research Grants, entry (G) 551

Siy Scholarship. *See* Arsenio and Co Bit Siy Scholarship, entry (U) 34

Smith Memorial Scholarship. *See* Mabel Smith Memorial Scholarship, entry (U) 232

Smith Scholarship. *See* Nora Stone Smith Scholarship, entry (U) 275, 314

Smith Scholarships. *See* John T. Smith Scholarships, entry (U) 196

Smithsonian Minority Awards Program, (U) 334, (G) 746

Snavely, Jr. Cascadia Research Fund Award. *See* Geological Society of America Graduate Student Research Grants, entry (G) 551

Social, Behavioral, and Economic Sciences Doctoral Dissertation Research Improvement Grants. *See* SBE Doctoral Dissertation Research Improvement Grants, entry (G) 735

Society for the Study of Social Problems Racial/Ethnic Minority Graduate Scholarship. *See* SSSP Racial/Ethnic Minority Graduate Scholarship, entry (G) 756

Society of Pediatric Psychology Diversity Research Grant, (G) 747, (P) 936

Sodexo Foundation APIASF Scholarship, (U) 335

Sonoda Memorial Scholarship. *See* Dr. Kiyoshi Sonoda Memorial Scholarship, entry (G) 518

Soo Yuen Benevolent Association Scholarships, (U) 336

Soongook Choi Scholarships, (G) 748

South Asian Journalists Association Scholarships. *See* SAJA Scholarships, entries (U) 321, (G) 734

South Asian Journalists Association Student Journalism Awards, (U) 337, (G) 749

Southern California Chinese Lawyers Association Scholarships, (G) 750

Southern Region Korean American Scholarships, (U) 338, (G) 751

Southern Regional Education Board Dissertation Awards, (G) 752

Southern Regional Education Board Doctoral Awards. *See* SREB Doctoral Awards, entry (G) 755

Southwestern Region Korean American Scholarships, (U) 339, (G) 753

Sparks Early Career Grant. *See* John and Polly Sparks Early Career Grant, entry (P) 880

Spaulding Memorial Scholarships. *See* Sandra R. Spaulding Memorial Scholarships, entry (U) 323

Spectrum Scholarship Program. *See* ALA Spectrum Scholarship Program, entry (G) 420

SPIE Scholarship Program, (U) 340, (G) 754

Spitzer Fellowship. *See* Hubble Fellowships, entry (P) 874

Spurlock Research Fellowship in Substance Abuse and Addiction for Minority Medical Students. *See* Jeanne Spurlock Research Fellowship in Substance Abuse and Addiction for Minority Medical Students, entry (G) 596

SREB Doctoral Awards, (G) 755

SSSP Racial/Ethnic Minority Graduate Scholarship, (G) 756

Stafford Scholarship in Architecture. *See* Gordon Stafford Scholarship in Architecture, entries (U) 156, (G) 554

Stan Beck Fellowship, (U) 341, (G) 757

Stanford Chen Internship Grants, (U) 342, (G) 758

Stanford Memorial WLMA Scholarship. *See* John Stanford Memorial WLMA Scholarship, entry (G) 602

Stanley and Mary Mu Scholarship. *See* Chinese American Citizens Alliance Foundation Scholarships, entry (U) 81

Stanley Minority and International Scholarship. *See* Alan Compton and Bob Stanley Minority and International Scholarship, entry (U) 15

STAR Fellowships for Graduate Environmental Study, (G) 759

State Council on Adapted Physical Education Cultural Diversity Student Scholarship, (U) 343

Stearns Fellowship Award. *See* Geological Society of America Graduate Student Research Grants, entry (G) 551

Stephen K. Tamura Scholarship. *See* Japanese American Bar Association Educational Foundation Scholarships, entry (G) 591

Stoel Rives First-Year Diversity Fellowships, (G) 760

Stone Research Fellowship. *See* Betty Lea Stone Research Fellowship, entry (G) 465

Stone Scholarship. *See* NSRCF Scholarships, entry (U) 283

Strait Minority Scholarship Endowment. *See* George A. Strait Minority Scholarship Endowment, entries (G) 552, (P) 862

Stratton/Tipton Scholarships, (U) 344

Student Affiliates in School Psychology Diversity Scholarships, (G) 761

Student Journalism Awards. *See* South Asian Journalists Association Student Journalism Awards, entries (U) 337, (G) 749

Student Opportunity Scholarships of the Presbyterian Church (USA), (U) 345

Substance Abuse and Mental Health Services Minority Fellowship Program. *See* APA/SAMHSA Minority Fellowship Program, entry (P) 815

Substance Abuse Fellowship Program. *See* APA Substance Abuse Fellowship Program, entry (P) 816

Sue Scholarship. *See* Chinese American Citizens Alliance Foundation Scholarships, entry (U) 81

Sumako Itano Memorial Scholarship. *See* High School Senior Scholarships of the Japanese American Citizens League, entry (U) 169

Summer Research Opportunities Program (SROP), (U) 346

Summer Undergraduate Research Fellowships in Organic Chemistry, (U) 347

SUNY Graduate Diversity Fellowship Program, (G) 762

U–Undergraduates   **G–Graduate Students**   **P–Professionals/Postdoctorates**

Sponsoring Organization Index

The Sponsoring Organization Index makes it easy to identify agencies that offer financial aid to Asian Americans. In this index, the sponsoring organizations are listed alphabetically, word by word. In addition, we've used an alphabetical code (within parentheses) to help you identify the intended recipients of the funding offered by the organizations: U = Undergraduates; G = Graduate Students; P = Professionals/Postdoctorates. For example, if the name of a sponsoring organization is followed by (U) 241, a program sponsored by that organization is described in the Undergraduate chapter, in entry 241. If that sponsoring organization's name is followed by another entry number—for example, (G) 915—the same or a different program sponsored by that organization is described in the Professionals/Postdoctorates chapter, in entry 915. Remember: the numbers cited here refer to program entry numbers, not to page numbers in the book.

U–Undergraduates   **G–Graduate Students**   **P–Professionals/Postdoctorates**

B

Baker, Donelson, Bearman, Caldwell & Berkowitz, P.C., (G) 459

BakerHostetler LLP, (G) 460, 704

Banner & Witcoff, Ltd., (G) 514

Baptist Communicators Association, (U) 15

Battelle Memorial Institute, (P) 864

Bay Area Lawyers for Individual Freedom, (G) 439

BBCN Bank, (U) 55

Bill and Melinda Gates Foundation, (U) 150

Black Data Processing Associates, (U) 123

Boehringer Ingelheim Pharmaceuticals, Inc., (G) 414

Booz Allen Hamilton, (G) 718

Brookhaven National Laboratory, (P) 864

Brown and Caldwell, (U) 61, (G) 471

Bullivant Houser Bailey PC, (G) 472

Butler Rubin Saltarelli & Boyd LLP, (G) 473

C

California Association for Health, Physical Education, Recreation and Dance, (U) 187, 343, (G) 589

California Dietetic Association, (U) 63, 73, 95, (G) 513, (P) 843

California Japanese American Alumni Association, (U) 64, (G) 476

California Library Association, (G) 491

California Nurses Association, (U) 323

California School Library Association, (U) 224, (G) 633

California State University. Office of the Chancellor, (G) 477

California Teachers Association, (U) 98, (G) 500, (P) 829

Cambodian Health Professionals Association of America, (U) 65

Capstone Corporation, (U) 69

Capture the Dream, Inc., (U) 152

Cargill, Inc., (U) 70

CDC Small Business Finance, (U) 35

Center for Advanced Study in the Behavioral Sciences, (P) 823

Center for Asian American Media, (P) 824, 892, 922

CH2M Hill, (G) 483, 571

Chen Foundation, (U) 77

Chen-Pai Lee Scholarship Fund, (U) 78

Chinese American Association of Minnesota, (U) 79, (G) 485

Chinese American Citizens Alliance, (U) 80, 383-384

Chinese American Citizens Alliance Foundation, (U) 81

Chinese American Citizens Alliance. Portland Lodge, (U) 149

Chinese American Librarians Association, (G) 486, 743, (P) 930

Chinese American Medical Society, (G) 487-488

Chinese American Physicians Society, (G) 489

Chinese Institute of Engineers/USA. Seattle Chapter, (U) 85

Choice Hotels International, (U) 252

Christian Church (Disciples of Christ), (G) 503, 748

Christian Reformed Church, (U) 97, (G) 499

Cincinnati Children's Hospital Medical Center, (U) 398, (G) 795

City University of New York. Bernard M. Baruch College, (G) 677, (P) 901

Cleveland Foundation, (U) 48, (P) 814

Coca-Cola Foundation, (U) 86

Colgate-Palmolive Company, (U) 88

College Now Greater Cleveland, Inc., (U) 231

Colorado Education Association, (U) 74

Colorado Educational Services and Development Association, (U) 89

Columbia University College of Physicians and Surgeons, (P) 871

Columbia University. Graduate School of Journalism, (P) 914

Committee on Institutional Cooperation, (U) 346

Communities-Adolescents-Nutrition-Fitness, (U) 67-68, (G) 478

Community Foundation of Greater New Britain, (U) 17

Community Foundation of Sarasota County, (G) 557

Conference of Minority Transportation Officials, (U) 50, 72, 148, 230, 293-294, 316, 358, 361, (G) 480, 548, 639, 729, 769, 772

Connecticut Administrators of Programs for English Language Learners, (U) 93

Connecticut Education Association, (U) 90-91

Connecticut Office of Financial and Academic Affairs for Higher Education, (U) 92, 392

Connecticut Teachers of English to Speakers of Other Languages, (U) 93

Consortium for Faculty Diversity at Liberal Arts Colleges, (G) 507, (P) 918

Constangy, Brooks & Smith LLC, (G) 494

Construction Management Association of America, (U) 147, (G) 547

Cooley LLP, (G) 496

Corporation for Public Broadcasting, (P) 824

Council for International Cooperation, (U) 84

Council on Social Work Education, (U) 71, (G) 479, 649

Courage Center, (U) 125

D

Darden Restaurants, (U) 75, 101, (G) 482

David Evans and Associates, Inc., (U) 102

Davis Wright Tremaine LLP, (G) 504

D&D Unlimited, (U) 370

DDB Worldwide, (U) 57, (G) 466

Deloitte LLP, (U) 244, (G) 650

Delta Kappa Gamma Society International. Alpha Kappa State Organization, (U) 160

Dickstein Shapiro LLP, (G) 505

Dinsmore & Shohl LLP, (G) 506

Djerassi Resident Artists Program, (P) 863

DLA Piper US LLP, (G) 546

Dong Ji Hoi Society, (U) 113

Dorsey & Whitney LLP, (G) 516

DRI-The Voice of the Defense Bar, (G) 521

E

East Ohio United Methodist Foundation, (U) 364, (G) 774

Edgar Allan Poe Literary Society, (U) 105

Educational Foundation for Women in Accounting, (U) 261, (G) 671

Educational Testing Service, (P) 856

Eli Lilly and Company, (U) 123

Elsevier Science Ltd., (P) 850-851

Embassy of the Republic of Korea in the USA, (U) 208, (G) 624

Enterprise Holdings, (U) 370

Entertainment Software Association, (U) 126

Entomological Society of America, (U) 341, (G) 757

Epilepsy Foundation, (U) 56, (G) 462, 561, 713, (P) 818, 853, 919, 924

Episcopal Church Center, (G) 529

Ernst & Young LLP, (U) 127, 244, (G) 650

Evangelical Lutheran Church in America, (G) 524

ExxonMobil Corporation, (U) 370

U–Undergraduates   **G–Graduate Students**   **P–Professionals/Postdoctorates**

U–Undergraduates   **G–Graduate Students**   **P–Professionals/Postdoctorates**

Kansas Board of Regents, (U) 199
Kappa Omicron Nu, (P) 899, 902
Katten Muchin Rosenman LLP, (G) 613
KATU-TV, (U) 203
Kegler, Brown, Hill & Ritter, (G) 614
Kentucky Association of Vocational Education Special Needs Personnel, (U) 344
Kentucky Community and Technical College System, (U) 196
Kentucky Department of Education, (U) 206, (G) 617
Kentucky Library Association, (U) 205, (G) 616
Kentucky United Methodist Foundation, (U) 364, (G) 774
Kimball International, Inc., (U) 207
King & Spalding, (G) 618
Kirkland & Ellis LLP, (G) 619
Korean American Bar Association of Southern California, (G) 615
Korean American Bar Association of Washington, (G) 620
Korean American Christian Scholarship Foundation of Greater Washington, (G) 621
Korean American Librarians and Information Professionals Association, (G) 622
Korean American Medical Association, (G) 623
Korean American Scholarship Foundation. Eastern Region, (U) 118, (G) 522
Korean American Scholarship Foundation. Mideastern Region, (U) 246, (G) 652
Korean American Scholarship Foundation. Midwestern Region, (U) 247, (G) 653
Korean American Scholarship Foundation. Northeastern Region, (U) 277, (G) 688
Korean American Scholarship Foundation. Southern Region, (U) 338, (G) 751
Korean American Scholarship Foundation. Southwestern Region, (U) 339, (G) 753
Korean American Scholarship Foundation. Western Region, (U) 395, (G) 792
Korean Institute of Toxicology, (G) 626, (P) 888
Korean Nurses Association of Southern California, (U) 209, (G) 625, (P) 887
Korean-American Adventist Scholarships, (U) 211, (G) 627
Korean-American Scientists and Engineers Association, (U) 83, 212, (G) 628
KPMG LLP, (U) 244, (G) 650

L
Ladies Professional Golf Association, (U) 302
Lagrant Foundation, (U) 214, (G) 629
Landmark Media Enterprises LLC, (U) 215
Landscape Architecture Foundation, (U) 120
Lane Powell PC, (G) 553
Lao American New Generation, Inc., (U) 217
Lao American Women Association, (U) 218, 380
Laotian American Scholarship Foundation, Inc., (U) 219
Latham & Watkins LLP, (G) 630
Latino Media Association. Seattle Chapter, (U) 279
LeClairRyan, (G) 696
Lee & Low Books, (P) 903-904
Legacy Park Foundation, (U) 225
Library Systems & Services, Inc., (G) 635
Lilly Endowment, Inc., (P) 857
Lim, Ruger & Kim, (G) 672
LIN Television Corporation, (U) 227

Lloyd G. Balfour Foundation, (G) 461
Louisville Institute, (P) 857
LTK Engineering Services, (U) 230, (G) 639
Lubrizol Corporation, (U) 231
The Lullaby Guild, Inc., (U) 221

M
Macy's, (U) 153
Marathon Oil Corporation, (U) 234, (G) 641
Marine Biological Laboratory, (P) 848
Massachusetts Mutual Life Insurance Company, (U) 239, (G) 714
Mayday Fund, (G) 702
Mayo Clinic, (U) 282, (G) 693
McAndrews, Held & Malloy, Ltd., (G) 646
McDermott Will & Emery, (G) 647
Medical College of Wisconsin, (U) 241
Medical Library Association, (G) 648, 669
Merck and Company, Inc., (U) 347
Meriter Health Services, (U) 242
Michael Baker Corporation, (U) 243
Michigan Association of Certified Public Accountants, (U) 244, (G) 650
Midwest Archives Conference, (G) 444
Midwest Sociological Society, (G) 435
Milbank, Tweed, Hadley & McCloy LLP, (G) 654
Miller Nash LLP, (G) 656
The Minerals, Metals & Materials Society, (G) 744, (P) 935
Minnesota Association for Korean Americans, (U) 249
Minnesota Broadcasters Association, (U) 188
Minority Corporate Counsel Association, (G) 638
Minority Educational Foundation of the United States of America, (U) 38
Minority Nurse Magazine, (U) 254, (G) 665
Missouri Department of Higher Education, (U) 259
Missouri Society of Certified Public Accountants, (U) 253, (G) 661
Missouri United Methodist Foundation, (U) 364, (G) 774
Mitsui USA, (G) 593, (P) 878
Montebello Plymouth Congregational Church, (U) 357, (G) 768
Moss Adams LLP, (U) 261, (G) 671
Ms. JD, (G) 437
Mutual of Omaha, (U) 262

N
Nashville Area United Methodist Foundation, (U) 364, (G) 774
National Asian Pacific American Bar Association, (G) 438, 468, 573, 672, 776
National Association of Asian American Professionals, (U) 264
National Association of Asian American Professionals. Phoenix Chapter, (U) 301
National Association of Asian American Professionals. Seattle Chapter, (G) 741
National Association of Black Journalists. Seattle Chapter, (U) 279
National Association of Collegiate Directors of Athletics, (G) 601, (P) 881
National Association of Geoscience Teachers, (U) 265
National Association of School Psychologists, (G) 673
National Association of Teacher Educators for Family and Consumer Sciences, (G) 532
National Athletic Trainers' Association, (G) 599
National Black MBA Association. Central Florida Chapter, (U) 75, (G) 482

U–Undergraduates   **G–Graduate Students**   **P–Professionals/Postdoctorates**

U–Undergraduates   **G–Graduate Students**   **P–Professionals/Postdoctorates**

Residency Index

Some programs listed in this book are set aside for Asian Americans who are residents of a particular state or region. Others are open to applicants wherever they may live. The Residency Index will help you pinpoint programs available in your area as well as programs that have no residency restrictions at all (these are listed under the term "United States"). To use this index, look up the geographic areas that apply to you (always check the listings under "United States"), jot down the entry numbers listed for the recipient level that applies to you (Undergraduates, Graduate Students, or Professionals/Postdoctorates), and use those numbers to find the program descriptions in the directory. To help you in your search, we've provided some "see" and "see also" references in the index entries. Remember: the numbers cited here refer to program entry numbers, not to page numbers in the book.

A

Alameda County, California: **Undergraduates,** 55. *See also* California

Alaska: **Undergraduates,** 52. *See also* Northwestern states; United States

Alexandria, Virginia: **Undergraduates,** 389. *See also* Virginia

American Samoa: **Undergraduates,** 53, 86, 101, 135, 146, 170, 268, 324, 335, 352, 363, 373, 393. *See also* United States territories

Arizona: **Undergraduates,** 28, 33, 35, 301. *See also* United States

Arkansas: **Undergraduates,** 354; **Graduate Students,** 766. *See also* United States

Arlington County, Virginia: **Undergraduates,** 389. *See also* Virginia

B

Belmont County, Ohio: **Undergraduates,** 351. *See also* Ohio

Bergen County, New Jersey: **Undergraduates,** 55. *See also* New Jersey

Bronx County, New York: **Undergraduates,** 55. *See also* New York

Bronx, New York. *See* Bronx County, New York

Brooklyn, New York. *See* Kings County, New York

Burnett County, Wisconsin: **Undergraduates,** 125. *See also* Wisconsin

C

California: **Undergraduates,** 28, 35, 41-42, 52, 63-64, 67-68, 73, 77, 81-82, 95, 98, 107, 152, 156, 187, 209, 220, 224, 323, 336, 343, 363, 373; **Graduate Students,** 457, 476, 478, 491, 500, 509, 513, 554, 589, 625, 633; **Professionals/Postdoctorates,** 829, 843, 887. *See also* United States

California, southern: **Graduate Students,** 493, 715. *See also* California

Chicago, Illinois: **Undergraduates,** 396. *See also* Illinois

Clark County, Washington: **Undergraduates,** 43, 149. *See also* Washington

Colorado: **Undergraduates,** 28, 74, 89, 104, 130-131. *See also* United States

Columbiana County, Ohio: **Undergraduates,** 351. *See also* Ohio

Connecticut: **Undergraduates,** 17, 90-91, 93, 134, 160, 182, 189, 217, 319; **Graduate Students,** 534, 733. *See also* New England states; Northeastern states; United States

Cook County, Illinois: **Undergraduates,** 55. *See also* Illinois

D

Delaware: **Undergraduates,** 215, 319; **Graduate Students,** 733. *See also* Northeastern states; Southeastern states; United States

Denver, Colorado: **Undergraduates,** 396. *See also* Colorado

District of Columbia. *See* Washington, D.C.

DuPage County, Illinois: **Undergraduates,** 55. *See also* Illinois

F

Fairfax County, Virginia: **Undergraduates,** 389. *See also* Virginia

Florida: **Undergraduates,** 96, 141-142, 373; **Graduate Students,** 541. *See also* Southeastern states; United States

Frederick County, Maryland: **Undergraduates,** 389. *See also* Maryland

G

Georgia: **Undergraduates,** 28, 176, 179. *See also* Southeastern states; United States

Guam: **Undergraduates,** 53, 86, 101, 135, 146, 170, 234, 239, 268, 324, 335, 352, 363, 373, 393; **Graduate Students,** 493, 571, 641. *See also* United States territories

H

Harbor City, California. *See* Los Angeles, California

Harrison County, Ohio: **Undergraduates,** 351. *See also* Ohio

Tenability Index

Some programs listed in this book can be used only in specific cities, counties, states, or regions. Others may be used anywhere in the United States. The Tenability Index will help you locate funding that is restricted to a specific area as well as funding that has no tenability restrictions (these are listed under the term "United States"). To use this index, look up the geographic areas where you'd like to go (always check the listings under "United States"), jot down the entry numbers listed for the recipient group that represents you (Undergraduates, Graduate Students, Professionals/Postdoctorates), and use those numbers to find the program descriptions in the directory. To help you in your search, we've provided some "see" and "see also" references in the index entries. Remember: the numbers cited here refer to program entry numbers, not to page numbers in the book.

A

Alabama: **Undergraduates,** 36, 338; **Graduate Students,** 494, 751-752, 755. *See also* United States; names of specific cities and counties

Alaska: **Undergraduates,** 395; **Graduate Students,** 792. *See also* United States; names of specific cities

Allentown, Pennsylvania: **Graduate Students,** 507; **Professionals/Postdoctorates,** 918. *See also* Pennsylvania

Amherst, Massachusetts: **Undergraduates,** 122; **Graduate Students,** 523, 539. *See also* Massachusetts

Anchorage, Alaska: **Graduate Students,** 760. *See also* Alaska

Ann Arbor, Michigan: **Undergraduates,** 346; **Professionals/Postdoctorates,** 926, 933. *See also* Michigan

Appleton, Wisconsin: **Graduate Students,** 507; **Professionals/Postdoctorates,** 918. *See also* Wisconsin

Arizona: **Undergraduates,** 35, 102, 301, 395; **Graduate Students,** 792. *See also* United States; names of specific cities and counties

Arkansas: **Undergraduates,** 339, 354; **Graduate Students,** 752-753, 755, 766. *See also* United States; names of specific cities and counties

Athens, Georgia: **Graduate Students,** 800. *See also* Georgia

Atlanta, Georgia: **Undergraduates,** 57, 289, 310; **Graduate Students,** 466, 537, 618, 698, 719, 773, 800. *See also* Georgia

Austin, Texas: **Undergraduates,** 57, 289; **Graduate Students,** 466, 618, 698, 783. *See also* Texas

B

Baltimore, Maryland: **Graduate Students,** 507, 800; **Professionals/Postdoctorates,** 918. *See also* Maryland

Baton Rouge, Louisiana: **Graduate Students,** 773. *See also* Louisiana

Berkeley, California: **Professionals/Postdoctorates,** 927, 933. *See also* California

Big Rapids, Michigan: **Undergraduates,** 304. *See also* Michigan

Blacksburg, Virginia: **Undergraduates,** 310; **Graduate Students,** 719. *See also* Virginia

Boise, Idaho: **Graduate Students,** 760. *See also* Idaho

Boston, Massachusetts: **Undergraduates,** 122; **Graduate Students,** 496, 523, 537, 647; **Professionals/Postdoctorates,** 869-870. *See also* Massachusetts

Boulder, Colorado: **Graduate Students,** 533; **Professionals/Postdoctorates,** 900. *See also* Colorado

Bronx, New York

Brooklyn, New York

Broomfield, Colorado: **Graduate Students,** 496. *See also* Colorado

Brunswick, Maine: **Graduate Students,** 507; **Professionals/Postdoctorates,** 918. *See also* Maine

Bryn Mawr, Pennsylvania: **Graduate Students,** 507; **Professionals/Postdoctorates,** 918. *See also* Pennsylvania

Buies Creek, North Carolina: **Undergraduates,** 304. *See also* North Carolina

C

California: **Undergraduates,** 3, 35, 41, 64, 67-68, 77, 81-82, 98, 102, 107, 187, 209, 220, 224, 240, 248, 323, 343, 363, 395; **Graduate Students,** 409, 475-476, 478, 494, 500, 509, 589, 625, 633, 657, 696, 792; **Professionals/Postdoctorates,** 829, 887. *See also* United States; names of specific cities and counties

California, northern: **Undergraduates,** 278; **Graduate Students,** 439, 448, 455, 647, 689, 780. *See also* California

California, southern: **Undergraduates,** 37, 394; **Graduate Students,** 447, 615, 750, 791. *See also* California

Cambridge, Massachusetts: **Graduate Students,** 463; **Professionals/Postdoctorates,** 819, 917, 923, 927, 933. *See also* Massachusetts

Carlisle, Pennsylvania: **Graduate Students,** 507; **Professionals/Postdoctorates,** 918. *See also* Pennsylvania

Champaign, Illinois: **Undergraduates,** 346. *See also* Illinois

Subject Index

There are hundreds of specific subject fields covered in this directory. Use the Subject Index to identify these topics, as well as the recipient level supported (Undergraduates, Graduate Students, or Professionals/Postdoctorates) by the available funding programs. To help you pinpoint your search, we've included many "see" and "see also" references. Since a large number of programs are not restricted by subject, be sure to check the references listed under the "General programs" heading in the subject index (in addition to the specific terms that directly relate to your interest areas); hundreds of funding opportunities are listed there that can be used to support activities in any subject area   although the programs may be restricted in other ways. Remember: the numbers cited in this index refer to program entry numbers, not to page numbers in the book.

Calendar Index

Since most funding programs have specific deadline dates, some may have already closed by the time you begin to look for money. You can use the Calendar Index to identify which programs are still open. To do that, go to the recipient category (Undergraduates, Graduate Students, or Professionals/Postdoctorates) that interests you, think about when you'll be able to complete your application forms, go to the appropriate months, jot down the entry numbers listed there, and use those numbers to find the program descriptions in the directory. Keep in mind that the numbers cited here refer to program entry numbers, not to page numbers in the book.

Undergraduates:

January: 19, 27, 41, 44, 53, 55, 78, 86, 88, 101, 122, 135, 146, 150, 170, 180, 182, 195, 209, 215, 233, 244, 252, 254, 258, 268, 282, 317, 324, 334-336, 343, 352, 363, 373, 393

February: 20-21, 28-29, 33, 42, 52, 60, 62, 80, 94, 98, 100, 105, 109, 116, 120, 138, 144, 158-159, 167-169, 173-174, 186, 202, 210, 214, 221-222, 228, 241, 248, 251, 253, 257, 260, 265-266, 275, 326, 340, 346-347, 356, 359-360, 364-365, 382, 399, 406

March: 4, 7, 9-10, 14-16, 34, 36, 40, 43, 47, 56, 67-69, 74, 83, 87, 89, 97, 107, 112, 114, 128, 137, 139-140, 143, 149, 160, 166, 172, 178, 183-185, 191, 198, 200-201, 204, 212-213, 220, 226-227, 231, 236-237, 240, 267, 273-274, 276, 281, 283, 286-288, 296, 298-299, 320-322, 327, 332-333, 337, 370-371, 374-375, 381, 385-388, 390-391, 404, 408

April: 1-2, 11-12, 30, 32, 38-39, 48, 58, 61, 63-64, 73, 77, 90-91, 93, 95, 99, 102, 104, 130-132, 134, 151, 157, 179, 192, 199, 203, 218, 225, 238, 242-243, 250, 261, 270, 279, 284-285, 290-291, 297, 307, 310, 312, 329-330, 342, 344, 348, 351, 353, 367-369, 380, 383-384, 389, 398, 400

May: 5, 8, 13, 35, 37, 49-50, 66, 70-72, 82, 84, 111, 115, 119, 125-127, 133, 141, 148, 161-162, 176, 189, 223-224, 230, 232, 239, 271, 292-294, 301-302, 305-306, 309, 314, 316, 318, 338, 345, 354, 357-358, 361, 376-377

June: 81, 85, 110, 113, 147, 156, 188, 194, 197, 205, 208, 211, 235, 259, 272, 277, 319, 339, 341, 379

July: 96, 118, 123, 129, 142, 152, 163, 219, 245, 247, 269, 280, 303, 311, 315, 323, 395

August: 24, 54, 246, 350, 394

September: 23, 25, 45, 117, 190, 234, 249, 349, 407

October: 3, 6, 17-18, 57, 75-76, 92, 103, 136, 145, 155, 181, 262, 278, 355, 378, 392, 396

November: 31, 46, 51, 59, 106, 108, 153-154, 164-165, 171, 187, 193, 216, 229, 255, 295, 300, 308, 313, 328, 331, 366, 372, 397, 405

December: 22, 79, 256, 264

Any time: 121, 177

Deadline not specified: 26, 65, 124, 175, 196, 206-207, 217, 263, 289, 304, 325, 362, 401-403

Graduate Students:

January: 429, 431, 435, 445, 448, 463, 465, 472, 481, 484, 504, 511, 516, 523, 527, 538-539, 541, 544, 551, 569, 571, 582, 591, 597, 600, 609, 614, 620, 625-626, 644, 646, 650, 656, 665, 668, 693, 702, 704, 707, 712, 720, 739, 742, 746, 756, 760, 775, 783, 804

February: 411, 417-418, 420, 423-424, 432, 437, 442, 444, 457-458, 470, 477, 489, 492, 497, 500, 520, 525, 536-537, 543, 559, 565-566, 568, 572, 586, 588, 596, 598-599, 606-607, 629, 631, 635, 649, 657-658, 661, 663-664, 666, 669-670, 677, 695, 718, 736, 754, 770-771, 774, 781, 787, 790

March: 412, 421-422, 449, 455, 462, 478, 490, 495, 499, 503, 509, 518, 531, 549, 552, 561, 564, 579-580, 587, 615, 622, 628, 632, 640, 642, 655, 662, 667, 682, 684-685, 687, 691, 699, 708, 717, 724, 728, 734, 737, 748-750, 752, 755, 778, 788-789, 803

April: 410, 443, 450-451, 454, 456, 471, 476, 486-488, 501-502, 513, 529-530, 534-535, 542, 558, 567, 581, 583-584, 592, 601-603, 645, 671, 680, 686, 694, 696-697, 700, 715, 719, 721-722, 730, 732, 738, 743, 758, 763, 794-796

May: 413-416, 419, 447, 464, 479-480, 498, 521, 540, 548, 555, 605, 610, 623, 633, 636, 638-639, 710, 726, 729, 741, 751, 766, 768-769, 772, 782, 784, 800

June: 436, 441, 459, 475, 496, 515, 547, 554, 604, 611, 616, 624, 627, 683, 688, 716, 727, 733, 744, 753, 757, 777, 780, 786, 798

July: 491, 522, 557, 560, 651, 653, 679, 703, 711, 792

August: 427, 433, 493, 553, 575, 612, 618-619, 652, 654, 676, 713, 723, 745, 765, 791

September: 428, 434, 438-439, 452, 468, 505-506, 524, 528, 533, 556, 573, 576, 590, 608, 613, 630, 637, 641, 672, 740, 747, 764, 776, 797, 802

October: 409, 430, 446, 460-461, 466-467, 482, 507, 514, 532, 545, 577, 585, 647, 673, 675, 681, 689-690, 701, 714, 731, 767, 773, 779, 785

November: 469, 483, 494, 508, 510, 526, 550, 562-563, 570, 574, 589, 594, 634, 643, 648, 659-660, 678, 692, 706, 709, 759, 793, 801

December: 425-426, 485, 512, 517, 519, 546, 593, 595, 674, 705

Any time: 578